CRIMINAL PROCEDURE

CONSTITUTIONAL LIMITS ON POLICING

BELLIN & GERSHOWITZ

This casebook is intended for use as part of a Criminal Procedure I course in an American law school. It incorporates judicial opinions, commentary, problems, statistics, and other materials to encourage an interactive approach to doctrine and theory.

#TeamCrimPro

Van Gogh, Prisoners' Round, 1890

Criminal Procedure: Constitutional Limits on Policing

Copyright © 2023

Jeffrey Bellin & Adam M. Gershowitz

Williamsburg, Virginia USA

Second Edition

ISBN: 979-8-37188-084-0

#TEAMCRIMPRO

Criminal Procedure: Constitutional Limits on Policing

PREFACE

———

There are many Criminal Procedure casebooks. This one stands out for three reasons. First, the book presents the relevant Supreme Court cases through an easy-to-follow, intuitive framework that helps students keep the big picture in mind. Organization is one of the most important things a casebook can offer, and we spent years working to get the organization right.

Second, the book gets to the point. It provides all the necessary material: the cases that shape the doctrine, explanatory cases that illustrate how the doctrine is applied, constitutional provisions, statutes, statistics, and other primary source materials. And it offers abundant narration to fill gaps and draw connections. But time is precious and attention spans are finite. You won't find notes with unanswerable questions; critiques of legal doctrine that generate rhetorical power through lack of nuance; anecdotes from our pre-professor careers; or other material that is not essential to learning.

Third, the book prioritizes readability. Casebooks are for teaching not research. Citations, internal quotation marks, and other legal formalities are reduced to the minimum necessary for pedagogical purposes. In addition, we feel no special obligation to the authors of the opinions we excerpt. Supreme Court opinions are important because they say what the law is, not because the Justices are unusually skilled or wise. We leave out the cases that no longer matter and carefully edit the remaining opinions to include only the portions necessary for learning criminal procedure. This allows students to focus on the complex constitutional doctrines that make up the course, developing a deep understanding of these doctrines before moving to analysis and critique.

Streamlining the course materials results in a cheaper, shorter, more readable book and improved student engagement. In addition, the criminal procedure instructors we know have fascinating perspectives and insights. Our approach lets those instructors tailor this important course to the needs of their students, prioritizing their voice, not ours.

We hope you enjoy the book.   – JB & AG

TABLE OF CONTENTS

Chapter 1

Chapter 2

Chapter 3

Reasonableness: Warrants...*110*

Chapter 4

Chapter 5

Reasonableness: Manner Of Searching and Seizing...................380

Chapter 6

The Exclusionary Rule and Standing 407

Chapter 7

Chapter 1

THE SCOPE OF POLICING AND REGULATION

A.   CRIME AND POLICING

Before we dive into legal doctrine, it is important to understand the context for the rules that the Supreme Court hands down in the opinions that make up this course.

At its core this course is about interactions between the police and the public. Data on these interactions can be found in the Department of Justice, Bureau of Justice Statistics' (BJS) publication "Contacts Between Police and The Public." The series was last published in November 2022 presenting data from 2020. The BJS collects this data by surveying "a nationally representative sample of U.S. households."

TABLE 1
U.S. residents age 16 or older who had police contact, by type of contact and demographic

Demographic characteristic	U.S. residents age 16 or older	Any police contact		Police-initiated contact		Resident-initiated contact	
		Number	Percent	Number	Percent	Number	Percent
Total	260,916,200	53,836,600	20.6%	25,463,700	9.8%	29,979,700	11.5%
Sex							
Male*	126,524,700	26,751,200	21.1%	13,887,200	11.0%	13,657,500	10.8%
Female	134,391,500	27,085,400	20.2 †	11,576,500	8.6 †	16,322,300	12.1 †
Race/Hispanic origin							
White[a]*	163,405,100	36,677,800	22.4%	16,863,900	10.3%	21,145,600	12.9%
Black[a]	31,382,000	5,656,300	18.0 †	2,895,000	9.2 ‡	2,747,100	8.8 †
Hispanic	44,074,400	7,283,900	16.5 †	3,627,800	8.2 †	3,914,900	8.9 †
Asian[a]	16,192,100	2,595,000	16.0 †	1,275,700	7.9 †	1,202,700	7.4 †
Other[a,b]	5,862,500	1,623,600	27.7 †	801,300	13.7 †	969,500	16.5 †

The original source (available at bjs.ojp.gov) presents some caveats to this data. You can probably think of additional caveats yourself. For purposes of this introduction, however, the data is intended solely to illustrate the broad reach of American policing. The next table from the report breaks down the types of police contact that Americans most frequently experience:

TABLE 2
U.S. residents age 16 or older who had police contact, by type of contact and reason, 2015, 2018, and 2020

Type of contact and reason	2015 Number	2015 Percent	2018 Number	2018 Percent	2020* Number	2020* Percent
Any police contact	53,469,300	21.1%	61,542,300 †	23.7% †	53,836,600	20.6%
Police-initiated contact	27,415,900 †	10.8% †	28,880,900 †	11.1% †	25,463,700	9.8%
Traffic stop, driver[a]	19,204,500 †	8.6 †	18,666,000 †	8.1 †	16,709,200	7.1
Traffic stop, passenger	5,964,100 †	2.4 †	5,702,600 †	2.2 †	4,918,700	1.9
Street stop[b]	2,503,700	1.0	3,528,100 †	1.4 †	2,626,500	1.0
Arrested[c]	814,800 †	0.3 †	386,000	0.1	412,500	0.2
Approached, other[d]	1,946,700 †	0.8 †	3,638,100 †	1.4 †	3,063,400	1.2
Resident-initiated contact	27,060,200 †	10.7% †	35,468,500 †	13.7% †	29,979,700	11.5%
Reported possible crime	16,928,100	6.7 †	19,109,200 †	7.4 †	16,177,200	6.2
Reported noncrime emergency[e]	8,841,900	3.5	9,971,500 †	3.8 †	8,573,900	3.3
Reported nonemergency[f]	...	...	10,068,700 †	3.9 †	8,076,900	3.1
Block watch	2,366,200 †	0.9 †	2,160,900 †	0.8 †	1,639,800	0.6
Sought help, other[g]	2,478,400 †	1.0 †	641,200 †	0.2 †	321,600	0.1
Traffic accident	7,950,500	3.1%	8,882,000 †	3.4% †	7,824,600	3.0%

Other tables in the report show that in 2020, 4.3% of drivers stopped in traffic stops were either searched or arrested, and 5.2% of pedestrians stopped by police were searched or arrested. Data like this illustrate the broad importance of the rules we will study and highlight which rules will be most frequently invoked. Consider, for example, the millions of annual police-initiated traffic stops as we cover the rules governing cars in the pages to come.

As we will see, the Constitution limits the type of actions police can take during encounters, including the use of force. The BJS report sets out the types of nonfatal force used by police during reported encounters.

TABLE 8
Percent of U.S. residents age 16 or older whose most recent police contact was police-initiated or related to a traffic accident, by race or Hispanic origin and police action, 2018 and 2020

	2018 Total	2018 White[a]*	2018 Black[a]	2018 Hispanic	2018 Other[a,b]	2020 Total	2020 White[a]*	2020 Black[a]	2020 Hispanic	2020 Other[a,b]
Any police action[c,d]	3.7%	2.7%	6.8% †	5.9% †	2.5%	3.7%	3.0%	7.0% †	4.5% †	2.6%
Shouting	1.7%	1.2%	2.9% †	3.0% †	1.5%	1.6%	1.4%	3.1% †	1.6%	1.4%
Cursing	0.6%	0.5%	1.7% †	0.7%	:	0.6%	0.5%	1.4%	:	:
Threat/nonfatal use of force[e]	2.8%	2.0%	5.3% †	4.8% †	1.9%	2.7%	2.1%	5.5% †	3.4% †	1.8%
Threat of force	0.7	0.5	2.0 †	1.2 ‡	:	0.6	0.3	2.2 †	0.8 ‡	:
Handcuffing[f]	2.3	1.6	4.4 †	3.5 †	1.9	2.1	1.9	2.9	2.8 ‡	1.7
Pushing/grabbing/hitting/kicking	0.7	0.4	1.6 †	1.4 †	0.8	0.7	0.5	1.6 †	0.7	:
Using weapon/other force[g]	0.4	0.2	0.9 †	0.8 ‡	:	0.2	0.1	:	0.0[h]	:

The BJS report emphasizes an increased use of force by police against certain demographic groups revealed in its data.

"In 2020, approximately 4% of residents experienced some type of police action during their most recent police-initiated or traffic accident-related contact, with 3% experiencing the threat or use of force (table 8). Persons most commonly experienced handcuffing (2.1%) or shouting (1.6%) by police. Residents were more likely to report that police displayed or used a weapon in 2018 than in 2020. Black persons (7%) and Hispanic persons (5%) were more likely to experience at least one type of police action than white persons (3%) in 2020. Black (6%) and Hispanic (3%) persons were also more likely than white persons (2%) to experience the threat or use of force. Black persons (3%) were more likely to be shouted at by police than white persons (1%)."

Crime is the most commonly cited justification for law enforcement in the United States. The BJS estimates annual crime using the National Crime Victimization Survey (NCVS). NCVS data are generated through interviews with members of the public and subsequent statistical modeling. The first two tables from the most recent NCVS report follow:

TABLE 1
Number and rate of violent victimizations, by type of crime, 2016–2020

Type of violent crime	2016		2017		2018		2019		2020*	
	Number	Rate per 1,000[a]	Number	Rate per 1,000[a]	Number	Rate per 1,000[a]	Number	Rate per 1,000[a]	Number	Rate per 1,000[a]
Violent crime[b]	5,353,820 †	19.7 †	5,612,670 †	20.6 †	6,385,520 †	23.2 †	5,813,410 †	21.0 †	4,558,150	16.4
Rape/sexual assault[c]	298,410	1.1	393,980	1.4	734,630 †	2.7 †	459,310	1.7	319,950	1.2
Robbery	458,810	1.7	613,840 †	2.3 †	573,100	2.1	534,420	1.9	437,260	1.6
Assault	4,596,600 †	16.9 †	4,604,850 †	16.9 †	5,077,790 †	18.4 †	4,819,680 †	17.4 †	3,800,950	13.7
Aggravated assault	1,040,580 †	3.8 †	993,170 ‡	3.6 ‡	1,058,040 †	3.8 †	1,019,490 †	3.7 ‡	812,180	2.9
Simple assault	3,556,020 †	13.1 †	3,611,680 †	13.3 †	4,019,750 †	14.6 †	3,800,190 †	13.7 †	2,988,770	10.7
Violent crime excluding simple assault[d]	1,797,790	6.6 ‡	2,000,990 †	7.3 †	2,365,770 †	8.6 †	2,013,220 †	7.3 †	1,569,390	5.6
Selected characteristics of violent crime										
Domestic violence[e]	1,068,120	3.9	1,237,960 †	4.5 †	1,333,050 †	4.8 †	1,164,540 †	4.2 ‡	856,750	3.1
Intimate partner violence[f]	597,200	2.2	666,310 ‡	2.4 ‡	847,230 †	3.1 †	695,060 †	2.5 ‡	484,830	1.7
Stranger violence	2,082,410	7.7	2,034,100	7.5	2,493,750	9.1 †	2,254,740	8.1	1,973,200	7.1

TABLE 2
Number and rate of property victimizations, by type of crime, 2016–2020

Type of property crime	2016		2017		2018		2019		2020*	
	Number	Rate per 1,000[a]	Number	Rate per 1,000[a]	Number	Rate per 1,000[a]	Number	Rate per 1,000[a]	Number	Rate per 1,000[a]
Total[b]	15,815,310	118.6 †	13,340,220 †	108.4 †	13,502,840 †	108.2 †	12,818,000 †	101.4 †	12,085,170	94.5
Burglary/trespassing[c]	3,160,450	23.7 †	2,538,170 †	20.6 †	2,639,620 †	21.1 †	2,178,400 †	17.2 †	1,741,250	13.6
Burglary[d]	2,205,180	16.5 †	1,688,890 †	13.7 †	1,867,620 †	15.0 †	1,484,730 †	11.7 †	1,210,640	9.5
Trespassing[e]	955,270	7.2 †	849,280 †	6.9 †	772,000 †	6.2 †	693,670 †	5.5 †	530,610	4.1
Motor vehicle theft	618,330	4.6	516,810	4.2	534,010	4.3	495,670	3.9	545,810	4.3
Other theft[f]	12,036,530	90.3 †	10,285,240	83.6 †	10,329,210 ‡	82.7 †	10,143,930	80.2	9,798,110	76.6

Again, those interested can explore the various caveats to the data at the BJS web site. For our purposes, it is enough to get a rough sense of the scale of crime in the United States.

Both crime and perceptions of crime influence police, lawmakers, courts, and the public. The next pair of graphs from the PEW Research Center show that perceptions of crime do not necessarily match the reality.

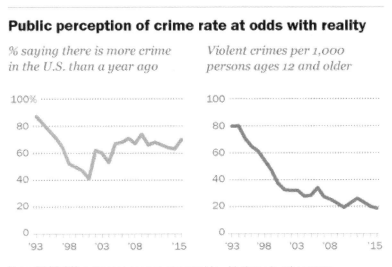

Public perception of crime rate at odds with reality

% saying there is more crime in the U.S. than a year ago

Violent crimes per 1,000 persons ages 12 and older

Note: 2006 BJS estimates are not comparable with those in other years.
Source: Gallup, Bureau of Justice Statistics.

PEW RESEARCH CENTER

Public dissatisfaction with policing takes two primary forms: (1) disapproval of police misconduct, such as police brutality, and (2) disapproval of police ineffectiveness, such as an inability to solve crimes.

With respect to the first topic, in summer 2020, police killings of unarmed Black men heightened public awareness of the need for policing reform, as this table from a recent Gallup poll reveals:

Americans' Support for Policing Reform Options, by Race/Ethnicity

Percentage who "strongly support" or "somewhat support" each reform idea

	All Americans	Black Americans	Asian Americans	Hispanic Americans	White Americans
	%	%	%	%	%
Changing management practices so officers with multiple incidents of abuse of power are not allowed to serve	98	99	98	99	97
Requiring officers to have good relations with the community	97	97	98	96	97
Changing management practices so officer abuses are punished	96	98	99	96	95
Promoting community-based alternatives such as violence intervention	82	94	91	83	80
Ending stop and frisk	74	93	89	76	70
Eliminating police unions	56	61	68	56	55
Eliminating officer enforcement of nonviolent crimes	50	72	72	55	44
Reducing the budgets of police departments and shifting the money to social programs	47	70	80	49	41
Abolishing police departments	15	22	27	20	12

GALLUP PANEL, JUNE 23-JULY 6, 2020

These criticisms of American policing are not new. In the wake of "racial disorders [in] American cities" in the summer of 1967, including a five-day riot that resulted in 43 dead, 1189 injured, and the deployment of thousands of Army paratroopers to the streets of Detroit, President Johnson established a high profile commission. This "Kerner Commission" issued a comprehensive report that highlighted arrests for minor offenses as the spark of the disorder in many of the impacted cities and cited oppressive policing of Black residents as a key contributor to the conditions that caused that spark to become a flame: "The atmosphere of hostility and cynicism [created by policing in American cities] is reinforced by a widespread belief … in the existence of police brutality and corruption and of a 'double standard' of justice and protection." In a Harris poll conducted in the wake of the unrest, 51% of Black respondents (but only 10% of white respondents) identified "police brutality" as a major cause of the riots. Almost all of the respondents (82%) agreed that American cities should diversify their police forces to include more Black officers.

Police are also criticized when they are unable to reduce or respond to crime effectively. As the next graphic from the Pew Research Center shows, a large percentage of crime is not reported to police, and a substantial portion of reported crimes are not solved.

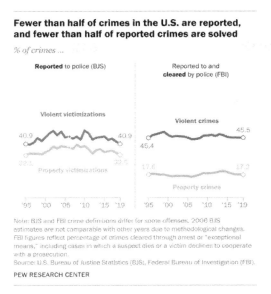

Fewer than half of crimes in the U.S. are reported, and fewer than half of reported crimes are solved

% of crimes ...

Note: BJS and FBI crime definitions differ for some offenses. 2006 BJS estimates are not comparable with other years due to methodological changes. FBI figures reflect percentage of crimes cleared through arrest or "exceptional means," including cases in which a suspect dies or a victim declines to cooperate with a prosecution.
Source: U.S. Bureau of Justice Statistics (BJS), Federal Bureau of Investigation (FBI).

PEW RESEARCH CENTER

The FBI published the following summary of the clearance rates (what percentage of reported crimes are solved) for major crimes. "Exceptional means" is an unusual event that makes an arrest unnecessary, like the suspect dies or the police conclude that the reported crime never happened.

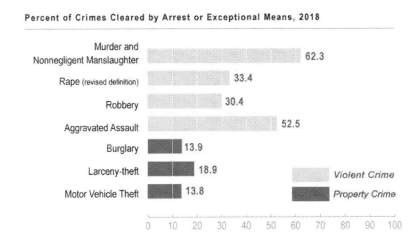

Percent of Crimes Cleared by Arrest or Exceptional Means, 2018

Crime	Percent
Murder and Nonnegligent Manslaughter	62.3
Rape (revised definition)	33.4
Robbery	30.4
Aggravated Assault	52.5
Burglary	13.9
Larceny-theft	18.9
Motor Vehicle Theft	13.8

Violent Crime
Property Crime

The primary means of clearing a reported crime is by arrest – one of the key aspects of policing covered in this course. An arrest is only the beginning of the process. This circle chart illustrates the progression of reported crime through the criminal justice system using estimates based on statistics in a typical American city.[1]

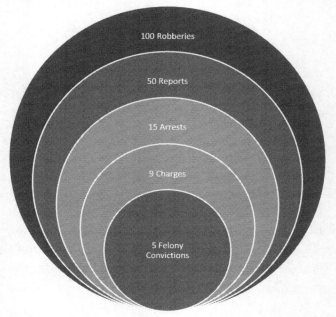

It may be helpful in thinking about the rules governing police conduct to have a sense of what kinds of crimes police most commonly make arrests for. The long table on the next page is created from data collected by the FBI to generate annual estimates of the number of arrests made by police in the United States. 2019 data is used to avoid distortions generated by the impact of Covid-19 on American policing.

---

[1] The chart and the discussion of incarceration trends is adapted from Bellin, MASS INCARCERATION NATION, HOW THE UNITED STATES BECAME ADDICTED TO PRISONS AND JAILS AND HOW IT CAN RECOVER (2023).

Estimated Number of Arrests US	2019
Total	10,085,207
Drug abuse violations	1,558,862
Driving under the influence	1,024,508
Larceny-theft	813,073
Aggravated assault	385,278
Other assaults	1,025,711
Drunkenness	316,032
Disorderly conduct	310,331
Vandalism	180,501
Liquor laws	175,548
Burglary	171,590
Weapons; carrying, possessing, etc.	153,161
Fraud	112,707
Stolen property; buying, receiving, possessing	88,272
Offenses against the family and children	85,687
Motor vehicle theft	80,636
Robbery	74,547
Forgery and counterfeiting	45,183
Sex offenses (except rape and prostitution)	40,796
Prostitution and commercialized vice	26,713
Rape	24,986
Vagrancy	21,896
Curfew and loitering law violations	14,653
Embezzlement	13,497
Murder and nonnegligent manslaughter	11,060
Arson	9,068
Gambling	2,458
All other offenses	3,318,453

"The FBI's Uniform Crime Reporting (UCR) Program counts one arrest for each separate instance in which a person is arrested, cited, or summoned for an offense. Because a person may be arrested multiple times during a year, the UCR arrest figures do not reflect the number of individuals who have been arrested; rather, the arrest data show the number of times that persons are arrested, as reported by law enforcement agencies to the UCR Program."

As the cases we explore in the upcoming pages unfolded, the United States simultaneously embarked on a path that led to "Mass Incarceration." The following graphs from the Pew Research Center reveal the scale of this phenomenon and its disproportionate racial impact. The first graph includes both jail and prison populations in the United States; the second graph only those held in prison.

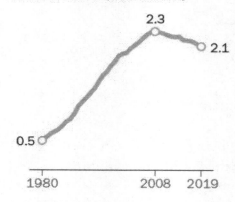

Estimated number of people incarcerated (in millions)

Source: Bureau of Justice Statistics.

PEW RESEARCH CENTER

Sentenced federal and state prisoners by race and Hispanic origin, 2007-2017

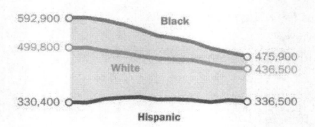

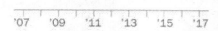

The final chart, based on 2020 data from the World Prison Brief, offers an international comparison. The second column shows each country's incarceration rate (per 100,000 population); the third column is the number of people incarcerated. The first five countries in the chart are the world's top incarcerators by rate (prior to 2020, the United States had the highest incarceration rate). The next entries represent notable examples from around the world, and include the top incarcerators in terms of numbers.[1]

Incarceration by Country - 2020

Country	Rate	Number
El Salvador	605	39,538
Rwanda	580	76,099
Turkmenistan	576	35,000
Cuba	510	57,337
U.S.	**505**	**1,690,000**
Brazil	389	835,643
Russia	304	439,453
Mexico	174	229,621
UK	137	82,839
China	119	1,675,400
France	106	72,350
India	40	554,034
Japan	36	45,714

As we will see, the Supreme Court often relies on assumptions about crime, policing and the public interest in crafting constitutional rules. As we analyze the Court's opinions, consider whether the Justices explicit and implicit assumptions (and your reactions to those assumptions) are supported by, inconsistent with, or unaffected by the empirical data summarized above.

---

[1] As the World Prison Brief acknowledges, there is significant uncertainty in the precise numbers for some of these countries due to a lack of transparency of the governments involved.

B.   THE FOURTEENTH AMENDMENT AND THE BILL OF RIGHTS

This course focuses on rights found in the first ten amendments to the United States Constitution (the "Bill of Rights"). In an 1833 case, *Barron v. City of Baltimore*, Chief Justice John Marshall, writing for the Supreme Court, explained that the provisions of the Bill of Rights limit the federal, not the state government:

> " The constitution was ordained and established by the people of the United States for themselves, for their own government, and not for the government of the individual states. Each state established a constitution for itself, and in that constitution, provided such limitations and restrictions on the powers of its particular government, as its judgment dictated. The people of the United States framed such a government for the United States as they supposed best adapted to their situation and best calculated to promote their interests. The powers they conferred on this government were to be exercised by itself; and the limitations on power, if expressed in general terms, are naturally, and, we think, necessarily, applicable to the government created by the instrument. They are limitations of power granted in the instrument itself; not of distinct governments, framed by different persons and for different purposes.

This proposition — that the Bill of Rights restrains only the federal government — is especially important in the criminal context. In the United States, criminal investigations are overwhelmingly conducted by state and local (not federal) police, and most criminal proceedings are conducted in state (not federal) courts.

In 1868, in the aftermath of the Civil War, the Fourteenth Amendment was added to the Constitution. The Amendment reads, in part:

> "Section 1.... No State shall make or enforce any law which shall abridge the privileges or immunities of citizens of the United States; nor shall any State deprive any person of life, liberty, or property, without due process of law; nor deny to any person within its jurisdiction the equal protection of the laws."

As its text makes clear, the Fourteenth Amendment places limits on the States. Over the next century, the Supreme Court decided a series of cases determining precisely what the Fourteenth Amendment's restrictions entailed.

BROWN v. MISSISSIPPI
297 U.S. 278 (1936)

Chief Justice HUGHES delivered the opinion of the unanimous Court.

The question in this case is whether convictions, which rest solely upon confessions shown to have been extorted by officers of the state by brutality and violence, are consistent with the due process of law required by the Fourteenth Amendment of the Constitution of the United States.

Petitioners were indicted for the murder of one Raymond Stewart, whose death occurred on March 30, 1934. They were indicted on April 4, 1934, and were then arraigned and pleaded not guilty. Counsel were appointed by the court to defend them. Trial was begun the next morning and was concluded on the following day, when they were found guilty and sentenced to death.

Aside from the confessions, there was no evidence sufficient to warrant the submission of the case to the jury.... On their appeal to the Supreme Court of the State, defendants assigned as error the inadmissibility of the confessions. The judgment was affirmed....

The opinion of the state court did not set forth the evidence as to the circumstances in which the confessions were procured. That the evidence established that they were procured by coercion was not questioned. The state court said: 'After the state closed its case on the merits, the appellants, for the first time, introduced evidence from which it appears that the confessions were not made voluntarily but were coerced.' There is no dispute as to the facts upon this point, and as they are clearly and adequately stated in the dissenting opinion of Judge Griffith (with whom Judge Anderson concurred), showing both the extreme brutality of the measures to extort the confessions and the participation of the state authorities, we quote this part of his opinion in full, as follows:

> '.... On [March 30] one Dial, a deputy sheriff, accompanied by others, came to the home of Yank Ellington, one of the defendants, and requested him to accompany them to the house of the deceased, and there

a number of white men were gathered, who began to accuse the defendant of the crime. Upon his denial they seized him, and with the participation of the deputy they hanged him by a rope to the limb of a tree, and, having let him down, they hung him again, and when he was let down the second time, and he still protested his innocence, he was tied to a tree and whipped, and, still declining to accede to the demands that he confess, he was finally released, and he returned with some difficulty to his home, suffering intense pain and agony. The record of the testimony shows that the signs of the rope on his neck were plainly visible during the so-called trial. A day or two thereafter the said deputy, accompanied by another, returned to the home of the said defendant and arrested him, and departed with the prisoner towards the jail in an adjoining county, but went by a route which led into the state of Alabama; and while on the way, in that state, the deputy stopped and again severely whipped the defendant, declaring that he would continue the whipping until he confessed, and the defendant then agreed to confess to such a statement as the deputy would dictate, and he did so, after which he was delivered to jail.

'The other two defendants, Ed Brown and Henry Shields, were also arrested and taken to the same jail. On Sunday night, April 1, 1934, the same deputy, accompanied by a number of white men, one of whom was also an officer, and by the jailer, came to the jail, and the two last named defendants were made to strip and they were laid over chairs and their backs were cut to pieces with a leather strap with buckles on it, and they were likewise made by the said deputy definitely to understand that the whipping would be continued unless and until they confessed…. When the confessions had been obtained in the exact form and contents as desired by the mob, they left with the parting admonition and warning that, if the defendants changed their story at any time in any respect from that last stated, the perpetrators of the outrage would administer the same or equally effective treatment.

'Further details of the brutal treatment to which these helpless prisoners were subjected need not be pursued. It is sufficient to say that in pertinent respects the transcript reads more like pages torn from some medieval account than a record made within the confines of a modern civilization which aspires to an enlightened constitutional government.

'All this having been accomplished, on the next day, that is, on Monday, April 2, when the defendants had been given time to recuperate somewhat from the tortures to which they had been subjected, the two sheriffs, one of the county where the crime was committed, and the other of the county of the jail in which the prisoners were confined, came to the jail [so that] the solemn farce of hearing the free and voluntary confessions was gone through with, and these two sheriffs and one other person then present were the three witnesses used in court to establish the so-called confessions, which were received by the court and admitted in evidence over the objections of the defendants ....

'The spurious confessions having been obtained—and the farce last mentioned having been gone through with on Monday, April 2—the court, then in session, on the following day, Tuesday, April 3, 1934, ordered the grand jury to reassemble on the succeeding day, April 4, 1934, at 9 o'clock, and on the morning of the day last mentioned the grand jury returned an indictment against the defendants for murder. Late that afternoon the defendants were brought from the jail in the adjoining county and arraigned, when one or more of them offered to plead guilty, which the court declined to accept, and, upon inquiry whether they had or desired counsel, they stated that they had none, and did not suppose that counsel could be of any assistance to them. The court thereupon appointed counsel, and set the case for trial for the following morning at 9 o'clock, and the defendants were returned to the jail in the adjoining county about thirty miles away.

'The defendants were brought to the courthouse of the county on the following morning, April 5th, and the so-called trial was opened, and was concluded on the next day, April 6, 1934, and resulted in a pretended conviction with death sentences. The evidence upon which the conviction was obtained was the so-called confessions. Without this evidence, a peremptory instruction to find for the defendants would have been inescapable. The defendants were put on the stand, and by their testimony the facts and the details thereof as to the manner by which the confessions were extorted from them were fully developed, and it is further disclosed by the record that the same deputy, Dial, under whose guiding hand and active participation the tortures to coerce the confessions were administered, was actively in the performance of the supposed duties of a court deputy in the courthouse and in the presence of the prisoners during what is denominated, in complimentary terms, the trial of these defendants…. The facts are not only undisputed, they are admitted, and admitted to have been done by officers of the state, in conjunction with other participants, and all this was definitely well known to everybody connected with the trial, and during the trial, including the state's prosecuting attorney and the trial judge presiding.'

The state stresses the statement in Twining v. New Jersey (1908) that 'exemption from compulsory self-incrimination in the courts of the states is not secured by any part of the Federal Constitution,' and the statement in Snyder v. Massachusetts (1934) that 'the privilege against self-incrimination may be withdrawn and the accused put upon the stand as a witness for the state.' But the question of the right of the state to withdraw the privilege against self-incrimination is not here involved. The compulsion to which the quoted statements refer is that of the processes of justice by which the accused may be called as a witness and required to testify. Compulsion by torture to extort a confession is a different matter.

The state is free to regulate the procedure of its courts in accordance with its own conceptions of policy, unless in so doing it 'offends some principle of justice so rooted in the traditions and conscience of our people as to be ranked as fundamental.' The state may abolish trial by jury. It may dispense with indictment by a grand jury and substitute complaint or information. But the freedom of the state in establishing its policy is the freedom of constitutional government and is limited by the requirement of due process of law. Because a state may dispense with a jury trial, it does not follow that it may substitute trial by ordeal. The rack and torture chamber may not be substituted for the witness stand. The state may not permit an accused to be hurried to conviction under mob domination—where the whole proceeding is but a mask—without supplying corrective process…. Nor may a state, through the action of its officers, contrive a conviction through the pretense of a trial which in truth is 'but used as a means of depriving a defendant of liberty through a deliberate deception of court and jury by the presentation of testimony known to be perjured.' And the trial equally is a mere pretense where the state authorities have contrived a conviction resting solely upon confessions obtained by violence…. It would be difficult to conceive of methods more revolting to the sense of justice than those taken to procure the confessions of these petitioners, and the use of the confessions thus obtained as the basis for conviction and sentence was a clear denial of due process….

[The courts of Mississippi in this case] denied a federal right fully established and specially set up and claimed, and the judgment must be reversed.

The Mississippi judge's opinion quoted by the Supreme Court emphasized that the defendants in the case were Black, situating Mississippi's "revolting" and "medieval" methods within the State's long history of slavery and racial oppression. The judge also quoted testimony from one of the deputies that discounted the severity of the whipping on the ground that the person whipped was Black.

In light of the racial animus exhibited by the Mississippi authorities in the case, the Supreme Court's application of the Fourteenth Amendment to reverse the convictions closely tracked the Court's description of the purpose of the Amendment: "the protection of the newly-made freeman and citizen from the oppressions of those who had formerly exercised unlimited dominion over him." *Slaughter-House Cases* (1872)

In later cases, the Supreme Court began to apply the Fourteenth Amendment outside this context, generating more difficult questions about the precise boundaries of the Amendment's reach.

DUNCAN v. LOUISIANA
391 U.S. 145 (1968)

Justice WHITE delivered the opinion of the Court.

Appellant, Gary Duncan, was convicted of simple battery in the Twenty-fifth Judicial District Court of Louisiana. Under Louisiana law simple battery is a misdemeanor, punishable by a maximum of two years' imprisonment and a $300 fine. Appellant sought trial by jury, but because the Louisiana Constitution grants jury trials only in cases in which capital punishment or imprisonment at hard labor may be imposed, the trial judge denied the request. Appellant was convicted and sentenced to serve 60 days in the parish prison and pay a fine of $150.

I

The Fourteenth Amendment denies the States the power to "deprive any person of life, liberty, or property, without due process of law." In resolving conflicting claims concerning the meaning of this spacious language, the Court has looked increasingly to the Bill of Rights for guidance; many of the rights guaranteed by the first eight Amendments to the Constitution have been held [in earlier Supreme Court cases] to be protected against state action by the Due Process Clause of the Fourteenth Amendment. That clause now protects the right to compensation for property taken by the State; the rights of speech, press, and religion covered by the First Amendment; the Fourth Amendment rights to be free from unreasonable searches and seizures and to have excluded from criminal trials any evidence illegally seized; the right guaranteed by the Fifth Amendment to be free of compelled self-incrimination; and the Sixth Amendment rights to counsel, to a speedy and public trial, to confrontation of opposing witnesses, and to compulsory process for obtaining witnesses.

The test for determining whether a right extended by the Fifth and Sixth Amendments with respect to federal criminal proceedings is also protected against state action by the Fourteenth Amendment has been phrased in a variety of ways in the opinions of this Court. The question has been asked whether a right is among those "fundamental principles of liberty and justice which lie at the base of all our civil and political institutions"; whether it is "basic in our system of jurisprudence"; and whether it is "a fundamental right, essential to a fair trial." The claim before us is that the right to trial by jury guaranteed by the Sixth Amendment meets these tests…. [*Ed. Note*: The Court then reviewed the history of the American jury trial and concluded:] Because we believe that trial by jury in criminal cases is fundamental to the American scheme of justice, we hold that the Fourteenth Amendment guarantees a right of jury trial in all criminal cases which—were they to be tried in a federal court—would come within the Sixth Amendment's guarantee. Since we consider the appeal before us to be such a case, we hold that the Constitution was violated when appellant's demand for jury trial was refused….

II

…. It is doubtless true that there is a category of petty crimes or offenses which is not subject to the Sixth Amendment jury trial provision and should not be subject to the Fourteenth Amendment jury trial requirement here applied to the

States…. We need not, however, settle in this case the exact location of the line between petty offenses and serious crimes. It is sufficient for our purposes to hold that a crime punishable by two years in prison is, based on past and contemporary standards in this country, a serious crime and not a petty offense. Consequently, appellant was entitled to a jury trial and it was error to deny it.

In *McDonald v. Chicago*, the Supreme Court ruled that the Second Amendment right to keep and bear arms applies to the States. The opinion includes a helpful summary of the Supreme Court's ongoing interpretation of the Fourteenth Amendment to apply the provisions of the Bill of Rights to the States.

MCDONALD v. CHICAGO
561 U.S. 742 (2010)

Justice ALITO delivered the opinion of the Court.

…. The Bill of Rights, including the Second Amendment, originally applied only to the Federal Government. In Barron v. Baltimore (1833), the Court, in an opinion by Chief Justice Marshall, explained that this question was "of great importance" but "not of much difficulty." In less than four pages, the Court firmly rejected the proposition that the first eight Amendments operate as limitations on the States, holding that they apply only to the Federal Government.

The constitutional Amendments adopted in the aftermath of the Civil War fundamentally altered our country's federal system. The provision at issue in this case, §1 of the Fourteenth Amendment, provides, among other things, that a State may not abridge "the privileges or immunities of citizens of the United States" or deprive "any person of life, liberty, or property, without due process of law."…

In the late 19th century, the Court began to consider whether the Due Process Clause prohibits the States from infringing rights set out in the Bill of Rights…. The Court explained that the only rights protected against state infringement by the Due Process Clause were those rights "of such a nature that they are included in the conception of due process of law." The Court used different formulations in describing the boundaries of due process. [For example,] the Court famously said that due process protects those rights that are "the very essence of a scheme of ordered liberty" and essential to "a fair and enlightened system of justice."

…An alternative theory regarding the relationship between the Bill of Rights and of the Fourteenth Amendment was championed by Justice Black. This theory held that §1 of the Fourteenth Amendment totally incorporated all of the provisions of the Bill of Rights. As Justice Black noted, the chief congressional proponents of the Fourteenth Amendment espoused the view that the Amendment made the Bill of Rights applicable to the States and, in so doing, overruled this Court's decision in Barron. Nonetheless, the Court never has embraced Justice Black's "total incorporation" theory.

While Justice Black's theory was never adopted, the Court eventually moved in that direction by initiating what has been called a process of "selective incorporation," i.e., the Court began to hold that the Due Process Clause fully incorporates particular rights contained in the first eight Amendments.

[In these cases,] the Court inquired whether a particular Bill of Rights guarantee is fundamental to our scheme of ordered liberty and system of justice…. The Court eventually incorporated almost all of the provisions of the Bill of Rights. Only a handful of the Bill of Rights protections remain unincorporated.

Finally, the Court abandoned "the notion that the Fourteenth Amendment applies to the States only a watered-down, subjective version of the individual guarantees of the Bill of Rights," stating that it would be "incongruous" to apply different standards "depending on whether the claim was asserted in a state or federal court." Instead, the Court decisively held that incorporated Bill of Rights protections "are all to be enforced against the States under the Fourteenth Amendment according to the same standards that protect those personal rights against federal encroachment."

In the United States, state and local law enforcement conduct the overwhelming majority of searches, seizures, and interrogations. The applicability of criminal procedure rights to the States, then, makes the precise content of those rights – the balance of this course – substantially more consequential.

As the preceding opinions suggest, the Fourth, Fifth, and Sixth Amendment restrictions covered in this course apply to the States through the Fourteenth Amendment's due process clause. This resulted from decisions like *Duncan v. Louisiana.* Short quotes from those decisions follow:

- "The security of one's privacy against arbitrary intrusion by the police—which is at the core of the Fourth Amendment—is basic to a free society. It is therefore implicit in 'the concept of ordered liberty' and as such enforceable against the States through the Due Process Clause." *Wolf v. Colorado* (1949)

- "We hold today that the Fifth Amendment's exception from compulsory self-incrimination is also protected by the Fourteenth Amendment against abridgment by the States." *Malloy v. Hogan* (1964)

- "In our adversary system of criminal justice, any person haled into court, who is too poor to hire a lawyer, cannot be assured a fair trial unless counsel is provided for him." *Gideon v. Wainwright* (1963) (Sixth Amendment right to counsel)

As the Supreme Court stated in *McDonald v. Chicago*, and further emphasized in *Timbs v. Indiana* (2019), every Supreme Court decision defining (or expanding) the contours of these rights binds the States just as it does the federal government: "If a Bill of Rights protection is incorporated, there is no daylight between the federal and state conduct it prohibits or requires."

In 2020, the Court followed this principle to eliminate a historical inconsistency that had permitted State (but not federal) courts to convict people of crimes through non-unanimous jury verdicts. In *Ramos v. Louisiana* (2020), the Supreme Court struck down this practice, explaining:

> "There can be no question … that the Sixth Amendment's unanimity requirement applies to state and federal criminal trials equally. This Court has long explained that the Sixth Amendment right to a jury trial is 'fundamental to the American scheme of justice' and incorporated against the States under the Fourteenth Amendment. See Duncan v. Louisiana. This Court has long explained, too, that incorporated provisions of the Bill of Rights bear the same content when asserted against States as they do when asserted against the federal government. So if the Sixth Amendment's right to a jury trial requires a unanimous verdict to support a conviction in federal court, it requires no less in state court."

Chapter 2

FOURTH AMENDMENT THRESHOLDS

"The right of the people to be secure in their persons, houses, papers, and effects, against unreasonable searches and seizures, shall not be violated, and no warrants shall issue, but upon probable cause, supported by oath or affirmation, and particularly describing the place to be searched, and the persons or things to be seized."

U.S. Const. Amend. IV

A. GOVERNMENT ACTION AND "THE PEOPLE"

The Fourth Amendment is only one sentence long, but that sentence raises numerous questions of interpretation. We begin with one of the most fundamental points about the Amendment's scope.

A key limitation on the Fourth Amendment's protections hinges on the identity of the person or entity who engages in a contested "search" or "seizure." To flesh out this point, representative quotes from the Supreme Court follow, along with a lengthier excerpt applying the principle involved:

- "The Fourth Amendment ... was intended as a restraint upon the activities of sovereign authority, and was not intended to be a limitation upon other than governmental agencies." *Burdeau v. McDowell* (1921)

- "Although the Fourth Amendment does not apply to a search or seizure, even an arbitrary one, effected by a private party on his own initiative, the Amendment protects against such intrusions if the private party acted as an instrument or agent of the Government." *Skinner v. Railway Labor Executives' Ass'n* (1989)

COOLIDGE v. NEW HAMPSHIRE
403 U.S. 443 (1971)

Justice STEWART delivered the opinion of the Court.

[Police visited Joanne Coolidge's home when her spouse Edward Coolidge came under suspicion in a kidnapping. Edward was not at home; police spoke to Joanne. During the conversation, Joanne sought out and produced evidence from inside the home (guns and clothing) that implicated her spouse in the kidnapping. Edward later challenged the admissibility of that evidence in court.]

Had Mrs. Coolidge, wholly on her own initiative, sought out her husband's guns and clothing and then taken them to the police station to be used as evidence against him, there can be no doubt under existing law that the articles would later have been admissible in evidence. The question presented here is whether the conduct of the police officers at the Coolidge house was such as to make her actions their actions for purposes of the Fourth and Fourteenth Amendments and their attendant exclusionary rules. The test ... is whether Mrs. Coolidge, in light of all the circumstances of the case, must be regarded as having acted as an 'instrument' or agent of the state when she produced her husband's belongings.

In a situation like the one before us there no doubt always exist forces pushing the spouse to cooperate with the police. Among these are the simple but often powerful convention of openness and honesty, the fear that secretive behavior will intensify suspicion, and uncertainty as to what course is most likely to be helpful to the absent spouse. But there is nothing constitutionally suspect in the existence, without more, of these incentives to full disclosure or active cooperation with the police. The exclusionary rules were fashioned to prevent, not to repair, and their target is official misconduct. They are to compel respect for the constitutional guaranty in the only effectively available way—by removing the incentive to disregard it. But it is no part of the policy underlying the Fourth and Fourteenth Amendments to discourage citizens from aiding to the utmost of their ability in the apprehension of criminals. If, then, the exclusionary rule is properly applicable to the evidence taken from the Coolidge house ... it must be upon the basis that some type of unconstitutional police conduct occurred.

Once Mrs. Coolidge had admitted them, the policemen were surely acting normally and properly when they asked her, as they had asked those questioned earlier in the investigation, including Edward Coolidge himself, about any guns there might be in the house. The question concerning the clothes Coolidge had been wearing on the night of the disappearance was logical and in no way coercive. Indeed, one might doubt the competence of the officers involved had they not asked exactly the questions they did ask. And surely when Mrs. Coolidge of her own accord produced the guns and clothes for inspection, rather than simply describing them, it was not incumbent on the police to stop her or avert their eyes.

The crux of the petitioner's argument must be that when Mrs. Coolidge asked the policemen whether they wanted the guns, they should have replied that they could not take them, or have first telephoned Coolidge … and asked his permission to take them, or have asked her whether she had been authorized by her husband to release them. Instead, after one policeman had declined the offer, the other turned and said, 'We might as well take them,' to which Mrs. Coolidge replied, 'If you would like them, you may take them.'

In assessing the claim that this course of conduct amounted to a search and seizure, it is well to keep in mind that Mrs. Coolidge described her own motive as that of clearing her husband, and that she believed that she had nothing to hide. She had seen her husband himself produce his guns for two other policemen earlier in the week, and there is nothing to indicate that she realized that he had offered only three of them for inspection on that occasion. The two officers who questioned her behaved, as her own testimony shows, with perfect courtesy. There is not the slightest implication of an attempt on their part to coerce or dominate her, or, for that matter, to direct her actions by the more subtle techniques of suggestion that are available to officials in circumstances like these. To hold that the conduct of the police here was a search and seizure would be to hold, in effect, that a criminal suspect has constitutional protection against the adverse consequences of a spontaneous, good-faith effort by his wife to clear him of suspicion....

In most cases, there is no question that a search or seizure is a consequence of state action, such as when police officers or other government officials conduct the search or seizure. As *Coolidge* suggests, even someone who is not employed by the government may be acting as an "instrument of the state" triggering Fourth Amendment protections.

Another less frequently invoked limit on the scope of the Fourth Amendment concerns the person or place that was searched or seized.

UNITED STATES v. VERDUGO-URQUIDEZ
494 U.S. 259 (1990)

Chief Justice REHNQUIST delivered the opinion of the Court.

The question presented by this case is whether the Fourth Amendment applies to the search and seizure by United States agents of property that is owned by a nonresident alien and located in a foreign country. We hold that it does not....

Respondent Rene Martin Verdugo–Urquidez is a citizen and resident of Mexico.... Based on a complaint charging respondent with various narcotics-related offenses, the Government obtained a warrant for his arrest on August 3, 1985. In January 1986, Mexican police officers, after discussions with United States marshals, apprehended Verdugo–Urquidez in Mexico and transported him to the United States Border Patrol station in Calexico, California. There, United States marshals arrested respondent and eventually moved him to a correctional center in San Diego, California, where he remains incarcerated pending trial.

Following respondent's arrest, Terry Bowen, a DEA agent assigned to the Calexico DEA office, decided to arrange for searches of Verdugo–Urquidez's Mexican residences located in Mexicali and San Felipe. Bowen telephoned Walter White, the Assistant Special Agent in charge of the DEA office in Mexico City, and asked him to seek authorization for the search from the Director General of the Mexican Federal Judicial Police (MFJP).... White eventually contacted the Director General, who authorized the searches and promised the cooperation of Mexican authorities. Thereafter, DEA agents working in concert with officers of the MFJP searched respondent's properties in Mexicali and San Felipe and seized certain documents.... The District Court granted respondent's motion to suppress evidence seized during the searches, concluding that the Fourth Amendment applied to the searches and that the DEA agents had failed to justify searching respondent's premises without a warrant....

[The Fourth Amendment] text, by contrast with the Fifth and Sixth Amendments, extends its reach only to "the people." Contrary to the suggestion of amici curiae that the Framers used this phrase "simply to avoid an awkward rhetorical redundancy," "the people" seems to have been a term of art employed in select parts of the Constitution. The Preamble declares that the Constitution is ordained and established by "the People of the United States." The Second Amendment protects "the right of the people to keep and bear Arms," and the Ninth and Tenth Amendments provide that certain rights and powers are retained by and reserved to "the people." While this textual exegesis is by no means conclusive, it suggests that "the people" protected by the Fourth Amendment, and by the First and Second Amendments, and to whom rights and powers are reserved in the Ninth and Tenth Amendments, refers to a class of persons who are part of a national community or who have otherwise developed sufficient connection with this country to be considered part of that community....

[Prior] cases ... establish only that aliens receive constitutional protections when they have come within the territory of the United States and developed substantial connections with this country. Respondent is an alien who has had no previous significant voluntary connection with the United States, so these cases avail him not.

... In INS v. Lopez–Mendoza (1984), ... a majority of Justices assumed that the Fourth Amendment applied to illegal aliens in the United States.... Even assuming such aliens would be entitled to Fourth Amendment protections, their situation is different from respondent's. The illegal aliens in Lopez–Mendoza were in the United States voluntarily and presumably had accepted some societal obligations; but respondent had no voluntary connection with this country that might place him among "the people" of the United States....

We think that the text of the Fourth Amendment, its history, and our cases discussing the application of the Constitution to aliens and extraterritorially require rejection of respondent's claim. At the time of the search, he was a citizen and resident of Mexico with no voluntary attachment to the United States, and the place searched was located in Mexico. Under these circumstances, the Fourth Amendment has no application.

B. DEFINING "SEARCH"

Perhaps the most substantial limitation on the Fourth Amendment's protections is its application to "searches" and "seizures." Government conduct that is not a "search" or "seizure" does not trigger the Fourth Amendment's protections. In a later section, we will consider "seizures," by which we typically mean the seizure of a person, such as an arrest. This section considers the definition of the term "search" under the Fourth Amendment. A few of the cases also touch on Fourth Amendment "seizures" of property.

Often it is obvious that the police conducted a "search." When the police enter a home or office and look through the rooms and closets for evidence of a crime, that is a "search." In other circumstances, such as when officers review footage from a surveillance camera, whether the police conducted a "search" is less clear. The modern Court's approach to defining "search" begins with *Katz v. United States*.

1. REASONABLE EXPECTATION OF PRIVACY

KATZ v. UNITED STATES
389 U.S. 347 (1967)

Justice STEWART delivered the opinion of the Court.

The petitioner, Charles Katz, was convicted in the District Court for the Southern District of California under an eight-count indictment charging him with transmitting wagering information by telephone from Los Angeles to Miami and Boston in violation of a federal statute.

At trial the Government was permitted, over the petitioner's objection, to introduce evidence of the petitioner's end of a telephone conversation, overheard by FBI agents who had attached an electronic listening and recording device to the outside of the public telephone booth from which he had placed his calls. In affirming his conviction, the Court of Appeals rejected the contention that the recordings had been obtained in violation of the Fourth Amendment, because 'there was no physical entrance into the area occupied by, the petitioner.' We granted certiorari in order to consider the constitutional questions thus presented....

The parties have attached great significance to the characterization of the telephone booth from which the petitioner placed his calls. The petitioner has strenuously argued that the booth was a 'constitutionally protected area.' The Government has maintained with equal vigor that it was not. But this effort to decide whether or not a given 'area,' viewed in the abstract, is 'constitutionally protected' deflects attention from the problem presented by this case. For the Fourth Amendment protects people, not places. What a person knowingly exposes to the public, even in his own home or office, is not a subject of Fourth Amendment protection. But what he seeks to preserve as private, even in an area accessible to the public, may be constitutionally protected.

The Government stresses the fact that the telephone booth from which the petitioner made his calls was constructed partly of glass, so that he was as visible after he entered it as he would have been if he had remained outside. But what he sought to exclude when he entered the booth was not the intruding eye—it was the uninvited ear. He did not shed his right to do so simply because he made his calls from a place where he might be seen. No less than an individual in a business office, in a friend's apartment, or in a taxicab, a person in a telephone booth may rely upon the protection of the Fourth Amendment. One who occupies it, shuts the door behind him, and pays the toll that permits him to place a call is surely entitled to assume that the words he utters into the mouthpiece will not be broadcast to the world. To read the Constitution more narrowly is to ignore the vital role that the public telephone has come to play in private communication.

The Government contends, however, that the activities of its agents in this case should not be tested by Fourth Amendment requirements, for the surveillance technique they employed involved no physical penetration of the telephone booth from which the petitioner placed his calls. It is true that the absence of such penetration was at one time thought to foreclose further Fourth Amendment inquiry, Olmstead v. United States (1928); Goldman v. United States (1942), for that Amendment was thought to limit only searches and seizures of tangible property. But the premise that property interests control the right of the Government to search and seize has been discredited. Thus, although a closely divided Court supposed in Olmstead that surveillance without any trespass and without the seizure of any material object fell outside the ambit of the

Constitution, we have since departed from the narrow view on which that decision rested....

We conclude that the underpinnings of Olmstead and Goldman have been so eroded by our subsequent decisions that the 'trespass' doctrine there enunciated can no longer be regarded as controlling. The Government's activities in electronically listening to and recording the petitioner's words violated the privacy upon which he justifiably relied while using the telephone booth and thus constituted a 'search and seizure' within the meaning of the Fourth Amendment. The fact that the electronic device employed to achieve that end did not happen to penetrate the wall of the booth can have no constitutional significance....

Justice HARLAN, concurring.

I join the opinion of the Court.... As the Court's opinion states, 'the Fourth Amendment protects people, not places.' The question, however, is what protection it affords to those people. Generally, as here, the answer to that question requires reference to a 'place.' My understanding of the rule that has emerged from prior decisions is that there is a twofold requirement, first that a person have exhibited an actual (subjective) expectation of privacy and, second, that the expectation be one that society is prepared to recognize as 'reasonable.'

Thus a man's home is, for most purposes, a place where he expects privacy, but objects, activities, or statements that he exposes to the 'plain view' of outsiders are not 'protected' because no intention to keep them to himself has been exhibited. On the other hand, conversations in the open would not be protected against being overheard, for the expectation of privacy under the circumstances would be unreasonable.

The critical fact in this case is that '(o)ne who occupies it, (a telephone booth) shuts the door behind him, and pays the toll that permits him to place a call is surely entitled to assume' that his conversation is not being intercepted. The point is not that the booth is 'accessible to the public' at other times, but that it is a temporarily private place whose momentary occupants' expectations of freedom from intrusion are recognized as reasonable....

To appreciate the implications of *Katz*, it is helpful to understand the doctrine that the case displaced – exemplified by the "physical penetration" cases referenced in the majority opinion. In *Olmstead v. U.S.* (1928), federal (alcohol) prohibition officers attached wires to phone lines running along the street outside the suspects' homes and in the basement of an office building, and then listened to the suspects' phone conversations. The Supreme Court held that this "wire tapping … did not amount to a search or seizure within the meaning of the Fourth Amendment." The Court explained this was because: "The [wire] insertions were made without trespass upon any property of the defendants." In *Goldman v. U.S.* (1942), federal agents held a "detectaphone" against the wall of a room adjoining the suspect's office, and listened to his conversations. Again, the Court held there was no trespass and thus no search.

Katz rejected this "trespass doctrine." Its replacement – the "reasonable expectation of privacy" test – appears most clearly in Justice Harlan's concurring opinion. As explained in a later case,

> "The touchstone of Fourth Amendment analysis is whether a person has a 'constitutionally protected reasonable expectation of privacy.' Katz v. United States (1967) (Harlan, J., concurring). Katz posits a two-part inquiry: first, has the individual manifested a subjective expectation of privacy in the object of the challenged search? Second, is society willing to recognize that expectation as reasonable?" *California v. Ciraolo* (1986)

See also *Kyllo v. United States* (2001) ("As Justice Harlan's oft-quoted concurrence described it, a Fourth Amendment search occurs when the government violates a subjective expectation of privacy that society recognizes as reasonable.").

The *Katz* test is regularly criticized. Here is Justice Thomas, dissenting in a recent Fourth Amendment case:

> "The … fundamental problem with the Court's opinion, however, is its use of the "reasonable expectation of privacy" test, which was first articulated by Justice Harlan in Katz v. United States (1967) (concurring opinion). The Katz test has no basis in the text or history of the Fourth Amendment. And, it invites courts to make judgments about policy, not law."

29

It can be difficult to obtain clear answers from the reasonable-expectation-of-privacy test itself. Instead, the Supreme Court tends to generate more concrete sub-rules using the *Katz* formula. The sub-rules can then point to an answer that resolves a case or set of cases.

The next Sections cover these sub-rules:

- Third-Party Doctrine
- Exposed to Public View
- Exposes Only Contraband
- Near Perfect Surveillance

2.   THIRD-PARTY DOCTRINE

> "This Court consistently has held that a person has no legitimate expectation of privacy in information he voluntarily turns over to third parties." *Smith v. Maryland*

UNITED STATES v. WHITE
401 U.S. 745 (1971)

Justice WHITE announced the judgment of the Court and an opinion in which three other Justices joined.

…. The issue before us is whether the Fourth Amendment bars from evidence the testimony of governmental agents who related certain conversations which had occurred between defendant James White and a government informant, Harvey Jackson, and which the agents overheard by monitoring the frequency of a radio transmitter carried by Jackson and concealed on his person. On four occasions the conversations took place in Jackson's home; each of these conversations was overheard by an agent concealed in a kitchen closet with Jackson's consent and by a second agent outside the house using a radio receiver. Four other conversations—one in respondent's home, one in a restaurant, and two in Jackson's car—were overheard by the use of radio equipment. The prosecution was unable to locate and produce Jackson at the trial and the trial court overruled objections to the testimony of the agents who conducted the electronic surveillance….

The Court of Appeals read Katz v. United States as … interpreting the Fourth Amendment to forbid the introduction of the agents' testimony in the circumstances of this case.... In our view, the Court of Appeals misinterpreted both the Katz case and the Fourth Amendment....

Katz v. United States ... swept away doctrines that electronic eavesdropping is permissible under the Fourth Amendment unless physical invasion of a constitutionally protected area produced the challenged evidence....

Hoffa v. United States (1966), which was left undisturbed by Katz, held that however strongly a defendant may trust an apparent colleague, his expectations in this respect are not protected by the Fourth Amendment when it turns out that the colleague is a government agent regularly communicating with the authorities. In these circumstances, 'no interest legitimately protected by the Fourth Amendment is involved,' for that amendment affords no protection to 'a wrongdoer's misplaced belief that a person to whom he voluntarily confides his wrongdoing will not reveal it.' No warrant to 'search and seize' is required in such circumstances, nor is it when the Government sends to defendant's home a secret agent who conceals his identity and makes a purchase of narcotics from the accused, Lewis v. United States (1966), or when the same agent, unbeknown to the defendant, carries electronic equipment to record the defendant's words and the evidence so gathered is later offered in evidence. Lopez v. United States (1963).

Conceding that Hoffa, Lewis, and Lopez remained unaffected by Katz, the Court of Appeals nevertheless read both Katz and the Fourth Amendment to require a different result if the agent not only records his conversations with the defendant but instantaneously transmits them electronically to other agents equipped with radio receivers. Where this occurs, the Court of Appeals held, the Fourth Amendment is violated and the testimony of the listening agents must be excluded from evidence.

.... [We have held that] a police agent who conceals his police connections may write down for official use his conversations with a defendant and testify concerning them, without a warrant authorizing his encounters with the defendant and without otherwise violating the latter's Fourth Amendment rights. Hoffa v. United States (1966). For constitutional purposes, no different result is required if the agent instead of immediately reporting and transcribing his conversations with defendant, either (1) simultaneously records them with electronic equipment which he is carrying on his person; (2) or carries radio equipment which simultaneously transmits the conversations either to recording equipment located elsewhere or to other agents monitoring the transmitting frequency. If the conduct and revelations of an agent operating without electronic equipment do not invade the defendant's constitutionally justifiable expectations of privacy, neither does a simultaneous recording of the same conversations made by the agent or by others from transmissions received from the agent to whom the defendant is talking and whose trustworthiness the defendant necessarily risks.

Our problem is not what the privacy expectations of particular defendants in particular situations may be or the extent to which they may in fact have relied on the discretion of their companions. Very probably, individual defendants neither know nor suspect that their colleagues have gone or will go to the police or are carrying recorders or transmitters. Otherwise, conversation would cease and our problem with these encounters would be nonexistent or far different from those now before us. Our problem, in terms of the principles announced in Katz, is what expectations of privacy are constitutionally 'justifiable'—what expectations the Fourth Amendment will protect in the absence of a warrant. So far, the law permits the frustration of actual expectations of privacy by permitting authorities to use the testimony of those associates who for one reason or another have determined to turn to the police, as well as by authorizing the use of informants in the manner exemplified by Hoffa and Lewis. If the law gives no protection to the wrongdoer whose trusted accomplice is or becomes a police agent, neither should it protect him when that same agent has recorded or transmitted the conversations which are later offered in evidence to prove the State's case....

[*Ed. Note*: Justice Black added a fifth vote, concurring on the grounds stated in his dissent in Katz, that the Fourth Amendment's text does not apply to this type of investigative activity. "A conversation overheard by eavesdropping, whether by plain snooping or wiretapping, is not tangible and, under the normally accepted meanings of the words, can neither be searched nor seized."]

SMITH v. MARYLAND
442 U.S. 735 (1979)

Justice BLACKMUN delivered the opinion of the Court.

This case presents the question whether the installation and use of a pen register[1] constitutes a "search" within the meaning of the Fourth Amendment, made applicable to the States through the Fourteenth Amendment.

I

On March 5, 1976, in Baltimore, Md., Patricia McDonough was robbed. She gave the police a description of the robber and of a 1975 Monte Carlo automobile she had observed near the scene of the crime. After the robbery, McDonough began receiving threatening and obscene phone calls from a man identifying himself as the robber. On one occasion, the caller asked that she step out on her front porch; she did so, and saw the 1975 Monte Carlo she had earlier described to police moving slowly past her home. On March 16, police spotted a man who met McDonough's description driving a 1975 Monte Carlo in her neighborhood. By tracing the license plate number, police learned that the car was registered in the name of petitioner, Michael Smith.

The next day, the telephone company, at police request, installed a pen register at its central offices to record the numbers dialed from the telephone at petitioner's home. The police did not get a warrant or court order before having the pen register installed. The register revealed that on March 17 a call was placed from petitioner's home to McDonough's phone. On the basis of this and other evidence, the police obtained a warrant to search petitioner's residence. The search revealed that a page in petitioner's phone book was turned down to the name and number of Patricia McDonough; the phone book was seized. Petitioner was arrested, and a six-man

---

[1] A pen register is a mechanical device that records the numbers dialed on a telephone by monitoring the electrical impulses caused when the dial on the telephone is released. It does not overhear oral communications and does not indicate whether calls are actually completed. A pen register is usually installed at a central telephone facility and records on a paper tape all numbers dialed from the line to which it is attached.
[*Ed. Note*: **Footnotes that appear within opinion excerpts are from the opinions themselves and retain the footnote numbering of the source.**]

lineup was held on March 19. McDonough identified petitioner as the man who had robbed her.

Petitioner was indicted in the Criminal Court of Baltimore for robbery. By pretrial motion, he sought to suppress "all fruits derived from the pen register" on the ground that the police had failed to secure a warrant prior to its installation. The trial court denied the suppression motion, holding that the warrantless installation of the pen register did not violate the Fourth Amendment. Petitioner then waived a jury, and the case was submitted to the court on an agreed statement of facts.... Petitioner was convicted, and was sentenced to six years....

II
A

The Fourth Amendment guarantees "[t]he right of the people to be secure in their persons, houses, papers, and effects, against unreasonable searches and seizures." In determining whether a particular form of government-initiated electronic surveillance is a "search" within the meaning of the Fourth Amendment, our lodestar is Katz v. United States....

Consistently with Katz, this Court uniformly has held that the application of the Fourth Amendment depends on whether the person invoking its protection can claim a "justifiable," a "reasonable," or a "legitimate expectation of privacy" that has been invaded by government action. This inquiry, as Justice Harlan aptly noted in his Katz concurrence, normally embraces two discrete questions. The first is whether the individual, by his conduct, has "exhibited an actual (subjective) expectation of privacy,"—whether, in the words of the Katz majority, the individual has shown that "he seeks to preserve [something] as private." The second question is whether the individual's subjective expectation of privacy is "one that society is prepared to recognize as 'reasonable,'" —whether, in the words of the Katz majority, the individual's expectation, viewed objectively, is "justifiable" under the circumstances.

B

In applying the Katz analysis to this case, it is important to begin by specifying precisely the nature of the state activity that is challenged. The activity here took the form of installing and using a pen register. Since the pen register was installed on telephone company property at the telephone company's central offices, petitioner obviously cannot claim that his "property" was invaded or that police intruded into a "constitutionally protected area." Petitioner's claim, rather, is that, notwithstanding the absence of a trespass, the State, as did the Government in Katz, infringed a "legitimate expectation of privacy" that petitioner held. Yet a pen register differs significantly from the listening device employed in Katz, for pen registers do not acquire the contents of communications. This Court recently noted:

> "Indeed, a law enforcement official could not even determine from the use of a pen register whether a communication existed. These devices do not hear sound. They disclose only the telephone numbers that have been dialed—a means of establishing communication. Neither the purport of any communication between the caller and the recipient of the call, their identities, nor whether the call was even completed is disclosed by pen registers."

Given a pen register's limited capabilities, therefore, petitioner's argument that its installation and use constituted a "search" necessarily rests upon a claim that he had a "legitimate expectation of privacy" regarding the numbers he dialed on his phone.

This claim must be rejected. First, we doubt that people in general entertain any actual expectation of privacy in the numbers they dial. All telephone users realize that they must "convey" phone numbers to the telephone company, since it is through telephone company switching equipment that their calls are completed. All subscribers realize, moreover, that the phone company has facilities for making permanent records of the numbers they dial, for they see a list of their long-distance (toll) calls on their monthly bills. In fact, pen registers and similar devices are routinely used by telephone companies "for the purposes of checking billing operations, detecting fraud and preventing violations of law."... Although most people may be oblivious to a pen register's esoteric functions, they presumably have some awareness of one common use: to aid in the identification of persons making annoying or obscene calls.... Although subjective expectations cannot be scientifically gauged, it is too much to believe that telephone subscribers, under these circumstances, harbor any general expectation that the numbers they dial will remain secret....

Second, even if petitioner did harbor some subjective expectation that the phone numbers he dialed would remain private, this expectation is not "one that society is prepared to recognize as 'reasonable.'" This Court consistently has held that a person has no legitimate expectation of privacy in information he voluntarily turns over to third parties. E.g., United States v. Miller (1976); United States v. White (1971); Hoffa v. United States (1966); Lopez v. United States (1963). In Miller, for example, the Court held that a bank depositor has no "legitimate 'expectation of privacy'" in financial information "voluntarily conveyed to … banks and exposed to their employees in the ordinary course of business." The Court explained:

> "The depositor takes the risk, in revealing his affairs to another, that the information will be conveyed by that person to the Government…. This Court has held repeatedly that the Fourth Amendment does not prohibit the obtaining of information revealed to a third party and conveyed by him to Government authorities, even if the information is revealed on the assumption that it will be used only for a limited purpose and the confidence placed in the third party will not be betrayed."

Because the depositor "assumed the risk" of disclosure, the Court held that it would be unreasonable for him to expect his financial records to remain private.

This analysis dictates that petitioner can claim no legitimate expectation of privacy here. When he used his phone, petitioner voluntarily conveyed numerical information to the telephone company and "exposed" that information to its equipment in the ordinary course of business. In so doing, petitioner assumed the risk that the company would reveal to police the numbers he dialed. The switching equipment that processed those numbers is merely the modern counterpart of the operator who, in an earlier day, personally completed calls for the subscriber. Petitioner concedes that if he had placed his calls through an operator, he could claim no legitimate expectation of privacy. We are not inclined to hold that a different constitutional result is required because the telephone company has decided to automate….

We therefore conclude that petitioner in all probability entertained no actual expectation of privacy in the phone numbers he dialed, and that, even if he did, his expectation was not "legitimate." The installation and use of a pen register, consequently, was not a "search," and no warrant was required.

CRITICISM OF THIRD-PARTY DOCTRINE

Third-party doctrine has come under substantial scholarly and judicial critique in recent years. In a concurrence in a 2012 case (*United States v. Jones*), Justice Sotomayor sketched out the core of this critique:

> It may be necessary to reconsider the premise that an individual has no reasonable expectation of privacy in information voluntarily disclosed to third parties. E.g., Smith v. Maryland (1979); United States v. Miller (1976). This approach is ill suited to the digital age, in which people reveal a great deal of information about themselves to third parties in the course of carrying out mundane tasks. People disclose the phone numbers that they dial or text to their cellular providers; the URLs that they visit and the e-mail addresses with which they correspond to their Internet service providers; and the books, groceries, and medications they purchase to online retailers. Perhaps, as Justice Alito notes, some people may find the 'tradeoff' of privacy for convenience 'worthwhile,' or come to accept this 'diminution of privacy' as 'inevitable,' and perhaps not. I for one doubt that people would accept without complaint the warrantless disclosure to the government of a list of every Web site they had visited in the last week, or month, or year. But whatever the societal expectations, they can attain constitutionally protected status only if our Fourth Amendment jurisprudence ceases to treat secrecy as a prerequisite for privacy. I would not assume that all information voluntarily disclosed to some member of the public for a limited purpose is, for that reason alone, disentitled to Fourth Amendment protection. See Smith (Marshall, J., dissenting) ("Privacy is not a discrete commodity, possessed absolutely or not at all. Those who disclose certain facts to a bank or phone company for a limited business purpose need not assume that this information will be released to other persons for other purposes.").

Lower courts sensitive to the concerns raised by Justice Sotomayor often highlight a distinction between a digital communication's content and non-content information. This distinction parallels a factor emphasized in *Smith v. Maryland*: "Although petitioner's conduct may have been calculated to keep the *contents* of his conversation private, his conduct was not and could not have been calculated to preserve the privacy of the number he dialed." Citing this distinction, courts typically resist arguments that third-party doctrine eliminates Fourth Amendment protection from the contents of an email or text message obtained from a service provider such as Verizon, as opposed to the non-content addressee information or the time and date the message was sent. That said, the courts have not clarified the precise role that the content/non-content distinction plays. And if the message's recipient (not Verizon) discloses the contents of a text message to the government, a court will likely apply third-party doctrine to conclude that there was no Fourth Amendment violation.

In addition, even non-content information can be revealing. And some information blurs the content and non-content categories, such as a Google search history or a URL that identifies both an Internet site address and (indirectly) its content. In light of this uncertainty, legislators have acted to fill the perceived gap in Fourth Amendment protection, enacting complex statutes like the federal Stored Communications Act (SCA). These laws regulate when and how companies like Google and Verizon can disclose user information even to the government.

As explained by one scholar:

> "The SCA addresses [the poor fit between the Fourth Amendment and digital communication] by offering network account holders a range of statutory privacy rights against access to stored account information held by network service providers. The statute creates a set of Fourth Amendment-like privacy protections by statute, regulating the relationship between government investigators and service providers in possession of users' private information. It does this in two ways. First, the statute creates limits on the government's ability to compel providers to disclose information in their possession about their customers and subscribers. Although the Fourth Amendment may require no more than a subpoena to obtain e-mails, the statute confers greater privacy protection. Second, the statute places limits on the ability of ISPs [Internet Service Providers] to voluntarily disclose information about their customers and subscribers to the government."[1]

---

[1] Orin Kerr, A User's Guide to the Stored Communications Act, 72 Geo. Wash. L. Rev. 1208 (2004).

As we will see in a later case, however, statutes like the SCA typically do not provide the same protection that would be available under the Fourth Amendment. Consequently, even when the government complies with a governing statute, the resulting disclosure may nevertheless violate the Fourth Amendment.

3. EXPOSED TO THE PUBLIC

> "What a person knowingly exposes to the public, even in his own home or office, is not a subject of Fourth Amendment protection." *Katz v. U.S.*

As the next cases illustrate, when police gather information that is exposed to the public, there is no "search" under the Reasonable Expectation of Privacy test.

UNITED STATES v. KARO
468 U.S. 705 (1984)

Justice WHITE delivered the opinion of the Court.

In United States v. Knotts (1983), we held that the warrantless monitoring of an electronic tracking device ("beeper") inside a container of chemicals did not violate the Fourth Amendment when it revealed no information that could not have been obtained through visual surveillance. In this case, we are called upon to address two questions left unresolved in Knotts: (1) whether installation of a beeper in a container of chemicals with the consent of the original owner constitutes a search or seizure within the meaning of the Fourth Amendment when the container is delivered to a buyer having no knowledge of the presence of the beeper, and (2) whether monitoring of a beeper falls within the ambit of the Fourth Amendment when it reveals information that could not have been obtained through visual surveillance.

I

In August 1980, Agent Rottinger of the Drug Enforcement Administration (DEA) learned that respondents James Karo, Richard Horton, and William Harley had ordered 50 gallons of ether from Government informant Carl Muehlenweg of Graphic Photo Design in Albuquerque, New Mexico. Muehlenweg told Rottinger that the ether was to be used to extract cocaine from clothing that had been imported into the United States. The Government obtained a court order authorizing the installation and monitoring of a beeper in one of the cans of ether.

With Muehlenweg's consent, agents substituted their own can containing a beeper for one of the cans in the shipment and then had all 10 cans painted to give them a uniform appearance.

On September 20, 1980, agents saw Karo pick up the ether from Muehlenweg. They then followed Karo to his house using visual and beeper surveillance. At one point later that day, agents determined by using the beeper that the ether was still inside the house, but they later determined that it had been moved undetected to Horton's house, where they located it using the beeper. Agent Rottinger could smell the ether from the public sidewalk near Horton's residence. Two days later, agents discovered that the ether had once again been moved, and, using the beeper, they located it at the residence of Horton's father. The next day, the beeper was no longer transmitting from Horton's father's house, and agents traced the beeper to a commercial storage facility....

...Respondents Karo, Horton, Harley, Steele, and Roth were indicted for conspiring to possess cocaine with intent to distribute it and with the underlying offense.... We granted the Government's petition for certiorari, which raised the question whether a warrant was required to authorize either the installation of the beeper or its subsequent monitoring....

II

Because the judgment below in favor of Karo rested in major part on the conclusion that the installation violated his Fourth Amendment rights and that any information obtained from monitoring the beeper was tainted by the initial illegality, we must deal with the legality of the warrantless installation. It is clear that the actual placement of the beeper into the can violated no one's Fourth Amendment rights. The can into which the beeper was placed belonged at the time to the DEA, and by no stretch of the imagination could it be said that respondents then had any legitimate expectation of privacy in it. The ether and the original 10 cans, on the other hand, belonged to, and were in the possession of, Muehlenweg, who had given his consent to any invasion of those items that occurred. Thus, even if there had been no substitution of cans and the agents had placed the beeper into one of the original 10 cans, Muehlenweg's consent was sufficient to validate the placement of the beeper in the can.

The Court of Appeals acknowledged that before Karo took control of the ether "the DEA and Muehlenweg presumably could do with the can and ether whatever they liked without violating Karo's rights." It did not hold that the actual placement of the beeper into the ether can violated the Fourth Amendment. Instead, it held that the violation occurred at the time the beeper-laden can was transferred to Karo....

Not surprisingly, the Court of Appeals did not describe the transfer as either a "search" or a "seizure," for plainly it is neither. A "search" occurs "when an expectation of privacy that society is prepared to consider reasonable is infringed." The mere transfer to Karo of a can containing an unmonitored beeper infringed no privacy interest. It conveyed no information that Karo wished to keep private, for it conveyed no information at all. To be sure, it created a potential for an invasion of privacy, but we have never held that potential, as opposed to actual, invasions of privacy constitute searches for purposes of the Fourth Amendment. A holding to that effect would mean that a policeman walking down the street carrying a parabolic microphone capable of picking up conversations in nearby homes would be engaging in a search even if the microphone were not turned on. It is the exploitation of technological advances that implicates the Fourth Amendment, not their mere existence.

We likewise do not believe that the transfer of the container constituted a seizure. A "seizure" of property occurs when "there is some meaningful interference with an individual's possessory interests in that property." Although the can may have contained an unknown and unwanted foreign object, it cannot be said that anyone's possessory interest was interfered with in a meaningful way. At most, there was a technical trespass on the space occupied by the beeper....

We conclude that no Fourth Amendment interest of Karo or of any other respondent was infringed by the installation of the beeper. Rather, any impairment of their privacy interests that may have occurred was occasioned by the monitoring of the beeper.

III

In United States v. Knotts, law enforcement officials, with the consent of the seller, installed a beeper in a 5–gallon can of chloroform and monitored the beeper after delivery of the can to the buyer in Minneapolis, Minn. Although there was partial visual surveillance as the automobile containing the can moved along the public highways, the beeper enabled the officers to locate the can in the area of a cabin near Shell Lake, Wis., and it was this information that provided the basis for the issuance of a search warrant. As the case came to us, the installation of the beeper was not challenged; only the monitoring was at issue. The Court held that since the movements of the automobile and the arrival of the can containing the beeper in the area of the cabin could have been observed by the naked eye, no Fourth Amendment violation was committed by monitoring the beeper during the trip to the cabin. In Knotts, the record did not show that the beeper was monitored while the can containing it was inside the cabin, and we therefore had no occasion to consider whether a constitutional violation would have occurred had the fact been otherwise.

Here, there is no gainsaying that the beeper was used to locate the ether in a specific house in Taos, N.M., and that that information was in turn used to secure a warrant for the search of the house. The affidavit supporting the application for a search warrant recited that the ether arrived at the residence in a motor vehicle that later departed and that:

> "For fear of detection, we did not maintain tight surveillance of the residence.... Using the 'beeper' locator, I positively determined that the 'beeper' can (5–gallon can of ether, described earlier in this affidavit) was now inside the above-described premises to be searched because the 'beeper' locator (direction finder) pinpointed the beeper signal as emanating from the above-described premises.... Again, later on Saturday (now in the daytime), 7 February 1981, my 'beeper' locator still shows a strong 'beeper' signal emanating from inside the above-described residence."

This case thus presents the question whether the monitoring of a beeper in a private residence, a location not open to visual surveillance, violates the Fourth Amendment rights of those who have a justifiable interest in the privacy of the residence. Contrary to the submission of the United States, we think that it does.

At the risk of belaboring the obvious, private residences are places in which the individual normally expects privacy free of governmental intrusion not authorized by a warrant, and that expectation is plainly one that society is prepared to recognize as justifiable.... In this case, had a DEA agent thought it useful to enter the Taos residence to verify that the ether was actually in the house and had he done so surreptitiously and without a warrant, there is little doubt that he would have engaged in an unreasonable search within the meaning of the Fourth Amendment.

For purposes of the Amendment, the result is the same where, without a warrant, the Government surreptitiously employs an electronic device to obtain information that it could not have obtained by observation from outside the curtilage of the house. The beeper tells the agent that a particular article is actually located at a particular time in the private residence and is in the possession of the person or persons whose residence is being watched. Even if visual surveillance has revealed that the article to which the beeper is attached has entered the house, the later monitoring not only verifies the officers' observations but also establishes that the article remains on the premises….

The monitoring of an electronic device such as a beeper is, of course, less intrusive than a full-scale search, but it does reveal a critical fact about the interior of the premises that the Government is extremely interested in knowing and that it could not have otherwise obtained without a warrant. The case is thus not like Knotts, for there the beeper told the authorities nothing about the interior of Knotts' cabin. The information obtained in Knotts was "voluntarily conveyed to anyone who wanted to look …"; here, as we have said, the monitoring indicated that the beeper was inside the house, a fact that could not have been visually verified….

In sum, we discern no reason for deviating from the general rule that a search of a house should be conducted pursuant to a warrant.

The distinction the Court draws between *Karo* and *Knotts* is critical to understanding this line of cases. Here is a brief excerpt from the *Knotts* opinion to further clarify that distinction.

United States v. Knotts
460 U.S. 276 (1983)

"A police car following [the car driven by one of the co-defendants] at a distance throughout his journey could have observed him leaving the public highway and arriving at the cabin owned by respondent, with the drum of chloroform still in the car. This fact, along with others, was used by the government in obtaining a search warrant which led to the discovery of the clandestine drug laboratory. But there is no indication that the beeper was used in any way to reveal information as to the

> movement of the drum within the cabin, or in any way that would not have been visible to the naked eye from outside the cabin...."

The next cases illustrate that "exposed to the public" is a broad concept capturing even observations that are unlikely to be made by members of the public, so long as they are (in the Court's view) hypothetically plausible.

CALIFORNIA v. GREENWOOD
486 U.S. 35 (1988)

Justice WHITE delivered the opinion of the Court.

The issue here is whether the Fourth Amendment prohibits the warrantless search and seizure of garbage left for collection outside the curtilage of a home. We conclude, in accordance with the vast majority of lower courts that have addressed the issue, that it does not.

I

In early 1984, Investigator Jenny Stracner of the Laguna Beach Police Department received information indicating that respondent Billy Greenwood might be engaged in narcotics trafficking. Stracner learned that a criminal suspect had informed a federal drug enforcement agent in February 1984 that a truck filled with illegal drugs was en route to the Laguna Beach address at which Greenwood resided. In addition, a neighbor complained of heavy vehicular traffic late at night in front of Greenwood's single-family home. The neighbor reported that the vehicles remained at Greenwood's house for only a few minutes.

Stracner sought to investigate this information by conducting a surveillance of Greenwood's home. She observed several vehicles make brief stops at the house during the late-night and early morning hours, and she followed a truck from the house to a residence that had previously been under investigation as a narcotics-trafficking location.

On April 6, 1984, Stracner asked the neighborhood's regular trash collector to pick up the plastic garbage bags that Greenwood had left on the curb in front of his house and to turn the bags over to her without mixing their contents with garbage from other houses. The trash collector cleaned his truck bin of other refuse, collected the garbage bags from the street in front of Greenwood's house, and turned the bags over to Stracner. The officer searched through the rubbish and found items indicative of narcotics use....

On May 4, Investigator Robert Rahaeuser obtained Greenwood's garbage from the regular trash collector in the same manner as had Stracner. The garbage again contained evidence of narcotics use....

II

The warrantless search and seizure of the garbage bags left at the curb outside the Greenwood house would violate the Fourth Amendment only if respondents manifested a subjective expectation of privacy in their garbage that society accepts as objectively reasonable. Respondents do not disagree with this standard. They assert, however, that they had, and exhibited, an expectation of privacy with respect to the trash that was searched by the police: The trash, which was placed on the street for collection at a fixed time, was contained in opaque plastic bags, which the garbage collector was expected to pick up, mingle with the trash of others, and deposit at the garbage dump. The trash was only temporarily on the street, and there was little likelihood that it would be inspected by anyone.

It may well be that respondents did not expect that the contents of their garbage bags would become known to the police or other members of the public. An expectation of privacy does not give rise to Fourth Amendment protection, however, unless society is prepared to accept that expectation as objectively reasonable.

Here, we conclude that respondents exposed their garbage to the public sufficiently to defeat their claim to Fourth Amendment protection. It is common knowledge that plastic garbage bags left on or at the side of a public street are readily accessible to animals, children, scavengers, snoops, and other members of the public. Moreover, respondents placed their refuse at the curb for the express purpose of conveying it to a third party, the trash collector, who might himself have sorted through respondents' trash or permitted others, such as the police, to do so. Accordingly, having deposited their garbage in an area particularly suited for public inspection and, in a manner of speaking, public consumption, for the express purpose of having strangers take it, respondents could have had no reasonable expectation of privacy in the inculpatory items that they discarded.

Furthermore, as we have held, the police cannot reasonably be expected to avert their eyes from evidence of criminal activity that could have been observed by any member of the public. Hence, "[w]hat a person knowingly exposes to the public, even in his own home or office, is not a subject of Fourth Amendment protection." Katz v. United States. We held in Smith v. Maryland (1979), for example, that the police did not violate the Fourth Amendment by causing a pen register to be installed at the telephone company's offices to record the telephone numbers dialed by a criminal suspect. An individual has no legitimate expectation of privacy in the numbers dialed on his telephone, we reasoned, because he voluntarily conveys those numbers to the telephone company when he uses the telephone. Again, we observed that "a person has no legitimate expectation of privacy in information he voluntarily turns over to third parties."... Our conclusion that society would not accept as reasonable respondents' claim to an expectation of privacy in trash left for collection in an area accessible to the public is reinforced by the unanimous rejection of similar claims by the Federal Courts of Appeals....

Justice BRENNAN, with whom Justice MARSHALL joins, dissenting.

Every week for two months, and at least once more a month later, the Laguna Beach police clawed through the trash that respondent Greenwood left in opaque, sealed bags on the curb outside his home. Complete strangers minutely scrutinized their bounty, undoubtedly dredging up intimate details of Greenwood's private life and habits. The intrusions proceeded without a warrant, and no court before or since has concluded that the police acted on probable cause to believe Greenwood was engaged in any criminal activity.

Scrutiny of another's trash is contrary to commonly accepted notions of civilized behavior. I suspect, therefore, that members of our society will be shocked to learn that the Court, the ultimate guarantor of liberty, deems unreasonable our expectation that the aspects of our private lives that are concealed safely in a trash bag will not become public....

CALIFORNIA v. CIRAOLO
476 U.S. 207 (1986)

Chief Justice BURGER delivered the opinion of the Court.

We granted certiorari to determine whether the Fourth Amendment is violated by aerial observation without a warrant from an altitude of 1,000 feet of a fenced-in backyard within the curtilage of a home.

I

On September 2, 1982, Santa Clara Police received an anonymous telephone tip that marijuana was growing in respondent, Dante Ciraolo's backyard. Police were unable to observe the contents of respondent's yard from ground level because of a 6-foot outer fence and a 10-foot inner fence completely enclosing the yard. Later that day, Officer Shutz, who was assigned to investigate, secured a private plane and flew over respondent's house at an altitude of 1,000 feet, within navigable airspace; he was accompanied by Officer Rodriguez. Both officers were trained in marijuana identification. From the overflight, the officers readily identified marijuana plants 8 feet to 10 feet in height growing in a 15- by 25-foot plot in respondent's yard; they photographed the area with a standard 35mm camera....

The State argues that respondent has "knowingly exposed" his backyard to aerial observation, because all that was seen was visible to the naked eye from any aircraft flying overhead. The State analogizes its mode of observation to a knothole or opening in a fence: if there is an opening, the police may look.

The California Court of Appeal … accepted the analysis that unlike the casual observation of a private person flying overhead, this flight was focused specifically on a small suburban yard, and was not the result of any routine patrol overflight. Respondent contends he has done all that can reasonably be expected to tell the world he wishes to maintain the privacy of his garden within the curtilage without covering his yard. Such covering, he argues, would defeat its purpose as an outside living area; he asserts he has not "knowingly" exposed himself to aerial views.

II

The touchstone of Fourth Amendment analysis is whether a person has a constitutionally protected reasonable expectation of privacy. Katz posits a two-part inquiry: first, has the individual manifested a subjective expectation of privacy in the object of the challenged search? Second, is society willing to recognize that expectation as reasonable?

Clearly—and understandably—respondent has met the test of manifesting his own subjective intent and desire to maintain privacy as to his unlawful agricultural pursuits.... It can reasonably be assumed that the 10-foot fence was placed to conceal the marijuana crop from at least street-level views. So far as the normal sidewalk traffic was concerned, this fence served that purpose, because respondent took normal precautions to maintain his privacy.

Yet a 10-foot fence might not shield these plants from the eyes of a citizen or a policeman perched on the top of a truck or a two-level bus. Whether respondent therefore manifested a subjective expectation of privacy from all observations of his backyard, or whether instead he manifested merely a hope that no one would observe his unlawful gardening pursuits, is not entirely clear in these circumstances. Respondent appears to challenge the authority of government to observe his activity from any vantage point or place if the viewing is motivated by a law enforcement purpose, and not the result of a casual, accidental observation.

We turn, therefore, to the second inquiry under Katz, i.e., whether that expectation is reasonable. In pursuing this inquiry, we must keep in mind that the test of legitimacy is not whether the individual chooses to conceal assertedly "private" activity, but instead whether the government's intrusion infringes upon the personal and societal values protected by the Fourth Amendment.

Respondent argues that because his yard was in the curtilage of his home, no governmental aerial observation is permissible under the Fourth Amendment without a warrant. The history and genesis of the curtilage doctrine are instructive. At common law, the curtilage is the area to which extends the intimate activity associated with the "sanctity of a man's home and the privacies of life." The protection afforded the curtilage is essentially a protection of families and personal privacy in an area intimately linked to the home, both physically and psychologically, where privacy expectations are most heightened. The claimed area here was immediately adjacent to a suburban home, surrounded by high double fences. This close nexus to the home would appear to encompass this small area within the curtilage. Accepting, as the State does, that this yard and its crop fall within the curtilage, the question remains whether naked-eye observation of the curtilage by police from an aircraft lawfully operating at an altitude of 1,000 feet violates an expectation of privacy that is reasonable.

That the area is within the curtilage does not itself bar all police observation. The Fourth Amendment protection of the home has never been extended to require law enforcement officers to shield their eyes when passing by a home on public thoroughfares. Nor does the mere fact that an individual has taken measures to restrict some views of his activities preclude an officer's observations from a public vantage point where he has a right to be and which renders the activities clearly visible. "What a person knowingly exposes to the public, even in his own home or office, is not a subject of Fourth Amendment protection."

The observations by Officers Shutz and Rodriguez in this case took place within public navigable airspace, in a physically nonintrusive manner; from this point they were able to observe plants readily discernible to the naked eye as marijuana. That the observation from aircraft was directed at identifying the plants and the officers were trained to recognize marijuana is irrelevant. Such observation is precisely what a judicial officer needs to provide a basis for a warrant. Any member of the public flying in this airspace who glanced down could have seen everything that these officers observed. On this record, we readily conclude that respondent's expectation that his garden was protected from such observation is unreasonable and is not an expectation that society is prepared to honor.

…. In an age where private and commercial flight in the public airways is routine, it is unreasonable for respondent to expect that his marijuana plants were constitutionally protected from being observed with the naked eye from an altitude of 1,000 feet. The Fourth Amendment simply does not require the police traveling in the public airways at this altitude to obtain a warrant in order to observe what is visible to the naked eye.

The Supreme Court considered a similar fact pattern in ***Florida v. Riley*** (1989). The facts were as follows:

> "This case originated with an anonymous tip to the Sheriff's office that marijuana was being grown on respondent's property. When an investigating officer discovered that he could not see the contents of the greenhouse from the road, he circled twice over respondent's property in a helicopter at the height of 400 feet. With his naked eye, he was able to see through the openings in the roof and one or more of the open sides of the greenhouse and to identify what he thought was marijuana growing in the structure."

The plurality opinion signed by four Justices found this not to be a search emphasizing the similarity to *Ciraolo*: "the helicopter in this case was not violating the law" and "there was no undue noise, and no wind, dust, or threat of injury" from the helicopter's overflight.

Justice O'Connor added the fifth vote deeming the observations obtained through the helicopter's circling not to be a search. She wrote a separate opinion, however, because, in her view, the plurality rested "too heavily on [the helicopter's] compliance with FAA regulations whose purpose is to promote air safety" not protect privacy. She explained that "Ciraolo's expectation of privacy was unreasonable not because the airplane was operating where it had a 'right to be,' but because public air travel at 1,000 feet is a sufficiently routine part of modern life that it is unreasonable for persons on the ground to expect that their curtilage will not be observed from the air at that altitude." Similarly, in *Riley*, Justice O'Connor felt there was no search "because there is reason to believe that there is considerable public use of airspace at altitudes of 400 feet and above, and because Riley introduced no evidence to the contrary."

There are limits to how far the Court will stretch the "exposed to the public" concept. As the next cases show, those limits typically parallel Justice O'Connor's suggestion in *Florida v. Riley*. At some point, a police officer's conduct strays so far from what we would expect members of the public to do, that the information obtained by the officer will not be deemed to have been "exposed to the public."

BOND v. UNITED STATES
529 U.S. 334 (2000)

Chief Justice REHNQUIST delivered the opinion of the Court.

This case presents the question whether a law enforcement officer's physical manipulation of a [Greyhound] bus passenger's carry-on luggage violated the Fourth Amendment's proscription against unreasonable searches. We hold that it did....

As Agent Cantu inspected the luggage in the compartment above petitioner Steven Bond's seat, he squeezed a green canvas bag and noticed that it contained a "brick-like" object....

Here, petitioner concedes that, by placing his bag in the overhead compartment, he could expect that it would be exposed to certain kinds of touching and handling. But petitioner argues that Agent Cantu's physical manipulation of his luggage "far exceeded the casual contact petitioner could have expected from other passengers." The Government counters that it did not.

Our Fourth Amendment analysis embraces two questions. First, we ask whether the individual, by his conduct, has exhibited an actual expectation of privacy; that is, whether he has shown that he sought to preserve something as private. Here, petitioner sought to preserve privacy by using an opaque bag and placing that bag directly above his seat. Second, we inquire whether the individual's expectation of privacy is one that society is prepared to recognize as reasonable. When a bus passenger places a bag in an overhead bin, he expects that other passengers or bus employees may move it for one reason or another. Thus, a bus passenger clearly expects that his bag may be handled. He does not expect that other passengers or bus employees will, as a matter of course, feel the bag in an exploratory manner. But this is exactly what the agent did here. We therefore hold that the agent's physical manipulation of petitioner's bag violated the Fourth Amendment. [*Ed. Note*: The agent did not have a warrant or any basis to believe the luggage contained evidence of a crime.]

KYLLO v. UNITED STATES
533 U.S. 27 (2001)

Justice SCALIA delivered the opinion of the Court.

This case presents the question whether the use of a thermal-imaging device aimed at a private home from a public street to detect relative amounts of heat within the home constitutes a "search" within the meaning of the Fourth Amendment.

I

In 1991 Agent William Elliott of the United States Department of the Interior came to suspect that marijuana was being grown in the home belonging to petitioner Danny Kyllo, part of a triplex on Rhododendron Drive in Florence, Oregon.

Indoor marijuana growth typically requires high-intensity lamps. In order to determine whether an amount of heat was emanating from petitioner's home consistent with the use of such lamps, at 3:20 a.m. on January 16, 1992, Agent Elliott and Dan Haas used an Agema Thermovision 210 thermal imager to scan the triplex.

Agema Thermovision Infrared Camera

Thermal imagers detect infrared radiation, which virtually all objects emit but which is not visible to the naked eye. The imager converts radiation into images based on relative warmth—black is cool, white is hot, shades of gray connote relative differences; in that respect, it operates somewhat like a video camera showing heat images. The scan of Kyllo's home took

Images at issue in Kyllo

only a few minutes and was performed from the passenger seat of Agent Elliott's vehicle across the street from the front of the house and also from the street in back of the house. The scan showed that the roof over the garage and a side wall of petitioner's home were relatively hot compared to the rest of the home and substantially warmer than neighboring homes in the triplex. Agent Elliott concluded that petitioner was using halide lights to grow marijuana in his house, which indeed he was. Based on tips from informants, utility bills, and the thermal imaging, a Federal Magistrate Judge issued a warrant authorizing a search of petitioner's home, and the agents found an indoor growing operation involving more than 100 plants. Petitioner was indicted on one count of manufacturing marijuana…. He unsuccessfully moved to suppress the evidence seized from his home and then entered a conditional guilty plea.

The Court of Appeals for the Ninth Circuit remanded the case for an evidentiary hearing regarding the intrusiveness of thermal imaging. On remand the District Court found that the Agema 210 "is a non-intrusive device which emits no rays or beams and shows a crude visual image of the heat being radiated from the outside of the house"; it "did not show any people or activity within the walls of the structure"; "the device used cannot penetrate walls or windows to reveal conversations or human activities"; and "no intimate details of the home were observed." Based on these findings, the District Court upheld the validity of the warrant that relied in part upon the thermal imaging, and reaffirmed its denial of the motion to suppress….

II

…. At the very core of the Fourth Amendment "stands the right of a man to retreat into his own home and there be free from unreasonable governmental intrusion." With few exceptions, the question whether a warrantless search of a home is reasonable and hence constitutional must be answered no.

On the other hand, the antecedent question whether or not a Fourth Amendment "search" has occurred is not so simple under our precedent. The permissibility of ordinary visual surveillance of a home used to be clear because, well into the 20th century, our Fourth Amendment jurisprudence was tied to common-law trespass. Visual surveillance was unquestionably lawful because "the eye cannot by the laws of England be guilty of a trespass." We have since decoupled violation of a person's Fourth Amendment rights from trespassory violation of his property, but the lawfulness of warrantless visual surveillance of a home has still been preserved. As we observed in California v. Ciraolo (1986), "the Fourth Amendment protection of the home has never been extended to require law enforcement officers to shield their eyes when passing by a home on public thoroughfares."

One might think that the new validating rationale would be that examining the portion of a house that is in plain public view, while it is a "search" despite the absence of trespass, is not an "unreasonable" one under the Fourth Amendment.

But in fact we have held that visual observation is no "search" at all—perhaps in order to preserve somewhat more intact our doctrine that warrantless searches are presumptively unconstitutional. In assessing when a search is not a search, we have applied somewhat in reverse the principle first enunciated in Katz.... As Justice Harlan's oft-quoted concurrence described it, a Fourth Amendment search occurs when the government violates a subjective expectation of privacy that society recognizes as reasonable. We have subsequently applied this principle to hold that a Fourth Amendment search does not occur—even when the explicitly protected location of a house is concerned—unless "the individual manifested a subjective expectation of privacy in the object of the challenged search," and "society is willing to recognize that expectation as reasonable."...

The present case involves officers on a public street engaged in more than naked-eye surveillance of a home. We have previously reserved judgment as to how much technological enhancement of ordinary perception from such a vantage point, if any, is too much....

III

It would be foolish to contend that the degree of privacy secured to citizens by the Fourth Amendment has been entirely unaffected by the advance of technology. For example, as the cases discussed above make clear, the technology enabling human flight has exposed to public view (and hence, we have said, to official observation) uncovered portions of the house and its curtilage that once were private. The question we confront today is what limits there are upon this power of technology to shrink the realm of guaranteed privacy.

The Katz test—whether the individual has an expectation of privacy that society is prepared to recognize as reasonable—has often been criticized as circular, and hence subjective and unpredictable. While it may be difficult to refine Katz when the search of areas such as telephone booths, automobiles, or even the curtilage and uncovered portions of residences is at issue, in the case of the search of the interior of homes—the prototypical and hence most commonly litigated area of protected privacy—there is a ready criterion, with roots deep in the common law, of the minimal expectation of privacy that exists, and that is acknowledged to be reasonable. To withdraw protection of this minimum expectation would be to permit police technology to erode the privacy guaranteed by the Fourth Amendment. We think that obtaining by sense-enhancing technology any information regarding the interior of the home that could not otherwise have been obtained without physical "intrusion into a constitutionally protected area," constitutes a search—at least where (as here) the technology in question is not in general public use. This assures preservation of that degree of privacy against government that existed when the Fourth Amendment was adopted. On the basis of this criterion, the information obtained by the thermal imager in this case was the product of a search.

The Government maintains, however, that the thermal imaging must be upheld because it detected "only heat radiating from the external surface of the house." The dissent makes this its leading point, contending that there is a fundamental difference between what it calls "off-the-wall" observations and "through-the-wall surveillance." But just as a thermal imager captures only heat emanating from a house, so also a powerful directional microphone picks up only sound emanating from a house-and a satellite capable of scanning from many miles away would pick up only visible light emanating from a house. We rejected such a mechanical interpretation of the Fourth Amendment in Katz, where the eavesdropping device picked up only sound waves that reached the exterior of the phone booth. Reversing that approach would leave the homeowner at the mercy of advancing technology—including imaging technology that could discern all human activity in the home. While the technology used in the present case was relatively crude, the rule we adopt must take account of more sophisticated systems that are already in use or in development....

The Government also contends that the thermal imaging was constitutional because it did not "detect private activities occurring in private areas."... The Fourth Amendment's protection of the home has never been tied to measurement of the quality or quantity of information obtained.... In the home, our cases show, all details are intimate details, because the entire area is held safe from prying government eyes....[6]

---

[6] The dissent argues that we have injected potential uncertainty into the constitutional analysis by noting that whether or not the technology is in general public use may be a factor. That quarrel, however, is not with us but with this Court's precedent. See California v. Ciraolo (1986) ("In an age where private and commercial flight in the public airways is routine, it is unreasonable for respondent to expect that his marijuana plants were constitutionally protected from being observed with the naked eye from an altitude of 1,000 feet"). Given that we can quite confidently say that thermal imaging is not "routine," we decline in this case to reexamine that factor.

We have said that the Fourth Amendment draws "a firm line at the entrance to the house." That line, we think, must be not only firm but also bright—which requires clear specification of those methods of surveillance that require a warrant. While it is certainly possible to conclude from the videotape of the thermal imaging that occurred in this case that no "significant" compromise of the homeowner's privacy has occurred, we must take the long view, from the original meaning of the Fourth Amendment forward.

The Fourth Amendment is to be construed in the light of what was deemed an unreasonable search and seizure when it was adopted, and in a manner which will conserve public interests as well as the interests and rights of individual citizens. Where, as here, the Government uses a device that is not in general public use, to explore details of the home that would previously have been unknowable without physical intrusion, the surveillance is a "search" and is presumptively unreasonable without a warrant....

It is important to consider the vantage point from which police make a challenged observation. For example, an officer standing on a public sidewalk could observe someone open the door to their home and walk inside; that would not be a "search" even if the officer, during that observation, saw items that were inside the home. But the officer could not follow the person into the home and then look around, claiming that the interior of the home had been "exposed to the public." This means that "exposed to the public" cases often turn on an assessment of whether the police violated the Fourth Amendment in arriving at the spot where they made their observations. And, as the next cases illustrate, that assessment often depends on whether the police were standing in the "curtilage" or an "open field."

OLIVER v. UNITED STATES
466 U.S. 170 (1984)

Justice POWELL delivered the opinion of the Court.

The "open fields" doctrine, first enunciated by this Court in Hester v. United States (1924), permits police officers to enter and search a field without a warrant. We granted certiorari ... to clarify confusion that has arisen as to the continued vitality of the doctrine.

I

Acting on reports that marihuana was being raised on the farm of petitioner Ray Oliver, two narcotics agents of the Kentucky State Police went to the farm to investigate. Arriving at the farm, they drove past petitioner's house to a locked gate with a "No Trespassing" sign. A footpath led around one side of the gate. The agents walked around the gate and along the road for several hundred yards, passing a barn and a parked camper. At that point, someone standing in front of the camper shouted: "No hunting is allowed, come back up here." The officers shouted back that they were Kentucky State Police officers, but found no one when they returned to the camper. The officers resumed their investigation of the farm and found a field of marihuana over a mile from petitioner's home.

Petitioner was arrested and indicted for manufacturing a controlled substance. After a pretrial hearing, the District Court suppressed evidence of the discovery of the marihuana field. Applying Katz v. United States (1967), the court found that petitioner had a reasonable expectation that the field would remain private because petitioner "had done all that could be expected of him to assert his privacy in the area of farm that was searched." He had posted "No Trespassing" signs at regular intervals and had locked the gate at the entrance to the center of the farm. Further, the court noted that the field itself is highly secluded: it is bounded on all sides by woods, fences, and embankments and cannot be seen from any point of public access. The court concluded that this was not an "open" field that invited casual intrusion. The Court of Appeals for the Sixth Circuit, sitting en banc, reversed the District Court. The court concluded that Katz, upon which the District Court relied, had not impaired the vitality of the open fields doctrine of Hester. Rather, the open fields doctrine was entirely compatible with Katz' emphasis on privacy. The court reasoned that the "human relations that create the need for privacy do not ordinarily take place" in open fields, and that the property owner's common-law right to exclude trespassers is insufficiently linked to privacy to warrant the Fourth Amendment's protection. We granted certiorari....

II

The rule announced in Hester v. United States was founded upon the explicit language of the Fourth Amendment. That Amendment indicates with some precision the places and things encompassed by its protections. As Justice Holmes explained for the Court in his characteristically laconic style: "The special protection accorded by the Fourth Amendment to the people in their 'persons, houses, papers, and effects,' is not extended to the open fields. The distinction between the latter and the house is as old as the common law." Nor are the open fields "effects" within the meaning of the Fourth Amendment. In this respect, it is suggestive that James Madison's proposed draft of what became the Fourth Amendment preserves "[t]he rights of the people to be secured in their persons, their houses, their papers, and their other property, from all unreasonable searches and seizures...." Although Congress' revisions of Madison's proposal broadened the scope of the Amendment in some respects, the term "effects" is less inclusive than "property" and cannot be said to encompass open fields.[7]

We conclude, as did the Court in deciding Hester v. United States, that the government's intrusion upon the open fields is not one of those "unreasonable searches" proscribed by the text of the Fourth Amendment.

III

This interpretation of the Fourth Amendment's language is consistent with the understanding of the right to privacy expressed in our Fourth Amendment jurisprudence. Since Katz v. United States (1967), the touchstone of Fourth Amendment analysis has been the question whether a person has a "constitutionally protected reasonable expectation of privacy." The Amendment does not protect the merely subjective expectation of privacy, but only those expectations that society is prepared to recognize as "reasonable."

.... Open fields do not provide the setting for those intimate activities that the Amendment is intended to shelter from government interference or surveillance. There is no societal interest in protecting the privacy of those activities, such as the cultivation of crops, that occur in open fields. Moreover, as a practical matter these lands usually are accessible to the public and the police in ways that a home, an office, or commercial structure would not be. It is not generally true that fences or "No Trespassing" signs effectively bar the public from viewing open fields in rural areas. And ... the public and police lawfully may survey lands from the air. For

---

[7] The Framers would have understood the term "effects" to be limited to personal, rather than real, property.

these reasons, the asserted expectation of privacy in open fields is not an expectation that "society recognizes as reasonable."

The historical underpinnings of the open fields doctrine also demonstrate that the doctrine is consistent with respect for "reasonable expectations of privacy." As Justice Holmes, writing for the Court, observed in Hester, the common law distinguished "open fields" from the "curtilage," the land immediately surrounding and associated with the home. The distinction implies that only the curtilage, not the neighboring open fields, warrants the Fourth Amendment protections that attach to the home. At common law, the curtilage is the area to which extends the intimate activity associated with the "sanctity of a man's home and the privacies of life," and therefore has been considered part of home itself for Fourth Amendment purposes. Thus, courts have extended Fourth Amendment protection to the curtilage; and they have defined the curtilage, as did the common law, by reference to the factors that determine whether an individual reasonably may expect that an area immediately adjacent to the home will remain private. Conversely, the common law implies, as we reaffirm today, that no expectation of privacy legitimately attaches to open fields.

We conclude, from the text of the Fourth Amendment and from the historical and contemporary understanding of its purposes, that an individual has no legitimate expectation that open fields will remain free from warrantless intrusion by government officers…. We therefore affirm [the ruling of the Court of Appeals for the Sixth Circuit].

In a footnote, the *Oliver* majority elaborated on the imprecise phrase "open fields":

"The term 'open fields' may include any unoccupied or undeveloped area outside of the curtilage. An open field need be neither 'open' nor a 'field' as those terms are used in common speech. For example, a thickly wooded area nonetheless may be an open field as that term is used in construing the Fourth Amendment."

CURTILAGE

One practical definition of an "open field" is any outdoor space that is not "curtilage." That definition is only helpful, however, if we can precisely define curtilage. Here are three short summaries/excerpts from Supreme Court cases offering guidance on that question.

United States v. Dunn
480 U.S. 294 (1987)
Summary

Ronald Dunn challenged the warrantless entry by a Drug Enforcement Agency (DEA) agent onto his ranch property which was surrounded by livestock fencing. As the Supreme Court explained:

"A DEA agent crossed over the perimeter fence and one interior fence. Standing approximately midway between the residence and the barns, the DEA agent smelled what he believed to be phenylacetic acid, the odor coming from the direction of the barns. The officer proceeded to the larger barn, crossing another barbed wire fence as well as a wooden fence that enclosed the front portion of the barn. The officer walked under the barn's overhang to the locked wooden gates and, shining a flashlight through the netting on top of the gates, peered into the barn, [observing] a phenylacetone laboratory. The officer did not enter the barn."

The case turned on "whether the barn lay within the curtilage of the house." The barn is the darkened structure ("Pole Barn") at the top right of the map (below) and the house is depicted at the bottom right. To determine whether the officer's intrusion invaded the curtilage of the house, the Court set forth the following considerations:

"Drawing upon the Court's own cases and the cumulative experience of the lower courts that have grappled with the task of defining the extent of a home's curtilage, we believe that curtilage questions should be resolved with particular reference to four factors: [1] the proximity of the area claimed to be curtilage to the home, [2] whether the area is included within an enclosure surrounding the home, [3] the nature of the uses to which the area is put, and [4] the steps taken by the resident to protect the area from observation by people passing by. We do not suggest that combining these factors produces a finely tuned formula that, when mechanically applied, yields a 'correct' answer to all extent-of-curtilage questions. Rather, these factors are useful analytical tools only to the degree that, in any given case, they bear upon the centrally relevant consideration—whether the area in question is so intimately tied to the home itself that it should be placed under the home's umbrella of Fourth Amendment protection."

Applying these factors, the Court concluded that the officer had not intruded upon the home's curtilage, meaning that he had only walked through "open fields":

"There is no constitutional difference between police observations conducted while in a public place and while standing in the open fields…. The officer lawfully viewed the interior of respondent's barn, and his observations were properly considered by the Magistrate in issuing a search warrant for respondent's premises."

The District Court's opinion included the following map to illustrate the property

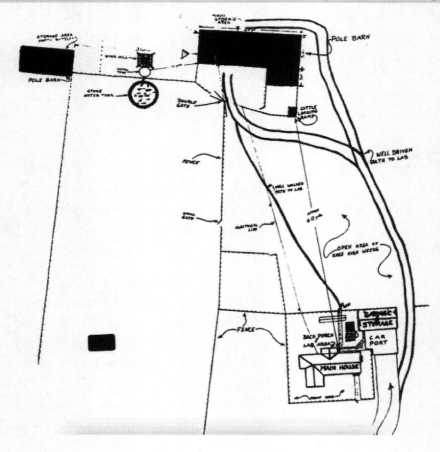

Florida v. Jardines
569 U.S. 1 (2013)

"When it comes to the Fourth Amendment, the home is first among equals. At the Amendment's very core stands 'the right of a man to retreat into his own home and there be free from unreasonable governmental intrusion.' This right would be of little practical value if the State's agents could stand in a home's porch or side garden and trawl for evidence with impunity; the right to retreat would be significantly diminished if the police could enter a man's property to observe his repose from just outside the front window.

We therefore regard the area immediately surrounding and associated with the home—what our cases call the curtilage—as part of the home itself for Fourth Amendment purposes. That principle has ancient and durable roots. Just as the distinction between the home and the open fields is 'as old as the common law,' so too is the identity of home and what Blackstone called the 'curtilage or homestall,' for the 'house protects and privileges all its branches and appurtenants.' This area around the home is 'intimately linked to the home, both physically and psychologically,' and is where 'privacy expectations are most heightened.' While the boundaries of the curtilage are generally clearly marked, the conception defining the curtilage is at any rate familiar enough that it is easily understood from our daily experience. Here there is no doubt that the officers entered it: The front porch is the classic exemplar of an area adjacent to the home and to which the activity of home life extends."

Collins v. Virginia
138 S.Ct. 1663 (2018)

"As an initial matter, we decide whether the part of the driveway where Collins' motorcycle was parked and subsequently searched is curtilage.

According to photographs in the record, the driveway runs alongside the front lawn and up a few yards past the front perimeter of the house. The top portion of the driveway that sits behind the front perimeter of the house is enclosed on two sides by a brick wall about the height of a car and on a third side by the house. A side door provides direct access between this partially enclosed section of the driveway and the house. A visitor endeavoring to reach the front door of the house would have to walk partway up the driveway, but would turn off before entering the enclosure and instead proceed up a set of steps leading to the front porch. When Officer Rhodes searched the motorcycle, it was parked inside this partially enclosed top portion of the driveway that abuts the house.

…. Just like the front porch, side garden, or area outside the front window, the driveway enclosure where Officer Rhodes searched the motorcycle constitutes 'an area adjacent to the home and to which the activity of home life extends,' and so is properly considered curtilage."

[*Ed. Note*: The photo below left is from the record in the case; the photo on the right (taken at a later time) shows the property from a wider angle.]

Here are some examples from lower courts discussing the curtilage concept:

- "Struckman's backyard—a small, enclosed yard adjacent to a home in a residential neighborhood—is unquestionably such a 'clearly marked' area 'to which the activity of home life extends,' and so is 'curtilage' subject to Fourth Amendment protection." *U.S. v. Struckman* (9th Cir. 2010)

- "We find that Moffitt's driveway and the yard in front of his house are not areas 'so intimately tied to the home' that they are protected curtilage. The first two [*Dunn*] factors weigh in favor of the area being curtilage, as the driveway was located directly next to the house, and Moffitt had enclosed the yard and house with a chain-link fence. However, the third factor-'the nature of uses to which the area is put'-weighs against this area being curtilage. Moffitt's driveway and front yard were access areas for visitors to enter and knock on the front door. With an open gate in an urban neighborhood, Moffitt could not have reasonably expected to keep neighbors, door-to-door salespeople, and trick or treaters from driving or walking to his house and approaching his front door. It follows therefrom that if he has a reasonable expectation that various members of society may enter his property, he should find it equally likely that the police, or a police-hired informant, will do so. We also find that Moffitt fails the fourth factor as he did not take 'steps ... to protect the area from outside observation.' While his yard is surrounded by a chain-link fence, on which hung four 'no trespassing' signs, this chain-link fence was see-through and did not protect the yard from outside observation." *U.S. v. Moffitt* (5th Cir. 2007)

4.   EXPOSING ONLY CONTRABAND

> "[G]overnmental conduct that *only* reveals the possession of contraband 'compromises no legitimate privacy interest.'" *Illinois v. Caballes*

ILLINOIS v. CABALLES
543 U.S. 405 (2005)

Justice STEVENS delivered the opinion of the Court.

Illinois State Trooper Daniel Gillette stopped respondent Roy Caballes for speeding on an interstate highway. When Gillette radioed the police dispatcher to report the stop, a second trooper, Craig Graham, a member of the Illinois State Police Drug Interdiction Team, overheard the transmission and immediately headed for the scene with his narcotics-detection dog. When they arrived, respondent's car was on the shoulder of the road and respondent was in Gillette's vehicle. While Gillette was in the process of writing a warning ticket, Graham walked his dog around respondent's car. The dog alerted at the trunk. Based on that alert, the officers searched the trunk, found marijuana, and arrested respondent. The entire incident lasted less than 10 minutes.

... The Illinois Supreme Court held that the initially lawful traffic stop became an unlawful seizure solely as a result of the canine sniff that occurred outside respondent's stopped car. That is, the court characterized the dog sniff as the cause rather than the consequence of a constitutional violation. In its view, the use of the dog converted the citizen-police encounter from a lawful traffic stop into a drug investigation, and because the shift in purpose was not supported by any reasonable suspicion that respondent possessed narcotics, it was unlawful. In our view, conducting a dog sniff would not change the character of a traffic stop that is lawful at its inception and otherwise executed in a reasonable manner, unless the dog sniff itself infringed respondent's constitutionally protected interest in privacy. Our cases hold that it did not.

Official conduct that does not "compromise any legitimate interest in privacy" is not a search subject to the Fourth Amendment. We have held that any interest in possessing contraband cannot be deemed "legitimate," and thus, governmental conduct that *only* reveals the possession of contraband compromises no legitimate privacy interest. This is because the expectation that certain facts will not come to the attention of the authorities is not the same as an interest in privacy that society is prepared to consider reasonable. In United States v. Place (1983), we treated a canine sniff by a well-trained narcotics-detection dog as "sui generis" because it "discloses only the presence or absence of narcotics, a contraband item." Respondent likewise concedes that "drug sniffs are designed, and if properly conducted are generally likely, to reveal only the presence of contraband." Although respondent argues that the error rates, particularly the existence of false positives, call into question the premise that drug-detection dogs alert only to contraband, the record contains no evidence or findings that support his argument. Moreover, respondent does not suggest that an erroneous alert, in and of itself, reveals any legitimate private information, and, in this case, the trial judge found that the dog sniff was sufficiently reliable to establish probable cause to conduct a full-blown search of the trunk. Accordingly, the use of a well-trained narcotics-detection dog—one that "does not expose noncontraband items that otherwise would remain hidden from public view"—during a lawful traffic stop, generally does not implicate legitimate privacy interests. In this case, the dog sniff was performed on the exterior of respondent's car while he was lawfully seized for a traffic violation. Any intrusion on respondent's privacy expectations does not rise to the level of a constitutionally cognizable infringement.

Before reading any further, think about how you might distinguish the dog sniff cases, *United States v. Place* and *Illinois v. Caballes*, from *Kyllo*.

Here is how the majority in *Caballes* distinguished *Kyllo*:

> " This conclusion [that the dog sniff is not a "search"] is entirely consistent with our recent decision that the use of a thermal-imaging device to detect the growth of marijuana in a home constituted an unlawful search. Kyllo v. United States (2001). Critical to that decision was the fact that the device was capable of detecting lawful activity—in that case, intimate details in a home, such as "at what hour each night the lady of the house takes her daily sauna and bath." The legitimate expectation that information about perfectly lawful activity will remain private is categorically distinguishable from respondent's hopes or expectations concerning the nondetection of contraband in the trunk of his car. A dog sniff conducted during a concededly lawful traffic stop that reveals no information other than the location of a substance that no individual has any right to possess does not violate the Fourth Amendment.

ARIZONA v. HICKS
480 U.S. 321 (1987)

Justice SCALIA delivered the opinion of the Court.

I[*]

On April 18, 1984, a bullet was fired through the floor of respondent James Hick's apartment, striking and injuring a man in the apartment below. Police officers arrived and entered respondent's apartment to search for the shooter, for other victims, and for weapons. They found and seized three weapons, including a sawed-off rifle, and in the course of their search also discovered a stocking-cap mask.

One of the policemen, Officer Nelson, noticed two sets of expensive stereo components, which seemed out of place in the squalid and otherwise ill-appointed four-room apartment. Suspecting that they were stolen, he read and recorded their serial numbers—moving some of the components, including a Bang and Olufsen turntable, in order to do so—which he then reported by phone to his headquarters.

---

[*] [*Ed. Note*: Unnecessary/redundant introductory material is omitted prior to the "I"; similar editing has occurred in subsequent opinion excerpts in this book that begin with a roman numeral.]

On being advised that the turntable had been taken in an armed robbery, he seized it immediately. It was later determined that some of the other serial numbers matched those on other stereo equipment taken in the same armed robbery, and a warrant was obtained and executed to seize that equipment as well. Respondent was subsequently indicted for the robbery.

The state trial court granted respondent's motion to suppress the evidence that had been seized. The Court of Appeals of Arizona affirmed. It was conceded that the initial entry and search, although warrantless, were justified by the exigent circumstance of the shooting. The Court of Appeals viewed the obtaining of the serial numbers, however, as an additional search, unrelated to that exigency. Relying upon a statement in Mincey v. Arizona (1978), that a "warrantless search must be 'strictly circumscribed by the exigencies which justify its initiation,'" the Court of Appeals held that the police conduct violated the Fourth Amendment, requiring the evidence derived from that conduct to be excluded....

II

As an initial matter, the State argues that Officer Nelson's actions constituted neither a "search" nor a "seizure" within the meaning of the Fourth Amendment. We agree that the mere recording of the serial numbers did not constitute a seizure. To be sure, that was the first step in a process by which respondent was eventually deprived of the stereo equipment. In and of itself, however, it did not "meaningfully interfere" with respondent's possessory interest in either the serial numbers or the equipment, and therefore did not amount to a seizure.

Officer Nelson's moving of the equipment, however, did constitute a "search" separate and apart from the search for the shooter, victims, and weapons that was the lawful objective of his entry into the apartment. Merely inspecting those parts of the turntable that came into view during the latter search would not have constituted an independent search, because it would have produced no additional invasion of respondent's privacy interest. But taking action, unrelated to the objectives of the authorized intrusion, which exposed to view concealed portions of the apartment or its contents, did produce a new invasion of respondent's privacy unjustified by the exigent circumstance that validated the entry. This is why, contrary to Justice Powell's suggestion, the "distinction between 'looking' at a suspicious object in plain view and 'moving' it even a few inches" is much more than trivial for purposes of the Fourth Amendment. It matters not that the search uncovered nothing of any great personal value to respondent—serial numbers rather than (what might conceivably have been hidden behind or under the equipment) letters or photographs. A search is a search, even if it happens to disclose nothing but the bottom of a turntable....

5. "NEAR PERFECT SURVEILLANCE"

CARPENTER v. UNITED STATES
138 S. Ct. 2206 (2018)

Chief Justice ROBERTS delivered the opinion of the Court.

This case presents the question whether the Government conducts a search under the Fourth Amendment when it accesses historical cell phone records that provide a comprehensive chronicle of the user's past movements.

I

A

There are 396 million cell phone service accounts in the United States—for a Nation of 326 million people. Cell phones perform their wide and growing variety of functions by connecting to a set of radio antennas called "cell sites." Although cell sites are usually mounted on a tower, they can also be found on light posts, flagpoles, church steeples, or the sides of buildings. Cell sites typically have several directional antennas that divide the covered area into sectors.

Cell phones continuously scan their environment looking for the best signal, which generally comes from the closest cell site. Most modern devices, such as smartphones, tap into the wireless network several times a minute whenever their signal is on, even if the owner is not using one of the phone's features. Each time the phone connects to a cell site, it generates a time-stamped record known as cell-site location information (CSLI). The precision of this information depends on the size of the geographic area covered by the cell site. The greater the concentration of cell sites, the smaller the coverage area....

Wireless carriers collect and store CSLI for their own business purposes, including finding weak spots in their network and applying "roaming" charges when another carrier routes data through their cell sites. In addition, wireless carriers often sell aggregated location records to data brokers, without individual identifying information of the sort at issue here. While carriers have long retained CSLI for the start and end of incoming calls, in recent years phone companies have also collected location information from the transmission of text messages and routine data connections. Accordingly, modern cell phones generate increasingly vast amounts of increasingly precise CSLI.

B

In 2011, police officers arrested four men suspected of robbing a series of Radio Shack and (ironically enough) T–Mobile stores in Detroit. One of the men confessed that, over the previous four months, the group (along with a rotating cast of getaway drivers and lookouts) had robbed nine different stores in Michigan and Ohio. The suspect identified 15 accomplices who had participated in the heists and gave the FBI some of their cell phone numbers; the FBI then reviewed his call records to identify additional numbers that he had called around the time of the robberies.

Based on that information, the prosecutors applied for court orders under the Stored Communications Act to obtain cell phone records for petitioner Timothy Carpenter and several other suspects. That statute, as amended in 1994, permits the Government to compel the disclosure of certain telecommunications records when it "offers specific and articulable facts showing that there are reasonable grounds to believe" that the records sought "are relevant and material to an ongoing criminal investigation." 18 U.S.C. § 2703(d). Federal Magistrate Judges issued two orders directing Carpenter's wireless carriers – MetroPCS and Sprint – to disclose "cell/site sector information for [Carpenter's] telephone at call origination and at call termination for incoming and outgoing calls" during the four-month period when the string of robberies occurred…. Altogether the Government obtained 12,898 location points cataloging Carpenter's movements—an average of 101 data points per day.

Carpenter was charged with six counts of robbery and an additional six counts of carrying a firearm during a federal crime of violence. Prior to trial, Carpenter moved to suppress the cell-site data provided by the wireless carriers. He argued that the Government's seizure of the records violated the Fourth Amendment because they had been obtained without a warrant supported by probable cause. The District Court denied the motion.

At trial, seven of Carpenter's confederates pegged him as the leader of the operation. In addition, FBI agent Christopher Hess offered expert testimony about the cell-site data. Hess explained that each time a cell phone taps into the wireless network, the carrier logs a time-stamped record of the cell site and particular sector that were used. With this information, Hess produced maps that placed Carpenter's phone near four of the charged robberies…. Carpenter was convicted on all but one of the firearm counts and sentenced to more than 100 years in prison….

Ed. Note: This is an excerpt of the map referenced by the Court. The S represents the location of one of the Radio Shacks that was robbed. The large dots represent two nearby Metro PCS towers. The robbery occurred at 10:35 a.m. on December 13. Agent Hess testified that the CSLI records showed that Carpenter's cell phone accessed the bottom left tower at 10:24 a.m. and the top right tower at 10:31 a.m.

II

A

The Fourth Amendment protects "[t]he right of the people to be secure in their persons, houses, papers, and effects, against unreasonable searches and seizures." The "basic purpose of this Amendment," our cases have recognized, "is to safeguard the privacy and security of individuals against arbitrary invasions by governmental officials." The Founding generation crafted the Fourth Amendment as a "response to the reviled 'general warrants' and 'writs of assistance' of the colonial era, which allowed British officers to rummage through homes in an unrestrained search for evidence of criminal activity."…

For much of our history, Fourth Amendment search doctrine was tied to common-law trespass and focused on whether the Government obtains information by physically intruding on a constitutionally protected area. More recently, the Court has recognized that property rights are not the sole measure of Fourth Amendment violations. In Katz v. United States (1967), we established that "the Fourth Amendment protects people, not places," and expanded our conception of the

Amendment to protect certain expectations of privacy as well. When an individual "seeks to preserve something as private," and his expectation of privacy is "one that society is prepared to recognize as reasonable," we have held that official intrusion into that private sphere generally qualifies as a search and requires a warrant supported by probable cause.

Although no single rubric definitively resolves which expectations of privacy are entitled to protection, the analysis is informed by historical understandings of what was deemed an unreasonable search and seizure when the Fourth Amendment was adopted. On this score, our cases have recognized some basic guideposts. First, that the Amendment seeks to secure "the privacies of life" against "arbitrary power." Second, and relatedly, that a central aim of the Framers was "to place obstacles in the way of a too permeating police surveillance."

We have kept this attention to Founding-era understandings in mind when applying the Fourth Amendment to innovations in surveillance tools. As technology has enhanced the Government's capacity to encroach upon areas normally guarded from inquisitive eyes, this Court has sought to "assure preservation of that degree of privacy against government that existed when the Fourth Amendment was adopted." For that reason, we rejected in Kyllo a "mechanical interpretation" of the Fourth Amendment and held that use of a thermal imager to detect heat radiating from the side of the defendant's home was a search. Because any other conclusion would leave homeowners "at the mercy of advancing technology," we determined that the Government—absent a warrant—could not capitalize on such new sense-enhancing technology to explore what was happening within the home....

B

The case before us involves the Government's acquisition of wireless carrier cell-site records revealing the location of Carpenter's cell phone whenever it made or received calls. This sort of digital data—personal location information maintained by a third party—does not fit neatly under existing precedents. Instead, requests for cell-site records lie at the intersection of two lines of cases, both of which inform our understanding of the privacy interests at stake.

The first set of cases addresses a person's expectation of privacy in his physical location and movements. In United States v. Knotts (1983), we considered the Government's use of a "beeper" to aid in tracking a vehicle through traffic.... Since the movements of the vehicle and its final destination had been "voluntarily conveyed to anyone who wanted to look," Knotts could not assert a privacy interest in the information obtained. This Court in Knotts, however, was careful to distinguish between the rudimentary tracking facilitated by the beeper and more sweeping modes of surveillance. The Court emphasized the "limited use which the government made of the signals from this particular beeper" during a discrete "automotive journey." Significantly, the Court reserved the question whether "different constitutional principles may be applicable" if "twenty-four hour surveillance of any citizen of this country were possible."…[3]

A person does not surrender all Fourth Amendment protection by venturing into the public sphere. To the contrary, what one seeks to preserve as private, even in an area accessible to the public, may be constitutionally protected…. Mapping a cell phone's location over the course of 127 days provides an all-encompassing record of the holder's whereabouts. As with GPS information, the time-stamped data provides an intimate window into a person's life, revealing not only his particular movements, but through them his familial, political, professional, religious, and sexual associations. These location records hold for many Americans the "privacies of life." And like GPS monitoring, cell phone tracking is remarkably easy, cheap, and efficient compared to traditional investigative tools. With just the click of a button, the Government can access each carrier's deep repository of historical location information at practically no expense…. When the Government tracks the location of a cell phone it achieves near perfect surveillance, as if it had attached an ankle monitor to the phone's user.

Moreover, the retrospective quality of the data here gives police access to a category of information otherwise unknowable. In the past, attempts to reconstruct a person's movements were limited by a dearth of records and the frailties of recollection. With access to CSLI, the Government can now travel back in time to retrace a person's whereabouts, subject only to the retention polices of the wireless carriers, which currently maintain records for up to five years. Critically, because location information is continually logged for all of the 400 million devices in the

---

[3] The parties suggest as an alternative to their primary submissions that the acquisition of CSLI becomes a search only if it extends beyond a limited period…. Contrary to Justice Kennedy's assertion, we need not decide whether there is a limited period for which the Government may obtain an individual's historical CSLI free from Fourth Amendment scrutiny, and if so, how long that period might be. It is sufficient for our purposes today to hold that accessing seven days of CSLI constitutes a Fourth Amendment search.

United States—not just those belonging to persons who might happen to come under investigation—this newfound tracking capacity runs against everyone.... Police need not even know in advance whether they want to follow a particular individual, or when.

Whoever the suspect turns out to be, he has effectively been tailed every moment of every day for five years, and the police may—in the Government's view—call upon the results of that surveillance without regard to the constraints of the Fourth Amendment. Only the few without cell phones could escape this tireless and absolute surveillance.

.... While the records in this case reflect the state of technology at the start of the decade, the accuracy of CSLI is rapidly approaching GPS-level precision. As the number of cell sites has proliferated, the geographic area covered by each cell sector has shrunk, particularly in urban areas. In addition, with new technology measuring the time and angle of signals hitting their towers, wireless carriers already have the capability to pinpoint a phone's location within 50 meters. Accordingly, when the Government accessed CSLI from the wireless carriers, it invaded Carpenter's reasonable expectation of privacy in the whole of his physical movements.

The Government's primary contention to the contrary is that the third-party doctrine governs this case. [*Ed. Note*: This is the second of the "two lines of cases" referenced earlier in the opinion.] In its view, cell-site records are fair game because they are "business records" created and maintained by the wireless carriers....

The Government's position fails to contend with the seismic shifts in digital technology that made possible the tracking of not only Carpenter's location but also everyone else's, not for a short period but for years and years. Sprint Corporation and its competitors are not your typical witnesses. Unlike the nosy neighbor who keeps an eye on comings and goings, they are ever alert, and their memory is nearly infallible. There is a world of difference between the limited types of personal information addressed in Smith v. Maryland and United States v. Miller and the exhaustive chronicle of location information casually collected by wireless carriers today....

The third-party doctrine partly stems from the notion that an individual has a reduced expectation of privacy in information knowingly shared with another. But the fact of diminished privacy interests does not mean that the Fourth Amendment falls out of the picture entirely. Smith and Miller, after all, did not rely solely on the act of sharing. Instead, they considered "the nature of the particular documents sought" to determine whether "there is a legitimate 'expectation of privacy' concerning their contents." Smith pointed out the limited capabilities of a pen register…. Miller likewise noted that checks were "not confidential communications but negotiable instruments to be used in commercial transactions." In mechanically applying the third-party doctrine to this case, the Government fails to appreciate that there are no comparable limitations on the revealing nature of CSLI.

Neither does the second rationale underlying the third-party doctrine—voluntary exposure—hold up when it comes to CSLI. Cell phone location information is not truly "shared" as one normally understands the term. In the first place, cell phones and the services they provide are such a pervasive and insistent part of daily life that carrying one is indispensable to participation in modern society. Second, a cell phone logs a cell-site record by dint of its operation, without any affirmative act on the part of the user beyond powering up. Virtually any activity on the phone generates CSLI, including incoming calls, texts, or e-mails and countless other data connections that a phone automatically makes when checking for news, weather, or social media updates. Apart from disconnecting the phone from the network, there is no way to avoid leaving behind a trail of location data. As a result, in no meaningful sense does the user voluntarily "assume the risk" of turning over a comprehensive dossier of his physical movements.

We therefore decline to extend Smith and Miller to the collection of CSLI. Given the unique nature of cell phone location information, the fact that the Government obtained the information from a third party does not overcome Carpenter's claim to Fourth Amendment protection. The Government's acquisition of the cell-site records was a search within the meaning of the Fourth Amendment.

Our decision today is a narrow one. We do not express a view on matters not before us: real-time CSLI or "tower dumps" (a download of information on all the devices that connected to a particular cell site during a particular interval). We do not disturb the application of Smith and Miller or call into question conventional surveillance techniques and tools, such as security cameras. Nor do we address other business records that might incidentally reveal location information. Further, our opinion does not consider other collection techniques involving foreign affairs or national security. As Justice Frankfurter noted when considering new innovations in airplanes and radios, the Court must tread carefully in such cases, to ensure that we do not "embarrass the future."

…. We decline to grant the state unrestricted access to a wireless carrier's database of physical location information. In light of the deeply revealing nature of CSLI, its depth, breadth, and comprehensive reach, and the inescapable and automatic nature of its collection, the fact that such information is gathered by a third party does not make it any less deserving of Fourth Amendment protection. The Government's acquisition of the cell-site records here was a search under that Amendment….

[*Ed. Note*: In another portion of the opinion, the Court concluded: "Having found that the acquisition of Carpenter's CSLI was a search, we also conclude that the Government must generally obtain a warrant supported by probable cause before acquiring such records." The Court, then, reversed and remanded the case.]

6. THE KATZ TEST'S FLEXIBILITY

While commentators generally applauded the result in *Carpenter*, critics pointed out that the majority's analysis strained Fourth Amendment "search" doctrine. For a flavor of this critique, here is a brief excerpt from a law review article:

Courts attempting to apply Katz generally skip over the unhelpful "reasonable expectation of privacy" test to the three broad categories of government intrusions that dominate post-Katz jurisprudence: (1) information exposed to the public; (2) information provided to a third party; and (3) information that reveals only the possession of contraband. When the government obtains information that falls into any of these three categories there is typically (but not always) no search because such conduct does not invade a "reasonable expectation of privacy."

When the government obtains information in a way that does not implicate these three "no-search" categories, the Supreme Court typically (but not always) deems the conduct a search. Thus, in Kyllo v. United States, (1) the defendant did not expose his marijuana grow-house to the public; (2) the government did not obtain knowledge of its existence through a third party; and (3) the government's "thermal-imaging device" revealed more than just the presence of contraband (e.g., "that someone left a closet light on"). That's a "search." Similarly, in Arizona v.

Hicks, the Court found a "search" when, suspecting it was stolen, an officer moved a stereo to expose its serial number. The serial number had not been exposed to public view or obtained from a third party, and the investigative technique was not restricted to discovering contraband. (There might have been a treasure map pinned to the back of the stereo or embarrassing dust bunnies.)

But that's just a descriptive guide. The three categories identified above do little analytical work. The engine driving modern "search" jurisprudence is an ever-expanding catalogue of Supreme Court opinions identifying which cases fall where--all striving to channel the elusive expectations of privacy that "society is prepared to recognize as 'reasonable.'" This means that the Court need not ever fully define the categories or adhere to their (unspecified) bounds. Instead, the Court embraces the free hand Katz provides to expand, contract, or ignore these categories to reach the "best" outcome. Perhaps no case illustrates this freedom more than Carpenter. The location information obtained by the government in Carpenter fit into both the first (exposed to public) and second (obtained from a third party) "no-search" categories. The Carpenter majority simply moved the goalposts, depositing the case into its own category of one, something Katz not only allows but demands.[4]

Lower courts must adapt to the changes to "search" analysis generated by both *Carpenter* and the new investigative techniques that are continually implemented by police. Consider the facts of *United States v. Tuggle* (7th Cir. 2021):

"Between 2013 and 2016, several law enforcement agencies investigated a large methamphetamine distribution conspiracy in central Illinois that resulted in Travis Tuggle's prosecution. The focus of this appeal is the government's warrantless use of three video cameras affixed to nearby utility poles to monitor Tuggle's residence.

The government installed three cameras on public property that viewed Tuggle's home. Agents mounted two cameras on a pole in an alley next to his residence and a third on a pole one block south of the other two cameras. The first two cameras viewed the front of Tuggle's home and an adjoining parking area. The third camera also viewed the outside of his home but primarily captured a shed owned by Tuggle's coconspirator and codefendant.

---

[4] Bellin, Fourth Amendment Textualism, 118 Mich. L. Rev. 233 (2019).

Together, the three cameras captured nearly eighteen months of footage by recording Tuggle's property between 2014 and 2016.... The cameras offered several advantages to the government's investigation of the drug conspiracy. While in use, the cameras recorded around the clock. Rudimentary lighting technology improved the quality of overnight footage, although the cameras did not have infrared or audio capabilities. Law enforcement agents could also remotely zoom, pan, and tilt the cameras and review the camera footage in real time, though the footage captured only the exterior of Tuggle's house. While officers frequently monitored the live feed during business hours, they could later review all the footage, which the government stored at the Federal Bureau of Investigation office in Springfield, Illinois. More generally, the cameras had the practical advantage of enabling the government to surveil Tuggle's home without conspicuously deploying agents to perform traditional visual or physical surveillance on the lightly traveled roads of Tuggle's residential neighborhood.

The cameras provided substantial video evidence that supported the government's eventual indictment of Tuggle (and others). The officers tallied over 100 instances of what they suspected were deliveries of methamphetamine to Tuggle's residence. Camera footage depicted individuals arriving at Tuggle's home, carrying various items inside, and leaving only with smaller versions of those items or sometimes nothing at all. After these alleged "drops," different individuals would soon arrive, enter the home, and purportedly pay for and pick up methamphetamine....

Relying heavily on the video evidence, the officers secured and executed search warrants on several locations, including Tuggle's house. A grand jury subsequently indicted him for conspiring to distribute at least 50 grams of methamphetamine, and for maintaining a drug-involved premises.

Before trial, Tuggle moved to suppress the evidence obtained from the pole cameras, arguing that the use of the cameras constituted a warrantless search in violation of the Fourth Amendment."

Since the government did not obtain a warrant, this conduct would violate the Fourth Amendment if it constituted a "search." Would a lower court have found the police conduct described above to be a search prior to *Carpenter*? After *Carpenter*?

7. TRESPASSORY SEARCHES

In *United States v. Jones* (2012), the Supreme Court added a new wrinkle to its "search" caselaw. The Court explained that *Katz*'s "reasonable expectation of privacy" test was not the sole test for determining whether a "search" occurred. A different kind of search, a "trespassory search" (which the Court found had occurred in *Jones*) could trigger Fourth Amendment protections even if an application of *Katz*'s reasonable expectation of privacy test would have concluded that there was no "search." The Court framed this seemingly-new, supplemental "search" test as a long-standing component of the doctrine, explaining that "the Katz reasonable-expectation-of-privacy test ha[d] been added to, not substituted for, the common-law trespassory test." The Court fine-tuned the new-old test in *Florida v. Jardines*.

FLORIDA v. JARDINES
569 U.S. 1 (2013)

Justice SCALIA delivered the opinion of the Court.

We consider whether using a drug-sniffing dog on a homeowner's porch to investigate the contents of the home is a "search" within the meaning of the Fourth Amendment.

I

In 2006, Detective William Pedraja of the Miami–Dade Police Department received an unverified tip that marijuana was being grown in the home of respondent Joelis Jardines.... Detective

"Franky"

Pedraja [later] approached Jardines' home accompanied by Detective Douglas Bartelt, a trained canine handler who had just arrived at the scene with his drug-sniffing dog[, "Franky"]. The dog was trained to detect the scent of marijuana, cocaine, heroin, and several other drugs, indicating the presence of any of these substances through particular behavioral changes recognizable by his handler.

Detective Bartelt had the dog on a six-foot leash, owing in part to the dog's "wild" nature, and tendency to dart around erratically while searching. As the dog approached Jardines' front porch, he apparently sensed one of the odors he had been trained to detect, and began energetically exploring the area for the strongest point source of that odor. As Detective Bartelt explained, the dog "began tracking that airborne odor by … tracking back and forth," engaging in what is called "bracketing," "back and forth, back and forth." Detective Bartelt gave the dog "the full six feet of the leash plus whatever safe distance [he could] give him" to do this—he testified that he needed to give the dog "as much distance as I can." And Detective Pedraja stood back while this was occurring, so that he would not "get knocked over" when the dog was "spinning around trying to find" the source.

After sniffing the base of the front door, the dog sat, which is the trained behavior upon discovering the odor's strongest point. Detective Bartelt then pulled the dog away from the door and returned to his vehicle. He left the scene after informing Detective Pedraja that there had been a positive alert for narcotics.

On the basis of what he had learned at the home, Detective Pedraja applied for and received a warrant to search the residence. When the warrant was executed later that day, Jardines attempted to flee and was arrested; the search revealed marijuana plants, and he was charged with trafficking in cannabis….

The home in *Jardines*

We granted certiorari, limited to the question of whether the officers' behavior was a search within the meaning of the Fourth Amendment.

II

The Fourth Amendment … establishes a simple baseline, one that for much of our history formed the exclusive basis for its protections: When "the Government obtains information by physically intruding" on persons, houses, papers, or effects, "a 'search' within the original meaning of the Fourth Amendment" has "undoubtedly occurred." United States v. Jones (2012). By reason of our decision in Katz v. United States (1967), property rights "are not the sole measure of Fourth Amendment violations"—but though Katz may add to the baseline, it does not subtract anything from the Amendment's protections when the Government does engage in a physical intrusion of a constitutionally protected area.

That principle renders this case a straightforward one. The officers were gathering information in an area belonging to Jardines and immediately surrounding his house—in the curtilage of the house, which we have held enjoys protection as part of the home itself. And they gathered that information by physically entering and occupying the area to engage in conduct not explicitly or implicitly permitted by the homeowner.

A

.... We ... regard the area immediately surrounding and associated with the home – what our cases call the curtilage – as part of the home itself for Fourth Amendment purposes.... The front porch is the classic exemplar of an area adjacent to the home and to which the activity of home life extends.

B

Since the officers' investigation took place in a constitutionally protected area, we turn to the question of whether it was accomplished through an unlicensed physical intrusion. While law enforcement officers need not "shield their eyes" when passing by the home "on public thoroughfares," an officer's leave to gather information is sharply circumscribed when he steps off those thoroughfares and enters the Fourth Amendment's protected areas. In permitting, for example, visual observation of the home from "public navigable airspace," we were careful to note that it was done "in a physically nonintrusive manner." California v. Ciraolo (1986). Entick v. Carrington (K.B. 1765), a case "undoubtedly familiar" to "every American statesman" at the time of the Founding, states the general rule clearly: "Our law holds the property of every man so sacred, that no man can set his foot upon his neighbour's close without his leave." As it is undisputed that the detectives had all four of their feet and all four of their companion's firmly planted on the constitutionally protected extension of Jardines' home, the only question is whether he had given his leave (even implicitly) for them to do so. He had not.

"A license may be implied from the habits of the country," notwithstanding the "strict rule of the English common law as to entry upon a close." We have accordingly recognized that "the knocker on the front door is treated as an invitation or license to attempt an entry, justifying ingress to the home by solicitors, hawkers and peddlers of all kinds." This implicit license typically permits the visitor to approach the home by the front path, knock promptly, wait briefly to be received, and then (absent invitation to linger longer) leave. Complying with the terms of that traditional invitation does not require fine-grained legal knowledge; it is generally managed without incident by the Nation's Girl Scouts and trick-or-treaters. Thus, a police officer not armed with a warrant may approach a home and knock, precisely because that is "no more than any private citizen might do." Kentucky v. King (2011).

But introducing a trained police dog to explore the area around the home in hopes of discovering incriminating evidence is something else. There is no customary invitation to do that. An invitation to engage in canine forensic investigation assuredly does not inhere in the very act of hanging a knocker. To find a visitor knocking on the door is routine (even if sometimes unwelcome); to spot that same visitor exploring the front path with a metal detector, or marching his bloodhound into the garden before saying hello and asking permission, would inspire most of us to—well, call the police. The scope of a license—express or implied—is limited not only to a particular area but also to a specific purpose. Consent at a traffic stop to an officer's checking out an anonymous tip that there is a body in the trunk does not permit the officer to rummage through the trunk for narcotics. Here, the background social norms that invite a visitor to the front door do not invite him there to conduct a search.

The State points to our decisions holding that the subjective intent of the officer is irrelevant[, including] Whren v. United States (1996). But those cases merely hold that a stop or search that is objectively reasonable is not vitiated by the fact that the officer's real reason for making the stop or search has nothing to do with the validating reason. Thus, the defendant will not be heard to complain that although he was speeding the officer's real reason for the stop was racial harassment. Here, however, the question before the court is precisely whether the officer's conduct was an objectively reasonable search. As we have described, that depends upon whether the officers had an implied license to enter the porch, which in turn depends upon the purpose for which they entered. Here, their behavior objectively reveals a purpose to conduct a search, which is not what anyone would think he had license to do.

III

The State argues that investigation by a forensic narcotics dog by definition cannot implicate any legitimate privacy interest. The State cites for authority our decisions in United States v. Place (1983), United States v. Jacobsen (1984), and Illinois v.

Caballes (2005), which held, respectively, that canine inspection of luggage in an airport, chemical testing of a substance that had fallen from a parcel in transit, and canine inspection of an automobile during a lawful traffic stop, do not violate the "reasonable expectation of privacy" described in Katz.

Just last Term, we considered an argument much like this. United States v. Jones (2012) held that tracking an automobile's whereabouts using a physically-mounted GPS receiver is a Fourth Amendment search. The Government argued that the Katz standard "showed that no search occurred," as the defendant had "no 'reasonable expectation of privacy'" in his whereabouts on the public roads—a proposition with at least as much support in our case law as the one the State marshals here. See, e.g., United States v. Knotts (1983). But because the GPS receiver had been physically mounted on the defendant's automobile (thus intruding on his "effects"), we held that tracking the vehicle's movements was a search: a person's "Fourth Amendment rights do not rise or fall with the Katz formulation." The Katz reasonable-expectations test "has been added to, not substituted for," the traditional property-based understanding of the Fourth Amendment, and so is unnecessary to consider when the government gains evidence by physically intruding on constitutionally protected areas.

Thus, we need not decide whether the officers' investigation of Jardines' home violated his expectation of privacy under Katz. One virtue of the Fourth Amendment's property-rights baseline is that it keeps easy cases easy. That the officers learned what they learned only by physically intruding on Jardines' property to gather evidence is enough to establish that a search occurred.

For a related reason we find irrelevant the State's argument (echoed by the dissent) that forensic dogs have been commonly used by police for centuries. This argument is apparently directed to our holding in Kyllo v. United States (2001), that surveillance of the home is a search where "the Government uses a device that is not in general public use" to "explore details of the home that would previously have been unknowable *without physical intrusion.*" But the implication of that statement (inclusio unius est exclusio alterius) is that when the government uses a physical intrusion to explore details of the home (including its curtilage), the antiquity of the tools that they bring along is irrelevant.

The government's use of trained police dogs to investigate the home and its immediate surroundings is a "search" within the meaning of the Fourth Amendment….

Florida v. Jardines recognizes that police officers can walk up to the door of a typical house and knock in an effort to speak to a resident "because that is 'no more than any private citizen might do.'" To support that statement, the Court quoted *Kentucky v. King* (2011), a case routinely cited to support the constitutionality of so-called "knock and talks." What if a resident did not want the police to be able to do even that?

Some law professors have suggested that posting a lawn sign might revoke the implied license referenced in *Jardines*.[5]

Here is a court's description of a person who successfully argued that the general license to approach a house did not apply to his property:

> " Unlike many homeowners, Defendant did not leave the entrance open to social and business guests. Instead, Defendant took pains to keep visitors out. He posted two guard dog warning signs on the gate. He kept a phone number on the business sign by the gate so that visitors would call him instead of entering his property without notice. He kept his mailbox across the street. Thus, while privacy expectations are generally diminished in common entrances and pathways, Defendant maintained his expectation of privacy by restricting access to this area and providing an alternative means for visitors to contact him.[6]

The trespassory-search/unlicensed-physical-intrusion test is in its infancy. The courts still have many questions to answer about its application.

---

[5] Andrew Ferguson & Stephen Henderson, Lawn Signs: A Fourth Amendment for Constitutional Curmudgeons, 13 Ohio St. J. Crim. L. 487 (2016).
[6] United States v. Hambelton (N.D. Fla. 2009).

Consider the following facts from *Taylor v. City of Saginaw* (6th Cir. 2019):

"The City of Saginaw uses a common parking enforcement practice known as 'chalking,' whereby City parking enforcement officers use chalk to mark the tires of parked vehicles to track how long they have been parked. Parking enforcement officers return to the car after the posted time for parking has passed, and if the chalk marks are still there—a sign that the vehicle has not moved—the officer issues a citation. Alison Taylor, a frequent recipient of parking tickets, sued the City and its parking enforcement officer Tabitha Hoskins, alleging that chalking violated her Fourth Amendment right to be free from unreasonable search."

Does the chalking constitute a search under the *Jones/Jardines* test?

C. DEFINING "SEIZURE"

The Fourth Amendment's protections can be triggered by two kinds of "seizures": seizures of property and seizures of people. Seizures of property play a relatively minor role in Fourth Amendment jurisprudence. As the Supreme Court noted in *United States v. Karo*, "a 'seizure' of property occurs when there is some meaningful interference with an individual's possessory interests in that property."

The question whether the government conducts a "seizure" of a person, by contrast, is a frequent topic of judicial opinions. The quintessential "seizure" is an arrest. When police command a person to stop, place that person in handcuffs, and transport them to a local jail, there is clearly a "seizure." When a driver pulls over to the side of the road in response to a police car turning on its lights and siren, the driver has also been "seized." In other circumstances, whether a seizure occurs is less clear. In *Brendlin v. California* (2007), the Supreme Court summarized the multi-layered tests it uses to resolve these close cases:

      "When the actions of the police do not show an unambiguous intent to restrain or when an individual's submission to a show of governmental authority takes the form of passive acquiescence, there needs to be some test for telling when a seizure occurs in response to authority, and when it does not. The test was devised by Justice Stewart in United States v. Mendenhall (1980), who wrote that a seizure occurs if "in view of all of the circumstances surrounding the incident, a reasonable person would have believed that he was not free to leave." Later on, the Court adopted Justice Stewart's touchstone, but added that when a person "has no desire to leave" for reasons unrelated to the police presence, the "coercive effect of the encounter" can be measured better by asking whether "a reasonable person would feel free to decline the officers' requests or otherwise terminate the encounter."

The following materials fill out the outline sketched in *Brendlin*.

<hr />

UNITED STATES v. MENDENHALL
446 U.S. 544 (1980)

Case Summary

Some of the most famous "seizure" cases did not produce any clear answer about whether a seizure occurred, such as *U.S. v. Mendenhall*, the source of the doctrine's famous "free to leave" test. Here are the facts of that case as recounted by Justice Stewart's lead opinion:

> .... The respondent arrived at the Detroit Metropolitan Airport on a commercial airline flight from Los Angeles.... As she disembarked from the airplane, she was observed by two agents of the DEA, who were present at the airport for the purpose of detecting unlawful traffic in narcotics. After observing the respondent's conduct, which appeared to the agents to be characteristic of persons unlawfully carrying narcotics,[1] the agents approached her as she was walking through the concourse, identified themselves as federal agents, and asked to see her identification and airline ticket. The respondent produced her driver's license, which was in the name of Sylvia Mendenhall, and, in answer to a question of one of the agents, stated that she resided at the address appearing on the license. The airline ticket was issued in the name of 'Annette Ford.' When asked why the ticket bore a name different from her own, the respondent

---

[1] The agent testified that the respondent's behavior fit the so-called "drug courier profile" – an informally compiled abstract of characteristics thought typical of persons carrying illicit drugs. In this case the agents thought it relevant that (1) the respondent was arriving on a flight from Los Angeles, a city believed by the agents to be the place of origin for much of the heroin brought to Detroit; (2) the respondent was the last person to leave the plane, "appeared to be very nervous," and "completely scanned the whole area where [the agents] were standing"; (3) after leaving the plane the respondent proceeded past the baggage area without claiming any luggage; and (4) the respondent changed airlines for her flight out of Detroit.

stated that she 'just felt like using that name.' In response to a further question, the respondent indicated that she had been in California only two days. Agent Anderson then specifically identified himself as a federal narcotics agent and, according to his testimony, the respondent 'became quite shaken, extremely nervous. She had a hard time speaking.'

After returning the airline ticket and driver's license to her, Agent Anderson asked the respondent if she would accompany him to the airport DEA office for further questions. She did so, although the record does not indicate a verbal response to the request. The office, which was located up one flight of stairs about 50 feet from where the respondent had first been approached, consisted of a reception area adjoined by three other rooms. At the office the agent asked the respondent if she would allow a search of her person and handbag and told her that she had the right to decline the search if she desired. She responded: 'Go ahead.' She then handed Agent Anderson her purse, which contained a receipt for an airline ticket that had been issued to 'F. Bush' three days earlier for a flight from Pittsburgh through Chicago to Los Angeles. The agent asked whether this was the ticket that she had used for her flight to California, and the respondent stated that it was.

A female police officer then arrived to conduct the search of the respondent's person. She asked the agents if the respondent had consented to be searched. The agents said that she had, and the respondent followed the policewoman into a private room. There the policewoman again asked the respondent if she consented to the search, and the respondent replied that she did. The policewoman explained that the search would require that the respondent remove her clothing. The respondent stated that she had a plane to catch and was assured by the policewoman that if she were carrying no narcotics, there would be no problem. The respondent then began to disrobe without further comment. As the respondent removed her clothing, she took from her undergarments two small packages, one of which appeared to contain heroin, and handed both to the policewoman. The agents then arrested the respondent for possessing heroin...."

Two Justices (Stewart and Rehnquist) ruled that there was no Fourth Amendment violation in this scenario because there was no seizure. Here is their reasoning:

" " A person has been 'seized' within the meaning of the Fourth Amendment only if, in view of all of the circumstances surrounding the incident, a reasonable person would have believed that he was not free to leave.[6] Examples of circumstances that might indicate a seizure, even where the person did not attempt to leave, would be the threatening presence of several officers, the display of a weapon by an officer, some physical touching of the person of the citizen, or the use of language or tone of voice indicating that compliance with the officer's request might be compelled. In the absence of some such evidence, otherwise inoffensive contact between a member of the public and the police cannot, as a matter of law, amount to a seizure of that person.

On the facts of this case, no 'seizure' of the respondent occurred. The events took place in the public concourse. The agents wore no uniforms and displayed no weapons. They did not summon the respondent to their presence, but instead approached her and identified themselves as federal agents. They requested, but did not demand to see the respondent's identification and ticket. Such conduct, without more, did not amount to an intrusion upon any constitutionally protected interest. The respondent was not seized simply by reason of the fact that the agents approached her, asked her if she would show them her ticket and identification, and posed to her a few questions. Nor was it enough to establish a seizure that the person asking the questions was a law enforcement official. In short, nothing in the record suggests that the respondent had any objective reason to believe that she was not free to end the conversation in the concourse and proceed on her way, and for that reason we conclude that the agents' initial approach to her was not a seizure....

Although we have concluded that the initial encounter between the DEA agents and the respondent on the concourse at the Detroit Airport did not constitute an unlawful seizure, it is still arguable that the respondent's Fourth Amendment protections were violated when she went from the concourse to the DEA office.... The question whether the respondent's

---

[6] We agree with the District Court that the subjective intention of the DEA agent in this case to detain the respondent, had she attempted to leave, is irrelevant except insofar as that may have been conveyed to the respondent.

consent to accompany the agents was in fact voluntary or was the product of duress or coercion, express or implied, is to be determined by the totality of all the circumstances, and is a matter which the Government has the burden of proving. The respondent herself did not testify at the hearing. The Government's evidence showed that the respondent was not told that she had to go to the office, but was simply asked if she would accompany the officers. There were neither threats nor any show of force. The respondent had been questioned only briefly, and her ticket and identification were returned to her before she was asked to accompany the officers.... The totality of the evidence in this case was plainly adequate to support the District Court's finding that the respondent voluntarily consented to accompany the officers to the DEA office."

Four Justices (White, Brennan, Marshall, Stevens) disagreed:

" Although it is undisputed that Ms. Mendenhall was not free to leave after the DEA agents stopped her and inspected her identification, Justice Stewart concludes that she was not 'seized' because he finds that, under the totality of the circumstances, a reasonable person would have believed that she was free to leave. While basing this finding on an alleged absence from the record of objective evidence indicating that Ms. Mendenhall was not free to ignore the officer's inquiries and continue on her way, Justice Stewart's opinion brushes off the fact that this asserted evidentiary deficiency may be largely attributable to the fact that the 'seizure' question was never raised below....

Whatever doubt there may be concerning whether Ms. Mendenhall's Fourth Amendment interests were implicated during the initial stages of her confrontation with the DEA agents, she undoubtedly was 'seized' within the meaning of the Fourth Amendment when the agents escorted her from the public area of the terminal to the DEA office for questioning and a strip-search of her person.... The nature of the intrusion to which Ms. Mendenhall was subjected when she was escorted by DEA agents to their office and detained there for questioning and a strip-search was so great that it 'was in important respects indistinguishable from a traditional arrest.' Although Ms. Mendenhall was not told that she was under arrest, she in fact was not free to refuse to go to the DEA office and was not told that she was. Furthermore, once inside the office, Ms. Mendenhall would not have been permitted to leave without submitting to a strip-search."

The remaining Justices (Powell, Blackmun, Burger) avoided the question whether there was a seizure, by concluding that even if there was a seizure, it was "reasonable," based on "careful and commendable police work" – a conclusion that the four Justices quoted above vigorously disputed.

Mendenhall highlights both the complex analysis required to determine whether a "seizure" occurred and the important point that an affirmative answer to that question does not end the inquiry. First, a court must decide if there was a "search" or "seizure." If not, the Fourth Amendment challenge fails. If there was a "search" or "seizure," the inquiry continues to the second and equally important question of reasonableness – the topic of Chapter 3.

FLORIDA v. ROYER
460 U.S. 491 (1983)

Case Summary

Another case decided a few years after *Mendenhall* similarly splintered the Court without any opinion gaining the support of five Justices. Here are the facts:

❝ On January 3, 1978, Mark Royer was observed at Miami International Airport by two plain-clothes detectives of the Dade County, Florida, Public Safety Department assigned to the County's Organized Crime Bureau, Narcotics Investigation Section. Detectives Johnson and Magdalena believed that Royer's appearance, mannerisms, luggage, and actions fit the so-called 'drug courier profile.' Royer, apparently unaware of the attention he had attracted, purchased a one-way ticket to New York City and checked his two suitcases, placing on each suitcase an identification tag bearing the name 'Holt' and the destination, 'LaGuardia.' As Royer made his way to the concourse which led to the airline boarding area, the two detectives approached him, identified themselves as policemen working out of the sheriff's office, and asked if Royer had a 'moment' to speak with them; Royer said 'Yes.'

Upon request, but without oral consent, Royer produced for the detectives his airline ticket and his driver's license. The airline ticket, like the baggage identification tags, bore the name 'Holt,' while the driver's license carried respondent's correct name, 'Royer.' When the detectives asked about the discrepancy, Royer explained that a friend had made the reservation in the name of 'Holt.' Royer became noticeably more nervous during this conversation, whereupon the detectives informed Royer that they were in fact narcotics investigators and that they had reason to suspect him of transporting narcotics.

The detectives did not return his airline ticket and identification but asked Royer to accompany them to a room, approximately forty feet away, adjacent to the concourse. Royer said nothing in response but went with the officers as he had been asked to do. The room was later described by Detective Johnson as a 'large storage closet,' located in the stewardesses' lounge and containing a small desk and two chairs. Without Royer's consent or agreement, Detective Johnson, using Royer's baggage check stubs, retrieved the 'Holt' luggage from the airline and brought it to the room where respondent and Detective Magdalena were waiting. Royer was asked if he would consent to a search of the suitcases. Without orally responding to this request, Royer produced a key and unlocked one of the suitcases, which the detective then opened without seeking further assent from Royer. Drugs were found in that suitcase. According to Detective Johnson, Royer stated that he did not know the combination to the lock on the second suitcase. When asked if he objected to the detective opening the second suitcase, Royer said 'no, go ahead,' and did not object when the detective explained that the suitcase might have to be broken open. The suitcase was pried open by the officers and more marihuana was found. Royer was then told that he was under arrest. Approximately fifteen minutes had elapsed from the time the detectives initially approached respondent until his arrest upon the discovery of the contraband...."

Four Justices (White, Marshall, Powell, Stevens) ruled that there was an unreasonable seizure. Their explanation of why this interaction constituted a seizure, which was not squarely disputed by any Justice, is as follows:

"[The State argues] that the entire encounter was consensual and hence Royer was not being held against his will at all. We find this submission untenable. Asking for and examining Royer's ticket and his driver's license were no doubt permissible in themselves, but when the officers identified themselves as narcotics agents, told Royer that he was suspected of transporting narcotics, and asked him to accompany them to the police room, while retaining his ticket and driver's license and without indicating in any way that he was free to depart, Royer was effectively seized for the purposes of the Fourth Amendment. These circumstances surely amount to a show of official authority such that 'a reasonable person would have believed he was not free to leave.' United States v. Mendenhall (Opinion of Stewart, J.)."

In a footnote, the plurality opinion distinguished *Mendenhal* as follows:

"The case before us differs in important respects. Here, Royer's ticket and identification remained in the possession of the officers throughout the encounter; the officers also seized and had possession of his luggage. As a practical matter, Royer could not leave the airport without them. In *Mendenhall*, no luggage was involved, the ticket and identification were immediately returned, and the officers were careful to advise that the suspect could decline to be searched. Here, the officers had seized Royer's luggage and made no effort to advise him that he need not consent to the search."

Justice Brennan concurred in the judgment and endorsed the opinion's conclusion – "that at some point after the initial stop the officers' seizure of Royer matured into an arrest unsupported by probable cause. Royer's consent to the search of his suitcases, therefore, was tainted by the illegal arrest"; Brennan wrote that he did not join the plurality opinion because "the plurality reaches certain issues that it clearly need not reach to support an affirmance." (The four dissenting Justices deemed the police conduct reasonable even if it constituted a seizure.)

The Supreme Court reached greater consensus in the next major seizure cases *Florida v. Bostick* (1991) and …

UNITED STATES v. DRAYTON
536 U.S. 194 (2002)

Justice KENNEDY delivered the opinion of the Court.

I

On February 4, 1999, respondents Christopher Drayton and Clifton Brown, Jr., were traveling on a Greyhound bus en route from Ft. Lauderdale, Florida, to

Detroit, Michigan. The bus made a scheduled stop in Tallahassee, Florida. The passengers were required to disembark so the bus could be refueled and cleaned. As the passengers reboarded, the driver checked their tickets and then left to complete paperwork inside the terminal. As he left, the driver allowed three members of the Tallahassee Police Department to board the bus as part of a routine drug and weapons interdiction effort. The officers were dressed in plain clothes and carried concealed weapons and visible badges.

Once onboard Officer Hoover knelt on the driver's seat and faced the rear of the bus. He could observe the passengers and ensure the safety of the two other officers without blocking the aisle or otherwise obstructing the bus exit. Officers Lang and Blackburn went to the rear of the bus. Blackburn remained stationed there, facing forward. Lang worked his way toward the front of the bus, speaking with individual passengers as he went. He asked the passengers about their travel plans and sought to match passengers with luggage in the overhead racks. To avoid blocking the aisle, Lang stood next to or just behind each passenger with whom he spoke.

According to Lang's testimony, passengers who declined to cooperate with him or who chose to exit the bus at any time would have been allowed to do so without argument. In Lang's experience, however, most people are willing to cooperate. Some passengers go so far as to commend the police for their efforts to ensure the safety of their travel. Lang could recall five to six instances in the previous year in which passengers had declined to have their luggage searched. It also was common for passengers to leave the bus for a cigarette or a snack while the officers were on board. Lang sometimes informed passengers of their right to refuse to cooperate. On the day in question, however, he did not.

Respondents were seated next to each other on the bus. Drayton was in the aisle seat, Brown in the seat next to the window. Lang approached respondents from the rear and leaned over Drayton's shoulder. He held up his badge long enough for respondents to identify him as a police officer. With his face 12–to–18 inches away from Drayton's, Lang spoke in a voice just loud enough for respondents to hear:

> "I'm Investigator Lang with the Tallahassee Police Department. We're conducting bus interdiction, attempting to deter drugs and illegal weapons being transported on the bus. Do you have any bags on the bus?"

Both respondents pointed to a single green bag in the overhead luggage rack. Lang asked, "Do you mind if I check it?," and Brown responded, "Go ahead." Lang handed the bag to Officer Blackburn to check. The bag contained no contraband.

Officer Lang noticed that both respondents were wearing heavy jackets and baggy pants despite the warm weather. In Lang's experience drug traffickers often use baggy clothing to conceal weapons or narcotics. The officer thus asked Brown if he had any weapons or drugs in his possession. And he asked Brown: "Do you mind if I check your person?" Brown answered, "Sure," and cooperated by leaning up in his seat, pulling a cell phone out of his pocket, and opening up his jacket. Lang reached across Drayton and patted down Brown's jacket and pockets, including his waist area, sides, and upper thighs. In both thigh areas, Lang detected hard objects similar to drug packages detected on other occasions. Lang arrested and handcuffed Brown. Officer Hoover escorted Brown from the bus.

Lang then asked Drayton, "Mind if I check you?" Drayton responded by lifting his hands about eight inches from his legs. Lang conducted a patdown of Drayton's thighs and detected hard objects similar to those found on Brown. He arrested Drayton and escorted him from the bus. A further search revealed that respondents had duct-taped plastic bundles of powder cocaine between several pairs of their boxer shorts. Brown possessed three bundles containing 483 grams of cocaine. Drayton possessed two bundles containing 295 grams of cocaine.... [Both defendants moved to suppress the evidence at trial. The District Court denied the motion. Convicted at trial of possessing cocaine with intent to distribute, Drayton was sentenced to 10 years in prison; Brown pled guilty and received a 7-year sentence. The Eleventh Circuit reversed.] We granted certiorari. The respondents, we conclude, were not seized and their consent to the search was voluntary; and we reverse.

II

Law enforcement officers do not violate the Fourth Amendment's prohibition of unreasonable seizures merely by approaching individuals on the street or in other public places and putting questions to them if they are willing to listen. Even when law enforcement officers have no basis for suspecting a particular individual, they may pose questions, ask for identification, and request consent to search luggage—provided they do not induce cooperation by coercive means. If a reasonable person would feel free to terminate the encounter, then he or she has not been seized.

The Court has addressed on a previous occasion the specific question of drug interdiction efforts on buses. In Florida v. Bostick (1991), two police officers requested a bus passenger's consent to a search of his luggage. The passenger agreed, and the resulting search revealed cocaine in his suitcase. The Florida Supreme Court suppressed the cocaine. In doing so it adopted a per se rule that due to the cramped confines onboard a bus the act of questioning would deprive a person of his or her freedom of movement and so constitute a seizure under the Fourth Amendment. This Court reversed. Bostick first made it clear that for the most part per se rules are inappropriate in the Fourth Amendment context. The proper inquiry necessitates a consideration of "all the circumstances surrounding the encounter." The Court noted next that the traditional rule, which states that a seizure does not occur so long as a reasonable person would feel free "to disregard the police and go about his business" is not an accurate measure of the coercive effect of a bus encounter. A passenger may not want to get off a bus if there is a risk it will depart before the opportunity to reboard. A bus rider's movements are confined in this sense, but this is the natural result of choosing to take the bus; it says nothing about whether the police conduct is coercive. The proper inquiry "is whether a reasonable person would feel free to decline the officers' requests or otherwise terminate the encounter."

Finally, the Court rejected Bostick's argument that he must have been seized because no reasonable person would consent to a search of luggage containing drugs. The reasonable person test, the Court explained, is objective and "presupposes an innocent person."

In light of the limited record, Bostick refrained from deciding whether a seizure occurred. The Court, however, identified two factors "particularly worth noting" on remand. First, although it was obvious that an officer was armed, he did not remove the gun from its pouch or use it in a threatening way. Second, the officer advised the passenger that he could refuse consent to the search.

.... Applying the Bostick framework to the facts of this particular case, we conclude that the police did not seize respondents when they boarded the bus and began questioning passengers. The officers gave the passengers no reason to believe that they were required to answer the officers' questions. When Officer Lang approached respondents, he did not brandish a weapon or make any intimidating movements. He left the aisle free so that respondents could exit. He spoke to passengers one by one and in a polite, quiet voice. Nothing he said would suggest to a reasonable person that he or she was barred from leaving the bus or otherwise terminating the encounter.

There were ample grounds for the District Court to conclude that "everything that took place between Officer Lang and [respondents] suggests that it was cooperative" and that there "was nothing coercive or confrontational" about the encounter. There was no application of force, no intimidating movement, no overwhelming show of force, no brandishing of weapons, no blocking of exits, no threat, no command, not even an authoritative tone of voice. It is beyond question that had this encounter occurred on the street, it would be constitutional. The fact that an encounter takes place on a bus does not on its own transform standard police questioning of citizens into an illegal seizure. Indeed, because many fellow passengers are present to witness officers' conduct, a reasonable person may feel even more secure in his or her decision not to cooperate with police on a bus than in other circumstances.

Respondents make much of the fact that Officer Lang displayed his badge.... Officers are often required to wear uniforms and in many circumstances this is cause for assurance, not discomfort. Much the same can be said for wearing sidearms. That most law enforcement officers are armed is a fact well known to the public. The presence of a holstered firearm thus is unlikely to contribute to the coerciveness of the encounter absent active brandishing of the weapon.

Officer Hoover's position at the front of the bus also does not tip the scale in respondents' favor. Hoover did nothing to intimidate passengers, and he said nothing to suggest that people could not exit and indeed he left the aisle clear....

Finally, the fact that in Officer Lang's experience only a few passengers have refused to cooperate does not suggest that a reasonable person would not feel free to terminate the bus encounter. In Lang's experience it was common for passengers to leave the bus for a cigarette or a snack while the officers were questioning passengers. And of more importance, bus passengers answer officers' questions and otherwise cooperate not because of coercion but because the passengers know that their participation enhances their own safety and the safety of those around them. While most citizens will respond to a police request, the fact that people do so, and do so without being told they are free not to respond, hardly eliminates the consensual nature of the response.

Drayton contends that even if Brown's cooperation with the officers was consensual, Drayton was seized because no reasonable person would feel free to terminate the encounter with the officers after Brown had been arrested…. The argument fails. The arrest of one person does not mean that everyone around him has been seized by police. If anything, Brown's arrest should have put Drayton on notice of the consequences of continuing the encounter by answering the officers' questions. Even after arresting Brown, Lang addressed Drayton in a polite manner and provided him with no indication that he was required to answer Lang's questions.

We turn now from the question whether respondents were seized to whether they were subjected to an unreasonable search, i.e., whether their consent to the suspicionless search was involuntary. In circumstances such as these, where the question of voluntariness pervades both the search and seizure inquiries, the respective analyses turn on very similar facts. And, as the facts above suggest, respondents' consent to the search of their luggage and their persons was voluntary. Nothing Officer Lang said indicated a command to consent to the search. Rather, when respondents informed Lang that they had a bag on the bus, he asked for their permission to check it. And when Lang requested to search Brown and Drayton's persons, he asked first if they objected, thus indicating to a reasonable person that he or she was free to refuse. Even after arresting Brown, Lang provided Drayton with no indication that he was required to consent to a search. To the contrary, Lang asked for Drayton's permission to search him ("Mind if I check you?"), and Drayton agreed.

The Court has rejected in specific terms the suggestion that police officers must always inform citizens of their right to refuse when seeking permission to conduct a warrantless consent search. "While knowledge of the right to refuse consent is one factor to be taken into account, the government need not establish such knowledge as the sine qua non of an effective consent." Nor do this Court's decisions suggest that even though there are no per se rules, a presumption of invalidity attaches if a citizen consented without explicit notification that he or she was free to refuse to cooperate. Instead, the Court has repeated that the totality of the circumstances must control, without giving extra weight to the absence of this type of warning. Although Officer Lang did not inform respondents of their right to refuse the search, he did request permission to search, and the totality of the circumstances indicates that their consent was voluntary, so the searches were reasonable.

In a society based on law, the concept of agreement and consent should be given a weight and dignity of its own. Police officers act in full accord with the law when they ask citizens for consent. It reinforces the rule of law for the citizen to advise the police of his or her wishes and for the police to act in reliance on that understanding. When this exchange takes place, it dispels inferences of coercion....

Justice SOUTER, dissenting.

.... A perfect example of police conduct that supports no colorable claim of seizure is the act of an officer who simply goes up to a pedestrian on the street and asks him a question. A pair of officers questioning a pedestrian, without more, would presumably support the same conclusion. Now consider three officers, one of whom stands behind the pedestrian, another at his side toward the open sidewalk, with the third addressing questions to the pedestrian a foot or two from his face. Finally, consider the same scene in a narrow alley. On such barebones facts, one may not be able to say a seizure occurred, even in the last case, but one can say without qualification that the atmosphere of the encounters differed significantly from the first to the last examples. In the final instance there is every reason to believe that the pedestrian would have understood, to his considerable discomfort, what Justice Stewart described as the "threatening presence of several officers." The police not only carry legitimate authority but also exercise power free from immediate check, and when the attention of several officers is brought to bear on one civilian the imbalance of immediate power is unmistakable. We all understand this, as well as we understand that a display of power rising to Justice Stewart's "threatening" level may overbear a normal person's ability to act freely, even in the absence of explicit commands or the formalities of detention. As common as this understanding is, however, there is little sign of it in the Court's opinion....

SEIZURES AND RACE

Justice Stewart's opinion in *Mendenhall* suggests that factors like race can play a role in the seizure analysis. Here is the critical passage from that opinion:

"It is argued that the incident would reasonably have appeared coercive to the respondent, who was 22 years old and had not been graduated from high school. It is additionally suggested that the respondent, [a Black woman], may have felt unusually threatened by the officers, who were white males. While these factors were not irrelevant, neither were they decisive, and the totality of the evidence in this case was plainly adequate to support the District Court's finding that the respondent voluntarily consented to accompany the officers to the DEA office."

Since *Mendenhall*, the Supreme Court has not offered further guidance on how lower courts should factor race into the seizure analysis. In *Royer*, Justice Blackmun noted that "unlike the suspect in *Mendenhall*, Royer was a well-educated, adult, Caucasian male," but none of the Justices explicitly incorporated this distinction into their seizure analysis.

Following the Supreme Court's lead, most lower courts ignore race in assessing whether a seizure has occurred. Or they recognize that race matters, but not in a way that meaningfully changes the seizure analysis. Here is an excerpt from *U.S. v. Smith* (7th Cir. 2015):

" Finally, we address Smith's argument that the reasonable person test should take into account Smith's race. Specifically, he contends that no reasonable person in his "position"—as a young black male confronted in a high-crime, high-poverty, minority-dominated urban area where police-citizen relations are strained—would have felt free to walk away from the encounter with Officers Flannery and Michalski.

The Supreme Court dealt with a similar argument in United States v. Mendenhall.... While the Court stated that these factors "were not irrelevant," it also found they were not "decisive," ruling that the totality of the evidence demonstrated voluntary consent to police questioning.

We do not deny the relevance of race in everyday police encounters with citizens in Milwaukee and around the country. Nor we do we ignore empirical data demonstrating the existence of racial profiling, police brutality, and other racial disparities in the criminal justice system. But today we echo the sentiments of the Court in Mendenhall that while Smith's race is "not irrelevant" to the question of whether a seizure occurred, it is not dispositive either. Even without taking into account

Smith's race, we are able to find on the strength of the other factors discussed that this encounter constituted a seizure.

Some courts explicitly reject race as a consideration. Here is an example from *U.S. v. Easley* (10th Cir. 2018):

> We reject Ms. Easley's argument that we should consider subjective characteristics like race as part of our reasonable person analysis....
>
> Requiring officers to determine how an individual's race affects her reaction to a police request would seriously complicate Fourth Amendment seizure law. As the government notes, there is no easily discernable principle to guide consideration of race in the reasonable person analysis. There is no uniform life experience for persons of color, and there are surely divergent attitudes toward law enforcement officers among members of the population. Thus, there is no uniform way to apply a reasonable person test that adequately accounts for racial differences consistent with an objective standard for Fourth Amendment seizures. This distinguishes race from the Supreme Court's consideration of age in the reasonable person analysis in J.D.B. v. North Carolina (2011). In J.D.B., the Court noted that age is distinct from subjective considerations because it is readily discernible by police and any considerations apply broadly to children as a class. In addition, the considerations applicable to children are "self-evident to anyone who was a child once himself, including any police officer or judge," eliminating the necessity of conjecture about the effect age has on one's perception of freedom to leave. In contrast, consideration of race undermines one of the chief benefits of an objective test for search and seizure law, namely, the ability it gives law enforcement to know ex ante what conduct implicates the Fourth Amendment. Furthermore, as the government correctly notes, a seizure analysis that differentiates on the basis of race raises serious equal protection concerns if it could result in different treatment for those who are otherwise similarly situated. In short, the categorical consideration of race in the reasonable person analysis is error, and we reject Ms. Easley's argument to the contrary.

Scholars have urged the courts to explicitly incorporate race into the seizure analysis. See, e.g., Tracey Maclin, "Black and Blue Encounters" – Some Preliminary

Thoughts About Fourth Amendment Seizures: Should Race Matter?, 26 Val. U. L. Rev. 243 (1991) ("For most black men, the typical police confrontation is not a consensual encounter…. Although many black men *know* of their right to walk away from a police encounter, I submit that most do not trust the police to respect their decision to do so."); Aliza Hochman Bloom, Long Overdue: Confronting Race in the Fourth Amendment's Free to Leave Analysis, 65 How. L.J. 1 (2021) ("Just as courts can consider that a minor is typically less likely to feel free to leave an interaction with police, courts can weigh the commonsense reality, backed by substantial evidence, that race is a relevant contextual factor for whether a reasonable person would feel free to ignore police presence.").

Chief Justice of the South Carolina Supreme Court, Donald Beatty echoed these arguments in a dissent in *State v. Spears* (S.C. 2020):

> " Eric Spears is an African-American male. Scholars have examined ad nauseam the dynamics between marginalized groups—particularly African-Americans—and law enforcement. African-Americans generally experience police misconduct and brutality at higher levels than other demographics. Consequently, it is no surprise that scholars have also found African-Americans often perceive their interactions with law enforcement differently than other demographics. For many members of minority communities … the sight of an officer in uniform evokes a sense of fear and trepidation, rather than security. Moreover, given the mistrust by certain racial, ethnic, and socioeconomic groups, an individual who has observed or experienced police brutality and disrespect will react differently to inquiries from law enforcement officers…. Unfortunately, under our existing framework, this can result in the evisceration of Fourth Amendment protections for many people of color.
>
> Courts have also noted the existence of racial disparities in policing…. United States Supreme Court Justice Sonia Sotomayor has intimated:
>
>> But it is no secret that people of color are disproportionate victims of this type of scrutiny. For generations, black and brown parents have given their children "the talk"—instructing them never to run down the street; always keep your hands where they can be seen; do not even think of talking back to a stranger—all out of fear of how an officer with a gun will react to them. Utah v. Strieff (2016) (Sotomayor, J., dissenting)

In spite of these academic findings and judicial observations, our current framework fails to meaningfully consider the ways in which a person's race can influence their experience with law enforcement. As a result, I fear minority groups are not always afforded the full protections of the Fourth Amendment. Given the interests at stake, one would expect our criminal justice system to forcefully resist marginalizing the experiences of people of color by insisting on a "color-blind" reasonable person standard. In my opinion, the seizure analysis should consider whether a reasonable Black person felt free to end an encounter with police. At the very least, I believe courts should consider a person's race (and other personal characteristics) in examining the totality of the circumstances in a seizure analysis....

The United States population includes 42 million Americans of African descent. Inexplicably, these Americans are basically invisible to those of us who apply the analytical framework for reasonable behavior or beliefs. Somehow the judiciary, intentionally or not, excludes these Americans' normal behaviors, responses, and beliefs in circumstances involving law enforcement agents. For most, the "totality of the circumstances" does not include consideration of the reasonable behavior or response of African-Americans when confronted with certain stimuli. Thus, the regrettable and unsettling conclusion is that the question of what is "reasonable" is viewed solely from the perspective of Americans who are White. I shudder to think about the probable result had [Spears] continued to walk and ignore the police.

This unassailable observation is not intended as an indictment of my colleagues who wear the robe. I do not believe their obliviousness is due to intentional disregard. I prefer to assign their selective blindness to a lifetime of being repeatedly subjected to episodes of minimizing the African-American experience. Life experiences influence the way that we all view the world and legal issues. We should be cognizant of this fact and attempt to view the issue truly with an objective eye. An objective eye would acknowledge the fact that African-Americans are being reasonable when they respond in accordance with their collective experiences gained over two hundred years.

Chief Justice Beatty's statement, "I shudder to think about the probable result had [Spears] continued to walk and ignore the police," hints at the disproportionate rate of killings of Black Americans by police.

The Washington Post tracks fatal shootings by police in the United States. Since 2015, there have been about 1000 such shootings per year. At the end of 2022, the breakdown by race of the victim was as follows:

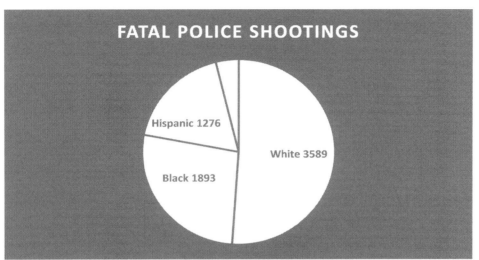

As the Post explains, "although half of the people shot and killed by police are White, Black Americans are shot at a disproportionate rate. They account for roughly 14 percent of the U.S. population and are killed by police at more than twice the rate of White Americans." Specifically, Black Americans are shot and killed by police at an annual rate of 5.9 per million contrasting with White Americans at 2.4 per million. The Post also notes that, "An overwhelming majority of people shot and killed by police are male – over 95 percent." And that most of those killed are between 20 and 40 years old.[7]

In *State v. Sum* (2022), the en banc Supreme Court of Washington concluded that race was relevant to the seizure calculus, explaining:

> "While it is true that there is no uniform life experience or perspective shared by all people of color, heightened police scrutiny of the BIPOC community is certainly common enough to establish that race and

---

[7] https://www.washingtonpost.com/graphics/investigations/police-shootings-database/

ethnicity have at least some relevance to the question of whether a person was seized. Cf. J.D.B. v. North Carolina (2011). The weight that should be given to the allegedly seized person's race and ethnicity will vary between cases based on the evidence presented, but the State cites no Washington authority holding that any objective circumstance is presumptively irrelevant to the seizure inquiry. The suggestion that we should do so with respect to race and ethnicity invites us to draw 'a strained and incorrect' distinction between race and ethnicity and all other circumstances, which we decline to do. Therefore, we hold that Sum's race is relevant to our determination of when he was seized by Deputy Rickerson."

SEIZURES AND INTENT

Sometimes police seize a person in unanticipated ways. For example, in *Brendlin v. California* (2007), the Supreme Court held that the passenger in a car was "seized" when the police pulled over the driver for a traffic violation. The Court explained:

"When a police officer makes a traffic stop, the driver of the car is seized within the meaning of the Fourth Amendment. The question in this case is whether the same is true of a passenger. We hold that a passenger is seized as well and so may challenge the constitutionality of the stop."

The *Brendlin* opinion also includes a useful summary that emphasizes a kind of intent requirement for seizures.

"A person is seized by the police and thus entitled to challenge the government's action under the Fourth Amendment when the officer, by means of physical force or show of authority, terminates or restrains his freedom of movement. Thus, an unintended person may be the object of the detention, so long as the detention is willful and not merely the consequence of an unknowing act. cf. County of Sacramento v. Lewis (1998) (no seizure where a police officer accidentally struck and killed a motorcycle passenger during a high-speed pursuit)."

Brendlin drew on *Brower v. County of Inyo* (1989), where the Supreme Court further elaborated on this intent requirement:

" Violation of the Fourth Amendment requires an intentional acquisition of physical control. A seizure occurs even when an unintended person or thing is the object of the detention or taking, but the detention or taking itself must be willful. This is implicit in the word "seizure," which can hardly be applied to an unknowing act....

Thus, if a parked and unoccupied police car slips its brake and pins a passerby against a wall, it is likely that a tort has occurred, but not a violation of the Fourth Amendment. And the situation would not change if the passerby happened, by lucky chance, to be a serial murderer for whom there was an outstanding arrest warrant—even if, at the time he was thus pinned, he was in the process of running away from two pursuing constables. It is clear, in other words, that a Fourth Amendment seizure does not occur whenever there is a governmentally caused termination of an individual's freedom of movement (the innocent passerby), nor even whenever there is a governmentally caused and governmentally desired termination of an individual's freedom of movement (the fleeing felon), but only when there is **a governmental termination of freedom of movement through means intentionally applied**. That is the reason there [is] no seizure [during "a police chase in which the suspect unexpectedly loses control of his car and crashes"]. The pursuing police car sought to stop the suspect only by the show of authority represented by flashing lights and continuing pursuit; and though he was in fact stopped, he was stopped by a different means—his loss of control of his vehicle and the subsequent crash. If, instead of that, the police cruiser had pulled alongside the fleeing car and sideswiped it, producing the crash, then the termination of the suspect's freedom of movement would have been a seizure.

The Court applied this reasoning in *Brower* to conclude that the police seized a suspect who, while fleeing, crashed into a police roadblock. Consider how the language bolded in the preceding excerpt applies to that scenario, as well as the passenger example in *Brendlin*.

The Supreme Court further elaborated on the details of seizures in the context of police pursuit in the next case which adds one last nuance to the "seizure" definition:

CALIFORNIA v. HODARI D.
499 U.S. 621 (1991)

Justice SCALIA delivered the opinion of the Court.

Late one evening in April 1988, Officers Brian McColgin and Jerry Pertoso were on patrol in a high-crime area of Oakland, California. They were dressed in street clothes but wearing jackets with "Police" embossed on both front and back. Their unmarked car proceeded west on Foothill Boulevard, and turned south onto 63rd Avenue. As they rounded the corner, they saw four or five youths huddled around a small red car parked at the curb. When the youths saw the officers' car approaching they apparently panicked, and took flight. The respondent here, Hodari D., and one companion ran west through an alley; the others fled south. The red car also headed south, at a high rate of speed.

The officers were suspicious and gave chase. McColgin remained in the car and continued south on 63rd Avenue; Pertoso left the car, ran back north along 63rd, then west on Foothill Boulevard, and turned south on 62nd Avenue. Hodari, meanwhile, emerged from the alley onto 62nd and ran north. Looking behind as he ran, he did not turn and see Pertoso until the officer was almost upon him, whereupon he tossed away what appeared to be a small rock. A moment later, Pertoso tackled Hodari, handcuffed him, and radioed for assistance. Hodari was found to be carrying $130 in cash and a pager; and the rock he had discarded was found to be crack cocaine.

.... As this case comes to us, the only issue presented is whether, at the time he dropped the drugs, Hodari had been "seized" within the meaning of the Fourth Amendment. If so, respondent argues, the drugs were the fruit of that seizure and the evidence concerning them was properly excluded. If not, the drugs were abandoned by Hodari and lawfully recovered by the police, and the evidence should have been admitted. (In addition, of course, Pertoso's seeing the rock of cocaine, at least if he recognized it as such, would provide reasonable suspicion for the unquestioned seizure that occurred when he tackled Hodari.)

We have long understood that the Fourth Amendment's protection against unreasonable seizures includes seizure of the person. From the time of the founding to the present, the word "seizure" has meant a "taking possession." For most purposes at common law, the word connoted not merely grasping, or applying physical force to, the animate or inanimate object in question, but actually bringing it within physical control. A ship still fleeing, even though under attack, would not be considered to have been seized as a war prize. A res capable of manual delivery was not seized until "taken into custody." To constitute an arrest, however—the quintessential "seizure of the person" under our Fourth Amendment jurisprudence—the mere grasping or application of physical force with lawful authority, whether or not it succeeded in subduing the arrestee, was sufficient. See, e.g., Whitehead v. Keyes, 85 Mass. 495 (1862) ("An officer effects an arrest of a person whom he has authority to arrest, by laying his hand on him for the purpose of arresting him, though he may not succeed in stopping and holding him"). As one commentator has described it:

> "There can be constructive detention, which will constitute an arrest, although the party is never actually brought within the physical control of the party making an arrest. This is accomplished by merely touching, however slightly, the body of the accused, by the party making the arrest and for that purpose, although he does not succeed in stopping or holding him even for an instant; as where the bailiff had tried to arrest one who fought him off by a fork, the court said, 'If the bailiff had touched him, that had been an arrest....'" A. Cornelius, Search and Seizure (2d ed. 1930).

To say that an arrest is effected by the slightest application of physical force, despite the arrestee's escape, is not to say that for Fourth Amendment purposes there is a continuing arrest during the period of fugitivity. If, for example, Pertoso had laid his hands upon Hodari to arrest him, but Hodari had broken away and had then cast away the cocaine, it would hardly be realistic to say that that disclosure had been made during the course of an arrest. Cf. Thompson v. Whitman, 18 Wall. 457 (1874) ("A seizure is a single act, and not a continuous fact"). The present case, however, is even one step further removed. It does not involve the application of any physical force; Hodari was untouched by Officer Pertoso at the time he discarded the cocaine. His defense relies instead upon the proposition that a seizure occurs "when the officer, by means of physical force or show of authority, has in some way restrained the liberty of a citizen." Hodari contends (and we accept as true for purposes of this decision) that Pertoso's pursuit qualified as a "show of authority" calling upon Hodari to halt. The narrow question before us is whether, with respect to a show of authority as with respect to application of physical force, a seizure occurs even though the subject does not yield. We hold that it does not.

The language of the Fourth Amendment, of course, cannot sustain respondent's contention. The word "seizure" readily bears the meaning of a laying on of hands or application of physical force to restrain movement, even when it is ultimately unsuccessful. ("She seized the purse-snatcher, but he broke out of her grasp.") It does not remotely apply, however, to the prospect of a policeman yelling "Stop, in the name of the law!" at a fleeing form that continues to flee. That is no seizure....

We do not think it desirable, even as a policy matter, to stretch the Fourth Amendment beyond its words and beyond the meaning of arrest, as respondent urges. Street pursuits always place the public at some risk, and compliance with police orders to stop should therefore be encouraged. Only a few of those orders, we must presume, will be without adequate basis, and since the addressee has no ready means of identifying the deficient ones it almost invariably is the responsible course to comply. Unlawful orders will not be deterred, moreover, by sanctioning through the exclusionary rule those of them that are not obeyed. Since policemen do not command "Stop!" expecting to be ignored, or give chase hoping to be outrun, it fully suffices to apply the deterrent to their genuine, successful seizures.

Respondent contends that his position is sustained by the so-called Mendenhall test, formulated by Justice Stewart's opinion in United States v. Mendenhall (1980), and adopted by the Court in later cases: "[A] person has been 'seized' within the meaning of the Fourth Amendment only if, in view of all the circumstances surrounding the incident, a reasonable person would have believed that he was not free to leave." In seeking to rely upon that test here, respondent fails to read it carefully. It says that a person has been seized "only if," not that he has been seized "whenever"; it states a necessary, but not a sufficient, condition for seizure—or, more precisely, for seizure effected through a "show of authority."

.... In sum, assuming that Pertoso's pursuit in the present case constituted a "show of authority" enjoining Hodari to halt, since Hodari did not comply with that injunction he was not seized until he was tackled. The cocaine abandoned while he was running was in this case not the fruit of a seizure, and his motion to exclude evidence of it was properly denied.

TORRES v. MADRID
141 S.Ct. 989 (2021)

Case Summary

In 2021, the Supreme Court revisited the question whether an unsuccessful effort to stop someone constitutes a seizure. The case is summarized below:

Facts

New Mexico state police officers Janice Madrid and Richard Williamson approached a Toyota FJ Cruiser that was backed into a parking spot with its engine running. The officers tried to speak to the driver, Roxanne Torres. Torres, who claimed she thought she was the victim of an attempted carjacking, drove off.

Madrid and Williamson, who claimed they feared for their safety, fired their weapons. Torres was hit twice but did not stop. She drove to a nearby parking lot, swapped her severely damaged FJ Cruiser for an unattended Kia Soul with its motor running, and drove 75 miles to Grants, New Mexico. Torres promptly checked into a hospital for treatment for bullet wounds and police arrested her there the next day.

Toyota FJ Cruiser

Procedural History and Argument

Torres later filed a civil rights lawsuit against Madrid and Williamson, alleging that the officers violated her constitutional rights because the shooting was an unreasonable Fourth Amendment "seizure." The lower courts granted summary judgment in favor of the officers, ruling that the shooting did not constitute a "seizure" at all.

In the Supreme Court, the officers' made the straightforward argument that to be seized means to be stopped, and Torres kept going. The officers contended: "The citizen's 'freedom of movement' must actually be physically restrained or controlled for a seizure to occur"? *Before continuing on, how do you think the Supreme Court resolved this question?*

Ruling

In a 5-3 opinion by Chief Justice Roberts, the Court reversed, concluding that the officers seized Torres even though she subsequently fled: "We hold that the (1) application of physical force to the body of a person (2) with intent to restrain is a seizure even if the person does not submit and is not subdued." Roberts added that "we largely covered this ground in California v. Hodari D." Can you point to language in *Hodari D.* that helps resolve the *Torres* case?

Although *Hodari D.* was the strongest influence on the Court's opinion, the *Torres* majority also sought guidance in the common law history of arrests. But by identifying the 1605 *Countess of Rutland's Case* as the "closest decision" the Court illustrated the difficulty of finding historical analogues to modern day policing. In the *Countess of Rutland's Case*, "serjeants-at-mace tracked down Isabel Holcroft, Countess of Rutland, to execute a writ for a judgment of debt. They 'shewed her their mace, and touching her body with it, said to her, we arrest you, madam.'" This pronouncement, the majority felt, supported the Court's ruling that the common law (and thus the Fourth Amendment) recognized a mere touching as a "seizure."

Apparently concerned that its ruling would be construed too broadly, the majority emphasized existing boundaries on what counts as a seizure, including that "a seizure requires the use of force *with intent to restrain*. Accidental force will not qualify." This means that an officer who accidentally bumps into someone, shakes their hand in greeting, or pats them on the shoulder, will not be deemed, by virtue of that physical contact alone, to have seized the person.

The Court summarized its "narrow" holding as follows:

> " The rule we announce today is narrow. In addition to the requirement of intent to restrain, a seizure by force—absent submission—lasts only as long as the application of force. That is to say that the Fourth Amendment does not recognize any "*continuing* arrest during the period of fugitivity." Hodari D. (1991). The fleeting nature of some seizures by force undoubtedly may inform what damages a civil plaintiff may recover, and what evidence a criminal defendant may exclude from trial. But brief seizures are seizures all the same.
>
> Applying these principles to the facts viewed in the light most favorable to Torres, the officers' shooting applied physical force to her body and objectively manifested an intent to restrain her from driving away. We therefore conclude that the officers seized Torres for the instant that the bullets struck her.

Chapter 3

REASONABLENESS: WARRANTS

The Fourth Amendment does not prohibit "searches" and "seizures." It requires that they be reasonable. See *Elkins v. United* States (1960) ("It must always be remembered that what the Constitution forbids is not all searches and seizures, but unreasonable searches and seizures.").

Outside formal legal contexts, assessing the "reasonableness" of a practice generally comes down to a rough balancing of the goal sought to be achieved by the practice against the potential harms generated in pursuit of that goal. While the Supreme Court sometimes interprets reasonableness in this ad hoc manner, more often it seeks to enforce certain rules or guidelines that stand in for reasonableness. One of the clearest rules comes from the Fourth Amendment itself: a search or seizure will generally be deemed reasonable if it is conducted pursuant to a valid warrant issued by a judicial officer.

Warrants are mentioned in the Fourth Amendment, but the reference is somewhat cryptic. The primary ambiguity has to do with the strength of the link between the first half of the Fourth Amendment (the "Reasonableness Clause") and the second half (the "Warrants Clause").

Reasonableness Clause

"The right of the people to be secure in their persons, houses, papers, and effects, against unreasonable searches and seizures, shall not be violated,

Warrants Clause

and no Warrants shall issue, but upon probable cause, supported by Oath or affirmation, and particularly describing the place to be searched, and the persons or things to be seized."

The Supreme Court generally articulates the link between the two clauses as establishing a default rule. Fourth Amendment reasonableness is established when the police act pursuant to a warrant supported by probable cause, but becomes open to question when police act without a warrant. Here are some representative quotes from the Court's cases:

- "The police must, whenever practicable, obtain advance judicial approval of searches and seizures through the warrant procedure." *Terry v. Ohio* (1968)

- "Searches conducted outside the judicial process, without prior approval by judge or magistrate, are per se unreasonable under the Fourth Amendment—subject only to a few specifically established and well-delineated exceptions." *Arizona v. Gant* (2009)

- "Although the text of the Fourth Amendment does not specify when a search warrant must be obtained, this Court has inferred that a warrant must generally be secured." *Kentucky v. King* (2011)

- "Searches and seizures inside a home without a warrant are presumptively unreasonable…." *United States v. Karo* (1984)

Taking this language at face value, police officers seeking to conduct a search or seizure must obtain a warrant based upon probable cause, unless the courts recognize an exception to the warrant requirement for the applicable scenario. This Chapter considers the standard ingredients of Fourth Amendment reasonableness (probable cause and warrants). The next Chapter covers the many exceptions – scenarios where the Supreme Court has ruled that one or both ingredients are not required.

A.　　PROBABLE CAUSE

One of the primary ingredients of reasonableness is a requisite degree of "individualized suspicion." See *City of Indianapolis v. Edmond* (2000) ("A search or seizure is ordinarily unreasonable in the absence of individualized suspicion of wrongdoing."). The inquiry into individualized suspicion asks: Why are the police searching *this* space or seizing *this* person? The Supreme Court operationalizes the concept through more specific articulations of the degree of suspicion that must support a particular search or seizure. The most commonly invoked standard of individualized suspicion is "probable cause," a phrase that appears in the text of the Fourth Amendment as a necessary ingredient of a valid warrant. The existence of "probable cause" governs not just the validity of warrants but also the authority to search and seize in a variety of scenarios without a warrant. This Section analyzes the legal guidance on what constitutes "probable cause," starting with one of the most-cited cases on that question.

1.   INFORMANTS

ILLINOIS v. GATES
462 U.S. 213 (1983)

Justice REHNQUIST delivered the opinion of the Court.

... On May 3, 1978, the Bloomingdale, Illinois Police Department received by mail an anonymous handwritten letter which read as follows:

> "This letter is to inform you that you have a couple in your town who strictly make their living on selling drugs. They are Sue and Lance Gates, they live on Greenway, off Bloomingdale Rd. in the condominiums. Most of their buys are done in Florida. Sue his wife drives their car to Florida, where she leaves it to be loaded up with drugs, then Lance flys down and drives it back. Sue flys back after she drops the car off in Florida. May 3 she is driving down there again and Lance will be flying down in a few days to drive it back. At the time Lance drives the car back he has the trunk loaded with over $100,000.00 in drugs. Presently they have over $100,000.00 worth of drugs in their basement.
>
> They brag about the fact they never have to work, and make their entire living on pushers.
>
> I guarantee if you watch them carefully you will make a big catch. They are friends with some big drugs dealers, who visit their house often.
>
> Lance & Susan Gates Greenway in Condominiums"

The letter was referred by the Chief of Police of the Bloomingdale Police Department to Detective Mader, who decided to pursue the tip. Mader learned, from the office of the Illinois Secretary of State, that an Illinois driver's license had been issued to one Lance Gates, residing at a stated address in Bloomingdale. He contacted a confidential informant, whose examination of certain financial records revealed a more recent address for the Gates, and he also learned from a police officer assigned to O'Hare Airport that "L. Gates" had made a reservation on Eastern Airlines flight 245 to West Palm Beach, Fla., scheduled to depart from Chicago on May 5 at 4:15 p.m.

Mader then made arrangements with an agent of the Drug Enforcement Administration for surveillance of the May 5 Eastern Airlines flight. The agent later reported to Mader that Gates had boarded the flight, and that federal agents in Florida had observed him arrive in West Palm Beach and take a taxi to the nearby Holiday Inn. They also reported that Gates went to a room registered to one Susan Gates and that, at 7:00 a.m. the next morning, Gates and an unidentified woman left the motel in a Mercury bearing Illinois license plates and drove northbound on an interstate frequently used by travelers to the Chicago area. In addition, the DEA agent informed Mader that the license plate number on the Mercury registered to a Hornet station wagon owned by Gates. The agent also advised Mader that the driving time between West Palm Beach and Bloomingdale was approximately 22 to 24 hours.

Mader signed an affidavit setting forth the foregoing facts, and submitted it to a judge of the Circuit Court of DuPage County, together with a copy of the anonymous letter. The judge of that court thereupon issued a search warrant for the Gates' residence and for their automobile. The judge, in deciding to issue the warrant, could have determined that the *modus operandi* of the Gates had been substantially corroborated. As the anonymous letter predicted, Lance Gates had flown from Chicago to West Palm Beach late in the afternoon of May 5th, had checked into a hotel room registered in the name of his wife, and, at 7:00 a.m. the following morning, had headed north, accompanied by an unidentified woman, out of West Palm Beach on an interstate highway used by travelers from South Florida to Chicago in an automobile bearing a license plate issued to him.

At 5:15 a.m. on March 7th, only 36 hours after he had flown out of Chicago, Lance Gates, and his wife, returned to their home in Bloomingdale, driving the car in which they had left West Palm Beach some 22 hours earlier. The Bloomingdale police were awaiting them, searched the trunk of the Mercury, and uncovered approximately 350 pounds of marijuana. A search of the Gates' home revealed marijuana, weapons, and other contraband. The Illinois Circuit Court ordered suppression of all these items, on the ground that the affidavit submitted to the

Circuit Judge failed to support the necessary determination of probable cause to believe that the Gates' automobile and home contained the contraband in question. This decision was affirmed in turn by the Illinois Appellate Court and by a divided vote of the Supreme Court of Illinois....

We agree with the Illinois Supreme Court that an informant's "veracity," "reliability" and "basis of knowledge" are all highly relevant in determining the value of his report. [*Ed. Note*: The quoted elements came from a line of Supreme Court cases.] We do not agree, however, that these elements should be understood as entirely separate and independent requirements to be rigidly exacted in every case, which the opinion of the Supreme Court of Illinois would imply. Rather, as detailed below, they should be understood simply as closely intertwined issues that may usefully illuminate the commonsense, practical question whether there is "probable cause" to believe that contraband or evidence is located in a particular place.

.... Probable cause is a fluid concept-turning on the assessment of probabilities in particular factual contexts-not readily, or even usefully, reduced to a neat set of legal rules. Informants' tips doubtless come in many shapes and sizes from many different types of persons.... Rigid legal rules are ill-suited to an area of such diversity.... For all these reasons, we ... reaffirm the totality-of-the-circumstances analysis that traditionally has informed probable cause determinations....

The showing of probable cause in the present case was [sufficient.]... Florida is well-known as a source of narcotics and other illegal drugs. Lance Gates' flight to Palm Beach, his brief, overnight stay in a motel, and apparent immediate return north to Chicago in the family car, conveniently awaiting him in West Palm Beach, is as suggestive of a pre-arranged drug run, as it is of an ordinary vacation trip.

In addition, the magistrate could rely on the anonymous letter, which had been corroborated in major part by Mader's efforts ... The corroboration of the letter's predictions that the Gates' car would be in Florida, that Lance Gates would fly to Florida in the next day or so, and that he would drive the car north toward Bloomingdale all indicated, albeit not with certainty, that the informant's other assertions also were true....

Finally, the anonymous letter contained a range of details relating not just to easily obtained facts and conditions existing at the time of the tip, but to future actions of third parties ordinarily not easily predicted. The letter writer's accurate information as to the travel plans of each of the Gates was of a character likely obtained only from the Gates themselves, or from someone familiar with their not entirely ordinary travel plans. If the informant had access to accurate information of this type a magistrate could properly conclude that it was not unlikely that he also had access to reliable information of the Gates' alleged illegal activities. Of course, the Gates' travel plans might have been learned from a talkative neighbor or travel agent.... But, as discussed previously, probable cause does not demand the certainty we associate with formal trials. It is enough that there was a fair probability that the writer of the anonymous letter had obtained his entire story either from the Gates or someone they trusted. And corroboration of major portions of the letter's predictions provides just this probability. It is apparent, therefore, that the judge issuing the warrant had a substantial basis for concluding that probable cause to search the Gates' home and car existed....

"Probable cause" can be based on physical evidence, surveillance footage, officers' personal observations, tips, and a multitude of other evidence. In each scenario, a "totality of the circumstances" approach guides the probable cause determination. As the Court explained in *Texas v. Brown* (1983):

> "Probable cause is a flexible, common-sense standard. It merely requires that the facts available to the officer would warrant a man of reasonable caution in the belief, that certain items may be contraband or stolen property or useful as evidence of a crime; it does not demand any showing that such a belief be correct or more likely true than false."

Subsequent Supreme Court opinions reiterate the totality of the circumstances approach while insisting on a kind of intentional imprecision. For instance, in *Maryland v. Pringle* (2003), the Court explained that: "The probable-cause standard is incapable of precise definition or quantification into percentages."

Two surveys of federal judges fixed the average self-reported numerical standard associated with probable cause at 44.5% and 51%, with the judges' individual responses revealing surprising variation around those averages.[8] As you read the cases that follow, reflect on whether it would be useful for the Supreme Court to set a precise numerical probability percentage to represent "probable cause" and, if so, what percentage the Court should select.

2. DRUG-SNIFFING DOGS

FLORIDA v. HARRIS
568 U.S. 237 (2013)

Justice KAGAN delivered the opinion of the Court.

In this case, we consider how a court should determine if the "alert" of a drug-detection dog during a traffic stop provides probable cause to search a vehicle. The Florida Supreme Court held that the State must in every case present an exhaustive set of records, including a log of the dog's performance in the field, to establish the dog's reliability. We think that demand inconsistent with the "flexible, common-sense standard" of probable cause. Illinois v. Gates (1983).

I

William Wheetley is a K–9 Officer in the Liberty County, Florida Sheriff's Office. On June 24, 2006, he was on a routine patrol with Aldo, a German shepherd trained to detect certain narcotics (methamphetamine, marijuana, cocaine, heroin, and ecstasy). Wheetley pulled over respondent Clayton Harris's  truck because it had an expired license plate. On approaching the driver's-side door, Wheetley saw that Harris was "visibly nervous," unable to sit still, shaking, and breathing rapidly. Wheetley also noticed an open can of beer in the truck's cup holder. Wheetley asked Harris for consent to search the truck, but Harris refused. At that point, Wheetley retrieved Aldo from the patrol car and walked him around Harris's truck for a "free air sniff." Aldo alerted at the driver's-side door handle— signaling, through a distinctive set of behaviors, that he smelled drugs there.

---

[8] See Ric Simmons, Smart Surveillance 76 (2019); C.M.A. McCauliff, Burdens of Proof: Degrees of Belief, Quanta of Evidence, or Constitutional Guarantees?, 35 Vand. L. Rev. 1293 (1982).

Wheetley concluded, based principally on Aldo's alert, that he had probable cause to search the truck. His search did not turn up any of the drugs Aldo was trained to detect. But it did reveal 200 loose pseudoephedrine pills, 8,000 matches, a bottle of hydrochloric acid, two containers of antifreeze, and a coffee filter full of iodine crystals—all ingredients for making methamphetamine. Wheetley accordingly arrested Harris, who admitted after proper Miranda warnings that he routinely "cooked" methamphetamine at his house and could not go "more than a few days without using" it. The State charged Harris with possessing pseudoephedrine for use in manufacturing methamphetamine.

While out on bail, Harris had another run-in with Wheetley and Aldo. This time, Wheetley pulled Harris over for a broken brake light. Aldo again sniffed the truck's exterior, and again alerted at the driver's-side door handle. Wheetley once more searched the truck, but on this occasion discovered nothing of interest.

Harris moved to suppress the evidence found in his truck on the ground that Aldo's alert had not given Wheetley probable cause for a search. At the hearing on that motion, Wheetley testified about both his and Aldo's training in drug detection....

The trial court concluded that Wheetley had probable cause to search Harris's truck and so denied the motion to suppress.... The Florida Supreme Court reversed, holding that Wheetley lacked probable cause to search Harris's vehicle under the Fourth Amendment. "When a dog alerts," the court wrote, "the fact that the dog has been trained and certified is simply not enough to establish probable cause." To demonstrate a dog's reliability, the State needed to produce a wider array of evidence:

> "The State must present the dog's training and certification records, an explanation of the meaning of the particular training and certification, field performance records (including any unverified alerts), and evidence concerning the experience and training of the officer handling the dog, as well as any other objective evidence known to the officer about the dog's reliability."

.... We granted certiorari, and now reverse.

II

A police officer has probable cause to conduct a search when "the facts available to him would warrant a person of reasonable caution in the belief" that contraband or evidence of a crime is present. Texas v. Brown (1983). The test for probable cause is not reducible to "precise definition or quantification." Finely tuned standards such as proof beyond a reasonable doubt or by a preponderance of the evidence have no place in the probable-cause decision. All we have required is the kind of "fair probability" on which "reasonable and prudent people, not legal technicians, act." Illinois v. Gates (1983).

In evaluating whether the State has met this practical and common-sensical standard, we have consistently looked to the totality of the circumstances. We have rejected rigid rules, bright-line tests, and mechanistic inquiries in favor of a more flexible, all-things-considered approach. In Gates, for example, we abandoned our old test for assessing the reliability of informants' tips because it had devolved into a "complex superstructure of evidentiary and analytical rules," any one of which, if not complied with, would derail a finding of probable cause. We lamented the development of a list of "inflexible, independent requirements applicable in every case." Probable cause, we emphasized, is "a fluid concept—turning on the assessment of probabilities in particular factual contexts—not readily, or even usefully, reduced to a neat set of legal rules."

The Florida Supreme Court flouted this established approach to determining probable cause. To assess the reliability of a drug-detection dog, the court created a strict evidentiary checklist, whose every item the State must tick off. Most prominently, an alert cannot establish probable cause under the Florida court's decision unless the State introduces comprehensive documentation of the dog's prior "hits" and "misses" in the field. (One wonders how the court would apply its test to a rookie dog.) No matter how much other proof the State offers of the dog's reliability, the absent field performance records will preclude a finding of probable cause. That is the antithesis of a totality-of-the-circumstances analysis. It is, indeed, the very thing we criticized in Gates when we overhauled our method for assessing the trustworthiness of an informant's tip. A gap as to any one matter, we explained, should not sink the State's case; rather, that "deficiency may be compensated for, in determining the overall reliability of a tip, by a strong showing as to other indicia of reliability." So too here, a finding of a drug-detection dog's reliability cannot depend on the State's satisfaction of multiple, independent evidentiary requirements. No more for dogs than for human informants is such an inflexible checklist the way to prove reliability, and thus establish probable cause.

Making matters worse, the decision below treats records of a dog's field performance as the gold standard in evidence, when in most cases they have relatively limited import…. The better measure of a dog's reliability thus comes away from the field, in controlled testing environments.

For that reason, evidence of a dog's satisfactory performance in a certification or training program can itself provide sufficient reason to trust his alert. If a bona fide organization has certified a dog after testing his reliability in a controlled setting, a court can presume (subject to any conflicting evidence offered) that the dog's alert provides probable cause to search. The same is true, even in the absence of formal certification, if the dog has recently and successfully completed a training program that evaluated his proficiency in locating drugs. After all, law enforcement units have their own strong incentive to use effective training and certification programs, because only accurate drug-detection dogs enable officers to locate contraband without incurring unnecessary risks or wasting limited time and resources.

A defendant, however, must have an opportunity to challenge such evidence of a dog's reliability, whether by cross-examining the testifying officer or by introducing his own fact or expert witnesses. The defendant, for example, may contest the adequacy of a certification or training program, perhaps asserting that its standards are too lax or its methods faulty. So too, the defendant may examine how the dog (or handler) performed in the assessments made in those settings. Indeed, evidence of the dog's (or handler's) history in the field, although susceptible to the kind of misinterpretation we have discussed, may sometimes be relevant…. And even assuming a dog is generally reliable, circumstances surrounding a particular alert may undermine the case for probable cause—if, say, the officer cued the dog (consciously or not), or if the team was working under unfamiliar conditions.

In short, a probable-cause hearing focusing on a dog's alert should proceed much like any other. The court should allow the parties to make their best case, consistent with the usual rules of criminal procedure. And the court should then evaluate the proffered evidence to decide what all the circumstances demonstrate. If the State has produced proof from controlled settings that a dog performs reliably in detecting drugs, and the defendant has not contested that showing, then the court should find probable cause. If, in contrast, the defendant has challenged the State's

119

case (by disputing the reliability of the dog overall or of a particular alert), then the court should weigh the competing evidence. In all events, the court should not prescribe, as the Florida Supreme Court did, an inflexible set of evidentiary requirements. The question—similar to every inquiry into probable cause—is whether all the facts surrounding a dog's alert, viewed through the lens of common sense, would make a reasonably prudent person think that a search would reveal contraband or evidence of a crime. A sniff is up to snuff when it meets that test.

III

And here, Aldo's did. The record in this case amply supported the trial court's determination that Aldo's alert gave Wheetley probable cause to search Harris's truck.

The State, as earlier described, introduced substantial evidence of Aldo's training and his proficiency in finding drugs. The State showed that two years before alerting to Harris's truck, Aldo had successfully completed a 120–hour program in narcotics detection, and separately obtained a certification from an independent company. And although the certification expired after a year, the Sheriff's Office required continuing training for Aldo and Wheetley. The two satisfied the requirements of another, 40–hour training program one year prior to the search at issue. And Wheetley worked with Aldo for four hours each week on exercises designed to keep their skills sharp. Wheetley testified, and written records confirmed, that in those settings Aldo always performed at the highest level….

And Harris's cross-examination of Wheetley, which focused on Aldo's field performance, failed to rebut the State's case. Harris principally contended in the trial court that because Wheetley did not find any of the substances Aldo was trained to detect, Aldo's two alerts must have been false. But we have already described the hazards of inferring too much from the failure of a dog's alert to lead to drugs; and here we doubt that Harris's logic does justice to Aldo's skills. Harris cooked and used methamphetamine on a regular basis; so as Wheetley later surmised, Aldo likely responded to odors that Harris had transferred to the driver's-side door handle of his truck. A well-trained drug-detection dog should alert to such odors; his response to them might appear a mistake, but in fact is not. And still more fundamentally, we do not evaluate probable cause in hindsight, based on what a search does or does not turn up. For the reasons already stated, Wheetley had good cause to view Aldo as a reliable detector of drugs. And no special circumstance here gave Wheetley reason to discount Aldo's usual dependability or distrust his response to Harris's truck.

Because training records established Aldo's reliability in detecting drugs and Harris failed to undermine that showing, we agree with the trial court that Wheetley had probable cause to search Harris's truck. We accordingly reverse the judgment of the Florida Supreme Court.

It is important when applying the concept of probable cause, to look for a logical connection between the evidence cited to support "probable cause" and the challenged search or seizure. The standard for a search is probable cause "that contraband or evidence of a crime will be found in a particular place." *Illinois v. Gates* (1983). The standard for a search is <u>not</u> probable cause that "something seems off" or even that a suspect committed a crime. See *United States v. Pitts*, 6 F.3d 1366 (9th Cir. 1993) ("Probable cause to believe that a suspect has committed a crime is not, however, by itself adequate to obtain a search warrant for the suspect's home. The affidavit must demonstrate reasonable cause to believe that the things listed as the objects of the search are located in the place to be searched."). Thus, in the *Harris* case, "the open can of beer in the truck's cup holder" provides no additional support for a search of the vehicle for drugs. As the Court's analysis reflected, everything in that case turned on the reliability of the dog's alert.

Probable cause can be established by inference. See *Ornelas v. United States* (1996) ("A police officer may draw inferences based on his own experience in deciding whether probable cause exists."). One commonly litigated question is how much can be inferred from the fact that a person possessed or sold illegal drugs. Here is a helpful discussion of the question from a California Court of Appeal opinion:[9]

> Cases throughout the country have considered whether an officer's opinion, or a logical inference, is sufficient to provide probable cause to search a residence for drugs where there is evidence that the occupant is a drug dealer, but no direct evidence of illegal activity connected with the home. There is a split of authority on the point. Some cases hold that an

---

[9] People v. Pressey, 102 Cal. App. 4th 1178 (2002).

opinion or logical inference is not enough, and that there must be some additional facts concerning the residence, such as that the seller went to his home prior to the sale, or that the sale occurred near the home, which would support the inference that the supply is probably located there. But in more recent times many courts have been disinclined to require such facts in the particular case to support that inference. Rather, it is commonly held that this gap can be filled merely on the basis of the affiant-officer's experience that drug dealers ordinarily keep their supply, records and monetary profits at home.

…. In U.S. v. Terry (9th Cir. 1990), for example, the defendant was stopped while driving a truck that contained plastic baggies with methamphetamine, a bottle with a precursor chemical for the manufacture of methamphetamine, and $10,000 in cash. A warrant to search the defendant's home was issued based on the property found in the truck, and an officer's opinion that "methamphetamine drug traffickers keep drugs, paraphernalia, records and money in their homes or adjoining structures." The court upheld the magistrate's finding of probable cause, citing the inference that "evidence is likely to be found where drug dealers live." The opposing approach is exemplified by the decision in State v. Thein, where a search warrant was issued based on evidence that the defendant was involved in drug dealing, and an officer's opinion that drug traffickers commonly keep drug inventory and paraphernalia, large sums of money, and weapons in their homes. The Washington Supreme Court found this showing insufficient to establish probable cause to search the defendant's residence, rejecting a "per se rule that if the magistrate determines a person is probably a drug dealer, then a finding of probable cause to search that person's residence automatically follows." The court concluded that "generalizations regarding the common habits of drug dealers" did not substitute for "specific facts linking such illegal activity to the residence searched… Although common sense and experience inform the inferences reasonably to be drawn from the facts, broad generalizations do not alone establish probable cause."

The People ask us to extend the approach of the California and Ninth Circuit cases involving drug dealers, and uphold the search warrant herein based on the evidence that appellant was a user of illegal drugs, and the officer's opinion that drug users will keep drugs "at their residence so they always have a source to satisfy their addiction." Since such an opinion or inference could be readily supplied or drawn in every case, the People are, to use the language of the Thein court, "essentially urging us to adopt a per se rule that if the magistrate determines a person is probably a drug user, then a finding of probable cause to search that person's residence automatically follows."

We will assume that the California decisions are correct insofar as they suggest that evidence of drug dealing, by itself, can furnish probable cause to search the dealer's residence. However, we decline to adopt a corresponding rule in cases involving only drug use…. We conclude that probable cause to search the residence of someone suspected of using illegal drugs requires more than an opinion or inference, available in every case, that drugs are likely to be present."

3. DRUG-SNIFFING HUMANS

UNITED STATES v. NIELSEN
(10th Cir. 1993)

LOGAN, Circuit Judge.

Defendant Douglas Merrill Nielsen entered a conditional guilty plea to possessing in excess of 500 grams of cocaine…. The only issue on appeal is whether a police officer's alleged smell of burnt marijuana gave probable cause to search the trunk of the car….

I

The district court succinctly summarized the facts as follows:

At approximately 4:30 p.m. on April 22, 1992, Bushnell stopped Nielsen for a speeding violation on I–35 near Nephi, Utah. Bushnell claimed that as he spoke with Nielsen, he immediately recognized the smell of burned marijuana coming from the open window of Nielsen's vehicle. According to Bushnell, he could not tell if the odor came from Nielsen's person or the vehicle. Bushnell asked Nielsen about the marijuana, and Nielsen said he had none. Bushnell then asked if he could search the interior of the vehicle, and

123

Nielsen consented. Bushnell searched the interior of the vehicle but found nothing that could have been the source of the odor.

Bushnell then ran a radio check on Nielsen which indicated that Nielsen had been arrested for a misdemeanor marijuana offense in 1977. Thereafter, Bushnell told Nielsen that he believed there was marijuana in the car and that he was going to search the trunk. Nielsen did not consent to the search of the trunk. Bushnell then removed the keys to Nielsen's car from the ignition, opened the trunk, and found a set of scales and approximately two kilograms of cocaine.

The district court believed Officer Bushnell's claims that he smelled marijuana emanating from defendant's vehicle and found Bushnell's testimony credible. The court then … determined that probable cause existed to search the trunk and denied defendant's motion to suppress. [*Ed. Note*: As we will discuss in Chapter 4, "probable cause" but not a warrant is required for car searches.]

II

In reviewing the denial of a motion to suppress evidence, we must accept the trial court's findings of fact unless they are clearly erroneous. The district court's factual findings are that the officer smelled burnt marijuana, obtained consent to search the passenger compartment and found nothing. When defendant refused consent to search the trunk, the officer conducted a warrantless search of the trunk in which he found only cocaine. Defendant introduced into evidence the negative results of a urine test that should have indicated whether he had used marijuana within the time frame of the stop.

… The rational explanations for these incongruous facts suggest the following possibilities: (1) Bushnell did smell marijuana–someone else had recently smoked marijuana in defendant's car, or, less likely, defendant (the sole occupant of the car at the time it was stopped) had smoked marijuana in the car, disposed the remains out the window, and the urine test result was invalid; (2) Bushnell thought he smelled marijuana, but was mistaken; or (3) Bushnell fabricated his testimony that he detected the smell of marijuana. The district court believed the officer's testimony, thus, apparently it accepted the first possibility. Based upon the cold record we would not have made the same determination; but, as is the case with essentially all factual findings based upon credibility, we cannot hold that the district court's factual finding is clearly erroneous.

III

We still must address the legal issue whether, based on the facts found by the district court, there was probable cause to search the trunk. We review de novo the trial court's legal conclusion that the search was reasonable under the Fourth Amendment. Probable cause to search a vehicle is established if, under the "totality of the circumstances" there is a "fair probability" that the car contains contraband or evidence. Illinois v. Gates (1983)....

The scope of a warrantless search of an automobile "is defined by the object of the search and the places in which there is probable cause to believe that it may be found." United States v. Ross (1982).... The smell of burnt marijuana would lead a person of ordinary caution to believe the passenger compartment might contain marijuana. In the instant case, Bushnell's consensual search of the passenger compartment revealed no marijuana or related contraband. We do not believe under the circumstances that there was a fair probability that the *trunk* contained marijuana.... Defendant's nervousness and a fifteen year old misdemeanor drug conviction do not persuade us otherwise. See United States v. Millan–Diaz (10th Cir.1992) (nervousness as basis for suspicion must be considered with caution and normally is not dispositive). We hold that under all of the circumstances there was no probable cause to search the trunk. The district court erred in denying defendant's motion to suppress the evidence. Reversed.

Sometimes the age of information police rely on (so called, "staleness") raises doubts about the existence of probable cause. Here is a discussion on this point from the New Hampshire Supreme Court:

> The defendants reveal the central weakness of their staleness claim when they state in their brief that the superior court "relied upon stale information" in reaching the probable cause determination. The quotation reflects a confusion between stale probable cause and stale information. Stale probable cause, so called, is probable cause that would have justified a warrant at some earlier moment that has already passed by the time the warrant is sought. Speaking of the probable cause as "stale" in such a case merely reflects the requirement that the police must show that at the time of the application for the warrant

there is a substantial likelihood of finding the evidentiary material specified.

There is not, however, any dispositive significance in the mere fact that some information offered to demonstrate probable cause may be called stale, in the sense that it concerns events that occurred well before the date of the application for the warrant. If such past fact contributes to an inference that probable cause exists at the time of the application, its age is no taint.[10]

See also *U.S. v. Encarnacion* (1st Cir. 2022) ("Information is stale if, for example, it established probable cause at some point in the past but does not support probable cause at the time of the warrant's issuance. Just as different kinds of produce will retain their freshness for varying periods, the timeliness of probable cause is context-dependent and will vary both with the nature of the information itself and with the nature of the suspected offense.").

4. TOTALITY OF THE CIRCUMSTANCES

DISTRICT OF COLUMBIA v. WESBY
138 S.Ct. 577 (2018)

Justice THOMAS delivered the opinion of the Court.

This case involves a civil suit against the District of Columbia and five of its police officers, brought by 16 individuals who were arrested for holding a raucous, late-night party in a house they did not have permission to enter. The United States Court of Appeals for the District of Columbia Circuit held that there was no probable cause to arrest the partygoers, and that the officers were not entitled to qualified immunity. We reverse on both grounds.

I

Around 1 a.m. on March 16, 2008, the District's Metropolitan Police Department received a complaint about loud music and illegal activities at a house in Northeast D.C. The caller, a former neighborhood commissioner, told police that the house

---

[10] State v. Valenzuela, 130 N.H. 175 (1987).

had been vacant for several months. When officers arrived at the scene, several neighbors confirmed that the house should have been empty. The officers approached the house and, consistent with the complaint, heard loud music playing inside.

After the officers knocked on the front door, they saw a man look out the window and then run upstairs. One of the partygoers opened the door, and the officers entered. They immediately observed that the inside of the house "was in disarray" and looked like "a vacant property." The officers smelled marijuana and saw beer bottles and cups of liquor on the floor.... Although the house had working electricity and plumbing, it had no furniture downstairs other than a few padded metal chairs. The only other signs of habitation were blinds on the windows, food in the refrigerator, and toiletries in the bathroom....

The officers found a total of 21 people in the house. After interviewing all 21, the officers did not get a clear or consistent story.... Two of the women working the party said that a woman named "Peaches" or "Tasty" was renting the house and had given them permission to be there.... An officer asked the woman to call Peaches on her phone so he could talk to her. Peaches answered and explained that she had just left the party to go to the store. When the officer asked her to return, Peaches refused because she was afraid of being arrested. The sergeant supervising the investigation also spoke with Peaches. At first, Peaches claimed to be renting the house from the owner, who was fixing it up for her. She also said that she had given the attendees permission to have the party. When the sergeant again asked her who had given her permission to use the house, Peaches became evasive and hung up. The sergeant called her back, and she began yelling and insisting that she had permission before hanging up a second time. The officers eventually got Peaches on the phone again, and she admitted that she did not have permission to use the house.

The officers then contacted the owner. He told them that he had been trying to negotiate a lease with Peaches, but they had not reached an agreement. He confirmed that he had not given Peaches (or anyone else) permission to be in the house—let alone permission to use it for a bachelor party. At that point, the officers arrested the 21 partygoers for unlawful entry. See D.C. Code § 22–3302 (2008). The police transported the partygoers to the police station, where the lieutenant decided

127

to charge them with disorderly conduct. See § 22–1321. The partygoers were released, and the charges were eventually dropped.[2]

II

Respondents, 16 of the 21 partygoers, sued the District and five of the arresting officers ... for false arrest under the Fourth Amendment, 42 U.S.C. § 1983, and [false arrest and negligent supervision] under District law.... The partygoers' claims were all "predicated upon the allegation that [they] were arrested without probable cause."

---

42 U.S.C. § 1983

"Every person who, under color of any statute, ordinance, regulation, custom, or usage, of any State or Territory or the District of Columbia, subjects, or causes to be subjected, any citizen of the United States or other person within the jurisdiction thereof to the deprivation of any rights, privileges, or immunities secured by the Constitution and laws, shall be liable to the party injured in an action at law, suit in equity, or other proper proceeding for redress...."

On cross-motions for summary judgment, the District Court awarded partial summary judgment to the partygoers. It concluded that the officers lacked probable cause to arrest the partygoers for unlawful entry. The officers were told that Peaches had invited the partygoers to the house, the District Court reasoned, and nothing the officers learned in their investigation suggested the partygoers "knew or should have known that [they were] entering against the [owner's] will." The District Court also concluded that the officers were not entitled to qualified immunity under §1983. It noted that, under District case law, "probable cause to arrest for unlawful entry requires evidence that the alleged intruder knew or should have known, upon entry, that such entry was against the will of the owner." And in its view, the officers had no such evidence.

---

[2] Because probable cause is an objective standard, an arrest is lawful if the officer had probable cause to arrest for any offense, not just the offense cited at the time of arrest or booking. Because unlawful entry is the only offense that the District and its officers discuss in their briefs to this Court, we likewise limit our analysis to that offense.

With liability resolved, the case proceeded to trial on damages. The jury awarded the partygoers a total of $680,000 in compensatory damages. After the District Court awarded attorney's fees, the total award was nearly $1 million.

On appeal, a divided panel of the D.C. Circuit affirmed....

III

The Fourth Amendment protects "[t]he right of the people to be secure in their persons, houses, papers, and effects, against unreasonable searches and seizures." Because arrests are "seizures" of "persons," they must be reasonable under the circumstances. A warrantless arrest is reasonable if the officer has probable cause to believe that the suspect committed a crime in the officer's presence.

To determine whether an officer had probable cause for an arrest, "we examine the events leading up to the arrest, and then decide 'whether these historical facts, viewed from the standpoint of an objectively reasonable police officer, amount to' probable cause." Because probable cause "deals with probabilities and depends on the totality of the circumstances," it is "a fluid concept" that is "not readily, or even usefully, reduced to a neat set of legal rules," Illinois v. Gates (1983). It "requires only a probability or substantial chance of criminal activity, not an actual showing of such activity." Probable cause is not a high bar.

A

There is no dispute that the partygoers entered the house against the will of the owner. Nonetheless, the partygoers contend that the officers lacked probable cause to arrest them because the officers had no reason to believe that they "knew or should have known" their "entry was unwanted." We disagree. Considering the totality of the circumstances, the officers made an entirely reasonable inference that the partygoers were knowingly taking advantage of a vacant house as a venue for their late-night party.

Consider first the condition of the house. Multiple neighbors, including a former neighborhood official, informed the officers that the house had been vacant for several months. The house had no furniture, except for a few padded metal chairs and a bare mattress. The rest of the house was empty, save for some fixtures and large appliances. The house had a few signs of inhabitance—working electricity and plumbing, blinds on the windows, toiletries in the bathroom, and food in the refrigerator. But those facts are not necessarily inconsistent with the house being unoccupied. The owner could have paid the utilities and kept the blinds while he looked for a new tenant, and the partygoers could have brought the food and toiletries. Although one woman told the officers that Peaches had recently moved in, the officers had reason to doubt that was true. There were no boxes or other moving supplies in the house; nor were there other possessions, such as clothes in the closet, suggesting someone lived there.

In addition to the condition of the house, consider the partygoers' conduct. The party was still going strong when the officers arrived after 1 a.m., with music so loud that it could be heard from outside. Upon entering the house, multiple officers smelled marijuana. The partygoers left beer bottles and cups of liquor on the floor, and they left the floor so dirty that one of them refused to sit on it. The living room had been converted into a makeshift strip club....

Taken together, the condition of the house and the conduct of the partygoers allowed the officers to make several common-sense conclusions about human behavior. Most homeowners do not live in near-barren houses. And most homeowners do not invite people over to use their living room as a strip club, to have sex in their bedroom, to smoke marijuana inside, and to leave their floors filthy. The officers could thus infer that the partygoers knew their party was not authorized.

The partygoers' reaction to the officers gave them further reason to believe that the partygoers knew they lacked permission to be in the house. Many scattered at the sight of the uniformed officers. Two hid themselves, one in a closet and the other in a bathroom. "Unprovoked flight upon noticing the police," we have explained, "is certainly suggestive" of wrongdoing and can be treated as "suspicious behavior" that factors into the totality of the circumstances. Illinois v. Wardlow (2000).... A reasonable officer could infer that the partygoers' scattering and hiding was an indication that they knew they were not supposed to be there.

The partygoers' answers to the officers' questions also suggested their guilty state of mind. When the officers asked who had given them permission to be there, the partygoers gave vague and implausible responses. They could not say who had invited them. Only two people claimed that Peaches had invited them, and they were working the party instead of attending it.... Additionally, some of the partygoers claimed the event was a bachelor party, but no one could identify the bachelor. The officers could have disbelieved them, since people normally do not throw a bachelor party without a bachelor. Based on the vagueness and implausibility of the partygoers' stories, the officers could have reasonably inferred that they were lying and that their lies suggested a guilty mind.

The panel majority relied heavily on the fact that Peaches said she had invited the partygoers to the house. But when the officers spoke with Peaches, she was nervous, agitated, and evasive. After initially insisting that she had permission to use the house, she ultimately confessed that this was a lie—a fact that the owner confirmed. Peaches' lying and evasive behavior gave the officers reason to discredit everything she had told them. For example, the officers could have inferred that Peaches lied to them when she said she had invited the others to the house, which was consistent with the fact that hardly anyone at the party knew her name. Or the officers could have inferred that Peaches told the partygoers (like she eventually told the police) that she was not actually renting the house, which was consistent with how the partygoers were treating it.

Viewing these circumstances as a whole, a reasonable officer could conclude that there was probable cause to believe the partygoers knew they did not have permission to be in the house.

B

In concluding otherwise, the panel majority engaged in an excessively technical dissection of the factors supporting probable cause. Indeed, the panel majority failed to follow two basic and well-established principles of law.

First, the panel majority viewed each fact in isolation, rather than as a factor in the totality of the circumstances. This was mistaken in light of our precedents. The "totality of the circumstances" requires courts to consider the whole picture. Our precedents recognize that the whole is often greater than the sum of its parts—especially when the parts are viewed in isolation. Instead of considering the facts as a whole, the panel majority took them one by one. For example, it dismissed the fact that the partygoers "scattered or hid when the police entered the house" because that fact was "not sufficient *standing alone* to create probable cause." Similarly, it found "nothing in the record suggesting that the condition of the house, *on its own*, should have alerted the [partygoers] that they were unwelcome." The totality-of-the-circumstances test precludes this sort of divide-and-conquer analysis.

Second, the panel majority mistakenly believed that it could dismiss outright any circumstances that were "susceptible of innocent explanation." For example, the panel majority brushed aside the drinking and the lap dances as "consistent with" the partygoers' explanation that they were having a bachelor party. And it similarly dismissed the condition of the house as "entirely consistent with" Peaches being a "new tenant." But probable cause does not require officers to rule out a suspect's innocent explanation for suspicious facts. As we have explained, "the relevant inquiry is not whether particular conduct is 'innocent' or 'guilty,' but the degree of suspicion that attaches to particular types of noncriminal acts." Thus, the panel majority should have asked whether a reasonable officer could conclude—considering all of the surrounding circumstances, including the plausibility of the explanation itself—that there was a substantial chance of criminal activity.

The circumstances here certainly suggested criminal activity. As explained, the officers found a group of people who claimed to be having a bachelor party with no bachelor, in a near-empty house, with strippers in the living room and sexual activity in the bedroom, and who fled at the first sign of police. The panel majority identified innocent explanations for most of these circumstances in isolation, but again, this kind of divide-and-conquer approach is improper. A factor viewed in isolation is often more readily susceptible to an innocent explanation than one viewed as part of a totality. And here, the totality of the circumstances gave the officers plenty of reasons to doubt the partygoers' protestations of innocence.

For all of these reasons, we reverse the D.C. Circuit's holding that the officers lacked probable cause to arrest. Accordingly, the District and its officers are entitled to summary judgment on all of the partygoers' claims....

As the Supreme Court repeatedly emphasizes, probable cause is assessed by reference to the time of the search or seizure, and thus does not depend on whether evidence is, in fact, found. This means officers can ultimately be wrong about whether a person is committing an offense or whether evidence will be found in a particular location but still have had probable cause to seize or search. In addition, the Supreme Court held in *Heien v. North Carolina* (2014) that when assessing probable cause (or related standards of individualized suspicion), an officer's reasonable mistake about the governing law should be treated similarly to a reasonable mistake about the perceived facts:

❝ The Fourth Amendment prohibits "unreasonable searches and seizures." Under this standard, a search or seizure may be permissible even though the justification for the action includes a reasonable factual mistake. An officer might, for example, stop a motorist for traveling alone in a high-occupancy vehicle lane, only to discover upon approaching the car that two children are slumped over asleep in the back seat. The driver has not violated the law, but neither has the officer violated the Fourth Amendment. But what if the police officer's reasonable mistake is not one of fact but of law? In this case, an officer stopped a vehicle because one of its two brake lights was out, but a court later determined that a single working brake light was all the law required. The question presented is whether such a mistake of law can nonetheless give rise to the reasonable suspicion necessary to uphold the seizure under the Fourth Amendment. We hold that it can. Because the officer's mistake about the brake-light law was reasonable, the stop in this case was lawful under the Fourth Amendment.

B.   WARRANTS

An important ingredient in determining the reasonableness of a "search" or "seizure" is whether the police first obtained a warrant.

> "The purpose of a warrant is to allow a neutral judicial officer to assess whether the police have probable cause to make an arrest or conduct a search. As we have often explained, the placement of this checkpoint between the Government and the citizen implicitly acknowledges that an 'officer engaged in the often competitive enterprise of ferreting out crime,' may lack sufficient objectivity to weigh correctly the strength of the evidence supporting the contemplated action against the individual's interests in protecting his own liberty and the privacy of his home."
> *Steagald v. United States* (1981)

1. ARREST WARRANTS v. SEARCH WARRANTS

There are two common types of warrants corresponding to the two primary concerns of the Fourth Amendment: arrest warrants and search warrants. The next cases discuss the purposes of each warrant and distinctions between them.

PAYTON v. NEW YORK
445 U.S. 573 (1980)

Case Summary

In *United States v. Watson* (1976), the Supreme Court ruled that police could make a warrantless arrest in a public place so long as they possessed probable cause to suspect that the person arrested had committed a felony. A New York statute sought to expand that rule to allow police to *enter a home* to make a warrantless arrest. The statute read:

> "A peace officer may, without a warrant, arrest a person, ... when a felony has in fact been committed, and he has reasonable cause for believing the person to be arrested to have committed it.... To make an arrest, ... the officer may break open an outer or inner door or window of a building, if, after notice of his office and purpose, he be refused admittance."

The Supreme Court considered the constitutionality of the New York statute in *Payton v. New York*. The Court's opinion consolidated two separate cases, with distinct facts:

❝ ❝ On January 14, 1970, after two days of intensive investigation, New York detectives had assembled evidence sufficient to establish probable cause to believe that Theodore Payton had murdered the manager of a gas station two days earlier. At about 7:30 a.m. on January 15, six officers went to Payton's apartment in the Bronx, intending to arrest him. They had not obtained a warrant. Although light and music emanated from the apartment, there was no response to their knock on the metal door. They summoned emergency assistance and, about 30 minutes later, used crowbars to break open the door and enter the apartment. No one was there. In plain view, however, was a .30-caliber shell casing that was seized and later admitted into evidence at Payton's murder trial....

[After] the commission of two armed robberies, Obie Riddick was identified by the victims ... and in January 1974 the police ... learned his address. They did not obtain a warrant for his arrest. At about noon on March 14, a detective, accompanied by three other officers, knocked on the door of the Queens house where Riddick was living. When his young son opened the door, they could see Riddick sitting in bed covered by a sheet. They entered the house and placed him under arrest. Before permitting him to dress, they opened a chest of drawers two feet from the bed in search of weapons and found narcotics and related paraphernalia. Riddick was subsequently indicted on narcotics charges....

The Supreme Court ruled that the police entries in both cases, while authorized by the New York statute, violated the Fourth Amendment. The Court began its analysis by noting that an analogous warrantless entry to locate and seize evidence would clearly violate the Fourth Amendment, suggesting that entry to locate and seize a person should be treated no differently:

> " The simple language of the Amendment applies equally to seizures of persons and to seizures of property. Our analysis in this case may therefore properly commence with rules that have been well established in Fourth Amendment litigation involving tangible items. As the Court reiterated just a few years ago, the 'physical entry of the home is the chief evil against which the wording of the Fourth Amendment is directed.' And we have long adhered to the view that the warrant procedure minimizes the danger of needless intrusions of that sort.
>
> .... Writing on the constitutional issue now before us ..., Judge Leventhal ... recognized that "a greater burden is placed on officials who enter a home or dwelling without consent. Freedom from intrusion into the home or dwelling is the archetype of the privacy protection secured by the Fourth Amendment."

His analysis of this question then focused on the long-settled premise that, absent exigent circumstances, a warrantless entry to search for weapons or contraband is unconstitutional even when a felony has been committed and there is probable cause to believe that incriminating evidence will be found within. He reasoned that the constitutional protection afforded to the individual's interest in the privacy of his own home is equally applicable to a warrantless entry for the purpose of arresting a resident of the house; for it is inherent in such an entry that a search for the suspect may be required before he can be apprehended. Judge Leventhal concluded that an entry to arrest and an entry to search for and to seize property implicate the same interest in preserving the privacy and the sanctity of the home, and justify the same level of constitutional protection…. We find this reasoning to be persuasive and in accord with this Court's Fourth Amendment decisions.

The Supreme Court also emphasized that while clear historical evidence supported the practice of warrantless public arrests, no such evidence supported warrantless home entries.

Finally, the Supreme Court offered a concession to the government. In assessing the practical impact of its ruling, the Court emphasized that a search warrant was not the only way to lawfully enter a home. The Court stated that an arrest warrant would also be sufficient in scenarios like those involved in *Payton*:

> "It is true that an arrest warrant requirement may afford less protection than a search warrant requirement, but it will suffice to interpose the magistrate's determination of probable cause between the zealous officer and the citizen. If there is sufficient evidence of a citizen's participation in a felony to persuade a judicial officer that his arrest is justified, it is constitutionally reasonable to require him to open his doors to the officers of the law. Thus, for Fourth Amendment purposes, an arrest warrant founded on probable cause implicitly carries with it the limited authority to enter a dwelling in which the suspect lives when there is reason to believe the suspect is within."

The Court concluded as follows: "Because no arrest warrant was obtained in either of these cases, the judgments must be reversed…."

STEAGALD v. UNITED STATES
451 U.S. 204 (1981)

Justice MARSHALL delivered the opinion of the Court.

The issue in this case is whether, under the Fourth Amendment, a law enforcement officer may legally search for the subject of an arrest warrant in the home of a third party without first obtaining a search warrant. Concluding that a search warrant must be obtained absent exigent circumstances or consent, we reverse the judgment of the United States Court of Appeals for the Fifth Circuit affirming petitioner's conviction.

I

In early January 1978, an agent of the Drug Enforcement Administration (DEA) was contacted in Detroit, Mich., by a confidential informant who suggested that he might be able to locate Ricky Lyons, a federal fugitive wanted on drug charges. On January 14, 1978, the informant called the agent again, and gave him a telephone number in the Atlanta, Ga., area where, according to the informant, Ricky Lyons could be reached during the next 24 hours. On January 16, 1978, the agent called fellow DEA Agent Kelly Goodowens in Atlanta and relayed the information he had obtained from the informant. Goodowens contacted Southern Bell Telephone Co., and secured the address corresponding to the telephone number obtained by the informant. Goodowens also discovered that Lyons was the subject of a 6-month-old arrest warrant.

Two days later, Goodowens and 11 other officers drove to the address supplied by the telephone company to search for Lyons. The officers observed two men standing outside the house to be searched. These men were Hoyt Gaultney and petitioner Gary Steagald. The officers approached with guns drawn, frisked both men, and, after demanding identification, determined that neither man was Lyons. Several agents proceeded to the house. Gaultney's wife answered the door, and informed the agents that she was alone in the house. She was told to place her hands against the wall and was guarded in that position while one agent searched the house. Ricky Lyons was not found, but during the search of the house the agent observed what he believed to be cocaine....

II

The question before us is a narrow one. The search at issue here took place in the absence of consent or exigent circumstances. Except in such special situations, we have consistently held that the entry into a home to conduct a search or make an arrest is unreasonable under the Fourth Amendment unless done pursuant to a warrant.... Here, of course, the agents had a warrant—one authorizing the arrest of Ricky Lyons. However, the Fourth Amendment claim here is not being raised by Ricky Lyons. Instead, the challenge to the search is asserted by a person not named in the warrant who was convicted on the basis of evidence uncovered during a search of his residence for Ricky Lyons. Thus, the narrow issue before us is whether an arrest warrant—as opposed to a search warrant—is adequate to protect the Fourth Amendment interests of persons not named in the warrant, when their homes are searched without their consent and in the absence of exigent circumstances.

.... While an arrest warrant and a search warrant both serve to subject the probable-cause determination of the police to judicial review, the interests protected by the two warrants differ. An arrest warrant is issued by a magistrate upon a showing that probable cause exists to believe that the subject of the warrant has committed an offense and thus the warrant primarily serves to protect an individual from an unreasonable seizure. A search warrant, in contrast is issued upon a showing of probable cause to believe that the legitimate object of a search is located in a particular place, and therefore safeguards an individual's interest in the privacy of his home and possessions against the unjustified intrusion of the police.

Thus, whether the arrest warrant issued in this case adequately safeguarded the interests protected by the Fourth Amendment depends upon what the warrant authorized the agents to do. To be sure, the warrant embodied a judicial finding that there was probable cause to believe the Ricky Lyons had committed a felony, and the warrant therefore authorized the officers to seize Lyons. However, the agents sought to do more than use the warrant to arrest Lyons in a public place or in his home; instead, they relied on the warrant as legal authority to enter the home of a third person based on their belief that Ricky Lyons might be a guest there. Regardless of how reasonable this belief might have been, it was never subjected to the detached scrutiny of a judicial officer. Thus, while the warrant in this case may have protected Lyons from an unreasonable seizure, it did absolutely nothing to protect petitioner's privacy interest in being free from an unreasonable invasion and search of his home. Instead, petitioner's only protection from an illegal entry and search was the agent's personal determination of probable cause. In the absence of exigent circumstances, we have consistently held that such judicially untested determinations are not reliable enough to justify an entry into a person's home to arrest him without a warrant, or a search of a home for objects in the absence of a search warrant. We see no reason to depart from this settled course when the search of a home is for a person rather than an object....

IV

.... The Government ... suggests that practical problems might arise if law enforcement officers are required to obtain a search warrant before entering the home of a third party to make an arrest. The basis of this concern is that persons, as opposed to objects, are inherently mobile, and thus officers seeking to effect an arrest may be forced to return to the magistrate several times as the subject of the arrest warrant moves from place to place. We are convinced, however, that a search warrant requirement will not significantly impede effective law enforcement efforts.

First, the situations in which a search warrant will be necessary are few. As noted in Payton v. New York, an arrest warrant alone will suffice to enter a suspect's own residence to effect his arrest. Furthermore, if probable cause exists, no warrant is required to apprehend a suspected felon in a public place. United States v. Watson (1976). Thus, the subject of an arrest warrant can be readily seized before entering or after leaving the home of a third party. Finally, the exigent-circumstances doctrine significantly limits the situations in which a search warrant would be needed. For example, a warrantless entry of a home would be justified if the police were in "hot pursuit" of a fugitive. See United States v. Santana (1976); Warden v. Hayden (1967). Thus, to the extent that searches for persons pose special problems, we believe that the exigent-circumstances doctrine is adequate to accommodate legitimate law enforcement needs. [*Ed. Note*: The case law concerning "exigent circumstances" is covered in Chapter 4.]

Moreover, in those situations in which a search warrant is necessary, the inconvenience incurred by the police is simply not that significant. First, if the police know of the location of the felon when they obtain an arrest warrant, the additional burden of obtaining a search warrant at the same time is miniscule. The inconvenience of obtaining such a warrant does not increase significantly when an outstanding arrest warrant already exists. In this case, for example, Agent Goodowens knew the address of the house to be searched two days in advance, and planned the raid from the federal courthouse in Atlanta where, we are informed, three full-time magistrates were on duty. In routine search cases such as this, the short time required to obtain a search warrant from a magistrate will seldom hinder efforts to apprehend a felon. Finally, if a magistrate is not nearby, a telephonic search warrant can usually be obtained.

Whatever practical problems remain, however, cannot outweigh the constitutional interests at stake....

2. OATH OR AFFIRMATION

The Fourth Amendment specifically references the prerequisites to the issuance of a warrant.

> "... [N]o warrants shall issue, but upon probable cause, **supported by oath or affirmation**, and particularly describing the place to be searched, and the persons or things to be seized."

The bolded text contemplates that someone must solemnly attest to the underlying facts supporting the issuance of a warrant. Some states employ a "four corners" rule in which judges may only consider statements that have been reduced to writing and sworn in an affidavit. Other states allow judges to consider oral testimony. Under either approach, a law enforcement officer will typically provide a sworn statement of the facts that support the warrant application. The magistrate then examines that application to determine whether the probable cause standard has been met. If so, the magistrate issues the requested warrant.

Importantly, it is not sufficient for the magistrate to merely defer to the officer's conclusions. The Supreme Court made this clear in *Illinois v. Gates* (1983):

❝ Our earlier cases illustrate the limits beyond which a magistrate may not venture in issuing a warrant. A sworn statement of an affiant that "he has cause to suspect and does believe that" liquor illegally brought into the United States is located on certain premises will not do. Nathanson v. United States (1933). An affidavit must provide the magistrate with a substantial basis for determining the existence of probable cause, and the wholly conclusory statement at issue in Nathanson failed to meet this requirement. An officer's statement that "affiants have received reliable information from a credible person and believe" that heroin is stored in a home, is likewise inadequate. Aguilar v. Texas (1964). As in Nathanson, this is a mere conclusory statement that gives the magistrate virtually no basis at all for making a judgment regarding probable cause. Sufficient information must be presented to the magistrate to allow that official to determine probable cause; his action cannot be a mere ratification of the bare conclusions of others. In order to ensure that such an abdication of the magistrate's duty does not occur, courts must continue to conscientiously review the sufficiency of affidavits on which warrants are issued. But when we move beyond the "bare bones" affidavits present in cases such as Nathanson and Aguilar, this area simply does not lend itself to a prescribed set of rules…. Instead, the flexible, common-sense standard … better serves the purposes of the Fourth Amendment's probable cause requirement.

Since the magistrate must rely on the affiant's factual assertions to determine whether probable cause exists, the truth of those statements becomes critical. The next case addresses the problem of false statements included in a warrant application.

FRANKS v. DELAWARE
438 U.S. 154 (1978)

Case Summary

Franks v. Delaware has unusually complicated facts, but the modern importance of the case comes from the standard it set out. The Supreme Court framed the question it faced as follows:

"Does a defendant in a criminal proceeding ever have the right, under the Fourth and Fourteenth Amendments, subsequent to the ex parte issuance of a search warrant, to challenge the truthfulness of factual statements made in an affidavit supporting the warrant?"

The Supreme Court of Delaware had held "that a defendant under no circumstances may … challenge the veracity of a sworn statement used by police to procure a search warrant." The United States Supreme Court reversed:

"We hold that, where the defendant makes a substantial preliminary showing that a false statement knowingly and intentionally, or with reckless disregard for the truth, was included by the affiant in the warrant affidavit, and if the allegedly false statement is necessary to the finding of probable cause, the Fourth Amendment requires that a hearing be held at the defendant's request. In the event that at that hearing the allegation of perjury or reckless disregard is established by the defendant by a preponderance of the evidence, and, with the affidavit's false material set to one side, the affidavit's remaining content is insufficient to establish probable cause, the search warrant must be voided and the fruits of the search excluded to the same extent as if probable cause was lacking on the face of the affidavit...."

The Court summarized the standard at the end of the opinion offering further clarity:

"In sum, and to repeat with some embellishment what we stated at the beginning of this opinion: There is, of course, a presumption of validity with respect to the affidavit supporting the search warrant. To mandate an evidentiary hearing, the challenger's attack must be more than conclusory and must be supported by more than a mere desire to cross-examine. There must be allegations of deliberate falsehood or of reckless disregard for the truth, and those allegations must be accompanied by an offer of proof. They should point out specifically the portion of the warrant affidavit that is claimed to be false; and they should be accompanied by a statement of supporting reasons. Affidavits or sworn or otherwise reliable statements of witnesses should be furnished, or their absence satisfactorily explained. Allegations of negligence or innocent mistake are insufficient. The deliberate falsity or reckless disregard whose impeachment is permitted today is only that of the affiant, not of any nongovernmental informant. Finally, if these requirements are met, and if, when material that is the subject of the alleged falsity or reckless disregard is set to one side, there remains sufficient content in the warrant affidavit to support a finding of probable cause, no hearing is required. On the other hand, if the remaining content is insufficient, the defendant is entitled, under the Fourth and Fourteenth Amendments, to his hearing. Whether he will prevail at that hearing is, of course, another issue."

What about omissions? Lower courts sometimes invoke *Franks'* "reckless disregard" language as authority for a rule that prohibits officers from omitting important exculpatory information in a warrant affidavit. The precise standard can be tricky to articulate. The Third Circuit's rule is that "omissions are made with reckless disregard if an officer withholds a fact in his ken that any reasonable person would have known that this was the kind of thing the judge would wish to know.":

"To determine the materiality of the misstatements and omissions, we excise the offending inaccuracies and insert the facts recklessly omitted, and then determine whether or not the 'corrected' warrant affidavit would establish probable cause." *Wilson v. Russo* (3d Cir. 2000); see also *Beauchamp v. City of Noblesville* (7th Cir. 2003) ("A 'reckless disregard for the truth' is demonstrated by showing that the officers entertained serious doubts as to the truth of their statements, had obvious reasons to doubt the accuracy of the information reported, or failed to inform the judicial officer of facts they knew would negate probable cause.").

Lying in a warrant application is not just a violation of the Fourth Amendment. Just like anyone else, police officers who make false statements under oath can be prosecuted for perjury and related crimes. In 2022, the Department of Justice (DOJ) brought federal charges against the officers who obtained the warrant that led, in 2020, to the death of Breonna Taylor – a killing that generated widespread media coverage and national outrage.

Announcing the charges, the DOJ explained that "Louisville Police Detective Joshua Jaynes and Sergeant Kyle Meany drafted and approved what they knew was a false affidavit to support a search warrant for Ms. Taylor's home" and "by preparing a false affidavit to secure a search warrant for Breonna Taylor's home, defendants Jaynes and Meany willfully deprived Ms. Taylor of her constitutional right to be free from unreasonable searches and seizures." Since the DOJ alleges that the constitutional violation caused Taylor's death, the charges are punishable by up to life in prison.

3. PARTICULARITY AND PLAIN VIEW

The Fourth Amendment also requires that warrants identify their targets with precision:

... [N]o warrants shall issue, but upon probable cause, supported by oath or affirmation, and **particularly describing the place to be searched, and the persons or things to be seized**."

Thus, a warrant to search a home and garage suspected to be involved in heroin sales could not authorize police to search "the house and nearby areas suspected by police of drug involvement" but instead:

> "the premises known as: 44 West 2700 South, South Salt Lake City, Utah, a white house, brown roof, front door faces south, small wood fence to the west of the door across the front, #44 on the wall to the right of the front door, a detached garage to the rear of the house on the east side."

Similarly, the warrant issued in September 2022 to search former President Donald Trump's property for classified documents, precisely identified the location to be searched as follows:

> "The premises to be searched, 1100 S Ocean Blvd, Palm Beach, FL 33480, is further described as a resort, club, and residence located near the intersection of Southern Blvd and S Ocean Blvd. It is described as a mansion with approximately 58 bedrooms, 33 bathrooms, on a 17-acre estate. The locations to be searched include the '45 Office,' all storage rooms, and all other rooms or areas within the premises used or available to be used by [Donald Trump] and his staff and in which boxes or documents could be stored, including all structures or buildings on the estate."

And it identified the "property to be seized" as follows:

> "All physical documents and records constituting evidence, contraband, fruits of crime, or other items illegally possessed in violation of 18 U.S.C. §§ 793, 2071, or 1519, including the following:
>
> > a. Any physical documents with classification markings, along with any containers/boxes (including any other contents) in which such documents are located, as well as any other containers/boxes that are collectively stored or found together with the aforementioned documents and containers/boxes;
> >
> > b. Information, including communications in any form, regarding the retrieval, storage, or transmission of national defense information or classified material;
> >
> > c. Any government and/or Presidential Records created between January 20, 2017, and January 20, 2021; or

144

d. Any evidence of the knowing alteration, destruction, or concealment of any government and/or Presidential Records, or of any documents with classification markings."

GROH v. RAMIREZ
540 U.S. 551 (2004)

Case Summary

In *Groh v. Ramirez*, the Supreme Court considered the following scenario:

"Respondents, Joseph Ramirez and members of his family, live on a large ranch in Butte–Silver Bow County, Montana. Petitioner, Jeff Groh, has been a Special Agent for the Bureau of Alcohol, Tobacco and Firearms (ATF) since 1989. In February 1997, a concerned citizen informed petitioner that on a number of visits to respondents' ranch the visitor had seen a large stock of weaponry, including an automatic rifle, grenades, a grenade launcher, and a rocket launcher. Based on that information, petitioner prepared and signed an application for a warrant to search the ranch. The application stated that the search was for 'any automatic firearms or parts to automatic weapons, destructive devices to include but not limited to grenades, grenade launchers, rocket launchers, and any and all receipts pertaining to the purchase or manufacture of automatic weapons or explosive devices or launchers.' Petitioner supported the application with a detailed affidavit, which he also prepared and executed, that set forth the basis for his belief that the listed items were concealed on the ranch. Petitioner then presented these documents to a Magistrate, along with a warrant form that petitioner also had completed. The Magistrate signed the warrant form."

The search turned up nothing illegal. Ramirez then sued the officers for violating his Fourth Amendment rights on the ground that the warrant was deficient. As the Supreme Court explained:

"Although the application particularly described the place to be searched and the contraband petitioner expected to find, the warrant itself was less specific; it failed to identify any of the items that petitioner intended to seize. In the portion of the form that called for a description of the "person or property" to be seized, petitioner typed a description of respondents' two-story blue house rather than the alleged stockpile of firearms. The warrant did not incorporate by reference the itemized list contained in the application."

As a consequence, the Supreme Court concluded that the search violated the Fourth Amendment.

"The warrant was plainly invalid. The Fourth Amendment states unambiguously that 'no Warrants shall issue, but upon probable cause, supported by Oath or affirmation, and *particularly describing* the place to be searched, and *the persons or things to be seized.*' The warrant in this case complied with the first three of these requirements: It was based on probable cause and supported by a sworn affidavit, and it described particularly the place of the search. On the fourth requirement, however, the warrant failed altogether."

The Court emphasized that the specificity of the *application* did not cure the *warrant's* failings.

"The fact that the application adequately described the 'things to be seized' does not save the warrant from its facial invalidity. The Fourth Amendment by its terms requires particularity in the warrant, not in the supporting documents. And for good reason: The presence of a search warrant serves a high function, and that high function is not necessarily vindicated when some other document, somewhere, says something about the objects of the search…. We do not say that the Fourth Amendment prohibits a warrant from cross-referencing other documents. Indeed, most Courts of Appeals have held that a court may construe a warrant with reference to a supporting application or affidavit if the warrant uses appropriate words of incorporation, and if the supporting document accompanies the warrant. But in this case the warrant did not incorporate other documents by reference, nor did either the affidavit or the application (which had been placed under seal) accompany the warrant. Hence, we need not further explore the matter of incorporation."

The Court also emphasized that these were not small errors.

"This warrant did not simply omit a few items from a list of many to be seized, or misdescribe a few of several items. Nor did it make what fairly could be characterized as a mere technical mistake or typographical error.

Rather, in the space set aside for a description of the items to be seized, the warrant stated that the items consisted of a 'single dwelling residence ... blue in color.' In other words, the warrant did not describe the items to be seized at all. In this respect the warrant was so obviously deficient that we must regard the search as 'warrantless' within the meaning of our case law."

Finally, the Supreme Court considered the claim that the search was nonetheless reasonable because the officers limited their search to the items listed in the application, and thus (Petitioner claimed) "the goals served by the particularity requirement" were satisfied. The Court disagreed, rejecting the premise of the claim:

"Unless the particular items described in the affidavit are also set forth in the warrant itself (or at least incorporated by reference, and the affidavit present at the search), there can be no written assurance that the Magistrate actually found probable cause to search for, and to seize, every item mentioned in the affidavit. In this case, for example, it is at least theoretically possible that the Magistrate was satisfied that the search for weapons and explosives was justified by the showing in the affidavit, but not convinced that any evidentiary basis existed for rummaging through respondents' files and papers for receipts pertaining to the purchase or manufacture of such items. Or, conceivably, the Magistrate might have believed that some of the weapons mentioned in the affidavit could have been lawfully possessed and therefore should not be seized. The mere fact that the Magistrate issued a warrant does not necessarily establish that he agreed that the scope of the search should be as broad as the affiant's request. Even though petitioner acted with restraint in conducting the search, the inescapable fact is that this restraint was imposed by the agents themselves, not by a judicial officer."

The exact degree of precision required in identifying the place to be searched and items to be seized can be a subject of controversy. The next case concerns a challenge to the language (specifically, the bolded phrase below) from a search warrant authorizing the seizure of:

"The following items pertaining to sale, purchase, settlement and conveyance of lot 13, block T, Potomac Woods subdivision, Montgomery County, Maryland:

title notes, title abstracts, title rundowns; contracts of sale and/or assignments from Raffaele Antonelli and Rocco Caniglia to Mount Vernon Development Corporation and/or others; lien payoff correspondence and lien pay-off memoranda to and from lienholders and noteholders; correspondence and memoranda to and from trustees of deeds of trust; lenders instructions for a construction loan or construction and permanent loan; disbursement sheets and disbursement memoranda; checks, check stubs and ledger sheets indicating disbursement upon settlement; correspondence and memoranda concerning disbursements upon settlement; settlement statements and settlement memoranda; fully or partially prepared deed of trust releases, whether or not executed and whether or not recorded; books, records, documents, papers, memoranda and correspondence, showing or tending to show a fraudulent intent, and/or knowledge as elements of the crime of false pretenses, in violation of Article 27, Section 140, of the Annotated Code of Maryland, **together with other fruits, instrumentalities and evidence of crime at this time unknown**."

ANDRESEN v. MARYLAND
427 U.S. 463 (1976)

Justice BLACKMUN delivered the opinion of the Court.

…. In early 1972, a Bi-County Fraud Unit, acting under the joint auspices of the State's Attorneys' Offices of Montgomery and Prince George's Counties, Md., began an investigation of real estate settlement activities in the Washington, D.C., area. At the time, petitioner Peter Andresen was an attorney who, as a sole practitioner, specialized in real estate settlements in Montgomery County. During the Fraud Unit's investigation, his activities came under scrutiny, particularly in connection with a transaction involving Lot 13T in the Potomac Woods subdivision of Montgomery County. The investigation, which included interviews with the purchaser, the mortgage holder, and other lienholders of Lot 13T, as well as an examination of county land records, disclosed that petitioner, acting as settlement attorney, had defrauded Standard-Young Associates, the purchaser of Lot 13T…. The investigators, concluding that there was probable cause to believe that petitioner had committed the state crime of false pretenses against Standard-Young, applied for warrants to search petitioner's law office and the separate office of Mount Vernon Development Corporation, of which petitioner was incorporator, sole shareholder, resident agent, and director. The application sought permission to search for specified documents pertaining to the sale and conveyance of Lot 13T. A judge of the Sixth Judicial Circuit of Montgomery County concluded that there was probable cause and issued the warrants.

…. We turn … to petitioner's contention that rights guaranteed him by the Fourth Amendment were violated because the descriptive terms of the search warrants were so broad as to make them impermissible "general" warrants….

The specificity of the search warrants. Although petitioner concedes that the warrants for the most part were models of particularity, he contends that they were rendered fatally "general" by the addition, in each warrant, to the exhaustive list of particularly described documents, of the phrase "together with other fruits, instrumentalities and evidence of crime at this time unknown." The quoted language, it is argued, must be read in isolation and without reference to the rest of the long sentence at the end of which it appears. When read "properly," petitioner contends, it permits the search for and seizure of any evidence of any crime.

General warrants, of course, are prohibited by the Fourth Amendment. The problem posed by the general warrant is not that of intrusion per se, but of a general, exploratory rummaging in a person's belongings. The Fourth Amendment addresses the problem by requiring a "particular description" of the things to be seized. This requirement makes general searches impossible and prevents the seizure of one thing under a warrant describing another. As to what is to be taken, nothing is left to the discretion of the officer executing the warrant.

In this case we agree with the determination of the Court of Special Appeals of Maryland that the challenged phrase must be read as authorizing only the search for and seizure of evidence relating to "the crime of false pretenses with respect to Lot 13T." The challenged phrase is not a separate sentence. Instead, it appears in each warrant at the end of a sentence containing a lengthy list of specified and particular items to be seized, all pertaining to Lot 13T. We think it clear from the context that the term "crime" in the warrants refers only to the crime of false pretenses with respect to the sale of Lot 13T. The "other fruits" clause is one of a series that follows the colon after the word "Maryland." All clauses in the series are limited by what precedes that colon, namely, "items pertaining to . . . lot 13, block T." The warrants, accordingly, did not authorize the executing officers to conduct a search for evidence of other crimes but only to search for and seize evidence relevant to the crime of false pretenses and Lot 13T.... [Thus, the warrant complied with the constitutional requirements.]

UNITED STATES v. BISHOP
910 F.3d 335 (7th Cir. 2018)

Easterbrook, Circuit Judge.

A drug deal went wrong. After receiving a dose of pepper spray from his customer, Edward Bishop shot her in the arm. A jury convicted him of discharging a firearm during a drug transaction and the judge sentenced him to 120 months' imprisonment. He presents one contention on appeal: that the warrant authorizing a search of his cell phone—a search that turned up incriminating evidence—violated the Fourth Amendment's requirement that every warrant "particularly describ[e] the place to be searched, and the persons or things to be seized."

This warrant described the "place to be searched" as the cell phone Bishop carried during the attempted sale, and it described the things to be seized as:

> any evidence (including all photos, videos, and/or any other digital files, including removable memory cards) of suspect identity, motive, scheme/plan along with DNA evidence of the crime of Criminal Recklessness with a deadly weapon which is hidden or secreted in the cellphone or related to the offense of Dealing illegal drugs.

That is too general, Bishop asserts, because it authorized the police to rummage through every application and file on the phone and left to the officers' judgment the decision which files met the description. The district court found the warrant valid, however, and denied the motion to suppress.

Bishop is right about the facts. This warrant *does* permit the police to look at every file on his phone and decide which files satisfy the description. But he is wrong to think that this makes a warrant too general. Criminals don't advertise where they keep evidence. A warrant authorizing a search of a house for drugs permits the police to search everywhere in the house, because "everywhere" is where the contraband may be hidden. And a warrant authorizing a search for documents that will prove a crime may authorize a search of every document the suspect has, because any of them might supply evidence. To see this, it isn't necessary to look beyond Andresen v. Maryland (1976), in which the Supreme Court considered a warrant that permitted a search of every document in a lawyer's files…. Andresen accepted the propriety of looking at every document in his possession but maintained that [certain portions of the warrant] entitled the agents to seize anything they wanted. The Justices concluded, however, that, when read in context, the contested language did no more than permit the seizure of any other evidence pertaining to real-estate fraud, the subject of the warrant.

Just so with this warrant. It permits the search of every document on the cell phone, which (like a computer) serves the same function as the filing cabinets in Andresen's office. And as with filing cabinets, the incriminating evidence may be in any file or folder. That's why courts routinely conclude that warrants with wording similar to the one at issue here are valid. It is enough, these decisions hold, if the warrant cabins the things being looked for by stating what crime is under investigation.

Andresen and its successors show that specificity is a relative matter. A warrant may be thought "too general" only if some more-specific alternative would have done better at protecting privacy while still permitting legitimate investigation. So if the police had known that Andresen kept all of his files about the real-estate deal in a particular cabinet, failure to identify that cabinet in the warrant would have violated the constitutional particularity requirement. But a warrant need not be more specific than knowledge allows. In *Andresen* the police did not know how the target organized his files, so the best they could do was the broad language the warrant used. Likewise here: the police did not know where on his phone Bishop kept his drug ledgers and gun videos—and, if he had told them, they would have been fools to believe him, for criminals often try to throw investigators off the trail. This warrant was as specific as circumstances allowed. The Constitution does not require more.

Importantly, the Supreme Court has also authorized the seizure of evidence of a crime or contraband that is in "plain view." The government can invoke this doctrine to justify the seizure of certain evidence or contraband not particularly identified in a warrant.

- "Notwithstanding the specificity of the constitutional prohibition, the courts [recognize] a narrow exception dictated by the practicalities of a particular situation as where in the course of a lawful search pursuant to a lawful arrest or the execution of a valid search warrant the officer uncovers evidence of another crime. In these circumstances the officer is not required to close his eyes to the realities of the situation. He may seize the fruits or the instruments of the crime or even that which is presumptively contraband." *Seymour v. United States* (10th Cir. 1966)
- "Law enforcement officers may seize evidence in plain view, provided that they have not violated the Fourth Amendment in arriving at the spot from which the observation of the evidence is made." *Kentucky v. King* (2011)

In *Horton v. California* (1990), the Supreme Court explained that the "plain view" doctrine concerns seizures, not searches:

❝ The "plain-view" doctrine is often considered an exception to the general rule that warrantless searches are presumptively unreasonable, but this characterization overlooks the important difference between searches and seizures. If an article is already in plain view, neither its observation nor its seizure would involve any invasion of privacy. A seizure of the article, however, would obviously invade the owner's possessory interest. If "plain view" justifies an exception from an otherwise applicable warrant requirement, therefore, it must be an exception that is addressed to the concerns that are implicated by seizures rather than by searches.

The Supreme Court in *Minnesota v. Dickerson* (1993) later summarized the "plain view" seizure doctrine as follows:

❝ Under that doctrine, if police are lawfully in a position from which they view an object, if its incriminating character is immediately apparent, and if the officers have a lawful right of access to the object, they may seize it without a warrant. If, however, the police lack probable cause to believe that an object in plain view is contraband without conducting some further search of the object—i.e., if its incriminating character is not "immediately apparent,"—the plain-view doctrine cannot justify its seizure.

The connection between broad search warrants and plain view has important implications for searches of electronic data. See *U.S. v. Perez* (3d Cir. 2017) ("Putting all information on a digital storage device that can hold data roughly equal to 16 billion thick books in plain view whenever law enforcement officers have a valid warrant to search for something that may exist in the storage substantially expands the aggregate quantity of material encompassed by the [plain view] exception. Conversely, because of individuals' ability to hide, mislabel, or manipulate files, there may be no practical substitute for actually looking in many (perhaps all) files and locations during a search of digital storage.").

The following excerpt from a law review article[11] illustrates the challenge of applying the particularity requirement to electronic searches:

> The Fourth Amendment requires not just that searches be based on probable cause and be reasonable, but also that "no Warrants shall issue" unless "particularly describing the place to be searched, and the persons or things to be seized." This so-called particularity requirement was designed to protect against the much-reviled "general warrants." Officers must describe what they are looking for and where they will find it so that magistrates will know they are not "indiscriminately rummaging through citizens' personal effects."
>
> In the physical world, the particularity requirement is not very complicated. If police approach a magistrate with an informant's testimony that Sally Suspect is involved in narcotics trafficking, the magistrate should not automatically issue a warrant for Sally's house, her office, her car, and her person.... [Instead,] the magistrate in Sally's case should demand more information about where the narcotics are likely to be found so that the search warrant can be tailored to a particular location where there is probable cause to believe narcotics will be located. The particularity guarantee applies within structures as well. If police have a search warrant for a stolen fifty-inch television, they cannot look in the microwave. If police only have probable cause for the trunk of an automobile, they cannot search in the car's glove compartment.
>
> In the context of computers, which house millions of pages of data, the particularity requirement should take on greater importance. Officers cannot procure a search warrant simply to engage in a "general search of all of the devices, records, files,

---

[11] Gershowitz, The Post-Riley Search Warrant, 69 VAND. L. REV. 585 (2016).

and data."... As one court explained by way of example, "A warrant to search a computer for evidence of narcotics trafficking cannot be used as a blank check to scour the computer for evidence of pornographic crimes."

Unfortunately, the particularity guarantee has provided little protection to defendants in the digital context. Because electronic data can be hidden anywhere on a computer or cell phone, it is very hard for officers to narrow down in advance the area that should be searched. Instead, courts typically let officers search through enormous amounts of data to find the needle in the haystack.... Thus, while one might expect that search warrants in computer or cell phone cases would specify in great detail what files or applications police may search, generally speaking that assumption would be wrong.

There are two fairly narrow categories of cases in which courts tend to find particularity violations in computer search warrants. First, courts will sustain particularity challenges when the search warrant does not state on its face what crime the search is being conducted to find evidence of. For instance, in *United States v. Galpin*, police submitted an affidavit indicating that Galpin--who was on parole for prior sex offenses--was using MySpace to lure young boys to his home for sexual activity. The warrant did not incorporate the application, however, and instead provided that police could search for evidence that Galpin had violated a sex offender registration statute requiring him to register online profiles. The warrant thus authorized a search for evidence of a registration offense, not the crimes of child pornography or luring minors. The forensic examiner, however, searched for evidence of the more serious crimes and located computer files containing child pornography. Because the search exceeded the scope of the named offense specified in the warrant, the court found a particularity violation.

Second, courts will also occasionally find a particularity violation when the search warrant contains overbroad, catch-all language. For instance, [the] Second Circuit ... concluded that a warrant to search "computer equipment" and "electronic digital storage media" lacked particularity in violation of the Fourth Amendment. Similarly, the Southern District of New York found a warrant that indiscriminately permitted the search of all "computers," "thumb drives," and various other electronic equipment to violate the particularity requirement. The Tenth Circuit found a poorly drafted warrant that authorized the search of "'any and all information and/or data' stored on a computer" to violate the particularity requirement in a mail fraud case...

[The cases above are the exception not the rule though.] Although particularity challenges are often made in computer search warrant cases, they are rarely successful....

Courts and scholars have begun debating whether search protocols -- ex ante regulations and restrictions on how police should execute search warrants -- should be imposed in computer and cell phone search warrants. Although the law and policy questions are complicated, they largely boil down to whether magistrates should impose tight restrictions up front so that officers will be guided from the outset, rather than litigating the reasonableness of an electronic search after it has already happened....

Not surprisingly, the Department of Justice has strongly resisted the introduction of search protocols that would limit how police search computers in executing a warrant. The Justice Department describes such restrictions as "burdensome," "unnecessary," and "inconsistent with Supreme Court precedent." In particular, the Justice Department has long argued against any restriction that limits officers to searching for particular keywords in files because not all types of files--PDF's are a good example--are searchable by keyword.

For the most part, courts have agreed with the Department of Justice and have declined to impose protocols specifying how a search warrant for a computer should be executed.... [As one federal court explained,] "this Court has never required warrants to contain a particularized computer search strategy.... It is unrealistic to expect a warrant to prospectively restrict the scope of a search by directory, filename or extension or attempt to structure search methods - that process must remain dynamic..."

While courts (so far) typically resist protocols, a recent Maryland opinion, *Richardson v. State*, 481 Md. 423 (2022), relied on the above-article to propose the following reasonableness-based framework for digital searches:

"There is no 'one size fits all' solution for ensuring particularity in cell phone search warrants. In submitting and ruling upon every application for a cell phone search warrant, the affiant and the issuing judge must think about how to effectively limit the discretion of the searching officers so as not to intrude on the phone owner's privacy interests any more than reasonably necessary to locate the evidence for which there is probable cause to search.... As discussed above, the affiant, in drafting the proposed warrant, and the issuing judge, in deciding what the warrant authorizes and requires, have a number of tools at their disposal. Among other things, affiants can suggest temporal restrictions as well as limitations on the applications that will be searched, with the understanding that they can later apply for a second, broader warrant if their initial search provides a basis to do so. Or the affiants can propose search protocols that will guide the agents in how to conduct their searches. If an issuing judge receives a proposed warrant that does not include any such suggested restrictions, the judge may require the affiant to add one or more of them in a revised warrant. Ultimately, the key point is that a search warrant for a cell phone must be specific enough so that the officers will only search for the items that are related to the probable cause that justifies the search in the first place."

4. NEW INFORMATION

MARYLAND v. GARRISON
480 U.S. 79 (1987)

Justice STEVENS delivered the opinion of the Court.

Baltimore police officers obtained and executed a warrant to search the person of Lawrence McWebb and "the premises known as 2036 Park Avenue third floor apartment." When the police applied for the warrant and when they conducted the search pursuant to the warrant, they reasonably believed that there was only one apartment on the premises described in the warrant. In fact, the third floor was divided into two apartments, one occupied by McWebb and one by respondent Harold Garrison. Before the officers executing the warrant became aware that they were in a separate apartment occupied by respondent, they had discovered the contraband that provided the basis for respondent's conviction for violating Maryland's Controlled Substances Act. The question presented is whether the seizure of that contraband was prohibited by the Fourth Amendment.

The trial court denied respondent's motion to suppress the evidence seized from his apartment.... The Court of Appeals of Maryland reversed and remanded with instructions to remand the case for a new trial.

There is no question that the warrant was valid and was supported by probable cause. The trial court found … that after making a reasonable investigation, including a verification of information obtained from a reliable informant, an exterior examination of the three-story building at 2036 Park Avenue, and an inquiry of the utility company, the officer who obtained the warrant reasonably concluded that there was only one apartment on the third floor and that it was occupied by McWebb. When six Baltimore police officers executed the warrant, they fortuitously encountered McWebb in front of the building and used his key to gain admittance to the first-floor hallway and to the locked door at the top of the stairs to the third floor. As they entered the vestibule on the third floor, they encountered respondent, who was standing in the hallway area. The police could see into the interior of both McWebb's apartment to the left and respondent's to the right, for the doors to both were open. Only after respondent's apartment had been entered and heroin, cash, and drug paraphernalia had been found did any of the officers realize that the third floor contained two apartments. As soon as they became aware of that fact, the search was discontinued. All of the officers reasonably believed that they were searching McWebb's apartment. No further search of respondent's apartment was made.

…. The Warrant Clause of the Fourth Amendment categorically prohibits the issuance of any warrant except one "particularly describing the place to be searched and the persons or things to be seized." The manifest purpose of this particularity requirement was to prevent general searches. By limiting the authorization to search to the specific areas and things for which there is probable cause to search, the requirement ensures that the search will be carefully tailored to its justifications, and will not take on the character of the wide-ranging exploratory searches the Framers intended to prohibit. Thus, the scope of a lawful search is defined by the object of the search and the places in which there is probable cause to believe that it may be found. Just as probable cause to believe that a stolen lawnmower may be found in a garage will not support a warrant to search an upstairs bedroom, probable cause to believe that undocumented aliens are being transported in a van will not justify a warrantless search of a suitcase.

In this case there is no claim that the "persons or things to be seized" were inadequately described or that there was no probable cause to believe that those things might be found in "the place to be searched" as it was described in the warrant. With the benefit of hindsight, however, we now know that the description of that place was broader than appropriate because it was based on the mistaken belief that there was only one apartment on the third floor of the building at 2036 Park Avenue. The question is whether that factual mistake invalidated a warrant that undoubtedly would have been valid if it had reflected a completely accurate understanding of the building's floor plan.

Plainly, if the officers had known, or even if they should have known, that there were two separate dwelling units on the third floor of 2036 Park Avenue, they would have been obligated to exclude respondent's apartment from the scope of the requested warrant. But we must judge the constitutionality of their conduct in light of the information available to them at the time they acted. Those items of evidence that emerge after the warrant is issued have no bearing on whether or not a warrant was validly issued. Just as the discovery of contraband cannot validate a warrant invalid when issued, so is it equally clear that the discovery of facts demonstrating that a valid warrant was unnecessarily broad does not retroactively invalidate the warrant. The validity of the warrant must be assessed on the basis of the information that the officers disclosed, or had a duty to discover and to disclose, to the issuing Magistrate. On the basis of that information, we agree with the conclusion of all three Maryland courts that the warrant, insofar as it authorized a search that turned out to be ambiguous in scope, was valid when it issued.

The question whether the execution of the warrant violated respondent's constitutional right to be secure in his home is somewhat less clear. We have no difficulty concluding that the officers' entry into the third-floor common area was legal; they carried a warrant for those premises, and they were accompanied by McWebb, who provided the key that they used to open the door giving access to the third-floor common area. If the officers had known, or should have known, that the third floor contained two apartments before they entered the living quarters on the third floor, and thus had been aware of the error in the warrant, they would have been obligated to limit their search to McWebb's apartment. Moreover, as the officers recognized, they were required to discontinue the search of respondent's apartment as soon as they discovered that there were two separate units on the third floor and therefore were put on notice of the risk that they might be in a unit erroneously included within the terms of the warrant. The officers' conduct and the limits of the search were based on the information available as the search proceeded. While the purposes justifying a police search strictly limit the permissible extent of the search, the Court has also recognized the need to allow some latitude for honest mistakes that are made by officers in the dangerous and difficult process of making arrests and executing search warrants.

…. The validity of the search of respondent's apartment pursuant to a warrant authorizing the search of the entire third floor depends on whether the officers' failure to realize the overbreadth of the warrant was objectively understandable and reasonable. Here it unquestionably was. The objective facts available to the officers at the time suggested no distinction between McWebb's apartment and the third-floor premises.

For that reason, the officers properly responded to the command contained in a valid warrant even if the warrant is interpreted as authorizing a search limited to McWebb's apartment rather than the entire third floor. Prior to the officers' discovery of the factual mistake, they perceived McWebb's apartment and the third-floor premises as one and the same; therefore their execution of the warrant reasonably included the entire third floor. Under either interpretation of the warrant, the officers' conduct was consistent with a reasonable effort to ascertain and identify the place intended to be searched within the meaning of the Fourth Amendment.

The judgment of the Court of Appeals is reversed….

5. WHO CAN ISSUE A WARRANT?

SHADWICK v. CITY OF TAMPA
407 U.S. 345 (1972)

Justice POWELL delivered the opinion for a unanimous Court.

The charter of Tampa, Florida, authorizes the issuance of certain arrest warrants by clerks of the Tampa Municipal Court. The sole question in this case is whether these clerks qualify as neutral and detached magistrates for purposes of the Fourth Amendment. We hold that they do….

A clerk of the municipal court is appointed by the city clerk from a classified list of civil servants and assigned to work in the municipal court. The statute does not specify the qualifications necessary for this job, but no law degree or special legal training is required. The clerk's duties are to receive traffic fines, prepare the court's dockets and records, fill out commitment papers and perform other routine clerical tasks. Apparently he may issue subpoenas. He may not, however, sit as a judge, and he may not issue a search warrant or even a felony or misdemeanor arrest warrant for violations of state laws. The only warrants he may issue are for the arrest of those charged with having breached municipal ordinances of the city of Tampa.

Appellant, contending that the Fourth Amendment requires that warrants be issued by 'judicial officers,' argues that even this limited warrant authority is constitutionally invalid. He reasons that warrant applications of whatever nature cannot be assured the discerning, independent review compelled by the Fourth Amendment when the review is performed by less than a judicial officer....

An examination of the Court's decisions reveals that the terms 'magistrate' and 'judicial officer' have been used interchangeably. Little attempt was made to define either term, to distinguish the one from the other, or to advance one as the definitive Fourth Amendment requirement. We find no commandment in either term, however, that all warrant authority must reside exclusively in a lawyer or judge.... The substance of the Constitution's warrant requirements does not turn on the labeling of the issuing party. The warrant traditionally has represented an independent assurance that a search and arrest will not proceed without probable cause to believe that a crime has been committed and that the person or place named in the warrant is involved in the crime. Thus, an issuing magistrate must meet two tests. He must be neutral and detached, and he must be capable of determining whether probable cause exists for the requested arrest or search. This Court long has insisted that inferences of probable cause be drawn by 'a neutral and detached magistrate instead of being judged by the officer engaged in the often competitive enterprise of ferreting out crime.' In Coolidge v. New Hampshire (1971), the Court last Term voided a search warrant issued by the state attorney general 'who was actively in charge of the investigation and later was to be chief prosecutor at trial.' If, on the other hand, detachment and capacity do conjoin, the magistrate has satisfied the Fourth Amendment's purpose.

The requisite detachment is present in the case at hand. Whatever else neutrality and detachment might entail, it is clear that they require severance and disengagement from activities of law enforcement. There has been no showing whatever here of partiality, or affiliation of these clerks with prosecutors or police. The record shows no connection with any law enforcement activity or authority which would distort the independent judgment the Fourth Amendment requires.

Appellant himself expressly refused to allege anything to that effect. The municipal court clerk is assigned not to the police or prosecutor but to the municipal court judge for whom he does much of his work. In this sense, he may well be termed a 'judicial officer.' While a statutorily specified term of office and appointment by someone other than 'an executive authority' might be desirable, the absence of such features is hardly disqualifying. Judges themselves take office under differing circumstances. Some are appointed, but many are elected by legislative bodies or by the people. Many enjoy but limited terms and are subject to re-appointment or re-election. Most depend for their salary level upon the legislative branch. We will not elevate requirements for the independence of a municipal clerk to a level higher than that prevailing with respect to many judges. The clerk's neutrality has not been impeached: he is removed from prosecutor or police and works within the judicial branch subject to the supervision of the municipal court judge.

Appellant likewise has failed to demonstrate that these clerks lack capacity to determine probable cause. The clerk's authority extends only to the issuance of arrest warrants for breach of municipal ordinances. We presume from the nature of the clerk's position that he would be able to deduce from the facts on an affidavit before him whether there was probable cause to believe a citizen guilty of impaired driving, breach of peace, drunkenness, trespass, or the multiple other common offenses covered by a municipal code. There has been no showing that this is too difficult a task for a clerk to accomplish. Our legal system has long entrusted nonlawyers to evaluate more complex and significant factual data than that in the case at hand. Grand juries daily determine probable cause prior to rendering indictments, and trial juries assess whether guilt is proved beyond a reasonable doubt. The significance and responsibility of these lay judgments betray any belief that the Tampa clerks could not determine probable cause for arrest.

…. States are entitled to some flexibility and leeway in their designation of magistrates, so long as all are neutral and detached and capable of the probable-cause determination required of them.

CONNALLY v. GEORGIA
429 U.S. 245 (1977)

PER CURIAM

…. Pursuant to a search warrant issued by a justice of the peace, appellant's house was raided and marihuana found there was seized. John Connally was arrested. At his trial he moved to suppress the evidence so seized on the ground that the justice who had issued the warrant was not "a neutral and detached magistrate" because he had a pecuniary interest in issuing the warrant….

Under Ga. Code Ann. § 24-1601 (1971), the fee for the issuance of a search warrant by a Georgia justice of the peace "shall be" $5, "and it shall be lawful for said (justice) of the peace to charge and collect the same." If the requested warrant is refused, the justice of the peace collects no fee for reviewing and denying the application. The fee so charged apparently goes into county funds and from there to the issuing justice as compensation.

At a pretrial hearing in Connally's case, the issuing justice testified on cross-examination that he was a justice primarily because he was "interested in a livelihood."; that he received no salary; that his compensation was "directly dependent on how many warrants" he issued; that since January 1, 1973, he had issued "some 10,000" warrants for arrests or searches; and that he had no legal background other than attendance at seminars and reading law….

[*Ed. Note*: At this point the Court's opinion includes a footnote with the following excerpt from the pretrial questioning of the issuing justice.]

"Q In the case of a search warrant, I believe you receive compensation ultimately in the amount of $5.00, if you issue the warrant, do you not?

"A That's true.

"Q If you choose not to issue the warrant, what compensation do you receive?

"A I don't know.

"Q You receive no compensation?

"A Well, I never have, I'll put it that way.

"Q Now with respect to issuing the search warrant, Mr. Murphy, does the $5.00, since that's the only way you get paid, does that enter your mind when you're sitting there contemplating whether or not to issue a search warrant?

"A It has.

"Q As a matter of fact, I believe you quite honestly and candidly told me [earlier] that you would be a liar if you said it didn't enter your mind?

"A That's what I said.

"Q Is that true now, you would be a liar if you said it didn't enter your mind?

"A It's only human nature to me.

…. The justice is not salaried. He is paid, so far as search warrants are concerned, by receipt of the fee prescribed by statute for his issuance of the warrant, and he receives nothing for his denial of the warrant. His financial welfare, therefore, is enhanced by positive action and is not enhanced by negative action. The situation, again, is one which offers "a possible temptation to the average man as a judge . . . or which might lead him not to hold the balance nice, clear and true between the State and the accused." It is, in other words, another situation where the defendant is subjected to what surely is judicial action by an officer of a court who has "a direct, personal, substantial, pecuniary interest" in his conclusion to issue or to deny the warrant.

…. We therefore hold that the issuance of the search warrant by the justice of the peace in Connally's case effected a violation of the protections afforded him by the Fourth and Fourteenth Amendments of the United States Constitution.

As the preceding excerpts explain, the Constitution requires police to obtain a warrant from a "neutral and detached" official "capable of determining whether probable cause exists for the requested arrest or search." Typically, this means a judge or magistrate. See *Coolidge v. New Hampshire* (1971) (warrant invalid where issued by the State's "Attorney General – who was actively in charge of the investigation and later was to be chief prosecutor at the trial" because "the whole point" of the warrant requirement "is that prosecutors and policemen simply cannot be asked to maintain the requisite neutrality with regard to their own investigations").

In large jurisdictions, there is a potential for police to engage in "magistrate shopping," selectively approaching judges who are friendly to their requests, or to apply for a warrant over and over until they find a willing judge. For example, in 2023, the federal Department of Justice (DOJ) published a report summarizing the findings from an investigation of the Louisville Metro Police Department (LMPD). Among several constitutional violations, the DOJ found that the LMPD's "search warrant applications routinely fail to demonstrate probable cause" – and yet were regularly approved. Part of the explanation for this appears to be that officers submitted warrant applications to the judges who were most likely to grant them. The DOJ reported: "Jefferson County has a rotating schedule for judges to review warrant applications, but LMPD does not follow the court's schedule. Of the warrants in our sample, officers rarely sought approval from 19 of the 30 judges who approved warrants in the sample. In fact, just six judges approved more than half of the warrants…."

The Supreme Court has never ruled on the propriety of these tactics, but here are two representative treatments of a related question from the lower courts:

- "The Fourth Amendment on its face does not prohibit the government from seeking a second magistrate's approval to search when another magistrate denies a search warrant. The Fourth Amendment commands only that a 'neutral and detached magistrate' determine that probable cause exists. Thus, the important questions, from a Fourth Amendment standpoint, are whether the magistrate really was 'neutral and detached,' and whether probable cause actually existed, not how many magistrates the government applied to before finally obtaining a warrant." *U.S. v. Pace* (7th Cir. 1990)

- "While the government is free to pursue warrants, subpoenas and other investigatory tools, and may do so in whichever judicial district is appropriate in light of the location of the information sought, it must fully disclose to each judicial officer prior efforts in other judicial fora to obtain the same or related information, and what those efforts have achieved." *U.S. v. Comprehensive Drug Testing* (9th Cir. 2010)

A seemingly neutral and detached magistrate may betray a lack of neutrality through conduct, as famously occurred in **Lo-Ji Sales, Inc. v. New York** (1979). In that case, the local magistrate issued a 2-page warrant authorizing the search of a "so-called 'adult' bookstore" for obscene material. The magistrate left blank the section of the warrant identifying the specific items to be seized; and then accompanied the police to the store to assist in identifying unlawful items. After the search, the items that had been seized were noted on the previously blank section of the warrant, which grew to 16 pages. The Supreme Court disapproved, explaining:

"The Town Justice did not manifest that neutrality and detachment demanded of a judicial officer when presented with a warrant application for a search and seizure. We need not question the subjective belief of the Town Justice in the propriety of his actions, but the objective facts of record manifest an erosion of whatever neutral and detached posture existed at the outset. He allowed himself to become a member, if not the leader, of the search party which was essentially a police operation. Once in the store, he conducted a generalized search under authority of an invalid warrant; he was not acting as a judicial officer but as an adjunct law enforcement officer."

As this excerpt hints, another problem with the search was that the warrant lacked particularity: "This search warrant and what followed the entry on petitioner's premises are reminiscent of the general warrant or writ of assistance of the 18th century against which the Fourth Amendment was intended to protect."

Chapter 4

REASONABLENESS: WARRANT EXCEPTIONS

Police officers conducting a search or seizure are on the firmest constituti ground when they possess a warrant supported by probable cause. But, as ι Chapter explains, there are numerous scenarios where the Supreme Court has rul that searches and seizures can be conducted without these ingredients. Eac scenario is typically accompanied by its own rules to limit the departure from th general default requirement of a warrant and probable cause. Illustrating the importance of these doctrines, one of the most comprehensive reports on warrant application processes across the country concluded that, "the overwhelming majority of criminal investigations are conducted without recourse to a search warrant."[12]

While this Chapter occupies the core of the Criminal Procedure course, be sure to layer the subsequent material onto the doctrines we have already learned. For example, there will be no need to analyze exceptions to the probable cause and warrant requirements unless a "search" or "seizure" has in fact occurred. And police can avoid challenges to their compliance with the warrant exceptions by … obtaining a warrant.

A. STOP AND FRISK

One exception to the warrant and probable cause requirements can be found in what the Supreme Court labels, "street encounters": a "rubric of police conduct— necessarily swift action predicated upon the on-the-spot observations of the officer on the beat—which historically has not been, and as a practical matter could not be, subjected to the warrant procedure."

---

[12] National Center for State Courts, The Search Warrant Process, 1985, https://ncsc.contentdm.oclc.org/digital/collection/criminal/id/3/

DOCTRINE

TERRY v. OHIO
392 U.S. 1 (1968)

delivered the opinion of the Court.

...ious questions concerning the role of the Fourth Amendment
...on on the street between the citizen and the policeman
...icious circumstances.

...i Terry was convicted of carrying a concealed weapon and sentenced
...orily prescribed term of one to three years in the penitentiary. Following
...of a pretrial motion to suppress, the prosecution introduced in evidence
...olvers and a number of bullets seized from Terry and a codefendant,
...d Chilton, by Cleveland Police Detective Martin McFadden. At the hearing
...ie motion to suppress this evidence, Officer McFadden testified that while he
...s patrolling in plain clothes in downtown Cleveland at approximately 2:30 in the
afternoon of October 31, 1963, his attention was attracted by two men, Chilton
and Terry, standing on the corner of Huron Road and Euclid Avenue. He had never
seen the two men before, and he was unable to say precisely what first drew his eye
to them. However, he testified that he had been a policeman for 39 years and a
detective for 35 and that he had been assigned to patrol this vicinity of downtown
Cleveland for shoplifters and pickpockets for 30 years. He explained that he had
developed routine habits of observation over the years and that he would 'stand
and watch people or walk and watch people at many intervals of the day.' He added:
'Now, in this case when I looked over they didn't look right to me at the time.'

His interest aroused, Officer McFadden took up a post of observation in the
entrance to a store 300 to 400 feet away from the two men. 'I get more purpose to
watch them when I seen their movements,' he testified. He saw one of the men
leave the other one and walk southwest on Huron Road, past some stores. The
man paused for a moment and looked in a store window, then walked on a short
distance, turned around and walked back toward the corner, pausing once again to
look in the same store window. He rejoined his companion at the corner, and the
two conferred briefly. Then the second man went through the same series of
motions, strolling down Huron Road, looking in the same window, walking on a
short distance, turning back, peering in the store window again, and returning to

confer with the first man at the corner. The two men repeated this ritual alternately between five and six times apiece—in all, roughly a dozen trips. At one point, while the two were standing together on the corner, a third man approached them and engaged them briefly in conversation. This man then left the two others and walked west on Euclid Avenue. Chilton and Terry resumed their measured pacing, peering and conferring. After this had gone on for 10 to 12 minutes, the two men walked off together, heading west on Euclid Avenue, following the path taken earlier by the third man.

By this time Officer McFadden had become thoroughly suspicious. He testified that after observing their elaborately casual and oft-repeated reconnaissance of the store window on Huron Road, he suspected the two men of 'casing a job, a stick-up,' and that he considered it his duty as a police officer to investigate further. He added that he feared 'they may have a gun.' Thus, Officer McFadden followed Chilton and Terry and saw them stop in front of Zucker's store to talk to the same man who had conferred with them earlier on the street corner. Deciding that the situation was ripe for direct action, Officer McFadden approached the three men, identified himself as a police officer and asked for their names. At this point his knowledge was confined to what he had observed. He was not acquainted with any of the three men by name or by sight, and he had received no information concerning them from any other source. When the men 'mumbled something' in response to his inquiries, Officer McFadden grabbed petitioner Terry, spun him around so that they were facing the other two, with Terry between McFadden and the others, and patted down the outside of his clothing. In the left breast pocket of Terry's overcoat Officer McFadden felt a pistol. He reached inside the overcoat pocket, but was unable to remove the gun. At this point, keeping Terry between himself and the others, the officer ordered all three men to enter Zucker's store. As they went in, he removed Terry's overcoat completely, removed a .38-caliber revolver from the pocket and ordered all three men to face the wall with their hands raised. Officer McFadden proceeded to pat down the outer clothing of Chilton and the third man, Katz. He discovered another revolver in the outer pocket of Chilton's overcoat, but no weapons were found on Katz. The officer testified that he only patted the men down to see whether they had weapons, and that he did not put his hands beneath the outer garments of either Terry or Chilton until he felt their guns. So far as appears from the record, he never placed his hands beneath Katz' outer garments. Officer McFadden seized Chilton's gun, asked the proprietor of the store to call a police wagon, and took all three men to the station, where Chilton and Terry were formally charged with carrying concealed weapons.

[The trial] court denied the defendants' motion [to suppress the evidence] on the ground that Officer McFadden, on the basis of his experience, 'had reasonable cause to believe that the defendants were conducting themselves suspiciously, and some interrogation should be made of their action.' Purely for his own protection, the court held, the officer had the right to pat down the outer clothing of these men, who he had reasonable cause to believe might be armed.... The frisk, it held, was essential to the proper performance of the officer's investigatory duties, for without it 'the answer to the police officer may be a bullet, and a loaded pistol discovered during the frisk is admissible.'

.... We granted certiorari to determine whether the admission of the revolvers in evidence violated petitioner's rights under the Fourth Amendment, made applicable to the States by the Fourteenth. We affirm the conviction.

I

.... Unquestionably petitioner was entitled to the protection of the Fourth Amendment as he walked down the street in Cleveland. The question is whether in all the circumstances of this on-the-street encounter, his right to personal security was violated by an unreasonable search and seizure.

We would be less than candid if we did not acknowledge that this question thrusts to the fore difficult and troublesome issues regarding a sensitive area of police activity—issues which have never before been squarely presented to this Court. Reflective of the tensions involved are the practical and constitutional arguments pressed with great vigor on both sides of the public debate over the power of the police to 'stop and frisk' —as it is sometimes euphemistically termed—suspicious persons....

In this context we approach the issues in this case mindful of the limitations of the judicial function in controlling the myriad daily situations in which policemen and citizens confront each other on the street.... Ever since its inception, the rule excluding evidence seized in violation of the Fourth Amendment has been recognized as a principal mode of discouraging lawless police conduct.... The exclusionary rule has its limitations, however, as a tool of judicial control. It cannot properly be invoked to exclude the products of legitimate police investigative techniques on the ground that much conduct which is closely similar involves unwarranted intrusions upon constitutional protections. Moreover, in some contexts the rule is ineffective as a deterrent. Street encounters between citizens and police officers are incredibly rich in diversity. They range from wholly friendly exchanges of pleasantries or mutually useful information to hostile confrontations of armed men involving arrests, or injuries, or loss of life. Moreover, hostile confrontations are not all of a piece. Some of them begin in a friendly enough manner, only to take a different turn upon the injection of some unexpected element into the conversation. Encounters are initiated by the police for a wide variety of purposes, some of which are wholly unrelated to a desire to prosecute for crime. Doubtless some police 'field interrogation' conduct violates the Fourth Amendment. But a stern refusal by this Court to condone such activity does not necessarily render it responsive to the exclusionary rule. Regardless of how effective the rule may be where obtaining convictions is an important objective of the police, it is powerless to deter invasions of constitutionally guaranteed rights where the police either have no interest in prosecuting or are willing to forgo successful prosecution in the interest of serving some other goal....

II

Our first task is to establish at what point in this encounter the Fourth Amendment becomes relevant. That is, we must decide whether and when Officer McFadden 'seized' Terry and whether and when he conducted a 'search.' There is some suggestion in the use of such terms as 'stop' and 'frisk' that such police conduct is outside the purview of the Fourth Amendment because neither action rises to the level of a 'search' or 'seizure' within the meaning of the Constitution. We emphatically reject this notion. It is quite plain that the Fourth Amendment governs 'seizures' of the person which do not eventuate in a trip to the station house and prosecution for crime – 'arrests' in traditional terminology. It must be recognized that whenever a police officer accosts an individual and restrains his freedom to walk away, he has 'seized' that person. And it is nothing less than sheer torture of the English language to suggest that a careful exploration of the outer surfaces of a person's clothing all over his or her body in an attempt to find weapons is not a 'search.' Moreover, it is simply fantastic to urge that such a procedure performed in public by a policeman while the citizen stands helpless, perhaps facing a wall with his hands raised, is a 'petty indignity.'[13] It is a serious intrusion upon the sanctity of the person, which may inflict great indignity and arouse strong resentment, and it is not to be undertaken lightly....

In this case there can be no question, then, that Officer McFadden 'seized' petitioner and subjected him to a 'search' when he took hold of him and patted down the outer surfaces of his clothing....

III

.... We do not retreat from our holdings that the police must, whenever practicable, obtain advance judicial approval of searches and seizures through the warrant procedure, or that in most instances failure to comply with the warrant requirement can only be excused by exigent circumstances. But we deal here with an entire rubric of police conduct—necessarily swift action predicated upon the on-the-spot observations of the officer on the beat—which historically has not been, and as a practical matter could not be, subjected to the warrant procedure. Instead, the conduct involved in this case must be tested by the Fourth Amendment's general proscription against unreasonable searches and seizures....

In order to assess the reasonableness of Officer McFadden's conduct as a general proposition, it is necessary first to focus upon the governmental interest which allegedly justifies official intrusion upon the constitutionally protected interests of the private citizen, for there is no ready test for determining reasonableness other than by balancing the need to search (or seize) against the invasion which the search (or seizure) entails. And in justifying the particular intrusion the police officer must be able to point to specific and articulable facts which, taken together with rational inferences from those facts, reasonably warrant that intrusion.[18] ... Anything less would invite intrusions upon constitutionally guaranteed rights based on nothing more substantial than inarticulate hunches, a result this Court has consistently refused to sanction. And simple good faith on the part of the arresting officer is not enough. If subjective good faith alone were the test, the protections of the

---

[13] Consider the following apt description: "The officer must feel with sensitive fingers every portion of the prisoner's body. A thorough search must be made of the prisoner's arms and armpits, waistline and back, the groin and area about the testicles, and entire surface of the legs down to the feet."

[18] This demand for specificity in the information upon which police action is predicated is the central teaching of this Court's Fourth Amendment jurisprudence.

Fourth Amendment would evaporate, and the people would be 'secure in their persons, houses, papers and effects,' only in the discretion of the police.

Applying these principles to this case, we consider first the nature and extent of the governmental interests involved. One general interest is of course that of effective crime prevention and detection; it is this interest which underlies the recognition that a police officer may in appropriate circumstances and in an appropriate manner approach a person for purposes of investigating possibly criminal behavior even though there is no probable cause to make an arrest. It was this legitimate investigative function Officer McFadden was discharging when he decided to approach petitioner and his companions....

The crux of this case, however, is not the propriety of Officer McFadden's taking steps to investigate petitioner's suspicious behavior, but rather, whether there was justification for McFadden's invasion of Terry's personal security by searching him for weapons in the course of that investigation. We are now concerned with more than the governmental interest in investigating crime; in addition, there is the more immediate interest of the police officer in taking steps to assure himself that the person with whom he is dealing is not armed with a weapon that could unexpectedly and fatally be used against him. Certainly it would be unreasonable to require that police officers take unnecessary risks in the performance of their duties. American criminals have a long tradition of armed violence, and every year in this country many law enforcement officers are killed in the line of duty, and thousands more are wounded. Virtually all of these deaths and a substantial portion of the injuries are inflicted with guns and knives.

In view of these facts, we cannot blind ourselves to the need for law enforcement officers to protect themselves and other prospective victims of violence in situations where they may lack probable cause for an arrest. When an officer is justified in believing that the individual whose suspicious behavior he is investigating at close range is armed and presently dangerous to the officer or to others, it would appear to be clearly unreasonable to deny the officer the power to take necessary measures to determine whether the person is in fact carrying a weapon and to neutralize the threat of physical harm.

We must still consider, however, the nature and quality of the intrusion on individual rights which must be accepted if police officers are to be conceded the right to search for weapons in situations where probable cause to arrest for crime is lacking. Even a limited search of the outer clothing for weapons constitutes a severe, though brief, intrusion upon cherished personal security, and it must surely be an annoying, frightening, and perhaps humiliating experience....

Our evaluation of the proper balance that has to be struck in this type of case leads us to conclude that there must be a narrowly drawn authority to permit a reasonable search for weapons for the protection of the police officer, where he has reason to believe that he is dealing with an armed and dangerous individual, regardless of whether he has probable cause to arrest the individual for a crime. The officer need not be absolutely certain that the individual is armed; the issue is whether a reasonably prudent man in the circumstances would be warranted in the belief that his safety or that of others was in danger. And in determining whether the officer acted reasonably in such circumstances, due weight must be given, not to his inchoate and unparticularized suspicion or 'hunch,' but to the specific reasonable inferences which he is entitled to draw from the facts in light of his experience.

IV

We must now examine the conduct of Officer McFadden in this case to determine whether his search and seizure of petitioner were reasonable, both at their inception and as conducted. He had observed Terry, together with Chilton and another man, acting in a manner he took to be preface to a 'stick-up.' We think on the facts and circumstances Officer McFadden detailed before the trial judge a reasonably prudent man would have been warranted in believing petitioner was armed and thus presented a threat to the officer's safety while he was investigating his suspicious behavior. The actions of Terry and Chilton were consistent with McFadden's hypothesis that these men were contemplating a daylight robbery— which, it is reasonable to assume, would be likely to involve the use of weapons— and nothing in their conduct from the time he first noticed them until the time he confronted them and identified himself as a police officer gave him sufficient reason to negate that hypothesis. Although the trio had departed the original scene, there was nothing to indicate abandonment of an intent to commit a robbery at some point. Thus, when Officer McFadden approached the three men gathered before the display window at Zucker's store he had observed enough to make it quite reasonable to fear that they were armed; and nothing in their response to his hailing them, identifying himself as a police officer, and asking their names served to dispel that reasonable belief. We cannot say his decision at that point to seize Terry and pat his clothing for weapons was the product of a volatile or inventive imagination, or was undertaken simply as an act of harassment; the record evidences the tempered act of a policeman who in the course of an investigation had to make a quick decision as to how to protect himself and others from possible danger, and took limited steps to do so.

The manner in which the seizure and search were conducted is, of course, as vital a part of the inquiry as whether they were warranted at all. The Fourth Amendment proceeds as much by limitations upon the scope of governmental action as by imposing preconditions upon its initiation. The entire deterrent purpose of the rule excluding evidence seized in violation of the Fourth Amendment rests on the assumption that 'limitations upon the fruit to be gathered tend to limit the quest itself.' Thus, evidence may not be introduced if it was discovered by means of a seizure and search which were not reasonably related in scope to the justification for their initiation.

We need not develop at length in this case, however, the limitations which the Fourth Amendment places upon a protective seizure and search for weapons. These limitations will have to be developed in the concrete factual circumstances of individual cases. Suffice it to note that such a search, unlike a search without a warrant incident to a lawful arrest, is not justified by any need to prevent the disappearance or destruction of evidence of crime. The sole justification of the search in the present situation is the protection of the police officer and others nearby, and it must therefore be confined in scope to an intrusion reasonably designed to discover guns, knives, clubs, or other hidden instruments for the assault of the police officer.

The scope of the search in this case presents no serious problem in light of these standards. Officer McFadden patted down the outer clothing of petitioner and his two companions. He did not place his hands in their pockets or under the outer surface of their garments until he had felt weapons, and then he merely reached for and removed the guns. He never did invade Katz' person beyond the outer surfaces of his clothes, since he discovered nothing in his patdown which might have been a weapon. Officer McFadden confined his search strictly to what was minimally necessary to learn whether the men were armed and to disarm them once he discovered the weapons. He did not conduct a general exploratory search for whatever evidence of criminal activity he might find.

V

We conclude that the revolver seized from Terry was properly admitted in evidence against him. At the time he seized petitioner and searched him for weapons, Officer McFadden had reasonable grounds to believe that petitioner was armed and dangerous, and it was necessary for the protection of himself and others to take swift measures to discover the true facts and neutralize the threat of harm if it materialized. The policeman carefully restricted his search to what was appropriate to the discovery of the particular items which he sought. Each case of this sort will, of course, have to be decided on its own facts. We merely hold today that where a police officer observes unusual conduct which leads him reasonably to conclude in light of his experience that criminal activity may be afoot and that the persons with whom he is dealing may be armed and presently dangerous, where in the course of investigating this behavior he identifies himself as a policeman and makes reasonable inquiries, and where nothing in the initial stages of the encounter serves to dispel his reasonable fear for his own or others' safety, he is entitled for the protection of himself and others in the area to conduct a carefully limited search of the outer clothing of such persons in an attempt to discover weapons which might be used to assault him. Such a search is a reasonable search under the Fourth Amendment, and any weapons seized may properly be introduced in evidence against the person from whom they were taken.

In cases like *Terry*, the Supreme Court relies on a perception of the dangers faced by police officers to support the reasonableness of permissive search and seizure rules. In 1997, the Bureau of Labor Statistics (BLS) published the following list of the most dangerous occupations:

Table 1. Occupations with largest number of fatalities, rates, relative risk, 1995

Occupation	Fatality count	Employment (in 1,000's)	Fatality rate[1]	Index of relative risk	Leading fatal event (percent)
Total	6,210	126,248	4.9	1.0	
Truckdriver	749	2,861	26.2	5.3	Highway crashes (68)
Farm occupations	579	2,282	25.3	5.1	Vehicular (50)
Construction laborers	309	780	39.5	8.1	Vehicular (28); Falls (27)
Supervisors, proprietors, sales	212	4,480	4.7	1.0	Homicide (63)
Nonconstruction laborers	212	1,337	15.8	3.2	Vehicular (36)
Police, detectives, and supervisors	174	1,051	16.6	3.4	Homicide (47); Highway (28)
Electricians	117	736	15.9	3.2	Electrocutions (59)
Cashiers	116	2,727	4.3	.9	Homicide (92)
Airplane pilots	111	114	97.4	19.9	Airplane crashes (98)
Guards	101	899	11.2	2.3	Homicide (58)
Taxicab drivers	99	213	46.5	9.5	Homicide (70)
Timber cutters	98	97	101.0	20.6	Struck by object (81)
Carpenters	96	1,255	7.6	1.6	Falls (43)
Groundkeepers and gardeners	77	832	9.3	1.9	Vehicular (31)
Welders and cutters	72	604	12.0	2.4	Falls (22); Fires (18)
Roofers	60	205	29.3	5.9	Falls (75)
Fishers	48	45	104.4	21.3	Drowning (81)
Auto mechanics	47	819	5.7	1.1	Highway (21); Homicide (13)
Structural metal workers	38	59	64.4	13.1	Falls (66)
Electric Power Install/rprs	35	126	27.8	5.7	Electrocutions (60)

The BLS finding of a relative risk of 3.4 for police represents a determination that police are 3.4 times "as likely to have a fatal work injury as the average worker." A more recent study based on updated BLS data found that police officers had the 25th most dangerous job behind loggers (#1 most dangerous), aircraft pilots (#2) and roofers (#3). Other common dangerous occupations included garbage collectors (#6), delivery drivers (#8), farmers (#10), and construction workers (#19).[13]

ILLINOIS v. WARDLOW
528 U.S. 119 (2000)

Chief Justice REHNQUIST delivered the opinion of the Court.

…. On September 9, 1995, Officers Nolan and Harvey were working as uniformed officers in the special operations section of the Chicago Police Department. The officers were driving the last car of a four car caravan converging on an area known for heavy narcotics trafficking in order to investigate drug transactions. The officers were traveling together because they expected to find a crowd of people in the area, including lookouts and customers.

---

[13] https://advisorsmith.com/data/most-dangerous-jobs/

As the caravan passed 4035 West Van Buren, Officer Nolan observed respondent William Wardlow standing next to the building holding an opaque bag. Respondent looked in the direction of the officers and fled. Nolan and Harvey turned their car southbound, watched him as he ran through the gangway and an alley, and eventually cornered him on the street. Nolan then exited his car and stopped respondent. He immediately conducted a protective patdown search for weapons because in his experience it was common for there to be weapons in the near vicinity of narcotics transactions. During the frisk, Officer Nolan squeezed the bag respondent was carrying and felt a heavy, hard object similar to the shape of a gun. The officer then opened the bag and discovered a .38–caliber handgun with five live rounds of ammunition. The officers arrested Wardlow [and he was convicted of unlawful possession of a firearm]....

The Illinois Supreme Court ... rejected the argument that flight combined with the fact that it occurred in a high crime area supported a finding of reasonable suspicion.... Finding no independently suspicious circumstances to support an investigatory detention, the court held that the stop and subsequent arrest violated the Fourth Amendment. We granted certiorari and now reverse.

.... This case, involving a brief encounter between a citizen and a police officer on a public street, is governed by the analysis we first applied in Terry v. Ohio. In Terry, we held that an officer may, consistent with the Fourth Amendment, conduct a brief, investigatory stop when the officer has a reasonable, articulable suspicion that criminal activity is afoot. While "reasonable suspicion" is a less demanding standard than probable cause and requires a showing considerably less than preponderance of the evidence, the Fourth Amendment requires at least a minimal level of objective justification for making the stop. The officer must be able to articulate more than an "inchoate and unparticularized suspicion or 'hunch'" of criminal activity.[2]

Nolan and Harvey were among eight officers in a four-car caravan that was converging on an area known for heavy narcotics trafficking, and the officers anticipated encountering a large number of people in the area, including drug customers and individuals serving as lookouts. It was in this context that Officer

---

[2] We granted certiorari solely on the question whether the initial stop was supported by reasonable suspicion. Therefore, we express no opinion as to the lawfulness of the frisk independently of the stop.

Nolan decided to investigate Wardlow after observing him flee. An individual's presence in an area of expected criminal activity, standing alone, is not enough to support a reasonable, particularized suspicion that the person is committing a crime. But officers are not required to ignore the relevant characteristics of a location in determining whether the circumstances are sufficiently suspicious to warrant further investigation. Accordingly, we have previously noted the fact that the stop occurred in a "high crime area" among the relevant contextual considerations in a Terry analysis.

In this case, moreover, it was not merely respondent's presence in an area of heavy narcotics trafficking that aroused the officers' suspicion, but his unprovoked flight upon noticing the police. Our cases have also recognized that nervous, evasive behavior is a pertinent factor in determining reasonable suspicion. Headlong flight—wherever it occurs—is the consummate act of evasion: It is not necessarily indicative of wrongdoing, but it is certainly suggestive of such. In reviewing the propriety of an officer's conduct, courts do not have available empirical studies dealing with inferences drawn from suspicious behavior, and we cannot reasonably demand scientific certainty from judges or law enforcement officers where none exists. Thus, the determination of reasonable suspicion must be based on commonsense judgments and inferences about human behavior. We conclude Officer Nolan was justified in suspecting that Wardlow was involved in criminal activity, and, therefore, in investigating further.

Such a holding is entirely consistent with our decision in Florida v. Royer (1983), where we held that when an officer, without reasonable suspicion or probable cause, approaches an individual, the individual has a right to ignore the police and go about his business. And any "refusal to cooperate, without more, does not furnish the minimal level of objective justification needed for a detention or seizure." But unprovoked flight is simply not a mere refusal to cooperate. Flight, by its very nature, is not "going about one's business"; in fact, it is just the opposite. Allowing officers confronted with such flight to stop the fugitive and investigate further is quite consistent with the individual's right to go about his business or to stay put and remain silent in the face of police questioning.

Respondent and amici also argue that there are innocent reasons for flight from police and that, therefore, flight is not necessarily indicative of ongoing criminal activity. This fact is undoubtedly true, but does not establish a violation of the Fourth Amendment. Even in Terry, the conduct justifying the stop was ambiguous and susceptible of an innocent explanation. The officer observed two individuals pacing back and forth in front of a store, peering into the window and periodically conferring. All of this conduct was by itself lawful, but it also suggested that the individuals were casing the store for a planned robbery. Terry recognized that the officers could detain the individuals to resolve the ambiguity.

In allowing such detentions, Terry accepts the risk that officers may stop innocent people. Indeed, the Fourth Amendment accepts that risk in connection with more drastic police action; persons arrested and detained on probable cause to believe they have committed a crime may turn out to be innocent. The Terry stop is a far more minimal intrusion, simply allowing the officer to briefly investigate further. If the officer does not learn facts rising to the level of probable cause, the individual must be allowed to go on his way. But in this case the officers found respondent in possession of a handgun, and arrested him for violation of an Illinois firearms statute. No question of the propriety of the arrest itself is before us.

The judgment of the Supreme Court of Illinois is reversed.

The *Wardlow* majority's assertion that "the fact that the stop occurred in a 'high crime area'" is "among the relevant contextual considerations in a Terry analysis" has led to "high crime area" becoming one of the most frequently cited stop justifications. See *Floyd v. City of New York* (S.D.N.Y. 2011) (noting that "55.4 percent of stops" in New York City over a five-year period "were based in whole or in part on 'high crime area'"). After all, there is some crime in virtually every densely populated area and the qualifier "high" is imprecise and subjective.

Importantly, Chief Justice Rehnquist's majority opinion recognizes that, "standing alone," presence in a high crime area will be insufficient to establish reasonable suspicion. But Justice Stevens, writing for three other Justices, didn't think the "high crime area" factor added anything at all: "Because many factors providing innocent motivations for unprovoked flight are concentrated in high crime areas, the character of the neighborhood arguably makes an inference of guilt less appropriate, rather than more so. Like unprovoked flight itself, presence in a high crime neighborhood is a fact too generic and susceptible to innocent explanation to satisfy the reasonable suspicion inquiry."

One way to reconcile these differing perspectives is to focus on the overarching inquiry: reasonable suspicion that the person stopped is committing a crime. Any use of the characteristics of a place to justify a stop must be connected to that inquiry. Thus, the fact that an area is plagued by auto thefts might support a stop of someone forcing open a car door, but not of a person engaged in hand-to-hand transactions. The fact that an area is known for drunk driving or drag racing might support a stop of a car driving erratically, but not of a pedestrian who runs in the other direction when police approach. And, in fact, the stop in *Wardlow* was not supported by a generic reference to "high crime" in that Chicago neighborhood. Rather Officer Nolan testified that the officers were targeting a specific location known for "heavy narcotics trafficking" and characterized by crowds of people buying and selling drugs, "including lookouts and customers." If the police suspected Wardlow of being involved in *that* specific criminal activity, the characteristics of the area where he was observed might be relevant to assessing whether their suspicion was reasonable. Of course, how much weight should be given to this factor in the circumstances of any case will still be subject to dispute. And contrary to the Supreme Court's presentation of the facts ("respondent's presence in an area of heavy narcotics trafficking"), the intermediate state appellate court concluded that the testimony at the suppression hearing did not establish that Wardlow was observed at the targeted drug trafficking location. People v. Wardlow, 287 Ill. App. 3d 367 (1997) ("From the evidence elicited at the hearing on the motion to suppress, it appears that the officers were simply driving by, on their way to some unidentified location, when they noticed defendant standing at 4035 West Van Buren.").

In June 2022, the Chicago police department issued a new policy restricting the circumstances under which its officers could conduct "foot pursuits" – instances where an officer "pursues (on foot or bicycle) a fleeing person who is attempting to evade detention by law enforcement." The policy was a response to the deaths of 13-year-old Adam Toledo and 22-year-old Anthony Alvarez who were both killed by police after being chased for minor offenses. An excerpt from the policy is below. *Would the Chicago police conduct in Wardlow violate Chicago's new policy?*

CHICAGO POLICE DEPARTMENT

★ ★ ★ ★

IV. DECISION TO PURSUE – DEPARTMENT MEMBER

B. Department members may only engage in or continue a Foot Pursuit if there is a valid law enforcement need to detain the person that Department members reasonably believe outweighs the threat to safety posed by pursuit....

1.   A valid law enforcement need to detain a person exists when the Department members establish reasonable articulable suspicion or probable cause to believe that (1) the person being pursued has committed, is committing, or is about to commit a Felony, a Class A misdemeanor, a traffic offense that endangers the physical safety of others, or (2) the person being pursued is committing or is about to commit an arrestable offense that poses an obvious physical threat to any person.

EXAMPLE:

> Some examples of Class A misdemeanor offenses where Foot Pursuits are permitted include aggravated assault, battery, domestic battery, unlawful use of weapon, criminal trespass to residence, theft, and retail theft.
>
> Some examples of less than a Class A misdemeanor offenses where Foot Pursuits are prohibited include business license offenses, parking violations, ordinance violations (e.g., curfew drinking on the public way), or Class B or C misdemeanors (e.g., simple assault or criminal trespass to land).
>
> Some examples of traffic offenses that endanger the physical safety of others where Foot Pursuits are permitted include driving under the influence, reckless driving, and street racing.
>
> Some examples of traffic offenses where Foot Pursuits are prohibited include licensing violations (e.g., fictitious, altered, suspended, revoked, or unlawful use of license), insurance violations, and other petty violations enforceable by citation only.

2. Under circumstances where Foot Pursuits are permissible, Department members are expected to weigh the seriousness of the offense against the immediate need to apprehend and the consideration of Department member and public safety. The decision to initiate or continue such a Foot Pursuit must

be continuously re-evaluated in light of the circumstances presented at the time.

C. A Department member may not conduct a Foot Pursuit based solely on a person's response to the presence of police, including a person's attempt to avoid contact with a Department member (e.g., walking away, declining to talk, running away, or crossing the street to avoid contact). People may avoid contact with a Department member for many reasons other than involvement in criminal activity.

D. Department members are prohibited from intentionally provoking or attempting to provoke flight in an effort to justify an Investigative Stop or a Foot Pursuit. For example, a Department member may not drive at a high rate of speed toward a group congregated on a corner, perform a threshold brake, and exit quickly with the intention of stopping anyone in the group who flees.

As with "probable cause," the Supreme Court resists efforts to precisely define the "reasonable suspicion" standard. In *United States v. Arvizu* (2002), the Court offered the following guidance:

> "Although an officer's reliance on a mere 'hunch' is insufficient to justify a [*Terry*] stop, the likelihood of criminal activity need not rise to the level required for probable cause, and it falls considerably short of satisfying a preponderance of the evidence standard.... Our cases have recognized that the concept of reasonable suspicion is somewhat abstract. But we have deliberately avoided reducing it to 'a neat set of legal rules.'"

The survey of federal judges referenced in Chapter 3 on "probable cause" also asked about "reasonable suspicion." The average percentage probability assigned by the federal judges to "reasonable suspicion" was 30%.[14]

---

[14] McCauliff, Burdens of Proof, 35 Vand. L. Rev. 1293 (1982).

KANSAS v. GLOVER
140 S.Ct. 1183 (2020)

Justice THOMAS delivered the opinion of the Court.

This case presents the question whether a police officer violates the Fourth Amendment by initiating an investigative traffic stop after running a vehicle's license plate and learning that the registered owner has a revoked driver's license. We hold that when the officer lacks information negating an inference that the owner is the driver of the vehicle, the stop is reasonable.

I

Kansas charged respondent Charles Glover, Jr., with driving as a habitual violator after a traffic stop revealed that he was driving with a revoked license. See Kan. Stat. Ann. § 8–285(a)(3). Glover filed a motion to suppress all evidence seized during the stop, claiming that the officer lacked reasonable suspicion. Neither Glover nor the police officer testified at the suppression hearing. Instead, the parties stipulated to the following facts:

"1. Deputy Mark Mehrer is a certified law enforcement officer employed by the Douglas County Kansas Sheriff's Office.

2. On April 28, 2016, Deputy Mehrer was on routine patrol in Douglas County when he observed a 1995 Chevrolet 1500 pickup truck with Kansas plate 295ATJ.

3. Deputy Mehrer ran Kansas plate 295ATJ through the Kansas Department of Revenue's file service. The registration came back to a 1995 Chevrolet 1500 pickup truck.

4. Kansas Department of Revenue files indicated the truck was registered to Charles Glover Jr. The files also indicated that Mr. Glover had a revoked driver's license in the State of Kansas.

5. Deputy Mehrer assumed the registered owner of the truck was also the driver, Charles Glover Jr.

6. Deputy Mehrer did not observe any traffic infractions, and did not attempt to identify the driver of the truck. Based solely on the information that the

registered owner of the truck was revoked, Deputy Mehrer initiated a traffic stop.

7. The driver of the truck was identified as the defendant, Charles Glover Jr."

The District Court granted Glover's motion to suppress. The Court of Appeals reversed [and] the Kansas Supreme Court reversed [the Court of Appeals]. According to the Kansas Supreme Court, Deputy Mehrer did not have reasonable suspicion because his inference that Glover was behind the wheel amounted to "only a hunch" that Glover was engaging in criminal activity....

II

Under this Court's precedents, the Fourth Amendment permits an officer to initiate a brief investigative traffic stop when he has a particularized and objective basis for suspecting the particular person stopped of criminal activity. See Terry v. Ohio (1968). Although a mere "hunch" does not create reasonable suspicion, the level of suspicion the standard requires is considerably less than proof of wrongdoing by a preponderance of the evidence, and obviously less than is necessary for probable cause.

Because it is a less demanding standard, reasonable suspicion can be established with information that is different in quantity or content than that required to establish probable cause. The standard depends on the factual and practical considerations of everyday life on which reasonable and prudent men, not legal technicians, act. Courts cannot reasonably demand scientific certainty where none exists. Rather, they must permit officers to make commonsense judgments and inferences about human behavior.

III

.... We turn to whether the facts known to Deputy Mehrer at the time of the stop gave rise to reasonable suspicion. We conclude that they did.

Before initiating the stop, Deputy Mehrer observed an individual operating a 1995 Chevrolet 1500 pickup truck with Kansas plate 295ATJ. He also knew that the registered owner of the truck had a revoked license and that the model of the truck matched the observed vehicle. From these three facts, Deputy Mehrer drew the commonsense inference that Glover was likely the driver of the vehicle, which provided more than reasonable suspicion to initiate the stop.

The fact that the registered owner of a vehicle is not always the driver of the vehicle does not negate the reasonableness of Deputy Mehrer's inference. Such is the case with all reasonable inferences. The reasonable suspicion inquiry falls considerably short of 51% accuracy, for, as we have explained, "to be reasonable is not to be perfect."

Glover's revoked license does not render Deputy Mehrer's inference unreasonable either. Empirical studies demonstrate what common experience readily reveals: Drivers with revoked licenses frequently continue to drive and therefore to pose safety risks to other motorists and pedestrians. See, e.g., 2 T. Neuman et al., National Coop. Hwy. Research Program Report 500: A Guide for Addressing Collisions Involving Unlicensed Drivers and Drivers With Suspended or Revoked Licenses, p. III–1 (2003) (noting that 75% of drivers with suspended or revoked licenses continue to drive); National Hwy. and Traffic Safety Admin., Research Note: Driver License Compliance Status in Fatal Crashes 2 (Oct. 2014) (noting that approximately 19% of motor vehicle fatalities from 2008–2012 "involved drivers with invalid licenses").

Although common sense suffices to justify this inference, Kansas law reinforces that it is reasonable to infer that an individual with a revoked license may continue driving. The State's license-revocation scheme covers drivers who have already demonstrated a disregard for the law or are categorically unfit to drive. The Division of Vehicles of the Kansas Department of Revenue (Division) "shall" revoke a driver's license upon certain convictions for involuntary manslaughter, vehicular homicide, battery, reckless driving, fleeing or attempting to elude a police officer, or conviction of a felony in which a motor vehicle is used. Kan. Stat. Ann. §§ 8–254(a), 8–252. Reckless driving is defined as "driving any vehicle in willful or wanton disregard for the safety of persons or property." § 8–1566(a). The Division also has discretion to revoke a license if a driver "has been convicted with such frequency of serious offenses against traffic regulations governing the movement of vehicles as to indicate a disrespect for traffic laws and a disregard for the safety of other persons on the highways," "has been convicted of three or more moving traffic violations committed on separate occasions within a 12-month period," "is incompetent to drive a motor vehicle," or "has been convicted of a moving traffic violation, committed at a time when the person's driving privileges were restricted, suspended, or revoked." §§ 8–255(a)(1)–(4). Other reasons include violating license restrictions, § 8–245(c), being under house arrest, § 21–6609(c), and being a habitual violator, § 8–286, which Kansas defines as a resident or nonresident who has been convicted three or more times within the past five years of certain enumerated driving offenses, § 8–285. The concerns motivating the State's various grounds for revocation lend further credence to the inference that a registered owner with a revoked Kansas driver's license might be the one driving the vehicle.

IV

…. Glover and the dissent … contend that adopting Kansas' view would eviscerate the need for officers to base reasonable suspicion on "specific and articulable facts" particularized to the individual, see Terry, because police could instead rely exclusively on probabilities. Their argument carries little force.

As an initial matter, we have previously stated that officers, like jurors, may rely on probabilities in the reasonable suspicion context. Moreover, as explained above, Deputy Mehrer did not rely exclusively on probabilities. He knew that the license plate was linked to a truck matching the observed vehicle and that the registered owner of the vehicle had a revoked license. Based on these minimal facts, he used common sense to form a reasonable suspicion that a specific individual was potentially engaged in specific criminal activity—driving with a revoked license. Traffic stops of this nature do not delegate to officers "broad and unlimited discretion" to stop drivers at random. Nor do they allow officers to stop drivers whose conduct is no different from any other driver's. Accordingly, combining database information and commonsense judgments in this context is fully consonant with this Court's Fourth Amendment precedents.

V

This Court's precedents have repeatedly affirmed that "the ultimate touchstone of the Fourth Amendment is 'reasonableness.'" Under the totality of the circumstances of this case, Deputy Mehrer drew an entirely reasonable inference that Glover was driving while his license was revoked.

We emphasize the narrow scope of our holding. Like all seizures, the officer's action must be justified at its inception. The standard takes into account the totality of the circumstances—the whole picture. As a result, the presence of additional facts might dispel reasonable suspicion. For example, if an officer knows that the registered owner of the vehicle is in his mid-sixties but observes that the driver is in her mid-twenties, then the totality of the circumstances would not raise a suspicion that the particular individual being stopped is engaged in wrongdoing. Here, Deputy Mehrer possessed no exculpatory information—let alone sufficient information to rebut the reasonable inference that Glover was driving his own truck—and thus the stop was justified.

Consider the facts of *Wisconsin v. Richey* (Wis. 2022):

> Officer Alexis Meier was on patrol on a Saturday night in late April. Over the radio, she heard a report [from] a sheriff's deputy ... to be on the lookout for a Harley-Davidson motorcycle driving erratically and speeding north on Alderson Street (near the intersection with Jelenik Avenue). The sheriff's deputy did not give any additional details. Officer Meier later said that she believed that the motorcycle the deputy saw on Alderson Street was fleeing police.
>
> Five minutes after the deputy's report, at 11:09 PM, Officer Meier spotted a motorcycle – about a half-mile from the reported location of the speeding Harley. Traffic was light at that time of night. Additionally, Officer Meier had seen relatively few motorcycles out that early in the year and none around the time of the deputy's report. Meier looked up the registration, which showed that it was a Harley-Davidson registered to Charles Richey. She followed the Harley-Davidson for several blocks, but did not see any erratic driving, speeding, or other traffic violations. Meier nevertheless performed a traffic stop, suspecting that this Harley-Davidson was the one seen driving erratically on Alderson Street five minutes earlier.
>
> [The Wisconsin Supreme Court included a map where] the north-pointing arrow and letter **D** marks the spot and direction of travel of the Harley-Davidson the sheriff's deputy saw driving erratically and at high speed at 11:04 PM; **A** identifies the place where Meier first saw Richey's Harley-Davidson at 11:09 PM; and **S** signifies the location of the stop moments later....

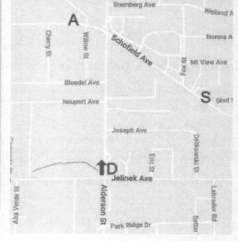

It is undisputed that the only reason Officer Meier pulled Richey over is she suspected he was the erratic driver the deputy saw five minutes earlier. The question is whether that suspicion was reasonable.

The Wisconsin Supreme Court deemed this a "close question" – how should they have ruled?

In *Dunaway v. N.Y.* (1979), Rochester police took a murder suspect to police headquarters for questioning. The government claimed that the officers did not need probable cause because the suspect was not told he was "under arrest" and was not "booked." The Supreme Court rejected that argument and held that the government conduct exceeded the bounds of *Terry*:

> "In contrast to the brief and narrowly circumscribed intrusions involved in [a valid *Terry* stop], the detention of petitioner was in important respects indistinguishable from a traditional arrest. Petitioner was not questioned briefly where he was found. Instead, he was taken from a neighbor's home to a police car, transported to a police station, and placed in an interrogation room. He was never informed that he was 'free to go.'… We accordingly hold that the Rochester police violated the Fourth and Fourteenth Amendments when, without probable cause, they seized petitioner and transported him to the police station for interrogation."

Terry v. Ohio authorizes a police officer with reasonable suspicion based upon articulable facts "that criminal activity may be afoot" to stop a suspect. But what if the officer suspects not that crime is "afoot," but that a crime already occurred? The Supreme Court addressed this question in *United States v. Hensley* (1985):

> "This is the first case we have addressed in which police stopped a person because they suspected he was involved in a completed crime. In our previous decisions involving investigatory stops on less than probable cause, police stopped or seized a person because they suspected he was about to commit a crime or was committing a crime at the moment of the stop.

We need not and do not decide today whether Terry stops to investigate all past crimes, however serious, are permitted. It is enough to say that, if police have a reasonable suspicion, grounded in specific and articulable facts, that a person they encounter was involved in or is wanted in connection with a completed felony, then a Terry stop may be made to investigate that suspicion.

2. EXPANSION OF TERRY DOCTRINE

The Supreme Court recognizes that *Terry* stops can occur outside the precise context considered in *Terry v. Ohio*. For example, *United States v. Place* (1983) considered an investigative seizure of a person's luggage at an airport. The Court explained that "because of the inherently transient nature of drug courier activity at airports, allowing police to make brief investigative stops of persons at airports on reasonable suspicion of drug-trafficking substantially enhances the likelihood that police will be able to prevent the flow of narcotics into distribution channels." And given that "police may confine their investigation to an on-the-spot inquiry— for example, immediate exposure of the luggage to a trained narcotics detection dog—or transport the property to another location ... some brief detentions of personal effects may be ... minimally intrusive of Fourth Amendment interests." The Court concluded that "when an officer's observations lead him reasonably to believe that a traveler is carrying luggage that contains narcotics, the principles of *Terry* and its progeny would permit the officer to detain the luggage briefly to investigate the circumstances that aroused his suspicion, provided that the investigative detention is properly limited in scope."

As illustrated in *Kansas v. Glover*, the Court has also concluded that *Terry* empowers police to detain vehicles and their occupants to conduct limited investigations. For example, the Court stated in *United States v. Hensley* (1985):

❝ In Terry, and subsequent cases, this Court has held that, consistent with the Fourth Amendment, police may stop persons in the absence of probable cause under limited circumstances. In particular, the Court has noted that law enforcement agents may briefly stop a moving automobile to investigate a reasonable suspicion that its occupants are involved in criminal activity. Although stopping a car and detaining its occupants constitute a seizure within the meaning of the Fourth Amendment, the governmental interest in investigating an officer's reasonable suspicion, based on specific and articulable facts, may outweigh the Fourth Amendment interest of the driver and passengers in remaining secure from the intrusion.

The next case considers the permissible boundaries of such a detention.

UNITED STATES v. SHARPE
470 U.S. 675 (1985)

Chief Justice BURGER delivered the opinion of the Court.

We granted certiorari to decide whether an individual reasonably suspected of engaging in criminal activity may be detained for a period of 20 minutes, when the detention is necessary for law enforcement officers to conduct a limited investigation of the suspected criminal activity.

I

On the morning of June 9, 1978, Agent Cooke of the Drug Enforcement Administration (DEA) was on patrol in an unmarked vehicle on a coastal road near Sunset Beach, North Carolina, an area under surveillance for suspected drug trafficking. At approximately 6:30 a.m., Cooke noticed a blue pickup truck with an attached camper shell traveling on the highway in tandem with a blue Pontiac Bonneville. Respondent Donald Savage was driving the pickup, and respondent William Sharpe was driving the Pontiac. The Pontiac also carried a passenger, Davis, the charges against whom were later dropped. Observing that the truck was riding low in the rear and that the camper did not bounce or sway appreciably when the truck drove over bumps or around curves, Agent Cooke concluded that it was heavily loaded. A quilted material covered the rear and side windows of the camper.

Cooke's suspicions were sufficiently aroused to follow the two vehicles for approximately 20 miles as they proceeded south into South Carolina. He then decided to make an "investigative stop" and radioed the State Highway Patrol for assistance. Officer Thrasher, driving a marked patrol car, responded to the call. Almost immediately after Thrasher caught up with the procession, the Pontiac and the pickup turned off the highway and onto a campground road. Cooke and Thrasher followed the two vehicles as the latter drove along the road at 55 to 60 miles an hour, exceeding the speed limit of 35 miles an hour. The road eventually looped back to the highway, onto which Savage and Sharpe turned and continued to drive south.

At this point, all four vehicles were in the middle lane of the three right-hand lanes of the highway. Agent Cooke asked Officer Thrasher to signal both vehicles to stop. Thrasher pulled alongside the Pontiac, which was in the lead, turned on his flashing light, and motioned for the driver of the Pontiac to stop. As Sharpe moved the Pontiac into the right lane, the pickup truck cut between the Pontiac and Thrasher's patrol car, nearly hitting the patrol car, and continued down the highway. Thrasher pursued the truck while Cooke pulled up behind the Pontiac.

Cooke approached the Pontiac and identified himself. He requested identification, and Sharpe produced a Georgia driver's license bearing the name of Raymond Pavlovich. Cooke then attempted to radio Thrasher to determine whether he had been successful in stopping the pickup truck, but he was unable to make contact for several minutes, apparently because Thrasher was not in his patrol car. Cooke radioed the local police for assistance, and two officers from the Myrtle Beach Police Department arrived about 10 minutes later. Asking the two officers to "maintain the situation," Cooke left to join Thrasher.

In the meantime, Thrasher had stopped the pickup truck about one-half mile down the road. After stopping the truck, Thrasher had approached it with his revolver drawn, ordered the driver, Savage, to get out and assume a "spread eagled" position against the side of the truck, and patted him down. Thrasher then holstered his gun and asked Savage for his driver's license and the truck's vehicle registration. Savage produced his own Florida driver's license and a bill of sale for the truck bearing the name of Pavlovich. In response to questions from Thrasher concerning the ownership of the truck, Savage said that the truck belonged to a friend and that he was taking it to have its shock absorbers repaired. When Thrasher told Savage that he would be held until the arrival of Cooke, whom Thrasher identified as a DEA agent, Savage became nervous, said that he wanted to leave, and requested the return of his driver's license. Thrasher replied that Savage was not free to leave at that time.

Agent Cooke arrived at the scene approximately 15 minutes after the truck had been stopped. Thrasher handed Cooke Savage's license and the bill of sale for the truck; Cooke noted that the bill of sale bore the same name as Sharpe's license. Cooke identified himself to Savage as a DEA agent and said that he thought the truck was loaded with marihuana. Cooke twice sought permission to search the camper, but Savage declined to give it, explaining that he was not the owner of the truck. Cooke then stepped on the rear of the truck and, observing that it did not sink any lower, confirmed his suspicion that it was probably overloaded. He put his nose against the rear window, which was covered from the inside, and reported that he could smell marihuana. Without seeking Savage's permission, Cooke removed the keys from the ignition, opened the rear of the camper, and observed a large number of burlap-wrapped bales resembling bales of marihuana that Cooke had seen in previous investigations. Agent Cooke then placed Savage under arrest and left him with Thrasher.

Cooke returned to the Pontiac and arrested Sharpe and Davis. Approximately 30 to 40 minutes had elapsed between the time Cooke stopped the Pontiac and the time he returned to arrest Sharpe and Davis. Cooke assembled the various parties and vehicles and led them to the Myrtle Beach police station. That evening, DEA agents took the truck to the Federal Building in Charleston, South Carolina. Several days later, Cooke supervised the unloading of the truck, which contained 43 bales [of marijuana] weighing a total of 2,629 pounds....

II

A

The Fourth Amendment is not, of course, a guarantee against all searches and seizures, but only against unreasonable searches and seizures. The authority and limits of the Amendment apply to investigative stops of vehicles such as occurred here. In Terry v. Ohio, we adopted a dual inquiry for evaluating the reasonableness of an investigative stop. Under this approach, we examine "whether the officer's action was justified at its inception, and whether it was reasonably related in scope to the circumstances which justified the interference in the first place."

As to the first part of this inquiry, the Court of Appeals assumed that the police had an articulable and reasonable suspicion that Sharpe and Savage were engaged in marihuana trafficking, given the setting and all the circumstances when the police attempted to stop the Pontiac and the pickup. That assumption is abundantly supported by the record. As to the second part of the inquiry, however, the court concluded that the 30- to 40-minute detention of Sharpe and the 20-minute detention of Savage "failed to meet the Fourth Amendment's requirement of brevity."

It is not necessary for us to decide whether the length of Sharpe's detention was unreasonable, because that detention bears no causal relation to Agent Cooke's discovery of the marihuana. The marihuana was in Savage's pickup, not in Sharpe's Pontiac; the contraband introduced at respondents' trial cannot logically be considered the "fruit" of Sharpe's detention. The only issue in this case, then, is whether it was reasonable under the circumstances facing Agent Cooke and Officer Thrasher to detain Savage, whose vehicle contained the challenged evidence, for approximately 20 minutes. We conclude that the detention of Savage clearly meets the Fourth Amendment's standard of reasonableness.

The Court of Appeals did not question the reasonableness of Officer Thrasher's or Agent Cooke's conduct during their detention of Savage. Rather, the court concluded that the length of the detention alone transformed it from a Terry stop into a de facto arrest. Counsel for respondents, as amicus curiae, assert that conclusion as their principal argument before this Court. That reliance is misplaced.

…. In Florida v. Royer, government agents stopped the defendant in an airport, seized his luggage, and took him to a small room used for questioning, where a search of the luggage revealed narcotics. The Court held that the defendant's detention constituted an arrest. As in Dunaway v. New York, though, the focus was primarily on facts other than the duration of the defendant's detention—particularly the fact that the police confined the defendant in a small airport room for questioning.

The plurality in Royer did note that "an investigative detention must be temporary and last no longer than is necessary to effectuate the purpose of the stop." The Court followed a similar approach in United States v. Place (1983). In that case, law enforcement agents stopped the defendant after his arrival in an airport and seized his luggage for 90 minutes to take it to a narcotics detection dog for a "sniff test." We decided that an investigative seizure of personal property could be justified under the Terry doctrine, but that "the length of the detention of respondent's luggage alone precludes the conclusion that the seizure was reasonable in the absence of probable cause." However, the rationale underlying that conclusion was premised on the fact that the police knew of respondent's arrival time for several hours beforehand, and the Court assumed that the police could have arranged for a trained narcotics dog in advance and thus avoided the necessity of holding respondent's luggage for 90 minutes. "In assessing the effect of the length of the detention, we take into account whether the police diligently pursue their investigation."

Here, the Court of Appeals did not conclude that the police acted less than diligently, or that they unnecessarily prolonged Savage's detention. Place and Royer thus provide no support for the Court of Appeals' analysis.

Admittedly, Terry, Dunaway, Royer, and Place, considered together, may in some instances create difficult line-drawing problems in distinguishing an investigative stop from a de facto arrest. Obviously, if an investigative stop continues indefinitely, at some point it can no longer be justified as an investigative stop. But our cases impose no rigid time limitation on Terry stops. While it is clear that "the brevity of the invasion of the individual's Fourth Amendment interests is an important factor in determining whether the seizure is so minimally intrusive as to be justifiable on reasonable suspicion," we have emphasized the need to consider the law enforcement purposes to be served by the stop as well as the time reasonably needed to effectuate those purposes. Much as a "bright line" rule would be desirable, in evaluating whether an investigative detention is unreasonable, common sense and ordinary human experience must govern over rigid criteria....

In Place, we expressly rejected the suggestion that we adopt a hard-and-fast time limit for a permissible Terry stop: "We understand the desirability of providing law enforcement authorities with a clear rule to guide their conduct. Nevertheless, we question the wisdom of a rigid time limitation. Such a limit would undermine the equally important need to allow authorities to graduate their responses to the demands of any particular situation."...

B

In assessing whether a detention is too long in duration to be justified as an investigative stop, we consider it appropriate to examine whether the police diligently pursued a means of investigation that was likely to confirm or dispel their suspicions quickly, during which time it was necessary to detain the defendant. A court making this assessment should take care to consider whether the police are acting in a swiftly developing situation, and in such cases the court should not indulge in unrealistic second-guessing. A creative judge engaged in post hoc evaluation of police conduct can almost always imagine some alternative means by which the objectives of the police might have been accomplished. But "the fact that the protection of the public might, in the abstract, have been accomplished by 'less intrusive' means does not, itself, render the search unreasonable." The question is not simply whether some other alternative was available, but whether the police acted unreasonably in failing to recognize or to pursue it.

We readily conclude that, given the circumstances facing him, Agent Cooke pursued his investigation in a diligent and reasonable manner. During most of Savage's 20-minute detention, Cooke was attempting to contact Thrasher and enlisting the help of the local police who remained with Sharpe while Cooke left to pursue Officer Thrasher and the pickup. Once Cooke reached Officer Thrasher and Savage, he proceeded expeditiously: within the space of a few minutes, he examined Savage's driver's license and the truck's bill of sale, requested (and was denied) permission to search the truck, stepped on the rear bumper and noted that the truck did not move, confirming his suspicion that it was probably overloaded. He then detected the odor of marihuana.

Clearly this case does not involve any delay unnecessary to the legitimate investigation of the law enforcement officers. Respondents presented no evidence that the officers were dilatory in their investigation. The delay in this case was attributable almost entirely to the evasive actions of Savage, who sought to elude the police as Sharpe moved his Pontiac to the side of the road. Except for Savage's maneuvers, only a short and certainly permissible pre-arrest detention would likely have taken place. The somewhat longer detention was simply the result of a graduated response to the demands of the particular situation.

We reject the contention that a 20-minute stop is unreasonable when the police have acted diligently and a suspect's actions contribute to the added delay about which he complains. The judgment of the Court of Appeals is reversed, and the case is remanded for further proceedings consistent with this opinion.

Consider the following facts from *Rodriguez v. United States* (2015):

> Just after midnight on March 27, 2012, police officer Morgan Struble observed a Mercury Mountaineer veer slowly onto the shoulder of Nebraska State Highway 275 for one or two seconds and then jerk back onto the road. Nebraska law prohibits driving on highway shoulders and on that basis, Struble pulled the Mountaineer over at 12:06 a.m. Struble is a K–9 officer

with the Valley Police Department in Nebraska, and his dog Floyd was in his patrol car that night. Two men were in the Mountaineer: the driver, Dennys Rodriguez, and a front-seat passenger, Scott Pollman.

Struble approached the Mountaineer on the passenger's side. After Rodriguez identified himself, Struble asked him why he had driven onto the shoulder. Rodriguez replied that he had swerved to avoid a pothole. Struble then gathered Rodriguez's license, registration, and proof of insurance, and asked Rodriguez to accompany him to the patrol car. Rodriguez asked if he was required to do so, and Struble answered that he was not. Rodriguez decided to wait in his own vehicle.

After running a records check on Rodriguez, Struble returned to the Mountaineer. Struble asked passenger Pollman for his driver's license and began to question him about where the two men were coming from and where they were going. Pollman replied that they had traveled to Omaha, Nebraska, to look at a Ford Mustang that was for sale and that they were returning to Norfolk, Nebraska. Struble returned again to his patrol car, where he completed a records check on Pollman, and called for a second officer. Struble then began writing a warning ticket for Rodriguez for driving on the shoulder of the road.

Struble returned to Rodriguez's vehicle a third time to issue the written warning. By 12:28 a.m., Struble had finished explaining the warning to Rodriguez, and had given back to Rodriguez and Pollman the documents obtained from them. As Struble later testified, at that point, Rodriguez and Pollman 'had all their documents back and a copy of the written warning. I got all the reasons for the stop out of the way, ... took care of all the business.'

Nevertheless, Struble did not consider Rodriguez 'free to leave.' Although justification for the traffic stop was 'out of the way,' Struble asked for permission to walk his dog around Rodriguez's vehicle. Rodriguez said no. Struble then instructed Rodriguez to turn off the ignition, exit the vehicle, and stand in front of the patrol car to wait for the second officer. Rodriguez complied. At 12:33 a.m., a deputy sheriff arrived. Struble retrieved his dog and led him twice around the Mountaineer. The dog alerted to the presence of drugs halfway through Struble's second pass. All told, seven or eight minutes had elapsed from the time Struble issued the written warning until

the dog indicated the presence of drugs. A search of the vehicle revealed a
large bag of methamphetamine.

*Before reading any further, what would you conclude as to the constitutionality of the police conduct
described above?*

The Supreme Court ruled that the Nebraska police violated the Fourth
Amendment, explaining: "An officer … may conduct certain unrelated checks
during an otherwise lawful traffic stop. But … he may not do so in a way that
prolongs the stop, absent the reasonable suspicion ordinarily demanded to justify
detaining an individual."

In an effort to apply *Rodriguez*, the Supreme Court of Idaho diagramed a challenged
stop using a precise timeline generated through the officers' body camera videos.
The diagram is included below:

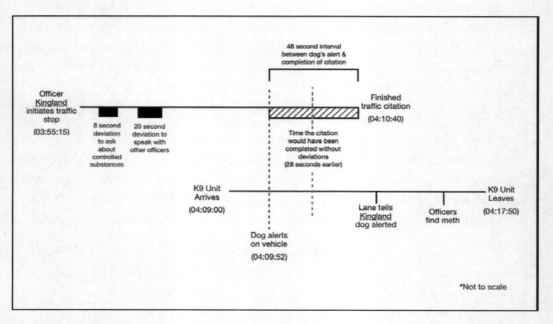

What does this timeline indicate in terms of whether the stop was prolonged in
violation of the standard set out in *Rodriguez*?

The Supreme Court in *Rodriguez* stated: "Like a Terry stop, the tolerable duration of police inquiries in the traffic-stop context is determined by the seizure's 'mission'—to address the traffic violation that warranted the stop, and attend to related safety concerns." This idea of permitting police conduct that forwards the mission of an otherwise lawful stop helps to fill out the contours of permitted police activity in a variety of contexts.

For example, in *Muehler v. Mena* (2005), police executed a search warrant for evidence related to a "gang-related, driveby shooting," detaining Iris Mena, one of the occupants of the searched address, during the search. Mena recognized that *Michigan v. Summers* (1981) [discussed in Chapter 5] gave the police the authority to detain her during the search but argued that the 2-3-hour detention in a garage using handcuffs exceeded that authority. The Supreme Court disagreed:

> "Inherent in *Summers*' authorization to detain an occupant of the place to be searched is the authority to use reasonable force to effectuate the detention…. [And] this was no ordinary search. The governmental interests in not only detaining, but using handcuffs, are at their maximum when, as here, a warrant authorizes a search for weapons and a wanted gang member resides on the premises. In such inherently dangerous situations, the use of handcuffs minimizes the risk of harm to both officers and occupants. Though this safety risk inherent in executing a search warrant for weapons was sufficient to justify the use of handcuffs, the need to detain multiple occupants made the use of handcuffs all the more reasonable.

> Mena argues that, even if the use of handcuffs to detain her in the garage was reasonable as an initial matter, the duration of the use of handcuffs made the detention unreasonable. The duration of a detention can, of course, affect the balance of interests. However, the 2– to 3–hour detention in handcuffs in this case does not outweigh the government's continuing safety interests. As we have noted, this case involved the detention of four detainees by two officers during a search of a gang house for dangerous weapons. We conclude that the detention of Mena in handcuffs during the search was reasonable."

The Supreme Court engages in similar analysis throughout its Fourth Amendment doctrine. For example, in *Pennsylvania v. Mimms* (1977), the Supreme Court created a "per se" rule that "once a motor vehicle has been lawfully detained for a traffic violation, the police officers may order the driver to get out of the vehicle without violating the Fourth Amendment's proscription of unreasonable seizures." In *Maryland v. Wilson* (1997), the Supreme Court extended this per se rule to passengers:

> "In summary, danger to an officer from a traffic stop is likely to be greater when there are passengers in addition to the driver in the stopped car. While there is not the same basis for ordering the passengers out of the car as there is for ordering the driver out, the additional intrusion on the passenger is minimal. We therefore hold that an officer making a traffic stop may order passengers to get out of the car pending completion of the stop."

The Supreme Court justifies granting broad powers to police officers on the grounds of public safety. But sometimes these powers have the opposite effect. For example, in 2015, Texas State Trooper Brian Encina pulled over Sandra Bland for failing to signal while changing lanes. The traffic stop escalated when Encina insisted that Bland put out her cigarette and, when she declined, ordered her out of the car, contending repeatedly that he was giving her "a lawful order." Encina arrested Bland for assault based (purportedly) on her resistance to being removed from the car and taken into custody. Three days later, while still in jail, Bland hanged herself. The incident received national attention when video footage of the stop and arrest revealed the officer's oppressive conduct. In response to the incident, Texas passed "the Sandra Bland Act," which mandates de-escalation training for police officers, funds measures to ensure regular cell checks in Texas jails, and requires outside investigation into all jail deaths. A grand jury indicted Encina for perjury based on his claim in an affidavit filed in connection with the case that he removed Bland from the car for safety reasons. The perjury charges were later dropped on the condition that Encina resign from the police force and never again seek a job in law enforcement.[15]

---

[15] For videos of the stop along with detailed analysis, see
https://www.nytimes.com/interactive/2015/07/20/us/sandra-bland-arrest-death-videos-maps.html

MINNESOTA v. DICKERSON
508 U.S. 366 (1993)

Justice WHITE delivered the opinion of the Court.

I

On the evening of November 9, 1989, two Minneapolis police officers were patrolling an area on the city's north side in a marked squad car. At about 8:15 p.m., one of the officers observed respondent, Timothy Dickerson, leaving a 12–unit apartment building on Morgan Avenue North. The officer, having previously responded to complaints of drug sales in the building's hallways and having executed several search warrants on the premises, considered the building to be a notorious "crack house." According to testimony credited by the trial court, respondent began walking toward the police but, upon spotting the squad car and making eye contact with one of the officers, abruptly halted and began walking in the opposite direction. His suspicion aroused, this officer watched as respondent turned and entered an alley on the other side of the apartment building. Based upon respondent's seemingly evasive actions and the fact that he had just left a building known for cocaine traffic, the officers decided to stop respondent and investigate further.

The officers pulled their squad car into the alley and ordered respondent to stop and submit to a patdown search. The search revealed no weapons, but the officer conducting the search did take an interest in a small lump in respondent's nylon jacket. The officer later testified: "As I pat-searched the front of his body, I felt a lump, a small lump, in the front pocket. I examined it with my fingers and it slid and it felt to be a lump of crack cocaine in cellophane."

The officer then reached into respondent's pocket and retrieved a small plastic bag containing one fifth of one gram of crack cocaine. Respondent was arrested and charged in Hennepin County District Court with possession of a controlled substance....

II

A

.... Terry v. Ohio ... held that "when an officer is justified in believing that the individual whose suspicious behavior he is investigating at close range is armed and presently dangerous to the officer or to others," the officer may conduct a patdown

200

search "to determine whether the person is in fact carrying a weapon." The purpose of this limited search is not to discover evidence of crime, but to allow the officer to pursue his investigation without fear of violence. Rather, a protective search— permitted without a warrant and on the basis of reasonable suspicion less than probable cause—must be strictly "limited to that which is necessary for the discovery of weapons which might be used to harm the officer or others nearby." If the protective search goes beyond what is necessary to determine if the suspect is armed, it is no longer valid under Terry and its fruits will be suppressed.

…. The question presented today is whether police officers may seize nonthreatening contraband detected during a protective patdown search of the sort permitted by Terry. We think the answer is clearly that they may, so long as the officers' search stays within the bounds marked by Terry.

B

We have already held that police officers, at least under certain circumstances, may seize contraband detected during the lawful execution of a Terry search. In Michigan v. Long (1983), for example, police approached a man who had driven his car into a ditch and who appeared to be under the influence of some intoxicant. As the man moved to reenter the car from the roadside, police spotted a knife on the floorboard. The officers stopped the man, subjected him to a patdown search, and then inspected the interior of the vehicle for other weapons. During the search of the passenger compartment, the police discovered an open pouch containing marijuana and seized it. This Court upheld the validity of the search and seizure under Terry. The Court held first that, in the context of a roadside encounter, where police have reasonable suspicion based on specific and articulable facts to believe that a driver may be armed and dangerous, they may conduct a protective search for weapons not only of the driver's person but also of the passenger compartment of the automobile. Of course, the protective search of the vehicle, being justified solely by the danger that weapons stored there could be used against the officers or bystanders, must be "limited to those areas in which a weapon may be placed or hidden." The Court then held: "If, while conducting a legitimate Terry search of the interior of the automobile, the officer should, as here, discover contraband other than weapons, he clearly cannot be required to ignore the contraband, and the Fourth Amendment does not require its suppression in such circumstances."

The Court in Long justified this latter holding by reference to our cases under the "plain-view" doctrine. Under that doctrine, if police are lawfully in a position from which they view an object, if its incriminating character is immediately apparent, and if the officers have a lawful right of access to the object, they may seize it without a warrant. If, however, the police lack probable cause to believe that an object in plain view is contraband without conducting some further search of the object—i.e., if its incriminating character is not "immediately apparent,"—the plain-view doctrine cannot justify its seizure.

We think that this doctrine has an obvious application by analogy to cases in which an officer discovers contraband through the sense of touch during an otherwise lawful search. The rationale of the plain-view doctrine is that if contraband is left in open view and is observed by a police officer from a lawful vantage point, there has been no invasion of a legitimate expectation of privacy and thus no "search" within the meaning of the Fourth Amendment—or at least no search independent of the initial intrusion that gave the officers their vantage point. The warrantless seizure of contraband that presents itself in this manner is deemed justified by the realization that resort to a neutral magistrate under such circumstances would often be impracticable and would do little to promote the objectives of the Fourth Amendment. The same can be said of tactile discoveries of contraband. If a police officer lawfully pats down a suspect's outer clothing and feels an object whose contour or mass makes its identity immediately apparent, there has been no invasion of the suspect's privacy beyond that already authorized by the officer's search for weapons; if the object is contraband, its warrantless seizure would be justified by the same practical considerations that inhere in the plain-view context....

III

It remains to apply these principles to the facts of this case. Respondent has not challenged the finding made by the trial court and affirmed by both the Court of Appeals and the State Supreme Court that the police were justified under Terry in stopping him and frisking him for weapons. Thus, the dispositive question before this Court is whether the officer who conducted the search was acting within the lawful bounds marked by Terry at the time he gained probable cause to believe that the lump in respondent's jacket was contraband. The State District Court did not make precise findings on this point, instead finding simply that the officer, after feeling "a small, hard object wrapped in plastic" in respondent's pocket, "formed the opinion that the object was crack cocaine." The District Court also noted that the officer made "no claim that he suspected this object to be a weapon," a finding affirmed on appeal. The Minnesota Supreme Court, after "a close examination of the record," held that the officer's own testimony "belies any notion that he 'immediately'" recognized the lump as crack cocaine. Rather, the court concluded, the officer determined that the lump was contraband only after "squeezing, sliding and otherwise manipulating the contents of the defendant's pocket"—a pocket which the officer already knew contained no weapon.

Under the State Supreme Court's interpretation of the record before it, it is clear that the court was correct in holding that the police officer in this case overstepped the bounds of the "strictly circumscribed" search for weapons allowed under Terry. Where, as here, "an officer who is executing a valid search for one item seizes a different item," this Court rightly "has been sensitive to the danger that officers will enlarge a specific authorization, furnished by a warrant or an exigency, into the equivalent of a general warrant to rummage and seize at will." Here, the officer's continued exploration of respondent's pocket after having concluded that it contained no weapon was unrelated to the sole justification of the search under Terry: the protection of the police officer and others nearby. It therefore amounted to the sort of evidentiary search that Terry expressly refused to authorize, and that we have condemned in subsequent cases.

Once again, the analogy to the plain-view doctrine is apt. In Arizona v. Hicks (1987), this Court held invalid the seizure of stolen stereo equipment found by police while executing a valid search for other evidence. Although the police were lawfully on the premises, they obtained probable cause to believe that the stereo equipment was contraband only after moving the equipment to permit officers to read its serial numbers. The subsequent seizure of the equipment could not be justified by the plain-view doctrine, this Court explained, because the incriminating character of the stereo equipment was not immediately apparent; rather, probable cause to believe that the equipment was stolen arose only as a result of a further search—the moving of the equipment—that was not authorized by a search warrant or by any exception to the warrant requirement. The facts of this case are very similar. Although the officer was lawfully in a position to feel the lump in respondent's pocket, because Terry entitled him to place his hands upon respondent's jacket, the court below determined that the incriminating character of the object was not immediately apparent to him. Rather, the officer determined that the item was contraband only after conducting a further search, one not authorized by Terry or by any other exception to the warrant requirement. Because this further search of respondent's pocket was constitutionally invalid, the seizure of the cocaine that followed is likewise unconstitutional.

3. MASS STOP AND FRISK

In 2007, New York City police officers stopped and frisked David Floyd, found no evidence of wrongdoing, and left. Floyd later became the lead plaintiff in a class action lawsuit against New York City that alleged that the city had a longstanding policy of unconstitutional searches and seizures. After extensive litigation, a federal district court ruled in Floyd's favor. A short excerpt from the court's lengthy opinion follows:

FLOYD v. CITY OF NEW YORK
959 F. Supp. 2d 540 (S.D.N.Y. 2013)

SHIRA SCHEINDLIN, District Judge

New Yorkers are rightly proud of their city and seek to make it as safe as the largest city in America can be. New Yorkers also treasure their liberty. Countless individuals have come to New York in pursuit of that liberty. The goals of liberty and safety may be in tension, but they can coexist—indeed the Constitution mandates it.

This case is about the tension between liberty and public safety in the use of a proactive policing tool called "stop and frisk." The New York City Police Department ("NYPD") made 4.4 million stops between January 2004 and June 2012. Over 80% of these 4.4 million stops were of blacks or Hispanics. In each of these stops a person's life was interrupted. The person was detained and questioned, often on a public street. More than half of the time the police subjected the person to a frisk.

Plaintiffs—blacks and Hispanics who were stopped—argue that the NYPD's use of stop and frisk violated their constitutional rights in two ways: (1) they were stopped without a legal basis in violation of the Fourth Amendment, and (2) they were targeted for stops because of their race in violation of the Fourteenth

Amendment. Plaintiffs do not seek to end the use of stop and frisk. Rather, they argue that it must be reformed to comply with constitutional limits. Two such limits are paramount here: first, that all stops be based on "reasonable suspicion" as defined by the Supreme Court of the United States; and second, that stops be conducted in a racially neutral manner.

I emphasize at the outset, as I have throughout the litigation, that this case is not about the effectiveness of stop and frisk in deterring or combating crime. This Court's mandate is solely to judge the constitutionality of police behavior, not its effectiveness as a law enforcement tool. Many police practices may be useful for fighting crime—preventive detention or coerced confessions, for example—but because they are unconstitutional they cannot be used, no matter how effective. "The enshrinement of constitutional rights necessarily takes certain policy choices off the table." District of Columbia v. Heller (2008).

This case is also not primarily about the nineteen individual stops that were the subject of testimony at trial. Rather, this case is about whether the City has a policy or custom of violating the Constitution by making unlawful stops and conducting unlawful frisks.

The Supreme Court has recognized that "the degree of community resentment aroused by particular practices is clearly relevant to an assessment of the quality of the intrusion upon reasonable expectations of personal security." In light of the very active and public debate on the issues addressed in this Opinion—and the passionate positions taken by both sides—it is important to recognize the human toll of unconstitutional stops. While it is true that any one stop is a limited intrusion in duration and deprivation of liberty, each stop is also a demeaning and humiliating experience. No one should live in fear of being stopped whenever he leaves his home to go about the activities of daily life. Those who are routinely subjected to stops are overwhelmingly people of color, and they are justifiably troubled to be singled out when many of them have done nothing to attract the unwanted attention. Some plaintiffs testified that stops make them feel unwelcome in some parts of the City, and distrustful of the police. This alienation cannot be good for the police, the community, or its leaders. Fostering trust and confidence between the police and the community would be an improvement for everyone....

Conclusions

…. Plaintiffs established the City's liability for the NYPD's violation of their Fourth Amendment rights under two theories, either of which is adequate …: first, plaintiffs showed that senior officials in the City and at the NYPD were deliberately indifferent to officers conducting unconstitutional stops and frisks; and second, plaintiffs showed that practices resulting in unconstitutional stops and frisks were sufficiently widespread that they had the force of law….

Plaintiffs have established the City's liability for the NYPD's violation of plaintiffs' Fourteenth Amendment [Equal Protection] rights under two theories, either of which is adequate …. First, plaintiffs showed that the City, through the NYPD, has a policy of indirect racial profiling based on local criminal suspect data. Second, plaintiffs showed that senior officials in the City and at the NYPD have been deliberately indifferent to the intentionally discriminatory application of stop and frisk at the managerial and officer levels….

A Historical Account of NYC Stop and Frisk[16]

…The voluminous scholarly literature and media reports critiquing NYC Stop and Frisk, the much-cited New York Attorney General's 1999 "Stop and Frisk" report, the 200-page opinion invalidating the program by Judge Shira Scheindlin, and NYPD Police Commissioner William Bratton's memoir, *Turnaround*, all share a curious omission. On the question of what exactly New York City's "stop and frisk" program is, and how it came into being, the accounts are conclusory and full of gaps. The elusive nature of NYC Stop and Frisk is perhaps best illustrated by the fact that Judge Scheindlin's recent ruling did not invalidate any tangible NYPD policy or procedure. Rather, the judge targeted the NYPD's "unwritten policy" of conducting race-conscious stops; "pressure" from senior NYPD officials to increase enforcement activity, including stops; and the NYPD's "deliberate indifference" to "constitutional deprivations caused by its employees."

The most powerful explanation for the skeletal nature of the existing narratives of NYC Stop and Frisk is that the notorious program is not a "program" at all, but

---

[16] Excerpted from: Bellin, *The Inverse Relationship Between the Constitutionality and Effectiveness of New York City "Stop And Frisk,"* 94 Boston Univ. Law Rev. 1495 (2014).

rather a widespread reaction of individual officers and midlevel supervisors to a variety of incentives. What came to be known as NYC Stop and Frisk appears to have grown idiosyncratically in ways perhaps never intended, and was only gradually and incidentally endorsed by high-level officials as a coherent (if unconstitutional) citywide approach to violent crime suppression.

The task of understanding NYC Stop and Frisk begins with Terry v. Ohio, the 1968 Supreme Court case that endorsed brief seizures ("stops") and cursory searches ("frisks") based only upon "reasonable suspicion" - a lower standard than the traditional "probable cause" standard required for an arrest. Specifically, Terry authorizes an officer to "conduct a brief, investigatory stop when the officer has a reasonable, articulable suspicion that criminal activity is afoot." A frisk may follow if there is reasonable suspicion to believe the person is armed and dangerous. There is, however, no direct connection between the spur of the moment "swift action" blessed by the Warren Court in Terry and the citywide efforts of thousands of NYPD officers to routinely stop and frisk pedestrians for the purpose of finding guns and discouraging gun carrying. The evolution of the relatively modest Terry stop into a core NYPD crime-fighting strategy is shrouded in mystery.

The origins of NYC Stop and Frisk can be traced to an epic crime wave that crested in New York City in the early 1990s. In 1990, the City hosted 2,245 homicides, a "record high."... In 1993, nearly half of the City's residents said they had been victimized by crime in the past year....

Homicides peaked in 1990, but the initial reductions were too modest and came too late for Mayor David Dinkins, who lost the November 1993 election to former prosecutor Rudolph Giuliani. As one of his first acts, Giuliani appointed William Bratton police commissioner. Bratton had garnered attention as NYC Transit Police Commissioner by embracing the increasingly popular Broken Windows theory of policing: pouring resources into arresting minor offenders, like subway fare evaders, in the hope that a decrease in low-level "disorder" would lead to fewer serious crimes....

While Bratton and his successors never explicitly embraced mass stop-and-frisk as a crime-fighting strategy in the 1990s, their general approach to policing, including a rhetorical embrace of Broken Windows, created the conditions under which stop-and-frisk would eventually thrive. First, Bratton and his successors called for putting large numbers of officers on the streets, interacting directly with civilians.

Second, Broken Windows theory endorsed low-level interdictions, often without formal arrest or prosecution, intended to prevent serious crimes before they occurred. Third, Bratton and his successors championed a data-driven approach to crime fighting, popularly referred to as "Compstat." Compstat entailed methodically gathering and computerizing data so that administrators could view crime trends and identify high-crime locations. Armed with this data, the Commissioner and his staff conducted twice-weekly, citywide sessions where precinct commanders were called to account for persistent crime in their jurisdiction. Accountability came with independence. Precinct commanders could address crime in whatever way they chose so long as the results were reflected in subsequent Compstat maps. Bratton explained, "I encouraged the precinct commanders to use their own initiative, and I told them I would judge them on their results."

The most direct connection between Bratton's approach to policing and NYC Stop and Frisk, however, has nothing to do with Broken Windows. Instead, it arose from a shared goal of eradicating unlawful public gun possession. Early in his tenure, Bratton seized upon statistics that revealed that the primary driver of the City's crime wave was surging gun crime. In one of the first policy documents issued by Bratton's NYPD, Police Strategy No. 1: Getting Guns off the Streets of New York, the Department announced a series of initiatives aimed at reducing gun violence. The document emphasized that between 1960 and 1992, the number of murders committed in New York City with a handgun increased by almost two thousand percent, growing from one-quarter to three-quarters of all murders. Tough restrictions on gun purchases seemed largely irrelevant to this problem, since "90% of the illegal guns came into the city from other states." Residents are "afraid for a reason," the document warned, "and that reason has mainly to do with handguns."

Although Police Strategy No. 1 does not refer to "stop and frisk" or related approaches to finding guns, it does announce the expansion of the elite "Street Crime Unit" ("SCU") and its deployment "in a concentrated approach" to high-crime areas to "increase firearms related arrests." As controversy engulfed the SCU in 1999, it came to light that the unit relied heavily on stop-and-frisks as part of its mission to find guns - at least 18,000 stops in 1997 and 27,000 in 1998. Although the precise directives SCU officers received are unclear, it appears that the unit was under pressure to generate gun arrests (perhaps including monthly quotas), and turned to Terry stop-and-frisks as a last-ditch means for finding guns when other tactics came up empty....

The NYPD disbanded the SCU in 2002, reabsorbing its members into other units, but the SCU experience can be viewed as a microcosm of the spread of "stop and frisk" citywide. Bratton and his successors' reliance on Compstat, and their underlying prioritization of gun crime, led to the saturation of high-crime areas, known as "putting cops on dots," with officers generically tasked with taking guns off the street. Directing officers (or units such as the SCU) to crime-plagued areas ("dots") is only part of the equation, however, since illegal guns do not turn themselves in. With thousands of officers walking the streets but few opportunities to catch gunmen in the act, beat cops predictably turned to (or, in Judge Scheindlin's view, were pushed towards) relatively mundane approaches to uncover concealed weapons: arresting minor offenders in order to search them and (when minor offenders were not in view) stopping and frisking pedestrians who might be carrying weapons. There was nothing inherently appealing about these tasks; officers embraced this "crap" work either because they believed it reduced crime or because they needed to demonstrate activity to their supervisors (or both). Since the NYPD tabulated "stop and frisks" in its database, commanders could point to increased stop activity (along with arrests) at Compstat meetings to highlight their assertive response to the "dots" in their precincts. Perhaps most important of all, the increased activity generally coincided with decreasing crime, generating support among administrators, precinct commanders and line officers for proactive policing tactics, like stop-and-frisk....

While the data reflect that the NYPD's escalating stops (and marijuana arrests) can most easily be explained as part of a quest for guns, there is a further piece to the puzzle. Once the City started documenting its stop-and-frisks, it came face-to-face with an uncomfortable truth. A tactic intended to find guns was not finding many guns at all. Critics of "stop and frisk" seized on this fact, and Judge Scheindlin emphasized in her opinion that only 1.5% of frisks found a weapon, with an even smaller percentage turning up guns. With "stop and frisk" under fire and the department's own statistics showing that it had become a citywide, crime-fighting behemoth, a justification other than finding weapons was needed. Although murky in its early phases, the theory comes into sharp relief over time, with individual NYPD officers articulating it as an explanation for the homicide decline as early as 1999, as related by Benjamin Bowling:

'In the view of many (but not all) of the police officers I interviewed, the result of persistent stop, frisk and arrests meant that young men thought twice before carrying their guns on their person .... That guns were not immediately accessible during routine confrontations was a frequently cited explanation for the reduction in murder in the mid-1990s.'

More recently, the deterrence theory of "stop and frisk" has been repeatedly articulated by the City's highest officials, and echoed in the media. In the recent Floyd trial, a state senator related statements he attributed to Commissioner Raymond Kelly from July 2010 that NYC Stop and Frisk worked by instilling a concern in (minority) youths "that they could be stopped and frisked every time they leave their homes so that they are less likely to carry weapons." Publicly, Mayor Bloomberg echoed this sentiment in a speech defending NYC Stop and Frisk in a Brooklyn church: "By making it 'too hot to carry,' the N.Y.P.D. is preventing guns from being carried on our streets.... That is our real goal - preventing violence before it occurs, not responding to the victims after the fact." Importantly, the deterrence theory validates "stop and frisk" regardless of its hit rate: if stops produce lots of weapons, the NYPD is successfully taking guns off the streets; when stops produce few weapons, the program is working to deter gun possession....

With crime plummeting and remaining low, the theory behind stop-and-frisk - deterring gun-carrying - gradually crystallized. Having early-on identified gun crimes as the driver of the City's violent-crime epidemic, and resigned to its inability to keep guns out of the City altogether, city officials came to justify NYC Stop and Frisk as part of an overarching strategy to deter people from unlawfully carrying guns in public. Far from apologizing for overuse of stop-and-frisk, Mayor Bloomberg, Commissioner Kelly and other luminaries warned of dire consequences if it were curtailed, imploring New Yorkers: "Stop-and-frisk works, and it should stay in place."...

The Fourth Amendment requires all police searches and seizures to be "reasonable." The main Fourth Amendment "reasonableness" hurdle to any deterrence-based crime-fighting strategy (like NYC Stop and Frisk) is the longstanding Supreme Court command that "a search or seizure is ordinarily unreasonable in the absence of individualized suspicion of wrongdoing." There are, in fact, few principles in Fourth Amendment doctrine as well established and widely trumpeted as the requirement of "individualized suspicion." The phrase "individualized suspicion" dates back only to the 1970s, but the underlying concept of requiring a showing that anyone searched or seized was (prior to the intrusion) reasonably suspected of an offense can be found in the constitutional text as well as in the history that animated it. The Court has even described this concept as "the central teaching" of its "Fourth Amendment jurisprudence."

NYC Stop and Frisk, if conceptualized as a program to deter gun-carrying, necessarily depends on stopping people without individualized suspicion. The theory justifying mass stop-and-frisk is that people will leave their guns at home to keep their weapons from being uncovered by an officer's frisk. In this scenario, the likelihood of a frisk determines the deterrent effect. If a frisk can be avoided by avoiding criminal activity such as trespassing, public marijuana smoking or public urination, people can comfortably carry guns unlawfully so long as they obey (or think they will obey) other laws while doing so. Thus, a high volume of arbitrary frisks is essential to effectively deterring gun possession. The knowledge that a stop-and-frisk is almost inevitable powerfully deters gun possession. The knowledge that police may stop you if they reasonably suspect you are committing or have committed a crime - the actual Terry standard - does not.

Viewing NYC Stop and Frisk as a crime-fighting strategy (as opposed to thousands of unrelated, isolated events) reveals not only its inability to fit within the Fourth Amendment's "individualized suspicion" framework, but also highlights its similarities to crime-fighting strategies previously rejected by American courts. Perhaps the most recent analogues involve vaguely worded loitering laws that the Supreme Court routinely struck down during the Civil Rights era (and in Chicago more recently) as riding too much on the "the moment-to-moment judgment of a policeman on his beat." Going further back in history, a legal regime that permits widespread, discretionary stops based on demographic characteristics or geographic location bears an unflattering resemblance to the "general warrant" - the primary historical evil targeted by the Fourth Amendment.

4. GUNS

In *New York State Rifle & Pistol Association v. Bruen* (2022), the Supreme Court extended its earlier ruling in *District of Columbia v. Heller* (2008) to hold that "the

Second and Fourteenth Amendments protect an individual's right to carry a handgun for self-defense." In concert with legislation easing restrictions on gun carrying, rulings like these are changing the Fourth Amendment landscape. It was once clear in cities with strict gun laws, like New York City, that gun possession constituted a lawful basis for a *Terry* stop, and that guns could be seized (at least temporarily) as part of a *Terry* frisk. These conclusions are now less clear as explained in the following excerpt from a law review article:[17]

> Weapons seizures are not an explicit part of the Terry framework, but a necessary implication of the case is that guns can be seized, at least temporarily, under both prongs: either as part of the stop, if the gun possession is unlawful, or as part of the frisk, if the firearm makes the person "presently dangerous."
>
> In the past, the assumption that a person carrying a concealed weapon was engaged in the crime of unlawful weapons possession allowed courts to uphold the disarming of an individual with little analysis. If police suspect that someone unlawfully possesses a firearm, it follows that the officer can remove the gun to discontinue the suspected crime. Critically, this means that confiscation of the weapon is justified under Terry's first analytical prong (suspicion of a crime), not necessarily the second (suspicion of dangerousness). The weapon, once detected, is suspected contraband, and contraband can be seized upon detection.
>
> [In light of recent judicial and legislative actions protecting gun carrying], the assumption that the mere possession of a firearm constitutes a crime is crumbling. This means that absent evidence that a person's firearm possession is unlicensed, the first prong of Terry no longer justifies the seizure of the firearm. Police authority to disarm persons, then, will regularly depend on Terry's second ("frisk") prong. Under this prong, a police officer interacting with an armed member of the public will need "reasonable suspicion" that the person is "presently dangerous to the officer or to others" to seize the firearm. Courts may agree that the inherent dangers of firearms make this showing essentially automatic whenever officers encounter armed persons in public. But given Terry's requirement of "specific and articulable facts" to justify a stop or frisk, that is hardly a foregone conclusion.

---

[17] Bellin, *The Right to Remain Armed*, 93 Wash. U.L. Rev. 1 (2015).

Pennsylvania v. Mimms (1977), referenced earlier in this Chapter, highlights the traditional reaction of courts (and police) to guns encountered during a police stop. In *Mimms*, the police stopped Harry Mimms for driving with an expired license plate. During the stop, and after the officer ordered Mimms out of the car, "the officer noticed a large bulge under respondent's sports jacket." The Court explained that,

> "The bulge in the jacket permitted the officer to conclude that Mimms was armed and thus posed a serious and present danger to the safety of the officer. In these circumstances, any man of reasonable caution would likely have conducted the pat down."

KILBURN v. STATE
297 So. 3d 671 (Fla. Dist. Ct. App. 2020)

…. Deputy Beach of the Escambia County Sheriff's Office testified that while he was patrolling the back parking lot of the Key West Motel at 8:30 in the morning, he noticed a Dodge Ram pickup truck parked with the driver's door open…. As Deputy Beach was approaching, the appellant got out of the truck holding a knife. When the appellant saw the deputy, he placed the knife on the front seat of the truck and raised his hands. When he raised his hands, Deputy Beach saw the butt of a handgun sticking out of the appellant's waistband. The deputy then "closed the distance and put [his] hands on him and kind of guided him up against the vehicle and began to detain him." After the appellant was handcuffed, placed in the back of the deputy's patrol car, and read the Miranda warning, the deputy asked the appellant if he had a concealed-weapons license, and the appellant responded in the negative. The appellant was then arrested for carrying a concealed weapon without a license in violation of Florida law. According to Deputy Beach, at the time of the appellant's initial seizure, "other than the firearm, [he] had no reason to detain him at that point."

…. At the suppression hearing, the trial court recognized that the sole basis for detention in this case was the presence of the handgun. The court looked to two [Florida] cases that seem to present a conflict, Regalado v. State and Mackey v. State.

In Regalado, a Fort Lauderdale police officer was approached by a citizen who reported "some guy was over there flashing his gun to a couple of friends." The officer was in the process of getting a description of the man when Regalado walked by. The informant identified Regalado to the officer as the man who had the gun. The officer began to follow Regalado. As the officer got within six or eight feet of Regalado, he observed a bulge in Regalado's waistband, which, from his training, he believed to be a handgun. The officer, concerned that Regalado was going to get lost in the crowd, drew his revolver and ordered Regalado to the ground. The officer then patted Regalado down and retrieved the handgun. At the suppression hearing, the officer admitted that Regalado had not threatened the officer nor had Regalado threatened anyone else. Furthermore, the informant did not report that Regalado threatened anyone. The officer had not observed any crime take place.

The Fourth District Court of Appeal reasoned that it was not illegal to possess a firearm in Florida if one has a concealed-weapons permit, a fact that cannot be determined by mere observation. The court ruled that unless the officer had a reasonable belief that some crime had been committed, was being committed, or was about to be committed, stopping someone solely based on possession of a firearm was a violation of the Fourth Amendment.

In Mackey, a Miami police officer was driving his patrol car when he saw Mackey standing on one side of a fence by an apartment complex. The officer slowed down. As he drove slowly by Mackey, he saw a solid object inside Mackey's pocket. As he drew closer, the officer saw a "piece of the handle sticking out. Not much, but a piece enough for [him] to identify a firearm." The officer got out of his car, approached Mackey, and asked whether Mackey had anything on him. Mackey replied "no." The officer conducted a pat-down of Mackey and recovered the firearm he had previously seen. The officer asked Mackey if he had a concealed-weapons license, and Mackey replied in the negative. The officer then arrested Mackey for carrying a concealed firearm without a license. The Third District Court of Appeal held that even without a reasonable suspicion that some crime had been or was about to be committed, an officer was entitled to stop someone based on mere possession of a firearm until the officer could confirm such firearm was legally carried....

In this case, Deputy Beach ... expressly stated that the only reason for the seizure and search of the appellant was the presence of the handgun. At the suppression hearing, the trial court stated that it agreed with the reasoning contained in Mackey. The trial court stated that it was illegal to carry a concealed weapon in Florida with an exception for those who possess a concealed-weapons license. It viewed this exception as an affirmative defense. The trial court found the search and seizure lawful.

The trial court's ruling is contrary to law. Terry v. Ohio (1968) clearly requires both a reasonable suspicion that criminal activity is afoot and a reasonable suspicion that the subject might be armed in order to do a stop-and-frisk. Without a reasonable suspicion of criminal activity, the officer cannot go further. Bearing arms is not only legal; it also is a specifically enumerated right in both the federal and Florida constitutions. The citizens of Florida have spoken through their Legislature and have stated that those who possess a license to carry a concealed weapon have the right to carry a concealed firearm.

…. In Florida, 2,074,782 residents were licensed to carry concealed weapons as of January 31, 2020…. Approximately one out of every seven persons over the age of twenty-one may lawfully carry a concealed weapon in Florida. The thought that these millions of people are subject to seizure by law enforcement until their licenses are verified is antithetical to our Fourth Amendment jurisprudence. No court would allow law enforcement to stop any motorist in order to check for a valid driver's license.

Based on the foregoing, we adopt the holding and rationale of Regalado and recognize conflict with the stated holding in Mackey. Because the ruling on the motion to suppress, which permitted the firearm to be admitted into evidence, was dispositive, we reverse the conviction and sentence of the appellant.

B. OTHER WARRANTLESS SEIZURES

As the cases so far suggest, the constitutional reasonableness of a seizure typically depends on an objective assessment of the level of suspicion possessed by the officer conducting the seizure that the seized person was engaged in unlawful activity. But questions remain about what types of crimes count for these purposes and whether police can make pretextual stops – stopping someone for one thing, while suspecting them of another. The next cases provide the Court's answers to these questions.

WHREN v. UNITED STATES
517 U.S. 806 (1996)

Justice SCALIA delivered the unanimous opinion of the Court.

In this case we decide whether the temporary detention of a motorist who the police have probable cause to believe has committed a civil traffic violation is inconsistent with the Fourth Amendment's prohibition against unreasonable seizures unless a reasonable officer would have been motivated to stop the car by a desire to enforce the traffic laws.

I

On the evening of June 10, 1993, plainclothes vice-squad officers of the District of Columbia Metropolitan Police Department were patrolling a "high drug area" of the city in an unmarked car. Their suspicions were aroused when they passed a dark Pathfinder truck with temporary license plates and youthful occupants waiting at a stop sign, the driver looking down into the lap of the passenger at his right. The truck remained stopped at the intersection for what seemed an unusually long time—more than 20 seconds. When the police car executed a U-turn in order to head back toward the truck, the Pathfinder turned suddenly to its right, without signaling, and sped off at an "unreasonable" speed. The policemen followed, and in a short while overtook the Pathfinder when it stopped behind other traffic at a red light. They pulled up alongside, and Officer Ephraim Soto stepped out and approached the driver's door, identifying himself as a police officer and directing the driver, petitioner James Brown, to put the vehicle in park. When Soto drew up to the driver's window, he immediately observed two large plastic bags of what appeared to be crack cocaine in petitioner Michael Whren's hands. Petitioners were arrested, and quantities of several types of illegal drugs were retrieved from the vehicle....

II

The Fourth Amendment guarantees "[t]he right of the people to be secure in their persons, houses, papers, and effects, against unreasonable searches and seizures." Temporary detention of individuals during the stop of an automobile by the police, even if only for a brief period and for a limited purpose, constitutes a "seizure" of "persons" within the meaning of this provision. An automobile stop is thus subject to the constitutional imperative that it not be "unreasonable" under the circumstances. As a general matter, the decision to stop an automobile is reasonable where the police have probable cause to believe that a traffic violation has occurred.

Petitioners accept that Officer Soto had probable cause to believe that various provisions of the District of Columbia traffic code had been violated. See 18 D.C. Mun. Regs. §§ 2213.4 (1995) ("An operator shall ... give full time and attention to the operation of the vehicle"); 2204.3 ("No person shall turn any vehicle ... without giving an appropriate signal"); 2200.3 ("No person shall drive a vehicle ... at a speed greater than is reasonable and prudent under the conditions"). They argue, however, that "in the unique context of civil traffic regulations" probable cause is not enough. Since, they contend, the use of automobiles is so heavily and minutely regulated that total compliance with traffic and safety rules is nearly impossible, a police officer will almost invariably be able to catch any given motorist in a technical violation. This creates the temptation to use traffic stops as a means of investigating other law violations, as to which no probable cause or even articulable suspicion exists. Petitioners, who are both black, further contend that police officers might decide which motorists to stop based on decidedly impermissible factors, such as the race of the car's occupants. To avoid this danger, they say, the Fourth Amendment test for traffic stops should be, not the normal one (applied by the Court of Appeals) of whether probable cause existed to justify the stop; but rather, whether a police officer, acting reasonably, would have made the stop for the reason given.

A

Petitioners contend that the standard they propose is consistent with our past cases' disapproval of police attempts to use valid bases of action against citizens as pretexts for pursuing other investigatory agendas. We are reminded that in Florida v. Wells (1990), we stated that "an inventory search must not be a ruse for a general rummaging in order to discover incriminating evidence"; ... and that in New York v. Burger (1987), we observed, in upholding the constitutionality of a warrantless administrative inspection, that the search did not appear to be "a 'pretext' for obtaining evidence of violation of penal laws." But only an undiscerning reader would regard these cases as endorsing the principle that ulterior motives can invalidate police conduct that is justifiable on the basis of probable cause to believe that a violation of law has occurred. In each case we were addressing the validity of a search conducted in the absence of probable cause. Our quoted statements simply explain that the exemption from the need for probable cause (and warrant), which is accorded to searches made for the purpose of inventory or administrative regulation, is not accorded to searches that are not made for those purposes.

…. Petitioners' difficulty is not simply a lack of affirmative support for their position. Not only have we never held, outside the context of inventory search or administrative inspection, that an officer's motive invalidates objectively justifiable behavior under the Fourth Amendment; but we have repeatedly held and asserted the contrary…. These cases foreclose any argument that the constitutional reasonableness of traffic stops depends on the actual motivations of the individual officers involved. We of course agree with petitioners that the Constitution prohibits selective enforcement of the law based on considerations such as race. But the constitutional basis for objecting to intentionally discriminatory application of laws is the Equal Protection Clause, not the Fourth Amendment. Subjective intentions play no role in ordinary, probable-cause Fourth Amendment analysis.

B

Recognizing that we have been unwilling to entertain Fourth Amendment challenges based on the actual motivations of individual officers, petitioners disavow any intention to make the individual officer's subjective good faith the touchstone of "reasonableness." They insist that the standard they have put forward—whether the officer's conduct deviated materially from usual police practices, so that a reasonable officer in the same circumstances would not have made the stop for the reasons given—is an "objective" one.

But although framed in empirical terms, this approach is plainly and indisputably driven by subjective considerations. Its whole purpose is to prevent the police from doing under the guise of enforcing the traffic code what they would like to do for different reasons. Petitioners' proposed standard may not use the word "pretext," but it is designed to combat nothing other than the perceived "danger" of the pretextual stop, albeit only indirectly and over the run of cases. Instead of asking whether the individual officer had the proper state of mind, the petitioners would have us ask, in effect, whether (based on general police practices) it is plausible to believe that the officer had the proper state of mind.

Why one would frame a test designed to combat pretext in such fashion that the court cannot take into account actual and admitted pretext is a curiosity that can only be explained by the fact that our cases have foreclosed the more sensible option. If those cases were based only upon the evidentiary difficulty of establishing subjective intent, petitioners' attempt to root out subjective vices through objective means might make sense. But they were not based only upon that, or indeed even principally upon that. Their principal basis—which applies equally to attempts to reach subjective intent through ostensibly objective means—is simply that the Fourth Amendment's concern with "reasonableness" allows certain actions to be taken in certain circumstances, whatever the subjective intent. But even if our concern had been only an evidentiary one, petitioners' proposal would by no means assuage it. Indeed, it seems to us somewhat easier to figure out the intent of an individual officer than to plumb the collective consciousness of law enforcement in order to determine whether a "reasonable officer" would have been moved to act upon the traffic violation. While police manuals and standard procedures may sometimes provide objective assistance, ordinarily one would be reduced to speculating about the hypothetical reaction of a hypothetical constable—an exercise that might be called virtual subjectivity.

Moreover, police enforcement practices, even if they could be practicably assessed by a judge, vary from place to place and from time to time. We cannot accept that the search and seizure protections of the Fourth Amendment are so variable, and can be made to turn upon such trivialities. The difficulty is illustrated by petitioners' arguments in this case. Their claim that a reasonable officer would not have made this stop is based largely on District of Columbia police regulations which permit plainclothes officers in unmarked vehicles to enforce traffic laws "only in the case of a violation that is so grave as to pose an immediate threat to the safety of others." This basis of invalidation would not apply in jurisdictions that had a different practice. And it would not have applied even in the District of Columbia, if Officer Soto had been wearing a uniform or patrolling in a marked police cruiser....

III

.... In what would appear to be an elaboration on the "reasonable officer" test, petitioners argue that the balancing inherent in any Fourth Amendment inquiry requires us to weigh the governmental and individual interests implicated in a traffic stop such as we have here. That balancing, petitioners claim, does not support investigation of minor traffic infractions by plainclothes police in unmarked vehicles; such investigation only minimally advances the government's interest in traffic safety, and may indeed retard it by producing motorist confusion and alarm—a view said to be supported by the Metropolitan Police Department's own regulations generally prohibiting this practice. And as for the Fourth Amendment interests of the individuals concerned, petitioners point out that our cases acknowledge that even ordinary traffic stops entail "a possibly unsettling show of authority"; that they at best "interfere with freedom of movement, are inconvenient, and consume time" and at worst "may create substantial anxiety." That anxiety is likely to be even more pronounced when the stop is conducted by plainclothes officers in unmarked cars.

It is of course true that in principle every Fourth Amendment case, since it turns upon a "reasonableness" determination, involves a balancing of all relevant factors. With rare exceptions not applicable here, however, the result of that balancing is not in doubt where the search or seizure is based upon probable cause....

Where probable cause has existed, the only cases in which we have found it necessary actually to perform the "balancing" analysis involved searches or seizures conducted in an extraordinary manner, unusually harmful to an individual's privacy or even physical interests—such as, for example, seizure by means of deadly force, see Tennessee v. Garner (1985), unannounced entry into a home, see Wilson v. Arkansas (1995), entry into a home without a warrant, see Welsh v. Wisconsin (1984), or physical penetration of the body, see Winston v. Lee (1985). The making of a traffic stop out of uniform does not remotely qualify as such an extreme practice, and so is governed by the usual rule that probable cause to believe the law has been broken "outbalances" private interest in avoiding police contact.

Petitioners urge as an extraordinary factor in this case that the "multitude of applicable traffic and equipment regulations" is so large and so difficult to obey perfectly that virtually everyone is guilty of violation, permitting the police to single out almost whomever they wish for a stop. But we are aware of no principle that would allow us to decide at what point a code of law becomes so expansive and so commonly violated that infraction itself can no longer be the ordinary measure of the lawfulness of enforcement. And even if we could identify such exorbitant codes, we do not know by what standard (or what right) we would decide, as petitioners would have us do, which particular provisions are sufficiently important to merit enforcement.

For the run-of-the-mine case, which this surely is, we think there is no realistic alternative to the traditional common-law rule that probable cause justifies a search and seizure.

Here the District Court found that the officers had probable cause to believe that petitioners had violated the traffic code. That rendered the stop reasonable under the Fourth Amendment, the evidence thereby discovered admissible, and the upholding of the convictions by the Court of Appeals for the District of Columbia Circuit correct.

The holdings of *Terry v. Ohio* and *Whren*, combined with the broad scope of modern traffic laws, grant police broad discretion to stop motorists. For example, many states have laws like VA. Code § 46.2-1054, which (until 2021) stated:

> It shall be unlawful for any person to drive a motor vehicle on a highway in the Commonwealth with any object or objects, other than a rear view mirror, sun visor, or other equipment of the motor vehicle approved by the Superintendent [of State Police], suspended from any part of the motor vehicle in such a manner as to obstruct the driver's clear view of the highway through the windshield ....

MASON v. COMMONWEALTH
64 Va. App. 292 (2015)

KELSEY, Judge.

.... In this case, a police officer testified that, while operating a stationary radar unit, he saw a sedan with a "dangling object" that was "hanging from the rearview mirror." The officer testified that he "saw it clearly" as the vehicle "went by" him at "approximately 2:30 in the afternoon." The object, reproduced below, was admitted into evidence. At the time of the traffic stop, Loren Mason, Jr. was a passenger in the sedan. The officer intended to issue the driver a summons for driving without a seatbelt and for violating Code § 46.2–1054. Prior to issuing the summons, however, the officer asked the driver if he would consent to a "weapons" pat down. The driver consented, and the officer found marijuana on the driver during the pat down.

The officer then searched the sedan and found a backpack containing cocaine, ecstasy pills, a "large sum of individually wrapped bags" of marijuana, a digital scale, and a box of plastic bags. Other evidence established that the backpack belonged to Mason. The officer then arrested Mason for possession of drugs....

Prior to trial, Mason moved to suppress the evidence, claiming that the traffic stop was unconstitutional. The trial court disagreed, denied the motion, and convicted Mason of the charged offenses.

On appeal, Mason challenges the trial court's denial of his motion to suppress. A divided panel of this Court agreed with Mason, reversed the trial court's ruling on the motion to suppress, and remanded the matter to the trial court. We granted the Commonwealth's petition for rehearing en banc, vacated the panel opinion, and now affirm the decision of the trial court....

In this case, the police officer testified that he "clearly" observed the parking pass prior to stopping the vehicle. The parking pass is an exhibit. We need no description of it from the officer. We are looking at the very thing that the officer said he clearly saw: an opaque plastic card that is five inches long and three inches wide. And the trial judge had something even better. He took a "view of the scene" to determine if the parking pass could obstruct a driver's vision in a vehicle similar to the one that the officer had stopped.

Given these facts, we agree with the trial court that a reasonable officer could suspect that the opaque, five-by-three-inch parking pass dangling from a rearview mirror might violate Code § 46.2–1054 and thus warrant an investigatory stop....

It bears repeating that an officer need not have proof beyond a reasonable doubt of any of these scenarios before he makes a vehicular stop. Nor does he need to be convinced by a preponderance of the evidence. To be sure, the quantum of confidence need not even rise to the level of probable cause. It is enough that the officer is aware of facts that, viewed objectively, could give rise to a reasonable suspicion that the parking pass may be non-compliant with Code § 46.2–1054.

.... Needless to say, our holding does not endorse any per se rule authorizing traffic stops whenever an object of any kind is observed dangling from a vehicle's rearview mirror.... Code § 46.2–1054, after all, does not uniformly forbid drivers from dangling objects from their rearview mirrors—only those positioned "in such a manner as to obstruct the driver's clear view of the highway." We thus limit our holding to the suspected obstruction in this case: a five-by-three-inch opaque parking pass hanging from a rearview mirror of a sedan.

HUMPHREYS, J. dissenting

…. Prior to Terry v. Ohio (1968) any restraint on the person amounting to a seizure for the purposes of the Fourth Amendment was invalid unless justified by probable cause. Terry created a limited exception to this general rule: certain seizures are justifiable under the Fourth Amendment if there is articulable suspicion that a person has committed or is about to commit a crime. After today and insofar as motor vehicles are concerned, this exception is no longer particularly limited and has now swallowed the general rule. Despite the majority's assertion to the contrary, I believe that the majority opinion in this case will be read to provide "automatic" reasonable articulable suspicion for any officer to pull a citizen over if he/she observes any object dangling from a rearview mirror….

The Fourth Amendment sets a minimum standard that police must follow – a floor, not a ceiling. Federal agencies, states, police departments, and individual officers can adopt more rigorous standards than the Constitution requires.

For example, Virginia enacted a package of laws in 2021 that prohibit law enforcement officers from making traffic stops based on a series of minor violations, including violations of the obstructed view statute at issue in *Mason*. The Va. Code Ann. § 46.2-1054 now includes this provision:

> "No law-enforcement officer shall stop a motor vehicle for a violation of this section. No evidence discovered or obtained as the result of a stop in violation of this subsection, including evidence discovered or obtained with the operator's consent, shall be admissible in any trial, hearing, or other proceeding."

As another example, in March 2022, the Los Angeles Police Department adopted a policy restricting pretextual stops. The Chief of Police explained the motivation for the policy as follows:

> "Members of our community and communities around the country have expressed concern regarding the manner and frequency with which

officers are stopping individuals (pedestrians, cyclists, and motorists) for perceived minor violations to investigate other crimes (a subset of which are known as and approved by the United States Supreme Court as "pretextual stops"). Their fears stem in large measure from a belief that such enforcement activities are arbitrary, capricious, and a reflection of an individual officer's implicit or explicit bias(es). Moreover, some community members question the impact such pretextual stops have on crime reduction."

The new policy is reprinted below:

240.06 POLICY - LIMITATION ON USE OF PRETEXTUAL STOPS

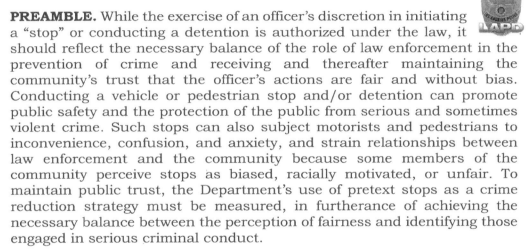

PREAMBLE. While the exercise of an officer's discretion in initiating a "stop" or conducting a detention is authorized under the law, it should reflect the necessary balance of the role of law enforcement in the prevention of crime and receiving and thereafter maintaining the community's trust that the officer's actions are fair and without bias. Conducting a vehicle or pedestrian stop and/or detention can promote public safety and the protection of the public from serious and sometimes violent crime. Such stops can also subject motorists and pedestrians to inconvenience, confusion, and anxiety, and strain relationships between law enforcement and the community because some members of the community perceive stops as biased, racially motivated, or unfair. To maintain public trust, the Department's use of pretext stops as a crime reduction strategy must be measured, in furtherance of achieving the necessary balance between the perception of fairness and identifying those engaged in serious criminal conduct.

Pretext Stops Defined. A pretextual or pretext stop is one where officers use reasonable suspicion or probable cause of a minor traffic or code violation (e.g., Municipal Code or Health and Safety Code) as a pretext to investigate another, more serious crime that is unrelated to that violation.

Policy.

Use of Traffic/Pedestrian Stops - General. Traffic or pedestrian stops made for the sole purpose of enforcing the Vehicle Code or other codes are intended to **protect public safety**. Therefore, officers should make stops for minor equipment violations or other infractions only when the officer believes that such a violation or infraction significantly interferes with public safety.

> **Note:** The public safety reason for all traffic/pedestrian stops, citations and warnings should be articulated on body-worn video (BWV) and should include an officer's response to any questions posed by the individual stopped.

Pretext Stops - Restricted. It is the Department's policy that pretextual stops shall not be conducted **unless** officers are acting upon articulable information in addition to the traffic violation, which may or may not amount to reasonable suspicion, regarding a serious crime (i.e., a crime with potential for great bodily injury or death), such as a Part I violent crime, driving under the influence (DUI), reckless driving, street racing, street takeovers, hit and run, human or narcotics trafficking, gun violence, burglary, or another similarly serious crime. Such decisions should not be based on a mere hunch or on generalized characteristics such as a person's race, gender, age, homeless circumstance, or presence in a high-crime location.

Department personnel seeking one or more specific persons who have been identified or described in part by one or more of these characteristics may rely on them only in combination with other appropriate identifying factors.

> **Note:** The reason for all pretext stops, and the citations and warnings resulting from them, should be articulated on BWV and should include an officer's response to any questions posed by the individual stopped.

> **Note:** An officer's training, experience and expertise may be used in articulating the additional information the officers used to initiate the stop.

> **Note:** A failure to sufficiently articulate the information which - in addition to the traffic violation - caused the officer to make the pretext stop, shall result in progressive discipline, beginning with counseling and retraining. Discipline shall escalate with successive violations of this mandate.

As the following graph shows, the Los Angeles Times found that the nature of LAPD stops changed after the policy was enacted.

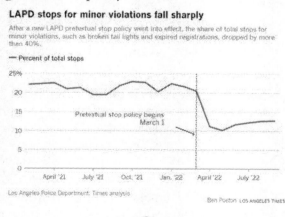

LAPD stops for minor violations fall sharply

After a new LAPD pretextual stop policy went into effect, the share of total stops for minor violations, such as broken tail lights and expired registrations, dropped by more than 40%.

Los Angeles Police Department; Times analysis

Ben Poston LOS ANGELES TIMES

225

The unanimous *Whren* opinion references the Equal Protection clause as an alternative source of authority that could prevent discriminatory stops. Commentators emphasize, however, that the Equal Protection clause has not proven to be an effective tool for addressing racial profiling. See, e.g., Kami Chavis, Beginning to End Racial Profiling: Definitive Solutions to an Elusive Problem, 18 Wash. & Lee J. Civil Rts. & Soc. Just. 25 (2011) ("While the Equal Protection Clause prohibits discrimination on the basis of race, in order to succeed on an Equal Protection claim, claimants have to show intentional discrimination and … substantiating these claims is extremely difficult."); David Harris, Racial Profiling Redux, 22 St. Louis U. Pub. L. Rev. 73 (2003) ("Far more common are cases in which courts slam the door on plaintiffs seeking to use the Equal Protection Clause (as suggested by Justice Scalia in *Whren*) or anti-discrimination statutes, usually by requiring that plaintiffs meet impossibly high standards to prove these claims.").

ATWATER v. CITY OF LAGO VISTA
532 U.S. 318 (2001)

Justice SOUTER delivered the opinion of the Court.

The question is whether the Fourth Amendment forbids a warrantless arrest for a minor criminal offense, such as a misdemeanor seatbelt violation punishable only by a fine. We hold that it does not.

I

A

In Texas, if a car is equipped with safety belts, a front-seat passenger must wear one, and the driver must secure any small child riding in front. Violation of either provision is "a misdemeanor punishable by a fine not less than $25 or more than $50." Texas law expressly authorizes "any peace officer to arrest without warrant a person found committing a violation" of these seatbelt laws, although it permits police to issue citations in lieu of arrest.

In March 1997, petitioner Gail Atwater was driving her pickup truck in Lago Vista, Texas, with her 3–year–old son and 5–year–old daughter in the front seat. None of them was wearing a seatbelt. Respondent Bart Turek, a Lago Vista police officer at the time, observed the seatbelt violations and pulled Atwater over. According to Atwater's complaint (the allegations of which we assume to be true for present purposes), Turek approached the truck and "yelled" something to the effect of "we've met before" and "you're going to jail." He then called for backup and asked to see Atwater's driver's license and insurance documentation, which state law required her to carry. When Atwater told Turek that she did not have the papers because her purse had been stolen the day before, Turek said that he had "heard that story two-hundred times."

Atwater asked to take her "frightened, upset, and crying" children to a friend's house nearby, but Turek told her, "you're not going anywhere." As it turned out, Atwater's friend learned what was going on and soon arrived to take charge of the children. Turek then handcuffed Atwater, placed her in his squad car, and drove her to the local police station, where booking officers had her remove her shoes, jewelry, and eyeglasses, and empty her pockets. Officers took Atwater's "mug shot" and placed her, alone, in a jail cell for about one hour, after which she was taken before a magistrate and released on $310 bond.

Atwater was charged with driving without her seatbelt fastened, failing to secure her children in seatbelts, driving without a license, and failing to provide proof of insurance. She ultimately pleaded no contest to the misdemeanor seatbelt offenses and paid a $50 fine; the other charges were dismissed.

B

Atwater and her husband, petitioner Michael Haas, filed suit in a Texas state court under 42 U.S.C. § 1983 against Turek and respondents City of Lago Vista and Chief of Police Frank Miller. So far as concerns us, petitioners (whom we will simply call Atwater) alleged that respondents (for simplicity, the City) had violated Atwater's Fourth Amendment "right to be free from unreasonable seizure," and sought compensatory and punitive damages…. We granted certiorari to consider whether the Fourth Amendment, either by incorporating common-law restrictions on misdemeanor arrests or otherwise, limits police officers' authority to arrest without warrant for minor criminal offenses.

II

The Fourth Amendment safeguards "[t]he right of the people to be secure in their persons, houses, papers, and effects, against unreasonable searches and seizures." In reading the Amendment, we are guided by "the traditional protections against unreasonable searches and seizures afforded by the common law at the time of the framing," since "an examination of the common-law understanding of an officer's authority to arrest sheds light on the obviously relevant, if not entirely dispositive, consideration of what the Framers of the Amendment might have thought to be reasonable." Thus, the first step here is to assess Atwater's claim that peace officers' authority to make warrantless arrests for misdemeanors was restricted at common law (whether "common law" is understood strictly as law judicially derived or, instead, as the whole body of law extant at the time of the framing). Atwater's specific contention is that "founding-era common-law rules" forbade peace officers to make warrantless misdemeanor arrests except in cases of "breach of the peace," a category she claims was then understood narrowly as covering only those nonfelony offenses "involving or tending toward violence." Although her historical argument is by no means insubstantial, it ultimately fails…. An examination of specifically American evidence is to the same effect [as that of English evidence]. Neither the history of the framing era nor subsequent legal development indicates that the Fourth Amendment was originally understood, or has traditionally been read, to embrace Atwater's position…. Today statutes in all 50 States and the District of Columbia permit warrantless misdemeanor arrests by at least some (if not all) peace officers without requiring any breach of the peace, as do a host of congressional enactments….

III

While it is true here that history, if not unequivocal, has expressed a decided, majority view that the police need not obtain an arrest warrant merely because a misdemeanor stopped short of violence or a threat of it, Atwater does not wager all on history. Instead, she asks us to mint a new rule of constitutional law on the understanding that when historical practice fails to speak conclusively to a claim grounded on the Fourth Amendment, courts are left to strike a current balance between individual and societal interests by subjecting particular contemporary circumstances to traditional standards of reasonableness. Atwater accordingly argues for a modern arrest rule, one not necessarily requiring violent breach of the peace, but nonetheless forbidding custodial arrest, even upon probable cause, when conviction could not ultimately carry any jail time and when the government shows no compelling need for immediate detention.

If we were to derive a rule exclusively to address the uncontested facts of this case, Atwater might well prevail. She was a known and established resident of Lago Vista with no place to hide and no incentive to flee, and common sense says she would almost certainly have buckled up as a condition of driving off with a citation. In her case, the physical incidents of arrest were merely gratuitous humiliations imposed by a police officer who was (at best) exercising extremely poor judgment. Atwater's claim to live free of pointless indignity and confinement clearly outweighs anything the City can raise against it specific to her case.

But we have traditionally recognized that a responsible Fourth Amendment balance is not well served by standards requiring sensitive, case-by-case determinations of government need, lest every discretionary judgment in the field be converted into an occasion for constitutional review. See, e.g., United States v. Robinson (1973). Often enough, the Fourth Amendment has to be applied on the spur (and in the heat) of the moment, and the object in implementing its command of reasonableness is to draw standards sufficiently clear and simple to be applied with a fair prospect of surviving judicial second-guessing months and years after an arrest or search is made. Courts attempting to strike a reasonable Fourth Amendment balance thus credit the government's side with an essential interest in readily administrable rules. See New York v. Belton (1981).

At first glance, Atwater's argument may seem to respect the values of clarity and simplicity, so far as she claims that the Fourth Amendment generally forbids warrantless arrests for minor crimes not accompanied by violence or some demonstrable threat of it (whether "minor crime" be defined as a fine-only traffic offense, a fine-only offense more generally, or a misdemeanor). But the claim is not ultimately so simple, nor could it be, for complications arise the moment we begin to think about the possible applications of the several criteria Atwater proposes for drawing a line between minor crimes with limited arrest authority and others not so restricted.

…. Accordingly, we confirm today what our prior cases have intimated: the standard of probable cause "applies to all arrests, without the need to balance the interests and circumstances involved in particular situations." If an officer has probable cause to believe that an individual has committed even a very minor criminal offense in his presence, he may, without violating the Fourth Amendment, arrest the offender.

IV

Atwater's arrest satisfied constitutional requirements. There is no dispute that Officer Turek had probable cause to believe that Atwater had committed a crime in his presence. She admits that neither she nor her children were wearing seatbelts, as required by [the] Texas Transportation Code. Turek was accordingly authorized (not required, but authorized) to make a custodial arrest without balancing costs and benefits or determining whether or not Atwater's arrest was in some sense necessary.

Nor was the arrest made in an "extraordinary manner, unusually harmful to [her] privacy or ... physical interests." As our citations in Whren make clear, the question whether a search or seizure is "extraordinary" turns, above all else, on the manner in which the search or seizure is executed. Atwater's arrest was surely "humiliating," as she says in her brief, but it was no more "harmful to privacy or physical interests" than the normal custodial arrest. She was handcuffed, placed in a squad car, and taken to the local police station, where officers asked her to remove her shoes, jewelry, and glasses, and to empty her pockets. They then took her photograph and placed her in a cell, alone, for about an hour, after which she was taken before a magistrate, and released on $310 bond. The arrest and booking were inconvenient and embarrassing to Atwater, but not so extraordinary as to violate the Fourth Amendment.

As noted throughout this book, state and local jurisdictions can provide more protection to their residents than the federal Constitution requires. For example, Virginia law prohibits arrest for most misdemeanor offenses:

Virginia Code Ann. § 19.2-74

"A.1. Whenever any person is detained by or is in the custody of an arresting officer for any violation committed in such officer's presence which offense is a violation of any ... ordinance or of any provision of this Code punishable as a ... misdemeanor ... the arresting officer shall take the name and address of such person and issue a summons or otherwise notify him in writing to appear at a time and place to be specified in such summons or notice. Upon the giving by such person of his written promise to appear at such time and place, the officer shall forthwith release him from custody. However, if any such person shall fail or refuse to discontinue the unlawful act, the officer may proceed according to the provisions of § 19.2-82 [setting out the procedures for an arrest].

> [I]f any person is believed by the arresting officer to be likely to disregard a summons issued under the provisions of this subsection, or if any person is reasonably believed by the arresting officer to be likely to cause harm to himself or to any other person, a magistrate or other issuing authority having jurisdiction shall proceed according to the provisions of § 19.2-82."

VIRGINIA v. MOORE
553 U.S. 164 (2008)

Justice SCALIA delivered the opinion of the Court.

We consider whether a police officer violates the Fourth Amendment by making an arrest based on probable cause but prohibited by state law.

On February 20, 2003, two city of Portsmouth police officers stopped a car driven by David Lee Moore. They had heard over the police radio that a person known as "Chubs" was driving with a suspended license, and one of the officers knew Moore by that nickname. The officers determined that Moore's license was in fact suspended, and arrested him for the misdemeanor of driving on a suspended license, which is punishable under Virginia law by a year in jail and a $2,500 fine. The officers subsequently searched Moore and found that he was carrying 16 grams of crack cocaine and $516 in cash.

Under state law, the officers should have issued Moore a summons instead of arresting him. Driving on a suspended license, like some other misdemeanors, is not an arrestable offense except as to those who "fail or refuse to discontinue" the violation, and those whom the officer reasonably believes to be likely to disregard a summons, or likely to harm themselves or others. Va. Code Ann. § 19.2–74 (2004). The intermediate appellate court found none of these circumstances applicable, and Virginia did not appeal that determination…. [The Virginia Supreme Court ruled that the search violated the Fourth Amendment.] The [Virginia Supreme] Court reasoned that since the arresting officers should have issued Moore a citation under state law, and the Fourth Amendment does not permit search incident to citation, the arrest search violated the Fourth Amendment. We granted certiorari [and now reverse the Virginia Supreme Court]….

In a long line of cases, we have said that when an officer has probable cause to believe a person committed even a minor crime in his presence, the balancing of private and public interests is not in doubt. The arrest is constitutionally reasonable. Our decisions counsel against changing this calculus when a State chooses to protect privacy beyond the level that the Fourth Amendment requires. We have treated additional protections exclusively as matters of state law....

We conclude that warrantless arrests for crimes committed in the presence of an arresting officer are reasonable under the Constitution, and that while States are free to regulate such arrests however they desire, state restrictions do not alter the Fourth Amendment's protections....

When officers have probable cause to believe that a person has committed a crime in their presence, the Fourth Amendment permits them to make an arrest, and to search the suspect in order to safeguard evidence and ensure their own safety....

Due to the perceived need for swift action in many arrest scenarios, the Supreme Court generally allows police to arrest suspects without judicial preclearance (i.e., a warrant). But after an arrest, the calculus changes. As the Court explained in *Gerstein v. Pugh* (1975):

> A policeman's on-the-scene assessment of probable cause provides legal justification for arresting a person suspected of crime, and for a brief period of detention to take the administrative steps incident to arrest. Once the suspect is in custody, however, the reasons that justify dispensing with the magistrate's neutral judgment evaporate. There no longer is any danger that the suspect will escape or commit further crimes while the police submit their evidence to a magistrate. And, while the State's reasons for taking summary action subside, the suspect's need for a neutral determination of probable cause increases significantly. The consequences of prolonged detention may be more serious than the interference occasioned by arrest.... When the stakes are this high, the detached judgment of a neutral magistrate is essential if the Fourth Amendment is to furnish meaningful protection from unfounded interference with liberty. Accordingly, we hold that the Fourth

Amendment requires a judicial determination of probable cause as a prerequisite to extended restraint of liberty following arrest.

The Court concluded that: "Whatever procedure a State may adopt, it must provide a fair and reliable determination of probable cause as a condition for any significant pretrial restraint of liberty, and this determination must be made by a judicial officer either before or promptly after arrest."

In *City of Riverside v. McLaughlin* (1991), the Court revisited the requirement of a "prompt" judicial assessment of probable cause to offer courts more specific guidance: "we believe that a jurisdiction that provides judicial determinations of probable cause within 48 hours of arrest will, as a general matter, comply with the promptness requirement of Gerstein."

UNCONSTITUTIONAL POLICING: FERGUSON, MISSOURI

In 1994, Congress authorized the Department of Justice (DOJ) to investigate local police departments alleged to be engaging in a "pattern or practice" of violating peoples' constitutional rights. If the DOJ finds such a pattern or practice, it can seek a "consent decree" whereby the police department agrees to reforms designed to eliminate continuing constitutional violations or, if no agreement is reached, sue the department in federal court to compel compliance. DOJ investigations often reveal unconstitutional police practices that avoid notice in reported case law.

In August 2014, a police officer in Ferguson, Missouri shot and killed an African American teenager, Michael Brown. In the wake of publicity surrounding the shooting (discussed in Chapter 5.B), the DOJ conducted an investigation of the Ferguson Police Department (FPD). The resulting report described a pattern and practice of constitutional rights violations. In addition, the investigation revealed that the City of Ferguson depended on its local criminal justice system for revenue. The DOJ concluded that, "Ferguson's law enforcement practices are shaped by the City's focus on revenue rather than by public safety needs."

> "The City budgets for sizeable increases in municipal fines and fees each year, exhorts police and court staff to deliver those revenue increases, and closely monitors whether those increases are achieved…. The importance of focusing on revenue generation is communicated to FPD officers. Ferguson police officers from all ranks told us that revenue generation is stressed heavily within the police department, and that the message comes from City

leadership…. Ferguson has allowed its focus on revenue generation to fundamentally compromise the role of Ferguson's municipal court. The municipal court does not act as a neutral arbiter of the law or a check on unlawful police conduct. Instead, the court primarily uses its judicial authority as the means to compel the payment of fines and fees that advance the City's financial interests."

The DOJ further explained that the FPD's improper use of the tools of law enforcement to generate revenue disproportionately impacted the City's African American population.

"Ferguson's law enforcement practices overwhelmingly impact African Americans. Data collected by the Ferguson Police Department from 2012 to 2014 shows that African Americans account for 85% of vehicle stops, 90% of citations, and 93% of arrests made by FPD officers, despite comprising only 67% of Ferguson's population. African Americans are more than twice as likely as white drivers to be searched during vehicle stops even after controlling for non-race based variables such as the reason the vehicle stop was initiated, but are found in possession of contraband 26% less often than white drivers, suggesting officers are impermissibly considering race as a factor when determining whether to search. African Americans are more likely to be cited and arrested following a stop regardless of why the stop was initiated and are more likely to receive multiple citations during a single incident. From 2012 to 2014, FPD issued four or more citations to African Americans on 73 occasions, but issued four or more citations to non-African Americans only twice. FPD appears to bring certain offenses almost exclusively against African Americans. For example, from 2011 to 2013, African Americans accounted for 95% of Manner of Walking in Roadway charges, and 94% of all Failure to Comply charges. Notably, with respect to speeding charges brought by FPD, the evidence shows not only that African Americans are represented at disproportionately high rates overall, but also that the disparate impact of FPD's enforcement practices on African Americans is 48% larger when citations are issued not on the basis of radar or laser, but by some other method, such as the officer's own visual assessment."

The report documents a series of examples of unconstitutional policing, including "a pattern of suspicionless, legally unsupportable stops ... described by FPD as 'ped checks' or 'pedestrian checks.'"

"Though at times officers use the term to refer to reasonable-suspicion-based pedestrian stops, or 'Terry stops,' they often use it when stopping a person with no objective, articulable suspicion. For example, one night in December 2013, officers went out and 'ped. checked those wandering around' in Ferguson's apartment complexes. In another case, officers responded to a call about a man selling drugs by stopping a group of six African-American youths who, due to their numbers, did not match the facts of the call. The youths were 'detained and ped checked.' Officers invoke the term 'ped check' as though it has some unique constitutional legitimacy. It does not. Officers may not detain a person, even briefly, without articulable reasonable suspicion. To the extent that the words 'ped check' suggest otherwise, the terminology alone is dangerous because it threatens to confuse officers' understanding of the law. Moreover, because FPD does not track or analyze pedestrian Terry stops—whether termed 'ped checks' or something else—in any reliable way, they are especially susceptible to discriminatory or otherwise unlawful use."

Another unconstitutional policing tactic involved citing residents for failing to comply with unlawful orders:

"Officers frequently arrest individuals under Section 29-16(1) on facts that do not meet the provision's elements. Section 29-16(1) makes it unlawful to 'fail to comply with the lawful order or request of a police officer in the discharge of the officer's official duties where such failure interfered with, obstructed or hindered the officer in the performance of such duties.' Many cases initiated under this provision begin with an officer ordering an individual to stop despite lacking objective indicia that the individual is engaged in wrongdoing. The order to stop is not a 'lawful order' under those circumstances because the officer lacks reasonable suspicion that criminal activity is afoot. Nonetheless, when individuals do not stop in those situations, FPD officers treat that conduct as a failure to comply with a lawful order, and make arrests. Such arrests violate the Fourth Amendment because they are not based on probable cause that the crime of Failure to Comply has been committed."

The DOJ report concludes that: "Addressing the deeply embedded constitutional deficiencies we found demands an entire reorientation of law enforcement in Ferguson. The City must replace revenue-driven policing with a system grounded in the principles of community policing and police legitimacy, in which people are equally protected and treated with compassion, regardless of race." The full report, as well as the consent decree entered into between the City of Ferguson and the DOJ, overseen by Federal District Court Judge Catherine Perry, is available online.

As of 2017, the DOJ had concluded 69 formal pattern and practice investigations. This map, courtesy of the DOJ, shows the locations of concluded investigations.

C. EXIGENT CIRCUMSTANCES

As the preceding sections demonstrate, warrants are typically not required for seizures of a person. By contrast, the Supreme Court regularly emphasizes the presumption that the Fourth Amendment requires searches to be authorized by a warrant. For example, in *Schneckloth v. Bustamonte* (1973), the Court stated: "It is well settled ... that a search conducted without a warrant issued upon probable cause is per se unreasonable . . . subject only to a few specifically established and well-delineated exceptions." The following sections address these exceptions, beginning with "exigent circumstances."

"Emergency Aid"

BRIGHAM CITY, UTAH v. STUART
547 U.S. 398 (2006)

Chief Justice ROBERTS delivered the opinion of the Court.

In this case we consider whether police may enter a home without a warrant when they have an objectively reasonable basis for believing that an occupant is seriously injured or imminently threatened with such injury. We conclude that they may.

I

This case arises out of a melee that occurred in a Brigham City, Utah, home in the early morning hours of July 23, 2000. At about 3 a.m., four police officers responded to a call regarding a loud party at a residence. Upon arriving at the house, they heard shouting from inside, and proceeded down the driveway to investigate. There, they observed two juveniles drinking beer in the backyard. They entered the backyard, and saw—through a screen door and windows—an altercation taking place in the kitchen of the home. According to the testimony of one of the officers, four adults were attempting, with some difficulty, to restrain a juvenile. The juvenile eventually "broke free, swung a fist and struck one of the adults in the face." The officer testified that he observed the victim of the blow spitting blood into a nearby sink. The other adults continued to try to restrain the juvenile, pressing him up against a refrigerator with such force that the refrigerator began moving across the floor. At this point, an officer opened the screen door and announced the officers' presence. Amid the tumult, nobody noticed. The officer entered the kitchen and again cried out, and as the occupants slowly became aware that the police were on the scene, the altercation ceased.

The officers subsequently arrested respondents and charged them with contributing to the delinquency of a minor, disorderly conduct, and intoxication. In the trial court, respondents filed a motion to suppress all evidence obtained after the officers entered the home, arguing that the warrantless entry violated the Fourth Amendment....

II

It is a basic principle of Fourth Amendment law that searches and seizures inside a home without a warrant are presumptively unreasonable. Nevertheless, because the ultimate touchstone of the Fourth Amendment is "reasonableness," the warrant requirement is subject to certain exceptions. We have held, for example, that law enforcement officers may make a warrantless entry onto private property to fight a fire and investigate its cause, to prevent the imminent destruction of evidence, or to engage in "hot pursuit" of a fleeing suspect. Warrants are generally required to search a person's home or his person unless the exigencies of the situation make the needs of law enforcement so compelling that the warrantless search is objectively reasonable under the Fourth Amendment.

One exigency obviating the requirement of a warrant is the need to assist persons who are seriously injured or threatened with such injury. The need to protect or preserve life or avoid serious injury is justification for what would be otherwise illegal absent an exigency or emergency. Accordingly, law enforcement officers may enter a home without a warrant to render emergency assistance to an injured occupant or to protect an occupant from imminent injury.

Respondents do not take issue with these principles, but instead advance two reasons why the officers' entry here was unreasonable. First, they argue that the officers were more interested in making arrests than quelling violence. They urge us to consider, in assessing the reasonableness of the entry, whether the officers were "indeed motivated primarily by a desire to save lives and property."... Our cases have repeatedly rejected this approach. An action is "reasonable" under the Fourth Amendment, regardless of the individual officer's state of mind, as long as the circumstances, viewed objectively, justify the action. The officer's subjective motivation is irrelevant. It therefore does not matter here—even if their subjective motives could be so neatly unraveled—whether the officers entered the kitchen to arrest respondents and gather evidence against them or to assist the injured and prevent further violence....

Respondents further contend that their conduct was not serious enough to justify the officers' intrusion into the home.... We think the officers' entry here was plainly reasonable under the circumstances. The officers were responding, at 3 o'clock in the morning, to complaints about a loud party. As they approached the house, they could hear from within "an altercation occurring, some kind of a fight." "It was loud and it was tumultuous." The officers heard "thumping and crashing" and people yelling "stop, stop" and "get off me." As the trial court found, "it was obvious that knocking on the front door" would have been futile. The noise seemed to be coming from the back of the house; after looking in the front window and seeing nothing, the officers proceeded around back to investigate further. They found two juveniles drinking beer in the backyard. From there, they could see that a fracas was taking place inside the kitchen. A juvenile, fists clenched, was being held back by several adults. As the officers watch, he breaks free and strikes one of the adults in the face, sending the adult to the sink spitting blood.

In these circumstances, the officers had an objectively reasonable basis for believing both that the injured adult might need help and that the violence in the kitchen was just beginning. Nothing in the Fourth Amendment required them to wait until another blow rendered someone unconscious or semi-conscious or worse before entering. The role of a peace officer includes preventing violence and restoring order, not simply rendering first aid to casualties; an officer is not like a boxing (or hockey) referee, poised to stop a bout only if it becomes too one-sided....

The "emergency aid" exception recognized in *Brigham City v. Stuart* allows police to enter a home without a warrant "to assist persons who are seriously injured or threatened with such injury." Consider whether that exception applies in the scenario presented by *Michigan v. Fisher* (2009)?

"" Police officers responded to a complaint of a disturbance near Allen Road in Brownstown, Michigan. Officer Christopher Goolsby later testified that, as he and his partner approached the area, a couple directed them to a residence where a man was "going crazy." Upon their arrival, the officers found a household in considerable chaos: a pickup truck in the driveway with its front smashed, damaged fenceposts along the side of the property, and three broken house windows, the glass still on the ground outside. The officers also noticed blood on the hood of the pickup and on clothes inside of it, as well as on one of the doors to the house.... Through a window, the officers could see respondent, Jeremy Fisher, inside the house, screaming and throwing things. The back door was locked, and a couch had been placed to block the front door.

The officers knocked, but Fisher refused to answer. They saw that Fisher had a cut on his hand, and they asked him whether he needed medical attention. Fisher ignored these questions and demanded, with accompanying profanity, that the officers go to get a search warrant. Officer Goolsby then pushed the front door partway open and ventured into the house.

Before reading any further, how do you think the Court answered the question: did the officers' entry of the house violate the Fourth Amendment?

In *Michigan v. Fisher*, the Supreme Court ruled that the officers did not violate the Fourth Amendment, explaining:

> " A straightforward application of the emergency aid exception, as in Brigham City, dictates that the officer's entry was reasonable. Just as in Brigham City, the police officers here were responding to a report of a disturbance. Just as in Brigham City, when they arrived on the scene they encountered a tumultuous situation in the house—and here they also found signs of a recent injury, perhaps from a car accident, outside. And just as in Brigham City, the officers could see violent behavior inside. Although Officer Goolsby and his partner did not see punches thrown, as did the officers in Brigham City, they did see Fisher screaming and throwing things. It would be objectively reasonable to believe that Fisher's projectiles might have a human target (perhaps a spouse or a child), or that Fisher would hurt himself in the course of his rage. In short, we find it as plain here as we did in Brigham City that the officer's entry was reasonable under the Fourth Amendment.

Much of what the police do is unconnected to the investigation of crime. For example, in *Cady v. Dombrowski* (1973), Wisconsin police responded to a traffic accident by arranging for a disabled car to be towed to a garage. Then, suspecting that a gun had been left in the car by the driver (a Chicago police officer who was in a coma as a result of the accident), they searched the car for the gun to prevent it from being found and potentially misused. The Supreme Court rejected a Fourth Amendment challenge to that search on the grounds that, "These officers in a rural area were simply reacting to the effect of an accident—one of the recurring practical situations that results from the operation of motor vehicles and with which local police officers must deal every day." The Court explained: "Local police officers, unlike federal officers, frequently investigate vehicle accidents in which there is no claim of criminal liability and engage in what, for want of a better term, may be described as community caretaking functions, totally divorced from the detection, investigation, or acquisition of evidence relating to the violation of a criminal statute."

The Supreme Court revisited *Cady* in **Caniglia v. Strom** (2021), where the police conducted a "welfare check" on Edward Caniglia, at the request of his wife, after he expressed suicidal thoughts. After speaking to Caniglia, the police called an ambulance; Caniglia voluntarily went to the hospital for psychiatric evaluation. The officers then entered Caniglia's home and seized his handguns. Caniglia later sued the officers for violating his Fourth Amendment rights. The U.S. Court of Appeals for the First Circuit, relying on *Cady*, dismissed the lawsuit since the police were not engaged in the investigation of any crime, but were engaged in "community caretaking."

The Supreme Court reversed, rejecting the suggestion that the Fourth Amendment did not apply whenever the police were motivated by something other than crime control. In an opinion by Justice Thomas, the Court explained:

> "The First Circuit's 'community caretaking' rule goes beyond anything this Court has recognized. The decision below assumed that respondents lacked a warrant or consent, and it expressly disclaimed the possibility that they were reacting to a crime. The court also declined to consider whether any recognized exigent circumstances were present because respondents had forfeited the point. Nor did it find that respondents' actions were akin to what a private citizen might have had authority to do if petitioner's wife had approached a neighbor for assistance instead of the police."

While the Court recognized that it had made exceptions to Fourth Amendment requirements for "community caretaking" functions in cases like *Cady*, the Court emphasized that those cases all took place outside the home. When it comes to warrantless *home* entries, the Court ruled, the police must follow the ordinary requirements of the Fourth Amendment.

"Hot Pursuit"

UNITED STATES v. SANTANA
427 U.S. 38 (1976)

Justice REHNQUIST delivered the opinion of the Court.

I

On August 16, 1974, Michael Gilletti, an undercover officer with the Philadelphia Narcotics Squad arranged a heroin "buy" with one Patricia McCafferty.... McCafferty told him it would cost $115 "and we will go down to Mom Santana's for the dope."... McCafferty took the money and went inside the house ... came out shortly afterwards and got into [Gilletti's] car... extracted from her bra several glassine envelopes containing a brownish-white powder and gave them to him.

Gilletti then stopped the car, displayed his badge, and placed McCafferty under arrest. He told her that the police were going back to 2311 North Fifth Street and that he wanted to know where the money was. She said, "Mom has the money." [With this information,] Sergeant Pruitt and other officers [returned] to 2311 North Fifth Street. They saw Dominga Santana standing in the doorway of the house with a brown paper bag in her hand. They pulled up to within 15 feet of Santana and got out of their van, shouting "police," and displaying their identification. As the officers approached, Santana retreated into the vestibule of her house.

The officers followed through the open door, catching her in the vestibule. As she tried to pull away, the bag tilted and "two bundles of glazed paper packets with a white powder" fell to the floor.... The white powder in the bag was later determined to be heroin....

II

In United States v. Watson (1976), we held that the warrantless arrest of an individual in a public place upon probable cause did not violate the Fourth Amendment. Thus the first question we must decide is whether, when the police first sought to arrest Santana, she was in a public place.

While it may be true that under the common law of property the threshold of one's dwelling is "private," as is the yard surrounding the house, it is nonetheless clear that under the cases interpreting the Fourth Amendment Santana was in a "public" place. She was not in an area where she had any expectation of privacy. "What a person knowingly exposes to the public, even in his own house or office, is not a subject of Fourth Amendment protection." Katz v. United States (1967). She was not merely visible to the public but was as exposed to public view, speech, hearing, and touch as if she had been standing completely outside her house. Thus, when the police, who concededly had probable cause to do so, sought to arrest her, they merely intended to perform a function which we have approved in Watson.

The only remaining question is whether her act of retreating into her house could thwart an otherwise proper arrest. We hold that it could not. In Warden v. Hayden (1967), we recognized the right of police, who had probable cause to believe that an armed robber had entered a house a few minutes before, to make a warrantless entry to arrest the robber and to search for weapons. This case, involving a true "hot pursuit," is clearly governed by Warden; the need to act quickly here is even greater than in that case while the intrusion is much less. The District Court was correct in concluding that "hot pursuit" means some sort of a chase, but it need not be an extended hue and cry "in and about the public streets." The fact that the pursuit here ended almost as soon as it began did not render it any the less a "hot pursuit" sufficient to justify the warrantless entry into Santana's house. Once Santana saw the police, there was likewise a realistic expectation that any delay would result in destruction of evidence…. We thus conclude that a suspect may not defeat an arrest which has been set in motion in a public place, and is therefore proper under Watson, by the expedient of escaping to a private place….

Santana references *Warden v. Hayden* (1967), but signals that *Hayden* was not a "true" hot pursuit case. Here are the facts of that case:

"About 8 a.m. on March 17, 1962, an armed robber entered the business premises of the Diamond Cab Company in Baltimore, Maryland. He took some $363 and ran. Two cab drivers in the vicinity, attracted by shouts of 'Holdup,' followed the man to 2111 Cocoa Lane. One driver notified the company dispatcher by radio that the man … had entered the house on Cocoa Lane. The dispatcher relayed the information to police who were proceeding to the scene of the robbery. Within minutes, police arrived at the house in a number of patrol cars. An officer knocked and announced their presence. Mrs. Hayden answered, and the officers told her they believed that a robber had entered the house, and asked to search the house. She offered no objection. The officers spread out through the first and second floors and the cellar in search of the robber. Hayden was found in an upstairs bedroom feigning sleep."

Without ever using the words "hot pursuit," the majority in *Hayden* ruled that the warrantless entry was constitutional:

"[The police] acted reasonably when they entered the house and began to search for a man of the description they had been given and for weapons which he had used in the robbery or might use against them. The Fourth Amendment does not require police officers to delay in the course of an investigation if to do so would gravely endanger their lives or the lives of others. Speed here was essential, and only a thorough search of the house for persons and weapons could have insured that Hayden was the only man present and that the police had control of all weapons which could be used against them or to effect an escape."

LANGE v. CALIFORNIA
141 S.Ct. 2011 (2021)

Justice KAGAN delivered the opinion of the Court.

The Fourth Amendment ordinarily requires that police officers get a warrant before entering a home without permission. But an officer may make a warrantless entry when the exigencies of the situation create a compelling law enforcement need. The question presented here is whether the pursuit of a fleeing misdemeanor suspect always—or more legally put, categorically—qualifies as an exigent circumstance. We hold it does not. A great many misdemeanor pursuits involve exigencies allowing warrantless entry. But whether a given one does so turns on the particular facts of the case.

I

This case began when petitioner Arthur Lange drove past a California highway patrol officer in Sonoma. Lange, it is fair to say, was asking for attention: He was listening to loud music with his windows down and repeatedly honking his horn. The officer began to tail Lange, and soon afterward turned on his overhead lights to signal that Lange should pull over. By that time, though, Lange was only about a hundred feet (some four-seconds drive) from his home. Rather than stopping, Lange continued to his driveway and entered his attached garage. The officer followed Lange in and began questioning him. Observing signs of intoxication, the officer put Lange through field sobriety tests. Lange did not do well, and a later blood test showed that his blood-alcohol content was more than three times the legal limit.

The State charged Lange with the misdemeanor of driving under the influence of alcohol, plus a (lower-level) noise infraction. Lange moved to suppress all evidence obtained after the officer entered his garage, arguing that the warrantless entry had violated the Fourth Amendment. The State contested the motion. It contended that the officer had probable cause to arrest Lange for the misdemeanor of failing to comply with a police signal. See, e.g., Cal. Veh. Code § 2800(a) (making it a misdemeanor to "willfully fail or refuse to comply with a lawful order, signal, or direction of a peace officer"). And it argued that the pursuit of a suspected misdemeanant always qualifies as an exigent circumstance authorizing a warrantless home entry. The Superior Court denied Lange's motion, and its appellate division affirmed.

II

…. "[T]he ultimate touchstone of the Fourth Amendment is 'reasonableness.'" That standard generally requires the obtaining of a judicial warrant before a law enforcement officer can enter a home without permission. But not always…. One important exception is for exigent circumstances…. The exception enables law enforcement officers to handle emergencies — situations presenting a compelling need for official action and no time to secure a warrant…. Our cases have generally applied the exigent-circumstances exception on a case-by-case basis…. That approach reflects the nature of emergencies. Whether a "now or never situation" actually exists—whether an officer has no time to secure a warrant—depends upon facts on the ground….

The question here is whether to use that approach, or instead apply a categorical warrant exception, when a suspected misdemeanant flees from police into his home. Under the usual case-specific view, an officer can follow the misdemeanant when, but only when, an exigency—for example, the need to prevent destruction of evidence—allows insufficient time to get a warrant. The appointed amicus asks us to replace that case-by-case assessment with a flat (and sweeping) rule finding exigency in every case of misdemeanor pursuit. In her view, those "entries are categorically reasonable, regardless of whether" any risk of harm (like, again, destruction of evidence) "materializes in a particular case." The fact of flight from the officer, she says, is itself enough to justify a warrantless entry. (The principal concurrence agrees.)...

The place to start is with our often-stated view of the constitutional interest at stake: the sanctity of a person's living space. "When it comes to the Fourth Amendment, the home is first among equals." Florida v. Jardines (2013). At the Amendment's "very core," we have said, "stands the right of a man to retreat into his own home and there be free from unreasonable government intrusion." Collins v. Virginia (2018).... So we are not eager—more the reverse—to print a new permission slip for entering the home without a warrant.

The amicus argues, though, that we have already created the rule she advocates. In United States v. Santana (1976) ... we upheld the warrantless entry as one involving a police "hot pursuit," even though the chase "ended almost as soon as it began." Citing "a realistic expectation that any delay would result in destruction of evidence," we recognized the officers' "need to act quickly." But we framed our holding in broader terms: Santana's "act of retreating into her house," we stated, could "not defeat an arrest" that had "been set in motion in a public place." The amicus takes that statement to support a flat rule permitting warrantless home entry when police officers (with probable cause) are pursuing any suspect—whether a felon or a misdemeanant. For support, she points to a number of later decisions describing Santana in dicta as allowing warrantless home entries when police are "in 'hot pursuit' of a fugitive" or "a fleeing suspect." The concurrence echoes her arguments.

We disagree with that broad understanding of Santana, as we have suggested before. In rejecting the amicus's view, we see no need to consider Lange's counterargument that Santana did not establish any categorical rule—even one for fleeing felons. Assuming Santana treated fleeing-felon cases categorically (that is, as always presenting exigent circumstances allowing warrantless entry), it still said nothing about fleeing misdemeanants....

Key to resolving that issue are two facts about misdemeanors: They vary widely, but they may be (in a word) "minor." In California and elsewhere, misdemeanors run the gamut of seriousness. As the amicus notes, some involve violence.... But calling an offense a misdemeanor usually limits prison time to one year. States thus tend to apply that label to less violent and less dangerous crimes. In California, it is a misdemeanor to litter on a public beach. And to "negligently cut" a plant "growing upon public land." And to "willfully disturb another person by loud and unreasonable noise." And (last one) to "artificially color any live chicks or rabbits." In forbidding such conduct, California is no outlier. Most States count as misdemeanors such offenses as traffic violations, public intoxication, and disorderly conduct. So the amicus's (and concurrence's) rule would cover lawbreakers of every type, including quite a few hard to think alarming.

This Court has held that when a minor offense alone is involved, police officers do not usually face the kind of emergency that can justify a warrantless home entry. In Welsh v. Wisconsin (1984), officers responded to a call about a drunk driver only to discover he had abandoned his vehicle and walked home. So no police pursuit was necessary, hot or otherwise. The officers just went to the driver's house, entered without a warrant, and arrested him for a "nonjailable" offense. The State contended that exigent circumstances supported the entry because the driver's "blood-alcohol level might have dissipated while the police obtained a warrant." We rejected that argument on the ground that the driver had been charged with only a minor offense. "The gravity of the underlying offense," we reasoned, is "an important factor to be considered when determining whether any exigency exists." "When only a minor offense has been committed" (again, without any flight), there is reason to question whether a compelling law enforcement need is present; so it is "particularly appropriate" to "hesitate in finding exigent circumstances." And we concluded: "Application of the exigent-circumstances exception in the context of a home entry should rarely be sanctioned when there is probable cause to believe that only a minor offense" is involved.

The concurrence is wrong to say that Welsh applies only to nonjailable offenses, and not to minor crimes that are labeled misdemeanors. No less than four times, Welsh framed its holding as applying to "minor offenses" generally…. And its essential rationale applies to all minor crimes, however labeled…. Add a suspect's flight and the calculus changes—but not enough to justify the amicus's categorical rule. We have no doubt that in a great many cases flight creates a need for police to act swiftly. A suspect may flee, for example, because he is intent on discarding evidence. Or his flight may show a willingness to flee yet again, while the police await a warrant. But no evidence suggests that every case of misdemeanor flight poses such dangers. Recall that misdemeanors can target minor, non-violent conduct. Welsh held that when that is so, officers can probably take the time to get a warrant. And at times that will be true even when a misdemeanant has forced the police to pursue him (especially given that "pursuit" may cover just a few feet of ground). Those suspected of minor offenses may flee for innocuous reasons and in non-threatening ways. Consider from the casebooks: the man with a mental disability who, in response to officers asking him about "fidgeting with a mailbox," retreated in "a hurried manner" to his nearby home. Or the teenager "driving without taillights" who on seeing a police signal "did not stop but drove two blocks to his parents' house, ran inside, and hid in the bathroom." In such a case, waiting for a warrant is unlikely to hinder a compelling law enforcement need. Those non-emergency situations may be atypical. But they reveal the overbreadth—fatal in this context—of the amicus's (and concurrence's) rule, which would treat a dangerous offender and the scared teenager the same. In misdemeanor cases, flight does not always supply the exigency that this Court has demanded for a warrantless home entry.

Our Fourth Amendment precedents thus point toward assessing case by case the exigencies arising from misdemeanants' flight. That approach will in many, if not most, cases allow a warrantless home entry. When the totality of circumstances shows an emergency—such as imminent harm to others, a threat to the officer himself, destruction of evidence, or escape from the home—the police may act without waiting. And those circumstances, as described just above, include the flight itself. But the need to pursue a misdemeanant does not trigger a categorical rule allowing home entry, even absent a law enforcement emergency. When the nature of the crime, the nature of the flight, and surrounding facts present no such exigency, officers must respect the sanctity of the home—which means that they must get a warrant.

…. Because the California Court of Appeal applied the categorical rule we reject today, we vacate its judgment and remand the case for further proceedings not inconsistent with this opinion.

MINNESOTA v. OLSON
495 U.S. 91 (1990)

Justice WHITE delivered the opinion of the Court.

[Shortly after a robbery and murder at an Amoco gas station in Minneapolis, Minnesota on July 18, police captured the suspected gunman but his accomplice escaped. They then developed substantial evidence that the accomplice was Rob Olson who resided at 2406 Fillmore with a friend, Julie, and her mother. On July 19 at 2:45 p.m., police received a tip that Olson was currently at the Fillmore residence.] The detective-in-charge instructed police officers to go to the house and surround it. He then telephoned Julie from headquarters and told her Rob should come out of the house. The detective heard a male voice say, "tell them I left." Julie stated that Rob had left, whereupon at 3 p.m. the detective ordered the police to enter the house. Without seeking permission and with weapons drawn, the police entered the upper unit and found respondent hiding in a closet....

It was held in Payton v. New York (1980), that a suspect should not be arrested in his house without an arrest warrant, even though there is probable cause to arrest him.... In Payton v. New York, the Court had no occasion to "consider the sort of emergency or dangerous situation, described in our cases as 'exigent circumstances,' that would justify a warrantless entry into a home for the purpose of either arrest or search." This case requires us to determine whether the Minnesota Supreme Court was correct in holding that there were no exigent circumstances that justified the warrantless entry into the house to make the arrest.

The Minnesota Supreme Court applied essentially the correct standard in determining whether exigent circumstances existed. The court observed that "a warrantless intrusion may be justified by hot pursuit of a fleeing felon, or imminent destruction of evidence, or the need to prevent a suspect's escape, or the risk of danger to the police or to other persons inside or outside the dwelling." The court also apparently thought that in the absence of hot pursuit there must be at least probable cause to believe that one or more of the other factors justifying the entry were present and that in assessing the risk of danger, the gravity of the crime and likelihood that the suspect is armed should be considered. Applying this standard, the state court determined that exigent circumstances did not exist.

We are not inclined to disagree with this fact-specific application of the proper legal standard. The court pointed out that although a grave crime was involved, respondent "was known not to be the murderer but thought to be the driver of the getaway car," and that the police had already recovered the murder weapon. "The police knew that Louanne and Julie were with the suspect in the upstairs duplex with no suggestion of danger to them. Three or four Minneapolis police squads surrounded the house. The time was 3 p.m., Sunday.... It was evident the suspect was going nowhere. If he came out of the house he would have been promptly apprehended." We do not disturb the state court's judgment that these facts do not add up to exigent circumstances.

Destruction of Evidence

KENTUCKY v. KING
563 U.S. 452 (2011)

Justice ALITO delivered the opinion of the Court.

It is well established that "exigent circumstances," including the need to prevent the destruction of evidence, permit police officers to conduct an otherwise permissible search without first obtaining a warrant. In this case, we consider whether this rule applies when police, by knocking on the door of a residence and announcing their presence, cause the occupants to attempt to destroy evidence. The Kentucky Supreme Court held that the exigent circumstances rule does not apply in the case at hand because the police should have foreseen that their conduct would prompt the occupants to attempt to destroy evidence. We reject this interpretation of the exigent circumstances rule. The conduct of the police prior to their entry into the apartment was entirely lawful. They did not violate the Fourth Amendment or threaten to do so. In such a situation, the exigent circumstances rule applies.

I

This case concerns the search of an apartment in Lexington, Kentucky. Police officers set up a controlled buy of crack cocaine outside an apartment complex. Undercover Officer Gibbons watched the deal take place from an unmarked car in a nearby parking lot. After the deal occurred, Gibbons radioed uniformed officers to move in on the suspect. He told the officers that the suspect was moving quickly toward the breezeway of an apartment building, and he urged them to "hurry up and get there" before the suspect entered an apartment.

In response to the radio alert, the uniformed officers drove into the nearby parking lot, left their vehicles, and ran to the breezeway. Just as they entered the breezeway, they heard a door shut and detected a very strong odor of burnt marijuana. At the end of the breezeway, the officers saw two apartments, one on the left and one on the right, and they did not know which apartment the suspect had entered. Gibbons had radioed that the suspect was running into the apartment on the right, but the officers did not hear this statement because they had already left their vehicles. Because they smelled marijuana smoke emanating from the apartment on the left, they approached the door of that apartment.

Officer Steven Cobb, one of the uniformed officers who approached the door, testified that the officers banged on the left apartment door "as loud as [they] could" and announced, "This is the police" or "Police, police, police." Cobb said that "as soon as [the officers] started banging on the door," they "could hear people inside moving," and "it sounded as though things were being moved inside the apartment." These noises, Cobb testified, led the officers to believe that drug-related evidence was about to be destroyed.

At that point, the officers announced that they "were going to make entry inside the apartment." Cobb then kicked in the door, the officers entered the apartment, and they found three people in the front room: respondent Hollis King, respondent's girlfriend, and a guest who was smoking marijuana. The officers performed a protective sweep of the apartment during which they saw marijuana and powder cocaine in plain view. In a subsequent search, they also discovered crack cocaine, cash, and drug paraphernalia.

Police eventually entered the apartment on the right. Inside, they found the suspected drug dealer who was the initial target of their investigation....

II

.... Although the text of the Fourth Amendment does not specify when a search warrant must be obtained, this Court has inferred that a warrant must generally be secured. "It is a basic principle of Fourth Amendment law," we have often said, "that searches and seizures inside a home without a warrant are presumptively unreasonable." But we have also recognized that this presumption may be overcome in some circumstances because the ultimate touchstone of the Fourth Amendment is "reasonableness." Accordingly, the warrant requirement is subject to certain reasonable exceptions.

One well-recognized exception applies when "the exigencies of the situation make the needs of law enforcement so compelling that a warrantless search is objectively reasonable under the Fourth Amendment." Mincey v. Arizona (1978). This Court has identified several exigencies that may justify a warrantless search of a home. Under the "emergency aid" exception, for example, "officers may enter a home without a warrant to render emergency assistance to an injured occupant or to protect an occupant from imminent injury." Brigham City v. Stuart (2006). Police officers may enter premises without a warrant when they are in hot pursuit of a fleeing suspect. See United States v. Santana (1976). And—what is relevant here— the need "to prevent the imminent destruction of evidence" has long been recognized as a sufficient justification for a warrantless search.

Over the years, lower courts have developed an exception to the exigent circumstances rule, the so-called "police-created exigency" doctrine. Under this doctrine, police may not rely on the need to prevent destruction of evidence when that exigency was "created" or "manufactured" by the conduct of the police…. In the vast majority of cases in which evidence is destroyed by persons who are engaged in illegal conduct, the reason for the destruction is fear that the evidence will fall into the hands of law enforcement…. [Consequently,] lower courts have held that the police-created exigency doctrine requires more than simple causation, but the lower courts have not agreed on the test to be applied….

III

As previously noted, warrantless searches are allowed when the circumstances make it reasonable, within the meaning of the Fourth Amendment, to dispense with the warrant requirement. Therefore, the answer to the question before us is that the exigent circumstances rule justifies a warrantless search when the conduct of the police preceding the exigency is reasonable in the same sense. Where, as here, the police did not create the exigency by engaging or threatening to engage in conduct that violates the Fourth Amendment, warrantless entry to prevent the destruction of evidence is reasonable and thus allowed….

When law enforcement officers who are not armed with a warrant knock on a door, they do no more than any private citizen might do. And whether the person who knocks on the door and requests the opportunity to speak is a police officer or a private citizen, the occupant has no obligation to open the door or to speak. When the police knock on a door but the occupants choose not to respond or to speak, the investigation will have reached a conspicuously low point, and the occupants will have the kind of warning that even the most elaborate security system cannot provide. And even if an occupant chooses to open the door and speak with the officers, the occupant need not allow the officers to enter the premises and may refuse to answer any questions at any time.

Occupants who choose not to stand on their constitutional rights but instead elect to attempt to destroy evidence have only themselves to blame for the warrantless exigent circumstances search that may ensue.

IV

We now apply our interpretation of the police-created exigency doctrine to the facts of this case.

A

We need not decide whether exigent circumstances existed in this case. Any warrantless entry based on exigent circumstances must, of course, be supported by a genuine exigency. The trial court and the Kentucky Court of Appeals found that there was a real exigency in this case, but the Kentucky Supreme Court expressed doubt on this issue, observing that there was "certainly some question as to whether the sound of persons moving inside the apartment was sufficient to establish that evidence was being destroyed." The Kentucky Supreme Court "assumed for the purpose of argument that exigent circumstances existed," and it held that the police had impermissibly manufactured the exigency.

We, too, assume for purposes of argument that an exigency existed. We decide only the question on which the Kentucky Supreme Court ruled and on which we granted certiorari: Under what circumstances do police impermissibly create an exigency? Any question about whether an exigency actually existed is better addressed by the Kentucky Supreme Court on remand.

B

In this case, we see no evidence that the officers either violated the Fourth Amendment or threatened to do so prior to the point when they entered the apartment. Officer Cobb testified without contradiction that the officers "banged on the door as loud as [they] could" and announced either "'Police, police, police'" or "'This is the police.'" This conduct was entirely consistent with the Fourth Amendment, and we are aware of no other evidence that might show that the officers either violated the Fourth Amendment or threatened to do so (for example, by announcing that they would break down the door if the occupants did not open the door voluntarily).... There is no evidence of a "demand" of any sort, much less a demand that amounts to a threat to violate the Fourth Amendment....

Finally, respondent claims that the officers "explained to the occupants that the officers were going to make entry inside the apartment," but the record is clear that the officers did not make this statement until after the exigency arose. As Officer Cobb testified, the officers "knew that there was possibly something that was going to be destroyed inside the apartment," and "at that point, ... [they] explained ... [that they] were going to make entry." Given that this announcement was made after the exigency arose, it could not have created the exigency.

Like the court below, we assume for purposes of argument that an exigency existed. Because the officers in this case did not violate or threaten to violate the Fourth Amendment prior to the exigency, we hold that the exigency justified the warrantless search of the apartment.

The judgment of the Kentucky Supreme Court is reversed, and the case is remanded for further proceedings not inconsistent with this opinion.

On remand, the Kentucky Supreme Court determined that there were, in fact, no exigent circumstances justifying a warrantless entry into King's apartment. Here is an excerpt from that opinion:

> " During the suppression hearing, Officer Cobb repeatedly referred to the "possible" destruction of evidence. He stated that he heard people moving inside the apartment, and that this was "the same kind of movements we've heard inside" when other suspects have destroyed evidence. Cobb never articulated the specific sounds he heard which led him to believe that evidence was about to be destroyed. In fact, the sounds as described at the suppression hearing were indistinguishable from ordinary household sounds, and were

consistent with the natural and reasonable result of a knock on the door. Nothing in the record suggests that the sounds officers heard were anything more than the occupants preparing to answer the door.

The police officers' subjective belief that evidence was being (or about to be) destroyed is not supported by the record, and this Court cannot conclude that the belief was objectively reasonable. No exigency is created simply because there is probable cause to believe that a serious crime has been committed. Exigent circumstances do not deal with mere possibilities, and the Commonwealth must show something more than a possibility that evidence is being destroyed to defeat the presumption of an unreasonable search and seizure.

Consistent with the instructions on remand from the United States Supreme Court, this Court concludes that exigent circumstances did not exist when police made a warrantless entry of the apartment occupied by Appellant King. Therefore, the denial of King's motion to suppress evidence is reversed, and King's judgment of conviction stands vacated.[18]

MISSOURI v. MCNEELY
569 U.S. 141 (2013)

Justice SOTOMAYOR delivered the opinion of the Court....

.... While on highway patrol at approximately 2:08 a.m., a Missouri police officer stopped Tyler McNeely's truck after observing it exceed the posted speed limit and repeatedly cross the centerline. The officer noticed several signs that McNeely was intoxicated, including McNeely's bloodshot eyes, his slurred speech, and the smell of alcohol on his breath. McNeely acknowledged to the officer that he had consumed "a couple of beers" at a bar, and he appeared unsteady on his feet when he exited the truck. After McNeely performed poorly on a battery of field-sobriety tests and declined to use a portable breath-test device to measure his blood alcohol concentration (BAC), the officer placed him under arrest.

---

[18] King v. Com., 386 S.W.3d 119 (Ky. 2012).

[The officer took him to a local hospital for a blood test.] The officer did not attempt to secure a warrant. Upon arrival at the hospital, the officer asked McNeely whether he would consent to a blood test…. McNeely … refused. The officer then directed a hospital lab technician to take a blood sample, and the sample was secured at approximately 2:35 a.m. Subsequent laboratory testing measured McNeely's BAC at 0.154 percent, which was well above the legal limit of 0.08 percent….

The State properly recognizes that the reasonableness of a warrantless search under the exigency exception to the warrant requirement must be evaluated based on the totality of the circumstances. But the State nevertheless seeks a per se rule for blood testing in drunk-driving cases. The State contends that whenever an officer has probable cause to believe an individual has been driving under the influence of alcohol, exigent circumstances will necessarily exist because BAC evidence is inherently evanescent….

It is true that as a result of the human body's natural metabolic processes, the alcohol level in a person's blood begins to dissipate once the alcohol is fully absorbed and continues to decline until the alcohol is eliminated. Testimony before the trial court in this case indicated that the percentage of alcohol in an individual's blood typically decreases by approximately 0.015 percent to 0.02 percent per hour once the alcohol has been fully absorbed. More precise calculations of the rate at which alcohol dissipates depend on various individual characteristics (such as weight, gender, and alcohol tolerance) and the circumstances in which the alcohol was consumed. Regardless of the exact elimination rate, it is sufficient for our purposes to note that because an individual's alcohol level gradually declines soon after he stops drinking, a significant delay in testing will negatively affect the probative value of the results….

But it does not follow that we should depart from careful case-by-case assessment of exigency and adopt the categorical rule proposed by the State and its amici. In those drunk-driving investigations where police officers can reasonably obtain a warrant before a blood sample can be drawn without significantly undermining the efficacy of the search, the Fourth Amendment mandates that they do so. We do not doubt that some circumstances will make obtaining a warrant impractical such that the dissipation of alcohol from the bloodstream will support an exigency justifying a properly conducted warrantless blood test. That, however, is a reason to decide each case on its facts … not to accept the considerable overgeneralization that a per se rule would reflect.

The context of blood testing is different in critical respects from other destruction-of-evidence cases in which the police are truly confronted with a "now or never" situation. In contrast to, for example, circumstances in which the suspect has control over easily disposable evidence, BAC evidence from a drunk-driving suspect naturally dissipates over time in a gradual and relatively predictable manner. Moreover, because a police officer must typically transport a drunk-driving suspect to a medical facility and obtain the assistance of someone with appropriate medical training before conducting a blood test, some delay between the time of the arrest or accident and the time of the test is inevitable regardless of whether police officers are required to obtain a warrant. This reality undermines the force of the State's contention, endorsed by the dissent, that we should recognize a categorical exception to the warrant requirement because BAC evidence "is actively being destroyed with every minute that passes."…

The State's proposed per se rule also fails to account for [technological] advances … that allow for the more expeditious processing of warrant applications, particularly in contexts like drunk-driving investigations where the evidence offered to establish probable cause is simple. The Federal Rules of Criminal Procedure were amended in 1977 to permit federal magistrate judges to issue a warrant based on sworn testimony communicated by telephone. As amended, the law now allows a federal magistrate judge to consider "information communicated by telephone or other reliable electronic means." States have also innovated. Well over a majority of States allow police officers or prosecutors to apply for search warrants remotely through various means, including telephonic or radio communication, electronic communication such as e-mail, and video conferencing. And in addition to technology-based developments, jurisdictions have found other ways to streamline the warrant process, such as by using standard-form warrant applications for drunk-driving investigations.

We by no means claim that telecommunications innovations have, will, or should eliminate all delay from the warrant-application process. Warrants inevitably take some time for police officers or prosecutors to complete and for magistrate judges to review. Telephonic and electronic warrants may still require officers to follow time-consuming formalities designed to create an adequate record, such as preparing a duplicate warrant before calling the magistrate judge. And improvements in communications technology do not guarantee that a magistrate judge will be available when an officer needs a warrant after making a late-night arrest. But technological developments that enable police officers to secure warrants more quickly, and do so without undermining the neutral magistrate judge's essential role as a check on police discretion, are relevant to an assessment of exigency. That is particularly so in this context, where BAC evidence is lost gradually and relatively predictably. Of course, there are important countervailing concerns. While experts can work backwards from the BAC at the time the sample was taken to determine the BAC at the time of the alleged offense, longer intervals may raise questions about the accuracy of the calculation. For that reason, exigent circumstances justifying a warrantless blood sample may arise in the regular course of law enforcement due to delays from the warrant application process. But adopting the State's per se approach would improperly ignore the current and future technological developments in warrant procedures, and might well diminish the incentive for jurisdictions to pursue progressive approaches to warrant acquisition that preserve the protections afforded by the warrant while meeting the legitimate interests of law enforcement.

In short, while the natural dissipation of alcohol in the blood may support a finding of exigency in a specific case... it does not do so categorically. Whether a warrantless blood test of a drunk-driving suspect is reasonable must be determined case by case based on the totality of the circumstances....

D. SEARCHES INCIDENT TO ARREST

1.   SITA

Searches incident to an arrest (SITA) are one of the most common "reasonable" warrantless searches. The Supreme Court articulated the general principle justifying these searches in *Chimel v. California* (1969):

> When an arrest is made, it is reasonable for the arresting officer to search the person arrested in order to remove any weapons that the latter might seek to use in order to resist arrest or effect his escape. Otherwise, the officer's safety might well be endangered, and the arrest itself frustrated. In addition, it is entirely reasonable for the arresting

officer to search for and seize any evidence on the arrestee's person in order to prevent its concealment or destruction. And the area into which an arrestee might reach in order to grab a weapon or evidentiary items must, of course, be governed by a like rule. A gun on a table or in a drawer in front of one who is arrested can be as dangerous to the arresting officer as one concealed in the clothing of the person arrested. There is ample justification, therefore, for a search of the arrestee's person and the area 'within his immediate control'— construing that phrase to mean the area from within which he might gain possession of a weapon or destructible evidence.

Subsequent cases clarified the boundaries of this important rule.

UNITED STATES v. ROBINSON
414 U.S. 218 (1973)

Justice REHNQUIST delivered the opinion of the Court.

.… On April 23, 1968, at approximately 11 p.m., Officer Richard Jenks, a 15-year veteran of the District of Columbia Metropolitan Police Department, observed the respondent driving a 1965 Cadillac near the intersection of 8th and C Streets, N.E., in the District of Columbia. Jenks, as a result of previous investigation following a check of respondent's operator's permit four days earlier, determined there was reason to believe that respondent was operating a motor vehicle after the revocation of his operator's permit. This is an offense defined by statute in the District of Columbia which carries a mandatory minimum jail term, a mandatory minimum fine, or both. Jenks signaled respondent to stop the automobile, which respondent did, and all three of the occupants emerged from the car. At that point Jenks informed respondent that he was under arrest for 'operating after revocation and obtaining a permit by misrepresentation.' It was assumed by the Court of Appeals, and is conceded by the respondent here, that Jenks had probable cause to arrest respondent, and that he effected a full custody arrest.

In accordance with procedures prescribed in police department instructions, Jenks then began to search respondent. He explained at a subsequent hearing that he was 'face-to-face' with the respondent, and 'placed (his) hands on (the respondent), my right-hand to his left breast like this (demonstrating) and proceeded to pat him down thus (with the right hand).' During this patdown, Jenks felt an object in the left breast pocket of the heavy coat respondent was wearing, but testified that he 'couldn't tell what it was' and also that he 'couldn't actually tell the size of it.' Jenks then reached into the pocket and pulled out the object, which turned out to be a 'crumpled up cigarette package.' Jenks testified that at this point he still did not know what was in the package: 'As I felt the package I could feel objects in the package but I couldn't tell what they were. I knew they weren't cigarettes.'

The officer then opened the cigarette pack and found 14 gelatin capsules of white powder which he thought to be, and which later analysis proved to be, heroin. Jenks then continued his search of respondent to completion, feeling around his waist and trouser legs, and examining the remaining pockets. The heroin seized from the respondent was admitted into evidence at the trial which resulted in his conviction in the District Court. [The Court of Appeals reversed Robinson's conviction for heroin possession, ruling that the search violated the Fourth Amendment.] We conclude that the search conducted by Jenks in this case did not offend the limits imposed by the Fourth Amendment, and we therefore reverse the judgment of the Court of Appeals.

It is well settled that a search incident to a lawful arrest is a traditional exception to the warrant requirement of the Fourth Amendment. This general exception has historically been formulated into two distinct propositions. The first is that a search may be made of the person of the arrestee by virtue of the lawful arrest. The second is that a search may be made of the area within the control of the arrestee.

Examination of this Court's decisions shows that these two propositions have been treated quite differently. The validity of the search of a person incident to a lawful arrest has been regarded as settled from its first enunciation, and has remained virtually unchallenged until the present case. The validity of the second proposition, while likewise conceded in principle, has been subject to differing interpretations as to the extent of the area which may be searched....

Our ... fundamental disagreement with the Court of Appeals arises from its suggestion that there must be litigated in each case the issue of whether or not there was present one of the reasons supporting the authority for a search of the person incident to a lawful arrest. We do not think the long line of authorities of this Court ..., or what we can glean from the history of practice in this country and in England, requires such a case-by-case adjudication. A police officer's determination as to how and where to search the person of a suspect whom he has arrested is necessarily a quick ad hoc judgment which the Fourth Amendment does not require to be broken down in each instance into an analysis of each step in the search. The authority to search the person incident to a lawful custodial arrest, while based upon the need to disarm and to discover evidence, does not depend on what a court may later decide was the probability in a particular arrest situation that weapons or evidence would in fact be found upon the person of the suspect. A custodial arrest of a suspect based on probable cause is a reasonable intrusion under the Fourth Amendment; that intrusion being lawful, a search incident to the arrest requires no additional justification. It is the fact of the lawful arrest which establishes the authority to search, and we hold that in the case of a lawful custodial arrest a full search of the person is not only an exception to the warrant requirement of the Fourth Amendment, but is also a 'reasonable' search under that Amendment.

The search of respondent's person conducted by Officer Jenks in this case and the seizure from him of the heroin, were permissible under established Fourth Amendment law. While thorough, the search partook of none of the extreme or patently abusive characteristics which were held to violate the Due Process Clause of the Fourteenth Amendment in Rochin v. California (1952). Since it is the fact of custodial arrest which gives rise to the authority to search, it is of no moment that Jenks did not indicate any subjective fear of the respondent or that he did not himself suspect that respondent was armed. Having in the course of a lawful search come upon the crumpled package of cigarettes, he was entitled to inspect it; and when his inspection revealed the heroin capsules, he was entitled to seize them as 'fruits, instrumentalities, or contraband' probative of criminal conduct....

As discussed in greater detail in Chapter 5, an initially "reasonable" search or seizure can become unconstitutional due to the unusually intrusive way that it is conducted. That is the point the Supreme Court was alluding to in referencing *Rochin v. California* (1952) – a case where the Court held that police methods that "shock[] the conscience" violate due process protections. Here are the facts of *Rochin*:

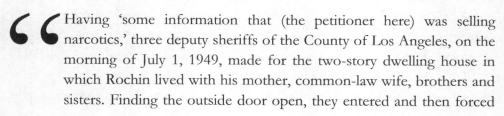

> Having 'some information that (the petitioner here) was selling narcotics,' three deputy sheriffs of the County of Los Angeles, on the morning of July 1, 1949, made for the two-story dwelling house in which Rochin lived with his mother, common-law wife, brothers and sisters. Finding the outside door open, they entered and then forced

open the door to Rochin's room on the second floor. Inside they found petitioner sitting partly dressed on the side of the bed, upon which his wife was lying. On a 'night stand' beside the bed the deputies spied two capsules. When asked 'Whose stuff is this?' Rochin seized the capsules and put them in his mouth. A struggle ensued, in the course of which the three officers 'jumped upon him' and attempted to extract the capsules. The force they applied proved unavailing against Rochin's resistance. He was handcuffed and taken to a hospital. At the direction of one of the officers a doctor forced an emetic solution through a tube into Rochin's stomach against his will. This 'stomach pumping' produced vomiting. In the vomited matter were found two capsules which proved to contain morphine.

In *Maryland v. Buie* (1990), the Supreme Court added a "**protective sweep**" enhancement to the search authority generated by an arrest, explaining:

"We hold that as an incident to the arrest [of Jerome Buie in his home] the officers could, as a precautionary matter and without probable cause or reasonable suspicion, look in closets and other spaces immediately adjoining the place of arrest from which an attack could be immediately launched. Beyond that, however, we hold that there must be articulable facts which, taken together with the rational inferences from those facts, would warrant a reasonably prudent officer in believing that the area to be swept harbors an individual posing a danger to those on the arrest scene…. We should emphasize that such a protective sweep, aimed at protecting the arresting officers, if justified by the circumstances, is nevertheless not a full search of the premises, but may extend only to a cursory inspection of those spaces where a person may be found. The sweep lasts no longer than is necessary to dispel the reasonable suspicion of danger and in any event no longer than it takes to complete the arrest and depart the premises."

KNOWLES v. IOWA
525 U.S. 113 (1998)

Chief Justice REHNQUIST delivered the opinion of the Court.

An Iowa police officer stopped petitioner Patrick Knowles for speeding, but issued him a citation rather than arresting him. The question presented is whether such a procedure authorizes the officer, consistently with the Fourth Amendment, to conduct a full search of the car. We answer this question "no."

Knowles was stopped in Newton, Iowa, after having been clocked driving 43 miles per hour on a road where the speed limit was 25 miles per hour. The police officer issued a citation to Knowles, although under Iowa law he might have arrested him. The officer then conducted a full search of the car, and under the driver's seat he found a bag of marijuana and a "pot pipe." Knowles was then arrested and charged with violation of state laws dealing with controlled substances.

Before trial, Knowles moved to suppress the evidence so obtained. He argued that the search could not be sustained under the "search incident to arrest" exception recognized in United States v. Robinson (1973), because he had not been placed under arrest....

Iowa Code Ann. § 321.485(1)(a) provides that Iowa peace officers having cause to believe that a person has violated any traffic or motor vehicle equipment law may arrest the person and immediately take the person before a magistrate. Iowa law also authorizes the far more usual practice of issuing a citation in lieu of arrest or in lieu of continued custody after an initial arrest. See Iowa Code Ann. § 805.1(1). Section 805.1(4) provides that the issuance of a citation in lieu of an arrest "does not affect the officer's authority to conduct an otherwise lawful search." The Iowa Supreme Court has interpreted this provision as providing authority to officers to conduct a full-blown search of an automobile and driver in those cases where police elect not to make a custodial arrest and instead issue a citation—that is, a search incident to citation....

In Robinson, we noted the two historical rationales for the "search incident to arrest" exception: (1) the need to disarm the suspect in order to take him into custody, and (2) the need to preserve evidence for later use at trial. But neither of these underlying rationales for the search incident to arrest exception is sufficient to justify the search in the present case.

…. The threat to officer safety from issuing a traffic citation is a good deal less than in the case of a custodial arrest…. This is not to say that the concern for officer safety is absent in the case of a routine traffic stop. It plainly is not…. [But] even without the search authority Iowa urges, officers have other, independent bases to search for weapons and protect themselves from danger. For example, they may order out of a vehicle both the driver, Pennsylvania v. Mimms (1977), and any passengers, Maryland v. Wilson (1997); perform a "patdown" of a driver and any passengers upon reasonable suspicion that they may be armed and dangerous, Terry v. Ohio (1968); conduct a "Terry patdown" of the passenger compartment of a vehicle upon reasonable suspicion that an occupant is dangerous and may gain immediate control of a weapon, Michigan v. Long (1983); and even conduct a full search of the passenger compartment, including any containers therein, pursuant to a custodial arrest, New York v. Belton (1981).

Nor has Iowa shown the second justification for the authority to search incident to arrest—the need to discover and preserve evidence. Once Knowles was stopped for speeding and issued a citation, all the evidence necessary to prosecute that offense had been obtained. No further evidence of excessive speed was going to be found either on the person of the offender or in the passenger compartment of the car.

…. In Robinson, we held that the authority to conduct a full field search as incident to an arrest was a "bright-line rule," which was based on the concern for officer safety and destruction or loss of evidence, but which did not depend in every case upon the existence of either concern. Here we are asked to extend that "bright-line rule" to a situation where the concern for officer safety is not present to the same extent and the concern for destruction or loss of evidence is not present at all. We decline to do so. The judgment of the Supreme Court of Iowa is reversed….

2.   CONTEMPORANEITY

A search incident to arrest must be contemporaneous with a lawful arrest. As the following excerpt from a law review article explains, however, a majority of the Court has never given firm guidance on what contemporaneous means.[19]

In United States v. Edwards (1974), police arrested Eugene Edwards at 11 p.m. for attempting to break into a government building. Edwards was promptly brought to jail, processed, and placed in a cell. Overnight, police discovered that the perpetrator had attempted to enter a wooden window and that he would likely have paint chips from the window on his clothing. The following morning, ten hours after his arrest, police took Edwards's clothing from him to search for paint chips. Edwards moved to suppress the evidence on the grounds that the search of his clothes occurred too long after arrest to fall within the search-incident-to-arrest exception. The Supreme Court rejected Edwards's argument and gave police wide authority to conduct the search incident to arrest well after the arrest was conducted.

Three years later, in the better-known case of United States v. Chadwick (1977), officers arrested Joseph Chadwick as he attempted to load a double-locked footlocker into his vehicle. One set of agents brought Chadwick to a federal building, and another group of agents followed behind with the footlocker. Approximately ninety minutes after the arrest, federal agents opened the footlocker and discovered a large quantity of marijuana. Unlike in Edwards, the Supreme Court rejected the Government's argument that the footlocker could be searched incident to arrest. In a brief footnote, the Court distinguished Edwards by explaining that "unlike searches of the person, searches of possessions within an arrestee's immediate control cannot be justified by any reduced expectations of privacy caused by the arrest." The Court further explained:

"Once law enforcement officers have reduced luggage or other personal property not immediately associated with the person of the arrestee to their exclusive control, and there is no longer any danger that the arrestee might gain

---

[19] Gershowitz, *Password Protected?* 96 Iowa L. Rev. 1125 (2011).

access to the property to seize a weapon or destroy evidence, a search of that property is no longer an incident of the arrest."

The Court's decisions in Edwards and Chadwick thus offer two different rules for the temporal scope of searches incident to arrest. If the search is of items associated with the person, police have great flexibility and can conduct the search many hours after arrest. If, however, the police search possessions that are not associated with the person and are merely nearby, then there is a more rigid time limitation. In the … decades since the Edwards and Chadwick decisions, the Supreme Court has offered no additional guidance on this distinction. There are, however, a few relatively clear, decipherable principles from lower court decisions.

Lower courts have repeatedly concluded that, in addition to clothing, police may search an arrestee's wallet incident to arrest at the station house because a wallet conceptually falls under Edwards as an item typically found on the person of an arrestee and thus closer to clothing than, for example, the footlocker in Chadwick. Similarly, courts have upheld station house searches incident to arrest of purses, duffle bags, and backpacks because they more closely resemble items on the person rather than nearby possessions. As [one scholar observed] courts have "rather consistently" held that under Edwards police can search incident to arrest the "pockets, wallet, and other containers on the person" at the station house following arrest. To the extent conflicting authority finds items as possessions falling under Chadwick, the cases typically involve purses and briefcases found in the arrestee's vehicle or otherwise not attached to the arrestee's body….

Although the Supreme Court has trumpeted the need for bright-line rules in the search-incident-to-arrest context, the Court has not adopted a bright-line rule dictating how long police can take to conduct such searches…. Accordingly, police must be guided by high-level principles offering little practical guidance. The overarching concept provides simply that police must conduct a search as soon as is practicable. Courts are willing to uphold searches taking longer periods of time when there are intervening events, like when police must wait for additional officers to secure the scene. If the search appears to be part of a "continuous series of events," rather than an afterthought, courts are more likely to uphold the search. Indeed, many courts will even give police leeway to conduct a search incident to arrest after officers remove an arrestee from the scene, so long as there is a good reason for the delay and the police conduct the search expeditiously.

3.   CELL PHONES

In the years after *Robinson*, lower courts applied the search incident to arrest doctrine to a wide variety of items found on arrestees, including wallets, envelopes, and aspirin bottles. Courts reasoned that these containers could hold contraband that might be destroyed if the police did not secure it. In the 1990s, lower courts confronted a new kind of container – electronic devices – that contained a new kind of evidence. Notably, drug dealers often coordinated their sales using pagers – a one-way remote communication device popularized by on-call medical doctors. Lower courts uniformly upheld the warrantless search incident to arrest of pagers on the grounds that they could contain evidence and that those devices held only a limited amount of data, some of which could be erased with each new incoming call. While lower courts upheld the search incident to arrest of pagers, they began to divide in cases involving cell phones. As wireless technology improved and flip phones that held only limited data gave way to smart phones, some courts began to reject cell phone searches conducted incident to arrest. While most lower courts concluded that cell phones were containers that could be searched under existing search incident to arrest doctrine, other courts were alarmed by the amount of data that police could review without a warrant, and those courts looked for a way to narrow the search incident to arrest doctrine. For background on the development of the law, see Gershowitz, *The iPhone Meets the Fourth Amendment*, 56 UCLA L. Rev. 27 (2008). With courts divided over whether cell phones could be searched incident to arrest without a warrant, the Supreme Court granted certiorari in *Riley v. California.*

RILEY v. CALIFORNIA
573 U.S. 373 (2014)

Chief Justice ROBERTS delivered the opinion of the Court.

These two cases raise a common question: whether the police may, without a warrant, search digital information on a cell phone seized from an individual who has been arrested.

I

A

In the first case, petitioner David Riley was stopped by a police officer for driving with expired registration tags. In the course of the stop, the officer also learned that

Riley's license had been suspended. The officer impounded Riley's car, pursuant to department policy, and another officer conducted an inventory search of the car. Riley was arrested for possession of concealed and loaded firearms when that search turned up two handguns under the car's hood.

An officer searched Riley incident to the arrest and found items associated with the "Bloods" street gang. He also seized a cell phone from Riley's pants pocket. According to Riley's uncontradicted assertion, the phone was a "smart phone," a cell phone with a broad range of other functions based on advanced computing capability, large storage capacity, and Internet connectivity. The officer accessed information on the phone and noticed that some words (presumably in text messages or a contacts list) were preceded by the letters "CK"—a label that, he believed, stood for "Crip Killers," a slang term for members of the Bloods gang.

At the police station about two hours after the arrest, a detective specializing in gangs further examined the contents of the phone. The detective testified that he "went through" Riley's phone "looking for evidence, because gang members will often video themselves with guns or take pictures of themselves with the guns." Although there was "a lot of stuff" on the phone, particular files that "caught [the detective's] eye" included videos of young men sparring while someone yelled encouragement using the moniker "Blood." The police also found photographs of Riley standing in front of a car they suspected had been involved in a shooting a few weeks earlier.

Riley was ultimately charged in connection with that earlier shooting.... At Riley's trial, police officers testified about the photographs and videos found on the phone, and some of the photographs were admitted into evidence. Riley was convicted ... and received an enhanced sentence of 15 years to life in prison....

B

In the second case, a police officer performing routine surveillance observed respondent Brima Wurie make an apparent drug sale from a car. Officers subsequently arrested Wurie and took him to the police station. At the station, the officers seized two cell phones from Wurie's person. The one at issue here was a "flip phone," a kind of phone that is flipped open for use and that generally has a smaller range of features than a smart phone. Five to ten minutes after arriving at the station, the officers noticed that the phone was repeatedly receiving calls from a source identified as "my house" on the phone's external screen. A few minutes later, they opened the phone and saw a photograph of a woman and a baby set as the phone's wallpaper. They pressed one button on the phone to access its call log, then another button to determine the phone number associated with the "my house" label. They next used an online phone directory to trace that phone number to an apartment building.

When the officers went to the building, they saw Wurie's name on a mailbox and observed through a window a woman who resembled the woman in the photograph on Wurie's phone. They secured the apartment while obtaining a search warrant and, upon later executing the warrant, found and seized 215 grams of crack cocaine, marijuana, drug paraphernalia, a firearm and ammunition, and cash.

Wurie was charged with distributing crack cocaine, possessing crack cocaine with intent to distribute, and being a felon in possession of a firearm and ammunition. He moved to suppress the evidence obtained from the search of the apartment, arguing that it was the fruit of an unconstitutional search of his cell phone. The District Court denied the motion. Wurie was convicted on all three counts and sentenced to 262 months in prison....

II

...The two cases before us concern the reasonableness of a warrantless search incident to a lawful arrest.... Although the existence of the exception for such searches has been recognized for a century, its scope has been debated for nearly as long. That debate has focused on the extent to which officers may search property found on or near the arrestee. Three related precedents set forth the rules governing such searches:

The first, Chimel v. California (1969), laid the groundwork for most of the existing search incident to arrest doctrine.... Four years later, in United States v. Robinson (1973), the Court applied the Chimel analysis in the context of a search of the arrestee's person. ... [In Robinson,] this Court ... reject[ed] the notion that "case-by-case adjudication" was required to determine "whether or not there was present one of the reasons supporting the authority for a search of the person incident to a lawful arrest." As the Court explained, "the authority to search the person incident to a lawful custodial arrest, while based upon the need to disarm and to discover evidence, does not depend on what a court may later decide was the probability in a particular arrest situation that weapons or evidence would in fact be found upon the person of the suspect."… The search incident to arrest trilogy concludes with Arizona v. Gant (2009), which analyzed searches of an arrestee's vehicle….

III

…. Absent more precise guidance from the founding era, we generally determine whether to exempt a given type of search from the warrant requirement by assessing, on the one hand, the degree to which it intrudes upon an individual's privacy and, on the other, the degree to which it is needed for the promotion of legitimate governmental interests. Such a balancing of interests supported the search incident to arrest exception in Robinson, and a mechanical application of Robinson might well support the warrantless searches at issue here….

We … decline to extend Robinson to searches of data on cell phones, and hold instead that officers must generally secure a warrant before conducting such a search.

A

We first consider each Chimel concern in turn. In doing so, we do not overlook Robinson's admonition that searches of a person incident to arrest, "while based upon the need to disarm and to discover evidence," are reasonable regardless of "the probability in a particular arrest situation that weapons or evidence would in fact be found." Rather than requiring the "case-by-case adjudication" that Robinson rejected, we ask instead whether application of the search incident to arrest doctrine to this particular category of effects would untether the rule from the justifications underlying the Chimel exception.

1

Digital data stored on a cell phone cannot itself be used as a weapon to harm an arresting officer or to effectuate the arrestee's escape. Law enforcement officers remain free to examine the physical aspects of a phone to ensure that it will not be used as a weapon—say, to determine whether there is a razor blade hidden between the phone and its case. Once an officer has secured a phone and eliminated any potential physical threats, however, data on the phone can endanger no one….

2

The United States and California focus primarily on the second Chimel rationale: preventing the destruction of evidence.

Both Riley and Wurie concede that officers could have seized and secured their cell phones to prevent destruction of evidence while seeking a warrant. That is a sensible concession. See Illinois v. McArthur (2001). And once law enforcement officers have secured a cell phone, there is no longer any risk that the arrestee himself will be able to delete incriminating data from the phone.

The United States and California argue that information on a cell phone may nevertheless be vulnerable to two types of evidence destruction unique to digital data—remote wiping and data encryption. Remote wiping occurs when a phone, connected to a wireless network, receives a signal that erases stored data. This can happen when a third party sends a remote signal or when a phone is preprogrammed to delete data upon entering or leaving certain geographic areas (so-called "geofencing"). Encryption is a security feature that some modern cell phones use in addition to password protection. When such phones lock, data becomes protected by sophisticated encryption that renders a phone all but "unbreakable" unless police know the password.

As an initial matter, these broader concerns about the loss of evidence are distinct from Chimel's focus on a defendant who responds to arrest by trying to conceal or destroy evidence within his reach. With respect to remote wiping, the Government's primary concern turns on the actions of third parties who are not present at the scene of arrest. And data encryption is even further afield. There, the Government focuses on the ordinary operation of a phone's security features, apart from any active attempt by a defendant or his associates to conceal or destroy evidence upon arrest.

We have also been given little reason to believe that either problem is prevalent. The briefing reveals only a couple of anecdotal examples of remote wiping triggered by an arrest. Similarly, the opportunities for officers to search a password-protected phone before data becomes encrypted are quite limited. Law enforcement officers are very unlikely to come upon such a phone in an unlocked state because most phones lock at the touch of a button or, as a default, after some very short period of inactivity.... In any event, as to remote wiping, law enforcement is not without specific means to address the threat. Remote wiping can be fully prevented by

271

disconnecting a phone from the network [either by turning it off or enclosing it in a "Faraday bag" – "essentially sandwich bags made of aluminum foil: cheap, lightweight, and easy to use"].

To the extent that law enforcement still has specific concerns about the potential loss of evidence in a particular case, there remain more targeted ways to address those concerns. If "the police are truly confronted with a 'now or never' situation,"—for example, circumstances suggesting that a defendant's phone will be the target of an imminent remote-wipe attempt—they may be able to rely on exigent circumstances to search the phone immediately. Or, if officers happen to seize a phone in an unlocked state, they may be able to disable a phone's automatic-lock feature in order to prevent the phone from locking and encrypting data. Such a preventive measure could be analyzed under the principles set forth in our decision in McArthur, which approved officers' reasonable steps to secure a scene to preserve evidence while they awaited a warrant.

B

The search incident to arrest exception rests not only on the heightened government interests at stake in a volatile arrest situation, but also on an arrestee's reduced privacy interests upon being taken into police custody.… [But] the fact that an arrestee has diminished privacy interests does not mean that the Fourth Amendment falls out of the picture entirely.…

Robinson is the only decision from this Court applying Chimel to a search of the contents of an item found on an arrestee's person. … Lower courts applying Robinson and Chimel, however, have approved searches of a variety of personal items carried by an arrestee. See, e.g., United States v. Carrion (C.A.5 1987) (billfold and address book); United States v. Watson (C.A.11 1982) (wallet); United States v. Lee (C.A.D.C.1974) (purse).

The United States asserts that a search of all data stored on a cell phone is "materially indistinguishable" from searches of these sorts of physical items. That is like saying a ride on horseback is materially indistinguishable from a flight to the moon. Both are ways of getting from point A to point B, but little else justifies lumping them together. Modern cell phones, as a category, implicate privacy concerns far beyond those implicated by the search of a cigarette pack, a wallet, or a purse. A conclusion that inspecting the contents of an arrestee's pockets works no substantial additional intrusion on privacy beyond the arrest itself may make sense as applied to physical items, but any extension of that reasoning to digital data has to rest on its own bottom.

1

Cell phones differ in both a quantitative and a qualitative sense from other objects that might be kept on an arrestee's person. The term "cell phone" is itself misleading shorthand; many of these devices are in fact minicomputers that also happen to have the capacity to be used as a telephone. They could just as easily be called cameras, video players, rolodexes, calendars, tape recorders, libraries, diaries, albums, televisions, maps, or newspapers.

One of the most notable distinguishing features of modern cell phones is their immense storage capacity. Before cell phones, a search of a person was limited by physical realities and tended as a general matter to constitute only a narrow intrusion on privacy. Most people cannot lug around every piece of mail they have received for the past several months, every picture they have taken, or every book or article they have read—nor would they have any reason to attempt to do so....

The storage capacity of cell phones has several interrelated consequences for privacy. First, a cell phone collects in one place many distinct types of information—an address, a note, a prescription, a bank statement, a video—that reveal much more in combination than any isolated record. Second, a cell phone's capacity allows even just one type of information to convey far more than previously possible. The sum of an individual's private life can be reconstructed through a thousand photographs labeled with dates, locations, and descriptions; the same cannot be said of a photograph or two of loved ones tucked into a wallet. Third, the data on a phone can date back to the purchase of the phone, or even earlier. A person might carry in his pocket a slip of paper reminding him to call Mr. Jones; he would not carry a record of all his communications with Mr. Jones for the past several months, as would routinely be kept on a phone.

Finally, there is an element of pervasiveness that characterizes cell phones but not physical records. Prior to the digital age, people did not typically carry a cache of sensitive personal information with them as they went about their day. Now it is the person who is not carrying a cell phone, with all that it contains, who is the exception. According to one poll, nearly three-quarters of smart phone users report being within five feet of their phones most of the time, with 12% admitting that they even use their phones in the shower. A decade ago police officers searching an arrestee might have occasionally stumbled across a highly personal item such as a diary. But those discoveries were likely to be few and far between. Today, by contrast, it is no exaggeration to say that many of the more than 90% of American adults who own a cell phone keep on their person a digital record of nearly every aspect of their lives—from the mundane to the intimate. Allowing the police to scrutinize such records on a routine basis is quite different from allowing them to search a personal item or two in the occasional case....

2

To further complicate the scope of the privacy interests at stake, the data a user views on many modern cell phones may not in fact be stored on the device itself. Treating a cell phone as a container whose contents may be searched incident to an arrest is a bit strained as an initial matter. But the analogy crumbles entirely when a cell phone is used to access data located elsewhere, at the tap of a screen. That is what cell phones, with increasing frequency, are designed to do by taking advantage of "cloud computing." ... The possibility that a search might extend well beyond papers and effects in the physical proximity of an arrestee is yet another reason that the privacy interests here dwarf those in Robinson....

IV

We cannot deny that our decision today will have an impact on the ability of law enforcement to combat crime. Cell phones have become important tools in facilitating coordination and communication among members of criminal enterprises, and can provide valuable incriminating information about dangerous criminals. Privacy comes at a cost.

Our holding, of course, is not that the information on a cell phone is immune from search; it is instead that a warrant is generally required before such a search, even when a cell phone is seized incident to arrest. Our cases have historically recognized that the warrant requirement is "an important working part of our machinery of government," not merely "an inconvenience to be somehow 'weighed' against the claims of police efficiency." Recent technological advances similar to those discussed here have, in addition, made the process of obtaining a warrant itself more efficient.

Moreover, even though the search incident to arrest exception does not apply to cell phones, other case-specific exceptions may still justify a warrantless search of a particular phone. One well-recognized exception applies when the exigencies of the situation make the needs of law enforcement so compelling that a warrantless search is objectively reasonable under the Fourth Amendment. Such exigencies could include the need to prevent the imminent destruction of evidence in individual cases, to pursue a fleeing suspect, and to assist persons who are seriously injured or are threatened with imminent injury....

In light of the availability of the exigent circumstances exception, there is no reason to believe that law enforcement officers will not be able to address some of the more extreme hypotheticals that have been suggested: a suspect texting an accomplice who, it is feared, is preparing to detonate a bomb, or a child abductor who may have information about the child's location on his cell phone. The defendants here recognize—indeed, they stress—that such fact-specific threats may justify a warrantless search of cell phone data. The critical point is that, unlike the search incident to arrest exception, the exigent circumstances exception requires a court to examine whether an emergency justified a warrantless search in each particular case.

Modern cell phones are not just another technological convenience. With all they contain and all they may reveal, they hold for many Americans the privacies of life. The fact that technology now allows an individual to carry such information in his hand does not make the information any less worthy of the protection for which the Founders fought. Our answer to the question of what police must do before searching a cell phone seized incident to an arrest is accordingly simple—get a warrant.

In *Birchfield v. North Dakota* (2016), the Supreme Court considered whether the police could conduct breath and blood tests incident to drunk driving arrests. The Court recognized at the outset that "the taking of a blood sample or the administration of a breath test is a search." It analogized these searches to the search of a cellphone in *Riley*:

"Blood and breath tests to measure BAC are not as new as searches of cell phones, but here, as in Riley, the founding era does not provide any definitive guidance as to whether they should be allowed incident to arrest. Lacking such guidance, we engage in the same mode of analysis as in Riley: We examine the degree to which they intrude upon an individual's privacy and the degree to which they are needed for the promotion of legitimate governmental interests."

After weighing the various interests involved, the Court concluded:

"Because breath tests are significantly less intrusive than blood tests and in most cases amply serve law enforcement interests, we conclude that a breath test, but not a blood test, may be administered as a search incident to a lawful arrest for drunk driving. As in all cases involving reasonable searches incident to arrest, a warrant is not needed in this situation."

4.   AUTOMOBILES

As this figure from the BJS survey referenced in the first Chapter reflects, traffic stops are the most reported form of police-initiated contact in this country.

FIGURE 1
U.S. residents age 16 or older who had police contact, by type of contact and reason, 2020

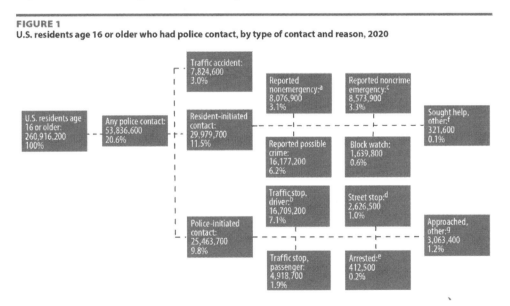

There are two separate and totally distinct exceptions to the warrant requirement that can come into play when police search vehicles, (1) the search of an automobile incident to an arrest; and (2) the vehicle exception. We will turn to the vehicle exception in Part E. First though, we focus on how the Supreme Court applies search-incident-to-arrest doctrine to automobiles.

In *New York v. Belton* (1981), the Supreme Court created what appeared to be a bright line rule:

> "We hold that when a policeman has made a lawful custodial arrest of the occupant of an automobile, he may, as a contemporaneous incident of that arrest, search the passenger compartment of that automobile."

The "passenger compartment" is the area of a vehicle that passengers have access to – under the seats, the glove compartment, the center console, etc.

In *Thornton v. United States* (2004), the Supreme Court applied the *Belton* rule to allow a search of a vehicle incident to arrest where the police first contacted the driver of the car after the driver exited the vehicle and closed the door. The Court explained: "So long as an arrestee is the sort of 'recent occupant' of a vehicle such as petitioner was here, officers may search that vehicle incident to the arrest."

The Court revisited and clarified/overruled *Belton*'s bright line rule in the next case.

ARIZONA v. GANT
556 U.S. 332 (2009)

Justice STEVENS delivered the opinion of the Court.

I

On August 25, 1999, acting on an anonymous tip that the residence at 2524 North Walnut Avenue was being used to sell drugs, Tucson police officers Griffith and Reed knocked on the front door and asked to speak to the owner. Rodney Gant answered the door and, after identifying himself, stated that he expected the owner to return later. The officers left the residence and conducted a records check, which revealed that Gant's driver's license had been suspended and there was an outstanding warrant for his arrest for driving with a suspended license.

When the officers returned to the house that evening, they found a man near the back of the house and a woman in a car parked in front of it. After a third officer arrived, they arrested the man for providing a false name and the woman for possessing drug paraphernalia. Both arrestees were handcuffed and secured in separate patrol cars when Gant arrived. The officers recognized his car as it entered the driveway, and Officer Griffith confirmed that Gant was the driver by shining a flashlight into the car as it drove by him. Gant parked at the end of the driveway, got out of his car, and shut the door. Griffith, who was about 30 feet away, called to Gant, and they approached each other, meeting 10-to-12 feet from Gant's car. Griffith immediately arrested Gant and handcuffed him.

Because the other arrestees were secured in the only patrol cars at the scene, Griffith called for backup. When two more officers arrived, they locked Gant in the backseat of their vehicle. After Gant had been handcuffed and placed in the back of a patrol car, two officers searched his car: One of them found a gun, and the other discovered a bag of cocaine in the pocket of a jacket on the backseat.

Gant was charged with two offenses—possession of a narcotic drug for sale and possession of drug paraphernalia (i.e., the plastic bag in which the cocaine was found). He moved to suppress the evidence seized from his car on the ground that the warrantless search violated the Fourth Amendment. Among other things, Gant argued that Belton did not authorize the search of his vehicle because he posed no threat to the officers after he was handcuffed in the patrol car and because he was arrested for a traffic offense for which no evidence could be found in his vehicle. When asked at the suppression hearing why the search was conducted, Officer Griffith responded: "Because the law says we can do it."

The trial court rejected the State's contention that the officers had probable cause to search Gant's car for contraband when the search began, but it denied the motion to suppress. Relying on the fact that the police saw Gant commit the crime of driving without a license and apprehended him only shortly after he exited his car, the court held that the search was permissible as a search incident to arrest. A jury found Gant guilty on both drug counts, and he was sentenced to a 3–year term of imprisonment....

II

.... In Chimel v. California (1969), we held that a search incident to arrest may only include "the arrestee's person and the area 'within his immediate control'— construing that phrase to mean the area from within which he might gain possession of a weapon or destructible evidence." That limitation, which continues to define the boundaries of the exception, ensures that the scope of a search incident to arrest is commensurate with its purposes of protecting arresting officers and safeguarding any evidence of the offense of arrest that an arrestee might conceal or destroy. If there is no possibility that an arrestee could reach into the area that law enforcement officers seek to search, both justifications for the search-incident-to-arrest exception are absent and the rule does not apply.

In Belton v. New York (1981), we considered Chimel's application to the automobile context. A lone police officer in that case stopped a speeding car in which Belton was one of four occupants. While asking for the driver's license and registration, the officer smelled burnt marijuana and observed an envelope on the car floor marked "Supergold"—a name he associated with marijuana. Thus having probable cause to believe the occupants had committed a drug offense, the officer ordered them out of the vehicle, placed them under arrest, and patted them down. Without handcuffing the arrestees, the officer "split them up into four separate areas of the Thruway ... so they would not be in physical touching area of each other" and searched the vehicle, including the pocket of a jacket on the backseat, in which he found cocaine.

[In Belton,] we held that when an officer lawfully arrests "the occupant of an automobile, he may, as a contemporaneous incident of that arrest, search the passenger compartment of the automobile" and any containers therein. That holding was based in large part on our assumption "that articles inside the relatively narrow compass of the passenger compartment of an automobile are in fact generally, even if not inevitably, within 'the area into which an arrestee might reach.'"...

III

Despite the textual and evidentiary support for [a narrower] reading of Belton, our opinion has been widely understood to allow a vehicle search incident to the arrest of a recent occupant even if there is no possibility the arrestee could gain access to the vehicle at the time of the search. This reading may be attributable to Justice Brennan's dissent in Belton, in which he characterized the Court's holding as resting on the "fiction ... that the interior of a car is always within the immediate control of an arrestee who has recently been in the car." Under the majority's approach, he argued, "the result would presumably be the same even if the officer had handcuffed Belton and his companions in the patrol car" before conducting the search.

Since we decided Belton, ... Justice Brennan's reading of the Court's opinion has predominated. As Justice O'Connor observed, "lower court decisions seem now to treat the ability to search a vehicle incident to the arrest of a recent occupant as a police entitlement rather than as an exception justified by the twin rationales of Chimel." Justice Scalia has similarly noted that, although it is improbable that an arrestee could gain access to weapons stored in his vehicle after he has been handcuffed and secured in the backseat of a patrol car, cases allowing a search in "this precise factual scenario are legion."…

Under this broad reading of Belton, a vehicle search would be authorized incident to every arrest of a recent occupant notwithstanding that in most cases the vehicle's passenger compartment will not be within the arrestee's reach at the time of the search. To read Belton as authorizing a vehicle search incident to every recent occupant's arrest would thus untether the rule from the justifications underlying the Chimel exception—a result clearly incompatible with our statement in Belton that it "in no way alters the fundamental principles established in the Chimel case regarding the basic scope of searches incident to lawful custodial arrests." Accordingly, we reject this reading of Belton and hold that the Chimel rationale authorizes police to search a vehicle incident to a recent occupant's arrest only when the arrestee is unsecured and within reaching distance of the passenger compartment at the time of the search.[4]

Although it does not follow from Chimel, we also conclude that circumstances unique to the vehicle context justify a search incident to a lawful arrest when it is reasonable to believe evidence relevant to the crime of arrest might be found in the vehicle. In many cases, as when a recent occupant is arrested for a traffic violation, there will be no reasonable basis to believe the vehicle contains relevant evidence. But in others, including Belton, the offense of arrest will supply a basis for searching the passenger compartment of an arrestee's vehicle and any containers therein.

Neither the possibility of access nor the likelihood of discovering offense-related evidence authorized the search in this case. Unlike in Belton, which involved a single officer confronted with four unsecured arrestees, the five officers in this case outnumbered the three arrestees, all of whom had been handcuffed and secured in

---

[4] Because officers have many means of ensuring the safe arrest of vehicle occupants, it will be the rare case in which an officer is unable to fully effectuate an arrest so that a real possibility of access to the arrestee's vehicle remains. Cf. 3 W. LaFave, Search and Seizure §7.1(c) (noting that the availability of protective measures "ensures the nonexistence of circumstances in which the arrestee's 'control' of the car is in doubt"). But in such a case a search incident to arrest is reasonable under the Fourth Amendment.

separate patrol cars before the officers searched Gant's car. Under those circumstances, Gant clearly was not within reaching distance of his car at the time of the search. An evidentiary basis for the search was also lacking in this case.... Gant was arrested for driving with a suspended license—an offense for which police could not expect to find evidence in the passenger compartment of Gant's car. Because police could not reasonably have believed either that Gant could have accessed his car at the time of the search or that evidence of the offense for which he was arrested might have been found therein, the search in this case was unreasonable....

E. THE VEHICLE EXCEPTION

Automobiles have been on the road in the United States for over one-hundred years. During prohibition, *Carroll v. United States* (1925) upheld a warrantless car search for bootlegged liquor, creating the "vehicle exception." The Supreme Court in *Maryland v. Dyson* (1999) explained the exception as follows:

> "The Fourth Amendment generally requires police to secure a warrant before conducting a search. As we recognized nearly 75 years ago ..., there is an exception to this requirement for searches of vehicles. And under our established precedent, the 'automobile exception' has no separate exigency requirement...: If a car is readily mobile and probable cause exists to believe it contains contraband, the Fourth Amendment ... permits police to search the vehicle without more."

1.   WARRANTLESS CAR SEARCHES

CALIFORNIA v. CARNEY
471 U.S. 386 (1985)

Chief Justice BURGER delivered the opinion of the Court.

I

On May 31, 1979, Drug Enforcement Agency Agent Robert Williams watched respondent, Charles Carney, approach a youth in downtown San Diego. The youth accompanied Carney to a Dodge Mini Motor Home parked in a nearby lot. Carney and the youth closed the window shades in the motor home, including one across the front window. Agent Williams had previously received uncorroborated information that the same motor home was used by another person who was exchanging marihuana for sex. Williams, with assistance from other agents, kept the motor home

1978 Dodge/Midas Motor Home

under surveillance for the entire one and one-quarter hours that Carney and the youth remained inside. When the youth left the motor home, the agents followed and stopped him. The youth told the agents that he had received marijuana in return for allowing Carney sexual contacts.

At the agents' request, the youth returned to the motor home and knocked on its door; Carney stepped out. The agents identified themselves as law enforcement officers. Without a warrant or consent, one agent entered the motor home and observed marihuana, plastic bags, and a scale of the kind used in weighing drugs on a table. Agent Williams took Carney into custody and took possession of the motor home. A subsequent search of the motor home at the police station revealed additional marihuana in the cupboards and refrigerator.

Respondent was charged with possession of marihuana for sale … pleaded nolo contendere to the charges against him, and was placed on probation for three years.

II

The Fourth Amendment protects the "right of the people to be secure in their persons, houses, papers, and effects, against unreasonable searches and seizures."

This fundamental right is preserved by a requirement that searches be conducted pursuant to a warrant issued by an independent judicial officer. There are, of course, exceptions to the general rule that a warrant must be secured before a search is undertaken; one is the so-called "automobile exception" at issue in this case. This exception to the warrant requirement was first set forth by the Court 60 years ago in Carroll v. United States (1925). There, the Court recognized that the privacy interests in an automobile are constitutionally protected; however, it held that the ready mobility of the automobile justifies a lesser degree of protection of those interests. The Court rested this exception on a long-recognized distinction between stationary structures and vehicles:

> "The guaranty of freedom from unreasonable searches and seizures by the Fourth Amendment has been construed, practically since the beginning of Government, as recognizing a necessary difference between a search of a store, dwelling house or other structure in respect of which a proper official warrant readily may be obtained, and a search of a ship, motor boat, wagon or automobile, for contraband goods, where it is not practicable to secure a warrant because the vehicle can be quickly moved out of the locality or jurisdiction in which the warrant must be sought."

…. Our cases have consistently recognized ready mobility as one of the principal bases of the automobile exception…. However, although ready mobility alone was perhaps the original justification for the vehicle exception, our later cases have made clear that ready mobility is not the only basis for the exception. The reasons for the vehicle exception, we have said, are twofold. "Besides the element of mobility, less rigorous warrant requirements govern because the expectation of privacy with respect to one's automobile is significantly less than that relating to one's home or office."…

These reduced expectations of privacy derive not from the fact that the area to be searched is in plain view, but from the pervasive regulation of vehicles capable of traveling on the public highways. As we explained in South Dakota v. Opperman (1976), an inventory search case:

> "Automobiles, unlike homes, are subjected to pervasive and continuing governmental regulation and controls, including periodic inspection and licensing requirements. As an everyday occurrence,

police stop and examine vehicles when license plates or inspection stickers have expired, or if other violations, such as exhaust fumes or excessive noise, are noted, or if headlights or other safety equipment are not in proper working order."

The public is fully aware that it is accorded less privacy in its automobiles because of this compelling governmental need for regulation. Historically, individuals always have been on notice that movable vessels may be stopped and searched on facts giving rise to probable cause that the vehicle contains contraband, without the protection afforded by a magistrate's prior evaluation of those facts. In short, the pervasive schemes of regulation, which necessarily lead to reduced expectations of privacy, and the exigencies attendant to ready mobility justify searches without prior recourse to the authority of a magistrate so long as the overriding standard of probable cause is met.

When a vehicle is being used on the highways, or if it is readily capable of such use and is found stationary in a place not regularly used for residential purposes – temporary or otherwise – the two justifications for the vehicle exception come into play. First, the vehicle is obviously readily mobile by the turn of an ignition key, if not actually moving. Second, there is a reduced expectation of privacy stemming from its use as a licensed motor vehicle subject to a range of police regulation inapplicable to a fixed dwelling. At least in these circumstances, the overriding societal interests in effective law enforcement justify an immediate search before the vehicle and its occupants become unavailable.

While it is true that respondent's vehicle possessed some, if not many of the attributes of a home, it is equally clear that the vehicle falls clearly within the scope of the exception laid down in Carroll and applied in succeeding cases. Like the automobile in Carroll, respondent's motor home was readily mobile. Absent the prompt search and seizure, it could readily have been moved beyond the reach of the police. Furthermore, the vehicle was licensed to operate on public streets; was serviced in public places; and was subject to extensive regulation and inspection. And the vehicle was so situated that an objective observer would conclude that it was being used not as a residence, but as a vehicle.

Respondent urges us to distinguish his vehicle from other vehicles within the exception because it was capable of functioning as a home. In our increasingly mobile society, many vehicles used for transportation can be and are being used not only for transportation but for shelter, i.e., as a "home" or "residence." To distinguish between respondent's motor home and an ordinary sedan for purposes of the vehicle exception would require that we apply the exception depending upon the size of the vehicle and the quality of its appointments. Moreover, to fail to apply the exception to vehicles such as a motor home ignores the fact that a motor home lends itself easily to use as an instrument of illicit drug traffic and other illegal activity. In United States v. Ross (1982), we declined to distinguish between "worthy" and "unworthy" containers, noting that "the central purpose of the Fourth Amendment forecloses such a distinction." We decline today to distinguish between "worthy" and "unworthy" vehicles which are either on the public roads and highways, or situated such that it is reasonable to conclude that the vehicle is not being used as a residence.

Our application of the vehicle exception has never turned on the other uses to which a vehicle might be put. The exception has historically turned on the ready mobility of the vehicle, and on the presence of the vehicle in a setting that objectively indicates that the vehicle is being used for transportation. These two requirements for application of the exception ensure that law enforcement officials are not unnecessarily hamstrung in their efforts to detect and prosecute criminal activity, and that the legitimate privacy interests of the public are protected. Applying the vehicle exception in these circumstances allows the essential purposes served by the exception to be fulfilled, while assuring that the exception will acknowledge legitimate privacy interests.

III

The question remains whether, apart from the lack of a warrant, this search was unreasonable. Under the vehicle exception to the warrant requirement, only the prior approval of the magistrate is waived; the search otherwise must be such as the magistrate could authorize. This search was not unreasonable; it was plainly one that the magistrate could authorize if presented with these facts. The DEA agents had fresh, direct, uncontradicted evidence that the respondent was distributing a controlled substance from the vehicle, apart from evidence of other possible offenses. The agents thus had abundant probable cause to enter and search the vehicle for evidence of a crime notwithstanding its possible use as a dwelling place.

Here is the language from *United States v. Ross* (1982) that the *Carney* opinion references as refusing to draw "a constitutional distinction between 'worthy' and 'unworthy' containers."

> "Even though such a distinction perhaps could evolve in a series of cases in which paper bags, locked trunks, lunch buckets, and orange crates were placed on one side of the line or the other, the central purpose of the Fourth Amendment forecloses such a distinction. For just as the most frail cottage in the kingdom is absolutely entitled to the same guarantees of privacy as the most majestic mansion, so also may a traveler who carries a toothbrush and a few articles of clothing in a paper bag or knotted scarf claim an equal right to conceal his possessions from official inspection as the sophisticated executive with the locked attaché case."

The Supreme Court loosely construes the permissible timing for a vehicle search. The following excerpt from a law review article explains that police can take hours or even days to search a vehicle and still need not get a warrant.[20]

❝The Court has upheld warrantless searches hours and even days after a vehicle was moved to the station. In *Florida v. Meyers* (1984), police searched a vehicle on the scene of an arrest and then towed the vehicle to the station. Eight hours later, a police officer went to the impound lot and searched the vehicle again and found incriminating evidence. The Court [upheld the search].

A year after *Meyers*, the Court went even further in giving police time to conduct a warrantless search under the automobile exception. In *United States v. Johns*, the Court addressed whether police could search packages without a warrant three days after they had been removed from a vehicle. The DEA had seized pickup trucks from a desert airstrip and brought them back to the DEA headquarters. The agents removed packages from the trucks and placed them in the DEA warehouse. The agents then immediately searched some of the packages, but waited three days before searching the other packages. At no point did the agents procure a warrant. The Supreme Court upheld the warrantless searches under the automobile exception, even though they occurred three days after the vehicle was impounded. The Court explained that there is simply no contemporaneousness requirement for

---

[20] Gershowitz, The Tesla Meets the Fourth Amendment, 48 BYU L. REV. (2023).

the automobile exception the way that there is for the search incident to arrest exception:

> "Our previous decisions indicate that the officers acted permissibly by waiting until they returned to DEA headquarters before they searched the vehicles and removed their contents. There is no requirement that the warrantless search of a vehicle occur contemporaneously with its lawful seizure. The justification to conduct such a warrantless search does not vanish once the car has been immobilized. A vehicle lawfully in police custody may be searched on the basis of probable cause to believe that it contains contraband, and there is no requirement of exigent circumstances to justify such a warrantless search."

The *Johns* Court did recognize that at some point a warrantless search would no longer be reasonable under the automobile exception. The Court noted that "[w]e do not suggest that police officers may indefinitely retain possession of a vehicle and its contents before they complete a vehicle search." And the Court further remarked "[n]or do we foreclose the possibility that the owner of a vehicle or its contents might attempt to prove that delay in the completion of a vehicle search was unreasonable because it adversely affected a privacy or possessory interest." Accordingly, it is clear that there are some temporal restrictions on when police can search a vehicle without a warrant. If police had no plausible basis to continue holding onto a vehicle, it seems quite possible that retaining the vehicle and conducting a warrantless search days after the seizure would be unconstitutional. But when police have probable cause to believe a vehicle contains evidence, the *Meyers* and *Johns* cases suggest that police can take their time in conducting a warrantless search.

See also *California v. Acevedo* (1991) ("If the police have probable cause to justify a warrantless seizure of an automobile on a public roadway, they may conduct either an immediate or a delayed search of the vehicle.").

In *Collins v. Virginia* (2018), the Supreme Court emphasized that "the automobile exception extends no further than the automobile itself." Virginia had argued that the exception permitted a police officer to enter the curtilage of a home to search a motorcycle. The Supreme Court disagreed, explaining:

> "Just as an officer must have a lawful right of access to any contraband he discovers in plain view in order to seize it without a warrant, and just as an officer must have a lawful right of access in order to arrest a person

in his home, so, too, an officer must have a lawful right of access to a vehicle in order to search it pursuant to the automobile exception. The automobile exception does not afford the necessary lawful right of access to search a vehicle parked within a home or its curtilage because it does not justify an intrusion on a person's separate and substantial Fourth Amendment interest in his home and curtilage."

2. CONTAINERS IN VEHICLES

When police officers search vehicles they often find closed containers. Crafting a clear rule for searching containers in cars vexed the Supreme Court for decades. The Court finally simplified the analysis in the following case.

CALIFORNIA v. ACEVEDO
500 U.S. 565 (1991)

Justice BLACKMUN delivered the opinion of the Court.

I

.... On October 28, 1987, Officer Coleman of the Santa Ana, Cal., Police Department received a telephone call from a federal drug enforcement agent in Hawaii. The agent informed Coleman that he had seized a package containing marijuana which was to have been delivered to the Federal Express Office in Santa Ana and which was addressed to J.R. Daza at 805 West Stevens Avenue in that city. The agent arranged to send the package to Coleman instead. Coleman then was to take the package to the Federal Express office and arrest the person who arrived to claim it.

Coleman received the package on October 29, verified its contents, and took it to the Senior Operations Manager at the Federal Express office. At about 10:30 a.m. on October 30, a man, who identified himself as Jamie Daza, arrived to claim the package. He accepted it and drove to his apartment on West Stevens. He carried the package into the apartment.

At 11:45 a.m., officers observed Daza leave the apartment and drop the box and paper that had contained the marijuana into a trash bin. Coleman at that point left the scene to get a search warrant. About 12:05 p.m., the officers saw Richard St. George leave the apartment carrying a blue knapsack which appeared to be half full. The officers stopped him as he was driving off, searched the knapsack, and found 1.5 pounds of marijuana.

At 12:30 p.m., respondent Charles Acevedo arrived. He entered Daza's apartment, stayed for about 10 minutes, and reappeared carrying a brown paper bag that looked full. The officers noticed that the bag was the size of one of the wrapped marijuana packages sent from Hawaii. Acevedo walked to a silver Honda in the parking lot. He placed the bag in the trunk of the car and started to drive away. Fearing the loss of evidence, officers in a marked police car stopped him. They opened the trunk and the bag, and found marijuana.

The California Court of Appeal concluded that the marijuana found in the paper bag in the car's trunk should have been suppressed. The court concluded that the officers had probable cause to believe that the paper bag contained drugs but lacked probable cause to suspect that Acevedo's car, itself, otherwise contained contraband. Because the officers' probable cause was directed specifically at the bag, the court held that the case was controlled by United States v. Chadwick (1977), rather than by United States v. Ross (1982). Although the court agreed that the officers could seize the paper bag, it held that, under Chadwick, they could not open the bag without first obtaining a warrant for that purpose. The court then recognized "the anomalous nature" of the dichotomy between the rule in Chadwick and the rule in Ross. That dichotomy dictates that if there is probable cause to search a car, then the entire car-including any closed container found therein-may be searched without a warrant, but if there is probable cause only as to a container in the car, the container may be held but not searched until a warrant is obtained.

…. We granted certiorari to reexamine the law applicable to a closed container in an automobile, a subject that has troubled courts and law enforcement officers since it was first considered in Chadwick.

II

In United States v. Ross, we held that a warrantless search of an automobile under the Carroll doctrine could include a search of a container or package found inside the car when such a search was supported by probable cause. The warrantless search of Ross' car occurred after an informant told the police that he had seen Ross complete a drug transaction using drugs stored in the trunk of his car. The police stopped the car, searched it, and discovered in the trunk a brown paper bag containing drugs. We decided that the search of Ross' car was not unreasonable under the Fourth Amendment: "The scope of a warrantless search based on probable cause is no narrower-and no broader-than the scope of a search authorized by a warrant supported by probable cause." Thus, "if probable cause justifies the search of a lawfully stopped vehicle, it justifies the search of every part of the vehicle and its contents that may conceal the object of the search." In Ross, therefore, we clarified the scope of the Carroll doctrine as properly including a "probing search" of compartments and containers within the automobile so long as the search is supported by probable cause.

In addition to this clarification, Ross distinguished the Carroll doctrine from the separate rule that governed the search of closed containers. The Court had announced this separate rule, unique to luggage and other closed packages, bags, and containers, in United States v. Chadwick (1977). In Chadwick, federal narcotics agents had probable cause to believe that a 200-pound double-locked footlocker contained marijuana. The agents tracked the locker as the defendants removed it from a train and carried it through the station to a waiting car. As soon as the defendants lifted the locker into the trunk of the car, the agents arrested them, seized the locker, and searched it. In this Court, the United States did not contend that the locker's brief contact with the automobile's trunk sufficed to make the Carroll doctrine applicable. Rather, the United States urged that the search of movable luggage could be considered analogous to the search of an automobile. The Court rejected this argument because, it reasoned, a person expects more privacy in his luggage and personal effects than he does in his automobile. Moreover, it concluded that as "may often not be the case when automobiles are seized," secure storage facilities are usually available when the police seize luggage.

In Arkansas v. Sanders (1979), the Court extended Chadwick's rule to apply to a suitcase actually being transported in the trunk of a car. In Sanders, the police had probable cause to believe a suitcase contained marijuana. They watched as the defendant placed the suitcase in the trunk of a taxi and was driven away. The police pursued the taxi for several blocks, stopped it, found the suitcase in the trunk, and searched it. Although the Court had applied the Carroll doctrine to searches of integral parts of the automobile itself, (indeed, in Carroll, contraband whiskey was in the upholstery of the seats), it did not extend the doctrine to the warrantless search of personal luggage "merely because it was located in an automobile lawfully stopped by the police." Again, the Sanders majority stressed the heightened privacy expectation in personal luggage and concluded that the presence of luggage in an automobile did not diminish the owner's expectation of privacy in his personal items.

In Ross, the Court endeavored to distinguish between Carroll, which governed the Ross automobile search, and Chadwick, which governed the Sanders automobile search. It held that the Carroll doctrine covered searches of automobiles when the police had probable cause to search an entire vehicle, but that the Chadwick doctrine governed searches of luggage when the officers had probable cause to search only a container within the vehicle. Thus, in a Ross situation, the police could conduct a reasonable search under the Fourth Amendment without obtaining a warrant, whereas in a Sanders situation, the police had to obtain a warrant before they searched....

IV

Dissenters in Ross asked why the suitcase in Sanders was "more private, less difficult for police to seize and store, or in any other relevant respect more properly subject to the warrant requirement, than a container that police discover in a probable-cause search of an entire automobile?" We now agree that a container found after a general search of the automobile and a container found in a car after a limited search for the container are equally easy for the police to store and for the suspect to hide or destroy. In fact, we see no principled distinction in terms of either the privacy expectation or the exigent circumstances between the paper bag found by the police in Ross and the paper bag found by the police here. Furthermore, by attempting to distinguish between a container for which the police are specifically searching and a container which they come across in a car, we have provided only minimal protection for privacy and have impeded effective law enforcement....

We conclude that it is better to adopt one clear-cut rule to govern automobile searches and eliminate the warrant requirement for closed containers set forth in Sanders.

The interpretation of the Carroll doctrine set forth in Ross now applies to all searches of containers found in an automobile. In other words, the police may search without a warrant if their search is supported by probable cause. The Court in Ross put it this way: "The scope of a warrantless search of an automobile is not defined by the nature of the container in which the contraband is secreted. Rather, it is defined by the object of the search and the places in which there is probable cause to believe that it may be found." It went on to note: "Probable cause to believe that a container placed in the trunk of a taxi contains contraband or evidence does not justify a search of the entire cab." We reaffirm that principle. In the case before us, the police had probable cause to believe that the paper bag in the automobile's trunk contained marijuana. That probable cause now allows a warrantless search of the paper bag. The facts in the record reveal that the police did not have probable cause to believe that contraband was hidden in any other part of the automobile and a search of the entire vehicle would have been without probable cause and unreasonable under the Fourth Amendment.

…. Until today, this Court has drawn a curious line between the search of an automobile that coincidentally turns up a container and the search of a container that coincidentally turns up in an automobile. The protections of the Fourth Amendment must not turn on such coincidences. We therefore interpret Carroll as providing one rule to govern all automobile searches. The police may search an automobile and the containers within it where they have probable cause to believe contraband or evidence is contained.

3. SCOPE

A search of a car under the vehicle exception most commonly involves a search of the passenger compartment and the trunk. As *Acevdeo* explained, police are also permitted to open containers when searching these areas. Keep in mind that for any of these actions, however, the police still must have probable cause to believe that evidence will be found in any area they search. The vehicle exception only eliminates the need for a warrant.

STATE v. WILLIAMS
462 So.2d 69 (Fla. App. 1985)

Mills, Judge

The State appeals from the trial court's order granting Vanessa Williams' motion to suppress evidence found after a search of the glove compartment of Williams' car. We affirm.

Williams was identified to the police by a confidential informant as the girlfriend of a cocaine supplier from whom the informant had obtained cocaine. The informant told police that the cocaine was kept in the supplier's apartment in a safe, which had been previously opened in the presence of both the informant and Williams, and appeared to contain cocaine.

Following their receipt of this information, the police set up a surveillance of the apartment. During the surveillance, the officer on duty observed Williams pull into the apartment parking lot in a car which had been described by the informant as belonging to her. After scanning the lot, Williams and a companion entered the apartment and emerged with a "brown box-like object" and a paper sack. Both items were placed in the car trunk, which was then shut. Williams re-entered the car and drove from the lot.

The surveillance vehicle followed her, and it became apparent from the evasiveness with which Williams drove that she was aware of the "tail." At this point, the driver of the surveillance vehicle, who had remained in radio contact with officers at the State Attorney's Office, was advised by those officers to stop and search Williams' car.

The car was blocked into a parking space by police vehicles. There is conflict over whether Williams next voluntarily opened the trunk or was forced to do so; in any case, the trunk was opened and a locked safe observed therein. Williams, who had not been placed under formal arrest at this time, was ordered to open the safe but could not do so. The contents of the safe therefore remained unknown to the police until it was later searched with a warrant at the police station.

Following the discovery of the safe, Williams still was not placed under formal arrest. The officers nevertheless proceeded to search the interior of the vehicle. Upon opening the glove compartment, the officers found small quantities of cocaine and marijuana. Williams was then placed under arrest on charges of possession of cocaine and cannabis.

She later moved to suppress both the evidence found in the trunk and that in the glove compartment. The trial court denied the motion as to the evidence from the trunk, and the propriety of that ruling is not before us. The motion was granted, however, as to the contraband found in the glove compartment, on the grounds that Williams was not under arrest at the time of the search nor was there any other exception to the warrant requirement justifying the search. It is from this latter ruling that the State appeals.

The State urges . . . reversal of the trial court's order [arguing] . . . that if probable cause justifies the search of a lawfully stopped vehicle, it justifies the search of every part of the vehicle and its contents that may conceal the object of the search. . . .

. . . Assuming without deciding that the police did have the requisite probable cause to stop Williams' car, the probable cause they had was to believe that a container placed in the car trunk contained the contraband, not that it was concealed somewhere in the vehicle. . . .

. . . The box was placed in the trunk, which was then shut. The police never lost sight of the car thereafter until the stop. Therefore, the trunk could not have been reopened and the safe's contents secreted elsewhere in the vehicle. . . . [As the Supreme Court in United States v. Ross explained:]

> The scope of a warrantless search of an automobile is defined by the object of the search and the place in which there is probable cause to believe that it may be found. Just as probable cause to believe that a stolen lawnmower may be found in a garage will not support a warrant to search an upstairs bedroom, probable cause to believe that undocumented aliens are being transported in a van will not justify a warrantless search of a suitcase. *Probable cause to believe that a container placed in the trunk of a vehicle contains contraband does not justify a search of the entire vehicle.*

Because police had probable cause only to search the container in the trunk of the car, that probable cause did not extend to the entire vehicle, and we therefore find that *Ross* cannot justify the search herein. . . .

Another "scope" problem arises with respect to passengers' belongings. In *Wyoming v. Houghton* (1999), police lawfully stopped a vehicle and saw that the driver had a syringe in his shirt pocket. When the officer asked what the syringe was for, the driver admitted that he used it to take drugs. This, the parties conceded, gave the officer probable cause to search the car for drugs. There was a purse on the back seat of the car that the officer determined belonged to a passenger. The officer then searched the purse and found methamphetamine inside. The Supreme Court rejected the passenger-Houghton's effort to suppress the evidence, explaining that:

> "When there is probable cause to search for contraband in a car, it is reasonable for police officers-like customs officials in the founding era-to examine packages and containers without a showing of individualized probable cause for each one. A passenger's personal belongings, just like the driver's belongings or containers attached to the car like a glove compartment, are 'in' the car, and the officer has probable cause to search for contraband *in* the car."

Courts have long upheld searches inside upholstery, gas tanks, engine blocks, beneath the floor board, and in other internal parts of the vehicle. Often these cases involves searches for drugs. As the Seventh Circuit has explained, "[u]nder the automobile exception . . . *all* parts of a vehicle may be searched without a warrant if there is probable cause to believe the car contains contraband or evidence." United States v. Patterson (7th Cir. 1995) (emphasis added).

F. INVENTORY SEARCHES

In addition to searching an arrestee, the government may conduct an additional search incident to jailing an arrested person.

> "It is not 'unreasonable' for police, as part of the routine procedure incident to incarcerating an arrested person, to search any container or article in his possession, in accordance with established inventory procedures." *Illinois v. Lafayette* (1983)

The Supreme Court later elaborated on permissible inventory searches in the context of impounded vehicles:

FLORIDA v. WELLS
495 U.S. 1 (1990)

Chief Justice REHNQUIST delivered the opinion of the Court.

A Florida Highway Patrol trooper stopped respondent Martin Wells for speeding. After smelling alcohol on Wells' breath, the trooper arrested Wells for driving under the influence. Wells then agreed to accompany the trooper to the station to take a breathalyzer test. The trooper informed Wells that the car would be impounded and obtained Wells' permission to open the trunk. At the impoundment facility, an inventory search of the car turned up two marijuana cigarette butts in an ashtray and a locked suitcase in the trunk. Under the trooper's direction, employees of the facility forced open the suitcase and discovered a garbage bag containing a considerable amount of marijuana.

The Supreme Court of Florida relied on the opinions in Colorado v. Bertine (1987) [to conclude that the search violated the Fourth Amendment]. Referring to language in the Bertine concurrence and a footnote in the majority opinion, the court held that "in the absence of a policy specifically requiring the opening of closed containers found during a legitimate inventory search, Bertine prohibits us from countenancing the procedure followed in this instance."… The court added: "The police under Bertine must mandate either that all containers will be opened during an inventory search, or that no containers will be opened. There can be no room for discretion."

While this latter statement of the Supreme Court of Florida derived support from a sentence in the Bertine concurrence taken in isolation, we think it is at odds with the thrust of both the concurrence and the opinion of the Court in that case. We said in Bertine: "Nothing in [our case law] prohibits the exercise of police discretion so long as that discretion is exercised according to standard criteria and on the basis of something other than suspicion of evidence of criminal activity."

Our view that standardized criteria, or established routine must regulate the opening of containers found during inventory searches is based on the principle that an inventory search must not be a ruse for a general rummaging in order to discover incriminating evidence. The policy or practice governing inventory searches should be designed to produce an inventory. The individual police officer must not be allowed so much latitude that inventory searches are turned into a purposeful and general means of discovering evidence of crime.

But in forbidding uncanalized discretion to police officers conducting inventory searches, there is no reason to insist that they be conducted in a totally mechanical "all or nothing" fashion. Inventory procedures serve to protect an owner's property while it is in the custody of the police, to insure against claims of lost, stolen, or vandalized property, and to guard the police from danger. A police officer may be allowed sufficient latitude to determine whether a particular container should or should not be opened in light of the nature of the search and characteristics of the container itself. Thus, while policies of opening all containers or of opening no containers are unquestionably permissible, it would be equally permissible, for example, to allow the opening of closed containers whose contents officers determine they are unable to ascertain from examining the containers' exteriors. The allowance of the exercise of judgment based on concerns related to the purposes of an inventory search does not violate the Fourth Amendment.

In the present case, the Supreme Court of Florida found that the Florida Highway Patrol had no policy whatever with respect to the opening of closed containers encountered during an inventory search. We hold that absent such a policy, the instant search was not sufficiently regulated to satisfy the Fourth Amendment and that the marijuana which was found in the suitcase, therefore, was properly suppressed by the Supreme Court of Florida. Its judgment is therefore affirmed.

The Supreme Court has not addressed the authority of the police to impound a vehicle, but such authority is regularly recognized in statutes and lower court rulings when the vehicle cannot be left unattended. For example, Virginia Code § 19.2-80.1 states,

> "In any case in which a police officer arrests the operator of a motor vehicle and there is no legal cause for the retention of the motor vehicle by the officer, the officer shall allow the person arrested to designate another person who is present at the scene of the arrest and a licensed driver to drive the motor vehicle from the scene to a place designated by the person arrested. If such a designation is not made, the officer may cause the vehicle to be taken to the nearest appropriate place for safekeeping."

G. SEARCHES BASED ON CONSENT

Consent is one of the most invoked exceptions to the warrant requirement. See National Center for State Courts, The Search Warrant Process, 1985 (concluding, based on comprehensive empirical study and interviews with police, that: "The vast majority of searches are conducted without a warrant, usually with the consent of the suspect (or someone in legal control of the area to be searched) or incident to the arrest of the suspect."); BJS, Police Contacts between Police and Public, 2008 (reporting that with respect to traffic stops, "50.8% of searches of both the driver and vehicle were conducted with consent"). This section explores the test for whether consent has been validly given; who is authorized to give that consent; how far the police can go in searching based on consent – i.e., the "scope" of consent; and revoking consent.

1. VOLUNTARINESS OF CONSENT

SCHNECKLOTH v. BUSTAMONTE
412 U.S. 218 (1973)

Justice STEWART delivered the opinion of the Court.

It is well settled under the Fourth and Fourteenth Amendments that a search conducted without a warrant issued upon probable cause is 'per se unreasonable ... subject only to a few specifically established and well-delineated exceptions.' It is equally well settled that one of the specifically established exceptions to the requirements of both a warrant and probable cause is a search that is conducted pursuant to consent. The constitutional question in the present case concerns the definition of 'consent' in this Fourth and Fourteenth Amendment context.

I

The respondent was brought to trial in a California court upon a charge of possessing a check with intent to defraud. He moved to suppress the introduction of certain material as evidence against him on the ground that the material had been acquired through an unconstitutional search and seizure. In response to the motion, the trial judge conducted an evidentiary hearing where it was established that the material in question had been acquired by the State under the following circumstances:

While on routine patrol in Sunnyvale, California, at approximately 2:40 in the morning, Police Officer James Rand stopped an automobile when he observed that one headlight and its license plate light were burned out. Six men were in the vehicle. Joe Alcala and the respondent, Robert Bustamonte, were in the front seat with Joe Gonzales, the driver. Three older men were seated in the rear. When, in response to the policeman's question, Gonzales could not produce a driver's license, Officer Rand asked if any of the other five had any evidence of identification. Only Alcala produced a license, and he explained that the car was his brother's. After the six occupants had stepped out of the car at the officer's request and after two additional policemen had arrived, Officer Rand asked Alcala if he could search the car. Alcala replied, 'Sure, go ahead.' Prior to the search no one was threatened with arrest and, according to Officer Rand's uncontradicted testimony, it 'was all very congenial at this time.' Gonzales testified that Alcala actually helped in the search of the car, by opening the trunk and glove compartment. In Gonzales' words: 'The police officer asked Joe Alcala, he goes, 'Does the trunk open?' And Joe said, 'Yes.' He went to the car and got the keys and opened up the trunk.' Wadded up under the left rear seat, the police officers found three checks that had previously been stolen from a car wash.

The trial judge denied the motion to suppress, and the checks in question were admitted in evidence at Bustamonte's trial. On the basis of this and other evidence he was convicted. [The California courts affirmed the conviction. Bustamonte then sought a writ of habeas corpus in a federal district court which was denied. On appeal, the Court of Appeals for the Ninth Circuit set aside the district court's order. The Court of Appeals] reasoned that a consent was a waiver of a person's Fourth and Fourteenth Amendment rights, and that the State was under an obligation to demonstrate, not only that the consent had been uncoerced, but that it had been given with an understanding that it could be freely and effectively withhold. Consent could not be found, the court held, solely from the absence of coercion and a verbal expression of assent. Since the District Court had not determined that Alcala had known that his consent could have been withheld and that he could have refused to have his vehicle searched, the Court of Appeals vacated the order denying the writ and remanded the case for further proceedings. We granted certiorari to determine whether the Fourth and Fourteenth Amendments require the showing thought necessary by the Court of Appeals.

II

.... The State concedes that 'when a prosecutor seeks to rely upon consent to justify the lawfulness of a search, he has the burden of proving that the consent was, in fact, freely and voluntarily given.' The precise question in this case, then, is what must the prosecution prove to demonstrate that a consent was 'voluntarily' given. And upon that question there is a square conflict of views between the state and federal courts that have reviewed the search involved in the case before us. The Court of Appeals for the Ninth Circuit concluded that it is an essential part of the State's initial burden to prove that a person knows he has a right to refuse consent.

The California courts have followed the rule that voluntariness is a question of fact to be determined from the totality of all the circumstances, and that the state of a defendant's knowledge is only one factor to be taken into account in assessing the voluntariness of a consent.

A

The most extensive judicial exposition of the meaning of 'voluntariness' has been developed in those cases in which the Court has had to determine the 'voluntariness' of a defendant's confession for purposes of the Fourteenth Amendment…. Those cases yield no talismanic definition of 'voluntariness,' mechanically applicable to the host of situations where the question has arisen. 'The notion of 'voluntariness,' Justice Frankfurter once wrote, 'is itself an amphibian.' It cannot be taken literally to mean a 'knowing' choice. 'Except where a person is unconscious or drugged or otherwise lacks capacity for conscious choice, all incriminating statements—even those made under brutal treatment—are 'voluntary' in the sense of representing a choice of alternatives. On the other hand, if 'voluntariness' incorporates notions of 'but for' cause, the question should be whether the statement would have been made even absent inquiry or other official action. Under such a test, virtually no statement would be voluntary because very few people give incriminating statements in the absence of official action of some kind.' It is thus evident that neither linguistics nor epistemology will provide a ready definition of the meaning of 'voluntariness.'

Rather, 'voluntariness' has reflected an accommodation of the complex of values implicated in police questioning of a suspect. At one end of the spectrum is the acknowledged need for police questioning as a tool for the effective enforcement of criminal laws…. At the other end of the spectrum is the set of values reflecting society's deeply felt belief that the criminal law cannot be used as an instrument of unfairness, and that the possibility of unfair and even brutal police tactics poses a real and serious threat to civilized notions of justice….

This Court's decisions reflect a frank recognition that the Constitution requires the sacrifice of neither security nor liberty. The Due Process Clause does not mandate that the police forgo all questioning, or that they be given carte blanche to extract what they can from a suspect. 'The ultimate test remains that which has been the only clearly established test in Anglo-American courts for two hundred years: the test of voluntariness. Is the confession the product of an essentially free and unconstrained choice by its maker? If it is, if he has willed to confess, it may be used against him. If it is not, if his will has been overborne and his capacity for self-determination critically impaired, the use of his confession offends due process.'

In determining whether a defendant's will was overborne in a particular case, the Court has assessed the totality of all the surrounding circumstances—both the characteristics of the accused and the details of the interrogation. Some of the factors taken into account have included the youth of the accused; his lack of education; or his low intelligence; the lack of any advice to the accused of his constitutional rights; the length of detention; the repeated and prolonged nature of the questioning; and the use of physical punishment such as the deprivation of food or sleep....

B

Similar considerations lead us to agree with the courts of California that the question whether a consent to a search was in fact 'voluntary' or was the product of duress or coercion, express or implied, is a question of fact to be determined from the totality of all the circumstances. While knowledge of the right to refuse consent is one factor to be taken into account, the government need not establish such knowledge as the sine qua non of an effective consent. As with police questioning, two competing concerns must be accommodated in determining the meaning of a 'voluntary' consent—the legitimate need for such searches and the equally important requirement of assuring the absence of coercion.

In situations where the police have some evidence of illicit activity, but lack probable cause to arrest or search, a search authorized by a valid consent may be the only means of obtaining important and reliable evidence. In the present case for example, while the police had reason to stop the car for traffic violations, the State does not contend that there was probable cause to search the vehicle or that the search was incident to a valid arrest of any of the occupants. Yet, the search yielded tangible evidence that served as a basis for a prosecution, and provided some assurance that others, wholly innocent of the crime, were not mistakenly brought to trial. And in those cases where there is probable cause to arrest or search, but where the police lack a warrant, a consent search may still be valuable. If the search is conducted and proves fruitless, that in itself may convince the police that an arrest with its possible stigma and embarrassment is unnecessary, or that a far more extensive search pursuant to a warrant is not justified. In short, a search pursuant to consent may result in considerably less inconvenience for the subject of the search, and, properly conducted, is a constitutionally permissible and wholly legitimate aspect of effective police activity.

But the Fourth and Fourteenth Amendments require that a consent not be coerced, by explicit or implicit means, by implied threat or covert force…. In examining all the surrounding circumstances to determine if in fact the consent to search was coerced, account must be taken of subtly coercive police questions, as well as the possibly vulnerable subjective state of the person who consents. Those searches that are the product of police coercion can thus be filtered out without undermining the continuing validity of consent searches. In sum, there is no reason for us to depart in the area of consent searches, from the traditional definition of 'voluntariness.'

The approach of the Court of Appeals for the Ninth Circuit finds no support in any of our decisions that have attempted to define the meaning of 'voluntariness.' Its ruling, that the State must affirmatively prove that the subject of the search knew that he had a right to refuse consent, would, in practice, create serious doubt whether consent searches could continue to be conducted…. One alternative that would go far toward proving that the subject of a search did know he had a right to refuse consent would be to advise him of that right before eliciting his consent. That, however, is a suggestion that has been almost universally repudiated by both federal and state courts, and, we think, rightly so. For it would be thoroughly impractical to impose on the normal consent search the detailed requirements of an effective warning. Consent searches are part of the standard investigatory techniques of law enforcement agencies. They normally occur on the highway, or in a person's home or office, and under informal and unstructured conditions. The circumstances that prompt the initial request to search may develop quickly or be a logical extension of investigative police questioning. The police may seek to investigate further suspicious circumstances or to follow up leads developed in questioning persons at the scene of a crime. These situations are a far cry from the structured atmosphere of a trial where, assisted by counsel if he chooses, a defendant is informed of his trial rights. And, while surely a closer question, these situations are still immeasurably, far removed from 'custodial interrogation' where, in Miranda v. Arizona (1966), we found that the Constitution required certain now familiar warnings as a prerequisite to police interrogation….

Consequently, we cannot accept the position of the Court of Appeals in this case that proof of knowledge of the right to refuse consent is a necessary prerequisite to demonstrating a 'voluntary' consent. Rather it is only by analyzing all the circumstances of an individual consent that it can be ascertained whether in fact it was voluntary or coerced. It is this careful sifting of the unique facts and circumstances of each case that is evidenced in our prior decisions involving consent searches.

…. In short, neither this Court's prior cases, nor the traditional definition of 'voluntariness' requires proof of knowledge of a right to refuse as the sine qua non of an effective consent to a search….

D

Much of what has already been said disposes of the argument that the Court's decision in the Miranda case requires the conclusion that knowledge of a right to refuse is an indispensable element of a valid consent…. In Miranda the Court found that the techniques of police questioning and the nature of custodial surroundings produce an inherently coercive situation….

In this case, there is no evidence of any inherently coercive tactics—either from the nature of the police questioning or the environment in which it took place. Indeed, since consent searches will normally occur on a person's own familiar territory, the specter of incommunicado police interrogation in some remote station house is simply inapposite. There is no reason to believe, under circumstances such as are present here, that the response to a policeman's question is presumptively coerced; and there is, therefore, no reason to reject the traditional test for determining the voluntariness of a person's response. Miranda, of course, did not reach investigative questioning of a person not in custody, which is most directly analogous to the situation of a consent search, and it assuredly did not indicate that such questioning ought to be deemed inherently coercive.

It is also argued that the failure to require the Government to establish knowledge as a prerequisite to a valid consent, will relegate the Fourth Amendment to the special province of 'the sophisticated, knowledgeable and the privileged.' We cannot agree. The traditional definition of voluntariness we accept today has always taken into account evidence of minimal schooling, low intelligence, and the lack of any effective warnings to a person of his rights; and the voluntariness of any statement taken under those conditions has been carefully scrutinized to determine whether it was in fact voluntarily given.

E

Our decision today is a narrow one. We hold only that when the subject of a search is not in custody and the State attempts to justify a search on the basis of his consent, the Fourth and Fourteenth Amendments require that it demonstrate that the consent was in fact voluntarily given, and not the result of duress or coercion, express or implied. Voluntariness is a question of fact to be determined from all the circumstances, and while the subject's knowledge of a right to refuse is a factor to be taken into account, the prosecution is not required to demonstrate such knowledge as a prerequisite to establishing a voluntary consent. Because the California court followed these principles in affirming the respondent's conviction, and because the Court of Appeals for the Ninth Circuit in remanding for an evidentiary hearing required more, its judgment must be reversed.

Justice MARSHALL, dissenting.

…. If consent to search means that a person has chosen to forgo his right to exclude the police from the place they seek to search, it follows that his consent cannot be considered a meaningful choice unless he knew that he could in fact exclude the police. The Court appears, however, to reject even the modest proposition that, if the subject of a search convinces the trier of fact that he did not know of his right to refuse assent to a police request for permission to search, the search must be held unconstitutional. For it says only that 'knowledge of the right to refuse consent is one factor to be taken into account.' I find this incomprehensible. I can think of no other situation in which we would say that a person agreed to some course of action if he convinced us that he did not know that there was some other course he might have pursued. I would therefore hold, at a minimum, that the prosecution may not rely on a purported consent to search if the subject of the search did not know that he could refuse to give consent….

I must conclude with some reluctance that when the Court speaks of practicality, what it really is talking of is the continued ability of the police to capitalize on the ignorance of citizens so as to accomplish by subterfuge what they could not achieve by relying only on the knowing relinquishment of constitutional rights. Of course it would be 'practical' for the police to ignore the commands of the Fourth Amendment, if by practicality we mean that more criminals will be apprehended, even though the constitutional rights of innocent people also go by the board. But such a practical advantage is achieved only at the cost of permitting the police to disregard the limitations that the Constitution places on their behavior, a cost that a constitutional democracy cannot long absorb....

In *Ohio v. Robinette* (1996), the Supreme Court considered an Ohio court's conclusion that a request for consent to search must be "preceded by the phrase 'At this time you legally are free to go' or by words of similar import." The Supreme Court concluded:

> We have previously rejected a per se rule very similar to that adopted by the Supreme Court of Ohio in determining the validity of a consent to search. In Schneckloth v. Bustamonte (1973), it was argued that such a consent could not be valid unless the defendant knew that he had a right to refuse the request. We rejected this argument: "While knowledge of the right to refuse consent is one factor to be taken into account, the government need not establish such knowledge as the sine qua non of an effective consent." And just as it "would be thoroughly impractical to impose on the normal consent search the detailed requirements of an effective warning," so too would it be unrealistic to require police officers to always inform detainees that they are free to go before a consent to search may be deemed voluntary.

One scholar, referencing the game show "Jeopardy" (where all answers must be phrased in the form of a question), critiques the Supreme Court's consent jurisprudence as follows:

> "The real standard applied in cases of this sort is ... a kind of Jeopardy rule: if the officer puts his command in the form of a question, consent is deemed voluntary and the evidence comes in."[21]

In light of police officers' broad discretion to decide when to ask for consent to search someone, researchers have examined consent-based searches for unwarranted disparities. A 2007 study conducted for the State of Illinois, for

---

[21] William Stuntz, Privacy's Problem and the Law of Criminal Procedure, 93 Mich. L. Rev. 1016 (1995).

example, found that Illinois police not only conducted more consent searches of racial minorities, but also that those searches found contraband less often. Specifically, police found contraband in 25% of consent searches of white drivers but only 13% of the time for non-white drivers. The authors noted that this finding – which commentators suggest indicates that officers ask for consent to search minorities with less justification – was "consistent with results found in other similar studies."

2. WHO CAN GRANT CONSENT?

The typical consent search involves individuals giving the police permission to search their own person or property. But sometimes police rely on consent from third parties such as spouses and roommates. For instance, consider the facts of *United States v. Matlock* (1974), where the defendant, William Matlock, lived in a house with Gayle Graff and Graff's young child:

> "Although the officers were aware at the time of the arrest that [Matlock] lived in the house, they did not ask him which room he occupied or whether he would consent to a search. Three of the arresting officers went to the door of the house and were admitted by Mrs. Graff, who was dressed in a robe and was holding her son in her arms. The officers told her they were looking for money and a gun and asked if they could search the house. Although denied by Mrs. Graff at the suppression hearings, it was found that she consented voluntarily to the search of the house, including the east bedroom on the second floor which she said was jointly occupied by Matlock and herself. The east bedroom was searched and the evidence at issue here, $4,995 in cash, was found in a diaper bag in the only closet in the room. The issue came to be whether Mrs. Graff's relationship to the east bedroom was sufficient to make her consent to the search valid against respondent Matlock."

The Court held that the police reasonably relied on Graff's consent to search the shared bedroom. The Court explained that "the consent of one who possesses common authority over premises or effects is valid as against the absent, nonconsenting person with whom that authority is shared." The absent party "assumed the risk" that the party in control of the property would grant consent. Thus, even though Matlock was not present when the police searched and even though Matlock himself was never asked for consent, the evidence found in his shared bedroom was admissible against him.

More recently, the Court considered a different co-occupant problem: What happens when police ask for consent to search and the co-occupants give different answers?

GEORGIA v. RANDOLPH
547 U.S. 103 (2006)

Justice SOUTER delivered the opinion of the Court.

I

Respondent Scott Randolph and his wife, Janet, separated in late May 2001, when she left the marital residence in Americus, Georgia, and went to stay with her parents in Canada, taking their son and some belongings. In July, she returned to the Americus house with the child, though the record does not reveal whether her object was reconciliation or retrieval of remaining possessions.

On the morning of July 6, she complained to the police that after a domestic dispute her husband took their son away, and when officers reached the house she told them that her husband was a cocaine user whose habit had caused financial troubles. She mentioned the marital problems and said that she and their son had only recently returned after a stay of several weeks with her parents. Shortly after the police arrived, Scott Randolph returned and explained that he had removed the child to a neighbor's house out of concern that his wife might take the boy out of the country again; he denied cocaine use, and countered that it was in fact his wife who abused drugs and alcohol.

One of the officers, Sergeant Murray, went with Janet Randolph to reclaim the child, and when they returned she not only renewed her complaints about her husband's drug use, but also volunteered that there were "items of drug evidence" in the house. Sergeant Murray asked Scott Randolph for permission to search the house, which he unequivocally refused.

The sergeant turned to Janet Randolph for consent to search, which she readily gave. She led the officer upstairs to a bedroom that she identified as Scott's, where the sergeant noticed a section of a drinking straw with a powdery residue he suspected was cocaine. He then left the house to get an evidence bag from his car and to call the district attorney's office, which instructed him to stop the search and apply for a warrant. When Sergeant Murray returned to the house, Janet Randolph withdrew her consent. The police took the straw to the police station, along with the Randolphs. After getting a search warrant, they returned to the house and seized further evidence of drug use, on the basis of which Scott Randolph was indicted for possession of cocaine.

He moved to suppress the evidence, as products of a warrantless search of his house unauthorized by his wife's consent over his express refusal. The trial court denied the motion, ruling that Janet Randolph had common authority to consent to the search.

The Court of Appeals of Georgia reversed, and was itself sustained by the State Supreme Court, principally on the ground that "the consent to conduct a warrantless search of a residence given by one occupant is not valid in the face of the refusal of another occupant who is physically present at the scene to permit a warrantless search."… We granted certiorari to resolve a split of authority on whether one occupant may give law enforcement effective consent to search shared premises, as against a co-tenant who is present and states a refusal to permit the search. We now affirm.

II

To the Fourth Amendment rule ordinarily prohibiting the warrantless entry of a person's house as unreasonable per se, one "jealously and carefully drawn" exception, recognizes the validity of searches with the voluntary consent of an individual possessing authority. That person might be the householder against whom evidence is sought, or a fellow occupant who shares common authority over property, when the suspect is absent, and the exception for consent extends even to entries and searches with the permission of a co-occupant whom the police reasonably, but erroneously, believe to possess shared authority as an occupant. None of our co-occupant consent-to-search cases, however, has presented the further fact of a second occupant physically present and refusing permission to search, and later moving to suppress evidence so obtained. The significance of such a refusal turns on the underpinnings of the co-occupant consent rule, as recognized since United States v. Matlock (1974).

A

…. The constant element in assessing Fourth Amendment reasonableness in the consent cases… is the great significance given to widely shared social expectations, which are naturally enough influenced by the law of property, but not controlled by its rules. [Our case law] accordingly not only holds that a solitary co-inhabitant may sometimes consent to a search of shared premises, but stands for the proposition that the reasonableness of such a search is in significant part a function of commonly held understanding about the authority that co-inhabitants may exercise in ways that affect each other's interests.

B

… It is … easy to imagine … facts on which, if known, no common authority could sensibly be suspected. A person on the scene who identifies himself, say, as a landlord or a hotel manager calls up no customary understanding of authority to admit guests without the consent of the current occupant. A tenant in the ordinary course does not take rented premises subject to any formal or informal agreement that the landlord may let visitors into the dwelling, and a hotel guest customarily has no reason to expect the manager to allow anyone but his own employees into his room. In these circumstances, neither state-law property rights, nor common contractual arrangements, nor any other source points to a common understanding of authority to admit third parties generally without the consent of a person occupying the premises. And when it comes to searching through bureau drawers, there will be instances in which even a person clearly belonging on premises as an occupant may lack any perceived authority to consent; a child of eight might well be considered to have the power to consent to the police crossing the threshold into that part of the house where any caller, such as a pollster or salesman, might well be admitted, but no one would reasonably expect such a child to be in a position to authorize anyone to rummage through his parents' bedroom.

C

…. It is fair to say that a caller standing at the door of shared premises would have no confidence that one occupant's invitation was a sufficiently good reason to enter when a fellow tenant stood there saying, "stay out." Without some very good reason, no sensible person would go inside under those conditions. Fear for the safety of the occupant issuing the invitation, or of someone else inside, would be thought to justify entry, but the justification then would be the personal risk, the threats to life or limb, not the disputed invitation.

The visitor's reticence without some such good reason would show not timidity but a realization that when people living together disagree over the use of their common quarters, a resolution must come through voluntary accommodation, not by appeals to authority. Unless the people living together fall within some recognized hierarchy, like a household of parent and child or barracks housing military personnel of different grades, there is no societal understanding of superior and inferior, a fact reflected in a standard formulation of domestic property law, that "each cotenant has the right to use and enjoy the entire property as if he or she were the sole owner, limited only by the same right in the other cotenants."… In sum, there is no common understanding that one co-tenant generally has a right or authority to prevail over the express wishes of another, whether the issue is the color of the curtains or invitations to outsiders.

D

Since the co-tenant wishing to open the door to a third party has no recognized authority in law or social practice to prevail over a present and objecting co-tenant, his disputed invitation, without more, gives a police officer no better claim to reasonableness in entering than the officer would have in the absence of any consent at all…. Disputed permission is thus no match for this central value of the Fourth Amendment, and the State's other countervailing claims do not add up to outweigh it….

Nor should this established policy of Fourth Amendment law be undermined by the principal dissent's claim that it shields spousal abusers and other violent co-tenants who will refuse to allow the police to enter a dwelling when their victims ask the police for help. It is not that the dissent exaggerates violence in the home; we recognize that domestic abuse is a serious problem in the United States.

But this case has no bearing on the capacity of the police to protect domestic victims. The dissent's argument rests on the failure to distinguish two different issues: when the police may enter without committing a trespass, and when the police may enter to search for evidence. No question has been raised, or reasonably could be, about the authority of the police to enter a dwelling to protect a resident from domestic violence; so long as they have good reason to believe such a threat exists, it would be silly to suggest that the police would commit a tort by entering, say, to give a complaining tenant the opportunity to collect belongings and get out safely, or to determine whether violence (or threat of violence) has just occurred or is about to (or soon will) occur, however much a spouse or other co-tenant objected. (And since the police would then be lawfully in the premises, there is no question that they could seize any evidence in plain view or take further action supported by any consequent probable cause.) Thus, the question whether the police might lawfully enter over objection in order to provide any protection that might be reasonable is easily answered yes. The undoubted right of the police to enter in order to protect a victim, however, has nothing to do with the question in this case, whether a search with the consent of one co-tenant is good against another, standing at the door and expressly refusing consent....

III

This case invites a straightforward application of the rule that a physically present inhabitant's express refusal of consent to a police search is dispositive as to him, regardless of the consent of a fellow occupant. Scott Randolph's refusal is clear, and nothing in the record justifies the search on grounds independent of Janet Randolph's consent. The State does not argue that she gave any indication to the police of a need for protection inside the house that might have justified entry into the portion of the premises where the police found the powdery straw (which, if lawfully seized, could have been used when attempting to establish probable cause for the warrant issued later). Nor does the State claim that the entry and search should be upheld under the rubric of exigent circumstances, owing to some apprehension by the police officers that Scott Randolph would destroy evidence of drug use before any warrant could be obtained.

The judgment of the Supreme Court of Georgia is therefore affirmed.

By emphasizing that the objecting occupant was "physically present," *Randolph* left open the possibility for police to strategically avoid its holding. For instance, in one case the police waited for a suspect to leave on a fishing trip before asking his spouse for consent to search. The Pennsylvania Supreme Court held that "by voluntarily absenting himself from the house he shared with" his spouse, the suspect "assumed the risk" that she would allow the agents to search. *Commonwealth v. Yancoskie* (Pa. 2006). In some cases, police went even further by themselves removing the non-consenting occupant from the scene, and then asking the remaining occupant to consent to a search. The Court provided further guidance on these scenarios in the next case.

FERNANDEZ v. CALIFORNIA
571 U.S. 292 (2014)

Justice ALITO delivered the opinion of the Court.

I

[Police responded to a building where they believed an armed robbery suspect had recently returned. As they arrived,] the officers heard sounds of screaming and fighting coming from that building.

After backup arrived, the officers knocked on the door of the apartment unit from which the screams had been heard. Roxanne Rojas answered the door. She was holding a baby and appeared to be crying. Her face was red, and she had a large bump on her nose. The officers also saw blood on her shirt and hand from what appeared to be a fresh injury. Rojas told the police that she had been in a fight. Officer Cirrito asked if anyone else was in the apartment, and Rojas said that her 4–year–old son was the only other person present.

After Officer Cirrito asked Rojas to step out of the apartment so that he could conduct a protective sweep, petitioner Walter Fernandez appeared at the door wearing only boxer shorts. Apparently agitated, petitioner stepped forward and said, "You don't have any right to come in here. I know my rights." Suspecting that petitioner had assaulted Rojas, the officers removed him from the apartment and then placed him under arrest. [The victim of the robbery] identified petitioner as his initial attacker, and petitioner was taken to the police station for booking.

Approximately one hour after petitioner's arrest, Detective Clark returned to the apartment and informed Rojas that petitioner had been arrested. Detective Clark requested and received both oral and written consent from Rojas to search the premises. In the apartment, the police found [evidence related to the robbery.]

II
A

…. "Consent searches are part of the standard investigatory techniques of law enforcement agencies" and are "a constitutionally permissible and wholly legitimate aspect of effective police activity." Schneckloth v. Bustamonte (1973). It would be unreasonable—indeed, absurd—to require police officers to obtain a warrant when the sole owner or occupant of a house or apartment voluntarily consents to a search. The owner of a home has a right to allow others to enter and examine the premises, and there is no reason why the owner should not be permitted to extend this same privilege to police officers if that is the owner's choice. Where the owner believes that he or she is under suspicion, the owner may want the police to search the premises so that their suspicions are dispelled. This may be particularly important where the owner has a strong interest in the apprehension of the perpetrator of a crime and believes that the suspicions of the police are deflecting the course of their investigation. An owner may want the police to search even where they lack probable cause, and if a warrant were always required, this could not be done. And even where the police could establish probable cause, requiring a warrant despite the owner's consent would needlessly inconvenience everyone involved—not only the officers and the magistrate but also the occupant of the premises, who would generally either be compelled or would feel a need to stay until the search was completed....

B

While consent by one resident of jointly occupied premises is generally sufficient to justify a warrantless search, we recognized a narrow exception to this rule in Georgia v. Randolph (2006) [where we] held that "*a physically present inhabitant's express refusal of consent to a police search of his home is dispositive as to him, regardless of the consent of a fellow occupant.*"...

III

In this case, petitioner was not present when Rojas consented, but petitioner still contends that Randolph is controlling. He advances two main arguments. First, he claims that his absence should not matter since he was absent only because the police had taken him away. Second, he maintains that it was sufficient that he objected to the search while he was still present. Such an objection, he says, should remain in effect until the objecting party "no longer wishes to keep the police out of his home." Neither of these arguments is sound.

A

We first consider the argument that the presence of the objecting occupant is not necessary when the police are responsible for his absence. In Randolph, the Court suggested in dictum that consent by one occupant might not be sufficient if "there is evidence that the police have removed the potentially objecting tenant from the entrance for the sake of avoiding a possible objection." We do not believe the statement should be read to suggest that improper motive may invalidate objectively justified removal. Hence, it does not govern here.

The Randolph dictum is best understood not to require an inquiry into the subjective intent of officers who detain or arrest a potential objector but instead to refer to situations in which the removal of the potential objector is not objectively reasonable. As petitioner acknowledges, our Fourth Amendment cases "have repeatedly rejected" a subjective approach…. Once it is recognized that the test is one of objective reasonableness, petitioner's argument collapses. He does not contest the fact that the police had reasonable grounds for removing him from the apartment so that they could speak with Rojas, an apparent victim of domestic violence, outside of petitioner's potentially intimidating presence. In fact, he does not even contest the existence of probable cause to place him under arrest. We therefore hold that an occupant who is absent due to a lawful detention or arrest stands in the same shoes as an occupant who is absent for any other reason.

This conclusion does not "make a mockery of Randolph," as petitioner protests. It simply accepts Randolph on its own terms. The Randolph holding unequivocally requires the presence of the objecting occupant in every situation other than the one mentioned in the dictum discussed above.

B

This brings us to petitioner's second argument that his objection, made at the threshold of the premises that the police wanted to search, remained effective until he changed his mind and withdrew his objection. This argument is inconsistent with Randolph's reasoning…. The argument cannot be squared with the "widely shared social expectations" or "customary social usage" upon which the Randolph holding was based. Explaining why consent by one occupant could not override an objection by a physically present occupant, the Randolph Court stated: "It is fair to say that a caller standing at the door of shared premises would have no confidence that one occupant's invitation was a sufficiently good reason to enter when a fellow tenant stood there saying, 'stay out.' Without some very good reason, no sensible person would go inside under those conditions." It seems obvious that the calculus of this hypothetical caller would likely be quite different if the objecting tenant was not standing at the door. When the objecting occupant is standing at the threshold saying "stay out," a friend or visitor invited to enter by another occupant can expect at best an uncomfortable scene and at worst violence if he or she tries to brush past the objector. But when the objector is not on the scene (and especially when it is known that the objector will not return during the course of the visit), the friend or visitor is much more likely to accept the invitation to enter. Thus, petitioner's argument is inconsistent with Randolph's reasoning....

What if the person who gives consent does not, in fact, have the right to authorize a search? In *Illinois v. Rodriguez* (1990), the Supreme Court considered a search of an apartment based upon the consent of an "infrequent visitor" to the apartment who "did not have common authority over the apartment." The Court emphasized that the visitor's consent could still be valid if the police "reasonably believed" that the consenting party "had the authority to consent." The Court added the following caveat:

> "What we hold today does not suggest that law enforcement officers may always accept a person's invitation to enter premises. Even when the invitation is accompanied by an explicit assertion that the person lives there, the surrounding circumstances could conceivably be such that a reasonable person would doubt its truth and not act upon it without further inquiry. As with other factual determinations bearing upon search and seizure, determination of consent to enter must be judged against an objective standard: would the facts available to the officer at the moment 'warrant a man of reasonable caution in the belief' that the consenting party had authority over the premises? If not, then warrantless entry without further inquiry is unlawful unless authority actually exists. But if so, the search is valid."

3. SCOPE OF CONSENT

How far does a consent to search extend? The basic answer, given in *Florida v. Jimeno* (1991) is that it depends on the consent given: "A suspect may of course delimit as he chooses the scope of the search to which he consents." But, as the Supreme Court explained in that case, the scope of consent will often be implicit (not explicit), and determined, after the fact, from context:

> " The scope of a search is generally defined by its expressed object. In this case, the terms of the search's authorization were simple. Respondent granted Officer Trujillo permission to search his car, and did not place any explicit limitation on the scope of the search. Trujillo had informed respondent that he believed respondent was carrying narcotics, and that he would be looking for narcotics in the car. We think that it was objectively reasonable for the police to conclude that the general consent to search respondent's car included consent to search containers within that car which might bear drugs. A reasonable person may be expected to know that narcotics are generally carried in some form of a container. Contraband goods rarely are strewn across the trunk or floor of a car. The authorization to search in this case, therefore, extended beyond the surfaces of the car's interior to the paper bag lying on the car's floor.
>
> The facts of this case are therefore different from those in State v. Wells, on which the Supreme Court of Florida relied in affirming the suppression order in this case. There the Supreme Court of Florida held that consent to search the trunk of a car did not include authorization to pry open a locked briefcase found inside the trunk. It is very likely unreasonable to think that a suspect, by consenting to the search of his trunk, has agreed to the breaking open of a locked briefcase within the trunk, but it is otherwise with respect to a closed paper bag.

While the Supreme Court endorsed the Florida court's finding that a general consent to search would not extend to locked containers, the analysis may change in the absence of a need for forcible entry. In *United States v. Jones* (4th Cir. 2004), police obtained consent to search a bag. Inside, they found a handgun, a locked metal box, and a set of keys. The officer used one of the keys to open the locked box and found drugs inside. The Fourth Circuit rejected the defendant's argument "that locked containers are different from closed containers and do not fall within the scope of a suspect's general consent to search a larger area." The court explained that

"As the ostensible owner of the bag, Jones knew that the keys to the metal box were inside the bag alongside the box. Since Jones did not qualify his consent in any way, an officer could reasonably conclude that Jones expected the officers to use the keys and open the box containing the illicit drugs. Moreover, Jones confirmed the propriety of the search by not objecting to [the officer's] use of the keys to open the locked box in Jones's presence."

Another question that arises in the case law is whether consent for the police to "search" a cell phone entails permission to answer the phone if it rings during the search. In *United States v. Lopez-Cruz* (9th Cir. 2013), the court found that answering the phone exceeded the scope of consent: "An individual who gives consent to the search of his phone does not, without more, give consent to his impersonation by a government agent, nor does he give the agent permission to carry on conversations in which the agent participates in his name in the conduct of criminal activity." The court held that the agent should have asked for specific consent to answer the phone.

Finally, consider whether a police officer's request to search a car for drugs includes not just human searches, but also the use of a drug-sniffing dog. In *Commonwealth v. Valdivia* (Pa. 2018), Randy Valdivia granted an officer permission to search his vehicle for drugs. Rather than search himself, however, the officer called for a drug-sniffing dog. Upon its arrival, the dog alerted to a package, which the officer then opened to find marijuana. The trial court concluded that the consent was valid even though the officer did not mention that the search would be conducted by a dog not a person, and the intermediate appellate court agreed: "nothing about a canine sniff strikes us as more intrusive than a vehicle search by humans, so when an individual consents to an official search of his vehicle, it is natural to assume that his consent includes both human and canine searches." The Supreme Court of Pennsylvania reversed:

"We disagree with the Superior Court ... that the level of intrusion involved with a canine sniff, as compared to a human search, has any relevance to the question before us.... Here, Valdivia gave his consent for two human officers to conduct a search of his vehicle. As Trooper Hoy testified at the suppression hearing, after asking Valdivia questions about his travel plans, he simply 'asked for consent to search the vehicle,' and that 'Valdivia agreed to allow us to search the vehicle.' There was no canine officer or handler present at the time, nor did the circumstances surrounding the interaction between Valdivia and the troopers suggest that a canine unit was going to be used to conduct the search. Under these circumstances, we cannot conclude that a reasonable person in Valdivia's position would have understood that his consent to allow two human officers to search his vehicle would somehow operate to permit the search to be conducted by a canine trained in drug detection."

4. REVOKING CONSENT

UNITED STATES v. SANDERS
424 F.3d 768 (8th Cir. 2005)

BYE, Circuit Judge.

I

…. Police officer Ryan Abodeely received telephone calls from an employee at a local motel regarding a guest, later identified as Craig Sanders, who was acting suspiciously. The caller indicated many people were coming and going from Sanders's room, and hotel employees suspected he might be dealing drugs....

Abodeely testified he and his colleague [went to the hotel,] identified themselves as Cedar Rapids police officers, asked permission to enter the room, and Sanders allowed them to enter…. Abodeely testified he told Sanders the officers suspected drug dealing and asked permission to search the room and Sanders's person. Sanders claims he was simply told to turn around and let the officers search him. Both agree Sanders raised his arms to facilitate a search of his person. Abodeely indicated he searched Sanders's upper body without incident but when he attempted to reach into one of his front pants pockets, Sanders lowered his hands and blocked Abodeely from going into his pockets….

At the suppression hearing, Abodeely testified:

"And I began to move down towards his front pockets on his pants; as I did that, he kept bringing his hands down and tried to block my hands from going into his pockets. I advised him that he needed to keep his hands up in the air. As I searched him, started to go once again to search the pockets, he did this (indicating) again where he put his hands down and tried to block my hands. This happened approximately five times at which time I became kind of concerned for Investigator Joecken and myself's safety."

At the suppression hearing, Sanders testified he felt compelled to submit to the search and brought his arms down to keep his pants from being pulled down as Abodeely reached into the pockets. While he repeatedly blocked Abodeely's hands, he did not verbally withdraw consent to search. Abodeely testified Sanders's refusal to cooperate with the search, and concerns about officer safety, led him to handcuff him.... After Sanders was handcuffed, Abodeely was able to complete the search which led to the discovery of eight small rocks of crack cocaine.

Sanders was indicted on one count of possession with intent to distribute crack cocaine. He moved to suppress the crack cocaine discovered in the search of his person, arguing he did not give consent. Alternatively, he also argued he withdrew his consent as evidenced by his repeated attempts to block Abodeely's hands from searching his pants pocket. The district court rejected Sanders's arguments holding he gave consent for the officers to enter the hotel room and to search his person. The court further held his actions did not communicate an intent to withdraw his consent. [The District Court sentenced Sanders to 210 months in prison.]

II

[After concluding that the district court's conclusion that Sanders consented to be searched was supported by the record, the Eighth Circuit turned to the question of withdrawal.]

.... Once given, consent to search may be withdrawn: Withdrawal of consent need not be effectuated through particular "magic words," but an intent to withdraw consent must be made by unequivocal act or statement. If equivocal, a defendant's attempt to withdraw consent is ineffective and police may reasonably continue their search pursuant to the initial grant of authority. "The standard for measuring the scope of a suspect's consent under the Fourth Amendment is that of 'objective' reasonableness—what would the typical reasonable person have understood by the exchange between the officer and the suspect?" Florida v. Jimeno (1991). Accordingly, we must determine whether a reasonable person would have concluded Sanders's repeated attempts to thwart Abodeely's attempts to search his pockets amounted to a withdrawal of consent.

Conduct withdrawing consent must be an act clearly inconsistent with the apparent consent to search, an unambiguous statement challenging the officer's authority to conduct the search, or some combination of both. For example, [in a Florida case,] a defendant who twice grabbed a deputy's hand in an attempt to stop him from searching a pack of cigarettes was held to have withdrawn his earlier consent, and it was improper for the officer to continue the search over the defendant's objections....

Conversely, when a defendant's actions are ambiguous or equivocal courts refuse to find an effective withdrawal of consent. Thus, [in a South Carolina case,] a defendant's act of merely lowering his hands as an officer searched his groin area was insufficient to demonstrate an unequivocal withdrawal of consent. Similarly, ... in United States v. Jones (D.C. Cir. 1990), the court held twisting away slightly during a consensual pat-down search was insufficient to communicate to the officer an unequivocal intent to withdraw consent....

It is undisputed that at least five times Sanders moved his hands down and prevented Abodeely from searching his pockets. Because this was a consensual search, he had every right to withdraw or limit the scope of his consent by taking actions clearly designed to prevent Abodeely from searching further. His actions made it apparent he did not intend to permit Abodeely to search his pockets, and Abodeely exceeded his authority by repeatedly ordering him to comply with the search. In the end, the only way Abodeely could complete the "consensual" search was to place Sanders in handcuffs. Based on these undisputed facts, we conclude the district court clearly erred when it held Sanders's actions, which so interfered with Abodeely's ability to search him he had to be handcuffed, communicated anything but a withdrawal of consent. Any objective observer watching this scenario would conclude he was not consenting to the search of his pockets. Stated another way, if a suspect has to be handcuffed to prevent interference with a search of his person, the search was not consensual.

III

The order and judgment of the district court denying Sanders's motion to suppress evidence seized during the search of his person is reversed.

H. ABANDONMENT

ABEL v. UNITED STATES
362 U.S. 217 (1960)

Justice FRANKFURTER delivered the opinion of the Court.

[The FBI suspected Rudolph Abel of espionage. Suspecting also that he was in the country illegally, they enlisted the assistance of the Immigration and Naturalization Service (INS). On June 21, FBI and INS agents, who had obtained "a warrant for petitioner's arrest and an order addressed to petitioner directing him to show cause why he should not be deported," entered his room at the Hotel Latham in New York City.]

After placing petitioner (Abel) under arrest, the four I.N.S. agents undertook a search of his person and of all of his belongings in the room, and the adjoining bathroom, which lasted for from fifteen to twenty minutes…. When the search was completed, petitioner was told to dress himself, to assemble his things and to choose what he wished to take with him. With the help of the I.N.S. agents almost everything in the room was packed into petitioner's baggage. A few things petitioner deliberately left on a window sill, indicating that he did not want to take them, and several other things which he chose not to pack up into his luggage he put into the room's wastepaper basket…. When petitioner's belongings had been completely packed, petitioner agreed to check out of the hotel. One of the F.B.I. agents obtained his bill from the hotel and petitioner paid it. Petitioner was then handcuffed and taken, along with his baggage, to a waiting automobile and thence to the headquarters of the I.N.S. in New York….

As soon as petitioner had been taken from the hotel an F.B.I. agent, Kehoe, who had been in the room adjoining petitioner's during the arrest and search and who, like the I.N.S. agents, had no search warrant, received permission from the hotel management to search the room just vacated by petitioner. Although the bill which petitioner had paid entitled him to occupy the room until 3 p.m. of that day, the hotel's practice was to consider a room vacated whenever a guest removed his baggage and turned in his key. Kehoe conducted a search of petitioner's room which lasted for about three hours. Among other things, he seized the contents of the wastepaper basket into which petitioner had put some things while packing his belongings. Two of the items thus seized were the challenged items of evidence we have designated (6) and (7): a hollow pencil containing microfilm and a block of wood containing a 'cipher pad.'…

These two items were found by an agent of the F.B.I. in the course of a search he undertook of petitioner's hotel room, immediately after petitioner had paid his bill and vacated the room. They were found in the room's wastepaper basket, where petitioner had put them while packing his belongings and preparing to leave. No pretense is made that this search by the F.B.I. was for any purpose other than to gather evidence of crime, that is, evidence of petitioner's espionage. As such, however, it was entirely lawful, although undertaken without a warrant. This is so for the reason that at the time of the search petitioner had vacated the room. The hotel then had the exclusive right to its possession, and the hotel management freely gave its consent that the search be made. Nor was it unlawful to seize the entire contents of the wastepaper basket, even though some of its contents had no connection with crime. So far as the record shows, petitioner had abandoned these articles. He had thrown them away. So far as he was concerned, they were bona vacantia. There can be nothing unlawful in the Government's appropriation of such abandoned property….

Unfortunately, *Abel* is the Supreme Court's most recent pronouncement on the important and complex question of whether an item has been "abandoned" for Fourth Amendment purposes and can, consequently, be seized and searched without a warrant (or individualized suspicion). Modern treatments of this concept in the lower courts typically adapt the abandonment inquiry to *Katz*'s "reasonable expectation of privacy." The Court of Appeals for the District of Columbia Circuit provides the following representative analysis:

Daniel Thomas fled into the entrance of an apartment building once he caught sight of police officers. When Officer Jones reached the door to the building, he observed that Thomas had mounted the stairs and was busying himself with the contents of the gym bag. Before Officer Jones opened the door, Thomas had turned from the bag and had started walking back down the stairs, leaving the bag behind him on the floor of a public hallway. Given these circumstances, we find no error in the district court's determination that Thomas intended for fourth amendment purposes to abandon the bag at the top of the stairs. His actions were in relevant respects similar to those of a person who tosses an object during police pursuit: in order to prevent discovery of his bag by the police, Thomas left it behind in a public place where he retained no reasonable expectation of privacy in it.[22]

Lower court decisions like this signal that *Abel* (a pre-*Katz* case) overstates the requirements for a showing of abandonment. *Abel* identifies the abandoned property in that case as "bona vacantia": "ownerless property" that "either belonged to the finder or escheated to the Crown." Black's Law Dictionary (2009)

In the case quoted above, the D.C. Circuit added a footnote to emphasize that abandonment in the Fourth Amendment context does not necessarily map onto property conceptions of ownerless property:

> "The legal significance of Thomas' acts is not altered by the fact that he might have intended to retrieve the bag later. His ability to do so would depend on the fortuity that other persons with access to the public hallway would not disturb his bag while it lay there unattended."

The Fourth Circuit similarly explains that:

> "A finding of abandonment is based not on whether all formal property rights have been relinquished, but whether the complaining party retains a reasonable expectation of privacy in the articles alleged to be abandoned. To determine whether the defendant maintains a reasonable expectation of privacy in an item, the court performs an objective analysis which considers the defendant's actions and intentions. Intent to abandon may be inferred from words spoken, acts done, and other objective facts."

Applying a *Katz* reasonable-expectation-of-privacy lens, lower courts can find that items are abandoned for Fourth Amendment purposes even if those items would not be considered "ownerless" as a matter of property law or social norms. This is because a person who discards something can lose a reasonable expectation of privacy in that thing while nonetheless retaining ownership of it. This could occur when, in context, members of the public would be expected to take possession or look through the item – assuming it had been discarded, lost, or forgotten. (If so, police would be able to engage in the same type of inquiry.) This remains true even

---

[22] United States v. Thomas, 864 F.2d 843 (D.C. Cir. 1989).

if the property's original possessor may by law and custom be able to later reclaim the property (for example, a lost purse or wallet).

STATE v. SAMALIA
375 P.3d 1082 (Wash. 2015)

Wiggins, J.

…. Yakima Police Officer Ryan Yates observed what he believed to be a stolen vehicle while on patrol. He confirmed with dispatch that the vehicle was stolen and began to follow it. Eventually, the driver stopped, got out of the vehicle, and faced Officer Yates. Officer Yates gave the driver various commands, but the driver did not obey and ran away. Officer Yates attempted to chase after the driver, but the driver successfully escaped.

Failing to apprehend the driver, Officer Yates returned to the stolen vehicle and began to search it without a warrant. Officer Yates found a cell phone somewhere near the vehicle's center console, but he did not know to whom it belonged. He then began calling some of the contacts listed in the cell phone.

From the cell phone's contacts, Officer Yates called Deylene Telles. He told Telles that he had found a cell phone and wanted to return it to its owner. Telles agreed to meet at a designated location. When Telles arrived at that location … [police] used the cell phone recovered by Officer Yates to call [Telles' phone]. Telles' cell phone displayed Samalia's name and photo, identifying him as the caller. Officer Yates then looked up Samalia's photo in a law enforcement database and identified Samalia as the driver who fled from the stolen vehicle.

On these facts, the State charged Samalia with possession of a stolen vehicle. Samalia moved to suppress the cell phone evidence, arguing that the officers violated his constitutional rights when they seized and searched his cell phone with neither a warrant nor a valid exception to the warrant requirement. The State responded that the warrantless search was valid under the abandonment doctrine….

Washington's Constitution states that, "No person shall be disturbed in his private affairs, or his home invaded, without authority of law." [This provision] encompasses the privacy expectations protected by the Fourth Amendment to the United States Constitution and, in some cases, may provide greater protection than the Fourth Amendment because its protections are not confined to the subjective privacy expectations of citizens. Under [the Washington Constitution] – in its protection of "private affairs" – a search occurs when the government disturbs those privacy interests which citizens of this state *have held, and should be entitled to hold*, safe from government trespass absent a warrant…. However, citizens may lose their constitutional protections in a private affair under the abandonment doctrine….

Based on the amount of private information that cell phones may hold, Samalia argues that [both the Washington Constitution and the federal Constitution as interpreted in Riley v. California (2014) require] that cell phones either be excluded from the abandonment doctrine or that we should require at least a heightened showing of intent to abandon….

Neither Riley nor [state case law] can be read for the proposition that the abandonment doctrine should not apply to cell phones or should be limited in its application to cell phones. The Riley holding that cell phones may not be searched incident to arrest without a warrant was based on the fact that such cell phone searches do not fall into the particular justifications for the search incident to arrest exception…. In this case and for the abandonment doctrine, there has been no advancement in technology to cause one to abandon property in stolen vehicles while attempting to flee from police. Moreover, the rationale driving the abandonment doctrine fits cell phone searches. When an individual voluntarily abandons an item, not as a facet of modern communication but to elude the police, that individual voluntarily exposes that item—and all information that it may contain—to anyone who may come across it. Cell phones are no different in this respect than for any other item; the abandonment doctrine applies to all personal property equally.

Therefore, we decline to find an exception to the abandonment doctrine for cell phones. We consider, then, whether the trial court properly found abandonment under these facts.

…. The trial court's finding that Samalia voluntarily abandoned his cell phone reasonably follows from the undisputed facts of the case: Samalia was driving a stolen vehicle, and when Samalia stopped, he got out of the vehicle and faced Officer Yates. Then, instead of obeying Officer Yates' commands, Samalia ran away, abandoning the vehicle and its contents. Officer Yates attempted to catch Samalia, but Samalia escaped, and Officer Yates returned to the stolen vehicle.

Inside the stolen vehicle, Officer Yates found the cell phone. Indeed, there is nothing in the record to suggest that Samalia protected the information on his cell phone by any security measures.

…. The information derived from Officer Yates' search of Samalia's cell phone was properly admitted as evidence under the abandonment doctrine….

Yu, J. (dissenting)

…. In the context of cell phones … the level of intrusion occasioned by an initial seizure pales in comparison to the level of intrusion occasioned by searching the phone's digital data…. It would be patently absurd to suggest that abandonment of a traditional key means that warrantless access is allowed to the house it locks; the same must be true of digital keys to electronic information.

…. The distinction between voluntarily abandoned property on one hand, and lost or mislaid property on the other, provides little practical protection against government intrusion into a person's private affairs in the context of digital data accessible through a cell phone. The owner of a lost or mislaid cell phone … can neither prevent nor undo the invasion of privacy that has already occurred when, as happened in this case, an investigating officer looks through a person's contact list for entries indicating an intimate or familial relation, such as "girlfriend" or "sweetheart."

In light of these facts, the majority's approach here effectively condones a practice of *assuming* that cell phones discovered without their owners are abandoned, and thus open to warrantless government searches for incriminating evidence (or, for that matter, any other information)…. I would hold that a search of digital data, even on an abandoned cell phone, must be pursuant to a lawfully issued warrant, supported by probable cause and subject to detached scrutiny by a neutral magistrate with precise limits established in advance by a specific court order.

The Supreme Court has not yet addressed searches of "abandoned" cell phones. A number of lower courts agree with *Samalia* and uphold such searches. This is particularly true when the owner of the phone flees from police as they are investigating a criminal offense. See, e.g., *Wiltz v. State* (Tex. App. 2020) ("As appellant stood handcuffed, before he fled, he retained the privacy protections to his cell phone the law affords. But appellant opted to flee the scene and leave his cell phone behind. In making that decision to abandon the cell phone, appellant intentionally gave up any privacy rights to information on the cell phone."). While agreeing that a cell phone was abandoned in similar circumstances, the Fourth Circuit, in *United States v. Small* (4th Cir. 2019), cautioned that, "Abandonment should not be casually inferred. People lose or misplace their cell phones all the time. But the simple loss of a cell phone does not entail the loss of a reasonable expectation of privacy. Thus, such ordinary mishaps do not constitute abandonments. Rather, there has to be some voluntary aspect to the circumstances that lead to the phone being what could be called abandoned."

Not all courts embrace the abandonment doctrine for cell phones. For instance, in *State v. K.C.* (Fla App. Ct. 2016), after police initiated a traffic stop, the car's occupants fled, leaving behind a cell phone that was password protected. Police seized the phone and several months later were able to unlock the phone and link it to K.C. Prosecutors argued that K.C. abandoned the phone and thus no search warrant was required. The Florida court disagreed and, relying in part on *Riley v. California*, held that "the abandonment exception does not apply to cell phones whose contents are protected by a password."

I. SPECIAL NEEDS AND RELATED BALANCING

In a long line of cases, the Supreme Court recognizes exceptions to the traditional Fourth Amendment requirements in "special needs" contexts. As explained by the Court in 2001,

> "The term 'special needs' first appeared in Justice Blackmun's opinion concurring in the judgment in New Jersey v. T.L.O. (1985). In his concurrence, Justice Blackmun agreed with the Court that there are limited exceptions to the probable-cause requirement, in which reasonableness is determined by 'a careful balancing of governmental and private interests,' but concluded that such a test should only be applied 'in those exceptional circumstances in which special needs, beyond the normal need for law enforcement, make the warrant and probable-cause requirement impracticable.' This Court subsequently adopted the 'special needs' terminology, … concluding that, in limited circumstances, a search unsupported by either warrant or probable cause can be constitutional

when 'special needs' other than the normal need for law enforcement provide sufficient justification."

As the next sections show, the Court applies this doctrine, or a variation of it, in a variety of contexts.

1. CLASSIC "SPECIAL NEEDS"

SKINNER v. RAILWAY LABOR EXECUTIVES' ASSOCIATION
489 U.S. 602 (1989)

Case Summary

In *Skinner v. Railway Labor Executives' Association*, the Supreme Court upheld a Federal Railroad Administration (FRA) regulation that required breath, blood, and urine tests of railroad employees who were involved in train accidents or violated safety rules. The Court explained,

> "Except in certain well-defined circumstances, a search or seizure … is not reasonable unless it is accomplished pursuant to a judicial warrant issued upon probable cause. We have recognized exceptions to this rule, however, 'when special needs, beyond the normal need for law enforcement, make the warrant and probable-cause requirement impracticable.' When faced with such special needs, we have not hesitated to balance the governmental and privacy interests to assess the practicality of the warrant and probable-cause requirements in the particular context."

Railroad safety presented this type of "special need":

> "The Government's interest in regulating the conduct of railroad employees to ensure safety, like its supervision of probationers or regulated industries, or its operation of a government office, school, or prison, likewise presents 'special needs' beyond normal law enforcement that may justify departures from the usual warrant and probable-cause requirements."

The Court then went on to balance the intrusion entailed by the searches, which it found particularly invasive with respect to the urine tests, against the government interest they furthered:

"We recognize … that the procedures for collecting the necessary samples, which require employees to perform an excretory function traditionally shielded by great privacy, raise [significant privacy] concerns…. [But] the expectations of privacy of covered employees are diminished by reason of their participation in an industry that is regulated pervasively to ensure safety, a goal dependent, in substantial part, on the health and fitness of covered employees….

We do not suggest, of course, that the interest in bodily security enjoyed by those employed in a regulated industry must always be considered minimal. Here, however, the covered employees have long been a principal focus of regulatory concern. As the dissenting judge below noted: "The reason is obvious. An idle locomotive, sitting in the roundhouse, is harmless. It becomes lethal when operated negligently by persons who are under the influence of alcohol or drugs." Though some of the privacy interests implicated by the toxicological testing at issue reasonably might be viewed as significant in other contexts, logic and history show that a diminished expectation of privacy attaches to information relating to the physical condition of covered employees and to this reasonable means of procuring such information. We conclude, therefore, that the testing procedures pose only limited threats to the justifiable expectations of privacy of covered employees.

By contrast, the Government interest in testing without a showing of individualized suspicion is compelling. Employees subject to the tests discharge duties fraught with such risks of injury to others that even a momentary lapse of attention can have disastrous consequences. Much like persons who have routine access to dangerous nuclear power facilities, employees who are subject to testing under the FRA regulations can cause great human loss before any signs of impairment become noticeable to supervisors or others. An impaired employee, the FRA found, will seldom display any outward "signs detectable by the lay person or, in many cases, even the physician."…

While no procedure can identify all impaired employees with ease and perfect accuracy, the FRA regulations supply an effective means of deterring employees engaged in safety-sensitive tasks from using controlled substances or alcohol in the first place. The railroad industry's experience with [existing drug and alcohol prohibitions] persuasively shows, and common sense confirms, that the customary dismissal sanction that threatens employees who use drugs or alcohol while on duty cannot serve as an effective deterrent unless violators know that they are likely to be discovered. By ensuring that employees in safety-sensitive positions know they will be tested upon the occurrence of a triggering event, the timing of which no employee can predict with certainty, the regulations significantly increase the deterrent effect of the administrative penalties associated with the prohibited conduct, concomitantly increasing the likelihood that employees will forgo using drugs or alcohol while subject to being called for duty....

The Court concluded: "We hold that the alcohol and drug tests contemplated by the FRA's regulations are reasonable within the meaning of the Fourth Amendment."

FERGUSON v. CITY OF CHARLESTON
532 U.S. 67 (2001)

Justice STEVENS delivered the opinion of the Court.

I

In the fall of 1988, staff members at the public hospital operated in the city of Charleston by the Medical University of South Carolina (MUSC) became concerned about an apparent increase in the use of cocaine by patients who were receiving prenatal treatment. In response to this perceived increase, MUSC began to order drug screens to be performed on urine samples from maternity patients who were suspected of using cocaine. If a patient tested positive, she was then referred by MUSC staff to the county substance abuse commission for counseling and treatment. However, despite the referrals, the incidence of cocaine use among the patients at MUSC did not appear to change.

[The hospital then coordinated with the local prosecutor's office to create a policy, Policy M-7, to further address the ongoing drug use.] The first three pages of Policy M–7 set forth the procedure to be followed by the hospital staff to "identify/assist pregnant patients suspected of drug abuse."... The threat of law enforcement involvement was set forth in two protocols, the first dealing with the identification of drug use during pregnancy, and the second with identification of drug use after labor. Under the latter protocol, the police were to be notified without delay and the patient promptly arrested. Under the former, after the initial positive drug test, the police were to be notified (and the patient arrested) only if the patient tested positive for cocaine a second time or if she missed an appointment with a substance abuse counselor. In 1990, however, the policy was modified at the behest of the [prosecutor's] office to give the patient who tested positive during labor, like the patient who tested positive during a prenatal care visit, an opportunity to avoid arrest by consenting to substance abuse treatment.

II

Petitioners are 10 women who received obstetrical care at MUSC and who were arrested after testing positive for cocaine. Four of them were arrested during the initial implementation of the policy; they were not offered the opportunity to receive drug treatment as an alternative to arrest. The others were arrested after the policy was modified in 1990; they either failed to comply with the terms of the drug treatment program or tested positive for a second time. Respondents include the city of Charleston, law enforcement officials who helped develop and enforce the policy, and representatives of MUSC.

Petitioners' complaint challenged the validity of the policy under various theories, including the claim that warrantless and nonconsensual drug tests conducted for criminal investigatory purposes were unconstitutional searches. Respondents advanced two principal defenses to the constitutional claim: (1) that, as a matter of fact, petitioners had consented to the searches; and (2) that, as a matter of law, the searches were reasonable, even absent consent, because they were justified by special non-law-enforcement purposes. [The District Court and Fourth Circuit Court of Appeals concluded that the hospital policies were permissible "special needs" searches.] We granted certiorari to review the appellate court's holding on the "special needs" issue. We conclude that the judgment should be reversed....

III

Because MUSC is a state hospital, the members of its staff are government actors, subject to the strictures of the Fourth Amendment. Moreover, the urine tests conducted by those staff members were indisputably searches within the meaning of the Fourth Amendment. Neither the District Court nor the Court of Appeals concluded that [the] criteria used to identify the women to be searched provided either probable cause to believe that they were using cocaine, or even the basis for a reasonable suspicion of such use. Rather, the District Court and the Court of Appeals viewed the case as one involving MUSC's right to conduct searches without warrants or probable cause....

Because the hospital seeks to justify its authority to conduct drug tests and to turn the results over to law enforcement agents without the knowledge or consent of the patients, this case differs from the four previous cases in which we have considered whether comparable drug tests "fit within the closely guarded category of constitutionally permissible suspicionless searches." In three of those cases, we sustained drug tests for railway employees involved in train accidents, Skinner v. Railway Labor Executives' Assn. (1989), for United States Customs Service employees seeking promotion to certain sensitive positions, Treasury Employees v. Von Raab (1989), and for high school students participating in interscholastic sports, Vernonia School Dist. 47J v. Acton (1995). In the fourth case, Chandler v. Miller (1997), we struck down such testing for candidates for designated state offices as unreasonable.

In each of those cases, we employed a balancing test that weighed the intrusion on the individual's interest in privacy against the "special needs" that supported the program. As an initial matter, we note that the invasion of privacy in this case is far more substantial than in those cases. In the previous four cases, there was no misunderstanding about the purpose of the test or the potential use of the test results, and there were protections against the dissemination of the results to third parties. The use of an adverse test result to disqualify one from eligibility for a particular benefit, such as a promotion or an opportunity to participate in an extracurricular activity, involves a less serious intrusion on privacy than the unauthorized dissemination of such results to third parties. The reasonable expectation of privacy enjoyed by the typical patient undergoing diagnostic tests in a hospital is that the results of those tests will not be shared with nonmedical personnel without her consent. In none of our prior cases was there any intrusion upon that kind of expectation.

The critical difference between those four drug-testing cases and this one, however, lies in the nature of the "special need" asserted as justification for the warrantless searches. In each of those earlier cases, the "special need" that was advanced as a justification for the absence of a warrant or individualized suspicion was one divorced from the State's general interest in law enforcement. In this case, however, the central and indispensable feature of the policy from its inception was the use of law enforcement to coerce the patients into substance abuse treatment. This fact distinguishes this case from circumstances in which physicians or psychologists, in the course of ordinary medical procedures aimed at helping the patient herself, come across information that under rules of law or ethics is subject to reporting requirements, which no one has challenged here.

Respondents argue in essence that their ultimate purpose—namely, protecting the health of both mother and child—is a beneficent one…. [But] a review of the M–7 policy plainly reveals that the purpose actually served by the MUSC searches "is ultimately indistinguishable from the general interest in crime control."

In looking to the programmatic purpose, we consider all the available evidence in order to determine the relevant primary purpose. In this case, as Judge Blake put it in her dissent below, "it is clear from the record that an initial and continuing focus of the policy was on the arrest and prosecution of drug-abusing mothers." Tellingly, the document codifying the policy incorporates the police's operational guidelines. It devotes its attention to the chain of custody, the range of possible criminal charges, and the logistics of police notification and arrests. Nowhere, however, does the document discuss different courses of medical treatment for either mother or infant, aside from treatment for the mother's addiction.

Moreover, throughout the development and application of the policy, the Charleston prosecutors and police were extensively involved in the day-to-day administration of the policy….

While the ultimate goal of the program may well have been to get the women in question into substance abuse treatment and off of drugs, the immediate objective of the searches was to generate evidence *for law enforcement purposes* in order to reach that goal. The threat of law enforcement may ultimately have been intended as a means to an end, but the direct and primary purpose of MUSC's policy was to ensure the use of those means. In our opinion, this distinction is critical. Because law enforcement involvement always serves some broader social purpose or objective, under respondents' view, virtually any nonconsensual suspicionless search could be immunized under the special needs doctrine by defining the search solely in terms of its ultimate, rather than immediate, purpose. Such an approach is inconsistent with the Fourth Amendment. Given the primary purpose of the Charleston program, which was to use the threat of arrest and prosecution in order to force women into treatment, and given the extensive involvement of law enforcement officials at every stage of the policy, this case simply does not fit within the closely guarded category of "special needs."…

Accordingly, the judgment of the Court of Appeals is reversed, and the case is remanded for further proceedings consistent with this opinion.

Government entities are one of the largest employers in the United States. And while the Fourth Amendment applies "when the Government acts in its capacity as an employer," "the 'special needs' of the workplace" reduce the justification required for searches. For example, in *City of Ontario v. Quon* (2010), the Supreme Court rejected a challenge by a California police officer to his employer's warrantless search of his government-issued pager. The Court applied generic reasonableness balancing to conclude that the search was reasonable because it "was motivated by a legitimate work-related purpose" and not "excessively intrusive."

2. SCHOOL SEARCHES

The Supreme Court relies on "special needs" to uphold searches of public school students. See *Vernonia School District v. Acton* (1995) ("We have found such 'special needs' to exist in the public school context."). Thus, in *New Jersey v. T.L.O.* (1985), the Supreme Court upheld the warrantless search of a student's purse by the school's vice principal. The Court explained that while the Fourth Amendment protected public school students, its protections were lessened in the school setting. First, "the warrant requirement … is unsuited to the school environment: requiring a teacher to obtain a warrant before searching a child suspected of an infraction of school rules (or of the criminal law) would unduly interfere with the maintenance of the swift and informal disciplinary procedures needed in the schools." Second, the "probable cause" standard did not apply. Instead, "the legality of a search of a student should depend simply on the reasonableness, under all the circumstances, of the search." The Court further detailed the applicable standard as follows:

> "Under ordinary circumstances, a search of a student by a teacher or other school official will be 'justified at its inception' when there are reasonable grounds for suspecting that the search will turn up evidence that the

student has violated or is violating either the law or the rules of the school. Such a search will be permissible in its scope when the measures adopted are reasonably related to the objectives of the search and not excessively intrusive in light of the age and sex of the student and the nature of the infraction."

The Court applied this standard in the next case.

SAFFORD UNIFIED SCH. DIST. v. REDDING
557 U.S. 364 (2009)

Justice SOUTER delivered the opinion of the Court.

The issue here is whether a 13–year–old student's Fourth Amendment right was violated when she was subjected to a search of her bra and underpants by school officials acting on reasonable suspicion that she had brought forbidden prescription and over-the-counter drugs to school. Because there were no reasons to suspect the drugs presented a danger or were concealed in her underwear, we hold that the search did violate the Constitution, but because there is reason to question the clarity with which the right was established, the official who ordered the unconstitutional search is entitled to qualified immunity from liability.

I

The events immediately prior to the search in question began in 13–year–old Savana Redding's math class at Safford Middle School one October day in 2003. The assistant principal of the school, Kerry Wilson, came into the room and asked Savana to go to his office. There, he showed her a day planner, unzipped and open flat on his desk, in which there were several knives, lighters, a permanent marker, and a cigarette. Wilson asked Savana whether the planner was hers; she said it was, but that a few days before she had lent it to her friend, Marissa Glines. Savana stated that none of the items in the planner belonged to her.

Wilson then showed Savana four white prescription-strength ibuprofen 400–mg pills, and one over-the-counter blue naproxen 200–mg pill, all used for pain and inflammation but banned under school rules without advance permission. He asked Savana if she knew anything about the pills. Savana answered that she did not. Wilson then told Savana that he had received a report that she was giving these pills to fellow students; Savana denied it and agreed to let Wilson search her belongings.

Helen Romero, an administrative assistant, came into the office, and together with Wilson they searched Savana's backpack, finding nothing.

At that point, Wilson instructed Romero to take Savana to the school nurse's office to search her clothes for pills. Romero and the nurse, Peggy Schwallier, asked Savana to remove her jacket, socks, and shoes, leaving her in stretch pants and a T-shirt (both without pockets), which she was then asked to remove. Finally, Savana was told to pull her bra out and to the side and shake it, and to pull out the elastic on her underpants, thus exposing her breasts and pelvic area to some degree. No pills were found.

Savana's mother filed suit against Safford Unified School District #1, Wilson, Romero, and Schwallier for conducting a strip search in violation of Savana's Fourth Amendment rights....

II

... In New Jersey v. T.L.O (1985), we recognized that the school setting "requires some modification of the level of suspicion of illicit activity needed to justify a search," and held that for searches by school officials "a careful balancing of governmental and private interests suggests that the public interest is best served by a Fourth Amendment standard of reasonableness that stops short of probable cause." We have thus applied a standard of reasonable suspicion to determine the legality of a school administrator's search of a student, and have held that a school search "will be permissible in its scope when the measures adopted are reasonably related to the objectives of the search and not excessively intrusive in light of the age and sex of the student and the nature of the infraction."...

III
A

In this case, the school's policies strictly prohibit the nonmedical use, possession, or sale of any drug on school grounds, including "any prescription or over-the-counter drug, except those for which permission to use in school has been granted pursuant to Board policy." A week before Savana was searched, another student ... told the principal and Assistant Principal Wilson that "certain students were bringing drugs and weapons on campus," and that he had been sick after taking some pills that "he got from a classmate." On the morning of October 8, the same boy handed Wilson a white pill that he said Marissa Glines had given him. He told Wilson that students were planning to take the pills at lunch.

Wilson learned from Peggy Schwallier, the school nurse, that the pill was Ibuprofen 400 mg, available only by prescription. Wilson then called Marissa out of class. Outside the classroom, Marissa's teacher handed Wilson the day planner, found within Marissa's reach, containing various contraband items. Wilson escorted Marissa back to his office.

In the presence of Helen Romero, Wilson requested Marissa to turn out her pockets and open her wallet. Marissa produced a blue pill, several white ones, and a razor blade. Wilson asked where the blue pill came from, and Marissa answered, "I guess it slipped in when SHE gave me the IBU 400s." When Wilson asked whom she meant, Marissa replied, "Savana Redding." Wilson then enquired about the day planner and its contents; Marissa denied knowing anything about them. Wilson did not ask Marissa any follow-up questions to determine whether there was any likelihood that Savana presently had pills: neither asking when Marissa received the pills from Savana nor where Savana might be hiding them.

Schwallier did not immediately recognize the blue pill, but information provided through a poison control hotline indicated that the pill was a 200–mg dose of an anti-inflammatory drug, generically called naproxen, available over the counter. At Wilson's direction, Marissa was then subjected to a search of her bra and underpants by Romero and Schwallier, as Savana was later on. The search revealed no additional pills.

It was at this juncture that Wilson called Savana into his office and showed her the day planner. Their conversation established that Savana and Marissa were on friendly terms: while she denied knowledge of the contraband, Savana admitted that the day planner was hers and that she had lent it to Marissa. Wilson had other reports of their friendship from staff members, who had identified Savana and Marissa as part of an unusually rowdy group at the school's opening dance in August, during which alcohol and cigarettes were found in the girls' bathroom. Wilson had reason to connect the girls with this contraband, for Wilson knew that Jordan Romero had told the principal that before the dance, he had been at a party at Savana's house where alcohol was served. Marissa's statement that the pills came from Savana was thus sufficiently plausible to warrant suspicion that Savana was involved in pill distribution.

This suspicion of Wilson's was enough to justify a search of Savana's backpack and outer clothing. If a student is reasonably suspected of giving out contraband pills, she is reasonably suspected of carrying them on her person and in the carryall that has become an item of student uniform in most places today. If Wilson's reasonable suspicion of pill distribution were not understood to support searches of outer clothes and backpack, it would not justify any search worth making. And the look into Savana's bag, in her presence and in the relative privacy of Wilson's office, was not excessively intrusive, any more than Romero's subsequent search of her outer clothing.

B

… Savana claim[s] that extending the search at Wilson's behest to the point of making her pull out her underwear was constitutionally unreasonable. The exact label for this final step in the intrusion is not important, though strip search is a fair way to speak of it. Romero and Schwallier directed Savana to remove her clothes down to her underwear, and then "pull out" her bra and the elastic band on her underpants. Although Romero and Schwallier stated that they did not see anything when Savana followed their instructions, we would not define strip search and its Fourth Amendment consequences in a way that would guarantee litigation about who was looking and how much was seen. The very fact of Savana's pulling her underwear away from her body in the presence of the two officials who were able to see her necessarily exposed her breasts and pelvic area to some degree, and both subjective and reasonable societal expectations of personal privacy support the treatment of such a search as categorically distinct, requiring distinct elements of justification on the part of school authorities for going beyond a search of outer clothing and belongings.

Savana's subjective expectation of privacy against such a search is inherent in her account of it as embarrassing, frightening, and humiliating. The reasonableness of her expectation (required by the Fourth Amendment standard) is indicated by the consistent experiences of other young people similarly searched, whose adolescent vulnerability intensifies the patent intrusiveness of the exposure. The common reaction of these adolescents simply registers the obviously different meaning of a search exposing the body from the experience of nakedness or near undress in other school circumstances. Changing for gym is getting ready for play; exposing for a search is responding to an accusation reserved for suspected wrongdoers and fairly understood as so degrading that a number of communities have decided that strip searches in schools are never reasonable and have banned them no matter what the facts may be.

The indignity of the search does not, of course, outlaw it, but it does implicate the rule of reasonableness as stated in T.L.O., that "the search as actually conducted be reasonably related in scope to the circumstances which justified the interference in the first place." The scope will be permissible, that is, when it is "not excessively intrusive in light of the age and sex of the student and the nature of the infraction."

Here, the content of the suspicion failed to match the degree of intrusion. Wilson knew beforehand that the pills were prescription-strength ibuprofen and over-the-counter naproxen, common pain relievers equivalent to two Advil, or one Aleve. He must have been aware of the nature and limited threat of the specific drugs he was searching for, and while just about anything can be taken in quantities that will do real harm, Wilson had no reason to suspect that large amounts of the drugs were being passed around, or that individual students were receiving great numbers of pills.

Nor could Wilson have suspected that Savana was hiding common painkillers in her underwear. Petitioners suggest, as a truth universally acknowledged, that "students hide contraband in or under their clothing," and cite a smattering of cases of students with contraband in their underwear. But when the categorically extreme intrusiveness of a search down to the body of an adolescent requires some justification in suspected facts, general background possibilities fall short; a reasonable search that extensive calls for suspicion that it will pay off. But nondangerous school contraband does not raise the specter of stashes in intimate places, and there is no evidence in the record of any general practice among Safford Middle School students of hiding that sort of thing in underwear; neither Jordan nor Marissa suggested to Wilson that Savana was doing that, and the preceding search of Marissa that Wilson ordered yielded nothing. Wilson never even determined when Marissa had received the pills from Savana; if it had been a few days before, that would weigh heavily against any reasonable conclusion that Savana presently had the pills on her person, much less in her underwear.

In sum, what was missing from the suspected facts that pointed to Savana was any indication of danger to the students from the power of the drugs or their quantity, and any reason to suppose that Savana was carrying pills in her underwear. We think that the combination of these deficiencies was fatal to finding the search reasonable.

…. The T.L.O. concern to limit a school search to reasonable scope requires the support of reasonable suspicion of danger or of resort to underwear for hiding evidence of wrongdoing before a search can reasonably make the quantum leap from outer clothes and backpacks to exposure of intimate parts. The meaning of such a search, and the degradation its subject may reasonably feel, place a search that intrusive in a category of its own demanding its own specific suspicions….

POLICE OFFICERS IN SCHOOLS

The dichotomy the Court implicitly crafted between school administrators and police officers in its school search cases became strained when, in the wake of high-profile school shootings in the 1990s, States staffed public schools with law enforcement officers ("School Resource Officers" or SROs). In 2015-16, about 65% of public secondary schools had police officers on site at least part of the time. The Bureau of Justice Statistics estimated that, as of 2019, there were almost 25,000 SROs in the United States.

Lower courts often apply the same deferential standard to SROs as to school administrators. See Josh Gupta-Kagan, *Reevaluating School Searches Following School-To-Prison Pipeline Reforms*, 87 Fordham L. Rev. 2013 (2019). The potential for police officers to become involved in routine school disciplinary matters also raises concerns about a "school to prison pipeline."

A chart published by the U.S. Department of Education reveals the breakdown by race for referrals from the nation's public schools to law enforcement in 2011-2012. The chart breaks down the 260,000 referrals and 92,000 arrests that school year.

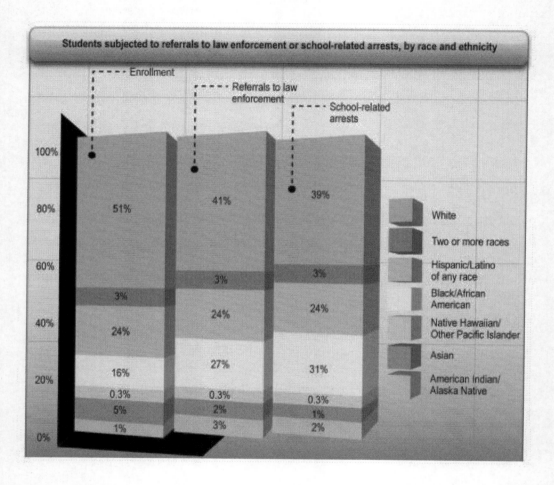

3. PROBATION AND PAROLE

The United States incarcerates a remarkable high percentage of its population, as compared to historical norms or other countries. In 2020, about 550,000 individuals were detained in America's jails awaiting trial or serving misdemeanor sentences. Another 1.2 million people were held in the nation's prisons, primarily for felonies. These figures pale in comparison however to the number of people under community supervision on

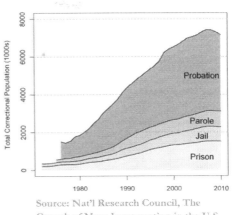

Source: Nat'l Research Council, The Growth of Mass Incarceration in the U.S.

probation and parole. There are almost 4 million people on probation or parole at any given time in the United States. This means that the rules governing searches of probationers and parolees (discussed in the next cases) are critically important.

GRIFFIN v. WISCONSIN
483 U.S. 868 (1987)

Justice SCALIA delivered the opinion of the Court.

…. On September 4, 1980, Joseph Griffin, who had previously been convicted of a felony, was convicted in Wisconsin state court of resisting arrest, disorderly conduct, and obstructing an officer. He was placed on probation.

Wisconsin law puts probationers in the legal custody of the State Department of Health and Social Services and renders them "subject to conditions set by the court and rules and regulations established by the department." One of the Department's regulations permits any probation officer to search a probationer's home without a warrant as long as his supervisor approves and as long as there are "reasonable grounds" to believe the presence of contraband—including any item that the probationer cannot possess under the probation conditions…. Another regulation makes it a violation of the terms of probation to refuse to consent to a home search. And still another forbids a probationer to possess a firearm without advance approval from a probation officer.

On April 5, 1983, while Griffin was still on probation, Michael Lew, the supervisor of Griffin's probation officer, received information from a detective on the Beloit Police Department that there were or might be guns in Griffin's apartment.... Lew, accompanied by another probation officer and three plainclothes policemen, went to the apartment. When Griffin answered the door, Lew told him who they were and informed him that they were going to search his home. During the subsequent search — carried out entirely by the probation officers under the authority of Wisconsin's probation regulation — they found a handgun.

Griffin was charged with possession of a firearm by a convicted felon, which is itself a felony. He moved to suppress the evidence seized during the search. [The trial court denied the motion and the Wisconsin Supreme Court affirmed.]

We think the Wisconsin Supreme Court correctly concluded that this warrantless search did not violate the Fourth Amendment.... A probationer's home, like anyone else's, is protected by the Fourth Amendment's requirement that searches be "reasonable." Although we usually require that a search be undertaken only pursuant to a warrant (and thus supported by probable cause, as the Constitution says warrants must be), we have permitted exceptions when "special needs, beyond the normal need for law enforcement, make the warrant and probable-cause requirement impracticable."

Thus, we have held that government employers and supervisors may conduct warrantless, work-related searches of employees' desks and offices without probable cause, O'Connor v. Ortega (1987), and that school officials may conduct warrantless searches of some student property, also without probable cause, New Jersey v. T.L.O. (1985). We have also held, for similar reasons, that in certain circumstances government investigators conducting searches pursuant to a regulatory scheme need not adhere to the usual warrant or probable-cause requirements as long as their searches meet "reasonable legislative or administrative standards." Camara v. Municipal Court (1967).

A State's operation of a probation system, like its operation of a school, government office or prison, or its supervision of a regulated industry, likewise presents "special needs" beyond normal law enforcement that may justify departures from the usual warrant and probable-cause requirements.... To a greater or lesser degree, it is always true of probationers (as we have said it to be true of parolees) that they do not enjoy the absolute liberty to which every citizen is entitled, but only conditional liberty properly dependent on observance of special probation restrictions.

These restrictions are meant to assure that the probation serves as a period of genuine rehabilitation and that the community is not harmed by the probationer's being at large. These same goals require and justify the exercise of supervision to assure that the restrictions are in fact observed.... Supervision, then, is a "special need" of the State permitting a degree of impingement upon privacy that would not be constitutional if applied to the public at large. That permissible degree is not unlimited, however, so we next turn to whether it has been exceeded here.

In determining whether the "special needs" of its probation system justify Wisconsin's search regulation, we must take that regulation as it has been interpreted by state corrections officials and state courts. The Wisconsin Supreme Court—the ultimate authority on issues of Wisconsin law—has held that a tip from a police detective that Griffin "had" or "may have had" an illegal weapon at his home constituted the requisite "reasonable grounds." Whether or not we would choose to interpret a similarly worded federal regulation in that fashion, we are bound by the state court's interpretation, which is relevant to our constitutional analysis only insofar as it fixes the meaning of the regulation. We think it clear that the special needs of Wisconsin's probation system make the warrant requirement impracticable and justify replacement of the standard of probable cause by "reasonable grounds," as defined by the Wisconsin Supreme Court.

.... It is both unrealistic and destructive of the whole object of the continuing probation relationship to insist upon the same degree of demonstrable reliability of particular items of supporting data, and upon the same degree of certainty of violation, as is required in other contexts. In some cases—especially those involving drugs or illegal weapons—the probation agency must be able to act based upon a lesser degree of certainty than the Fourth Amendment would otherwise require in order to intervene before a probationer does damage to himself or society. The agency, moreover, must be able to proceed on the basis of its entire experience with the probationer, and to assess probabilities in the light of its knowledge of his life, character, and circumstances.

To allow adequate play for such factors, we think it reasonable to permit information provided by a police officer whether or not on the basis of firsthand knowledge, to support a probationer search. The same conclusion is suggested by the fact that the police may be unwilling to disclose their confidential sources to probation personnel. For the same reason, and also because it is the very assumption of the institution of probation that the probationer is in need of rehabilitation and is more likely than the ordinary citizen to violate the law, we think it enough if the information provided indicates, as it did here, only the likelihood ("had or might have guns") of facts justifying the search.

The search of Griffin's residence was "reasonable" within the meaning of the Fourth Amendment because it was conducted pursuant to a valid regulation governing probationers. This conclusion makes it unnecessary to consider whether, as the court below held and the State urges, *any* search of a probationer's home by a probation officer is lawful when there are "reasonable grounds" to believe contraband is present.

UNITED STATES v. KNIGHTS
534 U.S. 112 (2001)

Chief Justice REHNQUIST delivered the opinion of the Court.

A California court sentenced respondent Mark Knights to summary probation for a drug offense. The probation order included the following condition: that Knights would "submit his person, property, place of residence, vehicle, personal effects, to search at anytime, with or without a search warrant, warrant of arrest or reasonable cause by any probation officer or law enforcement officer." Knights signed the probation order, which stated immediately above his signature that "I HAVE RECEIVED A COPY, READ AND UNDERSTAND THE ABOVE TERMS AND CONDITIONS OF PROBATION AND AGREE TO ABIDE BY SAME." In this case, we decide whether a search pursuant to this probation condition, and supported by reasonable suspicion, satisfied the Fourth Amendment.

Three days after Knights was placed on probation, a Pacific Gas & Electric (PG & E) power transformer and adjacent Pacific Bell telecommunications vault near the Napa County Airport were pried open and set on fire, causing an estimated $1.5 million in damage. Brass padlocks had been removed and a gasoline accelerant had been used to ignite the fire. This incident was the latest in more than 30 recent acts of vandalism against PG&E facilities in Napa County. Suspicion for these acts had long focused on Knights and his friend, Steven Simoneau…. Detective Hancock decided to set up surveillance of Knights' apartment. [After viewing suspicious activity,] Detective Hancock decided to conduct a search of Knights' apartment. Detective Hancock was aware of the search condition in Knights' probation order and thus believed that a warrant was not necessary. The search revealed a detonation cord, ammunition, liquid chemicals, instruction manuals on chemistry and electrical circuitry, bolt cutters, telephone pole-climbing spurs, drug paraphernalia, and a brass padlock stamped "PG&E."

Knights was arrested, and a federal grand jury subsequently indicted him for conspiracy to commit arson, for possession of an unregistered destructive device, and for being a felon in possession of ammunition. Knights moved to suppress the evidence obtained during the search of his apartment. The District Court held that Detective Hancock had "reasonable suspicion" to believe that Knights was involved with incendiary materials. The District Court nonetheless granted the motion to suppress on the ground that the search was for "investigatory" rather than "probationary" purposes....

Certainly nothing in the condition of probation suggests that it was confined to searches bearing upon probationary status and nothing more. The search condition provides that Knights will submit to a search "by any probation officer or law enforcement officer" and does not mention anything about purpose. The question then is whether the Fourth Amendment limits searches pursuant to this probation condition to those with a "probationary" purpose.

Knights argues that this limitation follows from our decision in Griffin v. Wisconsin (1987). In Griffin, we upheld a search of a probationer conducted pursuant to a Wisconsin regulation permitting "any probation officer to search a probationer's home without a warrant as long as his supervisor approves and as long as there are 'reasonable grounds' to believe the presence of contraband." The Wisconsin regulation that authorized the search was not an express condition of Griffin's probation; in fact, the regulation was not even promulgated at the time of Griffin's sentence. The regulation applied to all Wisconsin probationers, with no need for a judge to make an individualized determination that the probationer's conviction justified the need for warrantless searches. We held that a State's operation of its probation system presented a "special need" for the "exercise of supervision to assure that probation restrictions are in fact observed." That special need for supervision justified the Wisconsin regulation and the search pursuant to the regulation was thus reasonable.

In Knights' view, apparently shared by the Court of Appeals, a warrantless search of a probationer satisfies the Fourth Amendment only if it is just like the search at issue in Griffin – i.e., a "special needs" search conducted by a probation officer monitoring whether the probationer is complying with probation restrictions. This dubious logic – that an opinion upholding the constitutionality of a particular search implicitly holds unconstitutional any search that is not like it – runs contrary to Griffin's express statement that its "special needs" holding made it "unnecessary to consider whether" warrantless searches of probationers were otherwise reasonable within the meaning of the Fourth Amendment.

We now consider that question in assessing the constitutionality of the search of Knights' apartment…. The touchstone of the Fourth Amendment is reasonableness, and the reasonableness of a search is determined by assessing, on the one hand, the degree to which it intrudes upon an individual's privacy and, on the other, the degree to which it is needed for the promotion of legitimate governmental interests….

Inherent in the very nature of probation is that probationers do not enjoy the absolute liberty to which every citizen is entitled…. The judge who sentenced Knights to probation determined that it was necessary to condition the probation on Knights' acceptance of the search provision. It was reasonable to conclude that the search condition would further the two primary goals of probation-rehabilitation and protecting society from future criminal violations. The probation order clearly expressed the search condition and Knights was unambiguously informed of it. The probation condition thus significantly diminished Knights' reasonable expectation of privacy….

[As for the government interest,] the State has a dual concern with a probationer. On the one hand is the hope that he will successfully complete probation and be integrated back into the community. On the other is the concern, quite justified, that he will be more likely to engage in criminal conduct than an ordinary member of the community. The view of the Court of Appeals in this case would require the State to shut its eyes to the latter concern and concentrate only on the former. But we hold that the Fourth Amendment does not put the State to such a choice. Its interest in apprehending violators of the criminal law, thereby protecting potential victims of criminal enterprise, may therefore justifiably focus on probationers in a way that it does not on the ordinary citizen….

We hold that the balance of these considerations requires no more than reasonable suspicion to conduct a search of this probationer's house…. The District Court found, and Knights concedes, that the search in this case was supported by reasonable suspicion. We therefore hold that the warrantless search of Knights, supported by reasonable suspicion and authorized by a condition of probation, was reasonable within the meaning of the Fourth Amendment….

Probation and parole have distinct features. Often a person on probation has been spared the obligation, at least initially, to serve time in prison or jail. By contrast, parole is typically for individuals who have been incarcerated and are being permitted to serve the remainder of their sentences outside of prison. The Supreme Court explained in *Samson v. California* (2006) that:

> "Parolees have fewer expectations of privacy than probationers, because parole is more akin to imprisonment than probation is to imprisonment. As this Court has pointed out, 'parole is an established variation on imprisonment of convicted criminals. The essence of parole is release from prison, before the completion of sentence, on the condition that the prisoner abide by certain rules during the balance of the sentence.' In most cases, the State is willing to extend parole only because it is able to condition it upon compliance with certain requirements."

In *Samson*, Donald Samson had been informed upon his release from prison that California law required him to "submit to suspicionless searches by a parole officer or other peace officer at any time."

California Penal Code § 3067

"(a) Any inmate who is eligible for release on parole … shall be given notice that he or she is subject to terms and conditions of his or her release from prison.

(b) The notice shall include all of the following: …

> An advisement that he or she is subject to search or seizure by a probation or parole officer or other peace officer at any time of the day or night, with or without a search warrant or with or without cause."

A police officer later saw Samson walking down the street, knew he was on parole, searched him, and discovered drugs in his pocket.

Samson argued that the search violated the Fourth Amendment given that he had no outstanding warrants and that the officer had no individualized suspicion. The Court rejected that argument, explaining that the State has an "overwhelming interest in supervising parolees because parolees … are more likely to commit future criminal offenses" creating a state interest in supervision aimed at "reducing recidivism and thereby promoting reintegration and positive citizenship among probationers and parolees." Accordingly, the Court held that "the Fourth Amendment does not prohibit a police officer from conducting a suspicionless search of a parolee."

Given the holding in *Samson*, it should not be surprising that courts also grant prison and jail officials broad authority to search inmates without probable cause or reasonable suspicion. As the Supreme Court explained in *Florence v. Board of Chosen Freeholders of Burlington* (2012):

> "Maintaining safety and order at these institutions requires the expertise of correctional officials, who must have substantial discretion to devise reasonable solutions to the problems they face. The Court has confirmed the importance of deference to correctional officials and explained that a regulation impinging on an inmate's constitutional rights must be upheld if it is reasonably related to legitimate penological interests."

In *Florence*, the Court upheld the authority of correctional authorities to require strip searches of even pretrial detainees, including persons charged with minor offenses and not yet found guilty of any crime. The Court also permits prison and jail officials to conduct suspicionless searches of inmate lockers and cells. See *Hudson v. Palmer* (1984).

4. CHECKPOINTS

The Supreme Court applies a variant of the "special needs" doctrine to traffic checkpoints to uphold stops of motorists in certain circumstances without a warrant or individualized suspicion.

MICHIGAN DEP'T OF STATE POLICE v. SITZ
496 U.S. 444 (1990)

Case Summary

In *Sitz*, the Supreme Court considered "whether a State's use of highway sobriety checkpoints violates the Fourth and Fourteenth Amendments to the United States Constitution." In that case,

> The Michigan Department of State Police and its director, established a sobriety checkpoint pilot program in early 1986.... Under the guidelines [created under the program], checkpoints would be set up at selected sites along state roads. All vehicles passing through a checkpoint would be stopped and their drivers briefly examined for signs of intoxication. In cases where a checkpoint officer detected signs of intoxication, the motorist would be directed to a location out of the traffic flow where an officer would check the motorist's driver's license and car registration and, if warranted, conduct further sobriety tests. Should the field tests and the officer's observations suggest that the driver was intoxicated, an arrest would be made. All other drivers would be permitted to resume their journey immediately.

> The first – and to date the only – sobriety checkpoint operated under the program was conducted in Saginaw County with the assistance of the Saginaw County Sheriff's Department. During the 75–minute duration of the checkpoint's operation, 126 vehicles passed through the checkpoint. The average delay for each vehicle was approximately 25 seconds. Two drivers were detained for field sobriety testing, and one of the two was arrested for driving under the influence of alcohol. A third driver who drove through without stopping was pulled over by an officer in an observation vehicle and arrested for driving under the influence....

The Court started its analysis by acknowledging that "a Fourth Amendment 'seizure' occurs when a vehicle is stopped at a checkpoint." Consequently, the Court had to decide "whether such seizures are 'reasonable' under the Fourth Amendment." To answer this question, the Court did not apply the traditional warrant-and-probable-cause requirements but, instead, balanced the invasiveness of the stops against the government interests involved.

As for invasiveness, the Court stated that "the measure of the intrusion on motorists stopped briefly at sobriety checkpoints is slight,"

> "The circumstances surrounding a checkpoint stop and search are far less intrusive than those attending a roving-patrol stop. Roving patrols often operate at night on seldom-traveled roads, and their approach may frighten motorists. At traffic checkpoints the motorist can see that other vehicles are being stopped, he can see visible signs of the officers' authority, and he is much less likely to be frightened or annoyed by the intrusion. Here, checkpoints are selected pursuant to the guidelines, and uniformed police officers stop every approaching vehicle."

On the other side of the balance, the Court emphasized "the magnitude of the drunken driving problem" and "the States' interest in eradicating it," noting that "Drunk drivers cause an annual death toll of over 25,000 and in the same time span cause nearly one million personal injuries and more than five billion dollars in property damage." It also noted that the checkpoint was somewhat effective, since "approximately 1.6 percent of the drivers passing through the checkpoint were arrested for alcohol impairment" and "an expert witness testified at the trial that experience in other States demonstrated that, on the whole, sobriety checkpoints resulted in drunken driving arrests of around 1 percent of all motorists stopped."

The Court concluded:

> "In sum, the balance of the State's interest in preventing drunken driving, the extent to which this system can reasonably be said to advance that interest, and the degree of intrusion upon individual motorists who are briefly stopped, weighs in favor of the state program. We therefore hold that it is consistent with the Fourth Amendment."

INDIANAPOLIS v. EDMOND
531 U.S. 32 (2000)

Justice O'CONNOR delivered the opinion of the Court.

I

In August 1998, the city of Indianapolis began to operate vehicle checkpoints on Indianapolis roads in an effort to interdict unlawful drugs. The city conducted six such roadblocks between August and November that year, stopping 1,161 vehicles and arresting 104 motorists. Fifty-five arrests were for drug-related crimes, while 49 were for offenses unrelated to drugs. The overall "hit rate" of the program was thus approximately nine percent.

The parties stipulated to the facts concerning the operation of the checkpoints by the Indianapolis Police Department (IPD) for purposes of the preliminary injunction proceedings instituted below. At each checkpoint location, the police stop a predetermined number of vehicles. Approximately 30 officers are stationed at the checkpoint. Pursuant to written directives issued by the chief of police, at least one officer approaches the vehicle, advises the driver that he or she is being stopped briefly at a drug checkpoint, and asks the driver to produce a license and registration. The officer also looks for signs of impairment and conducts an open-view examination of the vehicle from the outside. A narcotics-detection dog walks around the outside of each stopped vehicle.

The directives instruct the officers that they may conduct a search only by consent or based on the appropriate quantum of particularized suspicion. The officers must conduct each stop in the same manner until particularized suspicion develops, and the officers have no discretion to stop any vehicle out of sequence. The city agreed in the stipulation to operate the checkpoints in such a way as to ensure that the total duration of each stop, absent reasonable suspicion or probable cause, would be five minutes or less.

The affidavit of Indianapolis Police Sergeant Marshall DePew, although it is technically outside the parties' stipulation, provides further insight concerning the operation of the checkpoints. According to Sergeant DePew, checkpoint locations are selected weeks in advance based on such considerations as area crime statistics and traffic flow. The checkpoints are generally operated during daylight hours and are identified with lighted signs reading, "NARCOTICS CHECKPOINT __ MILE

AHEAD, NARCOTICS K–9 IN USE, BE PREPARED TO STOP." Once a group of cars has been stopped, other traffic proceeds without interruption until all the stopped cars have been processed or diverted for further processing. Sergeant DePew also stated that the average stop for a vehicle not subject to further processing lasts two to three minutes or less.

Respondents James Edmond and Joell Palmer were each stopped at a narcotics checkpoint in late September 1998. Respondents then filed a lawsuit on behalf of themselves and the class of all motorists who had been stopped or were subject to being stopped in the future at the Indianapolis drug checkpoints. Respondents claimed that the roadblocks violated the Fourth Amendment of the United States Constitution and the search and seizure provision of the Indiana Constitution. Respondents requested declaratory and injunctive relief for the class, as well as damages and attorney's fees for themselves…. A divided panel of the United States Court of Appeals for the Seventh Circuit … held that the checkpoints contravened the Fourth Amendment….

II

The Fourth Amendment requires that searches and seizures be reasonable. A search or seizure is ordinarily unreasonable in the absence of individualized suspicion of wrongdoing. While such suspicion is not an "irreducible" component of reasonableness, we have recognized only limited circumstances in which the usual rule does not apply. For example, we have upheld certain regimes of suspicionless searches where the program was designed to serve "special needs, beyond the normal need for law enforcement." See, e.g., Vernonia School Dist. 47J v. Acton (1995) (random drug testing of student-athletes); Treasury Employees v. Von Raab (1989) (drug tests for United States Customs Service employees seeking transfer or promotion to certain positions); Skinner v. Railway Labor Executives' Assn. (1989) (drug and alcohol tests for railway employees involved in train accidents or found to be in violation of particular safety regulations). We have also allowed searches for certain administrative purposes without particularized suspicion of misconduct, provided that those searches are appropriately limited. See, e.g., New York v. Burger (1987) (warrantless administrative inspection of premises of "closely regulated" business); Michigan v. Tyler (1978) (administrative inspection of fire-damaged premises to determine cause of blaze); Camara v. Municipal Court of City and County of San Francisco (1967) (administrative inspection to ensure compliance with city housing code).

We have also upheld brief, suspicionless seizures of motorists at a fixed Border Patrol checkpoint designed to intercept illegal aliens, United States v. Martinez–Fuerte (1976), and at a sobriety checkpoint aimed at removing drunk drivers from the road, Michigan Dept. of State Police v. Sitz (1990). In addition, in Delaware v. Prouse (1979), we suggested that a similar type of roadblock with the purpose of verifying drivers' licenses and vehicle registrations would be permissible. In none of these cases, however, did we indicate approval of a checkpoint program whose primary purpose was to detect evidence of ordinary criminal wrongdoing.

…. In United States v. Montoya de Hernandez (1985), we counted Martinez–Fuerte as one of a number of Fourth Amendment cases that "reflect longstanding concern for the protection of the integrity of the border." Although the stops in Martinez–Fuerte did not occur at the border itself, the checkpoints were located near the border and served a border control function made necessary by the difficulty of guarding the border's entire length.

In Sitz, we evaluated the constitutionality of a Michigan highway sobriety checkpoint program…. This checkpoint program was clearly aimed at reducing the immediate hazard posed by the presence of drunk drivers on the highways, and there was an obvious connection between the imperative of highway safety and the law enforcement practice at issue. The gravity of the drunk driving problem and the magnitude of the State's interest in getting drunk drivers off the road weighed heavily in our determination that the program was constitutional.

In Prouse, we invalidated a discretionary, suspicionless stop for a spot check of a motorist's driver's license and vehicle registration. The officer's conduct in that case was unconstitutional primarily on account of his exercise of "standardless and unconstrained discretion." We nonetheless acknowledged the States' "vital interest in ensuring that only those qualified to do so are permitted to operate motor vehicles, that these vehicles are fit for safe operation, and hence that licensing, registration, and vehicle inspection requirements are being observed." Accordingly, we suggested that "questioning of all oncoming traffic at roadblock-type stops" would be a lawful means of serving this interest in highway safety.

We further indicated in Prouse that we considered the purposes of such a hypothetical roadblock to be distinct from a general purpose of investigating crime…. Not only does the common thread of highway safety thus run through

Sitz and Prouse, but Prouse itself reveals a difference in the Fourth Amendment significance of highway safety interests and the general interest in crime control.

III

It is well established that a vehicle stop at a highway checkpoint effectuates a seizure within the meaning of the Fourth Amendment. The fact that officers walk a narcotics-detection dog around the exterior of each car at the Indianapolis checkpoints does not transform the seizure into a search. See United States v. Place (1983). Just as in Place, an exterior sniff of an automobile does not require entry into the car and is not designed to disclose any information other than the presence or absence of narcotics. Like the dog sniff in Place, a sniff by a dog that simply walks around a car is "much less intrusive than a typical search." Rather, what principally distinguishes these checkpoints from those we have previously approved is their primary purpose.

As petitioners concede, the Indianapolis checkpoint program unquestionably has the primary purpose of interdicting illegal narcotics. In their stipulation of facts, the parties repeatedly refer to the checkpoints as "drug checkpoints" and describe them as "being operated by the City of Indianapolis in an effort to interdict unlawful drugs in Indianapolis." In addition, the first document attached to the parties' stipulation is entitled "DRUG CHECKPOINT CONTACT OFFICER DIRECTIVES BY ORDER OF THE CHIEF OF POLICE." These directives instruct officers to "advise the citizen that they are being stopped briefly at a drug checkpoint." The second document attached to the stipulation is entitled "1998 Drug Road Blocks" and contains a statistical breakdown of information relating to the checkpoints conducted. Further, according to Sergeant DePew, the checkpoints are identified with lighted signs reading, "NARCOTICS CHECKPOINT ___ MILE AHEAD, NARCOTICS K–9 IN USE, BE PREPARED TO STOP."

We have never approved a checkpoint program whose primary purpose was to detect evidence of ordinary criminal wrongdoing. Rather, our checkpoint cases have recognized only limited exceptions to the general rule that a seizure must be accompanied by some measure of individualized suspicion. We suggested in Prouse that we would not credit the "general interest in crime control" as justification for a regime of suspicionless stops. Consistent with this suggestion, each of the checkpoint programs that we have approved was designed primarily to serve purposes closely related to the problems of policing the border or the necessity of ensuring roadway safety. Because the primary purpose of the Indianapolis narcotics checkpoint program is to uncover evidence of ordinary criminal wrongdoing, the program contravenes the Fourth Amendment....

Of course, there are circumstances that may justify a law enforcement checkpoint where the primary purpose would otherwise, but for some emergency, relate to ordinary crime control. For example, as the Court of Appeals noted, the Fourth Amendment would almost certainly permit an appropriately tailored roadblock set up to thwart an imminent terrorist attack or to catch a dangerous criminal who is likely to flee by way of a particular route. The exigencies created by these scenarios are far removed from the circumstances under which authorities might simply stop cars as a matter of course to see if there just happens to be a felon leaving the jurisdiction. While we do not limit the purposes that may justify a checkpoint program to any rigid set of categories, we decline to approve a program whose primary purpose is ultimately indistinguishable from the general interest in crime control.

.... Petitioners argue that the Indianapolis checkpoint program is justified by its lawful secondary purposes of keeping impaired motorists off the road and verifying licenses and registrations. If this were the case, however, law enforcement authorities would be able to establish checkpoints for virtually any purpose so long as they also included a license or sobriety check. For this reason, we examine the available evidence to determine the primary purpose of the checkpoint program. While we recognize the challenges inherent in a purpose inquiry, courts routinely engage in this enterprise in many areas of constitutional jurisprudence as a means of sifting abusive governmental conduct from that which is lawful. As a result, a program driven by an impermissible purpose may be proscribed while a program impelled by licit purposes is permitted, even though the challenged conduct may be outwardly similar. While reasonableness under the Fourth Amendment is predominantly an objective inquiry, our special needs and administrative search cases demonstrate that purpose is often relevant when suspicionless intrusions pursuant to a general scheme are at issue.

It goes without saying that our holding today does nothing to alter the constitutional status of the sobriety and border checkpoints that we approved in Sitz and Martinez–Fuerte, or of the type of traffic checkpoint that we suggested would be lawful in Prouse. The constitutionality of such checkpoint programs still depends on a balancing of the competing interests at stake and the effectiveness of the program. When law enforcement authorities pursue primarily general crime control purposes at checkpoints such as here, however, stops can only be justified by some quantum of individualized suspicion.

Our holding also does not affect the validity of border searches or searches at places like airports and government buildings, where the need for such measures to ensure public safety can be particularly acute. Nor does our opinion speak to other intrusions aimed primarily at purposes beyond the general interest in crime control. Our holding also does not impair the ability of police officers to act appropriately upon information that they properly learn during a checkpoint stop justified by a lawful primary purpose, even where such action may result in the arrest of a motorist for an offense unrelated to that purpose. Finally, we caution that the purpose inquiry in this context is to be conducted only at the programmatic level and is not an invitation to probe the minds of individual officers acting at the scene.

Because the primary purpose of the Indianapolis checkpoint program is ultimately indistinguishable from the general interest in crime control, the checkpoints violate the Fourth Amendment....

Four years after *Edmond*, the Supreme Court decided another checkpoint case – an information-gathering checkpoint in **Illinois v. Lidster** (2004). That case concerned a checkpoint set up after a motorist killed a bicyclist in a hit-and-run accident around midnight. A week after the killing, police officers set up a checkpoint at the same location and same late hour. Officers stopped each car, leading to lines of up to fifteen cars in each lane. "As each vehicle drew up to the checkpoint, an officer would stop it for 10 to 15 seconds, ask the occupants whether they had seen anything happen there the previous weekend, and hand each driver a flyer." The flyer said:

ALERT ... FATAL HIT & RUN ACCIDENT

...

ASSISTANCE IN IDENTIFYING THE VEHICLE AND DRIVER INVOLVED IN THIS ACCIDENT WHICH KILLED A 70 YEAR OLD BICYCLIST.

As Robert Lidster approached the checkpoint, his van swerved and nearly hit one of the officers. After failing a sobriety test, Lidster was arrested for drunk driving.

Lidster argued that the information checkpoint was created for the primary purpose of general crime control and thus unconstitutional under *Indianapolis v. Edmond*. The Supreme Court rejected Lidster's challenge, explaining that:

> " The checkpoint stop here differs significantly from that in *Edmond*. The stop's primary law enforcement purpose was *not* to determine whether a vehicle's occupants were committing a crime, but to ask vehicle occupants, as members of the public, for their help in providing information about a crime in all likelihood committed by others. The police expected the information elicited to help them apprehend, not the vehicle's occupants, but other individuals....
>
> For another thing, information-seeking highway stops are less likely to provoke anxiety or to prove intrusive. The stops are likely brief. The police are not likely to ask questions designed to elicit self-incriminating information. And citizens will often react positively when police simply ask for their help as responsible citizens to give whatever information they may have to aid in law enforcement.
>
> The relevant public concern was grave. Police were investigating a crime that had resulted in a human death. No one denies the police's need to obtain more information at that time. And the stop's objective was to help find the perpetrator of a specific and known crime, not of unknown crimes of a general sort.
>
> The stop advanced this grave public concern to a significant degree. The police appropriately tailored their checkpoint stops to fit important criminal investigatory needs. The stops took place about one week after the hit-and-run accident, on the same highway near the location of the accident, and at about the same time of night. And police used the stops to obtain information from drivers, some of whom might well have been in the vicinity of the crime at the time it occurred.
>
> Most importantly, the stops interfered only minimally with liberty of the sort the Fourth Amendment seeks to protect. Viewed objectively, each stop required only a brief wait in line – a very few minutes at most. Contact with the police lasted only a few seconds. Police contact consisted simply of a request for information and the distribution of a flyer. Viewed subjectively, the contact provided little reason for anxiety or alarm. The

police stopped all vehicles systematically. And there is no allegation here that the police acted in a discriminatory or otherwise unlawful manner while questioning motorists during stops.

For these reasons we conclude that the checkpoint stop was constitutional.

5. BORDERS AND AIRPORTS

Another place the courts apply a special-needs-like analysis is to border searches.

UNITED STATES v. MONTOYA DE HERNANDEZ
473 U.S. 531 (1985)

Case Summary

Shortly after midnight on March 5, 1983, Rosa Montoya de Hernandez flew into Los Angeles Airport from Bogota, Columbia. As she went through customs, inspectors suspected that she "was a 'balloon swallower,' one who attempts to smuggle narcotics into this country hidden in her alimentary canal." The inspectors detained Montoya de Hernandez while waiting for her to use the bathroom. When she did not do so, they obtained a court order for a rectal examination. By the time they obtained the order, Montoya de Hernandez's detention had lasted almost 24 hours. Pursuant to the court order, "a physician conducted a rectal examination and removed from respondent's rectum a balloon containing a foreign substance. Respondent was then placed formally under arrest. By 4:10 a.m. respondent had passed 6 similar balloons; over the next four days she passed 88 balloons containing a total of 528 grams of 80% pure cocaine hydrochloride."

The Ninth Circuit reversed Montoya de Hernandez's subsequent conviction for narcotics smuggling, "holding that her detention violated the Fourth Amendment to the United States Constitution because the customs inspectors did not have a 'clear indication' of alimentary canal smuggling at the time she was detained." In reversing the Ninth Circuit, the Supreme Court emphasized the government's heightened interests at the international border:

"The Fourth Amendment's balance of reasonableness is qualitatively different at the international border than in the interior. Routine searches of the persons and effects of entrants are not subject to any requirement of reasonable suspicion, probable cause, or warrant, and first-class mail may be opened without a warrant on less than probable cause, Automotive travelers may be stopped at fixed checkpoints near the border without individualized suspicion even if the stop is based largely on ethnicity, and boats on inland waters with ready access to the sea may be hailed and boarded with no suspicion whatever."

The Court also emphasized that privacy expectations are diminished for someone crossing the border:

> "Balanced against the sovereign's interests at the border are the Fourth Amendment rights of respondent. Having presented herself at the border for admission, and having subjected herself to the criminal enforcement powers of the Federal Government, respondent was entitled to be free from unreasonable search and seizure. But not only is the expectation of privacy less at the border than in the interior, the Fourth Amendment balance between the interests of the Government and the privacy right of the individual is also struck much more favorably to the Government at the border."

The Supreme Court recognized that Montoya de Hernandez's lengthy detention was not one of the "routine" stops and searches that officials could undertake at the border without individualized suspicion. Nevertheless, the Court declined to adopt the Ninth Circuit's relatively strict "clear indication" standard for justifying this non-routine detention. Instead, the Court adopted the familiar "reasonable suspicion" standard: "We hold that the detention of a traveler at the border, beyond the scope of a routine customs search and inspection, is justified at its inception if customs agents, considering all the facts surrounding the traveler and her trip, reasonably suspect that the traveler is smuggling contraband in her alimentary canal." The Court then went on to hold that the standard had been met in the case.

Finally, as part of its general reasonableness analysis, the Court considered whether the detention, even if justified at its inception, exceeded permissible bounds:

" The final issue in this case is whether the detention of respondent was reasonably related in scope to the circumstances which justified it initially. In this regard we have cautioned that courts should not indulge in "unrealistic second-guessing," and we have noted that "creative judges, engaged in post hoc evaluations of police conduct can almost always imagine some alternative means by which the objectives of the police might have been accomplished."... Here, respondent was detained incommunicado for almost 16 hours before inspectors sought a warrant; the warrant then took a number of hours to procure, through no apparent fault of the inspectors. This length of time undoubtedly exceeds any other detention we have approved under reasonable suspicion. But we have also consistently rejected hard-and-fast time limits....

In the case of respondent the inspectors had available, as an alternative to simply awaiting her bowel movement, an x-ray. They offered her the alternative of submitting herself to that procedure. But when she refused that alternative, the customs inspectors were left with only two practical alternatives: detain her for such time as necessary to confirm their suspicions, a detention which would last much longer than the typical Terry stop, or turn her loose into the interior carrying the reasonably suspected contraband drugs.

The inspectors in this case followed this former procedure. They no doubt expected that respondent ... would produce a bowel movement without extended delay. But her visible efforts to resist the call of nature, which the court below labeled "heroic," disappointed this expectation and in turn caused her humiliation and discomfort. Our prior cases have refused to charge police with delays in investigatory detention attributable to the suspect's evasive actions and that principle applies here as well....

Under these circumstances, we conclude that the detention in this case was not unreasonably long. It occurred at the international border, where the Fourth Amendment balance of interests leans heavily to the Government.... Respondent's detention was long, uncomfortable, indeed, humiliating; but both its length and its discomfort resulted solely from the method by which she chose to smuggle illicit drugs into this country.... Her detention for the period of time necessary to either verify or dispel the suspicion was not unreasonable.

UNITED STATES v. FLORES-MONTANO
541 U.S. 149 (2004)

Chief Justice REHNQUIST delivered the opinion of the Court.

Customs officials seized 37 kilograms – a little more than 81 pounds – of marijuana from respondent Manuel Flores-Montano's gas tank at the international border. The Court of Appeals for the Ninth Circuit ... held that the Fourth Amendment forbade the fuel tank search absent reasonable suspicion. We hold that the search in question did not require reasonable suspicion.

Respondent, driving a 1987 Ford Taurus station wagon, attempted to enter the United States at the Otay Mesa Port of Entry in southern California. A customs inspector conducted an inspection of the station wagon, and requested respondent to leave the vehicle. The vehicle was then taken to a secondary inspection station.

At the secondary station, a second customs inspector inspected the gas tank by tapping it, and noted that the tank sounded solid. Subsequently, the inspector requested a mechanic under contract with Customs to come to the border station to remove the tank. Within 20 to 30 minutes, the mechanic arrived. He raised the car on a hydraulic lift, loosened the straps and unscrewed the bolts holding the gas tank to the undercarriage of the vehicle, and then disconnected some hoses and electrical connections. After the gas tank was removed, the inspector hammered off bondo (a putty-like hardening substance that is used to seal openings) from the top of the gas tank. The inspector opened an access plate underneath the bondo and found 37 kilograms of marijuana bricks. The process took 15 to 25 minutes.

A grand jury for the Southern District of California indicted respondent on one count of unlawfully importing marijuana, and one count of possession of marijuana with intent to distribute....

The Court of Appeals seized on language from our opinion in United States v. Montoya De Hernandez (1985), in which we used the word "routine" as a descriptive term in discussing border searches. ("Routine searches of the persons and effects of entrants are not subject to any requirement of reasonable suspicion, probable cause, or warrant."). The Court of Appeals took the term "routine," fashioned a new balancing test, and extended it to searches of vehicles. But the reasons that might support a requirement of some level of suspicion in the case of highly intrusive searches of the person – dignity and privacy interests of the person

362

being searched – simply do not carry over to vehicles. Complex balancing tests to determine what is a "routine" search of a vehicle, as opposed to a more "intrusive" search of a person, have no place in border searches of vehicles.

The Government's interest in preventing the entry of unwanted persons and effects is at its zenith at the international border. Time and again, we have stated that "searches made at the border, pursuant to the longstanding right of the sovereign to protect itself by stopping and examining persons and property crossing into this country, are reasonable simply by virtue of the fact that they occur at the border."...

Respondent asserts two main arguments with respect to his Fourth Amendment interests. First, he urges that he has a privacy interest in his fuel tank, and that the suspicionless disassembly of his tank is an invasion of his privacy. But on many occasions, we have noted that the expectation of privacy is less at the border than it is in the interior. We have long recognized that automobiles seeking entry into this country may be searched. It is difficult to imagine how the search of a gas tank, which should be solely a repository for fuel, could be more of an invasion of privacy than the search of the automobile's passenger compartment.

Second, respondent argues that the Fourth Amendment "protects property as well as privacy" and that the disassembly and reassembly of his gas tank is a significant deprivation of his property interest because it may damage the vehicle. He does not, and on the record cannot, truly contend that the procedure of removal, disassembly, and reassembly of the fuel tank in this case or any other has resulted in serious damage to, or destruction of, the property. According to the Government, for example, in fiscal year 2003, 348 gas tank searches conducted along the southern border were negative (i.e., no contraband was found), the gas tanks were reassembled, and the vehicles continued their entry into the United States without incident.

Respondent cites not a single accident involving the vehicle or motorist in the many thousands of gas tank disassemblies that have occurred at the border. A gas tank search involves a brief procedure that can be reversed without damaging the safety or operation of the vehicle. If damage to a vehicle were to occur, the motorist might be entitled to recovery. While the interference with a motorist's possessory interest is not insignificant when the Government removes, disassembles, and reassembles his gas tank, it nevertheless is justified by the Government's paramount interest in protecting the border.

For the reasons stated, we conclude that the Government's authority to conduct suspicionless inspections at the border includes the authority to remove, disassemble, and reassemble a vehicle's fuel tank. While it may be true that some searches of property are so destructive as to require a different result, this was not one of them. The judgment of the United States Court of Appeals for the Ninth Circuit is therefore reversed, and the case is remanded for further proceedings consistent with this opinion.

As the preceding cases suggest, unusually invasive searches of the person are more likely to be deemed "non-routine" and thus require individualized suspicion. See *Bustillos v. El Paso Hospital District* (5th Cir. 2018) ("Cavity searches, strip searches, and x-ray examinations are all 'non-routine.'"). Searches of cellphones and other electronic devices offer another candidate for special treatment. In fiscal year 2022, Customs and Border Patrol searched more than 45,000 electronic devices at the international border. Lower courts split on the question of whether border cellphone searches are non-routine. See *United States v. Cotterman* (9th Cir. 2013) (cell phones are non-routine searches requiring reasonable suspicion); *United States v. Touset* (11th Cir. 2018) (reasonable suspicion not required).

The majority opinion in *Montoya de Hernandez* states that border stops without individualized suspicion are permitted "even if the stop is based largely on ethnicity." For that proposition, the Court cited two earlier Supreme Court cases. In *U.S. v. Martinez-Fuerte* (1976), the Court upheld the constitutionality of fixed border checkpoints on major North-South highways approximately 70 miles north of the Mexican border. The Court ruled that "stops and questioning" designed to detect persons who crossed the border unlawfully "may be made in the absence of any individualized suspicion at reasonably located checkpoints." In addition, the Court stated that "it is constitutional to refer [stopped] motorists selectively to the secondary inspection area at the checkpoint on the basis of criteria that would not sustain a roving-patrol stop. Thus, even if it be assumed that such referrals are made largely on the basis of apparent Mexican ancestry, we perceive no constitutional violation." For this last point, the *Martinez-Fuerte* majority cited *United States v. Brignoni-Ponce* (1975). There, the Supreme Court considered a non-checkpoint stop of a car near the Mexican border that was based "on a single factor": "the apparent Mexican ancestry of the occupants." The Court ruled that the stop violated the Fourth Amendment, stating that "Mexican appearance" could be "a relevant factor" in this context, "but standing alone it does not justify stopping all Mexican-Americans to ask if they are aliens."

The Transportation Safety Administration (TSA) screens millions of domestic and international travelers at airports each year with advanced imaging technology and walk-through metal detectors. If the detectors alert, the TSA agents subject the passengers and their luggage to further scrutiny. Agents can rummage through suitcases, pat-down the passengers, force passengers to remove their jackets and shoes, and more.

Do these searches comply with the Fourth Amendment? If so, are they consent searches? And if airport searches are based on consent, can a passenger revoke that consent and walk away after walking through a metal detector and having it go off? The Supreme Court has never answered these questions. As the next case explains, the prevailing view is that airport searches are not based on consent, but instead fit in the "special needs" category.

UNITED STATES v. AUKAI
497 F.3d 955 (9th Cir. 2007)

BEA, Circuit Judge:

.... On February 1, 2003, Daniel Aukai arrived at the Honolulu International Airport intending to take a Hawaiian Airlines flight from Honolulu, Hawaii, to Kona, Hawaii. He proceeded to check in at the ticket counter but did not produce a government-issued picture identification. Accordingly, the ticket agent wrote the phrase "No ID" on Aukai's boarding pass.

Aukai then proceeded to the security checkpoint, at which signs were posted advising prospective passengers that they and their carry-on baggage were subject to search. He entered the security checkpoint at approximately 9:00 a.m., placed his shoes and a few other items into a plastic bin, and voluntarily walked through the metal detector or magnetometer. The parties agree that the magnetometer did not signal the presence of metal as Aukai walked through it. Nor did his belongings trigger an alarm or otherwise raise suspicion as they passed through the x-ray machine. After walking through the magnetometer, Aukai presented his boarding pass to TSA Officer Corrine Motonaga.

Pursuant to TSA procedures, a passenger who presents a boarding pass on which "No ID" has been written is subject to secondary screening even if he has passed through the initial screening without triggering an alarm or otherwise raising suspicion. As it was performed here, secondary screening consists of a TSA officer passing a handheld magnetometer, known as a "wand," near and around the passenger's body....

Because Aukai's boarding pass had the "No ID" notation, Motonaga directed Aukai to a nearby, roped-off area for secondary screening. Aukai initially complied but complained that he was in a hurry to catch his flight which, according to the boarding pass, was scheduled to leave at 9:05 a.m., just a few minutes later.... TSA Officer Andrew Misajon nonetheless had Aukai sit in a chair and proceeded to use the wand to detect metal objects. At some point, Misajon had Aukai stand, and when Misajon passed the wand across the front of Aukai's body, the wand alarm was triggered at Aukai's front right pants pocket. Misajon asked Aukai if he had anything in his pocket, and Aukai responded that he did not.... Misajon then felt the outside of Aukai's pocket and concluded that something was inside the pocket. Misajon could also see the outline of an unknown object in Aukai's pocket. At some point during this screening process, Aukai informed Misajon that he no longer wished to board a plane and wanted to leave the airport.

At this point, TSA Supervisor Joseph Vizcarra approached Misajon and asked whether he needed assistance. Misajon related the events and Vizcarra asked Misajon to pass the wand over Aukai's pocket again. When the wand alarm again was triggered, Vizcarra directed Aukai to empty his pocket. Aukai again protested that he had nothing in his pocket. Using the back of his hand, Vizcarra touched the outside of Aukai's pocket and felt something in the pocket. He again directed Aukai to empty his pocket. This time Aukai reached into his pocket and removed either his keys or change, but a bulge was still visible in his pocket. Vizcarra directed Aukai to remove all contents from his pocket. After claiming at first that there was nothing more, Aukai finally removed an object wrapped in some form of tissue paper and placed it on a tray in front of him.

Suspecting that the object might be a weapon, Vizcarra summoned a nearby law enforcement officer. Vizcarra then unwrapped the object and discovered a glass pipe used to smoke methamphetamine. The law enforcement officer escorted Aukai to a small office near the security checkpoint. Aukai was placed under arrest and was searched incident to his arrest. During the search, the police discovered in Aukai's front pants pockets several transparent bags containing a white crystal substance. Aukai eventually was taken into federal custody, where he was advised of and waived his Miranda rights, and then gave a statement in which he inculpated himself in the possession of methamphetamine.

Aukai was indicted for knowingly and intentionally possessing, with the intent to distribute, 50 grams or more of methamphetamine....

A search or seizure is ordinarily unreasonable in the absence of individualized suspicion of wrongdoing. While such suspicion is not an "irreducible" component of reasonableness, the Supreme Court has recognized only limited circumstances in which the usual rule does not apply. However, where the risk to public safety is substantial and real, blanket suspicionless searches calibrated to the risk may rank as "reasonable" – for example, searches now routine at airports and at entrances to courts and other official buildings. Thus, where a Fourth Amendment intrusion serves special governmental needs, beyond the normal need for law enforcement, it is necessary to balance the individual's privacy expectations against the Government's interests to determine whether it is impractical to require a warrant or some level of individualized suspicion in the particular context....

We have held that airport screening searches, like the one at issue here, are constitutionally reasonable administrative searches because they are conducted as part of a general regulatory scheme in furtherance of an administrative purpose, namely, to prevent the carrying of weapons or explosives aboard aircraft, and thereby to prevent hijackings. Our case law, however, has erroneously suggested that the reasonableness of airport screening searches is dependent upon consent, either ongoing consent or irrevocable implied consent.

The constitutionality of an airport screening search, however, does not depend on consent and requiring that a potential passenger be allowed to revoke consent to an ongoing airport security search makes little sense in a post-9/11 world. Such a rule would afford terrorists multiple opportunities to attempt to penetrate airport security by "electing not to fly" on the cusp of detection until a vulnerable portal is found. This rule would also allow terrorists a low-cost method of detecting systematic vulnerabilities in airport security, knowledge that could be extremely valuable in planning future attacks. Likewise, given that consent is not required, it makes little sense to predicate the reasonableness of an administrative airport screening search on an irrevocable implied consent theory. Rather, where an airport screening search is otherwise reasonable and conducted pursuant to statutory authority all that is required is the passenger's election to attempt entry into the secured area of an airport. Under current TSA regulations and procedures, that election occurs when a prospective passenger walks through the magnetometer or places items on the conveyor belt of the x-ray machine. The record establishes that Aukai elected to attempt entry into the posted secured area of Honolulu International Airport when he walked through the magnetometer, thereby subjecting himself to the airport screening process....

Although the constitutionality of airport screening searches is not dependent on consent, the scope of such searches is not limitless. A particular airport security screening search is constitutionally reasonable provided that it is no more extensive nor intensive than necessary, in the light of current technology, to detect the presence of weapons or explosives and that it is confined in good faith to that purpose. We conclude that the airport screening search of Aukai satisfied these requirements.

The search procedures used in this case were neither more extensive nor more intensive than necessary under the circumstances to rule out the presence of weapons or explosives. After passing through a magnetometer, Aukai was directed to secondary screening because his boarding pass was marked "No ID." Aukai then underwent a standard "wanding procedure." When the wand alarm sounded as the wand passed over Aukai's front right pants pocket, TSA Officer Misajon did not reach into Aukai's pocket or feel the outside of Aukai's pocket. Rather, Misajon asked Aukai if he had something in his pocket. When Aukai denied that there was anything in his pocket, Misajon repeated the wanding procedure. Only after the wand alarm again sounded and Aukai again denied having anything in his pocket did Misajon employ a more intrusive search procedure by feeling the outside of Aukai's pocket and determining that there was something in there.

.... We find these search procedures to be minimally intrusive. The duration of the detention associated with this airport screening search was also reasonable. Witnesses testified that Aukai entered the checkpoint area at approximately 9:00

a.m. and that the entire search at issue-starting from when Aukai walked through the checkpoint until the TSA's efforts to rule out the presence of a weapon resulted in the discovery of drug paraphernalia-took no more than 18 minutes. Although longer than detentions approved in other cases, the length of Aukai's detention was reasonable, especially in light of Aukai's conduct, because it was not prolonged beyond the time reasonably required to rule out the presence of weapons or explosives.

Accordingly, we hold that the airport screening search of Aukai was a constitutionally reasonable administrative search.

6. DNA COLLECTION

MARYLAND v. KING
569 U.S. 435 (2013)

Justice KENNEDY delivered the opinion of the Court.

I

When Alonzo King was arrested on April 10, 2009, for menacing a group of people with a shotgun and charged in state court with both first- and second-degree assault, he was processed for detention in custody at the Wicomico County Central Booking facility. Booking personnel used a cheek swab to take [a] DNA sample from him pursuant to provisions of the Maryland DNA Collection Act (or Act).

On July 13, 2009, King's DNA record was uploaded to the Maryland DNA database, and three weeks later, on August 4, 2009, his DNA profile was matched to the DNA sample collected in [an] unsolved 2003 rape case. Once the DNA was matched to King, detectives presented the forensic evidence to a grand jury, which indicted him for the rape. Detectives obtained a search warrant and took a second sample of DNA from King, which again matched the evidence from the rape. He moved to suppress the DNA match on the grounds that Maryland's DNA collection law violated the Fourth Amendment. The Circuit Court Judge upheld the statute as constitutional. King pleaded not guilty to the rape charges but was convicted and sentenced to life in prison without the possibility of parole.

In a divided opinion, the Maryland Court of Appeals struck down the portions of the Act authorizing collection of DNA from felony arrestees as unconstitutional....

Both federal and state courts have reached differing conclusions as to whether the Fourth Amendment prohibits the collection and analysis of a DNA sample from persons arrested, but not yet convicted, on felony charges. This Court granted certiorari to address the question....

II

The advent of DNA technology is one of the most significant scientific advancements of our era. The full potential for use of genetic markers in medicine and science is still being explored, but the utility of DNA identification in the criminal justice system is already undisputed....

A

The current standard for forensic DNA testing relies on an analysis of the chromosomes located within the nucleus of all human cells. The DNA material in chromosomes is composed of "coding" and "noncoding" regions. The coding regions are known as *genes* and contain the information necessary for a cell to make proteins. Non-protein-coding regions are not related directly to making proteins, and have been referred to as "junk" DNA. The adjective "junk" may mislead the layperson, for in fact this is the DNA region used with near certainty to identify a person. The term apparently is intended to indicate that this particular noncoding region, while useful and even dispositive for purposes like identity, does not show more far-reaching and complex characteristics like genetic traits.

Many of the patterns found in DNA are shared among all people, so forensic analysis focuses on repeated DNA sequences scattered throughout the human genome, known as "short tandem repeats" (STRs). The alternative possibilities for the size and frequency of these STRs at any given point along a strand of DNA are known as "alleles"; and multiple alleles are analyzed in order to ensure that a DNA profile matches only one individual. Future refinements may improve present technology, but even now STR analysis makes it possible to determine whether a biological tissue matches a suspect with near certainty.

The Act authorizes Maryland law enforcement authorities to collect DNA samples from "an individual who is charged with a crime of violence or an attempt to commit a crime of violence; or burglary or an attempt to commit burglary." Maryland law defines a crime of violence to include murder, rape, first-degree assault, kidnaping, arson, sexual assault, and a variety of other serious crimes. Once taken, a DNA sample may not be processed or placed in a database before the individual is arraigned (unless the individual consents). It is at this point that a judicial officer ensures that there is probable cause to detain the arrestee on a qualifying serious offense. If "all qualifying criminal charges are determined to be unsupported by probable cause the DNA sample shall be immediately destroyed." DNA samples are also destroyed if "a criminal action begun against the individual does not result in a conviction," "the conviction is finally reversed or vacated and no new trial is permitted," or "the individual is granted an unconditional pardon."

The Act also limits the information added to a DNA database and how it may be used. Specifically, "only DNA records that directly relate to the identification of individuals shall be collected and stored." No purpose other than identification is permissible: "A person may not willfully test a DNA sample for information that does not relate to the identification of individuals as specified in this subtitle." Tests for familial matches are also prohibited. The officers involved in taking and analyzing respondent's DNA sample complied with the Act in all respects.

Respondent's DNA was collected in this case using a common procedure known as a "buccal swab." Buccal cell collection involves wiping a small piece of filter paper or a cotton swab similar to a Q-tip against the inside cheek of an individual's mouth to collect some skin cells. The procedure is quick and painless. The swab touches inside an arrestee's mouth, but it requires no surgical intrusion beneath the skin, and it poses no threat to the health or safety of arrestees.

B

Respondent's identification as the rapist resulted in part through the operation of a national project to standardize collection and storage of DNA profiles. Authorized by Congress and supervised by the Federal Bureau of Investigation, the Combined DNA Index System (CODIS) connects DNA laboratories at the local, state, and national level. Since its authorization in 1994, the CODIS system has grown to include all 50 States and a number of federal agencies. CODIS collects DNA profiles provided by local laboratories taken from arrestees, convicted offenders, and forensic evidence found at crime scenes. To participate in CODIS, a local laboratory must sign a memorandum of understanding agreeing to adhere to quality standards and submit to audits to evaluate compliance with the federal standards for scientifically rigorous DNA testing.

One of the most significant aspects of CODIS is the standardization of the points of comparison in DNA analysis. The CODIS database is based on 13 loci at which the STR alleles are noted and compared. These loci make possible extreme accuracy in matching individual samples, with a random match probability of approximately 1 in 100 trillion (assuming unrelated individuals). The CODIS loci are from the non-protein coding junk regions of DNA, and are not known to have any association with a genetic disease or any other genetic predisposition. Thus, the information in the database is only useful for human identity testing....

All 50 States require the collection of DNA from felony convicts, and respondent does not dispute the validity of that practice. Twenty-eight States and the Federal Government have adopted laws similar to the Maryland Act authorizing the collection of DNA from some or all arrestees....

III

A

.... It can be agreed that using a buccal swab on the inner tissues of a person's cheek in order to obtain DNA samples is a search. Virtually any intrusion into the human body will work an invasion of cherished personal security that is subject to constitutional scrutiny.

The Court has applied the Fourth Amendment to police efforts to draw blood, scraping an arrestee's fingernails to obtain trace evidence, and even to a breathalyzer test, which generally requires the production of alveolar or "deep lung" breath for chemical analysis....

B

To say that the Fourth Amendment applies here is the beginning point, not the end of the analysis. The Fourth Amendment's proper function is to constrain, not against all intrusions as such, but against intrusions which are not justified in the circumstances, or which are made in an improper manner. As the text of the Fourth Amendment indicates, the ultimate measure of the constitutionality of a governmental search is "reasonableness." In giving content to the inquiry whether an intrusion is reasonable, the Court has preferred some quantum of individualized suspicion as a prerequisite to a constitutional search or seizure. But the Fourth Amendment imposes no irreducible requirement of such suspicion.

In some circumstances, such as when faced with special law enforcement needs, diminished expectations of privacy, minimal intrusions, or the like, the Court has found that certain general, or individual, circumstances may render a warrantless search or seizure reasonable. Those circumstances diminish the need for a warrant, either because the public interest is such that neither a warrant nor probable cause is required or because an individual is already on notice, for instance because of his employment, or the conditions of his release from government custody, that some reasonable police intrusion on his privacy is to be expected. The need for a warrant is perhaps least when the search involves no discretion that could properly be limited by the interpolation of a neutral magistrate between the citizen and the law enforcement officer.

The instant case can be addressed with this background. The Maryland DNA Collection Act provides that, in order to obtain a DNA sample, all arrestees charged with serious crimes must furnish the sample on a buccal swab applied, as noted, to the inside of the cheeks. The arrestee is already in valid police custody for a serious offense supported by probable cause. The DNA collection is not subject to the judgment of officers whose perspective might be colored by their primary involvement in "the often competitive enterprise of ferreting out crime.".... Here, the search effected by the buccal swab of respondent falls within the category of cases this Court has analyzed by reference to the proposition that "the touchstone of the Fourth Amendment is reasonableness, not individualized suspicion." Samson v. California.

Even if a warrant is not required, a search is not beyond Fourth Amendment scrutiny; for it must be reasonable in its scope and manner of execution. Urgent government interests are not a license for indiscriminate police behavior. To say that no warrant is required is merely to acknowledge that rather than employing a per se rule of unreasonableness, we balance the privacy-related and law enforcement-related concerns to determine if the intrusion was reasonable....

IV

A

The legitimate government interest served by the Maryland DNA Collection Act is one that is well established: the need for law enforcement officers in a safe and accurate way to process and identify the persons and possessions they must take into custody. It is beyond dispute that probable cause provides legal justification for arresting a person suspected of crime, and for a brief period of detention to take the administrative steps incident to arrest. Also uncontested is the right on the part of the Government, always recognized under English and American law, to search the person of the accused when legally arrested....

In every criminal case, it is known and must be known who has been arrested and who is being tried. An individual's identity is more than just his name or Social Security number, and the government's interest in identification goes beyond ensuring that the proper name is typed on the indictment. Identity has never been considered limited to the name on the arrestee's birth certificate. In fact, a name is of little value compared to the real interest in identification at stake when an individual is brought into custody. It is a well recognized aspect of criminal conduct that the perpetrator will take unusual steps to conceal not only his conduct, but also his identity. Disguises used while committing a crime may be supplemented or replaced by changed names, and even changed physical features. An arrestee may be carrying a false ID or lie about his identity, and criminal history records can be inaccurate or incomplete.

A suspect's criminal history is a critical part of his identity that officers should know when processing him for detention. It is a common occurrence that people detained for minor offenses can turn out to be the most devious and dangerous criminals. Hours after the Oklahoma City bombing, Timothy McVeigh was stopped by a state trooper who noticed he was driving without a license plate. Police stopped serial killer Joel Rifkin for the same reason....

The task of identification necessarily entails searching public and police records based on the identifying information provided by the arrestee to see what is already known about him. The DNA collected from arrestees is an irrefutable identification of the person from whom it was taken. Like a fingerprint, the 13 CODIS loci are not themselves evidence of any particular crime, in the way that a drug test can by itself be evidence of illegal narcotics use. A DNA profile is useful to the police because it gives them a form of identification to search the records already in their valid possession....

Because proper processing of arrestees is so important and has consequences for every stage of the criminal process, the Court has recognized that the "governmental interests underlying a station-house search of the arrestee's person and possessions may in some circumstances be even greater than those supporting a search immediately following arrest." Thus, the Court has been reluctant to circumscribe the authority of the police to conduct reasonable booking searches....

B

DNA identification represents an important advance in the techniques used by law enforcement to serve legitimate police concerns for as long as there have been arrests, concerns the courts have acknowledged and approved for more than a century....

Perhaps the most direct historical analogue to the DNA technology used to identify respondent is the familiar practice of fingerprinting arrestees. From the advent of this technique, courts had no trouble determining that fingerprinting was a natural part of the administrative steps incident to arrest....

DNA identification is an advanced technique superior to fingerprinting in many ways, so much so that to insist on fingerprints as the norm would make little sense to either the forensic expert or a layperson. The additional intrusion upon the arrestee's privacy beyond that associated with fingerprinting is not significant, and DNA is a markedly more accurate form of identifying arrestees. A suspect who has changed his facial features to evade photographic identification or even one who has undertaken the more arduous task of altering his fingerprints cannot escape the revealing power of his DNA.

.... In sum, there can be little reason to question the legitimate interest of the government in knowing for an absolute certainty the identity of the person arrested, in knowing whether he is wanted elsewhere, and in ensuring his identification in the event he flees prosecution. To that end, courts have confirmed that the Fourth Amendment allows police to take certain routine administrative steps incident to arrest—i.e., ... booking, photographing, and fingerprinting....

V
A

By comparison to this substantial government interest and the unique effectiveness of DNA identification, the intrusion of a cheek swab to obtain a DNA sample is a minimal one....

The reasonableness of any search must be considered in the context of the person's legitimate expectations of privacy. For example, when weighing the invasiveness of urinalysis of high school athletes, the Court noted that "legitimate privacy expectations are even less with regard to student athletes. Public school locker rooms, the usual sites for these activities, are not notable for the privacy they afford." Likewise, the Court has used a context-specific benchmark inapplicable to the public at large when "the expectations of privacy of covered employees are diminished by reason of their participation in an industry that is regulated pervasively," or when "the operational realities of the workplace may render entirely reasonable certain work-related intrusions by supervisors and co-workers that might be viewed as unreasonable in other contexts."

The expectations of privacy of an individual taken into police custody necessarily are of a diminished scope. Both the person and the property in his immediate possession may be searched at the station house. A search of the detainee's person when he is booked into custody may involve a relatively extensive exploration, including requiring at least some detainees to lift their genitals or cough in a squatting position.

In this critical respect, the search here at issue differs from the sort of programmatic searches of either the public at large or a particular class of regulated but otherwise law-abiding citizens that the Court has previously labeled as "special needs" searches. When the police stop a motorist at a checkpoint or test a political candidate for illegal narcotics, they intrude upon substantial expectations of privacy. So the Court has insisted on some purpose other than "to detect evidence of ordinary criminal wrongdoing" to justify these searches in the absence of individualized suspicion. Once an individual has been arrested on probable cause for a dangerous offense that may require detention before trial, however, his or her expectations of privacy and freedom from police scrutiny are reduced. DNA identification like that at issue here thus does not require consideration of any unique needs that would be required to justify searching the average citizen. The special needs cases, though in full accord with the result reached here, do not have a direct bearing on the issues presented in this case, because unlike the search of a citizen who has not been suspected of a wrong, a detainee has a reduced expectation of privacy....

B

In addition the processing of respondent's DNA sample's 13 CODIS loci did not intrude on respondent's privacy in a way that would make his DNA identification unconstitutional…. The CODIS loci come from noncoding parts of the DNA that do not reveal the genetic traits of the arrestee….

[Conclusion]

In light of the context of a valid arrest supported by probable cause respondent's expectations of privacy were not offended by the minor intrusion of a brief swab of his cheeks. By contrast, that same context of arrest gives rise to significant state interests in identifying respondent not only so that the proper name can be attached to his charges but also so that the criminal justice system can make informed decisions concerning pretrial custody. Upon these considerations the Court concludes that DNA identification of arrestees is a reasonable search that can be considered part of a routine booking procedure. When officers make an arrest supported by probable cause to hold for a serious offense and they bring the suspect to the station to be detained in custody, taking and analyzing a cheek swab of the arrestee's DNA is, like fingerprinting and photographing, a legitimate police booking procedure that is reasonable under the Fourth Amendment.

Justice SCALIA, dissenting.

The Fourth Amendment forbids searching a person for evidence of a crime when there is no basis for believing the person is guilty of the crime or is in possession of incriminating evidence. That prohibition is categorical and without exception; it lies at the very heart of the Fourth Amendment. Whenever this Court has allowed a suspicionless search, it has insisted upon a justifying motive apart from the investigation of crime.

It is obvious that no such noninvestigative motive exists in this case. The Court's assertion that DNA is being taken, not to solve crimes, but to identify those in the State's custody, taxes the credulity of the credulous. And the Court's comparison of Maryland's DNA searches to other techniques, such as fingerprinting, can seem apt only to those who know no more than today's opinion has chosen to tell them about how those DNA searches actually work….

While the Court is correct to note that there are instances in which we have permitted searches without individualized suspicion, "in none of these cases did we indicate approval of a search whose primary purpose was to detect evidence of ordinary criminal wrongdoing." Indianapolis v. Edmond (2000). That limitation is crucial. It is only when a governmental purpose aside from crime-solving is at stake that we engage in the free-form "reasonableness" inquiry that the Court indulges at length today. To put it another way, both the legitimacy of the Court's method and the correctness of its outcome hinge entirely on the truth of a single proposition: that the primary purpose of these DNA searches is something other than simply discovering evidence of criminal wrongdoing....

The Court elaborates at length the ways that the search here served the special purpose of "identifying" King. But that seems to me quite wrong—unless what one means by "identifying" someone is "searching for evidence that he has committed crimes unrelated to the crime of his arrest."...

The portion of the Court's opinion that explains the identification rationale is strangely silent on the actual workings of the DNA search at issue here. To know those facts is to be instantly disabused of the notion that what happened had anything to do with identifying King.

King was arrested on April 10, 2009, on charges unrelated to the case before us. That same day, April 10, the police searched him and seized the DNA evidence at issue here. What happened next? Reading the Court's opinion, particularly its insistence that the search was necessary to know "who [had] been arrested," one might guess that King's DNA was swiftly processed and his identity thereby confirmed—perhaps against some master database of known DNA profiles, as is done for fingerprints. After all, was not the suspicionless search here crucial to avoid "inordinate risks for facility staff" or to "existing detainee population"? Surely, then—surely—the State of Maryland got cracking on those grave risks immediately, by rushing to identify King with his DNA as soon as possible.

Nothing could be further from the truth. Maryland officials did not even begin the process of testing King's DNA that day. Or, actually, the next day. Or the day after that. And that was for a simple reason: Maryland law forbids them to do so. A "DNA sample collected from an individual charged with a crime may not be tested or placed in the statewide DNA data base system prior to the first scheduled arraignment date." And King's first appearance in court was not until three days after his arrest. (I suspect, though, that they did not wait three days to ask his name or take his fingerprints.)

.... Today's judgment will, to be sure, have the beneficial effect of solving more crimes; then again, so would the taking of DNA samples from anyone who flies on an airplane (surely the Transportation Security Administration needs to know the "identity" of the flying public), applies for a driver's license, or attends a public school. Perhaps the construction of such a genetic panopticon is wise. But I doubt that the proud men who wrote the charter of our liberties would have been so eager to open their mouths for royal inspection....

A noteworthy aspect of the majority opinion in *King* is the degree to which it tracks the "special needs" cases, without explicitly relying on those cases. The reason for this is alluded to in the dissenting opinion and articulated by scholar Erin Murphy:[23]

> Yet the "special needs" doctrine, despite its role as the traditional refuge of the warrantless, suspicionless search, did not quite work either. Indeed, the special needs cases proved problematic even for convicted offender DNA sampling, because they explicitly and importantly apply only to searches for purposes other than "ordinary criminal wrongdoing." Interestingly, however, the Court did not distinguish special needs on that ground. The majority conceded that the special needs cases "do not have a direct bearing on the issues presented in this case," but not because the DNA collection at issue was for "ordinary law enforcement." Rather, those cases were inapposite because they target "either the public at large or a particular class of regulated but otherwise law-abiding citizens." In contrast, arrestees have diminished privacy, and so the Constitution "does not require consideration of any unique needs that would be required to justify searching the average citizen."

---

[23] *License, Registration, Cheek Swab: DNA Testing and the Divided Court*, 127 HARV. L. REV. 161 (2013).

Chapter 5

REASONABLENESS: MANNER OF SEARCHING AND SEIZING

Ad hoc, reasonableness focused Fourth Amendment rules are often viewed as favorable to the government. But that is not always the case. In some circumstances, an overarching focus on reasonableness leads to a conclusion that the government is precluded from conducting a particularly invasive search or seizure even when the standard prerequisites of per se rules, such as "probable cause" and a warrant (or exigent circumstances), are present.

A. SURGICAL SEARCHES

WINSTON v. LEE
470 U.S. 753 (1985)

Justice BRENNAN delivered the opinion of the Court.

…. In this case, the Commonwealth of Virginia seeks to compel the respondent Rudolph Lee, who is suspected of attempting to commit armed robbery, to undergo a surgical procedure under a general anesthetic for removal of a bullet lodged in his chest. Petitioners allege that the bullet will provide evidence of respondent's guilt or innocence. We … hold that to permit the procedure would violate respondent's right to be secure in his person guaranteed by the Fourth Amendment.

I

At approximately 1 a.m. on July 18, 1982, Ralph Watkinson was closing his shop for the night. As he was locking the door, he observed someone armed with a gun coming toward him from across the street. Watkinson was also armed and when he drew his gun, the other person told him to freeze. Watkinson then fired at the other person, who returned his fire. Watkinson was hit in the legs, while the other individual, who appeared to be wounded in his left side, ran from the scene. The police arrived on the scene shortly thereafter, and Watkinson was taken by ambulance to the emergency room of the Medical College of Virginia (MCV) Hospital.

Approximately 20 minutes later, police officers responding to another call found respondent eight blocks from where the earlier shooting occurred. Respondent was suffering from a gunshot wound to his left chest area and told the police that he had been shot when two individuals attempted to rob him. An ambulance took respondent to the MCV Hospital. Watkinson was still in the MCV emergency room and, when respondent entered that room, said "that's the man that shot me." After an investigation, the police decided that respondent's story of having been himself the victim of a robbery was untrue and charged respondent with attempted robbery, malicious wounding, and two counts of using a firearm in the commission of a felony.

The Commonwealth shortly thereafter moved in state court for an order directing respondent to undergo surgery to remove an object thought to be a bullet lodged under his left collarbone. The court conducted several evidentiary hearings on the motion [and] granted the motion to compel surgery…. [After the Virginia Supreme Court affirmed, Respondent turned] to federal court, where he moved to alter or amend the judgment previously entered against him. After an evidentiary hearing, the District Court enjoined the threatened surgery. A divided panel of the Court of Appeals for the Fourth Circuit affirmed. We granted certiorari to consider whether a State may consistently with the Fourth Amendment compel a suspect to undergo surgery of this kind in a search for evidence of a crime.

II

…. Putting to one side the procedural protections of the warrant requirement, the Fourth Amendment generally protects the "security" of "persons, houses, papers, and effects" against official intrusions up to the point where the community's need for evidence surmounts a specified standard, ordinarily "probable cause." Beyond this point, it is ordinarily justifiable for the community to demand that the individual give up some part of his interest in privacy and security to advance the community's vital interests in law enforcement; such a search is generally "reasonable" in the Amendment's terms.

A compelled surgical intrusion into an individual's body for evidence, however, implicates expectations of privacy and security of such magnitude that the intrusion may be "unreasonable" even if likely to produce evidence of a crime…. The reasonableness of surgical intrusions beneath the skin depends on a case-by-case approach, in which the individual's interests in privacy and security are weighed against society's interests in conducting the procedure....

III

Applying the [requisite] balancing test in this case, we believe that the Court of Appeals reached the correct result. The Commonwealth plainly had probable cause to conduct the search. In addition, all parties apparently agree that respondent has had a full measure of procedural protections and has been able fully to litigate the difficult medical and legal questions necessarily involved in analyzing the reasonableness of a surgical incision of this magnitude. Our inquiry therefore must focus on the extent of the intrusion on respondent's privacy interests and on the State's need for the evidence.

The threats to the health or safety of respondent posed by the surgery are the subject of sharp dispute between the parties.... The Court of Appeals examined the medical evidence in the record and found that respondent would suffer some risks associated with the surgical procedure. One surgeon had testified that the difficulty of discovering the exact location of the bullet "could require extensive probing and retracting of the muscle tissue," carrying with it "the concomitant risks of injury to the muscle as well as injury to the nerves, blood vessels and other tissue in the chest and pleural cavity." The court further noted that "the greater intrusion and the larger incisions increase the risks of infection." Moreover, there was conflict in the testimony concerning the nature and the scope of the operation. One surgeon stated that it would take 15–20 minutes, while another predicted the procedure could take up to two and one-half hours. The court properly took the resulting uncertainty about the medical risks into account.

Both lower courts in this case believed that the proposed surgery, which for purely medical reasons required the use of a general anesthetic, would be an "extensive" intrusion on respondent's personal privacy and bodily integrity. When conducted with the consent of the patient, surgery requiring general anesthesia is not necessarily demeaning or intrusive. In such a case, the surgeon is carrying out the patient's own will concerning the patient's body and the patient's right to privacy is therefore preserved. In this case, however, the Court of Appeals noted that the Commonwealth proposes to take control of respondent's body, to "drug this citizen—not yet convicted of a criminal offense—with narcotics and barbiturates into a state of unconsciousness," and then to search beneath his skin for evidence of a crime. This kind of surgery involves a virtually total divestment of respondent's ordinary control over surgical probing beneath his skin.

The other part of the balance concerns the Commonwealth's need to intrude into respondent's body to retrieve the bullet. The Commonwealth claims to need the bullet to demonstrate that it was fired from Watkinson's gun, which in turn would show that respondent was the robber who confronted Watkinson. However, although we recognize the difficulty of making determinations in advance as to the strength of the case against respondent, petitioners' assertions of a compelling need for the bullet are hardly persuasive. The very circumstances relied on in this case to demonstrate probable cause to believe that evidence will be found tend to vitiate the Commonwealth's need to compel respondent to undergo surgery. The Commonwealth has available substantial additional evidence that respondent was the individual who accosted Watkinson on the night of the robbery. No party in this case suggests that Watkinson's entirely spontaneous identification of respondent at the hospital would be inadmissible. In addition, petitioners can no doubt prove that Watkinson was found a few blocks from Watkinson's store shortly after the incident took place. And petitioners can certainly show that the location of the bullet (under respondent's left collarbone) seems to correlate with Watkinson's report that the robber "jerked" to the left. The fact that the Commonwealth has available such substantial evidence of the origin of the bullet restricts the need for the Commonwealth to compel respondent to undergo the contemplated surgery.

In weighing the various factors in this case, we therefore reach the same conclusion as the courts below. The operation sought will intrude substantially on respondent's protected interests. The medical risks of the operation, although apparently not extremely severe, are a subject of considerable dispute; the very uncertainty militates against finding the operation to be "reasonable." In addition, the intrusion on respondent's privacy interests entailed by the operation can only be characterized as severe. On the other hand, although the bullet may turn out to be useful to the Commonwealth in prosecuting respondent, the Commonwealth has failed to demonstrate a compelling need for it. We believe that in these circumstances the Commonwealth has failed to demonstrate that it would be "reasonable" under the terms of the Fourth Amendment to search for evidence of this crime by means of the contemplated surgery....

B. DEADLY FORCE

TENNESSEE v. GARNER
471 U.S. 1 (1985)

Justice WHITE delivered the opinion of the Court.

This case requires us to determine the constitutionality of the use of deadly force to prevent the escape of an apparently unarmed suspected felon. We conclude that such force may not be used unless it is necessary to prevent the escape and the officer has probable cause to believe that the suspect poses a significant threat of death or serious physical injury to the officer or others.

I

At about 10:45 p.m. on October 3, 1974, Memphis Police Officers Elton Hymon and Leslie Wright were dispatched to answer a "prowler inside call." Upon arriving at the scene they saw a woman standing on her porch and gesturing toward the adjacent house. She told them she had heard glass breaking and that "they" or "someone" was breaking in next door. While Wright radioed the dispatcher to say that they were on the scene, Hymon went behind the house. He heard a door slam and saw someone run across the backyard. The fleeing suspect, Edward Garner, stopped at a 6-feet-high chain link fence at the edge of the yard. With the aid of a flashlight, Hymon was able to see Garner's face and hands. He saw no sign of a weapon, and, though not certain, was "reasonably sure" and "figured" that Garner was unarmed. He thought Garner was 17 or 18 years old and about 5'5" or 5'7" tall. While Garner was crouched at the base of the fence, Hymon called out "police, halt" and took a few steps toward him. Garner then began to climb over the fence. Convinced that if Garner made it over the fence he would elude capture, Hymon shot him. The bullet hit Garner in the back of the head. Garner was taken by ambulance to a hospital, where he died on the operating table. Ten dollars and a purse taken from the house were found on his body.

In using deadly force to prevent the escape, Hymon was acting under the authority of a Tennessee statute and pursuant to Police Department policy. The statute provides that "if, after notice of the intention to arrest the defendant, he either flee or forcibly resist, the officer may use all the necessary means to effect the arrest." The Department policy was slightly more restrictive than the statute, but still allowed the use of deadly force in cases of burglary. The incident was reviewed by the Memphis Police Firearm's Review Board and presented to a grand jury. Neither took any action.

Garner's father then brought this action in the Federal District Court for the Western District of Tennessee, seeking damages under 42 U.S.C. § 1983 for asserted violations of Garner's constitutional rights.... After a 3-day bench trial, the District Court entered judgment for all defendants....

IV

The District Court concluded that Hymon was justified in shooting Garner because state law allows, and the Federal Constitution does not forbid, the use of deadly force to prevent the escape of a fleeing felony suspect if no alternative means of apprehension is available. This conclusion made a determination of Garner's apparent dangerousness unnecessary. The court did find, however, that Garner appeared to be unarmed, though Hymon could not be certain that was the case. Restated in Fourth Amendment terms, this means Hymon had no articulable basis to think Garner was armed.

In reversing, the Court of Appeals accepted the District Court's factual conclusions and held that "the facts, as found, did not justify the use of deadly force." We agree. Officer Hymon could not reasonably have believed that Garner—young, slight, and unarmed—posed any threat. Indeed, Hymon never attempted to justify his actions on any basis other than the need to prevent an escape. The District Court stated in passing that "the facts of this case did not indicate to Officer Hymon that Garner was 'non-dangerous.'" This conclusion is not explained, and seems to be based solely on the fact that Garner had broken into a house at night. However, the fact that Garner was a suspected burglar could not, without regard to the other circumstances, automatically justify the use of deadly force. Hymon did not have probable cause to believe that Garner, whom he correctly believed to be unarmed, posed any physical danger to himself or others.

The dissent argues that the shooting was justified by the fact that Officer Hymon had probable cause to believe that Garner had committed a nighttime burglary. While we agree that burglary is a serious crime, we cannot agree that it is so dangerous as automatically to justify the use of deadly force. The FBI classifies burglary as a "property" rather than a "violent" crime. Although the armed burglar would present a different situation, the fact that an unarmed suspect has broken into a dwelling at night does not automatically mean he is physically dangerous. This case demonstrates as much. In fact, the available statistics demonstrate that burglaries only rarely involve physical violence. During the 10-year period from 1973-1982, only 3.8% of all burglaries involved violent crime…. The judgment of the Court of Appeals is affirmed, and the case is remanded for further proceedings consistent with this opinion.

FEDERAL PROSECUTIONS OF POLICE

The Supreme Court's interpretation of the Fourth Amendment plays a critical role not just in criminal cases where defendants seek to exclude evidence, but also in civil cases, like *Tennessee v. Garner*, where plaintiffs sue police officers in civil court for violations of their constitutional rights. Another context where these decisions play a role is in the determination of whether to bring federal criminal charges against police officers. A federal statute, 18 U.S.C. § 242, authorizes the Department of Justice (DOJ) to prosecute police officers for willful violations of a person's constitutional rights. The statute states that, "if death results from the acts committed in violation of this section" an officer convicted under the statute can be "imprisoned for any term of years or for life … or may be sentenced to death." The most clearly applicable right in police shootings is the Fourth Amendment's prohibition of unreasonable seizures.

In addition to investigating the Ferguson Police Department (FPD) as described in Chapter 4.B, the DOJ investigated the 2014 shooting of Michael Brown by FPD officer Darren Wilson. DOJ investigators applied the legal standard set down in *Tennessee v. Garner* to the evidence uncovered in their investigation to determine whether Wilson's use of deadly force violated the Fourth Amendment. Here is an excerpt from the DOJ report:

> " The use of deadly force is justified when the officer has 'probable cause to believe that the suspect pose[s] a threat of serious physical harm, either to the officer or to others.' Tennessee v. Garner (1985). As detailed throughout this report, the evidence does not establish that the shots fired by Wilson were objectively unreasonable under federal law. The physical evidence establishes that Wilson shot Brown once in the hand, at close range, while Wilson sat in his police SUV, struggling with Brown for

control of Wilson's gun. Wilson then shot Brown several more times from a distance of at least two feet after Brown ran away from Wilson and then turned and faced him. There are no witness accounts that federal prosecutors, and likewise a jury, would credit to support the conclusion that Wilson fired at Brown from behind. With the exception of the two wounds to Brown's right arm, which indicate neither bullet trajectory nor the direction in which Brown was moving when he was struck, the medical examiners' reports are in agreement that the entry wounds from the latter gunshots were to the front of Brown's body, establishing that Brown was facing Wilson when these shots were fired. This includes the fatal shot to the top of Brown's head. The physical evidence also establishes that Brown moved forward toward Wilson after he turned around to face him. The physical evidence is corroborated by multiple eyewitnesses.

Applying the well-established controlling legal authority, including binding precedent from the United States Supreme Court and Eighth Circuit Court of Appeals, the evidence does not establish that it was unreasonable for Wilson to perceive Brown as a threat while Brown was punching and grabbing him in the SUV and attempting to take his gun. Thereafter, when Brown started to flee, Wilson was aware that Brown had attempted to take his gun and suspected that Brown might have been part of a theft a few minutes before. Under the law, it was not unreasonable for Wilson to perceive that Brown posed a threat of serious physical harm, either to him or to others. When Brown turned around and moved toward Wilson, the applicable law and evidence do not support finding that Wilson was unreasonable in his fear that Brown would once again attempt to harm him and gain control of his gun. There are no credible witness accounts that state that Brown was clearly attempting to surrender when Wilson shot him. As detailed throughout this report, those witnesses who say so have given accounts that could not be relied upon in a prosecution because they are irreconcilable with the physical evidence, inconsistent with the credible accounts of other eyewitnesses, inconsistent with the witness's own prior statements, or in some instances, because the witnesses have acknowledged that their initial accounts were untrue....

Based on this investigation, the Department has concluded that Darren Wilson's actions do not constitute prosecutable violations under the applicable federal criminal civil rights statute, 18 U.S.C. § 242, which prohibits uses of deadly force that are "objectively unreasonable," as defined by the United States Supreme Court.[24]

In the next case, the Supreme Court clarified the *Garner* standard in the context of a claim that the police conducted an unreasonable seizure when they caused a fleeing suspect's car to crash into a ditch resulting in severe injuries.

SCOTT v. HARRIS
550 U.S. 372 (2007)

Justice SCALIA delivered the opinion of the Court.

In March 2001, a Georgia county deputy clocked respondent Victor Harris's vehicle traveling at 73 miles per hour on a road with a 55–mile–per–hour speed limit. The deputy activated his blue flashing lights indicating that respondent should pull over. Instead, respondent sped away, initiating a chase down what is in most portions a two-lane road, at speeds exceeding 85 miles per hour.... Petitioner, Deputy Timothy Scott, heard the radio communication and joined the pursuit along with other officers. In the midst of the chase, respondent pulled into the parking lot of a shopping center and was nearly boxed in by the various police vehicles. Respondent evaded the trap by making a sharp turn, colliding with Scott's police car, exiting the parking lot, and speeding off once again down a two-lane highway.

Following respondent's shopping center maneuvering, which resulted in slight damage to Scott's police car, Scott took over as the lead pursuit vehicle. Six minutes and nearly 10 miles after the chase had begun,... Scott applied his push bumper to the rear of respondent's vehicle. As a result, respondent lost control of his vehicle, which left the roadway, ran down an embankment, overturned, and crashed. Respondent was badly injured and was rendered a quadriplegic.

---

[24] The full report is available online at the following link:
https://www.justice.gov/sites/default/files/opa/press-releases/attachments/2015/03/04/doj_report_on_shooting_of_michael_brown_1.pdf

Respondent filed suit against Deputy Scott and others under … 42 U.S.C. § 1983, alleging, inter alia, a violation of his federal constitutional rights, viz. use of excessive force resulting in an unreasonable seizure under the Fourth Amendment.

Respondent urges us to analyze this case as we analyzed Tennessee v. Garner. We must first decide, he says, whether the actions Scott took constituted "deadly force."… If so, respondent claims that Garner prescribes certain preconditions that must be met before Scott's actions can survive Fourth Amendment scrutiny: (1) The suspect must have posed an immediate threat of serious physical harm to the officer or others; (2) deadly force must have been necessary to prevent escape; and (3) where feasible, the officer must have given the suspect some warning. Since these Garner preconditions for using deadly force were not met in this case, Scott's actions were per se unreasonable.

Respondent's argument falters at its first step; Garner did not establish a magical on/off switch that triggers rigid preconditions whenever an officer's actions constitute "deadly force." Garner was simply an application of the Fourth Amendment's "reasonableness" test to the use of a particular type of force in a particular situation. Garner held that it was unreasonable to kill a "young, slight, and unarmed" burglary suspect, by shooting him "in the back of the head" while he was running away on foot, and when the officer "could not reasonably have believed that the suspect posed any threat," and "never attempted to justify his actions on any basis other than the need to prevent an escape." Whatever Garner said about the factors that might have justified shooting the suspect in that case, such "preconditions" have scant applicability to this case, which has vastly different facts…. Nor is the threat posed by the flight on foot of an unarmed suspect even remotely comparable to the extreme danger to human life posed by respondent in this case. Although respondent's attempt to craft an easy-to-apply legal test in the Fourth Amendment context is admirable, in the end we must still slosh our way through the factbound morass of "reasonableness." Whether or not Scott's actions constituted application of "deadly force," all that matters is whether Scott's actions were reasonable.

In determining the reasonableness of the manner in which a seizure is effected, we must balance the nature and quality of the intrusion on the individual's Fourth Amendment interests against the importance of the governmental interests alleged to justify the intrusion. Scott defends his actions by pointing to the paramount governmental interest in ensuring public safety, and respondent nowhere suggests this was not the purpose motivating Scott's behavior. Thus, in judging whether Scott's actions were reasonable, we must consider the risk of bodily harm that Scott's actions posed to respondent in light of the threat to the public that Scott was trying to eliminate. Although there is no obvious way to quantify the risks on either side, it is clear from the [police dashcam] videotape that respondent posed an actual and imminent threat to the lives of any pedestrians who might have been present, to other civilian motorists, and to the officers involved in the chase. It is equally clear that Scott's actions posed a high likelihood of serious injury or death to respondent—though not the near certainty of death posed by, say, shooting a fleeing felon in the back of the head, or pulling alongside a fleeing motorist's car and shooting the motorist. So how does a court go about weighing the perhaps lesser probability of injuring or killing numerous bystanders against the perhaps larger probability of injuring or killing a single person? We think it appropriate in this process to take into account not only the number of lives at risk, but also their relative culpability. It was respondent, after all, who intentionally placed himself and the public in danger by unlawfully engaging in the reckless, high-speed flight that ultimately produced the choice between two evils that Scott confronted. Multiple police cars, with blue lights flashing and sirens blaring, had been chasing respondent for nearly 10 miles, but he ignored their warning to stop. By contrast, those who might have been harmed had Scott not taken the action he did were entirely innocent. We have little difficulty in concluding it was reasonable for Scott to take the action that he did.

But wait, says respondent: Couldn't the innocent public equally have been protected, and the tragic accident entirely avoided, if the police had simply ceased their pursuit? We think the police need not have taken that chance and hoped for the best. Whereas Scott's action—ramming respondent off the road—was certain to eliminate the risk that respondent posed to the public, ceasing pursuit was not. First of all, there would have been no way to convey convincingly to respondent that the chase was off, and that he was free to go. Had respondent looked in his rearview mirror and seen the police cars deactivate their flashing lights and turn around, he would have had no idea whether they were truly letting him get away, or simply devising a new strategy for capture. Perhaps the police knew a shortcut he didn't know, and would reappear down the road to intercept him; or perhaps they were setting up a roadblock in his path. Given such uncertainty, respondent might have been just as likely to respond by continuing to drive recklessly as by slowing down and wiping his brow.

Second, we are loath to lay down a rule requiring the police to allow fleeing suspects to get away whenever they drive so recklessly that they put other people's lives in danger. It is obvious the perverse incentives such a rule would create: Every fleeing motorist would know that escape is within his grasp, if only he accelerates to 90 miles per hour, crosses the double-yellow line a few times, and runs a few red lights. The Constitution assuredly does not impose this invitation to impunity-earned-by-recklessness. Instead, we lay down a more sensible rule: A police officer's attempt to terminate a dangerous high-speed car chase that threatens the lives of innocent bystanders does not violate the Fourth Amendment, even when it places the fleeing motorist at risk of serious injury or death.

The car chase that respondent initiated in this case posed a substantial and immediate risk of serious physical injury to others; no reasonable jury could conclude otherwise. Scott's attempt to terminate the chase by forcing respondent off the road was reasonable, and Scott is entitled to summary judgment.

In December 2021, the D.C. Police Department amended its internal policies governing vehicle chases. The new policy is excerpted below:

General Order - District of Columbia Police Department

A. Vehicle Pursuit Policy

> 1. Members may engage in a vehicle pursuit to apprehend a fleeing felon **only** when every other reasonable means of affecting the arrest or preventing the escape have been exhausted **and**:
>
> a. The suspect fleeing poses an immediate threat of death or serious bodily injury to the member or others; **or**
>
> b. There is probable cause to believe the crime committed or attempted involved an actual or threatened attack which resulted in or could have resulted in death or serious bodily injury; and
>
>> (1) There is probable cause to believe the subject committed, or attempted to commit, the crime; **and**
>>
>> (2) Failure to immediately apprehend the person places a member or the public in immediate danger of death or serious bodily injury; **and**
>>
>> (3) The lives of innocent people will not be endangered if the fleeing felon is pursued.

2. Members **shall not** pursue a vehicle for the sole purpose of affecting a stop for a traffic violation.

…

4. Members involved in a vehicle pursuit shall not intentionally cause physical contact between their vehicle and the fleeing vehicle, nor shall the member attempt to force the vehicle into another object or off the roadway.

C. KNOCK AND ANNOUNCE

When police execute a warrant to search a location, they typically bang on the door and yell "POLICE!" The ostensible goal is to alert the residents to open the door and peacefully acquiesce to the judicially-authorized search. Does the Constitution require that the police give notice in this manner?

In *Wilson v. Arkansas* (1995), the Supreme Court held that "the common-law knock and announce principle," which had been "woven … into the fabric of early American law," was a factor in determining whether an otherwise lawful entry of a building was reasonable under the Fourth Amendment. Subsequent cases offered further details on the constitutional knock-and-announce requirement.

UNITED STATES v. BANKS
540 U.S. 31 (2003)

Justice SOUTER delivered the opinion of the Court.

Officers executing a warrant to search for cocaine in respondent Lashawn Banks's apartment knocked and announced their authority. The question is whether their 15-to-20-second wait before a forcible entry satisfied the Fourth Amendment…. We hold that it did.

I

With information that Banks was selling cocaine at home, North Las Vegas Police Department officers and Federal Bureau of Investigation agents got a warrant to search his two-bedroom apartment. As soon as they arrived there, about 2 o'clock on a Wednesday afternoon, officers posted in front called out "police search warrant" and rapped hard enough on the door to be heard by officers at the back door. There was no indication whether anyone was home, and after waiting for 15 to 20 seconds with no answer, the officers broke open the front door with a battering ram. Banks was in the shower and testified that he heard nothing until the crash of the door, which brought him out dripping to confront the police. The search produced weapons, crack cocaine, and other evidence of drug dealing.

In response to drug and firearms charges, Banks moved to suppress evidence, arguing that the officers executing the search warrant waited an unreasonably short time before forcing entry, and so violated ... the Fourth Amendment....

II

There has never been a dispute that these officers were obliged to knock and announce their intentions when executing the search warrant, an obligation they concededly honored. Despite this agreement, we start with a word about standards for requiring or dispensing with a knock and announcement, since the same criteria bear on when the officers could legitimately enter after knocking.

The Fourth Amendment says nothing specific about formalities in exercising a warrant's authorization, speaking to the manner of searching as well as to the legitimacy of searching at all simply in terms of the right to be "secure ... against unreasonable searches and seizures."...

In Wilson v. Arkansas (1995), we held that the common law knock-and-announce principle is one focus of the reasonableness enquiry; and we subsequently decided that although the standard generally requires the police to announce their intent to search before entering closed premises, the obligation gives way when officers "have a reasonable suspicion that knocking and announcing their presence, under the particular circumstances, would be dangerous or futile, or would inhibit the effective investigation of the crime by, for example, allowing the destruction of evidence," Richards v. Wisconsin (1997). When a warrant applicant gives reasonable grounds to expect futility or to suspect that one or another such exigency already exists or will arise instantly upon knocking, a magistrate judge is acting within the Constitution to authorize a "no-knock" entry. And even when executing a warrant silent about that, if circumstances support a reasonable suspicion of exigency when the officers arrive at the door, they may go straight in.

.... At common law, the knock-and-announce rule was traditionally justified in part by the belief that announcement generally would avoid the destruction or breaking of any house by which great damage and inconvenience might ensue. One point in making an officer knock and announce, then, is to give a person inside the chance to save his door....

Since most people keep their doors locked, entering without knocking will normally do some damage, a circumstance too common to require a heightened justification when a reasonable suspicion of exigency already justifies an unwarned entry. We have accordingly held that police in exigent circumstances may damage premises so far as necessary for a no-knock entrance without demonstrating the suspected risk in any more detail than the law demands for an unannounced intrusion simply by lifting the latch. Either way, it is enough that the officers had a reasonable suspicion of exigent circumstances.

III

[In this case,] the Government claims that a risk of losing evidence arose shortly after knocking and announcing. Although the police concededly arrived at Banks's door without reasonable suspicion of facts justifying a no-knock entry, they argue that announcing their presence started the clock running toward the moment of apprehension that Banks would flush away the easily disposable cocaine, prompted by knowing the police would soon be coming in.... Banks does not, of course, deny that exigency may develop in the period beginning when officers with a warrant knock to be admitted, and the issue comes down to whether it was reasonable to suspect imminent loss of evidence after the 15 to 20 seconds the officers waited prior to forcing their way. Though we agree ... that this call is a close one, we think that after 15 or 20 seconds without a response, police could fairly suspect that cocaine would be gone if they were reticent any longer.

.... The fact that he [Banks] was actually in the shower and did not hear the officers is not to the point, and the same is true of the claim that it might have taken him longer than 20 seconds if he had heard the knock and headed straight for the door. As for the shower, it is enough to say that the facts known to the police are what count in judging reasonable waiting time, and there is no indication that the police knew that Banks was in the shower and thus unaware of an impending search that he would otherwise have tried to frustrate.

And the argument that 15 to 20 seconds was too short for Banks to have come to the door ignores the very risk that justified prompt entry. True, if the officers were to justify their timing here by claiming that Banks's failure to admit them fairly suggested a refusal to let them in, Banks could at least argue that no such suspicion can arise until an occupant has had time to get to the door, a time that will vary with the size of the establishment, perhaps five seconds to open a motel room door, or several minutes to move through a townhouse. In this case, however, the police claim exigent need to enter, and the crucial fact in examining their actions is not time to reach the door but the particular exigency claimed. On the record here, what matters is the opportunity to get rid of cocaine, which a prudent dealer will keep near a commode or kitchen sink. The significant circumstances include the arrival of the police during the day, when anyone inside would probably have been up and around, and the sufficiency of 15 to 20 seconds for getting to the bathroom or the kitchen to start flushing cocaine down the drain. That is, when circumstances are exigent because a pusher may be near the point of putting his drugs beyond reach, it is imminent disposal, not travel time to the entrance, that governs when the police may reasonably enter; since the bathroom and kitchen are usually in the interior of a dwelling, not the front hall, there is no reason generally to peg the travel time to the location of the door, and no reliable basis for giving the proprietor of a mansion a longer wait than the resident of a bungalow, or an apartment like Banks's. And 15 to 20 seconds does not seem an unrealistic guess about the time someone would need to get in a position to rid his quarters of cocaine....

Absent exigency, the police must knock and receive an actual refusal or wait out the time necessary to infer one. But in a case like this, where the officers knocked and announced their presence, and forcibly entered after a reasonable suspicion of exigency had ripened, their entry satisfied ... the Fourth Amendment.

While knock-and-announce is the default requirement, police sometimes obtain "no-knock" warrants to buttress their assessment that the likelihood of destruction of evidence or danger to the officers excuses the requirement to knock and announce. Here is an example of a no-knock warrant application.

The informant has reported that Guy is frequently armed with a handgun and accompanied by other individuals both known and unknown to your Affiant. Your Affiant knows that is not uncommon for individuals who deal in large quantities of controlled substance to employ others to sale and or protect their illegal substances and proceeds from the sale of these substances. Affiant asked that this warrant be issued authorizing a "No Knock" entry for the suspected place, 1104 Circle M Drive, Apartment C in Killeen.

Based on the foregoing facts, Affiant believes that there exists probable cause to believe that Marvin Guy is knowingly and intentionally in possession of a controlled substance to wit: cocaine at the premises described above and that the items described above constitute evidence of violations of the **TEXAS HEALTH AND SAFETY CODE**; there further exists probable cause to believe that the items described above are being concealed at the suspected premises, on the curtilage and on the person of Marvin Guy.

WHEREFORE, Affiant asks for issuance of a warrant that will authorize him to search said place, vehicles and premises for said property and seize the same and to arrest each said described and accused person (s).

AFFIANT

Subscribed and sworn to before me by said Affiant on this 8th day of May, 2014.

Judge, Killeen Municipal Court of Record
Bell County, Texas

For accounts of the raw power involved in warrant execution, see Kevin Sack, *Door-Busting Drug Raids Leave a Trail of Blood*, N.Y. Times, March 18, 2017.

CRITICISM OF NO-KNOCK WARRANTS

After nationwide publicity arising out of a nighttime raid when Kentucky police shot and killed Breonna Taylor, several jurisdictions moved to ban no-knock warrants. For example, a law enacted by Virginia in 2020 states:

"No law-enforcement officer shall seek, execute, or participate in the execution of a no-knock search warrant. A search warrant authorized under this section shall require that a law-enforcement officer be recognizable and identifiable as a uniformed law-enforcement officer and provide audible notice of his authority and purpose reasonably expected to be heard by occupants of such place to be searched prior to the execution of such search warrant.

Search warrants authorized under this section shall be executed only in the daytime unless a judge or magistrate ... authorizes the execution of such search warrant at another time for good cause shown. Any evidence obtained from a search warrant in violation of this subsection shall not be admitted into evidence for the Commonwealth in any prosecution."

In June 2020, the following federal legislation was introduced in Congress but never voted on.

A BILL

To prohibit no-knock warrants, and for other purposes.

Be it enacted by the Senate and House of Representatives of the United States of America in Congress assembled,

Section 1. Short Title.

This Act may be cited as the "Justice for Breonna Taylor Act".

Section 2. Prohibition on No-Knock Warrants.

(a) FEDERAL PROHIBITION. – Notwithstanding any other provision of law, a Federal law enforcement officer may not execute a warrant until after the officer provides notice of his or her authority and purpose.

(b) State And Local Law Enforcement Agencies.—Beginning in the first fiscal year beginning after the date of enactment of this Act, and each fiscal year thereafter, a State or local law enforcement agency that receive funds from the Department of Justice during the fiscal year may not execute a warrant that does not require the law enforcement officer serving the warrant to provide notice of his or her authority and purpose before forcibly entering a premises.

D. SEARCHES AND SEIZURES TO EXECUTE A WARRANT

ILLINOIS v. MCARTHUR
531 U.S. 326 (2001)

Justice BREYER delivered the opinion of the Court.

Police officers, with probable cause to believe that a man had hidden marijuana in his home, prevented that man from entering the home for about two hours while they obtained a search warrant. We must decide whether those officers violated the Fourth Amendment. We conclude that the officers acted reasonably. They did not violate the Amendment's requirements. And we reverse an Illinois court's holding to the contrary.

I

A

On April 2, 1997, Tera McArthur asked two police officers to accompany her to the trailer where she lived with her husband, Charles, so that they could keep the peace while she removed her belongings. The two officers, Assistant Chief John Love and Officer Richard Skidis, arrived with Tera at the trailer at about 3:15 p.m. Tera went inside, where Charles was present. The officers remained outside.

When Tera emerged after collecting her possessions, she spoke to Chief Love, who was then on the porch. She suggested he check the trailer because "Chuck had dope in there." She added (in Love's words) that she had seen Chuck "slide some dope underneath the couch." Love knocked on the trailer door, told Charles what Tera had said, and asked for permission to search the trailer, which Charles denied. Love then sent Officer Skidis with Tera to get a search warrant. Love told Charles, who by this time was also on the porch, that he could not reenter the trailer unless a police officer accompanied him. Charles subsequently reentered the trailer two or three times (to get cigarettes and to make phone calls), and each time Love stood just inside the door to observe what Charles did. Officer Skidis obtained the warrant by about 5 p.m. He returned to the trailer and, along with other officers, searched it. The officers found under the sofa a marijuana pipe, a box for marijuana (called a "one-hitter" box), and a small amount of marijuana. They then arrested Charles.

B

Illinois subsequently charged Charles McArthur with unlawfully possessing drug paraphernalia and marijuana (less than 2.5 grams), both misdemeanors. McArthur moved to suppress the pipe, box, and marijuana on the ground that they were the "fruit" of an unlawful police seizure, namely, the refusal to let him reenter the trailer unaccompanied, which would have permitted him, he said, to "have destroyed the marijuana."

The trial court granted McArthur's suppression motion. The Appellate Court of Illinois affirmed. We granted certiorari to determine whether the Fourth Amendment prohibits the kind of temporary seizure at issue here.

II

The Fourth Amendment says that the "right of the people to be secure in their persons, houses, papers, and effects, against unreasonable searches and seizures, shall not be violated." Its "central requirement" is one of reasonableness. In order to enforce that requirement, this Court has interpreted the Amendment as establishing rules and presumptions designed to control conduct of law enforcement officers that may significantly intrude upon privacy interests. Sometimes those rules require warrants. We have said, for example, that in "the ordinary case," seizures of personal property are "unreasonable within the meaning of the Fourth Amendment," without more, "unless accomplished pursuant to a judicial warrant," issued by a neutral magistrate after finding probable cause.

We nonetheless have made it clear that there are exceptions to the warrant requirement…. In the circumstances of the case before us, we cannot say that the warrantless seizure was *per se* unreasonable. It involves a plausible claim of specially pressing or urgent law enforcement need, i.e., "exigent circumstances." Moreover, the restraint at issue was tailored to that need, being limited in time and scope, and avoiding significant intrusion into the home itself. Consequently, rather than employing a *per se* rule of unreasonableness, we balance the privacy-related and law enforcement-related concerns to determine if the intrusion was reasonable.

We conclude that the restriction at issue was reasonable, and hence lawful, in light of the following circumstances, which we consider in combination. First, the police had probable cause to believe that McArthur's trailer home contained evidence of a crime and contraband, namely, unlawful drugs….

Second, the police had good reason to fear that, unless restrained, McArthur would destroy the drugs before they could return with a warrant…. Third, the police made reasonable efforts to reconcile their law enforcement needs with the demands of personal privacy. They neither searched the trailer nor arrested McArthur before obtaining a warrant. Rather, they imposed a significantly less restrictive restraint, preventing McArthur only from entering the trailer unaccompanied. They left his home and his belongings intact—until a neutral Magistrate, finding probable cause, issued a warrant. Fourth, the police imposed the restraint for a limited period of time, namely, two hours. As far as the record reveals, this time period was no longer than reasonably necessary for the police, acting with diligence, to obtain the warrant….

Our conclusion that the restriction was lawful finds significant support in this Court's case law…. In various other circumstances, this Court has upheld temporary restraints where needed to preserve evidence until police could obtain a warrant….

YBARRA v. ILLINOIS
444 U.S. 85 (1979)

Justice STEWART delivered the opinion of the Court.

…. On March 1, 1976, a special agent of the Illinois Bureau of Investigation presented a "Complaint for Search Warrant" to a judge of an Illinois Circuit Court. The complaint recited that the agent had spoken with an informant known to the police to be reliable and:

> "The informant related that over the weekend of 28 and 29 February he was in the Aurora Tap Tavern, located in the city of Aurora, Ill. and observed fifteen to twenty-five tin-foil packets on the person of the bartender 'Greg' and behind the bar. He also has been in the tavern on at least ten other occasions and has observed tin-foil packets on 'Greg' and in a drawer behind the bar. The informant has used heroin in the past and knows that tin-foil packets are a common method of packaging heroin. The informant advised that over the weekend of 28 and 29 February he had a conversation with 'Greg' and was advised that 'Greg' would have heroin for sale on Monday, March 1, 1976. This conversation took place in the tavern described."

On the strength of this complaint, the judge issued a warrant authorizing the search of "the following person or place: ... The Aurora Tap Tavern.... Also the person of 'Greg', the bartender, a male white with blondish hair appx. 25 years." The warrant authorized the police to search for "evidence of the offense of possession of a controlled substance," to wit, "heroin, contraband, other controlled substances, money, instrumentalities and narcotics, paraphernalia used in the manufacture, processing and distribution of controlled substances."

In the late afternoon of that day, seven or eight officers proceeded to the tavern. Upon entering it, the officers announced their purpose and advised all those present that they were going to conduct a "cursory search for weapons." One of the officers then proceeded to patdown each of the 9 to 13 customers present in the tavern, while the remaining officers engaged in an extensive search of the premises.

The police officer who frisked the patrons found the appellant, Ventura Ybarra, in front of the bar standing by a pinball machine. In his first patdown of Ybarra, the officer felt what he described as "a cigarette pack with objects in it." He did not remove this pack from Ybarra's pocket. Instead, he moved on and proceeded to patdown other customers. After completing this process the officer returned to Ybarra and frisked him once again. This second search of Ybarra took place approximately 2 to 10 minutes after the first. The officer relocated and retrieved the cigarette pack from Ybarra's pants pocket. Inside the pack he found six tinfoil packets containing a brown powdery substance which later turned out to be heroin.

Ybarra was subsequently indicted by an Illinois grand jury for the unlawful possession of a controlled substance. He filed a pretrial motion to suppress all the contraband that had been seized from his person at the Aurora Tap Tavern....

Each patron who walked into the Aurora Tap Tavern on March 1, 1976, was clothed with constitutional protection against an unreasonable search or an unreasonable seizure. That individualized protection was separate and distinct from the Fourth and Fourteenth Amendment protection possessed by the proprietor of the tavern or by "Greg." Although the search warrant, issued upon probable cause, gave the officers authority to search the premises and to search "Greg," it gave them no authority whatever to invade the constitutional protections possessed individually by the tavern's customers.... We conclude that the searches of Ybarra and the seizure of what was in his pocket contravened the Fourth and Fourteenth Amendments.

MICHIGAN v. SUMMERS
BAILEY v. UNITED STATES
Case Summaries

The Supreme Court set out rules for detaining people during the execution of search warrants in two cases decided over thirty years apart. In *Michigan v. Summers* (1981), the facts were as follows:

> "As Detroit police officers were about to execute a warrant to search a house for narcotics, they encountered respondent, George Summers, descending the front steps. They requested his assistance in gaining entry and detained him while they searched the premises. After finding narcotics in the basement and ascertaining that respondent owned the house, the police arrested him, searched his person, and found in his coat pocket an envelope containing 8.5 grams of heroin…."

These facts presented the question "whether the initial detention of respondent violated his constitutional right to be secure against an unreasonable seizure of his person."

On its way to answering the question in the negative, the Court emphasized that the search warrant already authorized a significant imposition:

> "Of prime importance in assessing the intrusion is the fact that the police had obtained a warrant to search respondent's house for contraband. A neutral and detached magistrate had found probable cause to believe that the law was being violated in that house and had authorized a substantial invasion of the privacy of the persons who resided there. The detention of one of the residents while the premises were searched, although admittedly a significant restraint on his liberty, was surely less intrusive than the search itself. Indeed, we may safely assume that most citizens—unless they intend flight to avoid arrest—would elect to remain in order to observe the search of their possessions. Furthermore, the type of detention imposed here is not likely to be exploited by the officer or unduly prolonged in order to gain more information, because the information the officers seek normally will be obtained through the search and not through the detention. Moreover,

because the detention in this case was in respondent's own residence, it could add only minimally to the public stigma associated with the search itself and would involve neither the inconvenience nor the indignity associated with a compelled visit to the police station."

The Court also highlighted the government interest in detaining Summers:

"Most obvious is the legitimate law enforcement interest in preventing flight in the event that incriminating evidence is found. Less obvious, but sometimes of greater importance, is the interest in minimizing the risk of harm to the officers. Although no special danger to the police is suggested by the evidence in this record, the execution of a warrant to search for narcotics is the kind of transaction that may give rise to sudden violence or frantic efforts to conceal or destroy evidence. The risk of harm to both the police and the occupants is minimized if the officers routinely exercise unquestioned command of the situation. Finally, the orderly completion of the search may be facilitated if the occupants of the premises are present. Their self-interest may induce them to open locked doors or locked containers to avoid the use of force that is not only damaging to property but may also delay the completion of the task at hand."

The Court summarized its holding as follows:

"If the evidence that a citizen's residence is harboring contraband is sufficient to persuade a judicial officer that an invasion of the citizen's privacy is justified, it is constitutionally reasonable to require that citizen to remain while officers of the law execute a valid warrant to search his home. Thus, for Fourth Amendment purposes, we hold that a warrant to search for contraband founded on probable cause implicitly carries with it the limited authority to detain the occupants of the premises while a proper search is conducted."

Finally, the Court distinguished *Ybarra* as follows:

"The 'seizure' issue in this case should not be confused with the 'search' issue presented in Ybarra v. Illinois. In Ybarra the police executing a search warrant for a public tavern detained and searched all of the customers who happened to be present. No question concerning the legitimacy of the detention was raised. Rather, the Court concluded that the search of Ybarra was invalid because the police had no reason to believe he had any special connection with the premises, and the police had no other basis for suspecting that he was armed or in possession of contraband. In this case, only the detention is at issue. The police knew respondent lived in the house, and they did not search him until after they had probable cause to arrest and had done so."

The government invoked *Summers*, in a subsequent case, *Bailey v. United States* (2013). The facts there were as follows:

" At 8:45 p.m. on July 28, 2005, local police obtained a warrant to search a [basement apartment on Lake Drive in Wyandanch, New York] for a .380–caliber handgun…. As the search unit began preparations for executing the warrant, two officers, Detectives Richard Sneider and Richard Gorbecki, were conducting surveillance in an unmarked car outside the residence. About 9:56 p.m., Sneider and Gorbecki observed two men – later identified as petitioner Chunon Bailey and Bryant Middleton – leave the gated area above the basement apartment and enter a car parked in the driveway. Both matched the general physical description of [the target of the search] provided by [an] informant. There was no indication that the men were aware of the officers' presence or had any knowledge of the impending search. The detectives watched the car leave the driveway. They waited for it to go a few hundred yards down the street and followed. The detectives informed the search team of their intent to follow and detain the departing occupants. The search team then executed the search warrant at the apartment.

Detectives Sneider and Gorbecki tailed Bailey's car for about a mile—and for about five minutes—before pulling the vehicle over in a parking lot by a fire station. They ordered Bailey and Middleton out of the car and did a patdown search of both men. The officers found no weapons but discovered a ring of keys in Bailey's pocket…. The officers put both men in handcuffs. When Bailey asked why, Gorbecki stated that they were being detained incident to the execution of a search warrant…. The detectives called for a patrol car to take Bailey and Middleton back to the Lake Drive apartment…. By the time the group returned to Lake Drive, the search team had discovered a gun and drugs in plain view inside the apartment. Bailey and Middleton were placed under arrest, and Bailey's keys were seized incident to the arrest. Officers later discovered that one of Bailey's keys opened the door of the basement apartment.

The Court began its analysis with the rule set out in *Summers*:

    " In Michigan v. Summers, the Court ... permitted officers executing a search warrant "to detain the occupants of the premises while a proper search is conducted.".... The rule announced in Summers allows detention incident to the execution of a search warrant "because the character of the additional intrusion caused by detention is slight and because the justifications for detention are substantial."

In Summers and later cases the occupants detained were found within or immediately outside a residence at the moment the police officers executed the search warrant. In Summers, the defendant was detained on a walk leading down from the front steps of the house. See also Muehler v. Mena (2005) (detention of occupant in adjoining garage); Los Angeles County v. Rettele (2007) (detention of occupants in bedroom). Here, however, petitioner left the apartment before the search began; and the police officers waited to detain him until he was almost a mile away. The issue is whether the reasoning in Summers can justify detentions beyond the immediate vicinity of the premises being searched....

Disagreeing with the Second Circuit, the Supreme Court concluded that *Summers* should not be expanded.

    " The Court of Appeals ... concluded that limiting the application of the authority to detain to the immediate vicinity would put law enforcement officers in a dilemma. They would have to choose between detaining an individual immediately (and risk alerting occupants still inside) or allowing the individual to leave (and risk not being able to arrest him later if incriminating evidence were discovered). Although the danger of alerting occupants who remain inside may be of real concern in some instances, as in the case when a no-knock warrant has been issued, this safety rationale rests on the false premise that a detention must take place. If the officers find that it would be dangerous to detain a departing individual in front of a residence, they are not required to stop him. And, where there are grounds to believe the departing occupant is dangerous, or involved in criminal activity, police will generally not need Summers to detain him at least for brief questioning, as they can rely instead on Terry v. Ohio (1968)....

Of the ... law enforcement interests identified to justify the detention in Summers, none applies with the same or similar force to the detention of recent occupants beyond the immediate vicinity of the premises to be searched. Any of the individual interests is also insufficient, on its own, to justify an expansion of the rule in Summers to permit the detention of a former occupant, wherever he may be found away from the scene of the search. This would give officers too much discretion. The categorical authority to detain incident to the execution of a search warrant must be limited to the immediate vicinity of the premises to be searched....

Chapter 6

THE EXCLUSIONARY RULE AND STANDING

The previous Chapters analyzed various types of Fourth Amendment violations. This Chapter pivots to the question of what, if any, remedy follows from a violation. The discussion is split into three parts: the Exclusionary Rule, exceptions to the Exclusionary Rule, and Standing.

A. THE EXCLUSIONARY RULE

Look back at the Fourth Amendment text and you will notice an important omission. The Amendment does not address the remedy, if any, for a violation of its commands. See *Davis v. United States* (2011) ("The Fourth Amendment protects the right to be free from 'unreasonable searches and seizures,' but it is silent about how this right is to be enforced."). As the cases in this section illustrate, this omission has given the Supreme Court broad leeway to craft the remedies (if any) for violations.

Weeks v. United States (1914) was among the first cases to recognize a so-called "exclusionary rule." In that case, police arrested Fremont Weeks for gambling. A federal marshal then went to Weeks' residence and, without a warrant, "searched the defendant's room and carried away certain letters and envelopes found in the drawer of a chiffonier."

> "Upon the introduction of such papers during the trial, the defendant objected on the ground that the papers had been obtained without a search warrant, and by breaking open his home, in violation of the 4th and 5th Amendments to the Constitution of the United States, which objection was overruled by the court."

The Supreme Court ruled that the trial court erred, explaining:

> ❝The tendency of those who execute the criminal laws of the country to obtain conviction by means of unlawful seizures and enforced confessions, the latter often obtained after subjecting accused persons to

unwarranted practices destructive of rights secured by the Federal Constitution, should find no sanction in the judgments of the courts, which are charged at all times with the support of the Constitution, and to which people of all conditions have a right to appeal for the maintenance of such fundamental rights....

If letters and private documents can thus be seized and held and used in evidence against a citizen accused of an offense, the protection of the 4th Amendment, declaring his right to be secure against such searches and seizures, is of no value, and, so far as those thus placed are concerned, might as well be stricken from the Constitution. The efforts of the courts and their officials to bring the guilty to punishment, praiseworthy as they are, are not to be aided by the sacrifice of those great principles established by years of endeavor and suffering which have resulted in their embodiment in the fundamental law of the land. The United States marshal could only have invaded the house of the accused when armed with a warrant issued as required by the Constitution, upon sworn information, and describing with reasonable particularity the thing for which the search was to be made. Instead, he acted without sanction of law, doubtless prompted by the desire to bring further proof to the aid of the government, and under color of his office undertook to make a seizure of private papers in direct violation of the constitutional prohibition against such action.... To sanction such proceedings would be to affirm by judicial decision a manifest neglect, if not an open defiance, of the prohibitions of the Constitution, intended for the protection of the people against such unauthorized action.

The Court concluded that the unlawfully obtained evidence should not have been admitted in Weeks' trial and reversed his conviction.

"We therefore reach the conclusion that the letters in question were taken from the house of the accused by an official of the United States, acting under color of his office, in direct violation of the constitutional rights of the defendant; that having made a seasonable application for their return, which was heard and passed upon by the court, there was involved in the order refusing the application a denial of the constitutional rights of the accused, and that the court should have restored these letters to the accused. In holding them and permitting their use upon the trial, we think prejudicial error was committed."

SILVERTHORNE LUMBER v. UNITED STATES
251 U.S. 385 (1920)

Justice HOLMES delivered the opinion of the Court.

This is a writ of error brought to reverse a judgment of the District Court fining the Silverthorne Lumber Company two hundred and fifty dollars for contempt of court and ordering Frederick Silverthorne to be imprisoned until he should purge himself of a similar contempt. The contempt in question was a refusal to obey subpoenas and an order of Court to produce books and documents of the company before the grand jury to be used in regard to alleged violation of the statutes of the United States by the said Silverthorne and his father. One ground of the refusal was that the order of the Court infringed the rights of the parties under the Fourth Amendment of the Constitution of the United States.

The facts are simple. An indictment upon a single specific charge having been brought against the two Silverthornes mentioned, they both were arrested at their homes early in the morning of February 25, and were detained in custody a number of hours. While they were thus detained representatives of the Department of Justice and the United States marshal without a shadow of authority went to the office of their company and made a clean sweep of all the books, papers and documents found there. All the employees were taken or directed to go to the office of the District Attorney of the United States to which also the books, &c., were taken at once. An application was made as soon as might be to the District Court for a return of what thus had been taken unlawfully. It was opposed by the District Attorney so far as he had found evidence against the plaintiffs in error, and it was stated that the evidence so obtained was before the grand jury. Color had been given by the District Attorney to the approach of those concerned in the act by an invalid subpoena for certain documents relating to the charge in the indictment then on file. Thus the case is not that of knowledge acquired through the wrongful act of a stranger, but it must be assumed that the Government planned or at all events ratified the whole performance. Photographs and copies of material papers were made and a new indictment was framed based upon the knowledge thus obtained. The District Court ordered a return of the originals but impounded the photographs and copies. Subpoenas to produce the originals then were served and on the refusal of the plaintiffs in error to produce them the Court made an order that the subpoenas should be complied with, although it had found that all the papers had been seized in violation of the parties' constitutional rights. The refusal to obey this order is the contempt alleged. The Government now, while in form repudiating and condemning the illegal seizure, seeks to maintain its right to avail itself of the knowledge obtained by that means which otherwise it would not have had.

The proposition could not be presented more nakedly. It is that although of course its seizure was an outrage which the Government now regrets, it may study the papers before it returns them, copy them, and then may use the knowledge that it has gained to call upon the owners in a more regular form to produce them; that the protection of the Constitution covers the physical possession but not any advantages that the Government can gain over the object of its pursuit by doing the forbidden act. Weeks v. United States (1914), to be sure, had established that laying the papers directly before the grand jury was unwarranted, but it is taken to mean only that two steps are required instead of one. In our opinion such is not the law. It reduces the Fourth Amendment to a form of words. The essence of a provision forbidding the acquisition of evidence in a certain way is that not merely evidence so acquired shall not be used before the Court but that it shall not be used at all. Of course this does not mean that the facts thus obtained become sacred and inaccessible. If knowledge of them is gained from an independent source they may be proved like any others, but the knowledge gained by the Government's own wrong cannot be used by it in the way proposed…. Judgment reversed.

MAPP v. OHIO
367 U.S. 643 (1961)

Justice CLARK delivered the opinion of the Court.

Appellant, Dollree Mapp, stands convicted of knowingly having had in her possession and under her control certain lewd and lascivious books, pictures, and photographs in violation of Ohio's Revised Code.

…. On May 23, 1957, three Cleveland police officers arrived at appellant's residence in that city pursuant to information that 'a person (was) hiding out in the home, who was wanted for questioning in connection with a recent bombing, and that there was a large amount of [gambling] paraphernalia being hidden in the home.' Miss Mapp and her daughter by a former marriage lived on the top floor of the two-family dwelling. Upon their arrival at that house, the officers knocked on the door and demanded entrance but appellant, after telephoning her attorney, refused to admit them without a search warrant. They advised their headquarters of the situation and undertook a surveillance of the house.

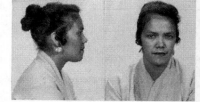

Booking photo: Dollree Mapp, 1957

The officers again sought entrance some three hours later when four or more additional officers arrived on the scene. When Miss Mapp did not come to the door immediately, at least one of the several doors to the house was forcibly opened and the policemen gained admittance. Meanwhile Miss Mapp's attorney arrived, but the officers, having secured their own entry, and continuing in their defiance of the law, would permit him neither to see Miss Mapp nor to enter the house. It appears that Miss Mapp was halfway down the stairs from the upper floor to the front door when the officers, in this highhanded manner, broke into the hall. She demanded to see the search warrant. A paper, claimed to be a warrant, was held up by one of the officers. She grabbed the 'warrant' and placed it in her bosom. A struggle ensued in which the officers recovered the piece of paper and as a result of which they handcuffed appellant because she had been 'belligerent' in resisting their official rescue of the 'warrant' from her person. Running roughshod over appellant, a policeman 'grabbed' her, 'twisted (her) hand,' and she 'yelled (and) pleaded with him' because 'it was hurting.' Appellant, in handcuffs, was then forcibly taken upstairs to her bedroom where the officers searched a dresser, a chest of drawers, a closet and some suitcases. They also looked into a photo album and through personal papers belonging to the appellant. The search spread to the rest of the second floor including the child's bedroom, the living room, the kitchen and a dinette. The basement of the building and a trunk found therein were also searched. The obscene materials for possession of which she was ultimately convicted were discovered in the course of that widespread search.

At the trial no search warrant was produced by the prosecution, nor was the failure to produce one explained or accounted for. At best, 'There is, in the record, considerable doubt as to whether there ever was any warrant for the search of defendant's home.' The Ohio Supreme Court believed a 'reasonable argument' could be made that the conviction should be reversed 'because the methods employed to obtain the evidence were such as to offend a sense of justice,' but the court found determinative the fact that the evidence had not been taken 'from defendant's person by the use of brutal or offensive physical force against defendant.'

The State says that even if the search were made without authority, or otherwise unreasonably, it is not prevented from using the unconstitutionally seized evidence at trial, citing Wolf v. Colorado (1949), in which this Court did indeed hold 'that in a prosecution in a State court for a State crime the Fourteenth Amendment does not forbid the admission of evidence obtained by an unreasonable search and seizure.' On this appeal, of which we have noted probable jurisdiction, it is urged once again that we review that holding.

… In Weeks v. United States (1914), this Court 'for the first time' held that in a federal prosecution the Fourth Amendment barred the use of evidence secured through an illegal search and seizure. This Court has ever since required of federal law officers a strict adherence to that command which this Court has held to be a clear, specific, and constitutionally required—even if judically implied—deterrent safeguard without insistence upon which the Fourth Amendment would have been reduced to 'a form of words.' It meant, quite simply, that 'conviction by means of unlawful seizures and enforced confessions should find no sanction in the judgments of the courts, and that such evidence 'shall not be used at all.'…

In Wolf v. Colorado … [this Court] discussed the effect of the Fourth Amendment upon the States through the operation of the Due Process Clause of the Fourteenth Amendment…. After declaring that the 'security of one's privacy against arbitrary intrusion by the police' is 'implicit in the concept of ordered liberty' and as such enforceable against the States through the Due Process Clause, and announcing that it 'stoutly adhered' to the Weeks decision, the Court decided that the Weeks exclusionary rule would not then be imposed upon the States as 'an essential ingredient of the right.' The Court's reasons for not considering essential to the right to privacy, as a curb imposed upon the States by the Due Process Clause, that which decades before had been posited as part and parcel of the Fourth Amendment's limitations upon federal encroachment of individual privacy, were bottomed on factual considerations.

While they are not basically relevant to a decision that the exclusionary rule is an essential ingredient of the Fourth Amendment as the right it embodies is vouchsafed against the States by the Due Process Clause, we will consider the current validity of the factual grounds upon which Wolf was based.... While in 1949, prior to the Wolf case, almost two-thirds of the States were opposed to the use of the exclusionary rule, now, despite the Wolf case, more than half of those since passing upon it, by their own legislative or judicial decision, have wholly or partly adopted or adhered to the Weeks rule. Significantly, among those now following the rule is California, which, according to its highest court, was 'compelled to reach that conclusion because other remedies have completely failed to secure compliance with the constitutional provisions.' In connection with this California case, we note that the second basis elaborated in Wolf in support of its failure to enforce the exclusionary doctrine against the States was that 'other means of protection' have been afforded 'the right to privacy.' The experience of California that such other remedies have been worthless and futile is buttressed by the experience of other States. The obvious futility of relegating the Fourth Amendment of the protection of other remedies has, moreover, been recognized by this Court since Wolf.

.... It, therefore, plainly appears that the factual considerations supporting the failure of the Wolf Court to include the Weeks exclusionary rule when it recognized the enforceability of the right to privacy against the States in 1949, while not basically relevant to the constitutional consideration, could not, in any analysis, now be deemed controlling.

.... Today we once again examine Wolf's constitutional documentation of the right to privacy free from unreasonable state intrusion, and, after its dozen years on our books, are led by it to close the only courtroom door remaining open to evidence secured by official lawlessness in flagrant abuse of that basic right, reserved to all persons as a specific guarantee against that very same unlawful conduct. We hold that all evidence obtained by searches and seizures in violation of the Constitution is, by that same authority, inadmissible in a state court.

Since the Fourth Amendment's right of privacy has been declared enforceable against the States through the Due Process Clause of the Fourteenth, it is enforceable against them by the same sanction of exclusion as is used against the Federal Government. Were it otherwise, then just as without the Weeks rule the assurance against unreasonable federal searches and seizures would be 'a form of

413

words,' valueless and undeserving of mention in a perpetual charter of inestimable human liberties, so too, without that rule the freedom from state invasions of privacy would be so ephemeral and so neatly severed from its conceptual nexus with the freedom from all brutish means of coercing evidence as not to merit this Court's high regard as a freedom 'implicit in 'the concept of ordered liberty.''

.... There are those who say, as did Justice (then Judge) Cardozo, that under our constitutional exclusionary doctrine 'the criminal is to go free because the constable has blundered.' In some cases this will undoubtedly be the result. But, as was said in [a prior case], 'there is another consideration—the imperative of judicial integrity.' The criminal goes free, if he must, but it is the law that sets him free. Nothing can destroy a government more quickly than its failure to observe its own laws, or worse, its disregard of the charter of its own existence. As Justice Brandeis, dissenting, said in Olmstead v. United States (1928): 'Our government is the potent, the omnipresent teacher. For good or for ill, it teaches the whole people by its example. If the government becomes a lawbreaker, it breeds contempt for law; it invites every man to become a law unto himself; it invites anarchy.' Nor can it lightly be assumed that, as a practical matter, adoption of the exclusionary rule fetters law enforcement.

.... The ignoble shortcut to conviction left open to the State tends to destroy the entire system of constitutional restraints on which the liberties of the people rest. Having once recognized that the right to privacy embodied in the Fourth Amendment is enforceable against the States, and that the right to be secure against rude invasions of privacy by state officers is, therefore, constitutional in origin, we can no longer permit that right to remain an empty promise.... Our decision, founded on reason and truth, gives to the individual no more than that which the Constitution guarantees him, to the police officer no less than that to which honest law enforcement is entitled, and, to the courts, that judicial integrity so necessary in the true administration of justice....

FRUIT OF THE POISONOUS TREE

As the preceding cases suggest, the exclusionary rule is not limited to evidence discovered as a direct consequence of unconstitutional police conduct; it also applies to evidence discovered indirectly through such conduct. The Supreme Court typically frames this point in terms of "fruits of a poisonous tree." Here is some illustrative language:

> • "The Government cannot violate the Fourth Amendment … and use the fruits of such unlawful conduct to secure a conviction. Nor can the Government make indirect use of such evidence for its case or support a conviction on evidence obtained through leads from the unlawfully obtained evidence. All these methods are outlawed, and convictions obtained by means of them are invalidated, because they encourage the kind of society that is obnoxious to free men." *Walder v. United States* (1954)

> • "The exclusionary sanction applies to any 'fruits' of a constitutional violation—whether such evidence be tangible, physical material actually seized in an illegal search, items observed or words overheard in the course of the unlawful activity, or confessions or statements of the accused obtained during an illegal arrest and detention." *United States v. Crews* (1980)

> • "Under the Court's precedents, the exclusionary rule encompasses both the primary evidence obtained as a direct result of an illegal search or seizure and … evidence later discovered and found to be derivative of an illegality, the so-called 'fruit of the poisonous tree.'" *Utah v. Strieff* (2016)

As Judge Learned Hand explained the concept, "limitations upon the fruit to be gathered tend to limit the quest itself."

The fruit of the poisonous tree doctrine applies in a variety of scenarios. For example, courts apply the doctrine to suppress fingerprint matches or lineup identifications generated through unlawful searches or seizures, as well as statements and physical evidence.

The Supreme Court has suggested that the existence of a witness, and thus that witness' testimony at trial, will rarely be suppressible as a fruit of the poisonous tree. See *United States v. Ceccolini* (1978) ("The exclusionary rule should be invoked with much greater reluctance where the claim is based on a causal relationship between a constitutional violation and the discovery of a live witness than when a similar claim is advanced to support suppression of an inanimate object.").

B. EXCEPTIONS TO THE EXCLUSIONARY RULE

The Supreme Court has carved out exceptions to the exclusionary rule when it believes suppressing evidence would fail to deter the police or would over-penalize the government for its errors. These exceptions fall into five basic categories: (1) Independent Source (the police found the same evidence lawfully); (2) Inevitable Discovery (the police *would* have found the evidence lawfully had they not discovered it through an illegal search); (3) Attenuation (the discovery of the evidence was far removed from the police misconduct); (4) Good Faith (the police acted unconstitutionally but in good faith reliance on other, typically non-police, officials); and (5) Impeachment (the evidence contradicts the defendant's trial testimony).

1. INDEPENDENT SOURCE

MURRAY v. UNITED STATES
487 U.S. 533 (1988)

Justice SCALIA delivered the opinion of the Court.

I

.... Based on information received from informants, federal law enforcement agents had been surveilling petitioner Michael Murray and several of his co-conspirators. At about 1:45 p.m. on April 6, 1983, they observed Murray drive a truck and James Carter drive a green camper, into a warehouse in South Boston. When the petitioners drove the vehicles out about 20 minutes later, the surveilling agents saw within the warehouse two individuals and a tractor-trailer rig bearing a long, dark container. Murray and Carter later turned over the truck and camper to other drivers, who were in turn followed and ultimately arrested, and the vehicles lawfully seized. Both vehicles were found to contain marijuana.

After receiving this information, several of the agents converged on the South Boston warehouse and forced entry. They found the warehouse unoccupied, but observed in plain view numerous burlap-wrapped bales that were later found to contain marijuana. They left without disturbing the bales, kept the warehouse under surveillance, and did not reenter it until they had a search warrant. In applying for the warrant, the agents did not mention the prior entry, and did not rely on any observations made during that entry. When the warrant was issued—at 10:40 p.m., approximately eight hours after the initial entry—the agents immediately reentered the warehouse and seized 270 bales of marijuana and notebooks listing customers for whom the bales were destined.

Before trial, petitioners moved to suppress the evidence found in the warehouse. The District Court denied the motion, rejecting petitioners' arguments that the warrant was invalid because the agents did not inform the Magistrate about their prior warrantless entry, and that the warrant was tainted by that entry....

II

The exclusionary rule prohibits introduction into evidence of tangible materials seized during an unlawful search and of testimony concerning knowledge acquired during an unlawful search. Beyond that, the exclusionary rule also prohibits the introduction of derivative evidence, both tangible and testimonial, that is the product of the primary evidence, or that is otherwise acquired as an indirect result of the unlawful search, up to the point at which the connection with the unlawful search becomes "so attenuated as to dissipate the taint."

Almost simultaneously with our development of the exclusionary rule, in the first quarter of this century, we also announced what has come to be known as the "independent source" doctrine. That doctrine, which has been applied to evidence acquired not only through Fourth Amendment violations but also through Fifth and Sixth Amendment violations, has recently been described as follows:

> "The interest of society in deterring unlawful police conduct and the
> public interest in having juries receive all probative evidence of a crime
> are properly balanced by putting the police in the same, not a worse,
> position that they would have been in if no police error or misconduct
> had occurred. When the challenged evidence has an independent
> source, exclusion of such evidence would put the police in a worse
> position than they would have been in absent any error or violation."

The dispute here is over the scope of this doctrine. Petitioners contend that it applies only to evidence obtained for the first time during an independent lawful

417

search. The Government argues that it applies also to evidence initially discovered during, or as a consequence of, an unlawful search, but later obtained independently from activities untainted by the initial illegality. We think the Government's view has better support in both precedent and policy.

Our cases have used the concept of "independent source" in a more general and a more specific sense. The more general sense identifies all evidence acquired in a fashion untainted by the illegal evidence-gathering activity. Thus, where an unlawful entry has given investigators knowledge of facts x and y, but fact z has been learned by other means, fact z can be said to be admissible because derived from an "independent source." This is how we used the term in Segura v. United States (1984). In that case, agents unlawfully entered the defendant's apartment and remained there until a search warrant was obtained. The admissibility of what they discovered while waiting in the apartment was not before us, but we held that the evidence found for the first time during the execution of the valid and untainted search warrant was admissible because it was discovered pursuant to an "independent source."

The original use of the term, however, and its more important use for purposes of these cases, was more specific. It was originally applied in the exclusionary rule context, by Justice Holmes, with reference to that particular category of evidence acquired by an untainted search which is identical to the evidence unlawfully acquired—that is, in the example just given, to knowledge of facts x and y derived from an independent source:

> "The essence of a provision forbidding the acquisition of evidence in a certain way is that not merely evidence so acquired shall not be used before the Court but that it shall not be used at all. Of course this does not mean that the facts thus obtained become sacred and inaccessible. If knowledge of them is gained from an independent source they may be proved like any others." Silverthorne Lumber v. United States.

As the First Circuit has observed, "in the classic independent source situation, information which is received through an illegal source is considered to be cleanly obtained when it arrives through an independent source."

…. Petitioners' asserted policy basis for excluding evidence which is initially discovered during an illegal search, but is subsequently acquired through an independent and lawful source, is that a contrary rule will remove all deterrence to, and indeed positively encourage, unlawful police searches. As petitioners see the incentives, law enforcement officers will routinely enter without a warrant to make sure that what they expect to be on the premises is in fact there. If it is not, they will have spared themselves the time and trouble of getting a warrant; if it is, they can get the warrant and use the evidence despite the unlawful entry. We see the incentives differently. An officer with probable cause sufficient to obtain a search warrant would be foolish to enter the premises first in an unlawful manner. By doing so, he would risk suppression of all evidence on the premises, both seen and unseen, since his action would add to the normal burden of convincing a magistrate that there is probable cause the much more onerous burden of convincing a trial court that no information gained from the illegal entry affected either the law enforcement officers' decision to seek a warrant or the magistrate's decision to grant it. Nor would the officer without sufficient probable cause to obtain a search warrant have any added incentive to conduct an unlawful entry, since whatever he finds cannot be used to establish probable cause before a magistrate....

III

To apply what we have said to the present cases: Knowledge that the marijuana was in the warehouse was assuredly acquired at the time of the unlawful entry. But it was also acquired at the time of entry pursuant to the warrant, and if that later acquisition was not the result of the earlier entry there is no reason why the independent source doctrine should not apply. Invoking the exclusionary rule would put the police (and society) not in the same position they would have occupied if no violation occurred, but in a worse one.

We think this is also true with respect to the tangible evidence, the bales of marijuana.... So long as a later, lawful seizure is genuinely independent of an earlier, tainted one (which may well be difficult to establish where the seized goods are kept in the police's possession) there is no reason why the independent source doctrine should not apply.

The ultimate question, therefore, is whether the search pursuant to warrant was in fact a genuinely independent source of the information and tangible evidence at issue here. This would not have been the case if the agents' decision to seek the warrant was prompted by what they had seen during the initial entry, or if information obtained during that entry was presented to the Magistrate and affected his decision to issue the warrant. On this point the Court of Appeals said the following:

> "We can be absolutely certain that the warrantless entry in no way contributed in the slightest either to the issuance of a warrant or to the discovery of the evidence during the lawful search that occurred pursuant to the warrant."

> "This is as clear a case as can be imagined where the discovery of the contraband in plain view was totally irrelevant to the later securing of a warrant and the successful search that ensued. As there was no causal link whatever between the illegal entry and the discovery of the challenged evidence, we find no error in the court's refusal to suppress."

Although these statements can be read to provide emphatic support for the Government's position, it is the function of the District Court rather than the Court of Appeals to determine the facts, and we do not think the Court of Appeals' conclusions are supported by adequate findings. The District Court found that the agents did not reveal their warrantless entry to the Magistrate, and that they did not include in their application for a warrant any recitation of their observations in the warehouse. It did not, however, explicitly find that the agents would have sought a warrant if they had not earlier entered the warehouse…. To be sure, the District Court did determine that the purpose of the warrantless entry was in part "to guard against the destruction of possibly critical evidence," and one could perhaps infer from this that the agents who made the entry already planned to obtain that "critical evidence" through a warrant-authorized search. That inference is not, however, clear enough to justify the conclusion that the District Court's findings amounted to a determination of independent source.

Accordingly, we vacate the judgment and remand these cases to the Court of Appeals with instructions that it remand to the District Court for determination whether the warrant-authorized search of the warehouse was an independent source of the challenged evidence in the sense we have described.

2.   INEVITABLE DISCOVERY

NIX v. WILLIAMS
467 U.S. 431 (1984)

Chief Justice BURGER delivered the opinion of the Court.

I

On December 24, 1968, 10-year-old Pamela Powers disappeared from a YMCA building in Des Moines, Iowa, where she had accompanied her parents to watch an athletic contest. [After investigation, a] warrant was issued for Robert Williams' arrest.

Police surmised that Williams had left Pamela Powers or her body somewhere between Des Moines and the Grinnell rest stop where some of the young girl's clothing had been found. On December 26, the Iowa Bureau of Criminal Investigation initiated a large-scale search. Two hundred volunteers divided into teams began the search 21 miles east of Grinnell, covering an area several miles to the north and south of Interstate 80. They moved westward from Poweshiek County, in which Grinnell was located, into Jasper County. Searchers were instructed to check all roads, abandoned farm buildings, ditches, culverts, and any other place in which the body of a small child could be hidden.

Meanwhile, Williams surrendered to local police in Davenport, where he was promptly arraigned. Williams contacted a Des Moines attorney who arranged for an attorney in Davenport to meet Williams at the Davenport police station. Des Moines police informed counsel they would pick Williams up in Davenport and return him to Des Moines without questioning him. Two Des Moines detectives then drove to Davenport, took Williams into custody, and proceeded to drive him back to Des Moines.

[*Ed. Note*: As we will discuss in Chapter 8, the detectives indirectly questioned Williams during this trip. That questioning violated Williams' Sixth Amendment right to counsel and made his subsequent statements inadmissible. In response to this questioning, Williams:] agreed to direct the officers to the child's body.... At that time, one search team near the Jasper County–Polk County line was only two and one-half miles from where Williams soon guided Detective Leaming and his party to the body....

At Williams' … trial …, the prosecution did not offer Williams' statements into evidence, nor did it seek to show that Williams had directed the police to the child's body. However, evidence of the condition of her body as it was found, articles and photographs of her clothing, and the results of post mortem medical and chemical tests on the body were admitted. The trial court concluded that the State had proved by a preponderance of the evidence that, if the search had not been suspended and Williams had not led the police to the victim, her body would have been discovered "within a short time" in essentially the same condition as it was actually found. The trial court also ruled that if the police had not located the body, "the search would clearly have been taken up again where it left off, given the extreme circumstances of this case and the body would have been found in short order."

In finding that the body would have been discovered in essentially the same condition as it was actually found, the court noted that freezing temperatures had prevailed and tissue deterioration would have been suspended. The challenged evidence was admitted and the jury … found Williams guilty of first-degree murder; he was sentenced to life in prison.…

II

…. The doctrine requiring courts to suppress evidence as the tainted "fruit" of unlawful governmental conduct had its genesis in Silverthorne Lumber Co. v. United States (1920); there, the Court held that the exclusionary rule applies not only to the illegally obtained evidence itself, but also to other incriminating evidence derived from the primary evidence.… Wong Sun v. United States (1963) extended the exclusionary rule to evidence that was the indirect product or "fruit" of unlawful police conduct.… Although Silverthorne and Wong Sun involved violations of the Fourth Amendment, the "fruit of the poisonous tree" doctrine has not been limited to cases in which there has been a Fourth Amendment violation. The Court has applied the doctrine where the violations were of the Sixth Amendment as well as of the Fifth Amendment.

The core rationale consistently advanced by this Court for extending the exclusionary rule to evidence that is the fruit of unlawful police conduct has been that this admittedly drastic and socially costly course is needed to deter police from violations of constitutional and statutory protections. This Court has accepted the argument that the way to ensure such protections is to exclude evidence seized as a result of such violations notwithstanding the high social cost of letting persons obviously guilty go unpunished for their crimes. On this rationale, the prosecution is not to be put in a better position than it would have been in if no illegality had transpired.

By contrast, the derivative evidence analysis ensures that the prosecution is not put in a worse position simply because of some earlier police error or misconduct. The independent source doctrine allows admission of evidence that has been discovered by means wholly independent of any constitutional violation. That doctrine, although closely related to the inevitable discovery doctrine, does not apply here; Williams' statements to [the detectives] indeed led police to the child's body, but that is not the whole story. The independent source doctrine teaches us that the interest of society in deterring unlawful police conduct and the public interest in having juries receive all probative evidence of a crime are properly balanced by putting the police in the same, not a worse, position that they would have been in if no police error or misconduct had occurred....

It is clear that the cases implementing the exclusionary rule begin with the premise that the challenged evidence is in some sense the product of illegal governmental activity. Of course, this does not end the inquiry. If the prosecution can establish by a preponderance of the evidence that the information ultimately or inevitably would have been discovered by lawful means—here the volunteers' search—then the deterrence rationale has so little basis that the evidence should be received.[5]

.... If the government can prove that the evidence would have been obtained inevitably and, therefore, would have been admitted regardless of any overreaching by the police, there is no rational basis to keep that evidence from the jury in order to ensure the fairness of the trial proceedings. In that situation, the State has gained no advantage at trial and the defendant has suffered no prejudice. Indeed, suppression of the evidence would operate to undermine the adversary system by putting the State in a worse position than it would have occupied without any police misconduct....

---

[5] As to the quantum of proof, we have already established some relevant guidelines. In United States v. Matlock (1974), we stated that "the controlling burden of proof at suppression hearings should impose no greater burden than proof by a preponderance of the evidence."...

The Court of Appeals did not find it necessary to consider whether the record fairly supported the finding that the volunteer search party would ultimately or inevitably have discovered the victim's body. However, three courts independently reviewing the evidence have found that the body of the child inevitably would have been found by the searchers. Williams challenges these findings, asserting that the record contains only the "post hoc rationalization" that the search efforts would have proceeded two and one-half miles into Polk County where Williams had led police to the body.

When that challenge was made at the suppression hearing preceding Williams' … trial, the prosecution offered the testimony of Agent Ruxlow of the Iowa Bureau of Criminal Investigation. Ruxlow had organized and directed some 200 volunteers who were searching for the child's body. The searchers were instructed "to check all the roads, the ditches, any culverts…. If they came upon any abandoned farm buildings, they were instructed to go onto the property and search those abandoned farm buildings or any other places where a small child could be secreted." Ruxlow testified that he marked off highway maps of Poweshiek and Jasper Counties in grid fashion, divided the volunteers into teams of four to six persons, and assigned each team to search specific grid areas. Ruxlow also testified that, if the search had not been suspended because of Williams' promised cooperation, it would have continued into Polk County, using the same grid system. Although he had previously marked off into grids only the highway maps of Poweshiek and Jasper Counties, Ruxlow had obtained a map of Polk County, which he said he would have marked off in the same manner had it been necessary for the search to continue.

The search had commenced at approximately 10 a.m. and moved westward through Poweshiek County into Jasper County. At approximately 3 p.m., after Williams had volunteered to cooperate with the police, Detective Leaming, who was in the police car with Williams, sent word to Ruxlow and the other Special Agent directing the search to meet him at the Grinnell truck stop and the search was suspended at that time. Ruxlow also stated that he was "under the impression that there was a possibility" that Williams would lead them to the child's body at that time. The search was not resumed once it was learned that Williams had led the police to the body, which was found two and one-half miles from where the search had stopped in what would have been the easternmost grid to be searched in Polk County. There was testimony that it would have taken an additional three to five hours to discover the body if the search had continued; the body was found near a culvert, one of the kinds of places the teams had been specifically directed to search.

On this record it is clear that the search parties were approaching the actual location of the body, and we are satisfied, along with three courts earlier, that the volunteer search teams would have resumed the search had Williams not earlier led the police to the body and the body inevitably would have been found....

3. ATTENUATION

Prior to *Utah v. Strieff*, the leading case on Attenuation was *Wong Sun v. United States* (1963). In *Wong Sun*, the Supreme Court summarized the doctrine and its application to the facts in that case as follows:

> "We have no occasion to disagree with the finding of the Court of Appeals that [Wong Sun's] arrest ... was without probable cause or reasonable grounds. At all events no evidentiary consequences turn upon that question. For Wong Sun's unsigned confession was not the fruit of that arrest, and was therefore properly admitted at trial. On the evidence that Wong Sun had been released on his own recognizance after a lawful arraignment, and had returned voluntarily several days later to make the statement, we hold that the connection between the arrest and the statement had 'become so attenuated as to dissipate the taint.'"

In *Utah v. Strieff*, the Supreme Court held that Attenuation doctrine provided an exception to the Exclusionary Rule in a more common and, as Justice Sotomayor points out in dissent, more controversial scenario.

UTAH v. STRIEFF
579 U.S. 232 (2016)

Justice THOMAS delivered the opinion of the Court.

To enforce the Fourth Amendment's prohibition against "unreasonable searches and seizures," this Court has at times required courts to exclude evidence obtained by unconstitutional police conduct. But the Court has also held that, even when there is a Fourth Amendment violation, this exclusionary rule does not apply when the costs of exclusion outweigh its deterrent benefits. In some cases, for example, the link between the unconstitutional conduct and the discovery of the evidence is too attenuated to justify suppression. The question in this case is whether this attenuation doctrine applies when an officer makes an unconstitutional investigatory stop; learns during that stop that the suspect is subject to a valid arrest warrant; and proceeds to arrest the suspect and seize incriminating evidence during a search incident to that arrest. We hold that the evidence the officer seized as part of the search incident to arrest is admissible because the officer's discovery of the arrest warrant attenuated the connection between the unlawful stop and the evidence seized incident to arrest.

I

This case began with an anonymous tip. In December 2006, someone called the South Salt Lake City police's drug-tip line to report "narcotics activity" at a particular residence. Narcotics detective Douglas Fackrell investigated the tip. Over the course of about a week, Officer Fackrell conducted intermittent surveillance of the home. He observed visitors who left a few minutes after arriving at the house. These visits were sufficiently frequent to raise his suspicion that the occupants were dealing drugs.

One of those visitors was respondent Edward Strieff. Officer Fackrell observed Strieff exit the house and walk toward a nearby convenience store. In the store's parking lot, Officer Fackrell detained Strieff, identified himself, and asked Strieff what he was doing at the residence.

As part of the stop, Officer Fackrell requested Strieff's identification, and Strieff produced his Utah identification card. Officer Fackrell relayed Strieff's information to a police dispatcher, who reported that Strieff had an outstanding arrest warrant for a traffic violation. Officer Fackrell then arrested Strieff pursuant to that warrant. When Officer Fackrell searched Strieff incident to the arrest, he discovered a baggie of methamphetamine and drug paraphernalia.

The State charged Strieff with unlawful possession of methamphetamine and drug paraphernalia. Strieff moved to suppress the evidence, arguing that the evidence was inadmissible because it was derived from an unlawful investigatory stop. At the suppression hearing, the prosecutor conceded that Officer Fackrell lacked reasonable suspicion for the stop but argued that the evidence should not be suppressed because the existence of a valid arrest warrant attenuated the connection between the unlawful stop and the discovery of the contraband.

The trial court agreed with the State and admitted the evidence.... Strieff conditionally pleaded guilty to reduced charges of attempted possession of a controlled substance and possession of drug paraphernalia, but reserved his right to appeal the trial court's denial of the suppression motion.... The Utah Supreme Court reversed.... We now reverse.

II

A

The Fourth Amendment protects "[t]he right of the people to be secure in their persons, houses, papers, and effects, against unreasonable searches and seizures." Because officers who violated the Fourth Amendment were traditionally considered trespassers, individuals subject to unconstitutional searches or seizures historically enforced their rights through tort suits or self-help. In the 20th century, however, the exclusionary rule—the rule that often requires trial courts to exclude unlawfully seized evidence in a criminal trial—became the principal judicial remedy to deter Fourth Amendment violations. See, e.g., Mapp v. Ohio (1961).

Under the Court's precedents, the exclusionary rule encompasses both the "primary evidence obtained as a direct result of an illegal search or seizure" and, relevant here, "evidence later discovered and found to be derivative of an illegality," the so-called "fruit of the poisonous tree." But the significant costs of this rule have led us to deem it applicable only where its deterrence benefits outweigh its substantial social costs. "Suppression of evidence has always been our last resort, not our first impulse." Hudson v. Michigan (2006).

We have accordingly recognized several exceptions to the rule. Three of these exceptions involve the causal relationship between the unconstitutional act and the discovery of evidence. First, the independent source doctrine allows trial courts to admit evidence obtained in an unlawful search if officers independently acquired it from a separate, independent source. See Murray v. United States (1988). Second, the inevitable discovery doctrine allows for the admission of evidence that would have been discovered even without the unconstitutional source. See Nix v. Williams (1984). Third, and at issue here, is the attenuation doctrine: Evidence is admissible when the connection between unconstitutional police conduct and the evidence is remote or has been interrupted by some intervening circumstance, so that "the interest protected by the constitutional guarantee that has been violated would not be served by suppression of the evidence obtained." Hudson v. Michigan (2006).

B

Turning to the application of the attenuation doctrine to this case, we first address a threshold question: whether this doctrine applies at all to a case like this, where the intervening circumstance that the State relies on is the discovery of a valid, pre-existing, and untainted arrest warrant. The Utah Supreme Court declined to apply the attenuation doctrine because it read our precedents as applying the doctrine only "to circumstances involving an independent act of a defendant's 'free will' in confessing to a crime or consenting to a search." In this Court, Strieff has not defended this argument, and we disagree with it, as well. The attenuation doctrine evaluates the causal link between the government's unlawful act and the discovery of evidence, which often has nothing to do with a defendant's actions. And the logic of our prior attenuation cases is not limited to independent acts by the defendant.

It remains for us to address whether the discovery of a valid arrest warrant was a sufficient intervening event to break the causal chain between the unlawful stop and the discovery of drug-related evidence on Strieff's person. The three factors articulated in Brown v. Illinois (1975) guide our analysis. First, we look to the "temporal proximity" between the unconstitutional conduct and the discovery of evidence to determine how closely the discovery of evidence followed the unconstitutional search. Second, we consider "the presence of intervening circumstances." Third, and "particularly" significant, we examine "the purpose and flagrancy of the official misconduct." In evaluating these factors, we assume without deciding (because the State conceded the point) that Officer Fackrell lacked reasonable suspicion to initially stop Strieff....

1

The first factor, temporal proximity between the initially unlawful stop and the search, favors suppressing the evidence. Our precedents have declined to find that this factor favors attenuation unless "substantial time" elapses between an unlawful act and when the evidence is obtained. Here, however, Officer Fackrell discovered drug contraband on Strieff's person only minutes after the illegal stop. As the Court explained in Brown, such a short time interval counsels in favor of suppression;

there, we found that the confession should be suppressed, relying in part on the "less than two hours" that separated the unconstitutional arrest and the confession.

In contrast, the second factor, the presence of intervening circumstances, strongly favors the State.... In this case, the warrant was valid, it predated Officer Fackrell's investigation, and it was entirely unconnected with the stop. And once Officer Fackrell discovered the warrant, he had an obligation to arrest Strieff. "A warrant is a judicial mandate to an officer to conduct a search or make an arrest, and the officer has a sworn duty to carry out its provisions." Officer Fackrell's arrest of Strieff thus was a ministerial act that was independently compelled by the pre-existing warrant. And once Officer Fackrell was authorized to arrest Strieff, it was undisputedly lawful to search Strieff as an incident of his arrest to protect Officer Fackrell's safety.

Finally, the third factor, "the purpose and flagrancy of the official misconduct," also strongly favors the State. The exclusionary rule exists to deter police misconduct. The third factor of the attenuation doctrine reflects that rationale by favoring exclusion only when the police misconduct is most in need of deterrence—that is, when it is purposeful or flagrant.

Officer Fackrell was at most negligent. In stopping Strieff, Officer Fackrell made two good-faith mistakes. First, he had not observed what time Strieff entered the suspected drug house, so he did not know how long Strieff had been there. Officer Fackrell thus lacked a sufficient basis to conclude that Strieff was a short-term visitor who may have been consummating a drug transaction.

Second, because he lacked confirmation that Strieff was a short-term visitor, Officer Fackrell should have asked Strieff whether he would speak with him, instead of demanding that Strieff do so. Officer Fackrell's stated purpose was to "find out what was going on in the house." Nothing prevented him from approaching Strieff simply to ask. See Florida v. Bostick (1991) ("A seizure does not occur simply because a police officer approaches an individual and asks a few questions"). But these errors in judgment hardly rise to a purposeful or flagrant violation of Strieff's Fourth Amendment rights.

While Officer Fackrell's decision to initiate the stop was mistaken, his conduct thereafter was lawful. The officer's decision to run the warrant check was a "negligibly burdensome precaution" for officer safety. And Officer Fackrell's actual search of Strieff was a lawful search incident to arrest.

429

Moreover, there is no indication that this unlawful stop was part of any systemic or recurrent police misconduct. To the contrary, all the evidence suggests that the stop was an isolated instance of negligence that occurred in connection with a bona fide investigation of a suspected drug house. Officer Fackrell saw Strieff leave a suspected drug house. And his suspicion about the house was based on an anonymous tip and his personal observations.

Applying these factors, we hold that the evidence discovered on Strieff's person was admissible because the unlawful stop was sufficiently attenuated by the pre-existing arrest warrant. Although the illegal stop was close in time to Strieff's arrest, that consideration is outweighed by two factors supporting the State. The outstanding arrest warrant for Strieff's arrest is a critical intervening circumstance that is wholly independent of the illegal stop. The discovery of that warrant broke the causal chain between the unconstitutional stop and the discovery of evidence by compelling Officer Fackrell to arrest Strieff. And, it is especially significant that there is no evidence that Officer Fackrell's illegal stop reflected flagrantly unlawful police misconduct.

2

… Strieff argues that, because of the prevalence of outstanding arrest warrants in many jurisdictions, police will engage in dragnet searches if the exclusionary rule is not applied. We think that this outcome is unlikely. Such wanton conduct would expose police to civil liability. See 42 U.S.C. § 1983; Monell v. New York City Dept. of Social Servs. (1978). And in any event, the Brown factors take account of the purpose and flagrancy of police misconduct. Were evidence of a dragnet search presented here, the application of the Brown factors could be different. But there is no evidence that the concerns that Strieff raises with the criminal justice system are present in South Salt Lake City, Utah.

We hold that the evidence Officer Fackrell seized as part of his search incident to arrest is admissible because his discovery of the arrest warrant attenuated the connection between the unlawful stop and the evidence seized from Strieff incident to arrest. The judgment of the Utah Supreme Court, accordingly, is reversed.

Justice SOTOMAYOR, with whom Justice GINSBURG joins as to Parts I, II, and III, dissenting.

The Court today holds that the discovery of a warrant for an unpaid parking ticket will forgive a police officer's violation of your Fourth Amendment rights. Do not be soothed by the opinion's technical language: This case allows the police to stop you on the street, demand your identification, and check it for outstanding traffic warrants—even if you are doing nothing wrong. If the officer discovers a warrant for a fine you forgot to pay, courts will now excuse his illegal stop and will admit into evidence anything he happens to find by searching you after arresting you on the warrant. Because the Fourth Amendment should prohibit, not permit, such misconduct, I dissent....

II

The Utah Supreme Court ... correctly rejected the State's argument that the officer's discovery of a traffic warrant unspoiled the poisonous fruit. The State analogizes finding the warrant to one of our earlier decisions, Wong Sun v. United States (1963). There, an officer illegally arrested a person who, days later, voluntarily returned to the station to confess to committing a crime. Even though the person would not have confessed "but for the illegal actions of the police," we noted that the police did not exploit their illegal arrest to obtain the confession. Because the confession was obtained by "means sufficiently distinguishable" from the constitutional violation, we held that it could be admitted into evidence. The State contends that the search incident to the warrant-arrest here is similarly distinguishable from the illegal stop.

But Wong Sun explains why Strieff's drugs must be excluded. We reasoned that a Fourth Amendment violation may not color every investigation that follows but it certainly stains the actions of officers who exploit the infraction. We distinguished evidence obtained by innocuous means from evidence obtained by exploiting misconduct after considering a variety of factors: whether a long time passed, whether there were "intervening circumstances," and whether the purpose or flagrancy of the misconduct was "calculated" to procure the evidence.

These factors confirm that the officer in this case discovered Strieff's drugs by exploiting his own illegal conduct. The officer did not ask Strieff to volunteer his name only to find out, days later, that Strieff had a warrant against him. The officer illegally stopped Strieff and immediately ran a warrant check. The officer's discovery of a warrant was not some intervening surprise that he could not have anticipated. Utah lists over 180,000 misdemeanor warrants in its database, and at the time of the arrest, Salt Lake County had a backlog of outstanding warrants so large that it faced the potential for civil liability.

The officer's violation was also calculated to procure evidence. His sole reason for stopping Strieff, he acknowledged, was investigative—he wanted to discover whether drug activity was going on in the house Strieff had just exited.

The warrant check, in other words, was not an "intervening circumstance" separating the stop from the search for drugs. It was part and parcel of the officer's illegal expedition for evidence in the hope that something might turn up. Under our precedents, because the officer found Strieff's drugs by exploiting his own constitutional violation, the drugs should be excluded....

IV

Writing only for myself, and drawing on my professional experiences, I would add that unlawful "stops" have severe consequences much greater than the inconvenience suggested by the name. This Court has given officers an array of instruments to probe and examine you. When we condone officers' use of these devices without adequate cause, we give them reason to target pedestrians in an arbitrary manner. We also risk treating members of our communities as second-class citizens.

Although many Americans have been stopped for speeding or jaywalking, few may realize how degrading a stop can be when the officer is looking for more. This Court has allowed an officer to stop you for whatever reason he wants—so long as he can point to a pretextual justification after the fact. Whren v. United States (1996). That justification must provide specific reasons why the officer suspected you were breaking the law, Terry, but it may factor in your ethnicity, United States v. Brignoni–Ponce (1975), where you live, Adams v. Williams (1972), what you were wearing, United States v. Sokolow (1989), and how you behaved, Illinois v. Wardlow (2000). The officer does not even need to know which law you might have broken so long as he can later point to any possible infraction—even one that is minor, unrelated, or ambiguous. Devenpeck v. Alford (2004); Heien v. North Carolina (2014).

The indignity of the stop is not limited to an officer telling you that you look like a criminal. The officer may next ask for your "consent" to inspect your bag or purse without telling you that you can decline. Florida v. Bostick (1991). Regardless of your answer, he may order you to stand "helpless, perhaps facing a wall with [your] hands raised." Terry v. Ohio (1968). If the officer thinks you might be dangerous, he may then "frisk" you for weapons. This involves more than just a pat down. As onlookers pass by, the officer may "feel with sensitive fingers every portion of [your] body. A thorough search [may] be made of [your] arms and armpits, waistline and back, the groin and area about the testicles, and entire surface of the legs down to the feet."

The officer's control over you does not end with the stop. If the officer chooses, he may handcuff you and take you to jail for doing nothing more than speeding, jaywalking, or "driving [your] pickup truck ... with [your] 3–year–old son and 5–year–old daughter ... without [your] seatbelt fastened." Atwater v. Lago Vista (2001). At the jail, he can fingerprint you, swab DNA from the inside of your mouth, and force you to "shower with a delousing agent" while you "lift [your] tongue, hold out [your] arms, turn around, and lift [your] genitals." Florence v. Board of Chosen Freeholders of County of Burlington (2012); Maryland v. King (2013). Even if you are innocent, you will now join the 65 million Americans with an arrest record and experience the "civil death" of discrimination by employers, landlords, and whoever else conducts a background check. And, of course, if you fail to pay bail or appear for court, a judge will issue a warrant to render you "arrestable on sight" in the future.

This case involves a suspicionless stop, one in which the officer initiated this chain of events without justification. As the Justice Department notes, many innocent people are subjected to the humiliations of these unconstitutional searches. The white defendant in this case shows that anyone's dignity can be violated in this manner. But it is no secret that people of color are disproportionate victims of this type of scrutiny. See M. Alexander, The New Jim Crow (2010). For generations, black and brown parents have given their children "the talk"—instructing them never to run down the street; always keep your hands where they can be seen; do not even think of talking back to a stranger—all out of fear of how an officer with a gun will react to them. See, e.g., W.E.B. Du Bois, The Souls of Black Folk (1903); J. Baldwin, The Fire Next Time (1963); T. Coates, Between the World and Me (2015).

By legitimizing the conduct that produces this double consciousness, this case tells everyone, white and black, guilty and innocent, that an officer can verify your legal status at any time. It says that your body is subject to invasion while courts excuse the violation of your rights. It implies that you are not a citizen of a democracy but the subject of a carceral state, just waiting to be cataloged.

We must not pretend that the countless people who are routinely targeted by police are "isolated." They are the canaries in the coal mine whose deaths, civil and literal, warn us that no one can breathe in this atmosphere. They are the ones who recognize that unlawful police stops corrode all our civil liberties and threaten all our lives. Until their voices matter too, our justice system will continue to be anything but.

HUDSON v. MICHIGAN

Case Note

In *Hudson v. Michigan* (2006), the Supreme Court held that the exclusionary rule does not apply to knock-and-announce violations (see Chapter 5). The Court summarized its ruling as follows:

> "The social costs of applying the exclusionary rule to knock-and-announce violations are considerable; the incentive to such violations is minimal to begin with, and the extant deterrences against them are substantial—incomparably greater than the factors deterring warrantless entries when Mapp was decided. Resort to the massive remedy of suppressing evidence of guilt is unjustified."

The lower courts interpret *Hudson* as a categorical rule removing the possibility of the suppression of evidence for a knock-and-announce violation. See, e.g., *United States v. Garcia-Hernandez* (1st Cir. 2011) ("We join these other courts in concluding that the holding in *Hudson* is categorical and that the amount of force used in effecting a no-knock entry does not alter that reality.").

4. "GOOD FAITH"

UNITED STATES v. LEON
468 U.S. 897 (1984)

Justice WHITE delivered the opinion of the Court.

This case presents the question whether the Fourth Amendment exclusionary rule should be modified so as not to bar the use in the prosecution's case in chief of evidence obtained by officers acting in reasonable reliance on a search warrant issued by a detached and neutral magistrate but ultimately found to be unsupported by probable cause. To resolve this question, we must consider once again the tension between the sometimes competing goals of, on the one hand, deterring official misconduct and removing inducements to unreasonable invasions of privacy and, on the other, establishing procedures under which criminal defendants are acquitted or convicted on the basis of all the evidence which exposes the truth.

I

[After an investigation into illegal drug sales,] Officer Cyril Rombach of the Burbank Police Department, an experienced and well-trained narcotics investigator, prepared an application for a warrant to search [three specified houses, including the home of Alberto Leon], and automobiles registered to each of the respondents for an extensive list of items believed to be related to respondents' drug-trafficking activities. Officer Rombach's extensive application was reviewed by several Deputy District Attorneys.

A facially valid search warrant was issued in September 1981 by a State Superior Court Judge. The ensuing searches produced large quantities of drugs at the [specified] addresses.... Other evidence was discovered at each of the residences and in [the specified] automobiles. Respondents were indicted by a grand jury in the District Court for the Central District of California and charged with conspiracy to possess and distribute cocaine....

The respondents then filed motions to suppress the evidence seized pursuant to the warrant. The District Court held an evidentiary hearing and, while recognizing that the case was a close one, granted the motions to suppress in part. It concluded that the affidavit was insufficient to establish probable cause, but did not suppress all of the evidence as to all of the respondents because none of the respondents had standing to challenge all of the searches. In response to a request from the Government, the court made clear that Officer Rombach had acted in good faith, but it rejected the Government's suggestion that the Fourth Amendment exclusionary rule should not apply where evidence is seized in reasonable, good-faith reliance on a search warrant. [The Court of Appeals affirmed.]

.... The Government's petition for certiorari expressly declined to seek review of the lower courts' determinations that the search warrant was unsupported by probable cause and presented only the question "whether the Fourth Amendment exclusionary rule should be modified so as not to bar the admission of evidence seized in reasonable, good-faith reliance on a search warrant that is subsequently held to be defective."…

The Fourth Amendment contains no provision expressly precluding the use of evidence obtained in violation of its commands, and an examination of its origin and purposes makes clear that the use of fruits of a past unlawful search or seizure works no new Fourth Amendment wrong. The wrong condemned by the Amendment is fully accomplished by the unlawful search or seizure itself, and the exclusionary rule is neither intended nor able to cure the invasion of the defendant's rights which he has already suffered. The rule thus operates as a judicially created remedy designed to safeguard Fourth Amendment rights generally through its deterrent effect, rather than a personal constitutional right of the party aggrieved.

Whether the exclusionary sanction is appropriately imposed in a particular case, our decisions make clear, is "an issue separate from the question whether the Fourth Amendment rights of the party seeking to invoke the rule were violated by police conduct." Only the former question is currently before us, and it must be resolved by weighing the costs and benefits of preventing the use in the prosecution's case in chief of inherently trustworthy tangible evidence obtained in reliance on a search warrant issued by a detached and neutral magistrate that ultimately is found to be defective.

The substantial social costs exacted by the exclusionary rule for the vindication of Fourth Amendment rights have long been a source of concern. Our cases have consistently recognized that unbending application of the exclusionary sanction to enforce ideals of governmental rectitude would impede unacceptably the truth-finding functions of judge and jury. An objectionable collateral consequence of this interference with the criminal justice system's truth-finding function is that some guilty defendants may go free or receive reduced sentences as a result of favorable plea bargains. Particularly when law enforcement officers have acted in objective good faith or their transgressions have been minor, the magnitude of the benefit conferred on such guilty defendants offends basic concepts of the criminal justice system. Indiscriminate application of the exclusionary rule, therefore, may well generate disrespect for the law and administration of justice. Accordingly, as with any remedial device, the application of the rule has been restricted to those areas where its remedial objectives are thought most efficaciously served.

…. Because a search warrant provides the detached scrutiny of a neutral magistrate, which is a more reliable safeguard against improper searches than the hurried judgment of a law enforcement officer "engaged in the often competitive enterprise of ferreting out crime," we have expressed a strong preference for warrants and declared that "in a doubtful or marginal case a search under a warrant may be sustainable where without one it would fall." Reasonable minds frequently may differ on the question whether a particular affidavit establishes probable cause, and we have thus concluded that the preference for warrants is most appropriately effectuated by according "great deference" to a magistrate's determination.

…. To the extent that proponents of exclusion rely on its behavioral effects on judges and magistrates in these areas, their reliance is misplaced. First, the exclusionary rule is designed to deter police misconduct rather than to punish the errors of judges and magistrates. Second, there exists no evidence suggesting that judges and magistrates are inclined to ignore or subvert the Fourth Amendment or that lawlessness among these actors requires application of the extreme sanction of exclusion.

Third, and most important, we discern no basis, and are offered none, for believing that exclusion of evidence seized pursuant to a warrant will have a significant deterrent effect on the issuing judge or magistrate. Many of the factors that indicate that the exclusionary rule cannot provide an effective "special" or "general" deterrent for individual offending law enforcement officers apply as well to judges or magistrates. And, to the extent that the rule is thought to operate as a "systemic" deterrent on a wider audience, it clearly can have no such effect on individuals empowered to issue search warrants. Judges and magistrates are not adjuncts to the law enforcement team; as neutral judicial officers, they have no stake in the outcome of particular criminal prosecutions. The threat of exclusion thus cannot be expected significantly to deter them. Imposition of the exclusionary sanction is not necessary meaningfully to inform judicial officers of their errors, and we cannot conclude that admitting evidence obtained pursuant to a warrant while at the same time declaring that the warrant was somehow defective will in any way reduce judicial officers' professional incentives to comply with the Fourth Amendment, encourage them to repeat their mistakes, or lead to the granting of all colorable warrant requests.

If exclusion of evidence obtained pursuant to a subsequently invalidated warrant is to have any deterrent effect, therefore, it must alter the behavior of individual law enforcement officers or the policies of their departments. One could argue that applying the exclusionary rule in cases where the police failed to demonstrate probable cause in the warrant application deters future inadequate presentations or "magistrate shopping" and thus promotes the ends of the Fourth Amendment. Suppressing evidence obtained pursuant to a technically defective warrant supported by probable cause also might encourage officers to scrutinize more closely the form of the warrant and to point out suspected judicial errors. We find such arguments speculative and conclude that suppression of evidence obtained pursuant to a warrant should be ordered only on a case-by-case basis and only in those unusual cases in which exclusion will further the purposes of the exclusionary rule.

…. This is particularly true, we believe, when an officer acting with objective good faith has obtained a search warrant from a judge or magistrate and acted within its scope. In most such cases, there is no police illegality and thus nothing to deter. It is the magistrate's responsibility to determine whether the officer's allegations establish probable cause and, if so, to issue a warrant comporting in form with the requirements of the Fourth Amendment. In the ordinary case, an officer cannot be expected to question the magistrate's probable-cause determination or his judgment that the form of the warrant is technically sufficient. Once the warrant issues, there is literally nothing more the policeman can do in seeking to comply with the law. Penalizing the officer for the magistrate's error, rather than his own, cannot logically contribute to the deterrence of Fourth Amendment violations.

We conclude that the marginal or nonexistent benefits produced by suppressing evidence obtained in objectively reasonable reliance on a subsequently invalidated search warrant cannot justify the substantial costs of exclusion. We do not suggest, however, that exclusion is always inappropriate in cases where an officer has obtained a warrant and abided by its terms. Searches pursuant to a warrant will rarely require any deep inquiry into reasonableness, for a warrant issued by a magistrate normally suffices to establish that a law enforcement officer has acted in good faith in conducting the search. Nevertheless, the officer's reliance on the magistrate's probable-cause determination and on the technical sufficiency of the warrant he issues must be objectively reasonable, and it is clear that in some circumstances the officer will have no reasonable grounds for believing that the warrant was properly issued.

Suppression therefore remains an appropriate remedy if the magistrate or judge in issuing a warrant was misled by information in an affidavit that the affiant knew was false or would have known was false except for his reckless disregard of the truth. Franks v. Delaware (1978). The exception we recognize today will also not apply in cases where the issuing magistrate wholly abandoned his judicial role in the manner condemned in Lo-Ji Sales, Inc. v. New York (1979); in such circumstances, no reasonably well trained officer should rely on the warrant. Nor would an officer manifest objective good faith in relying on a warrant based on an affidavit so lacking in indicia of probable cause as to render official belief in its existence entirely unreasonable. Finally, depending on the circumstances of the particular case, a warrant may be so facially deficient—i.e., in failing to particularize the place to be searched or the things to be seized—that the executing officers cannot reasonably presume it to be valid.

…. When the principles we have enunciated today are applied to the facts of this case, it is apparent that the judgment of the Court of Appeals cannot stand….

In the absence of an allegation that the magistrate abandoned his detached and neutral role, suppression is appropriate only if the officers were dishonest or reckless in preparing their affidavit or could not have harbored an objectively reasonable belief in the existence of probable cause…. Officer Rombach's application for a warrant clearly was supported by much more than a "bare bones" affidavit. The affidavit related the results of an extensive investigation and, as the opinions of the divided panel of the Court of Appeals make clear, provided evidence sufficient to create disagreement among thoughtful and competent judges as to the existence of probable cause. Under these circumstances, the officers' reliance on the magistrate's determination of probable cause was objectively reasonable, and application of the extreme sanction of exclusion is inappropriate.

HERRING v. UNITED STATES
555 U.S. 135 (2009)

Chief Justice ROBERTS delivered the opinion of the Court.

The Fourth Amendment forbids "unreasonable searches and seizures," and this usually requires the police to have probable cause or a warrant before making an arrest. What if an officer reasonably believes there is an outstanding arrest warrant, but that belief turns out to be wrong because of a negligent bookkeeping error by another police employee? The parties here agree that the ensuing arrest is still a violation of the Fourth Amendment, but dispute whether contraband found during a search incident to that arrest must be excluded in a later prosecution.

Our cases establish that such suppression is not an automatic consequence of a Fourth Amendment violation. Instead, the question turns on the culpability of the police and the potential of exclusion to deter wrongful police conduct. Here the error was the result of isolated negligence attenuated from the arrest. We hold that in these circumstances the jury should not be barred from considering all the evidence.

I

On July 7, 2004, Investigator Mark Anderson learned that Bennie Herring had driven to the Coffee County Sheriff's Department to retrieve something from his impounded truck. Herring was no stranger to law enforcement, and Anderson asked the county's warrant clerk, Sandy Pope, to check for any outstanding warrants for Herring's arrest. When she found none, Anderson asked Pope to check with Sharon Morgan, her counterpart in neighboring Dale County. After checking Dale County's computer database, Morgan replied that there was an active arrest warrant for Herring's failure to appear on a felony charge. Pope relayed the information to Anderson and asked Morgan to fax over a copy of the warrant as confirmation. Anderson and a deputy followed Herring as he left the impound lot, pulled him over, and arrested him. A search incident to the arrest revealed methamphetamine in Herring's pocket, and a pistol (which as a felon he could not possess) in his vehicle.

There had, however, been a mistake about the warrant. The Dale County sheriff's computer records are supposed to correspond to actual arrest warrants, which the office also maintains. But when Morgan went to the files to retrieve the actual warrant to fax to Pope, Morgan was unable to find it. She called a court clerk and learned that the warrant had been recalled five months earlier. Normally when a warrant is recalled the court clerk's office or a judge's chambers calls Morgan, who enters the information in the sheriff's computer database and disposes of the physical copy. For whatever reason, the information about the recall of the warrant for Herring did not appear in the database.

[*Ed. Note*: The District Court's opinion in this case includes this line: "Morgan admits the mistake was probably the fault of the Dale County Sheriff's Department, not that of the Dale County Clerk's Office."]

Morgan immediately called Pope to alert her to the mixup, and Pope contacted Anderson over a secure radio. This all unfolded in 10 to 15 minutes, but Herring had already been arrested and found with the gun and drugs, just a few hundred yards from the sheriff's office.

Herring was indicted in the District Court for the Middle District of Alabama for illegally possessing the gun and drugs. He moved to suppress the evidence on the ground that his initial arrest had been illegal because the warrant had been rescinded. The Magistrate Judge recommended denying the motion because the arresting officers had acted in a good-faith belief that the warrant was still outstanding. Thus, even if there were a Fourth Amendment violation, there was "no reason to believe that application of the exclusionary rule here would deter the occurrence of any future mistakes." The District Court adopted the Magistrate Judge's recommendation, and the Court of Appeals for the Eleventh Circuit affirmed....

II

.... For purposes of deciding this case ... we accept the parties' assumption that there was a Fourth Amendment violation. The issue is whether the exclusionary rule should be applied.

A

The Fourth Amendment protects "[t]he right of the people to be secure in their persons, houses, papers, and effects, against unreasonable searches and seizures," but contains no provision expressly precluding the use of evidence obtained in violation of its commands. Nonetheless, our decisions establish an exclusionary rule that, when applicable, forbids the use of improperly obtained evidence at trial. We have stated that this judicially created rule is "designed to safeguard Fourth Amendment rights generally through its deterrent effect."

In analyzing the applicability of the rule, Leon admonished that we must consider the actions of all the police officers involved. U.S. v. Leon (1984) ("It is necessary to consider the objective reasonableness, not only of the officers who eventually executed a warrant, but also of the officers who originally obtained it or who provided information material to the probable-cause determination."). The Coffee County officers did nothing improper. Indeed, the error was noticed so quickly because Coffee County requested a faxed confirmation of the warrant.

The Eleventh Circuit concluded, however, that somebody in Dale County should have updated the computer database to reflect the recall of the arrest warrant. The court also concluded that this error was negligent, but did not find it to be reckless or deliberate. That fact is crucial to our holding that this error is not enough by itself to require the extreme sanction of exclusion.

B

The fact that a Fourth Amendment violation occurred—i.e., that a search or arrest was unreasonable—does not necessarily mean that the exclusionary rule applies. Indeed, exclusion "has always been our last resort, not our first impulse," and our precedents establish important principles that constrain application of the exclusionary rule.

First, the exclusionary rule is not an individual right and applies only where it results in appreciable deterrence. We have repeatedly rejected the argument that exclusion is a necessary consequence of a Fourth Amendment violation. Instead we have focused on the efficacy of the rule in deterring Fourth Amendment violations in the future.

In addition, the benefits of deterrence must outweigh the costs. We have never suggested that the exclusionary rule must apply in every circumstance in which it might provide marginal deterrence. To the extent that application of the exclusionary rule could provide some incremental deterrent, that possible benefit must be weighed against its substantial social costs. The principal cost of applying the rule is, of course, letting guilty and possibly dangerous defendants go free— something that offends basic concepts of the criminal justice system. The rule's costly toll upon truth-seeking and law enforcement objectives presents a high obstacle for those urging its application.

These principles are reflected in the holding of Leon: When police act under a warrant that is invalid for lack of probable cause, the exclusionary rule does not apply if the police acted "in objectively reasonable reliance" on the subsequently invalidated search warrant. We (perhaps confusingly) called this objectively reasonable reliance "good faith." In a companion case, Massachusetts v. Sheppard (1984), we held that the exclusionary rule did not apply when a warrant was invalid because a judge forgot to make "clerical corrections" to it.

Shortly thereafter we extended these holdings to warrantless administrative searches performed in good-faith reliance on a statute later declared unconstitutional. Illinois v. Krull (1987). Finally, in Arizona v. Evans (1995), we applied this good-faith rule to police who reasonably relied on mistaken information in a court's database that an arrest warrant was outstanding. We held that a mistake made by a judicial employee could not give rise to exclusion for three reasons: The exclusionary rule was crafted to curb police rather than judicial misconduct; court employees were unlikely to try to subvert the Fourth Amendment; and "most important, there [was] no basis for believing that application of the exclusionary rule in [those] circumstances" would have any significant effect in deterring the errors. Evans left unresolved "whether the evidence should be suppressed if police personnel were responsible for the error," an issue not argued by the State in that case, but one that we now confront.

The extent to which the exclusionary rule is justified by these deterrence principles varies with the culpability of the law enforcement conduct. As we said in Leon, "an assessment of the flagrancy of the police misconduct constitutes an important step in the calculus" of applying the exclusionary rule. Similarly, in Krull we elaborated that "evidence should be suppressed only if it can be said that the law enforcement officer had knowledge, or may properly be charged with knowledge, that the search was unconstitutional under the Fourth Amendment."

Anticipating the good-faith exception to the exclusionary rule, Judge Friendly wrote that "the beneficent aim of the exclusionary rule to deter police misconduct can be sufficiently accomplished by a practice outlawing evidence obtained by flagrant or deliberate violation of rights." Indeed, the abuses that gave rise to the exclusionary rule featured intentional conduct that was patently unconstitutional. In Weeks v.

United States (1914), a foundational exclusionary rule case, the officers had broken into the defendant's home (using a key shown to them by a neighbor), confiscated incriminating papers, then returned again with a U.S. Marshal to confiscate even more. Not only did they have no search warrant, which the Court held was required, but they could not have gotten one had they tried. They were so lacking in sworn and particularized information that "not even an order of court would have justified such procedure." Silverthorne Lumber Co. v. United States (1920), on which petitioner repeatedly relies, was similar; federal officials "without a shadow of authority" went to the defendants' office and "made a clean sweep" of every paper they could find. Even the Government seemed to acknowledge that the "seizure was an outrage."

Equally flagrant conduct was at issue in Mapp v. Ohio (1961), which … extended the exclusionary rule to the States. Officers forced open a door to Ms. Mapp's house, kept her lawyer from entering, brandished what the court concluded was a false warrant, then forced her into handcuffs and canvassed the house for obscenity. An error that arises from nonrecurring and attenuated negligence is thus far removed from the core concerns that led us to adopt the rule in the first place. And in fact since Leon, we have never applied the rule to exclude evidence obtained in violation of the Fourth Amendment, where the police conduct was no more intentional or culpable than this.

To trigger the exclusionary rule, police conduct must be sufficiently deliberate that exclusion can meaningfully deter it, and sufficiently culpable that such deterrence is worth the price paid by the justice system. As laid out in our cases, the exclusionary rule serves to deter deliberate, reckless, or grossly negligent conduct, or in some circumstances recurring or systemic negligence. The error in this case does not rise to that level.

…. The pertinent analysis of deterrence and culpability is objective, not an inquiry into the subjective awareness of arresting officers. We have already held that "our good-faith inquiry is confined to the objectively ascertainable question whether a reasonably well trained officer would have known that the search was illegal" in light of "all of the circumstances." These circumstances frequently include a particular officer's knowledge and experience, but that does not make the test any more subjective than the one for probable cause, which looks to an officer's knowledge and experience, but not his subjective intent, Whren v. United States (1996).

We do not suggest that all recordkeeping errors by the police are immune from the exclusionary rule. In this case, however, the conduct at issue was not so objectively culpable as to require exclusion. In Leon, we held that "the marginal or nonexistent benefits produced by suppressing evidence obtained in objectively reasonable reliance on a subsequently invalidated search warrant cannot justify the substantial costs of exclusion." The same is true when evidence is obtained in objectively reasonable reliance on a subsequently recalled warrant.

If the police have been shown to be reckless in maintaining a warrant system, or to have knowingly made false entries to lay the groundwork for future false arrests, exclusion would certainly be justified under our cases should such misconduct cause a Fourth Amendment violation. We said as much in Leon, explaining that an officer could not "obtain a warrant on the basis of a 'bare bones' affidavit and then rely on colleagues who are ignorant of the circumstances under which the warrant was obtained to conduct the search." Petitioner's fears that our decision will cause police departments to deliberately keep their officers ignorant are thus unfounded.

Justice Ginsburg's dissent also adverts to the possible unreliability of a number of databases not relevant to this case. In a case where systemic errors were demonstrated, it might be reckless for officers to rely on an unreliable warrant system. But there is no evidence that errors in Dale County's system are routine or widespread. Officer Anderson testified that he had never had reason to question information about a Dale County warrant, and both Sandy Pope and Sharon Morgan testified that they could remember no similar miscommunication ever happening on their watch. That is even less error than in the database at issue in Evans, where we also found reliance on the database to be objectively reasonable. Because no such showings were made here, the Eleventh Circuit was correct to affirm the denial of the motion to suppress.

Petitioner's claim that police negligence automatically triggers suppression cannot be squared with the principles underlying the exclusionary rule, as they have been explained in our cases. In light of our repeated holdings that the deterrent effect of suppression must be substantial and outweigh any harm to the justice system, we conclude that when police mistakes are the result of negligence such as that described here, rather than systemic error or reckless disregard of constitutional requirements, any marginal deterrence does not "pay its way." In such a case, the criminal should not "go free because the constable has blundered."

DAVIS v. UNITED STATES
564 U.S. 229 (2011)

Case Summary

In *Davis v. United States*, the Supreme Court considered the application of the exclusionary rule to evidence found during a vehicle search. Here is the Court's description of the search:

> "On an April evening in 2007, police officers in Greenville, Alabama, conducted a routine traffic stop that eventually resulted in the arrests of driver Stella Owens (for driving while intoxicated) and passenger Willie Davis (for giving a false name to police). The police handcuffed both Owens and Davis, and they placed the arrestees in the back of separate patrol cars. [Before his arrest, Davis removed his jacket and left it in Owens' car.] The police then searched the passenger compartment of Owens' vehicle and found a revolver inside Davis' jacket pocket."

The Supreme Court decided *Arizona v. Gant* (2009) (see Chapter 4) while Davis' appeal was pending. Thus, when the Eleventh Circuit considered Davis' appeal, it was clear that the search of his jacket violated the Fourth Amendment. Yet, as the Supreme Court explained, there was a complication in applying the exclusionary rule to this Fourth Amendment violation:

> "At the time of the search at issue here, we had not yet decided Gant, and the Eleventh Circuit had interpreted our decision in Belton, to establish a bright-line rule authorizing the search of a vehicle's passenger compartment incident to a recent occupant's arrest."

Given this wrinkle, the Supreme Court emphasized that "we have said time and again that the *sole* purpose of the exclusionary rule is to deter misconduct by law enforcement" and that "about all that exclusion would deter in this case is conscientious police work." The Court then summarized its decision as follows:

> "The question here is whether to apply [the exclusionary rule] when the police conduct a search in compliance with binding precedent that is later overruled. Because suppression would do nothing to deter police misconduct in these circumstances, and because it would come

at a high cost to both the truth and the public safety, we hold that searches conducted in objectively reasonable reliance on binding appellate precedent are not subject to the exclusionary rule."

In a concurring opinion, Justice Sotomayor emphasized that the police in *Davis* acted in compliance with then-existing precedent that was directly on point. Consequently, she wrote:

"Whether exclusion would result in appreciable deterrence in the circumstances of this case is a different question from whether exclusion would appreciably deter Fourth Amendment violations when the governing law is unsettled. The Court's answer to the former question in this case thus does not resolve the latter one."

5. IMPEACHMENT

In 1950, federal agents received a tip that Sam Walder possessed heroin. They stopped and searched him but found no drugs. Officers then searched Walder's apartment and found a heroin capsule. The subsequent criminal case against Walder was dismissed after the trial judge suppressed the heroin capsule, ruling that the warrantless apartment search violated the Fourth Amendment.

Federal authorities prosecuted Walder again, this time for selling heroin to two government informants in 1951. At trial, Walder testified as follows:

'Q. Have you ever had any narcotics in your possession, other than what may have been given to you by a physician for an ailment? A. No.

The prosecution then sought to introduce an officer's testimony about the heroin capsule found in Walder's apartment in 1950. "The trial judge admitted this evidence, but carefully charged the jury that it was not to be used to determine whether the defendant had committed the crimes here charged, but solely for the purpose of impeaching the defendant's credibility." *Walder v. United States* (1954).

Walder was convicted and the Supreme Court affirmed, creating the "impeachment exception" to the exclusionary rule. The Court explained:

"It is one thing to say that the Government cannot make an affirmative use of evidence unlawfully obtained. It is quite another to say that the defendant can turn the illegal method by which evidence in the

Government's possession was obtained to his own advantage, and provide himself with a shield against contradiction of his untruths."

In *James v. Illinois* (1990), the Supreme Court acknowledged the continuing vitality of this exception but rejected an effort at expansion. The *James* Court explained:

"The impeachment exception to the exclusionary rule permits the prosecution in a criminal proceeding to introduce illegally obtained evidence to impeach the defendant's own testimony. The Illinois Supreme Court extended this exception to permit the prosecution to impeach the testimony of *all* defense witnesses with illegally obtained evidence. Finding this extension inconsistent with the balance of values underlying our previous applications of the exclusionary rule, we reverse."

C. "STANDING"

The following excerpt from a law review article introduces the topic of Standing:[25]

The Supreme Court has long held that "rights assured by the Fourth Amendment are personal rights" and "may be enforced … only at the instance of one whose own protection was infringed by the search and seizure." The Court's rationale for this requirement has shifted over time. From a textualist perspective, the principle follows from the use of the possessive "their" in the Amendment's text. The Fourth Amendment states: "The right of the people to be secure in *their* persons, houses, papers, and effects, against unreasonable searches and seizures, shall not be violated...."

The textual argument is strengthened by the analogous state constitutional provisions and proposals from which the Amendment was crafted. Both the Massachusetts Constitution and the Virginia proposal, from which [the Fourth Amendment's drafter, James] Madison drew, used wording that, while inelegant and gendered, made the possessive point explicit. For example, the Massachusetts Constitution stated (and still states), "Every subject has a right to be secure from all unreasonable searches and seizures, of his person, his houses, his papers, and all his possessions." In his proposal to the House, Madison replaced "[e]very subject" with "the people," and accordingly substituted a serial use of "their" for

---

[25] Bellin, Fourth Amendment Textualism, 118 Mich. L. Rev. 266 (2019).

Massachusetts's serial use of "his." The Committee of Eleven edited Madison's clunky serial "theirs" to a single "their" appearing at the head of the list of protected items in the final version of the Amendment. This same format (a single "their") appeared in the Pennsylvania and Vermont Constitutions. There is no suggestion in the historical sources or the academic literature that these facially stylistic changes were intended to alter the underlying nature of the protected right.

... The personal nature of Fourth Amendment rights means that a person cannot claim a Fourth Amendment violation based on the government's search of someone else's "person, houses, papers, and effects." Thus, a murder suspect cannot invoke the Fourth Amendment to object to an unreasonable search of the victim's fingernails or phone. In such a scenario, the police search the victim's person and effects, not those of the suspect.

The Supreme Court and commentators usually conceptualize the principle described above as a kind of "standing" requirement. Defendants must show not only a violation of the Fourth Amendment but also a violation of "their" own Fourth Amendment rights. In Supreme Court opinions, Fourth Amendment standing is sometimes dispositive and other times ignored.

Periodically, the Court signals a desire to incorporate "standing" into the substantive Fourth Amendment analysis, but commentators and judges resist. Merging the two inquiries [can lead to unnecessary] confusion....

RAKAS v. ILLINOIS
439 U.S. 128 (1978)

Justice REHNQUIST delivered the opinion of the Court.

I

Because we are not here concerned with the issue of probable cause, a brief description of the events leading to the [challenged] search of the automobile will suffice. A police officer on a routine patrol received a radio call notifying him of a robbery of a clothing store in Bourbonnais, Ill., and describing the getaway car. Shortly thereafter, the officer spotted an automobile which he thought might be the getaway car. After following the car for some time and after the arrival of assistance, he and several other officers stopped the vehicle. The occupants of the automobile, petitioners, Frank Rakas and Lonnie King, and two female companions, were ordered out of the car and, after the occupants had left the car, two officers searched the interior of the vehicle. They discovered a box of rifle shells in the glove compartment, which had been locked, and a sawed-off rifle under the front passenger seat. After discovering the rifle and the shells, the officers took petitioners to the station and placed them under arrest.

Before trial petitioners moved to suppress the rifle and shells seized from the car on the ground that the search violated the Fourth and Fourteenth Amendments. They conceded that they did not own the automobile and were simply passengers; the owner of the car had been the driver of the vehicle at the time of the search. Nor did they assert that they owned the rifle or the shells seized. The prosecutor challenged petitioners' standing to object to the lawfulness of the search of the car because neither the car, the shells nor the rifle belonged to them. The trial court agreed that petitioners lacked standing and denied the motion to suppress the evidence….

II

Petitioners first urge us to relax or broaden the rule of standing enunciated in Jones v. United States (1960) so that any criminal defendant at whom a search was "directed" would have standing to contest the legality of that search and object to the admission at trial of evidence obtained as a result of the search. Alternatively, petitioners argue that they have standing to object to the search under Jones because they were "legitimately on the premises" at the time of the search.

The concept of standing discussed in Jones focuses on whether the person seeking to challenge the legality of a search as a basis for suppressing evidence was himself the "victim" of the search or seizure. Adoption of the so-called "target" theory advanced by petitioners would in effect permit a defendant to assert that a violation of the Fourth Amendment rights of a third party entitled him to have evidence suppressed at his trial. If we reject petitioners' request for a broadened rule of standing such as this, and reaffirm the holding of Jones and other cases that Fourth Amendment rights are personal rights that may not be asserted vicariously, we will have occasion to re-examine the "standing" terminology emphasized in Jones. For we are not at all sure that the determination of a motion to suppress is materially aided by labeling the inquiry identified in Jones as one of standing, rather than simply recognizing it as one involving the substantive question of whether or not the proponent of the motion to suppress has had his own Fourth Amendment rights infringed by the search and seizure which he seeks to challenge. We shall therefore consider in turn petitioners' target theory, the necessity for continued adherence to the notion of standing discussed in Jones as a concept that is theoretically distinct from the merits of a defendant's Fourth Amendment claim, and, finally, the proper disposition of petitioners' ultimate claim in this case.

A

We decline to extend the rule of standing in Fourth Amendment cases in the manner suggested by petitioners. As we stated in Alderman v. United States (1969), "Fourth Amendment rights are personal rights which, like some other constitutional rights, may not be vicariously asserted." A person who is aggrieved by an illegal search and seizure only through the introduction of damaging evidence secured by a search of a third person's premises or property has not had any of his Fourth Amendment rights infringed. And since the exclusionary rule is an attempt to effectuate the guarantees of the Fourth Amendment, it is proper to permit only defendants whose Fourth Amendment rights have been violated to benefit from the rule's protections. There is no reason to think that a party whose rights have been infringed will not, if evidence is used against him, have ample motivation to move to suppress it. Even if such a person is not a defendant in the action, he may be able to recover damages for the violation of his Fourth Amendment rights, or seek redress under state law for invasion of privacy or trespass....

B

.... Having rejected petitioners' target theory and reaffirmed the principle that the rights assured by the Fourth Amendment are personal rights, which may be enforced by exclusion of evidence only at the instance of one whose own protection was infringed by the search and seizure, the question necessarily arises whether it serves any useful analytical purpose to consider this principle a matter of standing, distinct from the merits of a defendant's Fourth Amendment claim. We can think of no decided cases of this Court that would have come out differently had we concluded, as we do now, that the type of standing requirement discussed in Jones and reaffirmed today is more properly subsumed under substantive Fourth Amendment doctrine. Rigorous application of the principle that the rights secured by this Amendment are personal, in place of a notion of "standing," will produce no additional situations in which evidence must be excluded. The inquiry under either approach is the same. But we think the better analysis forthrightly focuses on the extent of a particular defendant's rights under the Fourth Amendment, rather than on any theoretically separate, but invariably intertwined concept of standing....

The question is whether the challenged search or seizure violated the Fourth Amendment rights of a criminal defendant who seeks to exclude the evidence obtained during it. That inquiry in turn requires a determination of whether the disputed search and seizure has infringed an interest of the defendant which the Fourth Amendment was designed to protect. We are under no illusion that by dispensing with the rubric of standing used in Jones we have rendered any simpler the determination of whether the proponent of a motion to suppress is entitled to contest the legality of a search and seizure. But by frankly recognizing that this aspect of the analysis belongs more properly under the heading of substantive Fourth Amendment doctrine than under the heading of standing, we think the decision of this issue will rest on sounder logical footing.

C

Here petitioners, who were passengers occupying a car which they neither owned nor leased, seek to analogize their position to that of the defendant in Jones v. United States. In Jones, petitioner was present at the time of the search of an apartment which was owned by a friend. The friend had given Jones permission to use the apartment and a key to it, with which Jones had admitted himself on the day of the search. He had a suit and shirt at the apartment and had slept there "maybe a night," but his home was elsewhere. At the time of the search, Jones was the only occupant of the apartment because the lessee was away for a period of several days. Under these circumstances, this Court stated that while one wrongfully on the premises could not move to suppress evidence obtained as a result of searching them, "anyone legitimately on premises where a search occurs may challenge its legality." Petitioners argue that their occupancy of the automobile in question was comparable to that of Jones in the apartment and that they therefore have standing to contest the legality of the search—or as we have rephrased the inquiry, that they, like Jones, had their Fourth Amendment rights violated by the search.

We do not question the conclusion in Jones that the defendant in that case suffered a violation of his personal Fourth Amendment rights if the search in question was unlawful. Nonetheless, we believe that the phrase "legitimately on premises" coined in Jones creates too broad a gauge for measurement of Fourth Amendment rights. For example, applied literally, this statement would permit a casual visitor who has never seen, or been permitted to visit, the basement of another's house to object to a search of the basement if the visitor happened to be in the kitchen of the house at the time of the search. Likewise, a casual visitor who walks into a house one minute before a search of the house commences and leaves one minute after the search ends would be able to contest the legality of the search. The first visitor would have absolutely no interest or legitimate expectation of privacy in the basement, the second would have none in the house, and it advances no purpose served by the Fourth Amendment to permit either of them to object to the lawfulness of the search.

We think that Jones on its facts merely stands for the unremarkable proposition that a person can have a legally sufficient interest in a place other than his own home so that the Fourth Amendment protects him from unreasonable governmental intrusion into that place. In defining the scope of that interest, we adhere to the view expressed in Jones and echoed in later cases that arcane distinctions developed in property and tort law between guests, licensees, invitees, and the like, ought not to control. But the Jones statement that a person need only be "legitimately on premises" in order to challenge the validity of the search of a dwelling place cannot be taken in its full sweep beyond the facts of that case....

D

Judged by the foregoing analysis, petitioners' claims must fail. They asserted neither a property nor a possessory interest in the automobile, nor an interest in the property seized. And as we have previously indicated, the fact that they were "legitimately on the premises" in the sense that they were in the car with the permission of its owner is not determinative of whether they had a legitimate expectation of privacy in the particular areas of the automobile searched. It is unnecessary for us to decide here whether the same expectations of privacy are warranted in a car as would be justified in a dwelling place in analogous circumstances. We have on numerous occasions pointed out that cars are not to be treated identically with houses or apartments for Fourth Amendment purposes. But here petitioners' claim is one which would fail even in an analogous situation in a dwelling place, since they made no showing that they had any legitimate expectation of privacy in the glove compartment or area under the seat of the car in which they were merely passengers. Like the trunk of an automobile, these are areas in which a passenger qua passenger simply would not normally have a legitimate expectation of privacy.

Jones v. United States (1960) and Katz v. United States (1967) involved significantly different factual circumstances. Jones not only had permission to use the apartment of his friend, but also had a key to the apartment with which he admitted himself on the day of the search and kept possessions in the apartment. Except with respect to his friend, Jones had complete dominion and control over the apartment and could exclude others from it. Likewise in Katz, the defendant occupied the telephone booth, shut the door behind him to exclude all others and paid the toll, which "entitled him to assume that the words he uttered into the mouthpiece would not be broadcast to the world." Katz and Jones could legitimately expect privacy in the areas which were the subject of the search and seizure each sought to contest. No such showing was made by these petitioners with respect to those portions of the automobile which were searched and from which incriminating evidence was seized.

III

The Illinois courts were therefore correct in concluding that it was unnecessary to decide whether the search of the car might have violated the rights secured to someone else by the Fourth and Fourteenth Amendments to the United States Constitution. Since it did not violate any rights of these petitioners, their judgment of conviction is Affirmed.

RAWLINGS v. KENTUCKY
448 U.S. 98 (1980)

Justice REHNQUIST delivered the opinion of the Court.

I

In the middle of the afternoon on October 18, 1976, six police officers armed with a warrant for the arrest of one Lawrence Marquess on charges of drug distribution arrived at Marquess' house in Bowling Green, Ky. In the house at the time the police arrived were one of Marquess' housemates, Dennis Saddler, and four visitors, Keith Northern, Linda Braden, Vanessa Cox, and petitioner David Rawlings. [About 45 minutes later, the officers also obtained a warrant to search the house.]

[One officer] approached petitioner and told him to stand. Officer Don Bivens simultaneously approached Cox and ordered her to empty the contents of her purse onto a coffee table in front of the couch. Among those contents were a jar containing 1,800 tablets of LSD and a number of smaller vials containing benzphetamine, methamphetamine, methyprylan, and pentobarbital, all of which are controlled substances under Kentucky law.

Upon pouring these objects out onto the coffee table, Cox turned to petitioner and told him "to take what was his." Petitioner, who was standing in response to Officer Railey's command, immediately claimed ownership of controlled substances....

Petitioner was indicted for possession with intent to sell the various controlled substances recovered from Cox's purse. At the suppression hearing, he testified that he had flown into Bowling Green about a week before his arrest to look for a job and perhaps to attend the local university. He brought with him at that time the drugs later found in Cox's purse. Initially, petitioner stayed in the house where the arrest took place as the guest of Michael Swank, who shared the house with Marquess and Saddler. While at a party at that house, he met Cox and spent at least two nights of the next week on a couch at Cox's house.

On the morning of petitioner's arrest, Cox had dropped him off at Swank's house where he waited for her to return from class. At that time, he was carrying the drugs in a green bank bag. When Cox returned to the house to meet him, petitioner dumped the contents of the bank bag into Cox's purse. Although there is dispute over the discussion that took place, petitioner testified that he "asked her if she would carry this for me, and she said, 'yes.'" Petitioner then left the room to use the bathroom and, by the time he returned, discovered that the police had arrived to arrest Marquess.....

II

In this Court, petitioner ... claims that he did have a reasonable expectation of privacy in Cox's purse so as to allow him to challenge the legality of the search of that purse.... In holding that petitioner could not challenge the legality of the search of Cox's purse, the Supreme Court of Kentucky looked primarily to our then recent decision in Rakas v. Illinois where we abandoned a separate inquiry into a defendant's "standing" to contest an allegedly illegal search in favor of an inquiry that focused directly on the substance of the defendant's claim that he or she possessed a "legitimate expectation of privacy" in the area searched. In the present case, the Supreme Court of Kentucky … held that petitioner "had not made a sufficient showing that his legitimate or reasonable expectations of privacy were violated" by the search of the purse.

We believe that the record in this case supports that conclusion…. At the time petitioner dumped thousands of dollars worth of illegal drugs into Cox's purse, he had known her for only a few days. According to Cox's uncontested testimony, petitioner had never sought or received access to her purse prior to that sudden bailment. Contrast Jones v. United States (1960). Nor did petitioner have any right to exclude other persons from access to Cox's purse…. Moreover, even assuming that petitioner's version of the bailment is correct and that Cox did consent to the transfer of possession, the precipitous nature of the transaction hardly supports a reasonable inference that petitioner took normal precautions to maintain his privacy….

Petitioner contends nevertheless that, because he claimed ownership of the drugs in Cox's purse, he should be entitled to challenge the search regardless of his expectation of privacy. We disagree. While petitioner's ownership of the drugs is undoubtedly one fact to be considered in this case, Rakas emphatically rejected the notion that "arcane" concepts of property law ought to control the ability to claim the protections of the Fourth Amendment….

The opinion describes Rawlings' provision of drugs to Cox using a property law concept, "**bailment**." Black's Law Dictionary defines that term as follows:

> "A delivery of personal property by one person (*the bailor*) to another (*the bailee*) who holds the property for a certain purpose usually under an express or implied in fact contract."

MINNESOTA v. CARTER
525 U.S. 83 (1998)

Chief Justice REHNQUIST delivered the opinion of the Court.

…. James Thielen, a police officer in the Twin Cities' suburb of Eagan, Minnesota, went to an apartment building to investigate a tip from a confidential informant. The informant said that he had walked by the window of a ground-floor apartment and had seen people putting a white powder into bags. The officer looked in the same window through a gap in the closed blind and observed the bagging operation for several minutes. He then notified headquarters, which began preparing affidavits for a search warrant while he returned to the apartment building. When two men left the building in a previously identified Cadillac, the police stopped the car. Inside were respondents Wayne Carter and Melvin Johns. As the police opened the door of the car to let Johns out, they observed a black, zippered pouch and a handgun, later determined to be loaded, on the vehicle's floor. Carter and Johns were arrested, and a later police search of the vehicle the next day discovered pagers, a scale, and 47 grams of cocaine in plastic sandwich bags.

After seizing the car, the police returned to Apartment 103 and arrested the occupant, Kimberly Thompson, who is not a party to this appeal. A search of the apartment pursuant to a warrant revealed cocaine residue on the kitchen table and plastic baggies similar to those found in the Cadillac. Thielen identified Carter, Johns, and Thompson as the three people he had observed placing the powder into baggies. The police later learned that while Thompson was the lessee of the apartment, Carter and Johns lived in Chicago and had come to the apartment for the sole purpose of packaging the cocaine. Carter and Johns had never been to the apartment before and were only in the apartment for approximately 2½ hours. In return for the use of the apartment, Carter and Johns had given Thompson one-eighth of an ounce of the cocaine.

Carter and Johns were charged with conspiracy to commit a controlled substance crime in the first degree and aiding and abetting in a controlled substance crime in the first degree. They moved to suppress all evidence obtained from the apartment and the Cadillac, as well as to suppress several postarrest incriminating statements they had made. They argued that Thielen's initial observation of their drug packaging activities was an unreasonable search in violation of the Fourth Amendment and that all evidence obtained as a result of this unreasonable search was inadmissible as fruit of the poisonous tree. The Minnesota trial court held that since, unlike the defendant in Minnesota v. Olson (1990), Carter and Johns were not overnight social guests but temporary out-of-state visitors, they were not entitled to claim the protection of the Fourth Amendment against the government intrusion into the apartment. The trial court also concluded that Thielen's observation was not a search within the meaning of the Fourth Amendment.... A divided Minnesota Supreme Court reversed, holding that respondents had "standing" to claim the protection of the Fourth Amendment because they had "a legitimate expectation of privacy in the invaded place."... Based upon its conclusion that respondents had "standing" to raise their Fourth Amendment claims, the court went on to hold that Thielen's observation constituted a search of the apartment under the Fourth Amendment, and that the search was unreasonable. We granted certiorari and now reverse.

The Minnesota courts analyzed whether respondents had a legitimate expectation of privacy under the rubric of "standing" doctrine, an analysis that this Court expressly rejected 20 years ago in Rakas. In that case, we held that automobile passengers could not assert the protection of the Fourth Amendment against the seizure of incriminating evidence from a vehicle where they owned neither the vehicle nor the evidence. Central to our analysis was the idea that in determining whether a defendant is able to show the violation of his (and not someone else's) Fourth Amendment rights, the definition of those rights is more properly placed within the purview of substantive Fourth Amendment law than within that of standing. Thus, we held that in order to claim the protection of the Fourth Amendment, a defendant must demonstrate that he personally has an expectation of privacy in the place searched, and that his expectation is reasonable; i.e., one that has "a source outside of the Fourth Amendment, either by reference to concepts of real or personal property law or to understandings that are recognized and permitted by society." Rakas v. Illinois (1978).

The Fourth Amendment ... protects persons against unreasonable searches of "their persons [and] houses" and thus indicates that the Fourth Amendment is a personal right that must be invoked by an individual. But the extent to which the Fourth Amendment protects people may depend upon where those people are. We have held that "capacity to claim the protection of the Fourth Amendment depends upon whether the person who claims the protection of the Amendment has a legitimate expectation of privacy in the invaded place." The text of the Amendment suggests that its protections extend only to people in "their" houses. But we have held that in some circumstances a person may have a legitimate expectation of privacy in the house of someone else. In Minnesota v. Olson (1990), for example, we decided that an overnight guest in a house had the sort of expectation of privacy that the Fourth Amendment protects. We said:

> "To hold that an overnight guest has a legitimate expectation of privacy in his host's home merely recognizes the every day

expectations of privacy that we all share. Staying overnight in another's home is a longstanding social custom that serves functions recognized as valuable by society. We stay in others' homes when we travel to a strange city for business or pleasure, when we visit our parents, children, or more distant relatives out of town, when we are in between jobs or homes, or when we house-sit for a friend.

From the overnight guest's perspective, he seeks shelter in another's home precisely because it provides him with privacy, a place where he and his possessions will not be disturbed by anyone but his host and those his host allows inside. We are at our most vulnerable when we are asleep because we cannot monitor our own safety or the security of our belongings. It is for this reason that, although we may spend all day in public places, when we cannot sleep in our own home we seek out another private place to sleep, whether it be a hotel room, or the home of a friend."

In Jones v. United States (1960), the defendant seeking to exclude evidence resulting from a search of an apartment had been given the use of the apartment by a friend. He had clothing in the apartment, had slept there "maybe a night," and at the time was the sole occupant of the apartment. But while the holding of Jones-that a search of the apartment violated the defendant's Fourth Amendment rights-is still valid, its statement that "anyone legitimately on the premises where a search occurs may challenge its legality," was expressly repudiated in Rakas v. Illinois (1978). Thus, an overnight guest in a home may claim the protection of the Fourth Amendment, but one who is merely present with the consent of the householder may not.

Respondents here were obviously not overnight guests, but were essentially present for a business transaction and were only in the home a matter of hours. There is no suggestion that they had a previous relationship with Thompson, or that there was any other purpose to their visit. Nor was there anything similar to the overnight guest relationship in Olson to suggest a degree of acceptance into the household. While the apartment was a dwelling place for Thompson, it was for these respondents simply a place to do business.

Property used for commercial purposes is treated differently for Fourth Amendment purposes from residential property. An expectation of privacy in commercial premises, however, is different from, and indeed less than, a similar expectation in an individual's home. And while it was a "home" in which respondents were present, it was not their home. Similarly, the Court has held that in some circumstances a worker can claim Fourth Amendment protection over his own workplace. See, e.g., O'Connor v. Ortega (1987). But there is no indication that respondents in this case had nearly as significant a connection to Thompson's apartment as the worker in O'Connor had to his own private office.

If we regard the overnight guest in Minnesota v. Olson as typifying those who may claim the protection of the Fourth Amendment in the home of another, and one merely "legitimately on the premises" as typifying those who may not do so, the present case is obviously somewhere in between. But the purely commercial nature of the transaction engaged in here, the relatively short period of time on the premises, and the lack of any previous connection between respondents and the householder, all lead us to conclude that respondents' situation is closer to that of one simply permitted on the premises. We therefore hold that any search which may have occurred did not violate their Fourth Amendment rights.

Because we conclude that respondents had no legitimate expectation of privacy in the apartment, we need not decide whether the police officer's observation constituted a "search." The judgments of the Supreme Court of Minnesota are accordingly reversed, and the cause is remanded for proceedings not inconsistent with this opinion.

In a dissenting opinion, Justice Ginsburg, joined by Justices Stevens and Souter, disagreed with the majority's analysis, explaining:

> "In my view, when a homeowner or lessee personally invites a guest into her home to share in a common endeavor, whether it be for conversation, to engage in leisure activities, or for business purposes licit or illicit, that guest should share his host's shelter against unreasonable searches and seizures."

Justice Breyer agreed with Justice Ginsburg but did not join the dissenting opinion because he felt it did not address a critical point. Instead, in a concurring opinion, Breyer explained:

I agree with Justice Ginsburg that respondents can claim the Fourth Amendment's protection. Petitioner, however, raises a second question, whether under the circumstances Officer Thielen's observation made "from a public area outside the curtilage of the residence" violated respondents' Fourth Amendment rights. In my view, it did not....

The majority opinions in *Rakas* and *Carter* discourage the most common framing of this type of analysis: as a type of "standing" requirement. In a later case, Justice Blackmun argued in a concurrence that "standing" terminology does, in fact, provide a helpful framework:

> In my view, Rakas v. Illinois (1978) recognized two analytically distinct but "invariably intertwined" issues of substantive Fourth Amendment jurisprudence. The first is "whether a disputed search or seizure has infringed an interest of the defendant which the Fourth Amendment was designed to protect," the second is whether "the challenged search or seizure violated that Fourth Amendment right." The first of these questions is answered by determining whether the defendant has a "legitimate expectation of privacy" that has been invaded by a governmental search or seizure. The second is answered by determining whether applicable cause and warrant requirements have been properly observed.

I agree with the Court that these two inquiries "merge into one," in the sense that both are to be addressed under the principles of Fourth Amendment analysis developed in Katz v. United States (1967), and its progeny. But I do not read today's decision, or Rakas, as holding that it is improper for lower courts to treat these inquiries as distinct components of a Fourth Amendment claim. Indeed, I am convinced that it would invite confusion to hold otherwise. It remains possible for a defendant to prove that his legitimate interest of privacy was invaded, and yet fail to prove that the police acted illegally in doing so. And it is equally possible for a defendant to prove that the police acted illegally, and yet fail to prove that his own privacy interest was affected.

Justice Kennedy, writing for the Court in the next case similarly recognizes the value of the "standing" conceptualization.

BYRD v. UNITED STATES
138 S. Ct. 1518 (2018)

Justice KENNEDY delivered the opinion of the Court.

In September 2014, Pennsylvania State Troopers pulled over a car driven by petitioner Terrence Byrd. Byrd was the only person in the car. In the course of the traffic stop the troopers learned that the car [had been rented by Byrd's friend, Latasha Reed] and that Byrd was not listed on the rental agreement as an authorized driver. For this reason, the troopers told Byrd they did not need his consent to search the car, including its trunk where he had stored personal effects. A search of the trunk uncovered body armor and 49 bricks of heroin…. Byrd moved to suppress the evidence as the fruit of an unlawful search….

The District Court denied Byrd's motion on the ground that Byrd lacked "standing" to contest the search as an initial matter. Byrd later entered a conditional guilty plea, reserving the right to appeal the suppression ruling. The Court of Appeals … recognized that a "circuit split exists as to whether the sole occupant of a rental vehicle has a Fourth Amendment expectation of privacy when that occupant is not named in the rental agreement"; but it noted that Circuit precedent already had "spoken as to this issue and determined such a person has no expectation of privacy and therefore no standing to challenge a search of the vehicle." This Court granted Byrd's petition for a writ of certiorari to address the conflict among the Courts of Appeals over whether an unauthorized driver has a reasonable expectation of privacy in a rental car….

It is worth noting that most courts analyzing the question presented in this case, including the Court of Appeals here, have described it as one of Fourth Amendment "standing," a concept the Court has explained is not distinct from the merits and "is more properly subsumed under substantive Fourth Amendment doctrine."

The concept of standing in Fourth Amendment cases can be a useful shorthand for capturing the idea that a person must have a cognizable Fourth Amendment interest in the place searched before seeking relief for an unconstitutional search; but it should not be confused with Article III standing, which is jurisdictional and must be assessed before reaching the merits….

[The] question … the Court addresses here … is whether the person claiming a constitutional violation has had his own Fourth Amendment rights infringed by the search and seizure which he seeks to challenge. Answering that question requires examination of whether the person claiming the constitutional violation had a "legitimate expectation of privacy in the premises" searched. Expectations of privacy protected by the Fourth Amendment, of course, need not be based on a common-law interest in real or personal property, or on the invasion of such an interest. Still, "property concepts" are instructive in determining the presence or absence of the privacy interests protected by that Amendment.

…. One who owns and possesses a car, like one who owns and possesses a house, almost always has a reasonable expectation of privacy in it. More difficult to define and delineate are the legitimate expectations of privacy of others.

On the one hand, as noted above, it is by now well established that a person need not always have a recognized common-law property interest in the place searched to be able to claim a reasonable expectation of privacy in it. On the other hand, it is also clear that legitimate presence on the premises of the place searched, standing alone, is not enough to accord a reasonable expectation of privacy, because it creates too broad a gauge for measurement of Fourth Amendment rights.

Although the Court has not set forth a single metric or exhaustive list of considerations to resolve the circumstances in which a person can be said to have a reasonable expectation of privacy, it has explained that "legitimation of expectations of privacy by law must have a source outside of the Fourth Amendment, either by reference to concepts of real or personal property law or to understandings that are recognized and permitted by society." Rakas v. Illinois (1978). The two concepts in cases like this one are often linked. One of the main rights attaching to property is the right to exclude others, and, in the main, one who owns or lawfully possesses or controls property will in all likelihood have a legitimate expectation of privacy by virtue of the right to exclude. This general property-based concept guides resolution of this case….

[This case is unlike Rakas] because [it] does not involve a passenger at all but instead the driver and sole occupant of a rental car…. This situation would be similar to the defendant in Jones v. United States (1960) who … had a reasonable expectation of privacy in his friend's apartment because he "had complete dominion and control over the apartment and could exclude others from it."…

The Court sees no reason why the expectation of privacy that comes from lawful possession and control and the attendant right to exclude would differ depending on whether the car in question is rented or privately owned by someone other than the person in current possession of it, much as it did not seem to matter whether the friend of the defendant in Jones owned or leased the apartment he permitted the defendant to use in his absence. Both would have the expectation of privacy that comes with the right to exclude....

The Government ... stresses that Byrd's driving the rental car violated the rental agreement that Reed signed, and it contends this violation meant Byrd could not have had any basis for claiming an expectation of privacy in the rental car at the time of the search.... The Government argues that permitting an unauthorized driver to take the wheel of a rental car is a breach ... so serious that the rental company would consider the agreement "void" the moment an unauthorized driver takes the wheel. To begin with, that is not what the contract says. It states: "Permitting an unauthorized driver to operate the vehicle is a violation of the rental agreement. This may result in any and all coverage otherwise provided by the rental agreement being void and my being fully responsible for all loss or damage, including liability to third parties."

Putting the Government's misreading of the contract aside, there may be countless innocuous reasons why an unauthorized driver might get behind the wheel of a rental car and drive it—perhaps the renter is drowsy or inebriated and the two think it safer for the friend to drive them to their destination. True, this constitutes a breach of the rental agreement, and perhaps a serious one, but the Government fails to explain what bearing this breach of contract, standing alone, has on expectations of privacy in the car....

Though new, the fact pattern here continues a well-traveled path in this Court's Fourth Amendment jurisprudence. Those cases support the proposition, and the Court now holds, that the mere fact that a driver in lawful possession or control of a rental car is not listed on the rental agreement will not defeat his or her otherwise reasonable expectation of privacy.... The judgment of the Court of Appeals is vacated, and the case is remanded for further proceedings consistent with this opinion.

Would a person who steals a car have Fourth Amendment standing to challenge a search of that car? The Supreme Court in *Byrd* suggested that wrongful possession changes the analysis:

> "Rakas v. Illinois makes clear that 'wrongful' presence at the scene of a search would not enable a defendant to object to the legality of the search. 'A burglar plying his trade in a summer cabin during the off season,' for example, 'may have a thoroughly justified subjective expectation of privacy, but it is not one which the law recognizes as legitimate.' Likewise, 'a person present in a stolen automobile at the time of the search may not object to the lawfulness of the search of the automobile.' No matter the degree of possession and control, the car thief would not have a reasonable expectation of privacy in a stolen car."

Focusing on that language from *Rakas*, the government had argued that "Byrd should have no greater expectation of privacy than a car thief because he intentionally used a third party as a strawman in a calculated plan to mislead the rental company from the very outset, all to aid him in committing a crime." But the Court declined to address that claim because the government had not raised it in the lower court proceedings and "it is unclear from the record whether the Government's inferences paint an accurate picture of what occurred."

On remand, the lower courts determined that the search was constitutional because it was based on probable cause – relying primarily on Byrd's statement, during his interaction with the officers, that he had a "blunt" in the car.

ROOMMATES

Many people live with relatives, friends or associates. If the police enter a shared residence, each resident has standing to challenge the entry. If police enter lawfully but conduct an unlawful search of the common areas (e.g. the kitchen or living room) each roommate will also generally have standing to challenge the search. The reason is that each roommate has a reasonable expectation of privacy (from the public at large) in the kitchen or living room. But what if the police enter lawfully, but conduct an illegal search of one of the bedrooms and discover evidence that incriminates both roommates? Would both roommates have standing to challenge the bedroom search? The answer is no, as the following excerpt from *United States v. Feliciano* (D. Ariz. 2009) explains:

❝❝ Around 3 p.m. on August 12, 2008, law enforcement officers arrested Julio Feliciano and others for armed robbery. Investigators, including local law enforcement and FBI officers, began questioning Feliciano and Marco Serrano, a co-defendant, late that night. Investigators learned that Serrano and Feliciano lived together in a trailer in Phoenix. Using this information, Detective Kathy Enriquez drafted a warrant affidavit for the search of the trailer.... Based on Detective Enriquez's affidavit, a superior court judge issued a warrant.... Officers seized 41 items from the trailer, some of which came from common areas or Feliciano's room and some of which came from Serrano's bedroom. Feliciano asks the Court to suppress all of the items seized from the trailer.

. . . Feliciano contends that he has standing because officers searched a place where he has a legitimate expectation of privacy—his home. The Court concludes, however, that Feliciano does not have standing to object to the search of Marco Serrano's bedroom. According to the Ninth Circuit, a defendant has no standing to contest the search of his roommate's bedroom unless he shares that bedroom or has permission to use it. See Northern v. United States (9th Cir. 1972). Feliciano has not asserted that he shared the bedroom with Serrano, that he had permission to enter the bedroom, or that he had an expectation of privacy in the items seized from the bedroom.

Feliciano argues in his reply that he has standing to object to the search of Serrano's bedroom because officers had to violate Feliciano's rights to get to the bedroom. Feliciano cites no authority holding that he can object to the search of Serrano's bedroom merely because law enforcement illegally walked through his living room. More importantly, as explained below, the Court finds that officers did not violate Feliciano's rights by their presence in the house. Feliciano later makes the same admission, stating that "the police were lawfully in Defendant's residence."

Because Feliciano has no standing to object to the items seized from Serrano's room the motion to suppress will be denied with respect to those items.

STANDING LOOSE ENDS

By requiring defendants to establish "standing" to contest a search, the Supreme Court places pressure on defendants to testify in suppression hearings – testimony that might prove damaging in a later trial. For example, if Frank Rakas had testified to owning the sawed-off shotgun, his suppression hearing testimony could hurt his defense at the later trial (if introduced into evidence by the prosecution). In *Simmons v. United States* (1968), the Court concluded that these practical implications necessitated a rule that limits the admissibility of a defendant's suppression hearing testimony at a later trial.

" A defendant who wishes to establish standing must do so at the risk that the words which he utters may later be used to incriminate him. Those courts which have allowed the admission of testimony given to establish standing have reasoned that there is no violation of the Fifth Amendment's Self-Incrimination Clause because the testimony was voluntary. As an abstract matter, this may well be true. A defendant is 'compelled' to testify in support of a motion to suppress only in the sense that if he refrains from testifying he will have to forego a benefit, and testimony is not always involuntary as a matter of law simply because it is given to obtain a benefit. However, the assumption which underlies this reasoning is that the defendant has a choice: he may refuse to testify and give up the benefit. When this assumption is applied to a situation in which the 'benefit' to be gained is that afforded by another provision of the Bill of Rights, an undeniable tension is created. Thus, in this case [the defendant] was obliged either to give up what he believed, with advice of counsel, to be a valid Fourth Amendment claim or, in legal effect, to waive his Fifth Amendment privilege against self-incrimination. In these circumstances, we find it intolerable that one constitutional right should have to be surrendered in order to assert another. We therefore hold that when a defendant testifies in support of a motion to suppress evidence on Fourth Amendment grounds, his testimony may not thereafter be admitted against him at trial on the issue of guilt unless he makes no objection.

Chapter 7

THE FIFTH AMENDMENT AND OFFICIAL QUESTIONING

> "No person shall be held to answer for a capital, or otherwise infamous crime, unless on a presentment or indictment of a Grand Jury, ...; nor shall any person be subject for the same offence to be twice put in jeopardy of life or limb; **nor shall be compelled in any criminal case to be a witness against himself**, nor be deprived of life, liberty, or property, without due process of law; nor shall private property be taken for public use, without just compensation."
>
> **U.S. Const. Amend. V**

A. A NARROW PRIVILEGE

There are few rights that the Supreme Court speaks about in as glowing terms as the Fifth Amendment prohibition on compelled self-incrimination (bolded above). Here is some famous language from *Murphy v. Waterfront Commission* (1964):

> "The privilege against self-incrimination registers an important advance in the development of our liberty—one of the great landmarks in man's struggle to make himself civilized. It reflects many of our fundamental values and most noble aspirations: our unwillingness to subject those suspected of crime to the cruel trilemma of self-accusation, perjury or contempt; our preference for an accusatorial rather than an inquisitorial system of criminal justice; our fear that self-incriminating statements will be elicited by inhumane treatment and abuses; our sense of fair play which dictates a fair state-individual balance by requiring the government to leave the individual alone until good cause is shown for disturbing him and by requiring the government in its contest with the individual to shoulder the entire load; our respect for the inviolability of the human personality and of the right of each individual to a private enclave where he may lead a private life; our distrust of self-deprecatory statements; and our

realization that the privilege, while sometimes a shelter to the guilty, is often a protection to the innocent."

It is no simple task to turn these aspirations into concrete constitutional doctrine. The Court attempts to do so by distilling three important touchstones for invoking the Fifth Amendment's protection from the constitutional text: no one can be (1) "compelled" (2) "to be a witness" (3) "against himself" "in [a] criminal case." These touchstones – compulsion, testimony, and self-incrimination – are discussed separately in the sections below, starting with self-incrimination.

1.   SELF-INCRIMINATION

To understand the protection provided by the Fifth Amendment, it is important to recognize the broad default power of the government to compel testimony. That power serves as the backdrop for the next case:

KASTIGAR v. UNITED STATES
406 U.S. 441 (1972)

Justice POWELL delivered the opinion of the Court.

This case presents the question whether the United States Government may compel testimony from an unwilling witness, who invokes the Fifth Amendment privilege against compulsory self-incrimination, by conferring on the witness immunity from use of the compelled testimony in subsequent criminal proceedings, as well as immunity from use of evidence derived from the testimony.

Petitioners, Charles Kastigar and Michael Stewart, were subpoenaed to appear before a United States grand jury in the Central District of California on February 4, 1971. The Government believed that petitioners were likely to assert their Fifth Amendment privilege. Prior to the scheduled appearances, the Government applied to the District Court for an order directing petitioners to answer questions and produce evidence before the grand jury under a grant of immunity conferred pursuant to 18 U.S.C. §§ 6002, 6003. Petitioners opposed issuance of the order, contending primarily that the scope of the immunity provided by the statute was not coextensive with the scope of the privilege against self-incrimination, and therefore was not sufficient to supplant the privilege and compel their testimony. The District Court rejected this contention, and ordered petitioners to appear before the grand jury and answer its questions under the grant of immunity.

Petitioners appeared but refused to answer questions, asserting their privilege against compulsory self-incrimination.

Ed. Note: Here is an excerpt of the grand jury testimony pulled from the trial record:

Q. Mr. Kastigar, the Grand Jury has received a great deal of information concerning a situation in which you had orthodontic braces placed on your teeth just prior to reporting for military induction and had them removed just afterword by a Dr. Bernard Bender, with offices at 8328 De Soto in Canoga Park.

Would you tell us, please, how that came about?

A. I'm sorry, I decline to say anything about that on the basis that my answer may tend to incriminate me and on the advice of counsel.

Q. Do you intend to take that same position with respect to all questions concerning this subject matter, so we don't waste your time or our time?

A. I intend to take the Fifth Amendment.

They were brought before the District Court, and each persisted in his refusal to answer the grand jury's questions, notwithstanding the grant of immunity. The court found both in contempt, and committed them to the custody of the Attorney General [i.e., incarceration] until either they answered the grand jury's questions or the term of the grand jury expired. The Court of Appeals for the Ninth Circuit affirmed. This Court granted certiorari to resolve the important question whether testimony may be compelled by granting immunity from the use of compelled testimony and evidence derived therefrom ('use and derivative use' immunity), or whether it is necessary to grant immunity from prosecution for offenses to which compelled testimony relates ('transactional' immunity).

The power of government to compel persons to testify in court or before grand juries and other governmental agencies is firmly established in Anglo-American jurisprudence. The power with respect to courts was established by statute in England as early as 1562, and Lord Bacon observed in 1612 that all subjects owed the King their 'knowledge and discovery.' While it is not clear when grand juries first resorted to compulsory process to secure the attendance and testimony of witnesses, the general common-law principle that 'the public has a right to every man's evidence' was considered an 'indubitable certainty' that 'cannot be denied' by 1742. The power to compel testimony, and the corresponding duty to testify, are recognized in the Sixth Amendment requirements that an accused be confronted with the witnesses against him, and have compulsory process for obtaining witnesses in his favor. The first Congress recognized the testimonial duty in the Judiciary Act of 1789, which provided for compulsory attendance of witnesses in the federal courts. Justice White noted the importance of this essential power of government in his concurring opinion in Murphy v. Waterfront Comm'n (1964):

> 'Among the necessary and most important of the powers of the States as well as the Federal Government to assure the effective functioning of government in an ordered society is the broad power to compel residents to testify in court or before grand juries or agencies. Such testimony constitutes one of the Government's primary sources of information.'

But the power to compel testimony is not absolute. There are a number of exemptions from the testimonial duty, the most important of which is the Fifth Amendment privilege against compulsory self-incrimination. The privilege reflects a complex of our fundamental values and aspirations, and marks an important advance in the development of our liberty. It can be asserted in any proceeding, civil or criminal, administrative or judicial, investigatory or adjudicatory; and it protects against any disclosures which the witness reasonably believes could be used in a criminal prosecution or could lead to other evidence that might be so used. This Court has been zealous to safeguard the values which underlie the privilege....

Petitioners' ... contention is that the scope of immunity provided by the federal witness immunity statute, 18 U.S.C. § 6002, is not coextensive with the scope of the Fifth Amendment privilege against compulsory self-incrimination, and therefore is not sufficient to supplant the privilege and compel testimony over a claim of the privilege. The statute provides that when a witness is compelled by district court order to testify over a claim of the privilege:

> 'the witness may not refuse to comply with the order on the basis of his privilege against self-incrimination; but no testimony or other information compelled under the order (or any information directly or indirectly derived from such testimony or other information) may be used against the witness in any criminal case, except a prosecution for

perjury, giving a false statement, or otherwise failing to comply with the order.' 18 U.S.C. § 6002.

The constitutional inquiry, rooted in logic and history, as well as in the decisions of this Court, is whether the immunity granted under this statute is coextensive with the scope of the privilege. If so, petitioners' refusals to answer based on the privilege were unjustified, and the judgments of contempt were proper, for the grant of immunity has removed the dangers against which the privilege protects. If, on the other hand, the immunity granted is not as comprehensive as the protection afforded by the privilege, petitioners were justified in refusing to answer, and the judgments of contempt must be vacated.

Petitioners draw a distinction between statutes that provide transactional immunity and those that provide, as does the statute before us, immunity from use and derivative use. They contend that a statute must at a minimum grant full transactional immunity in order to be coextensive with the scope of the privilege. In support of this contention, they rely on Counselman v. Hitchcock (1892) [where the Court] made the following statement, on which petitioners heavily rely:

> 'We are clearly of opinion that no statute which leaves the party or witness subject to prosecution after he answers the criminating question put to him, can have the effect of supplanting the privilege conferred by the Constitution of the United States. The immunity statute under consideration does not supply a complete protection from all the perils against which the constitutional prohibition was designed to guard, and is not a full substitute for that prohibition. In view of the constitutional provision, a statutory enactment, to be valid, must afford absolute immunity against future prosecution for the offence to which the question relates.'

Sixteen days after the Counselman decision, a new immunity bill was introduced by Senator Cullom, who urged that enforcement of the Interstate Commerce Act would be impossible in the absence of an effective immunity statute. The bill, which became the Compulsory Testimony Act of 1893, was drafted specifically to meet the broad language in Counselman set forth above. The new Act removed the privilege against self-incrimination in hearings before the Interstate Commerce Commission and provided that:

> 'no person shall be prosecuted or subjected to any penalty or forfeiture for or on account of any transaction, matter or thing, concerning which he may testify, or produce evidence, documentary or otherwise . . .'

This transactional immunity statute became the basic form for the numerous federal immunity statutes until 1970, when, after re-examining applicable constitutional principles and the adequacy of existing law, Congress enacted the statute here under consideration. The new statute, which does not 'afford the absolute immunity against future prosecution' referred to in Counselman, was drafted to meet what Congress judged to be the conceptual basis of Counselman, as elaborated in subsequent decisions of the Court, namely, that immunity from the use of compelled testimony and evidence derived therefrom is coextensive with the scope of the privilege.

The statute [18 U.S.C. § 6002]'s explicit proscription of the use in any criminal case of 'testimony or other information compelled under the order (or any information directly or indirectly derived from such testimony or other information)' is consonant with Fifth Amendment standards. We hold that such immunity from use and derivative use is coextensive with the scope of the privilege against self-incrimination, and therefore is sufficient to compel testimony over a claim of the privilege. While a grant of immunity must afford protection commensurate with that afforded by the privilege, it need not be broader. Transactional immunity, which accords full immunity from prosecution for the offense to which the compelled testimony relates, affords the witness considerably broader protection than does the Fifth Amendment privilege. The privilege has never been construed to mean that one who invokes it cannot subsequently be prosecuted. Its sole concern is to afford protection against being forced to give testimony leading to the infliction of penalties affixed to criminal acts. Immunity from the use of compelled testimony, as well as evidence derived directly and indirectly therefrom, affords this protection. It prohibits the prosecutorial authorities from using the compelled testimony in any respect, and it therefore insures that the testimony cannot lead to the infliction of criminal penalties on the witness.

Our holding is consistent with the conceptual basis of Counselman. The Counselman statute, as construed by the Court, was plainly deficient in its failure to prohibit the use against the immunized witness of evidence derived from his compelled testimony.

.... A person accorded this immunity under 18 U.S.C. § 6002, and subsequently prosecuted, is not dependent for the preservation of his rights upon the integrity and good faith of the prosecuting authorities. As stated in Murphy:

> 'Once a defendant demonstrates that he has testified, under a state grant of immunity, to matters related to the federal prosecution, the federal authorities have the burden of showing that their evidence is not tainted by establishing that they had an independent, legitimate source for the disputed evidence.'

This burden of proof, which we reaffirm as appropriate, is not limited to a negation of taint; rather, it imposes on the prosecution the affirmative duty to prove that the evidence it proposes to use is derived from a legitimate source wholly independent of the compelled testimony.

This is very substantial protection, commensurate with that resulting from invoking the privilege itself. The privilege assures that a citizen is not compelled to incriminate himself by his own testimony. It usually operates to allow a citizen to remain silent when asked a question requiring an incriminatory answer. This statute, which operates after a witness has given incriminatory testimony, affords the same protection by assuring that the compelled testimony can in no way lead to the infliction of criminal penalties. The statute, like the Fifth Amendment, grants neither pardon nor amnesty. Both the statute and the Fifth Amendment allow the government to prosecute using evidence from legitimate independent sources.... Affirmed.

Kastigar illustrates that the government can, in fact, compel a person to testify. It cannot, however, compel a person's testimony for use "against himself" in a criminal case. By granting immunity from prosecution that paralleled the protection offered by the Fifth Amendment, the government could compel the *Kastigar* defendants' testimony and, therefore, punish them for refusing to testify.

2.   TESTIMONY

In *Schmerber v. California* (1966), the Supreme Court highlighted another important limit on the Fifth Amendment's protections. The Amendment does not prevent people from being compelled to provide evidence that can be used against them in a criminal case. It only prevents being compelled "to be a witness" against oneself in a criminal case. The *Schmerber* Court summarized its ruling as follows:

> "We therefore must now decide whether the withdrawal of the blood and admission in evidence of the analysis involved in this case violated petitioner's [Fifth Amendment] privilege. We hold that the privilege protects an accused only from being compelled to testify against himself, or otherwise provide the State with evidence of a testimonial or communicative nature, and that the withdrawal of blood and use of the analysis in question in this case did not involve compulsion to these ends."

The Supreme Court elaborated on the "testimonial" requirement in the next case:

PENNSYLVANIA v. MUNIZ
496 U.S. 582 (1990)

Justice BRENNAN delivered the opinion of the Court.

We must decide in this case whether various incriminating utterances of a drunken-driving suspect, made while performing a series of sobriety tests, constitute testimonial responses to custodial interrogation for purposes of the Self–Incrimination Clause of the Fifth Amendment.

I

During the early morning hours of November 30, 1986, a patrol officer spotted respondent Inocencio Muniz and a passenger parked in a car on the shoulder of a highway. When the officer inquired whether Muniz needed assistance, Muniz replied that he had stopped the car so he could urinate. The officer smelled alcohol on Muniz's breath and observed that Muniz's eyes were glazed and bloodshot and his face was flushed. The officer then directed Muniz to remain parked until his condition improved, and Muniz gave assurances that he would do so. But as the officer returned to his vehicle, Muniz drove off. After the officer pursued Muniz down the highway and pulled him over, the officer asked Muniz to perform three standard field sobriety tests: a "horizontal gaze nystagmus" test, a "walk and turn" test, and a "one leg stand" test. Muniz performed these tests poorly, and he informed the officer that he had failed the tests because he had been drinking.

The patrol officer arrested Muniz and transported him to the West Shore facility of the Cumberland County Central Booking Center. Following its routine practice for receiving persons suspected of driving while intoxicated, the booking center videotaped the ensuing proceedings. Muniz was informed that his actions and voice were being recorded, but he was not at this time (nor had he been previously) advised of his rights under Miranda v. Arizona. Officer Hosterman first asked Muniz his name, address, height, weight, eye color, date of birth, and current age. He responded to each of these questions, stumbling over his address and age. The officer then asked Muniz, "Do you know what the date was of your sixth birthday?" After Muniz offered an inaudible reply, the officer repeated, "When you turned six years old, do you remember what the date was?" Muniz responded, "No, I don't."

Officer Hosterman next requested Muniz to perform each of the three sobriety tests that Muniz had been asked to perform earlier during the initial roadside stop. The videotape reveals that his eyes jerked noticeably during the gaze test, that he did not walk a very straight line, and that he could not balance himself on one leg for more than several seconds. During the latter two tests, he did not complete the requested verbal counts from 1 to 9 and from 1 to 30. Moreover, while performing these tests, Muniz "attempted to explain his difficulties in performing the various tasks, and often requested further clarification of the tasks he was to perform."

…. Both the video and audio portions of the videotape were admitted into evidence at Muniz' bench trial, along with the arresting officer's testimony that Muniz failed the roadside sobriety tests and made incriminating remarks at that time. Muniz was convicted of driving under the influence of alcohol…. On appeal, the Superior Court of Pennsylvania reversed…. Concluding that the audio portion of the videotape should have been suppressed in its entirety, the court reversed Muniz's conviction and remanded the case for a new trial….

II

The Self–Incrimination Clause of the Fifth Amendment provides that no "person … shall be compelled in any criminal case to be a witness against himself." Although the text does not delineate the ways in which a person might be made a "witness against himself," we have long held that the privilege does not protect a suspect from being compelled by the State to produce "real or physical evidence." Rather, the privilege "protects an accused only from being compelled to testify against himself, or otherwise provide the State with evidence of a testimonial or communicative nature." In order to be testimonial, an accused's communication must itself, explicitly or implicitly, relate a factual assertion or disclose information. Only then is a person compelled to be a "witness" against himself.

III

…. In the initial phase of the recorded proceedings, Officer Hosterman asked Muniz his name, address, height, weight, eye color, date of birth, current age, and the date of his sixth birthday. Both the delivery and content of Muniz's answers were incriminating. As the state court found, "Muniz's videotaped responses certainly led the finder of fact to infer that his confusion and failure to speak clearly indicated a state of drunkenness that prohibited him from safely operating his vehicle."…

We agree with the Commonwealth's contention that Muniz's answers are not rendered inadmissible … merely because the slurred nature of his speech was incriminating. The physical inability to articulate words in a clear manner due to the lack of muscular coordination of his tongue and mouth, is not itself a testimonial component of Muniz's responses to Officer Hosterman's introductory questions. In Schmerber v. California (1966), we drew a distinction between "testimonial" and "real or physical evidence" for purposes of the privilege against self-incrimination. We noted that in Holt v. United States (1910), Justice Holmes had written for the Court that "the prohibition of compelling a man in a criminal court to be witness against himself is a prohibition of the use of physical or moral compulsion to extort communications from him, not an exclusion of his body as evidence when it may be material." We also acknowledged that "both federal and state courts have usually held that it offers no protection against compulsion to submit to fingerprinting, photographing, or measurements, to write or speak for identification, to appear in court, to stand, to assume a stance, to walk, or to make a particular gesture." Embracing this view of the privilege's contours, we held that "the privilege is a bar against compelling 'communications' or 'testimony,' but that compulsion which makes a suspect or accused the source of 'real or physical evidence' does not violate it." Using this "helpful framework for analysis," we held that a person suspected of driving while intoxicated could be forced to provide a blood sample, because that sample was "real or physical evidence" outside the scope of the privilege and the sample was obtained in a manner by which "petitioner's testimonial capacities were in no way implicated."

We have since applied the distinction between "real or physical" and "testimonial" evidence in other contexts where the evidence could be produced only through some volitional act on the part of the suspect. In United States v. Wade (1967), we held that a suspect could be compelled to participate in a lineup and to repeat a phrase provided by the police so that witnesses could view him and listen to his voice. We explained that requiring his presence and speech at a lineup reflected "compulsion of the accused to exhibit his physical characteristics, not compulsion to disclose any knowledge he might have." In Gilbert v. California (1967), we held that a suspect could be compelled to provide a handwriting exemplar, explaining that such an exemplar, "in contrast to the content of what is written, like the voice or body itself, is an identifying physical characteristic outside the privilege's protection." And in United States v. Dionisio (1973), we held that suspects could be compelled to read a transcript in order to provide a voice exemplar, explaining that the "voice recordings were to be used solely to measure the physical properties of the witnesses' voices, not for the testimonial or communicative content of what was to be said."

Under Schmerber and its progeny, we agree with the Commonwealth that any slurring of speech and other evidence of lack of muscular coordination revealed by Muniz's responses to Officer Hosterman's direct questions constitute nontestimonial components of those responses. Requiring a suspect to reveal the physical manner in which he articulates words, like requiring him to reveal the physical properties of the sound produced by his voice, does not, without more, compel him to provide a "testimonial" response for purposes of the privilege.

This does not end our inquiry, for Muniz's answer to the sixth birthday question was incriminating, not just because of his delivery, but also because of his answer's content; the trier of fact could infer from Muniz's answer (that he did not know the proper date) that his mental state was confused. The Commonwealth and the United States as amicus curiae argue that this incriminating inference does not trigger the protections of the Fifth Amendment privilege because the inference concerns "the physiological functioning of Muniz's brain," which is asserted to be every bit as "real or physical" as the physiological makeup of his blood and the timbre of his voice.

But this characterization addresses the wrong question; that the "fact" to be inferred might be said to concern the physical status of Muniz's brain merely describes the way in which the inference is incriminating. The correct question for present purposes is whether the incriminating inference of mental confusion is drawn from a testimonial act or from physical evidence. In Schmerber, for example, we held that the police could compel a suspect to provide a blood sample in order to determine the physical makeup of his blood and thereby draw an inference about whether he was intoxicated. This compulsion was outside of the Fifth Amendment's protection, not simply because the evidence concerned the suspect's physical body, but rather because the evidence was obtained in a manner that did not entail any testimonial act on the part of the suspect: "Not even a shadow of testimonial compulsion upon or enforced communication by the accused was involved either in the extraction or in the chemical analysis." In contrast, had the police instead asked the suspect directly whether his blood contained a high concentration of alcohol, his affirmative response would have been testimonial even though it would have been used to draw the same inference concerning his physiology. In this case, the question is not whether a suspect's impaired mental faculties can fairly be characterized as an aspect of his physiology, but rather whether Muniz's response to the sixth birthday question that gave rise to the inference of such an impairment was testimonial in nature.

We recently explained in Doe v. United States (1988) that "in order to be testimonial, an accused's communication must itself, explicitly or implicitly, relate a factual assertion or disclose information." We reached this conclusion after addressing our reasoning in Schmerber, and its progeny:

> "The Court accordingly held that the privilege was not implicated in the line of cases beginning with Schmerber, because the suspect was not required 'to disclose any knowledge he might have,' or 'to speak his guilt.' It is the extortion of information from the accused, the attempt to force him 'to disclose the contents of his own mind,' that implicates the Self–Incrimination Clause. Unless some attempt is made to secure a communication—written, oral or otherwise—upon which reliance is to be placed as involving the accused's consciousness of the facts and the operations of his mind in expressing it, the demand made upon him is not a testimonial one."

After canvassing the purposes of the privilege recognized in prior cases, we concluded that "these policies are served when the privilege is asserted to spare the accused from having to reveal, directly or indirectly, his knowledge of facts relating him to the offense or from having to share his thoughts and beliefs with the Government."

This definition of testimonial evidence reflects an awareness of the historical abuses against which the privilege against self-incrimination was aimed. Historically, the privilege was intended to prevent the use of legal compulsion to extract from the accused a sworn communication of facts which would incriminate him. Such was the process of the ecclesiastical courts and the Star Chamber—the inquisitorial method of putting the accused upon his oath and compelling him to answer questions designed to uncover uncharged offenses, without evidence from another source. The major thrust of the policies undergirding the privilege is to prevent such compulsion. At its core, the privilege reflects our fierce "unwillingness to subject those suspected of crime to the cruel trilemma of self-accusation, perjury or contempt," that defined the operation of the Star Chamber, wherein suspects were forced to choose between revealing incriminating private thoughts and forsaking their oath by committing perjury.

We need not explore the outer boundaries of what is "testimonial" today, for our decision flows from the concept's core meaning. Because the privilege was designed primarily to prevent a recurrence of the Inquisition and the Star Chamber, even if not in their stark brutality, it is evident that a suspect is "compelled ... to be a witness against himself" at least whenever he must face the modern-day analog of the historic trilemma—either during a criminal trial where a sworn witness faces the identical three choices, or during custodial interrogation where, as we explained in Miranda, the choices are analogous and hence raise similar concerns. Whatever else it may include, therefore, the definition of "testimonial" evidence ... must encompass all responses to questions that, if asked of a sworn suspect during a criminal trial, could place the suspect in the "cruel trilemma." This conclusion is consistent with our recognition ... that "the vast majority of verbal statements thus will be testimonial" because "there are very few instances in which a verbal statement, either oral or written, will not convey information or assert facts." Whenever a suspect is asked for a response requiring him to communicate an express or implied assertion of fact or belief, the suspect confronts the "trilemma" of truth, falsity, or silence, and hence the response (whether based on truth or falsity) contains a testimonial component….

The sixth birthday question in this case required a testimonial response. When Officer Hosterman asked Muniz if he knew the date of his sixth birthday and

Muniz, for whatever reason, could not remember or calculate that date, he was confronted with the trilemma. By hypothesis, the inherently coercive environment created by the custodial interrogation precluded the option of remaining silent. Muniz was left with the choice of incriminating himself by admitting that he did not then know the date of his sixth birthday, or answering untruthfully by reporting a date that he did not then believe to be accurate (an incorrect guess would be incriminating as well as untruthful). The content of his truthful answer supported an inference that his mental faculties were impaired, because his assertion (he did not know the date of his sixth birthday) was different from the assertion (he knew the date was (correct date)) that the trier of fact might reasonably have expected a lucid person to provide. Hence, the incriminating inference of impaired mental faculties stemmed, not just from the fact that Muniz slurred his response, but also from a testimonial aspect of that response.

The state court held that the sixth birthday question constituted an unwarned interrogation for purposes of the privilege against self-incrimination, and that Muniz's answer was incriminating. The Commonwealth does not question either conclusion. Therefore, because we conclude that Muniz's response to the sixth birthday question was testimonial, the response should have been suppressed....

We agree with the state court's conclusion [requiring] suppression of Muniz's response to the question regarding the date of his sixth birthday, but we do not agree that the entire audio portion of the videotape must be suppressed. Accordingly, the court's judgment reversing Muniz's conviction is vacated, and the case is remanded for further proceedings not inconsistent with this opinion.

Problem: *State v. Meek*

In the early morning hours, Officer Hofeldt pulled over Delmas Meek on suspicion of drunk driving. Their subsequent conversation was recorded:

"Hofeldt: OK. It does appear that you've been drinking. I'm going to ask you to do some sobriety tests. The first thing I would like you to do is just to recite the alphabet start with A and go through Z. Can you do that for me?

Meek: No. I plead the Fifth Amendment.

Hofeldt: Well, Sir. I think it would probably be to your advantage to try to do some tests for me. Would you try to recite the alphabet for me?"

Meek then attempted the alphabet recital, performing poorly. At a later trial for drunk driving, Meek filed a motion to suppress the recorded conversation, including Meek's poor performance reciting the alphabet. *Did the State's introduction of the recording described above at Meek's trial violate the Fifth Amendment?*

Some scholars interpret cases like *Muniz* to suggest a "comprehensive positive theory of the Fifth Amendment right: the government may not compel disclosure of the incriminating substantive results of cognition."[26] Consider whether that description helps to analyze the previous problem and the cases that follow?

HIIBEL v. SIXTH JUDICIAL DISTRICT COURT OF NEVADA
542 U.S. 177 (2004)

Case Summary

In May 2000, Deputy Sheriff Lee Dove encountered Larry Hiibel while investigating a reported assault. Dove asked Hiibel for identification, but Hiibel refused to provide any and refused to state his name. Dove eventually arrested

---

[26] Ronald Allen & M. Kristin Mace, The Self-Incrimination Clause Explained and Its Future Predicted, 94 J. Crim. L. & Criminology 243 (2004).

Hiibel pursuant to a Nevada "stop and identify" statute. As the Supreme Court explained,

> "These statutes vary from State to State, but all permit an officer to ask or require a suspect to disclose his identity. A few States model their statutes on the Uniform Arrest Act, a model code that permits an officer to stop a person reasonably suspected of committing a crime and 'demand of him his name, address, business abroad and whither he is going.'... In some States, a suspect's refusal to identify himself is a misdemeanor offense or civil violation; in others, it is a factor to be considered in whether the suspect has violated loitering laws. In other States, a suspect may decline to identify himself without penalty."

In the first part of its opinion, the Court concluded that there was no Fourth Amendment violation. The officer had reasonable suspicion to stop Hiibel. And although a *Terry* stop does not create any authority to require an answer to an investigative inquiry, "the source of the legal obligation [to do so in this case] arises from Nevada state law, not the Fourth Amendment." The Court concluded that the state law, requiring a person lawfully stopped to identify themselves, was reasonable. Thus, "the stop, the request, and the State's requirement of a response did not contravene the guarantees of the Fourth Amendment."

Hiibel also contended that his conviction for refusing to disclose his name violated the Fifth Amendment. The Court began its analysis with the basics: "To qualify for the Fifth Amendment privilege, a communication must be testimonial, incriminating, and compelled." While the government argued that divulging one's name is not testimonial, the Court disagreed, explaining:

> "Stating one's name may qualify as an assertion of fact relating to identity. Production of identity documents might meet the definition as well. As we noted in U.S. v. Hubbell (2000), acts of production may yield testimony establishing 'the existence, authenticity, and custody of items the police seek.'"

Nevertheless, the Court resolved the case against Hiibel on the ground that the disclosure of his name was not sufficiently **incriminating** to trigger the Fifth Amendment's protections.

" Even if these required actions [disclosing one's name or producing an identity document] are testimonial, however, petitioner's challenge must fail because in this case disclosure of his name presented no reasonable danger of incrimination.

The Fifth Amendment prohibits only compelled testimony that is incriminating. See Brown v. Walker (1896) (noting that where "the answer of the witness will not directly show his infamy, but only tend to disgrace him, he is bound to answer"). A claim of Fifth Amendment privilege must establish reasonable ground to apprehend danger to the witness from his being compelled to answer. The danger to be apprehended must be real and appreciable, with reference to the ordinary operation of law in the ordinary course of things, – not a danger of an imaginary and unsubstantial character, having reference to some extraordinary and barely possible contingency, so improbable that no reasonable man would suffer it to influence his conduct.

As we stated in Kastigar v. United States (1972), the Fifth Amendment privilege against compulsory self-incrimination "protects against any disclosures that the witness reasonably believes could be used in a criminal prosecution or could lead to other evidence that might be so used." Suspects who have been granted immunity from prosecution may, therefore, be compelled to answer; with the threat of prosecution removed, there can be no reasonable belief that the evidence will be used against them.

In this case petitioner's refusal to disclose his name was not based on any articulated real and appreciable fear that his name would be used to incriminate him, or that it would furnish a link in the chain of evidence needed to prosecute him. As best we can tell, petitioner refused to identify himself only because he thought his name was none of the officer's business. Even today, petitioner does not explain how the disclosure of his name could have been used against him in a criminal case....

The narrow scope of the disclosure requirement is also important. One's identity is, by definition, unique; yet it is, in another sense, a universal characteristic. Answering a request to disclose a name is likely to be so insignificant in the scheme of things as to be incriminating only in unusual circumstances…. Even witnesses who plan to invoke the Fifth Amendment privilege answer when their names are called to take the stand. Still, a case may arise where there is a substantial allegation that furnishing identity at the time of a stop would have given the police a link in the chain of evidence needed to convict the individual of a separate offense. In that case, the court can then consider whether the privilege applies, and, if the Fifth Amendment has been violated, what remedy must follow. We need not resolve those questions here.

ACT OF PRODUCTION AND FOREGONE CONCLUSIONS

As *Hiibel* suggests, Justice Brennan's statement in *Muniz* that "the privilege does not protect a suspect from being compelled by the State to produce real or physical evidence" obscures the testimonial nature of "acts of production." Compelling a person to produce physical evidence, such as a stolen painting, would violate the Fifth Amendment if, by producing the evidence, the suspect implicitly acknowledges incriminating facts (e.g., possession of the painting). Thus, the Court has long held that in those circumstances: "A party is privileged from producing evidence but not from its production." This means that, as far as the Fifth Amendment is concerned, the government can compel the production of the painting by seizing it from the suspect's warehouse, but not by ordering the suspect to hand it over.

Sometimes, as in *Hiibel*, a disclosure or act of production will be deemed so trivial as to not be incriminating. An additional wrinkle arises when the government argues that any testimonial aspect of a compelled act (such as the suspect's possession of physical evidence), while significant, is not incriminating because it is already known. The Supreme Court labels this wrinkle, "a foregone conclusion."

The concept first appeared in *Fisher v. United States* (1976) where the Supreme Court considered a Fifth Amendment objection to a "subpoena served on a taxpayer requiring him to produce an accountant's workpapers in his possession." The papers themselves were incriminating, of course, but had been prepared voluntarily and so did not count as compelled incrimination. *Fisher* ("private incriminating statements of an accused may be overheard and used in evidence, if they are not compelled at the time they were uttered"). The only question was whether the compelled **production** of those papers violated the Fifth Amendment. While recognizing that producing papers in response to the subpoena has a testimonial element, the Court nevertheless rejected this particular Fifth Amendment claim.

> "It is doubtful that implicitly admitting the existence and possession of the papers rises to the level of testimony within the protection of the Fifth Amendment. The papers belong to the accountant, were prepared by him, and are the kind usually prepared by an accountant working on the tax returns of his client. Surely the Government is in no way relying on the "truth-telling" of the taxpayer to prove the existence of or his access to the documents. The existence and location of the papers are a **foregone conclusion** and the taxpayer adds little or nothing to the sum total of the Government's information by conceding that he in fact has the papers. Under these circumstances by enforcement of the summons no constitutional rights are touched. The question is not of testimony but of surrender.

> When an accused is required to submit a handwriting exemplar he admits his ability to write and impliedly asserts that the exemplar is his writing. But in common experience, the first would be a near truism and the latter self-evident. In any event, although the exemplar may be incriminating to the accused and although he is compelled to furnish it, his Fifth Amendment privilege is not violated because nothing he has said or done is deemed to be sufficiently testimonial for purposes of the privilege."

Here is a lower court's discussion of the overarching framework:

> "The Court has marked out two ways in which an act of production is not testimonial. First, the Fifth Amendment privilege is not triggered where the Government merely compels some physical act, i.e. where the individual is not called upon to make use of the contents of his or her mind. The most famous example is the key to the lock of a strongbox containing documents, but the Court has also used this rationale in a variety of other contexts. Second, under the "foregone conclusion" doctrine, an act of production is not testimonial—even if the act conveys a fact regarding the existence or location, possession, or authenticity of the subpoenaed materials—if the Government can show with 'reasonable particularity' that, at the time it sought to

compel the act of production, it already knew of the materials, thereby making any testimonial aspect a 'foregone conclusion.'"[27]

The "strongbox" example has become particularly important in the context of requests for suspects to provide government access to things like smartphones. The reference comes from a dissent in *Doe v. United States* (1988). There, Justice Stevens explained that a suspect "may in some cases be forced to surrender a key to a strongbox containing incriminating

17th Century German Strongbox

documents, but I do not believe he can be compelled to reveal the combination to his wall safe—by word or deed." The Supreme Court majority in *Doe* and later cases appeared to adopt this distinction. *See United States v. Hubbell* (2000) ("The assembly of those documents was like telling an inquisitor the combination to a wall safe, not like being forced to surrender the key to a strongbox."). Notice the importance to this reasoning of the verb "surrender." If it is known that there is a key *and* that the defendant possesses it, **surrendering** the key does not have testimonial aspects. The example would not work nearly as well if the government knew only that there was a strongbox and compelled the defendant to **produce** a key.

STATE v. ANDREWS
243 N.J. 447 (2020)

Justice SOLOMON delivered the opinion of the Court.

[FACTS]

[Robert Andrews was indicted on a variety of corruption charges. The indictment arose after] the target of a State narcotics investigation advised detectives that defendant, a law enforcement officer, had provided him with information about the investigation and advice to avoid criminal exposure. The target gave statements to investigators, confirmed in part by his cellphone, about photographs, cellphone calls, text message exchanges, and conversations with defendant during which defendant recommended that the target remove a tracking device that may have been placed on his car by the police; recommended that the target discard

---

[27] In re Grand Jury Subpoena Duces Tecum (11th Cir. 2012).

cellphones he and his cohorts used; and revealed the identity of an undercover officer and an undercover police vehicle.

The State obtained an arrest warrant for defendant and search warrants for defendant's iPhones, which were seized. Because the contents of the iPhones were inaccessible to investigators without the iPhones' passcodes, the State moved for an order compelling defendant to disclose the passcodes.

Defendant claimed the United States Constitution and New Jersey's common law and statutory protections against compelled self-incrimination protected his disclosure of the passcodes. The motion court and Appellate Division concluded that defendant's disclosure of the passcodes could be compelled. We agree and affirm.

[ANALYSIS]

Andrews does not challenge the search warrants issued for his cellphones. He does not claim that the phones were unlawfully seized or that the search warrants authorizing the State to comb their contents were unsupported by probable cause. Neither does defendant challenge the particularity with which the search warrants describe the "things subject to seizure." Thus, the State is permitted to access the phones' contents, as limited by the trial court's order, in the same way that the State may survey a home, vehicle, or other place that is the subject of a search warrant.

But a lawful seizure does not allow compelled disclosure of facts otherwise protected by the Fifth Amendment.

Andrews objects here to the means by which the State seeks to effectuate the searches authorized by the lawfully issued search warrants -- compelled disclosure of his cellphones' passcodes -- which Andrews claims violate federal and state protections against compelled self-incrimination. We therefore consider whether the Fifth Amendment protects Andrews from being compelled to disclose his passcodes....

The Fifth Amendment to the United States Constitution provides that "[n]o person ... shall be compelled in any criminal case to be a witness against himself." That right against self-incrimination applies only when the accused is compelled to make a testimonial communication that is incriminating. Testimonial communications may take any form but must imply assertions of fact for the Fifth Amendment privilege against self-incrimination to attach....

Accordingly, criminal defendants may lawfully be compelled to display their physical characteristics and commit physical acts because the display of physical characteristics is not coterminous with communications that relay facts. Among those acts are creating handwriting samples, and voice samples; providing blood, hair, and saliva samples, standing in a lineup, and donning particular articles of clothing. Also, consistent with the Fifth Amendment, individuals may be compelled to execute an authorization directing a foreign bank to disclose account records because neither the form, nor its execution, communicates any factual assertions, implicit or explicit, or conveys any information to the Government.

A handful of courts have held that compelled State access to electronic devices through the use of biometric features does not violate the Fifth Amendment. As those examples suggest, the Fifth Amendment is not an absolute bar to a defendant's forced assistance of the defendant's own criminal prosecution. In contrast to physical communications, however, if an individual is compelled to disclose the contents of his own mind, such disclosure implicates the Fifth Amendment privilege against self-incrimination.

In a series of cases, the United States Supreme Court has considered when an act of production constitutes a protected testimonial communication rather than a non-testimonial and therefore unprotected communication. In advancing that distinction, the Court has also developed an exception to the Fifth Amendment privilege against self-incrimination for acts of production that are testimonial in nature but of minimal testimonial value because the information they convey is a "foregone conclusion."...

From those cases, which all addressed the compelled production of documents, the following principles can be inferred: For purposes of the Fifth Amendment privilege against self-incrimination, the act of production must be considered in its own right, separate from the documents sought. And even production that is of a testimonial nature can be compelled if the Government can demonstrate it already knows the information that act will reveal -- if, in other words, the existence of the requested documents, their authenticity, and the defendant's possession of and control over them -- are a "foregone conclusion."...

Considering the foregoing in light of the facts of this case, we note first that the State correctly asserts that the lawfully issued search warrants -- the sufficiency of which Andrews does not challenge -- give it the right to the cellphones' purportedly incriminating contents as specified in the trial court's order. And neither those contents -- which are voluntary, not compelled, communications, -- nor the phones themselves -- which are physical objects, not testimonial communications -- are protected by the Fifth Amendment privilege against self-incrimination. Therefore, production of Andrews's cellphones and their contents is not barred; indeed, had the State succeeded in its efforts to access the phones, this case would not be before us.

But access to the cellphones' contents depends here upon entry of their passcodes. A cellphone's passcode is analogous to the combination to a safe, not a key. Communicating or entering a passcode requires facts contained within the holder's mind -- the numbers, letters, or symbols composing the passcode. It is a testimonial act of production.

The inquiry does not end there, however, because, if the foregone conclusion exception applies, production of the passcodes may still be compelled. To determine the exception's applicability, we must first determine to what it might apply -- the act of producing the passcodes, or the act of producing the cellphones' contents through the passcodes. To be consistent with the Supreme Court case law that gave rise to the exception, we find that the foregone conclusion test applies to the production of the passcodes themselves, rather than to the phones' contents.

The relevant Supreme Court cases explicitly predicate the applicability of the foregone conclusion doctrine on the fundamental distinction between the act of production and the documents to be produced. The documents may be entitled to no Fifth Amendment protection at all -- and, indeed, they were not so entitled in Fisher v. United States (1976) -- but the act of producing them may nevertheless be protected....

In sum, we view the compelled act of production in this case to be that of producing the passcodes. Although that act of production is testimonial, we note that passcodes are a series of characters without independent evidentiary significance and are therefore of "minimal testimonial value" -- their value is limited to communicating the knowledge of the passcodes. Thus, although the act of producing the passcodes is presumptively protected by the Fifth Amendment, its testimonial value and constitutional protection may be overcome if the passcodes' existence, possession, and authentication are foregone conclusions.

Based on the record before us, we have little difficulty concluding that compelled production of the passcodes falls within the foregone conclusion exception. The State established that the passcodes exist -- they determined the cellphones' contents are passcode-protected. Also, the trial court record reveals that the cellphones were in Andrews's possession when seized and that he owned and operated the cellphones, establishing his knowledge of the passcodes and that the passcodes enable access to the cellphones' contents....

The State's demonstration of the passcodes' existence [and] Andrews's previous possession and operation of the cellphones render the issue here one of surrender, not testimony, and the foregone conclusion exception to the Fifth Amendment privilege against self-incrimination thus applies. Therefore, the Fifth Amendment does not protect Andrews from compelled disclosure of the passcodes to his cellphones.

Justice LaVECCHIA, dissenting.

In a world where the right to privacy is constantly shrinking, the Constitution provides shelter to our innermost thoughts -- the contents of our minds -- from the prying eyes of the government. The right of individuals to be free from the forced disclosure of the contents of their minds to assist law enforcement in a criminal investigation, until now, has been an inviolate principle of our law, protected by the Fifth Amendment and our state common law. No United States Supreme Court case presently requires otherwise. That protection deserves utmost respect and should not be lessened to authorize courts to compel a defendant to reveal the passcode to a smartphone so law enforcement can access its secured contents.

We are at a crossroads in our law. Will we allow law enforcement -- and our courts as their collaborators -- to compel a defendant to disgorge undisclosed private thoughts -- presumably memorized numbers or letters -- so that the government can obtain access to encrypted smartphones? In my view, compelling the disclosure of a person's mental thoughts is anathema to fundamental principles under our Constitution and state common law....

3. COMPULSION

The Fifth Amendment prohibits being "compelled" to be a witness against oneself. That means that criminal defendants cannot be ordered to testify before a grand jury or at trial (or punished for not doing so). But since defendants' out-of-court statements can be introduced against them, these protections become largely ceremonial if the government has already obtained a confession prior to trial. As scholar Yale Kamisar pointed out in 1965,

> "The courtroom is a splendid place where defense attorneys bellow and strut and prosecuting attorneys are hemmed in at many turns. But what happens before an accused reaches the safety and enjoys the comfort of this veritable mansion? Ah, there's the rub. Typically he must pass through a much less pretentious edifice, a police station with bare back rooms and locked doors."

As Kamisar suggests, the most important applications of the Fifth Amendment prohibition on compelled self-incrimination arise during police questioning. Most obviously, the Amendment prohibits police from obtaining a confession by physically abusing suspects or threating them with physical harm during questioning. But what about less obviously coercive police tactics?

If police question a suspect, who is handcuffed to a desk, for hours in the middle of the night, is the resulting confession compelled? What if police provide one short break to use the bathroom over the span of 8 hours of questioning? What if the officers trick a suspect into confessing by lying about the evidence, the likely punishment, or about purported confessions by the suspect's accomplices? How much physical discomfort or deceit can police rely on before an interrogation becomes coercive and the resulting confession becomes inadmissible? The next case, *Spano v. New York*, addresses these questions.

In *Spano*, the Supreme Court relies on the due process clause of the Fourteenth Amendment rather than the Fifth Amendment. At the time the case was decided, the Court had not yet applied the Fifth Amendment to the States. Later cases merge the Fourteenth Amendment voluntariness and Fifth Amendment compulsion analysis.

SPANO v. NEW YORK
360 U.S. 315 (1959)

Chief Justice WARREN delivered the opinion of the Court.

This is another in the long line of cases presenting the question whether a confession was properly admitted into evidence under the Fourteenth Amendment....

The State's evidence reveals the following: Petitioner Vincent Spano is a derivative citizen of this country, having been born in Messina, Italy. He was 25 years old at the time of the shooting in question and had graduated from junior high school. He had a record of regular employment. The shooting took place on January 22, 1957.

On that day, petitioner was drinking in a bar. The decedent, a former professional boxer weighing almost 200 pounds who had fought in Madison Square Garden, took some of petitioner's money from the bar. Petitioner followed him out of the bar to recover it. A fight ensued, with the decedent knocking petitioner down and then kicking him in the head three or four times. Shock from the force of these blows caused petitioner to vomit. After the bartender applied some ice to his head, petitioner left the bar, walked to his apartment, secured a gun, and walked eight or nine blocks to a candy store where the decedent was frequently to be found. He entered the store in which decedent, three friends of decedent, at least two of whom were ex-convicts, and a boy who was supervising the store were present. He fired five shots, two of which entered the decedent's body, causing his death. The boy was the only eyewitness; the three friends of decedent did not see the person who fired the shot. Petitioner then disappeared for the next week or so.

On February 1, 1957, the Bronx County Grand Jury returned an indictment for first-degree murder against petitioner. Accordingly, a bench warrant was issued for his arrest, commanding that he be forthwith brought before the court to answer the indictment, or, if the court had adjourned for the term, that he be delivered into the custody of the Sheriff of Bronx County.

On February 3, 1957, petitioner called one Gaspar Bruno, a close friend of 8 or 10 years' standing who had attended school with him. Bruno was a fledgling police officer, having at that time not yet finished attending police academy. According to Bruno's testimony, petitioner told him 'that he took a terrific beating, that the

493

deceased hurt him real bad and he dropped him a couple of times and he was dazed; he didn't know what he was doing and that he went and shot at him.' Petitioner told Bruno that he intended to get a lawyer and give himself up. Bruno relayed this information to his superiors.

The following day, February 4, at 7:10 p.m., petitioner, accompanied by counsel, surrendered himself to the authorities in front of the Bronx County Building, where both the office of the Assistant District Attorney who ultimately prosecuted his case and the court-room in which he was ultimately tried were located. His attorney had cautioned him to answer no questions, and left him in the custody of the officers. He was promptly taken to the office of the Assistant District Attorney and at 7:15 p.m. the questioning began.... The record reveals that the questioning was both persistent and continuous. Petitioner, in accordance with his attorney's instructions, steadfastly refused to answer....

At 12:15 a.m. on the morning of February 5, after five hours of questioning in which it became evident that petitioner was following his attorney's instructions, on the Assistant District Attorney's orders petitioner was transferred to the 46th Squad, Ryer Avenue Police Station. The Assistant District Attorney also went to the police station and to some extent continued to participate in the interrogation.... But petitioner persisted in his refusal to answer, and again requested permission to see his attorney.... His request was again denied.

It was then that those in charge of the investigation decided that petitioner's close friend, Bruno, could be of use. He had been called out on the case around 10 or 11 p.m., although he was not connected with the 46th Squad or Precinct in any way. Although, in fact, his job was in no way threatened, Bruno was told to tell petitioner that petitioner's telephone call had gotten him 'in a lot of trouble,' and that he should seek to extract sympathy from petitioner for Bruno's pregnant wife and three children. Bruno developed this theme with petitioner without success, and petitioner, also without success, again sought to see his attorney, a request which Bruno relayed unavailingly to his superiors.... Inevitably, in the fourth [interrogation] ... lasting a full hour, petitioner succumbed to his friend's prevarications and agreed to make a statement. Accordingly, at 3:25 a.m. the Assistant District Attorney, a stenographer, and several other law enforcement officials entered the room where petitioner was being questioned, and took his statement in question and answer form with the Assistant District Attorney asking the questions. The statement was completed at 4:05 a.m.

But this was not the end. At 4:30 a.m. three detectives took petitioner to Police Headquarters in Manhattan. On the way they attempted to find the bridge from which petitioner said he had thrown the murder weapon. They crossed the Triborough Bridge into Manhattan, arriving at Police Headquarters at 5 a.m., and left Manhattan for the Bronx at 5:40 a.m. via the Willis Avenue Bridge. When petitioner recognized neither bridge as the one from which he had thrown the weapon, they re-entered Manhattan via the Third Avenue Bridge, which petitioner stated was the right one, and then returned to the Bronx well after 6 a.m. During that trip the officers also elicited a statement from petitioner that the deceased was always 'on (his) back,' 'always pushing' him and that he was 'not sorry' he had shot the deceased. All three detectives testified to that statement at the trial....

.... We find use of the confession obtained here inconsistent with the Fourteenth Amendment under traditional principles.

The abhorrence of society to the use of involuntary confessions does not turn alone on their inherent untrustworthiness. It also turns on the deep-rooted feeling that the police must obey the law while enforcing the law; that in the end life and liberty can be as much endangered from illegal methods used to convict those thought to be criminals as from the actual criminals themselves.... The facts of no case recently in this Court have quite approached the brutal beatings in Brown v. Mississippi (1936), or the 36 consecutive hours of questioning present in Ashcraft v. Tennessee (1944). But as law enforcement officers become more responsible, and the methods used to extract confessions more sophisticated, our duty to enforce federal constitutional protections does not cease. It only becomes more difficult because of the more delicate judgments to be made. Our judgment here is that, on all the facts, this conviction cannot stand.

Petitioner was a foreign-born young man of 25 with no past history of law violation or of subjection to official interrogation, at least insofar as the record shows. He had progressed only one-half year into high school and the record indicates that he had a history of emotional instability. He did not make a narrative statement, but was subject to the leading questions of a skillful prosecutor in a question and answer confession. He was subjected to questioning not by a few men, but by many....

Petitioner was questioned for virtually eight straight hours before he confessed, with his only respite being a transfer to an arena presumably considered more appropriate by the police for the task at hand. Nor was the questioning conducted during normal business hours, but began in early evening, continued into the night, and did not bear fruition until the not-too-early morning.... In such circumstances slowly mounting fatigue does, and is calculated to, play its part. The questioners persisted in the face of his repeated refusals to answer on the advice of his attorney, and they ignored his reasonable requests to contact the local attorney whom he had already retained and who had personally delivered him into the custody of these officers in obedience to the bench warrant.

The use of Bruno, characterized in this Court by counsel for the State as a 'childhood friend' of petitioner's, is another factor which deserves mention in the totality of the situation. Bruno's was the one face visible to petitioner in which he could put some trust. There was a bond of friendship between them going back a decade into adolescence. It was with this material that the officers felt that they could overcome petitioner's will. They instructed Bruno falsely to state that petitioner's telephone call had gotten him into trouble, that his job was in jeopardy, and that loss of his job would be disastrous to his three children, his wife and his unborn child. And Bruno played this part of a worried father, harried by his superiors, in not one, but four different acts, the final one lasting an hour....

We conclude that petitioner's will was overborne by official pressure, fatigue and sympathy falsely aroused after considering all the facts in their post-indictment setting.... The police were not therefore merely trying to solve a crime, or even to absolve a suspect. They were rather concerned primarily with securing a statement from defendant on which they could convict him. The undeviating intent of the officers to extract a confession from petitioner is therefore patent. When such an intent is shown, this Court has held that the confession obtained must be examined with the most careful scrutiny, and has reversed a conviction on facts less compelling than these. Accordingly, we hold that petitioner's conviction cannot stand under the Fourteenth Amendment.... Reversed.

Here is how the Supreme Court summarized the due process test applied in *Spano* in *Schneckloth v. Bustamonte* (1973):

"The Due Process Clause does not mandate that the police forgo all questioning, or that they be given carte blanche to extract what they can from a suspect. 'The ultimate test remains that which has been the only clearly established test in Anglo-American courts for two hundred years: the test of voluntariness. Is the confession the product of an essentially free and unconstrained choice by its maker? If it is, if he has willed to confess, it may be used against him. If it is not, if his will has been overborne and his capacity for self-determination critically impaired, the use of his confession offends due process.'"

COLORADO v. CONNELLY
479 U.S. 157 (1986)

Case Summary

In August 1983, Francis Connelly approached Officer Patrick Anderson, who was in uniform in downtown Denver, and stated that he had killed someone a year earlier. After police investigation corroborated this claim, Connelly was prosecuted for the murder. At trial, Connelly sought to suppress his confession to Anderson on the grounds that it was involuntary. According to a defense expert, Connelly believed he was hearing the "voice of God"; and that voice had told him "either to confess to the killing or to commit suicide. Reluctantly following the command of the voices, respondent approached Officer Anderson and confessed." The Colorado courts agreed that the confession was not a product of Connelly's "free will" and thus involuntary and inadmissible.

The Supreme Court reversed, emphasizing that its involuntary confession cases "focused upon the crucial element of police overreaching." And while it was true that the Court sometimes emphasized the weakened mental condition of a suspect, that factor became relevant only where "police exploited this weakness with coercive tactics." Focusing on involuntariness caused by police conduct, rather than other sources, the Court emphasized, respected "the settled law requiring some sort of state action" for a Constitutional violation. "Respondent's perception of coercion flowing from the 'voice of God'... is a matter to which the United States Constitution does not speak." The Court concluded:

> "We hold that coercive police activity is a necessary predicate to the finding that a confession is not "voluntary" [and] also conclude that the taking of respondent's statements, and their admission into evidence, constitute no violation of [the Constitution]."

DASSEY v. DITTMANN
877 F.3d 297 (7th Cir. 2017)

Case Summary

One of the most prominent modern applications of the voluntariness case law came in the courts' treatment of the confession of 16-year-old Brendan Dassey. Dassey's confession was called into doubt in the 2015 Netflix documentary, *Making a Murderer*. Popular support for Dassey generated by the documentary, however, did not ultimately translate into success in the courts.

In 2006, police interrogated Dassey at a local police station about a recent murder. Dassey's uncle, Steven Avery, was the primary suspect. The officers obtained Dassey's mother's permission for the interview, but she was not present during questioning. Dassey and Avery were later convicted. Dassey's confession was the primary evidence against him.

After the Wisconsin appellate courts rejected legal challenges to the confession, both a federal district court and a panel of the Seventh Circuit deemed its admission unconstitutional. The panel opinion by Judge Rovner emphasized Dassey's age and "extreme social anxiety and social avoidant characteristics" that made him particularly susceptible to the interrogation tactics adopted by the police:

> "The investigators' 'honesty is the only thing that will set you free' theme established a pattern whereby Dassey, seeking the promised result—freedom, or avoidance of conflict—searched for the narrative that the investigators would accept as 'the truth.' Dassey found 'the truth' either by stumbling upon it or by using the information the investigators had fed him. The promise of freedom became linked to the idea of truth which became defined as that which the investigators wanted to hear. Once this prompt-and-response pattern is noticed, it is impossible to read or view Dassey's interrogation and have any confidence that Dassey's confession was the product of his own free will rather than his will being overborne. Any reader who doubts that this pattern casts insurmountable

doubt on the voluntariness of Dassey's confession need only watch or read the interrogation with this 'key' in hand."[28]

The en banc Seventh Circuit reversed. Here is how Judge Hamilton's opinion for the en banc court described the factors on both sides of the question:[29]

" A number of relevant factors, we recognize, tend to support Dassey's claims about the March 1st confession. He was young. He was alone with the police. He was somewhat limited intellectually. The officers' questioning included general assurances of leniency if he told the truth, and Dassey may have believed they promised more than they did. At times it appeared as though Dassey simply did not grasp the gravity of his confession—after confessing to rape and murder, he asked the officers if he would be back at school that afternoon in time to turn in a project. Portions of the questioning also included leading and suggestive questions, and throughout the interrogation Dassey faced follow–up inquiries when the investigators were not satisfied with what he had told them, leading him at times to seem to guess. In addition, the confusion and contradictions in Dassey's account of the crimes of October 31st lend support to the view that his confession was the product of suggestions and/or a desire to tell the police what they wanted to hear.

At the same time, many other factors support the finding that Dassey's confession was indeed voluntary. Start with the circumstances of the interrogation. As stipulated by both sides, Dassey was not in custody when he admitted participating in the crimes of October 31st. He went with the officers voluntarily and with his mother's knowledge and consent. He was given Miranda warnings and understood them sufficiently. The interrogation was conducted during school hours and in a comfortable setting. Dassey showed no signs of physical distress. He had access to food, drinks, and restroom breaks. The interrogation was not particularly lengthy, especially with the breaks that were taken every hour.

Dassey was not subject to physical coercion or any sort of threats at all.... The investigators stayed calm and never even raised their voices....

---

[28] Dassey v. Dittmann, 860 F.3d 933 (7th Cir. 2017).
[29] Dassey v. Dittmann, 877 F.3d 297 (7th Cir. 2017).

Turning to the techniques used in the interrogation, the investigators told Dassey many times that they already knew what had happened when in fact they did not. Such deception is a common interview technique. To our knowledge, it has not led courts (and certainly not the Supreme Court) to find that a subject's incriminating answers were involuntary. Also, most of the incriminating details in Dassey's confession were not suggested by the questioners. He volunteered them in response to open–ended questions.

When Dassey's story did not make sense, seemed incomplete, or seemed to conflict with other evidence, the questioners pressed Dassey with further questions. Those techniques are not coercive. Dassey responded to such questioning by modifying his story on some points, but he stuck to his story on others. Those passages support the view that he was not being pushed to provide a false story against his will. For example, Dassey resisted repeated suggestions that he had participated in shooting Teresa. He denied repeated suggestions that he and Avery had used wires and cables in the garage to restrain or harm her. In one telling instance, the questioners tested Dassey by falsely telling him that Teresa had a tattoo on her stomach and asking him if he had seen it. He told them no. When the questioners pushed harder, he was not willing to say he knew they were wrong, but he stuck to his recollection that he had not seen a tattoo.

Given the factors on both sides, and the deferential standard of review of state court rulings, the en banc Seventh Circuit vacated the panel decision, allowing Dassey's state court conviction to stand.

Chief Judge Wood, writing for the dissenting judges on the en banc court, disagreed:

"Psychological coercion, questions to which the police furnished the answers, and ghoulish games of '20 Questions,' in which Brendan Dassey guessed over and over again before he landed on the 'correct' story (i.e., the one the police wanted), led to the 'confession' that furnished the only serious evidence supporting his murder conviction in the Wisconsin courts…. Dassey at the relevant time was 16 years old and had an IQ in the low 80s. His confession was coerced, and thus it should not have been admitted into evidence…. Dassey will spend the rest of his life in prison because of the injustice this court has decided to leave unredressed. I respectfully dissent."

The contrasting opinions in the *Dassey* case illustrate the malleability of the constitutional voluntariness inquiry. This long ago led the Supreme Court to became frustrated with regulating the admission of confessions solely through a voluntariness test.

B. POLICE INTERROGATION AND MIRANDA

The Supreme Court has approached the problem of coercive law enforcement questioning from a variety of angles, including the Fifth, Sixth, and Fourteenth Amendments. In the modern era, the most prominent approach is set out in the next case.

1. MIRANDA WARNINGS

MIRANDA v. ARIZONA
384 U.S. 436 (1966)

Chief Justice WARREN delivered the opinion of the Court.

I

The constitutional issue we decide in each of these cases is the admissibility of statements obtained from a defendant questioned while in custody or otherwise deprived of his freedom of action in any significant way. In each, the defendant was questioned by police officers, detectives, or a prosecuting attorney in a room in which he was cut off from the outside world. In none of these cases was the defendant given a full and effective warning of his rights at the outset of the interrogation process. In all the cases, the questioning elicited oral admissions, and in three of them, signed statements as well which were admitted at their trials. They all thus share salient features—incommunicado interrogation of individuals in a police-dominated atmosphere, resulting in self-incriminating statements without full warnings of constitutional rights.

An understanding of the nature and setting of this in-custody interrogation is essential to our decisions today. The difficulty in depicting what transpires at such interrogations stems from the fact that in this country they have largely taken place incommunicado. From extensive factual studies undertaken in the early 1930's, including the famous Wickersham Report to Congress by a Presidential Commission, it is clear that police violence and the 'third degree' flourished at that time. In a series of cases decided by this Court long after these studies, the police resorted to physical brutality—beatings, hanging, whipping—and to sustained and protracted questioning incommunicado in order to extort confessions. The Commission on Civil Rights in 1961 found much evidence to indicate that 'some policemen still resort to physical force to obtain confessions.' The use of physical brutality and violence is not, unfortunately, relegated to the past or to any part of the country…. The examples given above are undoubtedly the exception now, but they are sufficiently widespread to be the object of concern. Unless a proper limitation upon custodial interrogation is achieved—such as these decisions will advance—there can be no assurance that practices of this nature will be eradicated in the foreseeable future.

The conclusion of the Wickersham Commission Report, made over 30 years ago, is still pertinent:

> 'To the contention that the third degree is necessary to get the facts, the reporters aptly reply in the language of the present Lord Chancellor of England: 'It is not admissible to do a great right by doing a little wrong. It is not sufficient to do justice by obtaining a proper result by irregular or improper means.' Not only does the use of the third degree involve a flagrant violation of law by the officers of the law, but it involves also the dangers of false confessions, and it tends to make police and prosecutors less zealous in the search for objective evidence. As the New York prosecutor quoted in the report said, 'It is a short cut and makes the police lazy and unenterprising.'…'

Again we stress that the modern practice of in-custody interrogation is psychologically rather than physically oriented. As we have stated before … 'this Court has recognized that coercion can be mental as well as physical, and that the blood of the accused is not the only hallmark of an unconstitutional inquisition.' Interrogation still takes place in privacy. Privacy results in secrecy and this in turn results in a gap in our knowledge as to what in fact goes on in the interrogation rooms. A valuable source of information about present police practices, however, may be found in various police manuals and texts which document procedures employed with success in the past, and which recommend various other effective tactics. These texts are used by law enforcement agencies themselves as guides. It should be noted that these texts professedly present the most enlightened and effective means presently used to obtain statements through custodial interrogation. By considering these texts and other data, it is possible to describe procedures observed and noted around the country.

The officers are told by the manuals that the 'principal psychological factor contributing to a successful interrogation is privacy—being alone with the person under interrogation.'…

To highlight the isolation and unfamiliar surroundings, the manuals instruct the police to display an air of confidence in the suspect's guilt and from outward appearance to maintain only an interest in confirming certain details. The guilt of the subject is to be posited as a fact. The interrogator should direct his comments toward the reasons why the subject committed the act, rather than court failure by asking the subject whether he did it. Like other men, perhaps the subject has had a bad family life, had an unhappy childhood, had too much to drink, had an unrequited desire for women. The officers are instructed to minimize the moral seriousness of the offense, to cast blame on the victim or on society. These tactics are designed to put the subject in a psychological state where his story is but an elaboration of what the police purport to know already—that he is guilty. Explanations to the contrary are dismissed and discouraged.

The texts thus stress that the major qualities an interrogator should possess are patience and perseverance. One writer describes the efficacy of these characteristics in this manner:

> 'In the preceding paragraphs emphasis has been placed on kindness and stratagems. The investigator will, however, encounter many situations where the sheer weight of his personality will be the deciding factor. Where emotional appeals and tricks are employed to no avail, he must rely on an oppressive atmosphere of dogged persistence. He must interrogate steadily and without relent, leaving the subject no prospect of surcease. He must dominate his subject and overwhelm him with his inexorable will to obtain the truth. He should interrogate for a spell of several hours pausing only for the subject's necessities in acknowledgment of the need to avoid a charge of duress that can be technically substantiated. In a serious case, the interrogation may continue for days, with the required intervals for food and sleep, but with no respite from the atmosphere of domination. It is possible in this way to induce the subject to talk without resorting to duress or

coercion. The method should be used only when the guilt of the subject appears highly probable.'

The manuals suggest that the suspect be offered legal excuses for his actions in order to obtain an initial admission of guilt. Where there is a suspected revenge-killing, for example, the interrogator may say:

> 'Joe, you probably didn't go out looking for this fellow with the purpose of shooting him. My guess is, however, that you expected something from him and that's why you carried a gun—for your own protection. You knew him for what he was, no good. Then when you met him he probably started using foul, abusive language and he gave some indication that he was about to pull a gun on you, and that's when you had to act to save your own life. That's about it, isn't it, Joe?'

Having then obtained the admission of shooting, the interrogator is advised to refer to circumstantial evidence which negates the self-defense explanation. This should enable him to secure the entire story. One text notes that 'Even if he fails to do so, the inconsistency between the subject's original denial of the shooting and his present admission of at least doing the shooting will serve to deprive him of a self-defense 'out' at the time of trial.'...

From these representative samples of interrogation techniques, the setting prescribed by the manuals and observed in practice becomes clear. In essence, it is this: To be alone with the subject is essential to prevent distraction and to deprive him of any outside support. The aura of confidence in his guilt undermines his will to resist. He merely confirms the preconceived story the police seek to have him describe. Patience and persistence, at times relentless questioning, are employed. To obtain a confession, the interrogator must 'patiently maneuver himself or his quarry into a position from which the desired objective may be attained.' When normal procedures fail to produce the needed result, the police may resort to deceptive stratagems such as giving false legal advice. It is important to keep the subject off balance, for example, by trading on his insecurity about himself or his surroundings. The police then persuade, trick, or cajole him out of exercising his constitutional rights.

Even without employing brutality, the 'third degree' or the specific stratagems described above, the very fact of custodial interrogation exacts a heavy toll on individual liberty and trades on the weakness of individuals....

In the cases before us today, given this background, we concern ourselves primarily with this interrogation atmosphere and the evils it can bring. In No. 759, Miranda v. Arizona, the police arrested the defendant and took him to a special interrogation room where they secured a confession. In No. 760, Vignera v. New York, the defendant made oral admissions to the police after interrogation in the afternoon, and then signed an inculpatory statement upon being questioned by an assistant district attorney later the same evening. In No. 761, Westover v. United States, the defendant was handed over to the Federal Bureau of Investigation by local authorities after they had detained and interrogated him for a lengthy period, both at night and the following morning. After some two hours of questioning, the federal officers had obtained signed statements from the defendant. Lastly, in No. 584, California v. Stewart, the local police held the defendant five days in the station and interrogated him on nine separate occasions before they secured his inculpatory statement.

In these cases, we might not find the defendants' statements to have been involuntary in traditional terms. Our concern for adequate safeguards to protect precious Fifth Amendment rights is, of course, not lessened in the slightest. In each of the cases, the defendant was thrust into an unfamiliar atmosphere and run through menacing police interrogation procedures.... To be sure, the records do not evince overt physical coercion or patent psychological ploys. The fact remains that in none of these cases did the officers undertake to afford appropriate safeguards at the outset of the interrogation to insure that the statements were truly the product of free choice.

It is obvious that such an interrogation environment is created for no purpose other than to subjugate the individual to the will of his examiner. This atmosphere carries its own badge of intimidation. To be sure, this is not physical intimidation, but it is equally destructive of human dignity. The current practice of incommunicado interrogation is at odds with one of our Nation's most cherished principles—that the individual may not be compelled to incriminate himself. Unless adequate protective devices are employed to dispel the compulsion inherent in custodial surroundings, no statement obtained from the defendant can truly be the product of his free choice. From the foregoing, we can readily perceive an intimate connection between the privilege against self-incrimination and police custodial questioning....

III

There can be no doubt that the Fifth Amendment privilege is available outside of criminal court proceedings and serves to protect persons in all settings in which their freedom of action is curtailed in any significant way from being compelled to incriminate themselves. We have concluded that without proper safeguards the process of in-custody interrogation of persons suspected or accused of crime contains inherently compelling pressures which work to undermine the individual's will to resist and to compel him to speak where he would not otherwise do so freely. In order to combat these pressures and to permit a full opportunity to exercise the privilege against self-incrimination, the accused must be adequately and effectively apprised of his rights and the exercise of those rights must be fully honored.

It is impossible for us to foresee the potential alternatives for protecting the privilege which might be devised by Congress or the States in the exercise of their creative rule-making capacities. Therefore we cannot say that the Constitution necessarily requires adherence to any particular solution for the inherent compulsions of the interrogation process as it is presently conducted. Our decision in no way creates a constitutional straitjacket which will handicap sound efforts at reform, nor is it intended to have this effect. We encourage Congress and the States to continue their laudable search for increasingly effective ways of protecting the rights of the individual while promoting efficient enforcement of our criminal laws. However, unless we are shown other procedures which are at least as effective in apprising accused persons of their right of silence and in assuring a continuous opportunity to exercise it, the following safeguards must be observed.

At the outset, if a person in custody is to be subjected to interrogation, he must first be informed in clear and unequivocal terms that he has the right to remain silent. For those unaware of the privilege, the warning is needed simply to make them aware of it—the threshold requirement for an intelligent decision as to its exercise. More important, such a warning is an absolute prerequisite in overcoming the inherent pressures of the interrogation atmosphere. It is not just the subnormal or woefully ignorant who succumb to an interrogator's imprecations, whether implied or expressly stated, that the interrogation will continue until a confession is obtained or that silence in the face of accusation is itself damning and will bode ill when presented to a jury. Further, the warning will show the individual that his interrogators are prepared to recognize his privilege should he choose to exercise it.

The Fifth Amendment privilege is so fundamental to our system of constitutional rule and the expedient of giving an adequate warning as to the availability of the privilege so simple, we will not pause to inquire in individual cases whether the defendant was aware of his rights without a warning being given. Assessments of the knowledge the defendant possessed, based on information as to his age, education, intelligence, or prior contact with authorities, can never be more than speculation; a warning is a clearcut fact. More important, whatever the background of the person interrogated, a warning at the time of the interrogation is indispensable to overcome its pressures and to insure that the individual knows he is free to exercise the privilege at that point in time.

The warning of the right to remain silent must be accompanied by the explanation that anything said can and will be used against the individual in court. This warning is needed in order to make him aware not only of the privilege, but also of the consequences of forgoing it. It is only through an awareness of these consequences that there can be any assurance of real understanding and intelligent exercise of the privilege. Moreover, this warning may serve to make the individual more acutely aware that he is faced with a phase of the adversary system—that he is not in the presence of persons acting solely in his interest.

The circumstances surrounding in-custody interrogation can operate very quickly to overbear the will of one merely made aware of his privilege by his interrogators. Therefore, the right to have counsel present at the interrogation is indispensable to the protection of the Fifth Amendment privilege under the system we delineate today. Our aim is to assure that the individual's right to choose between silence and speech remains unfettered throughout the interrogation process. A once-stated warning, delivered by those who will conduct the interrogation, cannot itself suffice to that end among those who most require knowledge of their rights.... Even preliminary advice given to the accused by his own attorney can be swiftly overcome by the secret interrogation process. Thus, the need for counsel to protect the Fifth Amendment privilege comprehends not merely a right to consult with counsel prior to questioning, but also to have counsel present during any questioning if the defendant so desires.

The presence of counsel at the interrogation may serve several significant subsidiary functions as well. If the accused decides to talk to his interrogators, the assistance of counsel can mitigate the dangers of untrustworthiness. With a lawyer present the likelihood that the police will practice coercion is reduced, and if coercion is nevertheless exercised the lawyer can testify to it in court. The presence of a lawyer can also help to guarantee that the accused gives a fully accurate statement to the police and that the statement is rightly reported by the prosecution at trial.

…. Accordingly we hold that an individual held for interrogation must be clearly informed that he has the right to consult with a lawyer and to have the lawyer with him during interrogation under the system for protecting the privilege we delineate today. As with the warnings of the right to remain silent and that anything stated can be used in evidence against him, this warning is an absolute prerequisite to interrogation. No amount of circumstantial evidence that the person may have been aware of this right will suffice to stand in its stead. Only through such a warning is there ascertainable assurance that the accused was aware of this right.

If an individual indicates that he wishes the assistance of counsel before any interrogation occurs, the authorities cannot rationally ignore or deny his request on the basis that the individual does not have or cannot afford a retained attorney. The financial ability of the individual has no relationship to the scope of the rights involved here. The privilege against self-incrimination secured by the Constitution applies to all individuals. The need for counsel in order to protect the privilege exists for the indigent as well as the affluent. In fact, were we to limit these constitutional rights to those who can retain an attorney, our decisions today would be of little significance. The cases before us as well as the vast majority of confession cases with which we have dealt in the past involve those unable to retain counsel. While authorities are not required to relieve the accused of his poverty, they have the obligation not to take advantage of indigence in the administration of justice….

In order fully to apprise a person interrogated of the extent of his rights under this system then, it is necessary to warn him not only that he has the right to consult with an attorney, but also that if he is indigent a lawyer will be appointed to represent him. Without this additional warning, the admonition of the right to consult with counsel would often be understood as meaning only that he can consult with a lawyer if he has one or has the funds to obtain one. The warning of a right to counsel would be hollow if not couched in terms that would convey to the indigent—the person most often subjected to interrogation—the knowledge that he too has a right to have counsel present. As with the warnings of the right to remain silent and of the general right to counsel, only by effective and express explanation to the indigent of this right can there be assurance that he was truly in a position to exercise it.

Once warnings have been given, the subsequent procedure is clear. If the individual indicates in any manner, at any time prior to or during questioning, that he wishes to remain silent, the interrogation must cease. At this point he has shown that he intends to exercise his Fifth Amendment privilege; any statement taken after the person invokes his privilege cannot be other than the product of compulsion, subtle or otherwise. Without the right to cut off questioning, the setting of in-custody interrogation operates on the individual to overcome free choice in producing a statement after the privilege has been once invoked. If the individual states that he wants an attorney, the interrogation must cease until an attorney is present. At that time, the individual must have an opportunity to confer with the attorney and to have him present during any subsequent questioning. If the individual cannot obtain an attorney and he indicates that he wants one before speaking to police, they must respect his decision to remain silent.

This does not mean, as some have suggested, that each police station must have a 'station house lawyer' present at all times to advise prisoners. It does mean, however, that if police propose to interrogate a person they must make known to him that he is entitled to a lawyer and that if he cannot afford one, a lawyer will be provided for him prior to any interrogation. If authorities conclude that they will not provide counsel during a reasonable period of time in which investigation in the field is carried out, they may refrain from doing so without violating the person's Fifth Amendment privilege so long as they do not question him during that time.

If the interrogation continues without the presence of an attorney and a statement is taken, a heavy burden rests on the government to demonstrate that the defendant knowingly and intelligently waived his privilege against self-incrimination and his right to retained or appointed counsel....

Whatever the testimony of the authorities as to waiver of rights by an accused, the fact of lengthy interrogation or incommunicado incarceration before a statement is made is strong evidence that the accused did not validly waive his rights. In these circumstances the fact that the individual eventually made a statement is consistent with the conclusion that the compelling influence of the interrogation finally forced him to do so. It is inconsistent with any notion of a voluntary relinquishment of the privilege. Moreover, any evidence that the accused was threatened, tricked, or cajoled into a waiver will, of course, show that the defendant did not voluntarily waive his privilege. The requirement of warnings and waiver of rights is a fundamental with respect to the Fifth Amendment privilege and not simply a preliminary ritual to existing methods of interrogation.

The warnings required and the waiver necessary in accordance with our opinion today are, in the absence of a fully effective equivalent, prerequisites to the admissibility of any statement made by a defendant. No distinction can be drawn between statements which are direct confessions and statements which amount to 'admissions' of part or all of an offense. The privilege against self-incrimination protects the individual from being compelled to incriminate himself in any manner; it does not distinguish degrees of incrimination. Similarly, for precisely the same reason, no distinction may be drawn between inculpatory statements and statements alleged to be merely 'exculpatory.' If a statement made were in fact truly exculpatory it would, of course, never be used by the prosecution....

Our decision is not intended to hamper the traditional function of police officers in investigating crime. When an individual is in custody on probable cause, the police may, of course, seek out evidence in the field to be used at trial against him. Such investigation may include inquiry of persons not under restraint. General on-the-scene questioning as to facts surrounding a crime or other general questioning of citizens in the fact-finding process is not affected by our holding. It is an act of responsible citizenship for individuals to give whatever information they may have to aid in law enforcement. In such situations the compelling atmosphere inherent in the process of in-custody interrogation is not necessarily present....

To summarize, we hold that when an individual is taken into custody or otherwise deprived of his freedom by the authorities in any significant way and is subjected to questioning, the privilege against self-incrimination is jeopardized. Procedural safeguards must be employed to protect the privilege and unless other fully effective means are adopted to notify the person of his right of silence and to assure that the exercise of the right will be scrupulously honored, the following measures are required. He must be warned prior to any questioning that he has the right to remain silent, that anything he says can be used against him in a court of law, that he has the right to the presence of an attorney, and that if he cannot afford an attorney one will be appointed for him prior to any questioning if he so desires. Opportunity to exercise these rights must be afforded to him throughout the interrogation. After such warnings have been given, and such opportunity afforded him, the individual may knowingly and intelligently waive these rights and agree to answer questions or make a statement. But unless and until such warnings and waiver are demonstrated by the prosecution at trial, no evidence obtained as a result of interrogation can be used against him....

V

Because of the nature of the problem and because of its recurrent significance in numerous cases, we have to this point discussed the relationship of the Fifth Amendment privilege to police interrogation without specific concentration on the facts of the cases before us. We turn now to these facts to consider the application to these cases of the constitutional principles discussed above....

No. 759. Miranda v. Arizona.

On March 13, 1963, petitioner, Ernesto Miranda, was arrested at his home and taken in custody to a Phoenix police station. He was there identified by the complaining witness. The police then took him to 'Interrogation Room No. 2' of the detective bureau. There he was questioned by two police officers. The officers admitted at trial that Miranda was not advised that he had a right to have an attorney present. Two hours later, the officers emerged from the interrogation room with a written confession signed by Miranda. At the top of the statement was a typed paragraph stating that the confession was made voluntarily, without threats or promises of immunity and 'with full knowledge of my legal rights, understanding any statement I make may be used against me.'

At his trial before a jury, the written confession was admitted into evidence over the objection of defense counsel, and the officers testified to the prior oral confession made by Miranda during the interrogation. Miranda was found guilty of kidnapping and rape. He was sentenced to 20 to 30 years' imprisonment on each count, the sentences to run concurrently. On appeal, the Supreme Court of Arizona held that Miranda's constitutional rights were not violated in obtaining the confession and affirmed the conviction. In reaching its decision, the court emphasized heavily the fact that Miranda did not specifically request counsel.

We reverse. From the testimony of the officers and by the admission of respondent, it is clear that Miranda was not in any way apprised of his right to consult with an attorney and to have one present during the interrogation, nor was his right not to be compelled to incriminate himself effectively protected in any other manner. Without these warnings the statements were inadmissible. The mere fact that he signed a statement which contained a typed-in clause stating that he had 'full knowledge' of his 'legal rights' does not approach the knowing and intelligent waiver required to relinquish constitutional rights....

After the Supreme Court's reversal of the conviction in *Miranda v. Arizona*, investigators interviewed additional witnesses. They located Ernesto Miranda's former roommate who told them that Miranda had admitted to her that he committed the charged kidnapping and rape. With the roommate's testimony about Miranda's admission taking the place of the suppressed confession, the prosecution again tried Miranda. Again, a jury convicted and a judge sentenced Miranda to the same term he had originally received. *See* Richard Carelli, *The Law and Ernesto Miranda*, Albany Times Union, June 8, 1986.

To the extent the Court intended that *Miranda* would replace the involuntariness inquiry, it largely succeeded. While defendants can still argue that their statements were obtained involuntarily (Fourteenth Amendment) or through compulsion (Fifth Amendment), these doctrines have, in practice, been largely subsumed by *Miranda*. In *Dickerson v. United States* (2000), the Supreme Court emphasized that while voluntariness is a separate inquiry from *Miranda*, "cases in which a defendant can make a colorable argument that a self-incriminating statement was 'compelled' despite the fact that the law enforcement authorities adhered to the dictates of Miranda are rare." The *Dassey* case summarized above illustrates the point.

The *Miranda* opinion sets forth the now-famous warnings. A suspect questioned in custody must be warned prior to any questioning that:

> "[1] he has the right to remain silent, [2] that anything he says can be used against him in a court of law, [3] that he has the right to the presence of an attorney, and [4] that if he cannot afford an attorney one will be appointed for him prior to any questioning if he so desires."

In a later case, *Duckworth v. Eagan* (1989), the Court noted that these warnings need not be given verbatim. Instead, a reviewing court will inquire "whether the warnings reasonably convey to a suspect his rights as required by Miranda."

Consider the following facts drawn from *Florida v. Powell* (2010). *Did the police comply with* Miranda?

"On August 10, 2004, law enforcement officers in Tampa, Florida, seeking to apprehend respondent Kevin Powell in connection with a robbery investigation, entered an apartment rented by Powell's girlfriend. After spotting Powell coming from a bedroom, the officers searched the room and discovered a loaded nine-millimeter handgun under the bed.

The officers arrested Powell and transported him to the Tampa police headquarters. Once there, and before asking Powell any questions, the officers read Powell the standard Tampa Police Department Consent and Release Form 310. The form states:

> 'You have the right to remain silent. If you give up the right to remain silent, anything you say can be used against you in court. You have the right to talk to a lawyer before answering any of our questions. If you cannot afford to hire a lawyer, one will be appointed for you without cost and before any questioning. You have the right to use any of these rights at any time you want during this interview.'

Acknowledging that he had been informed of his rights, that he 'understood them,' and that he was 'willing to talk' to the officers, Powell signed the form. He then admitted that he owned the handgun found in the apartment. Powell knew he was prohibited from possessing a gun because he had previously been convicted of a felony, but said he had nevertheless purchased and carried the firearm for his protection."

The *Miranda* decision does not require warnings during every police-citizen interaction. Instead, police must provide the warnings "when an individual is taken into custody or otherwise deprived of his freedom by the authorities in any significant way and is subjected to questioning." As a result, courts must analyze whether a suspect was "in custody" and "subject to questioning" to determine if *Miranda* warnings were required. The next cases elaborate on these inquiries.

2. MIRANDA CUSTODY

In many cases, it is obvious that a person is in custody for purposes of *Miranda*. The most common example involves a suspect who has been arrested and is interrogated at a police station. That person is clearly in custody. But what about less imposing situations? The next case addresses the common scenario when police conduct a traffic stop and question a vehicle's occupants on the side of the road.

BERKEMER v. MCCARTY
468 U.S. 420 (1984)

Justice MARSHALL delivered the opinion of the Court.

This case presents [the question], does the roadside questioning of a motorist detained pursuant to a traffic stop constitute custodial interrogation for the purposes of the doctrine enunciated in Miranda?

I
A

The parties have stipulated to the essential facts. On the evening of March 31, 1980, Trooper Williams of the Ohio State Highway Patrol observed respondent's car weaving in and out of a lane on Interstate Highway 270. After following the car for two miles, Williams forced respondent to stop and asked him to get out of the vehicle. When respondent complied, Williams noticed that he was having difficulty standing. At that point, "Williams concluded that Richard McCarty would be charged with a traffic offense and, therefore, his freedom to leave the scene was terminated." However, respondent was not told that he would be taken into custody. Williams then asked respondent to perform a field sobriety test, commonly known as a "balancing test." Respondent could not do so without falling.

While still at the scene of the traffic stop, Williams asked respondent whether he had been using intoxicants. Respondent replied that "he had consumed two beers and had smoked several joints of marijuana a short time before." Respondent's speech was slurred, and Williams had difficulty understanding him. Williams thereupon formally placed respondent under arrest and transported him in the patrol car to the Franklin County Jail.

At the jail, respondent was given an intoxilyzer test to determine the concentration of alcohol in his blood. The test did not detect any alcohol whatsoever in respondent's system. Williams then resumed questioning respondent in order to obtain information for inclusion in the State Highway Patrol Alcohol Influence Report. Respondent answered affirmatively a question whether he had been drinking. When then asked if he was under the influence of alcohol, he said, "I guess, barely." Williams next asked respondent to indicate on the form whether the marihuana he had smoked had been treated with any chemicals. In the section of the report headed "Remarks," respondent wrote, "No angel dust or PCP in the pot. Rick McCarty."

At no point in this sequence of events did Williams or anyone else tell respondent that he had a right to remain silent, to consult with an attorney, and to have an attorney appointed for him if he could not afford one.

B

Respondent was charged with operating a motor vehicle while under the influence of alcohol and/or drugs. Under Ohio law, that offense is a first-degree misdemeanor and is punishable by fine or imprisonment for up to six months. Incarceration for a minimum of three days is mandatory.

Respondent moved to exclude the various incriminating statements he had made to Trooper Williams on the ground that introduction into evidence of those statements would violate the Fifth Amendment insofar as he had not been informed of his constitutional rights prior to his interrogation. When the trial court denied the motion, respondent pleaded "no contest" and was found guilty. He was sentenced to 10 days in jail and fined $200.

II

.... In Miranda v. Arizona (1966), the Court addressed the problem of how the privilege against compelled self-incrimination guaranteed by the Fifth Amendment could be protected from the coercive pressures that can be brought to bear upon a suspect in the context of custodial interrogation.... In the years since the decision in Miranda, we have frequently reaffirmed the central principle established by that case: if the police take a suspect into custody and then ask him questions without informing him of the rights enumerated above, his responses cannot be introduced into evidence to establish his guilt.

… One of the principal advantages of the doctrine that suspects must be given warnings before being interrogated while in custody is the clarity of that rule. Miranda's holding has the virtue of informing police and prosecutors with specificity as to what they may do in conducting custodial interrogation, and of informing courts under what circumstances statements obtained during such interrogation are not admissible. This gain in specificity, which benefits the accused and the State alike, has been thought to outweigh the burdens that the decision in Miranda imposes on law enforcement agencies and the courts by requiring the suppression of trustworthy and highly probative evidence even though the confession might be voluntary under traditional Fifth Amendment analysis.

…. There can be no question that respondent was "in custody" at least as of the moment he was formally placed under arrest and instructed to get into the police car. Because he was not informed of his constitutional rights at that juncture, respondent's subsequent admissions should not have been used against him.

III

To assess the admissibility of the self-incriminating statements made by respondent prior to his formal arrest, we are obliged to address [an] issue concerning the scope of our decision in Miranda: whether the roadside questioning of a motorist detained pursuant to a routine traffic stop should be considered "custodial interrogation." Respondent urges that it should, on the ground that Miranda by its terms applies whenever "a person has been taken into custody or otherwise deprived of his freedom of action in any significant way." Petitioner contends that a holding that every detained motorist must be advised of his rights before being questioned would constitute an unwarranted extension of the Miranda doctrine.

It must be acknowledged at the outset that a traffic stop significantly curtails the "freedom of action" of the driver and the passengers, if any, of the detained vehicle. Under the law of most States, it is a crime either to ignore a policeman's signal to stop one's car or, once having stopped, to drive away without permission. Certainly few motorists would feel free either to disobey a directive to pull over or to leave the scene of a traffic stop without being told they might do so. Partly for these reasons, we have long acknowledged that "stopping an automobile and detaining its occupants constitute a 'seizure' within the meaning of the Fourth Amendment, even though the purpose of the stop is limited and the resulting detention quite brief."

However, we decline to accord talismanic power to the phrase in the Miranda opinion emphasized by respondent. Fidelity to the doctrine announced in Miranda requires that it be enforced strictly, but only in those types of situations in which the concerns that powered the decision are implicated. Thus, we must decide whether a traffic stop exerts upon a detained person pressures that sufficiently impair his free exercise of his privilege against self-incrimination to require that he be warned of his constitutional rights.

Two features of an ordinary traffic stop mitigate the danger that a person questioned will be induced "to speak where he would not otherwise do so freely." First, detention of a motorist pursuant to a traffic stop is presumptively temporary and brief. The vast majority of roadside detentions last only a few minutes. A motorist's expectations, when he sees a policeman's light flashing behind him, are that he will be obliged to spend a short period of time answering questions and waiting while the officer checks his license and registration, that he may then be given a citation, but that in the end he most likely will be allowed to continue on his way. In this respect, questioning incident to an ordinary traffic stop is quite different from stationhouse interrogation, which frequently is prolonged, and in which the detainee often is aware that questioning will continue until he provides his interrogators the answers they seek.

Second, circumstances associated with the typical traffic stop are not such that the motorist feels completely at the mercy of the police. To be sure, the aura of authority surrounding an armed, uniformed officer and the knowledge that the officer has some discretion in deciding whether to issue a citation, in combination, exert some pressure on the detainee to respond to questions. But other aspects of the situation substantially offset these forces. Perhaps most importantly, the typical traffic stop is public, at least to some degree. Passersby, on foot or in other cars, witness the interaction of officer and motorist. This exposure to public view both reduces the ability of an unscrupulous policeman to use illegitimate means to elicit self-incriminating statements and diminishes the motorist's fear that, if he does not cooperate, he will be subjected to abuse. The fact that the detained motorist typically is confronted by only one or at most two policemen further mutes his sense of vulnerability. In short, the atmosphere surrounding an ordinary traffic stop is substantially less "police dominated" than that surrounding the kinds of interrogation at issue in Miranda itself, and in the subsequent cases in which we have applied Miranda.

In both of these respects, the usual traffic stop is more analogous to a so-called "Terry stop," see Terry v. Ohio (1968), than to a formal arrest.... The comparatively nonthreatening character of detentions of this sort explains the absence of any suggestion in our opinions that Terry stops are subject to the dictates of Miranda. The similarly noncoercive aspect of ordinary traffic stops prompts us to hold that persons temporarily detained pursuant to such stops are not "in custody" for the purposes of Miranda.

Respondent contends that to "exempt" traffic stops from the coverage of Miranda will open the way to widespread abuse. Policemen will simply delay formally arresting detained motorists, and will subject them to sustained and intimidating interrogation at the scene of their initial detention. The net result, respondent contends, will be a serious threat to the rights that the Miranda doctrine is designed to protect.

We are confident that the state of affairs projected by respondent will not come to pass. It is settled that the safeguards prescribed by Miranda become applicable as soon as a suspect's freedom of action is curtailed to a "degree associated with formal arrest." If a motorist who has been detained pursuant to a traffic stop thereafter is subjected to treatment that renders him "in custody" for practical purposes, he will be entitled to the full panoply of protections prescribed by Miranda.

Admittedly, our adherence to the doctrine just recounted will mean that the police and lower courts will continue occasionally to have difficulty deciding exactly when a suspect has been taken into custody. Either a rule that Miranda applies to all traffic stops or a rule that a suspect need not be advised of his rights until he is formally placed under arrest would provide a clearer, more easily administered line. However, each of these two alternatives has drawbacks that make it unacceptable. The first would substantially impede the enforcement of the Nation's traffic laws— by compelling the police either to take the time to warn all detained motorists of their constitutional rights or to forgo use of self-incriminating statements made by those motorists—while doing little to protect citizens' Fifth Amendment rights.

The second would enable the police to circumvent the constraints on custodial interrogations established by Miranda.

Turning to the case before us, we find nothing in the record that indicates that respondent should have been given Miranda warnings at any point prior to the time Trooper Williams placed him under arrest. For the reasons indicated above, we reject the contention that the initial stop of respondent's car, by itself, rendered him "in custody." And respondent has failed to demonstrate that, at any time between the initial stop and the arrest, he was subjected to restraints comparable to those associated with a formal arrest. Only a short period of time elapsed between the stop and the arrest. At no point during that interval was respondent informed that his detention would not be temporary. Although Trooper Williams apparently decided as soon as respondent stepped out of his car that respondent would be taken into custody and charged with a traffic offense, Williams never communicated his intention to respondent. A policeman's unarticulated plan has no bearing on the question whether a suspect was "in custody" at a particular time; the only relevant inquiry is how a reasonable man in the suspect's position would have understood his situation. Nor do other aspects of the interaction of Williams and respondent support the contention that respondent was exposed to "custodial interrogation" at the scene of the stop. From aught that appears in the stipulation of facts, a single police officer asked respondent a modest number of questions and requested him to perform a simple balancing test at a location visible to passing motorists. Treatment of this sort cannot fairly be characterized as the functional equivalent of formal arrest.

We conclude, in short, that respondent was not taken into custody for the purposes of Miranda until Williams arrested him. Consequently, the statements respondent made prior to that point were admissible against him.

In *Oregon v. Mathiason* (1977), a police officer suspected Carl Mathiason of committing a burglary:

❝ About 25 days after the burglary, the officer left his card at defendant's apartment with a note asking him to call because 'I'd like to discuss something with you.' The next afternoon the defendant did call. The officer asked where it would be convenient to meet. The defendant had no preference; so the officer asked if the defendant could meet him at the state patrol office in about an hour and a half, about 5:00 p.m. The patrol office was about two blocks from defendant's apartment. The building housed several state agencies.

The officer met defendant in the hallway, shook hands and took him into an office. The defendant was told he was not under arrest. The door was closed. The two sat across a desk. The police radio in another room could be heard. The officer told defendant he wanted to talk to him about a burglary and that his truthfulness would possibly be considered by the district attorney or judge. The officer further advised that the police believed defendant was involved in the burglary and (falsely stated that) defendant's fingerprints were found at the scene. The defendant sat for a few minutes and then said he had taken the property. This occurred within five minutes after defendant had come to the office. The officer then advised defendant of his Miranda rights and took a taped confession.

Before you read on, consider whether Mathiason was "in custody" for purposes of Miranda.

The Supreme Court ruled that he was not, explaining:

> "There is no indication that the questioning took place in a context where respondent's freedom to depart was restricted in any way. He came voluntarily to the police station, where he was immediately informed that he was not under arrest. At the close of a ½-hour interview respondent did in fact leave the police station without hindrance. It is clear from these facts that Mathiason was not in custody 'or otherwise deprived of his freedom of action in any significant way.'"

In later cases, the Supreme Court would distill the *Miranda* "in-custody" analysis as follows:

> "Although the circumstances of each case must certainly influence a determination of whether a suspect is 'in custody' for purposes of receiving Miranda protection, the ultimate inquiry is simply whether there is a 'formal arrest or restraint on freedom of movement' of the degree associated with a formal arrest." *California v. Beheler* (1983)

In *J.D.B. v. North Carolina* (2011), the Supreme Court further analyzed the "in-custody" question:

> Because [Miranda warnings] protect the individual against the coercive nature of custodial interrogation, they are required only where there has been such a restriction on a person's freedom as to render him "in custody." As we have repeatedly emphasized, whether a suspect is "in custody" is an objective inquiry.
>
> Two discrete inquiries are essential to the determination: first, what were the circumstances surrounding the interrogation; and second, given those circumstances, would a reasonable person have felt he or she was at liberty to terminate the interrogation and leave. Once the scene is set and the players' lines and actions are reconstructed, the court must apply an objective test to resolve the ultimate inquiry: was there a formal arrest or restraint on freedom of movement of the degree associated with formal arrest.
>
> Rather than demarcate a limited set of relevant circumstances, we have required police officers and courts to "examine all of the circumstances surrounding the interrogation," including any circumstance that "would have affected how a reasonable person" in the suspect's position "would perceive his or her freedom to leave." On the other hand, the "subjective views harbored by either the interrogating officers or the person being questioned" are irrelevant. The test, in other words, involves no consideration of the "actual mindset" of the particular suspect subjected to police questioning.

The suspect in *J.D.B.* was a 13-year old who was questioned about an unsolved burglary by school administrators in the presence of two police officers in a conference room at his middle school. The case centered on how a suspect's age fit into the *Miranda* "in-custody" calculus. The Supreme Court held that age could be considered, explaining:

> A child's age differs from other personal characteristics that, even when known to police, have no objectively discernible relationship to a reasonable person's understanding of his freedom of action. Yarborough v. Alvarado (2004) holds, for instance, that a suspect's prior interrogation history with law enforcement has no role to play in the custody analysis

because such experience could just as easily lead a reasonable person to feel free to walk away as to feel compelled to stay in place. Because the effect in any given case would be "contingent on the psychology" of the individual suspect, the Court explained, such experience cannot be considered without compromising the objective nature of the custody analysis. A child's age, however, is different. Precisely because childhood yields objective conclusions like those we have drawn ourselves—among others, that children are "most susceptible to influence," and "outside pressures" — considering age in the custody analysis in no way involves a determination of how youth "subjectively affects the mindset" of any particular child....

We hold that so long as the child's age was known to the officer at the time of police questioning, or would have been objectively apparent to a reasonable officer, its inclusion in the custody analysis is consistent with the objective nature of that test....

Justice Alito worried in his dissenting opinion that "today's decision will soon be cited by defendants—and perhaps by prosecutors as well—for the proposition that all manner of other individual characteristics should be treated like age and taken into account in the Miranda custody calculus."

Recall that the discussion about race and seizures in Chapter 2 drew on the *J.D.B.* opinion; that discussion applies to the *Miranda* custody question as well.

3. MIRANDA INTERROGATION

RHODE ISLAND v. INNIS
446 U.S. 291 (1980)

Justice STEWART delivered the opinion of the Court.

In Miranda v. Arizona, the Court held that, once a defendant in custody asks to speak with a lawyer, all interrogation must cease until a lawyer is present. The issue in this case is whether the respondent was "interrogated" in violation of the standards promulgated in the Miranda opinion.

I

On the night of January 12, 1975, John Mulvaney, a Providence, R.I., taxicab driver, disappeared after being dispatched to pick up a customer. His body was discovered four days later buried in a shallow grave in Coventry, R.I. He had died from a shotgun blast aimed at the back of his head.

On January 17, 1975, shortly after midnight, the Providence police received a telephone call from Gerald Aubin, also a taxicab driver, who reported that he had just been robbed by a man wielding a sawed-off shotgun. Aubin further reported that he had dropped off his assailant near Rhode Island College in a section of Providence known as Mount Pleasant. While at the Providence police station waiting to give a statement, Aubin noticed a picture of his assailant on a bulletin board. Aubin so informed one of the police officers present. The officer prepared a photo array, and again Aubin identified a picture of the same person. That person was the respondent, Thomas Innis. Shortly thereafter, the Providence police began a search of the Mount Pleasant area.

At approximately 4:30 a. m. on the same date, Patrolman Lovell, while cruising the streets of Mount Pleasant in a patrol car, spotted the respondent standing in the street facing him. When Patrolman Lovell stopped his car, the respondent walked towards it. Patrolman Lovell then arrested the respondent, who was unarmed, and advised him of his so-called Miranda rights. While the two men waited in the patrol car for other police officers to arrive, Patrolman Lovell did not converse with the respondent other than to respond to the latter's request for a cigarette.

Within minutes, Sergeant Sears arrived at the scene of the arrest, and he also gave the respondent the Miranda warnings. Immediately thereafter, Captain Leyden and other police officers arrived. Captain Leyden advised the respondent of his Miranda rights. The respondent stated that he understood those rights and wanted to speak with a lawyer. Captain Leyden then directed that the respondent be placed in a "caged wagon," a four-door police car with a wire screen mesh between the front and rear seats, and be driven to the central police station. Three officers, Patrolmen Gleckman, Williams, and McKenna, were assigned to accompany the respondent to the central station. They placed the respondent in the vehicle and shut the doors. Captain Leyden then instructed the officers not to question the respondent or intimidate or coerce him in any way. The three officers then entered the vehicle, and it departed.

While en route to the central station, Patrolman Gleckman initiated a conversation with Patrolman McKenna concerning the missing shotgun. As Patrolman Gleckman later testified:

> "At this point, I was talking back and forth with Patrolman McKenna stating that I frequent this area while on patrol and that because a school for handicapped children is located nearby, there's a lot of handicapped children running around in this area, and God forbid one of them might find a weapon with shells and they might hurt themselves."

Patrolman McKenna apparently shared his fellow officer's concern:

> "I more or less concurred with him [Gleckman] that it was a safety factor and that we should, you know, continue to search for the weapon and try to find it."

While Patrolman Williams said nothing, he overheard the conversation between the two officers:

> "He [Gleckman] said it would be too bad if the little—I believe he said a girl—would pick up the gun, maybe kill herself."

The respondent then interrupted the conversation, stating that the officers should turn the car around so he could show them where the gun was located. At this point, Patrolman McKenna radioed back to Captain Leyden that they were returning to the scene of the arrest and that the respondent would inform them of the location of the gun. At the time the respondent indicated that the officers should turn back, they had traveled no more than a mile, a trip encompassing only a few minutes.

The police vehicle then returned to the scene of the arrest where a search for the shotgun was in progress. There, Captain Leyden again advised the respondent of his Miranda rights. The respondent replied that he understood those rights but that he "wanted to get the gun out of the way because of the kids in the area in the school." The respondent then led the police to a nearby field, where he pointed out the shotgun under some rocks by the side of the road.

On March 20, 1975, a grand jury returned an indictment charging the respondent with the kidnaping, robbery, and murder of John Mulvaney. Before trial, the respondent moved to suppress the shotgun and the statements he had made to the police regarding it. After an evidentiary hearing at which the respondent elected not to testify, the trial judge ... sustained the admissibility of the shotgun and testimony related to its discovery. That evidence was later introduced at the respondent's trial, and the jury returned a verdict of guilty on all counts.

.... We granted certiorari to address for the first time the meaning of "interrogation" under Miranda v. Arizona.

II

.... In the present case, the parties are in agreement that the respondent was fully informed of his Miranda rights and that he invoked his Miranda right to counsel when he told Captain Leyden that he wished to consult with a lawyer. It is also uncontested that the respondent was "in custody" while being transported to the police station.

The issue, therefore, is whether the respondent was "interrogated" by the police officers in violation of the respondent's undisputed right under Miranda to remain silent until he had consulted with a lawyer. In resolving this issue, we first define the term "interrogation" under Miranda before turning to a consideration of the facts of this case.

A

The starting point for defining "interrogation" in this context is, of course, the Court's Miranda opinion. There the Court observed that "by custodial interrogation, we mean *questioning* initiated by law enforcement officers after a person has been taken into custody or otherwise deprived of his freedom of action in any significant way." This passage and other references throughout the opinion to "questioning" might suggest that the Miranda rules were to apply only to those police interrogation practices that involve express questioning of a defendant while in custody.

We do not, however, construe the Miranda opinion so narrowly....

We conclude that the Miranda safeguards come into play whenever a person in custody is subjected to either express questioning or its functional equivalent. That is to say, the term "interrogation" under Miranda refers not only to express questioning, but also to any words or actions on the part of the police (other than those normally attendant to arrest and custody) that the police should know are reasonably likely to elicit an incriminating response from the suspect. The latter portion of this definition focuses primarily upon the perceptions of the suspect, rather than the intent of the police. This focus reflects the fact that the Miranda safeguards were designed to vest a suspect in custody with an added measure of protection against coercive police practices, without regard to objective proof of the underlying intent of the police. A practice that the police should know is reasonably likely to evoke an incriminating response from a suspect thus amounts to interrogation.[7]

But, since the police surely cannot be held accountable for the unforeseeable results of their words or actions, the definition of interrogation can extend only to words or actions on the part of police officers that they should have known were reasonably likely to elicit an incriminating response.

B

Turning to the facts of the present case, we conclude that the respondent was not "interrogated" within the meaning of Miranda. It is undisputed that the first prong of the definition of "interrogation" was not satisfied, for the conversation between Patrolmen Gleckman and McKenna included no express questioning of the respondent. Rather, that conversation was, at least in form, nothing more than a dialogue between the two officers to which no response from the respondent was invited.

Moreover, it cannot be fairly concluded that the respondent was subjected to the "functional equivalent" of questioning. It cannot be said, in short, that Patrolmen Gleckman and McKenna should have known that their conversation was reasonably likely to elicit an incriminating response from the respondent. There is nothing in the record to suggest that the officers were aware that the respondent was peculiarly susceptible to an appeal to his conscience concerning the safety of handicapped children. Nor is there anything in the record to suggest that the police

---

[7] This is not to say that the intent of the police is irrelevant, for it may well have a bearing on whether the police should have known that their words or actions were reasonably likely to evoke an incriminating response. In particular, where a police practice is designed to elicit an incriminating response from the accused, it is unlikely that the practice will not also be one which the police should have known was reasonably likely to have that effect.

knew that the respondent was unusually disoriented or upset at the time of his arrest.

The case thus boils down to whether, in the context of a brief conversation, the officers should have known that the respondent would suddenly be moved to make a self-incriminating response. Given the fact that the entire conversation appears to have consisted of no more than a few off hand remarks, we cannot say that the officers should have known that it was reasonably likely that Innis would so respond. This is not a case where the police carried on a lengthy harangue in the presence of the suspect. Nor does the record support the respondent's contention that, under the circumstances, the officers' comments were particularly "evocative." It is our view, therefore, that the respondent was not subjected by the police to words or actions that the police should have known were reasonably likely to elicit an incriminating response from him.

The Rhode Island Supreme Court erred, in short, in equating "subtle compulsion" with interrogation. That the officers' comments struck a responsive chord is readily apparent. Thus, it may be said, as the Rhode Island Supreme Court did say, that the respondent was subjected to "subtle compulsion." But that is not the end of the inquiry. It must also be established that a suspect's incriminating response was the product of words or actions on the part of the police that they should have known were reasonably likely to elicit an incriminating response. This was not established in the present case.

MARSHALL, J. dissenting:

I am substantially in agreement with the Court's definition of "interrogation" within the meaning of Miranda v. Arizona…. The Court requires an objective inquiry into the likely effect of police conduct on a typical individual, taking into account any special susceptibility of the suspect to certain kinds of pressure of which the police know or have reason to know.

I am utterly at a loss, however, to understand how this objective standard as applied to the facts before us can rationally lead to the conclusion that there was no interrogation…. Gleckman's remarks would obviously have constituted interrogation if they had been explicitly directed to respondent, and the result should not be different because they were nominally addressed to McKenna. This is not a case where police officers speaking among themselves are accidentally overheard by a suspect. These officers were "talking back and forth" in close quarters with the handcuffed suspect, traveling past the very place where they believed the weapon was located. They knew respondent would hear and attend to their conversation, and they are chargeable with knowledge of and responsibility for the pressures to speak which they created....

In *Innis,* the Supreme Court explained that: "The concern of the Court in *Miranda* was that the 'interrogation environment' created by the interplay of interrogation and custody would 'subjugate the individual to the will of his examiner' and thereby undermine the privilege against compulsory self-incrimination." The next case further illustrates how interrogation and custody work together to trigger the Fifth Amendment's prohibition of **compelled** self-incrimination.

ILLINOIS v. PERKINS
496 U.S. 292 (1990)

Justice KENNEDY delivered the opinion of the Court.

An undercover government agent was placed in the cell of respondent Lloyd Perkins, who was incarcerated on charges unrelated to the subject of the agent's investigation. Respondent made statements that implicated him in the crime that the agent sought to solve. Respondent claims that the statements should be inadmissible because he had not been given Miranda warnings by the agent. We hold that the statements are admissible. Miranda warnings are not required when the suspect is unaware that he is speaking to a law enforcement officer and gives a voluntary statement....

It is the premise of Miranda that the danger of coercion results from the interaction of custody and official interrogation. We reject the argument that Miranda warnings are required whenever a suspect is in custody in a technical sense and converses with someone who happens to be a government agent. Questioning by captors, who appear to control the suspect's fate, may create mutually reinforcing pressures that the Court has assumed will weaken the suspect's will, but where a suspect does not know that he is conversing with a government agent, these pressures do not exist. The state court here mistakenly assumed that because the suspect was in custody, no undercover questioning could take place. When the suspect has no reason to think that the listeners have official power over him, it should not be assumed that his words are motivated by the reaction he expects from his listeners.

When the agent carries neither badge nor gun and wears not "police blue," but the same prison gray as the suspect, there is no interplay between police interrogation and police custody.

Miranda forbids coercion, not mere strategic deception by taking advantage of a suspect's misplaced trust in one he supposes to be a fellow prisoner. As we recognized in Miranda: "Confessions remain a proper element in law enforcement. Any statement given freely and voluntarily without any compelling influences is, of course, admissible in evidence." Ploys to mislead a suspect or lull him into a false sense of security that do not rise to the level of compulsion or coercion to speak are not within Miranda's concerns.

Miranda was not meant to protect suspects from boasting about their criminal activities in front of persons whom they believe to be their cellmates....

ROUTINE BOOKING QUESTIONS

Justice Brennan's opinion in *Pennsylvania v. Muniz* (1990) recognized a: "'routine booking question' exception which exempts from Miranda's coverage questions to secure the biographical data necessary to complete booking or pretrial services." Only four Justices endorsed that part of the opinion. Four other Justices deemed it "unnecessary to determine whether the questions fall within the 'routine booking question' exception to *Miranda* Justice Brennan recognizes." One Justice explicitly disagreed that there was such an exception.

The majority opinion in *Rhode Island v. Innis*, however, appears to endorse something like the booking question exception in the bolded language in the following sentence:

> "That is to say, the term 'interrogation' under Miranda refers not only to express questioning, but also to any words or actions on the part of the police **(other than those normally attendant to arrest and custody)** that the police should know are reasonably likely to elicit an incriminating response from the suspect."

The reference in *Innis* is cursory, however, and likely incomplete. For instance, Justice Brennan, in a footnote in *Muniz*, recognized an important caveat to any booking question exception:

> "Recognizing a 'booking exception' to Miranda does not mean, of course, that any question asked during the booking process falls within that exception. Without obtaining a waiver of the suspect's Miranda rights, the police may not ask questions, even during booking, that are designed to elicit incriminatory admissions."

This caveat resonates with the Supreme Court's analysis in *Hiibel v. Sixth Judicial District Court of Nevada* (2004), discussed earlier, where the Court recognized that, "a case may arise where there is a substantial allegation that furnishing identity at the time of a stop would have given the police a link in the chain of evidence needed to convict the individual of a separate offense." The same would presumably be true for booking questions.

Putting these pieces together, it seems that any booking question exception to *Miranda*, like the Fifth Amendment generally, must turn on the likelihood that a particular question will elicit incriminating information. And that inquiry will depend on the facts of the particular case. One lower court, adapting the "interrogation" definition from *Innis* without the parenthetical, frames the inquiry as follows:

> "Ultimately, the booking exception's applicability turns on an 'objective' test that asks whether the questions and circumstances were such that the officer should have reasonably expected the questions to elicit an incriminating response."[30]

4. MIRANDA INVOCATION AND WAIVER

Miranda requires police officers, prior to any questioning, to communicate to an in-custody suspect that the suspect can sit silently in the face of police questioning without penalty. This section addresses the related, but distinct, questions of: (1)

---

[30] United States v. Sanchez, 817 F.3d 38 (1st Cir. 2016).

when the police must stop questioning a suspect altogether ("invocation"), and (2) what constitutes a valid waiver of the *Miranda* rights ("waiver").

EDWARDS v. ARIZONA
451 U.S. 477 (1981)

Justice WHITE delivered the opinion of the Court.

. . . On January 19, 1976, a sworn complaint was filed against Robert Edwards in Arizona state court charging him with robbery, burglary, and first-degree murder. An arrest warrant was issued pursuant to the complaint, and Edwards was arrested at his home later that same day. At the police station, he was informed of his rights as required by Miranda v. Arizona. Petitioner stated that he understood his rights, and was willing to submit to questioning. After being told that another suspect already in custody had implicated him in the crime, Edwards denied involvement and gave a taped statement presenting an alibi defense. He then sought to "make a deal." The interrogating officer told him that he wanted a statement, but that he did not have the authority to negotiate a deal. The officer provided Edwards with the telephone number of a county attorney. Petitioner made the call, but hung up after a few moments. Edwards then said: "I want an attorney before making a deal." At that point, questioning ceased and Edwards was taken to county jail.

At 9:15 the next morning, two detectives, colleagues of the officer who had interrogated Edwards the previous night, came to the jail and asked to see Edwards. When the detention officer informed Edwards that the detectives wished to speak with him, he replied that he did not want to talk to anyone. The guard told him that "he had" to talk and then took him to meet with the detectives. The officers identified themselves, stated they wanted to talk to him, and informed him of his Miranda rights. Edwards was willing to talk, but he first wanted to hear the taped statement of the alleged accomplice who had implicated him. After listening to the tape for several minutes, petitioner said that he would make a statement so long as it was not tape-recorded. The detectives informed him that the recording was irrelevant since they could testify in court concerning whatever he said. Edwards replied: "I'll tell you anything you want to know, but I don't want it on tape." He thereupon implicated himself in the crime.

Prior to trial, Edwards moved to suppress his confession on the ground that his Miranda rights had been violated when the officers returned to question him after he had invoked his right to counsel.... [The trial court denied the motion and] evidence concerning his confession was admitted at trial.

Because the use of Edwards' confession against him at his trial violated his rights under the Fifth and Fourteenth Amendments as construed in Miranda v. Arizona, we reverse....

Although we have held that after initially being advised of his Miranda rights, the accused may himself validly waive his rights and respond to interrogation, the Court has strongly indicated that additional safeguards are necessary when the accused asks for counsel; and we now hold that when an accused has invoked his right to have counsel present during custodial interrogation, a valid waiver of that right cannot be established by showing only that he responded to further police-initiated custodial interrogation even if he has been advised of his rights. We further hold that an accused, such as Edwards, having expressed his desire to deal with the police only through counsel, is not subject to further interrogation by the authorities until counsel has been made available to him, unless the accused himself initiates further communication, exchanges, or conversations with the police.

Miranda itself indicated that the assertion of the right to counsel was a significant event and that once exercised by the accused, "the interrogation must cease until an attorney is present." Our later cases have not abandoned that view. In Michigan v. Mosley (1975), the Court noted that Miranda had distinguished between the procedural safeguards triggered by a request to remain silent and a request for an attorney and had required that interrogation cease until an attorney was present only if the individual stated that he wanted counsel. In Fare v. Michael C. (1979), the Court referred to Miranda's "rigid rule that an accused's request for an attorney is per se an invocation of his Fifth Amendment rights, requiring that all interrogation cease." And just last Term, in a case where a suspect in custody had invoked his Miranda right to counsel, the Court again referred to the "undisputed right" under Miranda to remain silent and to be free of interrogation "until he had consulted with a lawyer." Rhode Island v. Innis (1980). We reconfirm these views and, to lend them substance, emphasize that it is inconsistent with Miranda and its progeny for the authorities, at their instance, to reinterrogate an accused in custody if he has clearly asserted his right to counsel.

In concluding that the fruits of the interrogation initiated by the police on January 20 could not be used against Edwards, we do not hold or imply that Edwards was powerless to countermand his election or that the authorities could in no event use any incriminating statements made by Edwards prior to his having access to counsel. Had Edwards initiated the meeting on January 20, nothing in the Fifth and Fourteenth Amendments would prohibit the police from merely listening to his voluntary, volunteered statements and using them against him at the trial. The Fifth Amendment right identified in Miranda is the right to have counsel present at any custodial interrogation. Absent such interrogation, there would have been no infringement of the right that Edwards invoked and there would be no occasion to determine whether there had been a valid waiver.

But this is not what the facts of this case show. Here, the officers conducting the interrogation on the evening of January 19 ceased interrogation when Edwards requested counsel as he had been advised he had the right to do. The Arizona Supreme Court was of the opinion that this was a sufficient invocation of his Miranda rights, and we are in accord. It is also clear that without making counsel available to Edwards, the police returned to him the next day. This was not at his suggestion or request. Indeed, Edwards informed the detention officer that he did not want to talk to anyone. At the meeting, the detectives told Edwards that they wanted to talk to him and again advised him of his Miranda rights. Edwards stated that he would talk, but what prompted this action does not appear. He listened at his own request to part of the taped statement made by one of his alleged accomplices and then made an incriminating statement, which was used against him at his trial. We think it is clear that Edwards was subjected to custodial interrogation on January 20 and that this occurred at the instance of the authorities. His statement made without having had access to counsel, did not amount to a valid waiver and hence was inadmissible.

In a later case, the Supreme Court summarized *Edwards* as follows:

> "The rationale of Edwards is that once a suspect indicates that he is not capable of undergoing custodial questioning without advice of counsel, any subsequent waiver that has come at the authorities' behest, and not at the suspect's own instigation, is itself the product of the inherently compelling pressures and not the purely voluntary choice of the suspect. Under this rule, a voluntary Miranda waiver is sufficient at the time of an initial attempted interrogation to protect a suspect's right to have counsel

present, but it is not sufficient at the time of subsequent attempts if the suspect initially requested the presence of counsel."

Edwards briefly distinguishes *Michigan v. Mosley* (1975) as a case that involved "a request to remain silent" rather than "a request for an attorney." In *Mosley*, the Supreme Court ruled that the police did not violate *Miranda* when they questioned a suspect in police custody about a murder, even though the suspect had earlier invoked his *Miranda* rights when questioned about a series of robberies. The Court explained that "the admissibility of statements obtained after the person in custody has decided to remain silent depends under Miranda on whether his right to cut off questioning was 'scrupulously honored.'" The Court applied that test to the circumstances of the case as follows:

> A review of the circumstances leading to Mosley's confession reveals that his "right to cut off questioning" was fully respected in this case. Before his initial interrogation, Mosley was carefully advised that he was under no obligation to answer any questions and could remain silent if he wished.... When Mosley stated that he did not want to discuss the robberies, Detective Cowie immediately ceased the interrogation and did not try either to resume the questioning or in any way to persuade Mosley to reconsider his position. After an interval of more than two hours, Mosley was questioned by another police officer at another location about an unrelated holdup murder. He was given full and complete Miranda warnings at the outset of the second interrogation. He was thus reminded again that he could remain silent and could consult with a lawyer, and was carefully given a full and fair opportunity to exercise these options. The subsequent questioning did not undercut Mosley's previous decision not to answer Detective Cowie's inquiries. Detective Hill did not resume the interrogation about the [robberies], but instead focused exclusively on the Leroy Williams homicide, a crime different in nature and in time and place of occurrence from the robberies for which Mosley had been arrested and interrogated by Detective Cowie. Although it is not clear from the record how much Detective Hill knew about the earlier interrogation, his questioning of Mosley about an unrelated homicide was quite consistent with a reasonable interpretation of Mosley's earlier refusal to answer any questions about the robberies.

The *Mosley* opinion emphasized that "at no time during the questioning did Mosley indicate a desire to consult with a lawyer."

Even an invocation of the *Miranda* right to counsel will not last forever. In *Maryland v. Shatzer* (2010), the Supreme Court held that police could reapproach a suspect who invoked the *Miranda* right to an attorney during questioning if there had been a break in *Miranda* custody of at least 14 days.

DAVIS v. UNITED STATES
512 U.S. 452 (1994)

Justice O'CONNOR delivered the opinion of the Court.

In Edwards v. Arizona (1981), we held that law enforcement officers must immediately cease questioning a suspect who has clearly asserted his right to have counsel present during custodial interrogation. In this case we decide how law enforcement officers should respond when a suspect makes a reference to counsel that is insufficiently clear to invoke the Edwards prohibition on further questioning.

... Petitioner Robert Davis, a member of the United States Navy, spent the evening of October 2, 1988, shooting pool at a club on the base. Another sailor, Keith Shackleton, lost a game and a $30 wager to petitioner, but Shackleton refused to pay. After the club closed, Shackleton was beaten to death with a pool cue on a loading dock behind the commissary. The body was found early the next morning.

The investigation by the Naval Investigative Service (NIS) gradually focused on petitioner. Investigative agents determined that petitioner was at the club that evening, and that he was absent without authorization from his duty station the next morning. The agents also learned that only privately owned pool cues could be removed from the club premises, and that petitioner owned two cues—one of which had a bloodstain on it. The agents were told by various people that petitioner either had admitted committing the crime or had recounted details that clearly indicated his involvement in the killing.

On November 4, 1988, petitioner was interviewed at the NIS office. As required by military law, the agents advised petitioner that he was a suspect in the killing, that he was not required to make a statement, that any statement could be used against him at a trial by court-martial, and that he was entitled to speak with an attorney and have an attorney present during questioning. Petitioner waived his rights to remain silent and to counsel, both orally and in writing.

About an hour and a half into the interview, petitioner said, "Maybe I should talk to a lawyer." According to the uncontradicted testimony of one of the interviewing agents, the interview then proceeded as follows:

> "We made it very clear that we're not here to violate his rights, that if he wants a lawyer, then we will stop any kind of questioning with him, that we weren't going to pursue the matter unless we have it clarified is he asking for a lawyer or is he just making a comment about a lawyer, and he said, 'No, I'm not asking for a lawyer,' and then he continued on, and said, 'No, I don't want a lawyer.'"

After a short break, the agents reminded petitioner of his rights to remain silent and to counsel. The interview then continued for another hour, until petitioner said, "I think I want a lawyer before I say anything else." At that point, questioning ceased.

At his general court-martial, petitioner moved to suppress statements made during the November 4 interview. The Military Judge denied the motion, holding that "the mention of a lawyer by [petitioner] during the course of the interrogation was not in the form of a request for counsel and ... the agents properly determined that [petitioner] was not indicating a desire for or invoking his right to counsel." Petitioner was convicted . . . of unpremeditated murder....

The applicability of the rigid prophylactic rule of Edwards requires courts to determine whether the accused *actually invoked* his right to counsel. To avoid difficulties of proof and to provide guidance to officers conducting interrogations, this is an objective inquiry. Invocation of the Miranda right to counsel requires, at a minimum, some statement that can reasonably be construed to be an expression of a desire for the assistance of an attorney. But if a suspect makes a reference to an attorney that is ambiguous or equivocal in that a reasonable officer in light of the circumstances would have understood only that the suspect *might* be invoking the right to counsel, our precedents do not require the cessation of questioning.

Rather, the suspect must unambiguously request counsel. As we have observed, "a statement either is such an assertion of the right to counsel or it is not." Although a suspect need not "speak with the discrimination of an Oxford don," he must articulate his desire to have counsel present sufficiently clearly that a reasonable police officer in the circumstances would understand the statement to be a request for an attorney. If the statement fails to meet the requisite level of clarity, Edwards does not require that the officers stop questioning the suspect.

…. The rationale underlying Edwards is that the police must respect a suspect's wishes regarding his right to have an attorney present during custodial interrogation. But when the officers conducting the questioning reasonably do not know whether or not the suspect wants a lawyer, a rule requiring the immediate cessation of questioning would transform the Miranda safeguards into wholly irrational obstacles to legitimate police investigative activity, because it would needlessly prevent the police from questioning a suspect in the absence of counsel even if the suspect did not wish to have a lawyer present. Nothing in Edwards requires the provision of counsel to a suspect who consents to answer questions without the assistance of a lawyer. In Miranda itself, we expressly rejected the suggestion "that each police station must have a 'station house lawyer' present at all times to advise prisoners," and held instead that a suspect must be told of his right to have an attorney present and that he may not be questioned after invoking his right to counsel. We also noted that if a suspect is "indecisive in his request for counsel," the officers need not always cease questioning.

We recognize that requiring a clear assertion of the right to counsel might disadvantage some suspects who—because of fear, intimidation, lack of linguistic skills, or a variety of other reasons—will not clearly articulate their right to counsel although they actually want to have a lawyer present. But the primary protection afforded suspects subject to custodial interrogation is the Miranda warnings themselves. Full comprehension of the rights to remain silent and request an attorney is sufficient to dispel whatever coercion is inherent in the interrogation process. A suspect who knowingly and voluntarily waives his right to counsel after having that right explained to him has indicated his willingness to deal with the police unassisted. Although Edwards provides an additional protection—if a suspect subsequently requests an attorney, questioning must cease—it is one that must be affirmatively invoked by the suspect.

In considering how a suspect must invoke the right to counsel, we must consider the other side of the Miranda equation: the need for effective law enforcement. Although the courts ensure compliance with the Miranda requirements through the exclusionary rule, it is police officers who must actually decide whether or not they can question a suspect. The Edwards rule—questioning must cease if the suspect asks for a lawyer—provides a bright line that can be applied by officers in the real world of investigation and interrogation without unduly hampering the gathering of information. But if we were to require questioning to cease if a suspect makes a statement that *might* be a request for an attorney, this clarity and ease of application would be lost. Police officers would be forced to make difficult judgment calls about whether the suspect in fact wants a lawyer even though he has not said so, with the threat of suppression if they guess wrong. We therefore hold that, after a knowing and voluntary waiver of the Miranda rights, law enforcement officers may continue questioning until and unless the suspect clearly requests an attorney.

Of course, when a suspect makes an ambiguous or equivocal statement it will often be good police practice for the interviewing officers to clarify whether or not he actually wants an attorney. That was the procedure followed by the NIS agents in this case. Clarifying questions help protect the rights of the suspect by ensuring that he gets an attorney if he wants one, and will minimize the chance of a confession being suppressed due to subsequent judicial second-guessing as to the meaning of the suspect's statement regarding counsel. But we decline to adopt a rule requiring officers to ask clarifying questions. If the suspect's statement is not an unambiguous or unequivocal request for counsel, the officers have no obligation to stop questioning him.

To recapitulate: We held in Miranda that a suspect is entitled to the assistance of counsel during custodial interrogation even though the Constitution does not provide for such assistance. We held in Edwards that if the suspect invokes the right to counsel at any time, the police must immediately cease questioning him until an attorney is present. But we are unwilling to create a third layer of prophylaxis to prevent police questioning when the suspect *might* want a lawyer. Unless the suspect actually requests an attorney, questioning may continue.

The courts below found that petitioner's remark to the NIS agents—"Maybe I should talk to a lawyer"—was not a request for counsel, and we see no reason to disturb that conclusion....

BERGHUIS v. THOMPKINS
560 U.S. 370 (2010)

Justice KENNEDY delivered the opinion of the Court.

I

On January 10, 2000, a shooting occurred outside a mall in Southfield, Michigan. Among the victims was Samuel Morris, who died from multiple gunshot wounds. The other victim, Frederick France, recovered from his injuries and later testified. Van Chester Thompkins, who was a suspect, fled. About one year later he was found in Ohio and arrested there.

Two Southfield police officers traveled to Ohio to interrogate Thompkins, then awaiting transfer to Michigan. The interrogation began around 1:30 p.m. and lasted about three hours. The interrogation was conducted in a room that was 8 by 10 feet, and Thompkins sat in a chair that resembled a school desk (it had an arm on it that swings around to provide a surface to write on). At the beginning of the interrogation, one of the officers, Detective Helgert, presented Thompkins with a form derived from the Miranda rule. It stated:

"NOTIFICATION OF CONSTITUTIONAL RIGHTS AND STATEMENT

"1. You have the right to remain silent.

"2. Anything you say can and will be used against you in a court of law.

"3. You have a right to talk to a lawyer before answering any questions and you have the right to have a lawyer present with you while you are answering any questions.

"4. If you cannot afford to hire a lawyer, one will be appointed to represent you before any questioning, if you wish one.

"5. You have the right to decide at any time before or during questioning to use your right to remain silent and your right to talk with a lawyer while you are being questioned."

Helgert asked Thompkins to read the fifth warning out loud. Thompkins complied. Helgert later said this was to ensure that Thompkins could read, and Helgert concluded that Thompkins understood English. Helgert then read the other four Miranda warnings out loud and asked Thompkins to sign the form to demonstrate that he understood his rights. Thompkins declined to sign the form. The record contains conflicting evidence about whether Thompkins then verbally confirmed that he understood the rights listed on the form.

Officers began an interrogation. At no point during the interrogation did Thompkins say that he wanted to remain silent, that he did not want to talk with the police, or that he wanted an attorney. Thompkins was "largely" silent during the interrogation, which lasted about three hours. He did give a few limited verbal responses, however, such as "yeah," "no," or "I don't know." And on occasion he communicated by nodding his head. Thompkins also said that he "didn't want a peppermint" that was offered to him by the police and that the chair he was "sitting in was hard."

About 2 hours and 45 minutes into the interrogation, Helgert asked Thompkins, "Do you believe in God?" Thompkins made eye contact with Helgert and said "Yes," as his eyes "welled up with tears." Helgert asked, "Do you pray to God?" Thompkins said "Yes." Helgert asked, "Do you pray to God to forgive you for shooting that boy down?" Thompkins answered "Yes" and looked away. Thompkins refused to make a written confession, and the interrogation ended about 15 minutes later. Thompkins was charged with first-degree murder, assault with intent to commit murder, and certain firearms-related offenses. He moved to suppress the statements made during the interrogation. He argued that he had invoked his Fifth Amendment right to remain silent, requiring police to end the interrogation at once, that he had not waived his right to remain silent, and that his inculpatory statements were involuntary. The trial court denied the motion....

[After a trial, the] jury found Thompkins guilty on all counts. He was sentenced to life in prison without parole....

III

A

The Miranda Court formulated a warning that must be given to suspects before they can be subjected to custodial interrogation. The substance of the warning still must be given to suspects today.... All concede that the warning given in this case was in full compliance with these requirements. The dispute centers on the response—or nonresponse—from the suspect.

Thompkins makes various arguments that his answers to questions from the detectives were inadmissible. He first contends that he "invoked his privilege" to remain silent by not saying anything for a sufficient period of time, so the interrogation should have "ceased" before he made his inculpatory statements.

This argument is unpersuasive. In the context of invoking the Miranda right to counsel, the Court in Davis v. United States (1994) held that a suspect must do so "unambiguously." If an accused makes a statement concerning the right to counsel "that is ambiguous or equivocal" or makes no statement, the police are not required to end the interrogation or ask questions to clarify whether the accused wants to invoke his or her Miranda rights.

The Court has not yet stated whether an invocation of the right to remain silent can be ambiguous or equivocal, but there is no principled reason to adopt different standards for determining when an accused has invoked the Miranda right to remain silent and the Miranda right to counsel at issue in Davis. Both protect the privilege against compulsory self-incrimination by requiring an interrogation to cease when either right is invoked.

There is good reason to require an accused who wants to invoke his or her right to remain silent to do so unambiguously. A requirement of an unambiguous invocation of Miranda rights results in an objective inquiry that avoids difficulties of proof and provides guidance to officers on how to proceed in the face of ambiguity. If an ambiguous act, omission, or statement could require police to end the interrogation, police would be required to make difficult decisions about an accused's unclear intent and face the consequence of suppression if they guess wrong. Suppression of a voluntary confession in these circumstances would place a significant burden on society's interest in prosecuting criminal activity. Treating an ambiguous or equivocal act, omission, or statement as an invocation of Miranda rights might add marginally to Miranda's goal of dispelling the compulsion inherent in custodial interrogation. But as Miranda holds, full comprehension of the rights to remain silent and request an attorney are sufficient to dispel whatever coercion is inherent in the interrogation process.

Thompkins did not say that he wanted to remain silent or that he did not want to talk with the police. Had he made either of these simple, unambiguous statements,

541

he would have invoked his "right to cut off questioning." Here he did neither, so he did not invoke his right to remain silent.

B

We next consider whether Thompkins waived his right to remain silent. Even absent the accused's invocation of the right to remain silent, the accused's statement during a custodial interrogation is inadmissible at trial unless the prosecution can establish that the accused in fact knowingly and voluntarily waived Miranda rights when making the statement. The waiver inquiry has two distinct dimensions: waiver must be voluntary in the sense that it was the product of a free and deliberate choice rather than intimidation, coercion, or deception, and made with a full awareness of both the nature of the right being abandoned and the consequences of the decision to abandon it.

Some language in Miranda could be read to indicate that waivers are difficult to establish absent an explicit written waiver or a formal, express oral statement. Miranda said "a valid waiver will not be presumed simply from the silence of the accused after warnings are given or simply from the fact that a confession was in fact eventually obtained." In addition, the Miranda Court stated that "a heavy burden rests on the government to demonstrate that the defendant knowingly and intelligently waived his privilege against self-incrimination and his right to retained or appointed counsel."

The course of decisions since Miranda, informed by the application of Miranda warnings in the whole course of law enforcement, demonstrates that waivers can be established even absent formal or express statements of waiver that would be expected in, say, a judicial hearing to determine if a guilty plea has been properly entered. The main purpose of Miranda is to ensure that an accused is advised of and understands the right to remain silent and the right to counsel. Thus, if anything, our subsequent cases have reduced the impact of the Miranda rule on legitimate law enforcement while reaffirming the decision's core ruling that unwarned statements may not be used as evidence in the prosecution's case in chief.

One of the first cases to decide the meaning and import of Miranda with respect to the question of waiver was North Carolina v. Butler (1979). The Butler Court, after discussing some of the problems created by the language in Miranda, established certain important propositions. Butler interpreted the Miranda language concerning the "heavy burden" to show waiver, in accord with usual principles of determining waiver, which can include waiver implied from all the circumstances. And in a later case, the Court stated that this "heavy burden" is not more than the burden to establish waiver by a preponderance of the evidence.

The prosecution therefore does not need to show that a waiver of Miranda rights was express. An "implicit waiver" of the right to remain silent is sufficient to admit a suspect's statement into evidence. Butler made clear that a waiver of Miranda rights may be implied through "the defendant's silence, coupled with an understanding of his rights and a course of conduct indicating waiver." The Court in Butler therefore "retreated" from the "language and tenor of the Miranda opinion," which "suggested that the Court would require that a waiver be 'specifically made.'"

If the State establishes that a Miranda warning was given and the accused made an uncoerced statement, this showing, standing alone, is insufficient to demonstrate "a valid waiver" of Miranda rights. The prosecution must make the additional showing that the accused understood these rights. Where the prosecution shows that a Miranda warning was given and that it was understood by the accused, an accused's uncoerced statement establishes an implied waiver of the right to remain silent.

…. The record in this case shows that Thompkins waived his right to remain silent. There is no basis in this case to conclude that he did not understand his rights; and on these facts it follows that he chose not to invoke or rely on those rights when he did speak. First, there is no contention that Thompkins did not understand his rights; and from this it follows that he knew what he gave up when he spoke. There was more than enough evidence in the record to conclude that Thompkins understood his Miranda rights. Thompkins received a written copy of the Miranda warnings; Detective Helgert determined that Thompkins could read and understand English; and Thompkins was given time to read the warnings. Thompkins, furthermore, read aloud the fifth warning, which stated that "you have the right to decide at any time before or during questioning to use your right to remain silent and your right to talk with a lawyer while you are being questioned." He was thus aware that his right to remain silent would not dissipate after a certain amount of time and that police would have to honor his right to be silent and his right to counsel during the whole course of interrogation. Those rights, the warning made clear, could be asserted at any time. Helgert, moreover, read the warnings aloud.

Second, Thompkins' answer to Detective Helgert's question about whether Thompkins prayed to God for forgiveness for shooting the victim is a "course of conduct indicating waiver" of the right to remain silent. If Thompkins wanted to remain silent, he could have said nothing in response to Helgert's questions, or he could have unambiguously invoked his Miranda rights and ended the interrogation. The fact that Thompkins made a statement about three hours after receiving a Miranda warning does not overcome the fact that he engaged in a course of conduct indicating waiver. Police are not required to rewarn suspects from time to time. Thompkins' answer to Helgert's question about praying to God for forgiveness for shooting the victim was sufficient to show a course of conduct indicating waiver. This is confirmed by the fact that before then Thompkins had given sporadic answers to questions throughout the interrogation.

Third, there is no evidence that Thompkins' statement was coerced. Thompkins does not claim that police threatened or injured him during the interrogation or that he was in any way fearful. The interrogation was conducted in a standard-sized room in the middle of the afternoon. It is true that apparently he was in a straight-backed chair for three hours, but there is no authority for the proposition that an interrogation of this length is inherently coercive. Indeed, even where interrogations of greater duration were held to be improper, they were accompanied, as this one was not, by other facts indicating coercion, such as an incapacitated and sedated suspect, sleep and food deprivation, and threats. The fact that Helgert's question referred to Thompkins' religious beliefs also did not render Thompkins' statement involuntary. The Fifth Amendment privilege is not concerned with moral and psychological pressures to confess emanating from sources other than official coercion. In these circumstances, Thompkins knowingly and voluntarily made a statement to police, so he waived his right to remain silent....

D

In sum, a suspect who has received and understood the Miranda warnings, and has not invoked his Miranda rights, waives the right to remain silent by making an uncoerced statement to the police. Thompkins did not invoke his right to remain silent and stop the questioning. Understanding his rights in full, he waived his right to remain silent by making a voluntary statement to the police. The police, moreover, were not required to obtain a waiver of Thompkins' right to remain silent before interrogating him. The state court's decision rejecting Thompkins' Miranda claim was thus correct....

Justice SOTOMAYOR dissenting.

.... Today's decision turns Miranda upside down. Criminal suspects must now unambiguously invoke their right to remain silent—which, counterintuitively, requires them to speak. At the same time, suspects will be legally presumed to have waived their rights even if they have given no clear expression of their intent to do so. Those results, in my view, find no basis in Miranda or our subsequent cases and are inconsistent with the fair-trial principles on which those precedents are grounded....

Problem: Police Deception

Consider the question presented in *Moran v. Burbine* (1986):

> "After being informed of his rights pursuant to Miranda v. Arizona, and after executing a series of written waivers, Brian Burbine confessed to the murder of a young woman. At no point during the course of the interrogation, which occurred prior to arraignment, did he request an attorney. While he was in police custody, his sister attempted to retain a lawyer to represent him. The attorney telephoned the police station and received assurances that Burbine would not be questioned further until the next day. In fact, the interrogation session that yielded the inculpatory statements began later that evening. The question presented is whether either the conduct of the police or Burbine's ignorance of the attorney's efforts to reach him taints the validity of the waivers and therefore requires exclusion of the confessions."

Was the Fifth Amendment violated by the introduction of the confession obtained as described above?

5. PUBLIC SAFETY EXCEPTION

NEW YORK v. QUARLES
467 U.S. 649 (1984)

Justice REHNQUIST delivered the opinion of the Court.

…. On September 11, 1980, at approximately 12:30 a.m., … a woman approached [Officers Frank Kraft and Sal Scarring to report that "she had just been raped." She informed Kraft that the perpetrator] had just entered an A&P supermarket located nearby and that the man was carrying a gun.

The officers drove the woman to the supermarket, and Officer Kraft entered the store while Officer Scarring radioed for assistance. Officer Kraft quickly spotted respondent Benjamin Quarles, who matched the description given by the woman, approaching a checkout counter. Apparently upon seeing the officer, respondent turned and ran toward the rear of the store, and Officer Kraft pursued him with a drawn gun. When respondent turned the corner at the end of an aisle, Officer Kraft lost sight of him for several seconds, and upon regaining sight of respondent, ordered him to stop and put his hands over his head.

Although more than three other officers had arrived on the scene by that time, Officer Kraft was the first to reach respondent. He frisked him and discovered that he was wearing a shoulder holster which was then empty. After handcuffing him, Officer Kraft asked him where the gun was. Respondent nodded in the direction of some empty cartons and responded, "the gun is over there." Officer Kraft thereafter retrieved a loaded .38–caliber revolver from one of the cartons, formally placed respondent under arrest, and read him his Miranda rights from a printed card. Respondent indicated that he would be willing to answer questions without an attorney present. Officer Kraft then asked respondent if he owned the gun and where he had purchased it. Respondent answered that he did own it and that he had purchased it in Miami, Fla.

In the subsequent prosecution of respondent for criminal possession of a weapon, the judge excluded the statement, "the gun is over there," and the gun because the officer had not given respondent the warnings required by our decision in Miranda v. Arizona before asking him where the gun was located. The judge excluded the other statements about respondent's ownership of the gun and the place of purchase, as evidence tainted by the prior Miranda violation. The Appellate

Division of the Supreme Court of New York affirmed .... For the reasons which follow, we believe that this case presents a situation where concern for public safety must be paramount to adherence to the literal language of the prophylactic rules enunciated in Miranda.

The Fifth Amendment guarantees that "[n]o person ... shall be compelled in any criminal case to be a witness against himself." In Miranda this Court for the first time extended the Fifth Amendment privilege against compulsory self-incrimination to individuals subjected to custodial interrogation by the police. The Fifth Amendment itself does not prohibit all incriminating admissions; absent some officially coerced self-accusation, the Fifth Amendment privilege is not violated by even the most damning admissions. The Miranda Court, however, presumed that interrogation in certain custodial circumstances is inherently coercive and held that statements made under those circumstances are inadmissible unless the suspect is specifically informed of his Miranda rights and freely decides to forgo those rights. The prophylactic Miranda warnings therefore are not themselves rights protected by the Constitution but are instead measures to insure that the right against compulsory self-incrimination is protected. Requiring Miranda warnings before custodial interrogation provides practical reinforcement for the Fifth Amendment right.

In this case we have before us no claim that respondent's statements were actually compelled by police conduct which overcame his will to resist. Thus the only issue before us is whether Officer Kraft was justified in failing to make available to respondent the procedural safeguards associated with the privilege against compulsory self-incrimination since Miranda.[5]

The New York Court of Appeals was undoubtedly correct in deciding that the facts of this case come within the ambit of the Miranda decision as we have subsequently interpreted it. We agree that respondent was in police custody because we have noted that "the ultimate inquiry is simply whether there is a 'formal arrest or

---

[5] The dissent curiously takes us to task for "endorsing the introduction of coerced self-incriminating statements in criminal prosecutions," and for "sanctioning sub silentio criminal prosecutions based on compelled self-incriminating statements." Of course our decision today does nothing of the kind. As the Miranda Court itself recognized, the failure to provide Miranda warnings in and of itself does not render a confession involuntary, and respondent is certainly free on remand to argue that his statement was coerced under traditional due process standards....

restraint on freedom of movement' of the degree associated with a formal arrest." Here Quarles was surrounded by at least four police officers and was handcuffed when the questioning at issue took place....

We hold that on these facts there is a "public safety" exception to the requirement that Miranda warnings be given before a suspect's answers may be admitted into evidence, and that the availability of that exception does not depend upon the motivation of the individual officers involved. In a kaleidoscopic situation such as the one confronting these officers, where spontaneity rather than adherence to a police manual is necessarily the order of the day, the application of the exception which we recognize today should not be made to depend on post hoc findings at a suppression hearing concerning the subjective motivation of the arresting officer. Undoubtedly most police officers, if placed in Officer Kraft's position, would act out of a host of different, instinctive, and largely unverifiable motives—their own safety, the safety of others, and perhaps as well the desire to obtain incriminating evidence from the suspect.

Whatever the motivation of individual officers in such a situation, we do not believe that the doctrinal underpinnings of Miranda require that it be applied in all its rigor to a situation in which police officers ask questions reasonably prompted by a concern for the public safety....

The police in this case, in the very act of apprehending a suspect, were confronted with the immediate necessity of ascertaining the whereabouts of a gun which they had every reason to believe the suspect had just removed from his empty holster and discarded in the supermarket. So long as the gun was concealed somewhere in the supermarket, with its actual whereabouts unknown, it obviously posed more than one danger to the public safety: an accomplice might make use of it, a customer or employee might later come upon it.

In such a situation, if the police are required to recite the familiar Miranda warnings before asking the whereabouts of the gun, suspects in Quarles' position might well be deterred from responding. Procedural safeguards which deter a suspect from responding were deemed acceptable in Miranda in order to protect the Fifth Amendment privilege; when the primary social cost of those added protections is the possibility of fewer convictions, the Miranda majority was willing to bear that cost. Here, had Miranda warnings deterred Quarles from responding to Officer Kraft's question about the whereabouts of the gun, the cost would have been something more than merely the failure to obtain evidence useful in convicting Quarles. Officer Kraft needed an answer to his question not simply to make his case against Quarles but to insure that further danger to the public did not result from the concealment of the gun in a public area.

We conclude that the need for answers to questions in a situation posing a threat to the public safety outweighs the need for the prophylactic rule protecting the Fifth Amendment's privilege against self-incrimination. We decline to place officers such as Officer Kraft in the untenable position of having to consider, often in a matter of seconds, whether it best serves society for them to ask the necessary questions without the Miranda warnings and render whatever probative evidence they uncover inadmissible, or for them to give the warnings in order to preserve the admissibility of evidence they might uncover but possibly damage or destroy their ability to obtain that evidence and neutralize the volatile situation confronting them.

In recognizing a narrow exception to the Miranda rule in this case, we acknowledge that to some degree we lessen the desirable clarity of that rule.... As we have in other contexts, we recognize here the importance of a workable rule "to guide police officers, who have only limited time and expertise to reflect on and balance the social and individual interests involved in the specific circumstances they confront." But as we have pointed out, we believe that the exception which we recognize today lessens the necessity of that on-the-scene balancing process. The exception will not be difficult for police officers to apply because in each case it will be circumscribed by the exigency which justifies it. We think police officers can and will distinguish almost instinctively between questions necessary to secure their own safety or the safety of the public and questions designed solely to elicit testimonial evidence from a suspect.

The facts of this case clearly demonstrate that distinction and an officer's ability to recognize it. Officer Kraft asked only the question necessary to locate the missing gun before advising respondent of his rights. It was only after securing the loaded revolver and giving the warnings that he continued with investigatory questions about the ownership and place of purchase of the gun. The exception which we recognize today, far from complicating the thought processes and the on-the-scene judgments of police officers, will simply free them to follow their legitimate instincts when confronting situations presenting a danger to the public safety.[8]

We hold that the Court of Appeals in this case erred in excluding the statement, "the gun is over there," and the gun because of the officer's failure to read respondent his Miranda rights before attempting to locate the weapon. Accordingly we hold that it also erred in excluding the subsequent statements as illegal fruits of a Miranda violation. We therefore reverse and remand for further proceedings not inconsistent with this opinion.

Justice MARSHALL, dissenting:

…. The irony of the majority's decision is that the public's safety can be perfectly well protected without abridging the Fifth Amendment. If a bomb is about to explode or the public is otherwise imminently imperiled, the police are free to interrogate suspects without advising them of their constitutional rights. Such unconsented questioning may take place not only when police officers act on instinct but also when higher faculties lead them to believe that advising a suspect of his constitutional rights might decrease the likelihood that the suspect would reveal life-saving information…. While the Fourteenth Amendment sets limits on such behavior, nothing in the Fifth Amendment or our decision in Miranda v. Arizona proscribes this sort of emergency questioning. All the Fifth Amendment forbids is the introduction of coerced statements at trial….

---

[8] Although it involves police questions in part relating to the whereabouts of a gun, Orozco v. Texas (1969), is in no sense inconsistent with our disposition of this case. In Orozco four hours after a murder had been committed at a restaurant, four police officers entered the defendant's boardinghouse and awakened the defendant, who was sleeping in his bedroom. Without giving him Miranda warnings, they began vigorously to interrogate him about whether he had been present at the scene of the shooting and whether he owned a gun. The defendant eventually admitted that he had been present at the scene and directed the officers to a washing machine in the backroom of the boardinghouse where he had hidden the gun. We held that all the statements should have been suppressed. In Orozco, however, the questions about the gun were clearly investigatory; they did not in any way relate to an objectively reasonable need to protect the police or the public from any immediate danger associated with the weapon. In short there was no exigency requiring immediate action by the officers beyond the normal need expeditiously to solve a serious crime.

6. UNWARNED v. COMPELLED STATEMENTS

By commanding that a person cannot be compelled "to be a witness against himself" in a criminal case, the Fifth Amendment's text contains an implicit remedial provision. The text itself suggests that any compelled statement must be suppressed, along with any fruit of the poisonous tree. One consequence of this textual command is that sometimes the remedy for an unlawful interrogation will turn on the precise nature of the violation.

The Supreme Court in *Quarles* states that the requirements set out in *Miranda* are "not themselves rights protected by the Constitution," but instead "prophylactic" rules that sweep more broadly than the Constitution itself. Employing this distinction, the Supreme Court has, in various contexts, distinguished true Fifth Amendment violations ("actually compelled statements") from mere *Miranda* violations ("unwarned statements"). The primary implication of this distinction is that there are some scenarios where statements and evidence obtained through Fifth Amendment violations will be suppressed, but similar statements and evidence obtained through "mere" *Miranda* violations would not be.

For example, in *United States v. Patane* (2004), the Supreme Court held that the physical fruits of a *Miranda* violation (for example the gun in a case like *Quarles*) should not be suppressed. Here is the Court's announcement of its holding in *Patane*'s first paragraph:

> "In this case we must decide whether a failure to give a suspect the warnings prescribed by Miranda v. Arizona, requires suppression of the physical fruits of the suspect's unwarned but voluntary statements.... We answer the question presented in the negative."

While the above opinion was joined by only three Justices (Thomas, Rehnquist, and Scalia), two more Justices (Kennedy and O'Connor) concurred in the ruling that *Miranda* violations do not warrant suppression "of nontestimonial physical fruits."

The plurality opinion in *Patane* pointed out, as consistent with its ruling, that "statements taken without Miranda warnings (though not actually compelled) can be used to impeach a defendant's testimony at trial, Harris v. New York (1971), though the fruits of actually compelled testimony cannot, see New Jersey v. Portash (1979)." To buttress this last point, the plurality noted that:

"The Self–Incrimination Clause contains its own exclusionary rule. It provides that '[n]o person ... shall be compelled in any criminal case to be a witness against himself.' Unlike the Fourth Amendment's bar on unreasonable searches, the Self–Incrimination Clause is self-executing. We have repeatedly explained that those subjected to coercive police interrogations have an automatic protection from the use of their involuntary statements (or evidence derived from their statements) in any subsequent criminal trial."

When identifying "actually compelled" statements (as opposed to those obtained only in violation of *Miranda*), the Supreme Court typically references its involuntariness caselaw, suggesting that the Court views the modifiers "involuntary" and "compelled" as synonyms in this context. *See* George C. Thomas III, *Separated at Birth but Siblings Nonetheless: Miranda and the Due Process Notice Cases*, 99 Mich. L. Rev. 1081 (2001) ("Commentators have sought to draw differences between involuntary, compelled, and coerced statements. Whatever the common law approach, or the best philosophical approach, the Court today treats all three as synonymous."). For example, in *Quarles*, the Court emphasized the absence of any "claim that respondent's statements were actually **compelled** by police conduct which overcame his will to resist." In a subsequent footnote, the *Quarles* Court explained this point, stating that "the failure to provide Miranda warnings in and of itself does not render a confession **involuntary**, and respondent is certainly free on remand to argue that his statement was coerced under traditional due process standards."

Another distinction between compelled and unwarned statements arises in the "standing" context. Paralleling the discussion in Chapter 6, courts treat Fifth Amendment rights as "personal." See *Bellis v. United States* (1974) ("the Fifth Amendment privilege is a purely personal one"). This means that a defendant cannot suppress statements made by a witness to police on the ground that the police violated *the witness's* Fifth Amendment rights. This is most clearly recognized in the case law with respect to statements obtained in violation of *Miranda*. See, e.g., *United States v. Escobar* (8th Cir. 1995) ("[The witness's] Miranda rights are personal to him, and [the defendants] have no standing to assert this alleged violation."). But some lower courts suggest that a defendant could exclude a witness's compelled or involuntary statement on the ground that *introduction* of that statement at the defendant's trial violates the defendant's due process rights. See *Buckley v.*

Fitzsimmons (7th Cir. 1994) ("Confessions wrung out of their makers may be less reliable than voluntary confessions, so that using one person's coerced confession at another's trial violates his rights under the due process clause.").

Consistent distinctions in Supreme Court opinions between the Fifth Amendment and *Miranda* called into question the nature of *Miranda* itself, leading to *Dickerson v. United States* (2000). In that case, the Supreme Court considered a Congressional effort to override *Miranda* by statute. See 18 U.S.C. § 3501(a) ("In any criminal prosecution brought by the United States or by the District of Columbia, a confession ... shall be admissible in evidence if it is voluntarily given."). In *Dickerson*, the Fourth Circuit had ruled that the statute overrode *Miranda*. The Supreme Court reversed. The majority explained its ruling as follows:

> Congress may not legislatively supersede our decisions interpreting and applying the Constitution. This case therefore turns on whether the Miranda Court announced a constitutional rule or merely exercised its supervisory authority to regulate evidence in the absence of congressional direction. Recognizing this point, the Court of Appeals surveyed Miranda and its progeny to determine the constitutional status of the Miranda decision. Relying on the fact that we have created several exceptions to Miranda's warnings requirement and that we have repeatedly referred to the Miranda warnings as "prophylactic," and "not themselves rights protected by the Constitution," the Court of Appeals concluded that the protections announced in Miranda are not constitutionally required.
>
> We disagree with the Court of Appeals' conclusion, although we concede that there is language in some of our opinions that supports the view taken by that court. But first and foremost of the factors on the other side— that Miranda is a constitutional decision—is that both Miranda and two of its companion cases applied the rule to proceedings in state courts— to wit, Arizona, California, and New York. Since that time, we have consistently applied Miranda's rule to prosecutions arising in state courts. It is beyond dispute that we do not hold a supervisory power over the courts of the several States. With respect to proceedings in state courts, our "authority is limited to enforcing the commands of the United States Constitution."...

In sum, we conclude that Miranda announced a constitutional rule that Congress may not supersede legislatively. Following the rule of stare decisis, we decline to overrule Miranda ourselves....

Justice Scalia's dissent in the case emphasized the ambiguity, even in the majority opinion, about *Miranda*'s status:

"In light of [cases like *Quarles* and *Oregon v. Elstad*], it is simply no longer possible for the Court to conclude, even if it wanted to, that a violation of Miranda's rules is a violation of the Constitution. But as I explained at the outset, that is what is required before the Court may disregard a law of Congress governing the admissibility of evidence in federal court. The Court today insists that the decision in Miranda is a 'constitutional' one; that it has 'constitutional underpinnings'; a 'constitutional basis' and a 'constitutional origin'; that it was 'constitutionally based'; and that it announced a 'constitutional rule.' It is fine to play these word games; but what makes a decision 'constitutional' in the only sense relevant here—in the sense that renders it impervious to supersession by congressional legislation such as § 3501—is the determination that the Constitution requires the result that the decision announces and the statute ignores. By disregarding congressional action that concededly does not violate the Constitution, the Court flagrantly offends fundamental principles of separation of powers, and arrogates to itself prerogatives reserved to the representatives of the people."

The most recent challenge to *Miranda*'s hybrid status came in *Vega v. Tekoh* (2022), where the Supreme Court ruled that a *Miranda* violation alone could not support a federal civil rights claim. In Justice Alito's majority opinion, the Court explained that this was because "a violation of *Miranda* does not necessarily constitute a violation of the Constitution, and therefore such a violation does not constitute 'the deprivation of [a] right ... secured by the Constitution.' 42 U.S.C. § 1983."

In *Tekoh*, the Justices continued to walk a doctrinal fine line. The Court's ruling depended on its view that the rule set out in *Miranda* was not dictated by the Constitution. The majority opinion even emphasized that this made the *Miranda* decision "a bold and controversial claim of authority." Yet the opinion also stated, "we do not disturb [*Miranda*] in any way" and instead "accept it on its own terms, and for the purpose of deciding this case, we follow its rationale." The Court then echoed *Dickerson* in explaining that,

> "The *Miranda* rules are prophylactic rules that the Court found to be necessary to protect the Fifth Amendment right against compelled self-incrimination. In that sense, *Miranda* was a 'constitutional decision' and it adopted a 'constitutional rule' because the decision was based on the Court's judgment about what is required to safeguard that constitutional right. And when the Court adopts a constitutional prophylactic rule of this nature, *Dickerson* concluded, the rule has the status of a 'law of the United States' that is binding on the States under the Supremacy Clause."

7. TWO-STEP INTERROGATIONS

A final wrinkle involves the appropriate analysis for a two-step interrogation. In *Oregon v. Elstad* (1985), the Supreme Court considered a scenario where an admission of guilt obtained in violation of *Miranda*, was followed by the provision of *Miranda* warnings and a subsequent confession. The Court explained:

> "It is an unwarranted extension of Miranda to hold that a simple failure to administer the warnings, unaccompanied by any actual coercion or other circumstances calculated to undermine the suspect's ability to exercise his free will, so taints the investigatory process that a subsequent voluntary and informed waiver is ineffective for some indeterminate period. Though Miranda requires that the unwarned admission must be suppressed, the admissibility of any subsequent statement should turn in these circumstances solely on whether it is knowingly and voluntarily made....

> We hold today that a suspect who has once responded to unwarned yet uncoercive questioning is not thereby disabled from waiving his rights and confessing after he has been given the requisite Miranda warnings."

In *Missouri v. Seibert* (2004), the Supreme Court revisited a similar fact pattern involving an unwarned statement followed by a warned statement. But in *Seibert*, the Court reached a different result:

" Missouri argues that a confession repeated at the end of an interrogation sequence envisioned in a question-first strategy is admissible on the authority of Oregon v. Elstad (1985), but the argument disfigures that case. In Elstad, the police went to the young suspect's house to take him into custody on a charge of burglary. Before the arrest, one officer spoke with the suspect's mother, while the other one joined the suspect in a "brief stop in the living room," where the officer said he "felt" the young man was involved in a burglary. The suspect acknowledged he had been at the scene. This Court noted that the pause in the living room "was not to interrogate the suspect but to notify his mother of the reason for his arrest," and described the incident as having "none of the earmarks of coercion." The Court, indeed, took care to mention that the officer's initial failure to warn was an "oversight" that "may have been the result of confusion as to whether the brief exchange qualified as 'custodial interrogation' or may simply have reflected reluctance to initiate an alarming police procedure before an officer had spoken with respondent's mother." At the outset of a later and systematic station house interrogation going well beyond the scope of the laconic prior admission, the suspect was given Miranda warnings and made a full confession.

In holding the second statement admissible and voluntary, Elstad rejected the "cat out of the bag" theory that any short, earlier admission, obtained in arguably innocent neglect of Miranda, determined the character of the later, warned confession; on the facts of that case, the Court thought any causal connection between the first and second responses to the police was "speculative and attenuated." Although the Elstad Court expressed no explicit conclusion about either officer's state of mind, it is fair to read Elstad as treating the living room conversation as a good-faith Miranda mistake, not only open to correction by careful warnings before systematic questioning in that particular case, but posing no threat to warn-first practice generally.

The contrast between Elstad and this case reveals a series of relevant facts that bear on whether Miranda warnings delivered midstream could be effective enough to accomplish their object: the completeness and detail of the questions and answers in the first round of interrogation, the overlapping content of the two statements, the timing and setting of the first and the second, the continuity of police personnel, and the degree to which the interrogator's questions treated the second round as continuous with the first. In Elstad, it was not unreasonable to see the occasion for questioning at the station house as presenting a markedly different experience from the short conversation at home; since a reasonable person in the suspect's shoes could have seen the station house questioning as a new and distinct experience, the Miranda warnings could have made sense as presenting a genuine choice whether to follow up on the earlier admission.

At the opposite extreme are the facts here, which by any objective measure reveal a police strategy adapted to undermine the Miranda warnings. The unwarned interrogation was conducted in the station house, and the questioning was systematic, exhaustive, and managed with psychological skill. When the police were finished there was little, if anything, of incriminating potential left unsaid. The warned phase of questioning proceeded after a pause of only 15 to 20 minutes, in the same place as the unwarned segment. When the same officer who had conducted the first phase recited the Miranda warnings, he said nothing to counter the probable misimpression that the advice that anything Patrice Seibert said could be used against her also applied to the details of the inculpatory statement previously elicited. In particular, the police did not advise that her prior statement could not be used. Nothing was said or done to dispel the oddity of warning about legal rights to silence and counsel right after the police had led her through a systematic interrogation, and any uncertainty on her part about a right to stop talking about matters previously discussed would only have been aggravated by the way Officer Hanrahan set the scene by saying "we've been talking for a little while about what happened on Wednesday the twelfth, haven't we?" The impression that the further questioning was a mere continuation of the earlier questions and responses was fostered by references back to the confession already given. It would have been reasonable to regard the two sessions as parts of a continuum, in which it would have been unnatural to refuse to repeat at the second stage what had been said before. These circumstances must be seen as challenging the comprehensibility and efficacy of the Miranda warnings to the point that a reasonable person in the suspect's shoes would not have understood them to convey a message that she retained a choice about continuing to talk.

The plurality opinion (quoted above) garnered four votes. Justice Kennedy added a fifth vote, noting that, in his view, the departure from *Elstad* was only required because "the interrogation technique used in this case is designed to circumvent Miranda v. Arizona."

Chapter 8

THE SIXTH AMENDMENT AND OFFICIAL QUESTIONING

The Sixth Amendment contains several constitutional rights. This section discusses the Sixth Amendment right to counsel (bolded below) as it pertains to police questioning.

> "In all criminal prosecutions, the accused shall enjoy the right to a speedy and public trial, by an impartial jury of the state and district wherein the crime shall have been committed, which district shall have been previously ascertained by law, and to be informed of the nature and cause of the accusation; to be confronted with the witnesses against him; to have compulsory process for obtaining witnesses in his favor, and **to have the assistance of counsel for his defense**." **U.S. Const. Amend. VI**

A. ADVERSARY JUDICIAL PROCEEDINGS

Constitutional challenges to police interrogations most commonly invoke the Fifth Amendment, discussed in Chapter 7. That is because the Fifth Amendment applies prior to the start of formal adversary proceedings, when most police interrogations occur. By contrast, the Sixth Amendment's protections apply only after "a prosecution is commenced." As the Supreme Court explained in *Rothgery v. Gillespie County* (2008):

> "The Sixth Amendment right of the 'accused' to assistance of counsel in 'all criminal prosecutions' is limited by its terms: it does not attach until a prosecution is commenced. We have, for purposes of the right to counsel, pegged commencement to 'the initiation of adversary judicial criminal proceedings—whether by way of formal charge, preliminary hearing, indictment, information, or arraignment.' The rule is not mere formalism, but a recognition of the point at which the government has committed itself to prosecute, the adverse positions of government and defendant have solidified, and the accused finds himself faced with the prosecutorial

forces of organized society, and immersed in the intricacies of substantive and procedural criminal law."

Rothgery goes on to pinpoint the time at which the Sixth Amendment right attaches, stating: "a criminal defendant's initial appearance before a judicial officer, where he learns the charge against him and his liberty is subject to restriction, marks the start of adversary judicial proceedings that trigger attachment of the Sixth Amendment right to counsel."

To illustrate this point, think back to the police deception problem, *Moran v. Burbine* (1986), discussed in the previous chapter. There the Supreme Court held not only that there was no *Miranda* violation when the police deliberately prevented Burbine's lawyer from being present during their interrogation of his client, but also that the police did not violate Burbine's Sixth Amendment right to counsel in doing so, "because, as respondent acknowledges, the events that led to the inculpatory statements preceded the formal initiation of adversary judicial proceedings."

"Once the adversary judicial process has been initiated, the Sixth Amendment guarantees a defendant the right to have counsel present at all 'critical' stages of the criminal proceedings. Interrogation by the State is such a stage." *Montejo v. Louisiana* (2009).

BREWER v. WILLIAMS
430 U.S. 387 (1977)

Justice STEWART delivered the opinion of the Court.

I

.... On the afternoon of December 24, 1968, a 10-year-old girl named Pamela Powers went with her family to the YMCA in Des Moines, Iowa, to watch a wrestling tournament in which her brother was participating. When she failed to return from a trip to the washroom, a search for her began. The search was unsuccessful.

Robert Williams, who had recently escaped from a mental hospital, was a resident of the YMCA. Soon after the girl's disappearance Williams was seen in the YMCA lobby carrying some clothing and a large bundle wrapped in a blanket. He obtained help from a 14-year-old boy in opening the street door of the YMCA and the door to his automobile parked outside. When Williams placed the bundle in the front seat of his car the boy "saw two legs in it and they were skinny and white." Before anyone could see what was in the bundle Williams drove away. His abandoned car was found the following day in Davenport, Iowa, roughly 160 miles east of Des Moines. A warrant was then issued in Des Moines for his arrest on a charge of abduction.

On the morning of December 26, a Des Moines lawyer named Henry McKnight went to the Des Moines police station and informed the officers present that he had just received a long-distance call from Williams, and that he had advised Williams to turn himself in to the Davenport police. Williams did surrender that morning to the police in Davenport, and they booked him on the charge specified in the arrest warrant and gave him the warnings required by Miranda v. Arizona. The Davenport police then telephoned their counterparts in Des Moines to inform them that Williams had surrendered. McKnight, the lawyer, was still at the Des Moines police headquarters, and Williams conversed with McKnight on the telephone. In the presence of the Des Moines chief of police and a police detective named Leaming, McKnight advised Williams that Des Moines police officers would be driving to Davenport to pick him up, that the officers would not interrogate him or mistreat him, and that Williams was not to talk to the officers about Pamela Powers until after consulting with McKnight upon his return to Des Moines. As a result of these conversations, it was agreed between McKnight and the Des Moines police officials that Detective Leaming and a fellow officer would drive to Davenport to pick up Williams, that they would bring him directly back to Des Moines, and that they would not question him during the trip.

In the meantime Williams was arraigned before a judge in Davenport on the outstanding arrest warrant. The judge advised him of his Miranda rights and committed him to jail. Before leaving the courtroom, Williams conferred with a lawyer named Kelly, who advised him not to make any statements until consulting with McKnight back in Des Moines.

Detective Leaming and his fellow officer arrived in Davenport about noon to pick up Williams and return him to Des Moines. Soon after their arrival they met with Williams and Kelly, who, they understood, was acting as Williams' lawyer. Detective Leaming repeated the Miranda warnings, and told Williams:

> "We both know that you're being represented here by Mr. Kelly and you're being represented by Mr. McKnight in Des Moines, and . . . I

want you to remember this because we'll be visiting between here and Des Moines."

Williams then conferred again with Kelly alone, and after this conference Kelly reiterated to Detective Leaming that Williams was not to be questioned about the disappearance of Pamela Powers until after he had consulted with McKnight back in Des Moines.... Kelly was denied permission to ride in the police car back to Des Moines with Williams and the two officers.

The two detectives, with Williams in their charge, then set out on the 160-mile drive. At no time during the trip did Williams express a willingness to be interrogated in the absence of an attorney. Instead, he stated several times that "when I get to Des Moines and see Mr. McKnight, I am going to tell you the whole story." Detective Leaming knew that Williams was a former mental patient, and knew also that he was deeply religious.

The detective and his prisoner soon embarked on a wide-ranging conversation covering a variety of topics, including the subject of religion. Then, not long after leaving Davenport and reaching the interstate highway, Detective Leaming delivered what has been referred to in the briefs and oral arguments as the "Christian burial speech." Addressing Williams as "Reverend," the detective said:

> "I want to give you something to think about while we're traveling down the road.... Number one, I want you to observe the weather conditions, it's raining, it's sleeting, it's freezing, driving is very treacherous, visibility is poor, it's going to be dark early this evening. They are predicting several inches of snow for tonight, and I feel that you yourself are the only person that knows where this little girl's body is, that you yourself have only been there once, and if you get a snow on top of it you yourself may be unable to find it. And, since we will be going right past the area on the way into Des Moines, I feel that we could stop and locate the body, that the parents of this little girl should be entitled to a Christian burial for the little girl who was snatched away from them on Christmas Eve and murdered. And I feel we should stop and locate it on the way in rather than waiting until morning and trying to come back out after a snow storm and possibly not being able to find it at all."

Williams asked Detective Leaming why he thought their route to Des Moines would be taking them past the girl's body, and Leaming responded that he knew the body was in the area of Mitchellville a town they would be passing on the way to Des Moines. Leaming then stated: "I do not want you to answer me. I don't want to discuss it any further. Just think about it as we're riding down the road."

As the car approached Grinnell, a town approximately 100 miles west of Davenport, Williams asked whether the police had found the victim's shoes. When Detective Leaming replied that he was unsure, Williams directed the officers to a service station where he said he had left the shoes; a search for them proved unsuccessful. As they continued towards Des Moines, Williams asked whether the police had found the blanket, and directed the officers to a rest area where he said he had disposed of the blanket. Nothing was found. The car continued towards Des Moines, and as it approached Mitchellville, Williams said that he would show the officers where the body was. He then directed the police to the body of Pamela Powers.

Williams was indicted for first-degree murder. Before trial, his counsel moved to suppress all evidence relating to or resulting from any statements Williams had made during the automobile ride from Davenport to Des Moines. After an evidentiary hearing the trial judge denied the motion. He found that "an agreement was made between defense counsel and the police officials to the effect that the Defendant was not to be questioned on the return trip to Des Moines," and that the evidence in question had been elicited from Williams during "a critical stage in the proceedings requiring the presence of counsel on his request." The judge ruled, however, that Williams had "waived his right to have an attorney present during the giving of such information."

The evidence in question was introduced over counsel's continuing objection at the subsequent trial. The jury found Williams guilty of murder, and the judgment of conviction was affirmed by the Iowa Supreme Court…. Williams then petitioned for a writ of habeas corpus in the United States District Court for the Southern District of Iowa…. The District Court made findings of fact as summarized above, and concluded as a matter of law that the evidence in question had been wrongly admitted at Williams' trial. The Court of Appeals for the Eighth Circuit, with one judge dissenting affirmed. We granted certiorari to consider the constitutional issues presented.

II

…. There is no need to review in this case the doctrine of Miranda v. Arizona, a doctrine designed to secure the constitutional privilege against compulsory self-incrimination. It is equally unnecessary to evaluate the ruling of the District Court that Williams' self-incriminating statements were, indeed, involuntarily made. For it is clear that the judgment before us must in any event be affirmed upon the ground that Williams was deprived of a different constitutional right the right to the assistance of counsel.

This right, guaranteed by the Sixth and Fourteenth Amendments, is indispensable to the fair administration of our adversary system of criminal justice…. Whatever else it may mean, the right to counsel granted by the Sixth and Fourteenth Amendments means at least that a person is entitled to the help of a lawyer at or after the time that judicial proceedings have been initiated against him whether by way of formal charge, preliminary hearing, indictment, information, or arraignment.

There can be no doubt in the present case that judicial proceedings had been initiated against Williams before the start of the automobile ride from Davenport to Des Moines. A warrant had been issued for his arrest, he had been arraigned on that warrant before a judge in a Davenport courtroom, and he had been committed by the court to confinement in jail. The State does not contend otherwise.

There can be no serious doubt, either, that Detective Leaming deliberately and designedly set out to elicit information from Williams just as surely as and perhaps more effectively than if he had formally interrogated him. Detective Leaming was fully aware before departing for Des Moines that Williams was being represented in Davenport by Kelly and in Des Moines by McKnight. Yet he purposely sought during Williams' isolation from his lawyers to obtain as much incriminating information as possible. Indeed, Detective Leaming conceded as much when he testified at Williams' trial:

> "Q. In fact, Captain, whether he was a mental patient or not, you were trying to get all the information you could before he got to his lawyer, weren't you?
>
> "A. I was sure hoping to find out where that little girl was, yes, sir.

"Q. Well, I'll put it this way: You was (sic) hoping to get all the information you could before Williams got back to McKnight, weren't you?

"A. Yes, sir."

The state courts clearly proceeded upon the hypothesis that Detective Leaming's 'Christian burial speech' had been tantamount to interrogation. Both courts recognized that Williams had been entitled to the assistance of counsel at the time he made the incriminating statements. Yet no such constitutional protection would have come into play if there had been no interrogation.

The circumstances of this case are thus constitutionally indistinguishable from those presented in Massiah v. United States (1964). The petitioner in that case was indicted for violating the federal narcotics law. He retained a lawyer, pleaded not guilty, and was released on bail. While he was free on bail a federal agent succeeded by surreptitious means in listening to incriminating statements made by him. [*Ed. Note*: The agent worked with Massiah's co-defendant to use a covert listening device to transmit the co-defendant's conversations with Massiah to the agent.] Evidence of these statements was introduced against the petitioner at his trial, and he was convicted. This Court reversed the conviction, holding "that the petitioner was denied the basic protections of that guarantee (the right to counsel) when there was used against him at his trial evidence of his own incriminating words, which federal agents had deliberately elicited from him after he had been indicted and in the absence of his counsel." That the incriminating statements were elicited surreptitiously in the Massiah case, and otherwise here, is constitutionally irrelevant. Rather, the clear rule of Massiah is that once adversary proceedings have commenced against an individual, he has a right to legal representation when the government interrogates him. It thus requires no wooden or technical application of the Massiah doctrine to conclude that Williams was entitled to the assistance of counsel guaranteed to him by the Sixth and Fourteenth Amendments.

III

The Iowa courts recognized that Williams had been denied the constitutional right to the assistance of counsel. They held, however, that he had waived that right during the course of the automobile trip from Davenport to Des Moines.

.... The District Court and the Court of Appeals were ... correct in their understanding of the proper standard to be applied in determining the question of waiver as a matter of federal constitutional law—that it was incumbent upon the State to prove "an intentional relinquishment or abandonment of a known right or privilege." That standard has been reiterated in many cases. We have said that the right to counsel does not depend upon a request by the defendant, and that courts indulge in every reasonable presumption against waiver. This strict standard applies equally to an alleged waiver of the right to counsel whether at trial or at a critical stage of pretrial proceedings.

We conclude, finally, that the Court of Appeals was correct in holding that, judged by these standards, the record in this case falls far short of sustaining petitioner's burden. It is true that Williams had been informed of and appeared to understand his right to counsel. But waiver requires not merely comprehension but relinquishment, and Williams' consistent reliance upon the advice of counsel in dealing with the authorities refutes any suggestion that he waived that right.... Despite Williams' express and implicit assertions of his right to counsel, Detective Leaming proceeded to elicit incriminating statements from Williams. Leaming did not preface this effort by telling Williams that he had a right to the presence of a lawyer, and made no effort at all to ascertain whether Williams wished to relinquish that right. The circumstances of record in this case thus provide no reasonable basis for finding that Williams waived his right to the assistance of counsel.

IV

The crime of which Williams was convicted was senseless and brutal, calling for swift and energetic action by the police to apprehend the perpetrator and gather evidence with which he could be convicted. No mission of law enforcement officials is more important. Yet disinterested zeal for the public good does not assure either wisdom or right in the methods it pursues. Although we do not lightly affirm the issuance of a writ of habeas corpus in this case, so clear a violation of the Sixth and Fourteenth Amendments as here occurred cannot be condoned. The pressures on state executive and judicial officers charged with the administration of the criminal law are great, especially when the crime is murder and the victim a small child. But it is precisely the predictability of those pressures that makes imperative a resolute loyalty to the guarantees that the Constitution extends to us all.

As we will see, there are numerous limits on the Sixth Amendment protections in this context, causing one scholar to suggest that "law enforcement easily can work around an existing attorney-client relationship to question a charged defendant about nearly anything, up to and including the precise factual subject of filed charges."[31] These limits are that the right: (1) only applies after a prosecution has formally commenced, (2) is "offense specific," (3) must be invoked, and (4) can be waived.

Given all these limits it is useful at the outset to recognize one of the most important scenarios where the Sixth Amendment does add to a suspect's protections from police questioning, illustrated by *Massiah v. United States* (1964). Recall that in *Illinois v. Perkins* (1990) (Chapter 7), the Supreme Court found that there was no *Miranda* violation when the police sent an undercover operative into a suspect's jail cell to elicit information. However, in *Massiah*, the Court found a Sixth Amendment violation in a similar scenario. The Court also found Sixth Amendment violations in two subsequent cases.

In **United States v. Henry** (1980), Billy Henry was indicted for bank robbery, appointed counsel, and remanded to jail pending trial. An FBI agent instructed a paid informant (Nichols) who was being held in the same cellblock as Henry "to be alert to any statements made by [Henry], but not to initiate any conversation with or question Henry regarding the [charged] bank robbery." The Supreme Court deemed the resulting incriminating statements made by Henry to Nichols to have been obtained in violation of the Sixth Amendment: "Even if the agent's statement that he did not intend that Nichols would take affirmative steps to secure incriminating information is accepted, he must have known that such propinquity likely would lead to that result." In **Maine v. Moulton** (1985), Perley Moulton was indicted on auto theft charges, appointed counsel, and released on bail pending trial. The Supreme Court ruled that the police violated the Sixth Amendment by, then, having Moulton's associate wear a wire to surreptitiously record a conversation, initiated by the associate, about the thefts for which Moulton had been indicted.

---

[31] Brooks Holland, A Relational Sixth Amendment During Interrogation, 99 J. Crim. L. & Criminology 381 (2009).

In *Moulton*, the Court rejected the government's argument that the Sixth Amendment only applied when "the police set up the confrontation between the accused and a police agent at which incriminating statements were elicited." The Court explained:

> "The Sixth Amendment guarantees the accused, at least after the initiation of formal charges, the right to rely on counsel as a 'medium' between him and the State. As noted above, this guarantee includes the State's affirmative obligation not to act in a manner that circumvents the protections accorded the accused by invoking this right. The determination whether particular action by state agents violates the accused's right to the assistance of counsel must be made in light of this obligation. Thus, the Sixth Amendment is not violated whenever—by luck or happenstance—the State obtains incriminating statements from the accused after the right to counsel has attached. However, knowing exploitation by the State of an opportunity to confront the accused without counsel being present is as much a breach of the State's obligation not to circumvent the right to the assistance of counsel as is the intentional creation of such an opportunity. Accordingly, the Sixth Amendment is violated when the State obtains incriminating statements by knowingly circumventing the accused's right to have counsel present in a confrontation between the accused and a state agent."

The Supreme Court later elaborated on its "by luck or happenstance" proviso in *Kuhlmann v. Wilson* (1986), explaining:

> "A defendant does not make out a violation of [the right to counsel] simply by showing that an informant, either through prior arrangement or voluntarily, reported his incriminating statements to the police. Rather, the defendant must demonstrate that the police and their informant took some action, beyond merely listening, that was designed deliberately to elicit incriminating remarks."

Applying the "merely listening" principle, the Court found no violation in *Kuhlmann* even though the case was similar to *Henry*. The Court distinguished *Henry* by pointing out that, in *Henry*, "Although the informant had not questioned the defendant, the informant had 'stimulated' conversations with the defendant in order to 'elicit' incriminating information" – and that this "amounted to indirect and surreptitious interrogation." By contrast, in *Kuhlmann*, the informant "at no time asked any questions of respondent concerning the pending charges, and that he only listened to respondent's spontaneous and unsolicited statements."

In October 2022, the Civil Rights Division of the Department of Justice issued a report on the use of custodial informants by the Orange County (California) District Attorney's Office (OCDA) and Orange County Sheriff's Department (OCSD). Among other things, the report documented numerous Sixth Amendment violations. As the DOJ explained:

"The Sixth Amendment prohibits law enforcement from using informants to elicit statements from defendants about conduct that defendants have been charged with and for which they are represented by counsel. But this is exactly what OCDA and OCSD did: custodial informants in the Orange County Jail worked as agents of law enforcement to elicit incriminating statements from represented defendants while they were housed together in the jail. OCSD placed informants in proximity to represented defendants so that the informants could elicit inculpatory statements in the absence of the defendant's counsel. OCSD hid records for tracking and managing the informants inside the jail. The informants sought and expected benefits for their in-custody informant work, and informants were directly or impliedly promised by law enforcement that such benefits would be forthcoming. The way that OCDA and OCSD used custodial informants repeatedly violated defendants' Sixth Amendment right to counsel."

B. OFFENSE SPECIFIC

MCNEIL v. WISCONSIN
501 U.S. 171 (1991)

Justice SCALIA delivered the opinion of the Court.

This case presents the question whether an accused's invocation of his Sixth Amendment right to counsel during a judicial proceeding constitutes an invocation of his Miranda right to counsel.

I

Petitioner Paul McNeil was arrested in Omaha, Nebraska, in May 1987, pursuant to a warrant charging him with an armed robbery in West Allis, Wisconsin, a suburb of Milwaukee. Shortly after his arrest, two Milwaukee County deputy sheriffs arrived in Omaha to retrieve him. After advising him of his Miranda rights, the deputies sought to question him. He refused to answer any questions, but did not request an attorney. [*Ed. Note*: McNeil's brief in the Supreme Court states that "McNeil said nothing more than no."] The deputies promptly ended the interview.

Once back in Wisconsin, petitioner was brought before a Milwaukee County Court Commissioner on the armed robbery charge. The Commissioner set bail and scheduled a preliminary examination. An attorney from the Wisconsin Public Defender's Office represented petitioner at this initial appearance.

Later that evening, Detective Joseph Butts of the Milwaukee County Sheriff's Department visited petitioner in jail. Butts had been assisting the Racine County, Wisconsin, police in their investigation of a murder, attempted murder, and armed burglary in the town of Caledonia; petitioner was a suspect. Butts advised petitioner of his Miranda rights, and petitioner signed a form waiving them. In this first interview, petitioner did not deny knowledge of the Caledonia crimes, but said that he had not been involved.

Butts returned two days later with detectives from Caledonia. He again began the encounter by advising petitioner of his Miranda rights and providing a waiver form. Petitioner placed his initials next to each of the warnings and signed the form. This time, petitioner admitted that he had been involved in the Caledonia crimes, which he described in detail….

The following day, petitioner was formally charged with the Caledonia crimes and transferred to that jurisdiction. His pretrial motion to suppress the three incriminating statements was denied. He was convicted of second-degree murder, attempted first-degree murder, and armed robbery, and sentenced to 60 years in prison.

On appeal, petitioner argued that the trial court's refusal to suppress the statements was reversible error. He contended that his courtroom appearance with an attorney for the West Allis crime constituted an invocation of the Miranda right to counsel, and that any subsequent waiver of that right during police-initiated questioning regarding any offense was invalid. Observing that the State's Supreme Court had never addressed this issue, the Court of Appeals certified to that court the following question:

"Does an accused's request for counsel at an initial appearance on a charged offense constitute an invocation of his fifth amendment right to counsel that precludes police-initiated interrogation on unrelated, uncharged offenses?" The Wisconsin Supreme Court answered "no." We granted certiorari.

II

The Sixth Amendment provides that "[i]n all criminal prosecutions, the accused shall enjoy the right ... to have the Assistance of Counsel for his defence." In Michigan v. Jackson (1986), we held that once this right to counsel has attached and has been invoked, any subsequent waiver during a police-initiated custodial interview is ineffective. It is undisputed, and we accept for purposes of the present case, that at the time petitioner provided the incriminating statements at issue, his Sixth Amendment right had attached and had been invoked with respect to the West Allis armed robbery, for which he had been formally charged.

The Sixth Amendment right, however, is offense specific. It cannot be invoked once for all future prosecutions, for it does not attach until a prosecution is commenced, that is, "at or after the initiation of adversary judicial criminal proceedings—whether by way of formal charge, preliminary hearing, indictment, information, or arraignment." And just as the right is offense specific, so also its Michigan v. Jackson effect of invalidating subsequent waivers in police-initiated interviews is offense specific.

> "The police have an interest in investigating new or additional crimes after an individual is formally charged with one crime. To exclude evidence pertaining to charges as to which the Sixth Amendment right to counsel had not attached at the time the evidence was obtained, simply because other charges were pending at that time, would unnecessarily frustrate the public's interest in the investigation of criminal activities."

Incriminating statements pertaining to other crimes, as to which the Sixth Amendment right has not yet attached, are, of course, admissible at a trial of those offenses. Because petitioner provided the statements at issue here before his Sixth

Amendment right to counsel with respect to the Caledonia offenses had been (or even could have been) invoked, that right poses no bar to the admission of the statements in this case.

Petitioner relies, however, upon a different "right to counsel," found not in the text of the Sixth Amendment, but in this Court's jurisprudence relating to the Fifth Amendment guarantee that "[n]o person ... shall be compelled in any criminal case to be a witness against himself." In Miranda v. Arizona (1966), we established a number of prophylactic rights designed to counteract the "inherently compelling pressures" of custodial interrogation, including the right to have counsel present. Miranda did not hold, however, that those rights could not be waived. On the contrary, the opinion recognized that statements elicited during custodial interrogation would be admissible if the prosecution could establish that the suspect "knowingly and intelligently waived his privilege against self-incrimination and his right to retained or appointed counsel."

In Edwards v. Arizona (1981), we established a second layer of prophylaxis for the Miranda right to counsel: Once a suspect asserts the right, not only must the current interrogation cease, but he may not be approached for further interrogation "until counsel has been made available to him," —which means, we have most recently held, that counsel must be present. If the police do subsequently initiate an encounter in the absence of counsel (assuming there has been no break in custody), the suspect's statements are presumed involuntary and therefore inadmissible as substantive evidence at trial, even where the suspect executes a waiver and his statements would be considered voluntary under traditional standards. This is designed to prevent police from badgering a defendant into waiving his previously asserted Miranda rights. The Edwards rule, moreover, is not offense specific: Once a suspect invokes the Miranda right to counsel for interrogation regarding one offense, he may not be reapproached regarding any offense unless counsel is present.

Having described the nature and effects of both the Sixth Amendment right to counsel and the Miranda–Edwards "Fifth Amendment" right to counsel, we come at last to the issue here: Petitioner seeks to prevail by combining the two of them. He contends that, although he expressly waived his Miranda right to counsel on every occasion he was interrogated, those waivers were the invalid product of impermissible approaches, because his prior invocation of the offense specific Sixth Amendment right with regard to the West Allis burglary was also an invocation of the non-offense-specific Miranda–Edwards right. We think that is false as a matter of fact and inadvisable (if even permissible) as a contrary-to-fact presumption of policy.

As to the former: The purpose of the Sixth Amendment counsel guarantee—and hence the purpose of invoking it—is to protect the unaided layman at critical confrontations with his expert adversary, the government, after the adverse positions of government and defendant have solidified with respect to a particular alleged crime. The purpose of the Miranda–Edwards guarantee, on the other hand—and hence the purpose of invoking it—is to protect a quite different interest: the suspect's "desire to deal with the police only through counsel." This is in one respect narrower than the interest protected by the Sixth Amendment guarantee (because it relates only to custodial interrogation) and in another respect broader (because it relates to interrogation regarding any suspected crime and attaches whether or not the "adversarial relationship" produced by a pending prosecution has yet arisen). To invoke the Sixth Amendment interest is, as a matter of fact, not to invoke the Miranda–Edwards interest. One might be quite willing to speak to the police without counsel present concerning many matters, but not the matter under prosecution. It can be said, perhaps, that it is likely that one who has asked for counsel's assistance in defending against a prosecution would want counsel present for all custodial interrogation, even interrogation unrelated to the charge. That is not necessarily true, since suspects often believe that they can avoid the laying of charges by demonstrating an assurance of innocence through frank and unassisted answers to questions. But even if it were true, the likelihood that a suspect would wish counsel to be present is not the test for applicability of Edwards. The rule of that case applies only when the suspect has expressed his wish for the particular sort of lawyerly assistance that is the subject of Miranda. It requires, at a minimum, some statement that can reasonably be construed to be an expression of a desire for the assistance of an attorney in dealing with custodial interrogation by the police. Requesting the assistance of an attorney at a bail hearing does not bear that construction. To find that the defendant invoked his Fifth Amendment right to counsel on the present charges merely by requesting the appointment of counsel at his arraignment on the unrelated charge is to disregard the ordinary meaning of that request.

…. There remains to be considered the possibility that, even though the assertion of the Sixth Amendment right to counsel does not in fact imply an assertion of the

Miranda "Fifth Amendment" right, we should declare it to be such as a matter of sound policy. Assuming we have such an expansive power under the Constitution, it would not wisely be exercised.... The Sixth Amendment right to counsel attaches at the first formal proceeding against an accused, and in most States, at least with respect to serious offenses, free counsel is made available at that time and ordinarily requested. Thus, if we were to adopt petitioner's rule, most persons in pretrial custody for serious offenses would be *unapproachable* by police officers suspecting them of involvement in other crimes, *even though they have never expressed any unwillingness to be questioned*. Since the ready ability to obtain uncoerced confessions is not an evil but an unmitigated good, society would be the loser.... Petitioner's proposal would in our view do much more harm than good, and is not contained within, or even in furtherance of, the Sixth Amendment's right to counsel or the Fifth Amendment's right against compelled self-incrimination.... The judgment of the Wisconsin Supreme Court is *Affirmed*.

Because the Sixth Amendment right to counsel is "offense specific," there was no Sixth Amendment violation in *Illinois v. Perkins* (1990) [Chapter 7]. The *Perkins* opinion notes, "In the instant case no charges had been filed on the subject of the interrogation, and our Sixth Amendment precedents are not applicable."

After *McNeil v. Wisconsin*, many lower courts interpreted the phrase "offense specific" loosely. For example, in *Cobb v. State* (Tex. Crim. App. 2000), a suspect who had been indicted for a burglary was later questioned about a double murder that occurred during that burglary. The Texas courts deemed this to be unconstitutional, ruling that, when the Sixth Amendment right attaches it applies not only to questioning about the charged offense but also to questioning about "any other offense that is very closely related factually to the offense charged": "This rule prevents the government from circumventing the Sixth Amendment right to counsel merely by charging a defendant with additional crimes after questioning him without counsel present, or by charging predicate crimes with the purpose of questioning a suspect on an aggravated crime."

The U.S. Supreme Court reversed, holding in **Texas v. Cobb** (2001) that "our decision in McNeil v. Wisconsin meant what it said ... the Sixth Amendment right is 'offense specific.'" Thus, the Court rejected Texas' "closely related factually" test. Instead, it adopted a narrower test that it had long used "to delineate the scope of the Fifth Amendment's Double Jeopardy Clause, which prevents multiple or successive prosecutions for the 'same offence.'" That test, set out in *Blockburger v. United States* (1932), is: "where the same act or transaction constitutes a violation of two distinct statutory provisions, the test to be applied to determine whether there are two offenses or only one, is whether each provision requires proof of a fact which the other does not." The Court then applied the test as follows:

> "As defined by Texas law, burglary and capital murder are not the same offense under Blockburger. Compare Tex. Penal Code §30.02(a) (requiring entry into or continued concealment in a habitation or building) with §19.03(a)(7)(A) (requiring murder of more than one person during a single criminal transaction). Accordingly, the Sixth Amendment right to counsel did not bar police from interrogating respondent regarding the murders, and respondent's confession was therefore admissible."

C. INVOCATION AND WAIVER

As with the Fifth Amendment rights referenced in the preceding chapter, the Sixth Amendment right to have counsel present during questioning must be **invoked**. Thus, in **Patterson v. Illinois** (1988), the Supreme Court held that there was no Sixth Amendment violation when police questioned a suspect after his indictment and without counsel present. The Court explained:

> "Petitioner's first claim is that because his Sixth Amendment right to counsel arose with his indictment, the police were thereafter barred from initiating a meeting with him…. Petitioner, however, at no time sought to exercise his right to have counsel present. The fact that petitioner's Sixth Amendment right came into existence with his indictment, i.e., that he had such a right at the time of his questioning, does not distinguish him from the preindictment interrogatee whose right to counsel is in existence and available for his exercise while he is questioned. Had petitioner indicated he wanted the assistance of counsel, the authorities' interview with him would have stopped, and further questioning would have been forbidden (unless petitioner called for such a meeting)."

Since Patterson had not invoked his Sixth Amendment right to counsel, the Court ruled, police could question him without counsel.

The second claim at issue in *Patterson* was whether, despite the lack of an invocation, Patterson **waived** his right to counsel when he spoke to police. Indeed, whether a waiver had occurred was the critical question in *Brewer v. Williams* although the Court's waiver analysis (as opposed to its conclusion) was somewhat unclear. In subsequent case law, the Court suggested that, after the right to counsel had been invoked at an initial appearance, the right to have counsel present during subsequent critical stages (like questioning) could not be waived by the suspect unilaterally (i.e., without counsel). See Katharine Tinto, *Wavering on Waiver: Montejo v. Louisiana and the Sixth Amendment Right to Counsel*, 48 Am. Crim. L. Rev. 1335 (2011) ("until *Montejo v. Louisiana*, the police were essentially prohibited under the Sixth Amendment from initiating interrogation after a defendant had been arraigned on criminal charges and a lawyer had been appointed"). The Court retreated from that position in *Patterson* and rejected it entirely in **Montejo v. Louisiana** (2009). In *Montejo*, the Court explained the waiver rules as follows:

> "Our precedents also place beyond doubt that the Sixth Amendment right to counsel may be waived by a defendant, so long as relinquishment of the right is voluntary, knowing, and intelligent. The defendant may waive the right whether or not he is already represented by counsel; the decision to waive need not itself be counseled. And when a defendant is read his Miranda rights (which include the right to have counsel present during interrogation) and agrees to waive those rights, that typically does the trick, even though the Miranda rights purportedly have their source in the Fifth Amendment."

The Court's description of the rules for waiver in *Montejo* may seem more permissive than those referenced in *McNeil*. That is because *McNeil* relied on *Michigan v. Jackson* (1986) a case that *Montejo* explicitly overruled.

The upshot of *Montejo* is that the police can approach a defendant after the right to counsel has attached *and* after the defendant has invoked that right and been appointed counsel. Defendants who seek to invoke their Sixth Amendment right to prevent such questioning must do so when approached for interrogation, not "anticipatorily" at an arraignment or other preliminary hearing.

Since prosecutors sometimes participate directly or indirectly in interrogations it is important to be aware that such involvement can violate professional ethics codes. Justice Stevens, dissenting in *Patterson v. Illinois* (1988), emphasized this point:

> "An attempt to obtain evidence for use at trial by going behind the back of one's adversary would be not only a serious breach of professional ethics but also a manifestly unfair form of trial practice. In the criminal context, the same ethical rules apply and, in my opinion, notions of fairness that are at least as demanding should also be enforced."

Among the rules Justice Stevens cited is Model ABA Rule of Professional Responsibility 4.2, which states:

> **"In representing a client, a lawyer shall not communicate about the subject of the representation with a person the lawyer knows to be represented by another lawyer in the matter, unless the lawyer has the consent of the other lawyer or is authorized to do so by law or a court order."**

As Justice Stevens indicated, courts typically interpret this rule, or local variations of it, to apply to prosecutors.

The federal Department of Justice (DOJ) highlights Rule 4.2 in offering formal guidance to its prosecutors as they navigate their professional ethics in this context. The DOJ's guidance also cautions its prosecutors to be wary of contacts made by others with represented persons on their behalf:

> **"Department attorneys should be aware that agents and informants who communicate with represented persons as part of a law enforcement investigation may be deemed, for the purpose of the relevant professional responsibility rule, to be acting as the 'alter ego' of the Department attorney supervising the investigation. In such a circumstance, the attorney's professional conduct rules may be imputed to the law enforcement agents or informants." Justice Manual CRM 298.**

D. OTHER LIMITS ON INTERROGATION

The focus of this course is on *constitutional* limits on investigations, but statutes and rules also restrict the government's investigative authority. For example, the Supreme Court's *Miranda* opinion noted that the Federal Rules of Criminal Procedure require that an arrestee be brought "without unnecessary delay before a magistrate." The Court explained that:

> "These supervisory rules, requiring production of an arrested person before a commissioner 'without unnecessary delay' and [as effectuated in McNabb v. United States (1943) and Mallory v. United States (1957)] excluding evidence obtained in default of that statutory obligation, were ... responsive to the same considerations of Fifth Amendment policy that unavoidably face us now as to the States."

Under this authority or state analogues, a defendant who makes a statement while in custody during a period of time when the defendant should have, but was not, presented to a judicial officer (in the federal system, any time longer than six hours after the arrest absent extenuating circumstances) can move to exclude that statement, even if the statement was voluntary and made in compliance with *Miranda*. See, e.g., *United States v. Boche-Perez* (5th Cir. 2014).

More recent restrictions on the introduction of confessions include state laws that mandate the recording of interrogations. For example, in 2014, Connecticut passed a law stating that:

> "An oral, written or sign language statement of a person under investigation for or accused of a capital felony or a class A or B felony made as a result of a custodial interrogation at a place of detention shall be presumed to be inadmissible as evidence against the person in any criminal proceeding unless: (1) An electronic recording is made of the custodial interrogation, and (2) such recording is substantially accurate and not intentionally altered."

In addition to allowing jurors to better evaluate the weight to be given to an alleged confession, the availability of a recording helps courts to measure compliance with the rules regarding police interrogation. As we have already seen, police-worn body cameras can have a similar effect in helping courts to evaluate stops and other uses of force.

Chapter 9

EYEWITNESS IDENTIFICATIONS

To obtain a criminal conviction, the government must establish that the defendant, as opposed to some other person, committed the charged offense. This Chapter considers constitutional constraints under the Sixth and Fourteenth Amendments on police efforts to generate this important identification evidence through lineups or other means.

Identification Evidence[32]

There are two potential moments when the prosecution presents an eyewitness identification to the factfinder. One occurs during the trial itself when the prosecutor asks the witness to point out the perpetrator in court.

It has long been recognized, however, that in-court identifications are "unsatisfactory and inconclusive." Given the defendant's prominent place in the courtroom, a witness' selection of the person sitting where the defendant sits during trial is pro forma. John Henry Wigmore articulated the received wisdom as follows:

> "Ordinarily, when a witness is asked to identify the assailant, or thief, or other person who is the subject of his testimony, the witness' act of pointing out the accused (or other person), then and there, is of little testimonial force. After all that has intervened, it would seldom happen that the witness would not have come to believe in that person's identity."

As a result of the superficial nature of an in-court identification, prosecutors often introduce more compelling identification evidence in the form of the witness's pre-litigation identification of the defendant, typically in some kind of lineup.

Testimony about prior identifications can take two forms: (1) the witness describes the prior identification procedure and its outcome; or (2) a police officer who participated in the earlier procedure testifies about what transpired. The prosecution may present both forms of the evidence to maximize its impact.

---

[32] Excerpt from Bellin, The Evidence of Wrongful Convictions, 106 Cornell L. R. 305 (2021).

A. SIXTH AMENDMENT

UNITED STATES v. WADE
388 U.S. 218 (1967)

Justice BRENNAN delivered the opinion of the Court.

The federally insured bank in Eustace, Texas, was robbed on September 21, 1964. A man with a small strip of tape on each side of his face entered the bank, pointed a pistol at the female cashier and the vice president, the only persons in the bank at the time, and forced them to fill a pillowcase with the bank's money. The man then drove away with an accomplice who had been waiting in a stolen car outside the bank. On March 23, 1965, an indictment was returned against respondent, Billy Wade, and two others for conspiring to rob the bank, and against Wade and the accomplice for the robbery itself. Wade was arrested on April 2, and counsel was appointed to represent him on April 26. Fifteen days later an FBI agent, without notice to Wade's lawyer, arranged to have the two bank employees observe a lineup made up of Wade and five or six other prisoners and conducted in a courtroom of the local county courthouse. Each person in the line wore strips of tape such as allegedly worn by the robber and upon direction each said something like 'put the money in the bag,' the words allegedly uttered by the robber. Both bank employees identified Wade in the lineup as the bank robber.

At trial the two employees, when asked on direct examination if the robber was in the courtroom, pointed to Wade. The prior lineup identification was then elicited from both employees on cross-examination. At the close of testimony, Wade's counsel moved for a judgment of acquittal or, alternatively, to strike the bank officials' courtroom identifications on the ground that conduct of the lineup, without notice to and in the absence of his appointed counsel, violated his Fifth Amendment privilege against self-incrimination and his Sixth Amendment right to the assistance of counsel. The motion was denied, and Wade was convicted....

IV.

...The confrontation compelled by the State between the accused and the victim or witnesses to a crime to elicit identification evidence is peculiarly riddled with innumerable dangers and variable factors which might seriously, even crucially, derogate from a fair trial. The vagaries of eyewitness identification are well-known;

the annals of criminal law are rife with instances of mistaken identification. Justice Frankfurter once said: "What is the worth of identification testimony even when uncontradicted? The identification of strangers is proverbially untrustworthy. The hazards of such testimony are established by a formidable number of instances in the records of English and American trials. These instances are recent—not due to the brutalities of ancient criminal procedure."

A major factor contributing to the high incidence of miscarriage of justice from mistaken identification has been the degree of suggestion inherent in the manner in which the prosecution presents the suspect to witnesses for pretrial identification. A commentator has observed that "the influence of improper suggestion upon identifying witnesses probably accounts for more miscarriages of justice than any other single factor—perhaps it is responsible for more such errors than all other factors combined." Suggestion can be created intentionally or unintentionally in many subtle ways. And the dangers for the suspect are particularly grave when the witness' opportunity for observation was insubstantial, and thus his susceptibility to suggestion the greatest.

Moreover, it is a matter of common experience that, once a witness has picked out the accused at the line-up, he is not likely to go back on his word later on, so that in practice the issue of identity may (in the absence of other relevant evidence) for all practical purposes be determined there and then, before the trial.

The pretrial confrontation for purpose of identification may take the form of a lineup, also known as an "identification parade" or "showup," as in the present case, or presentation of the suspect alone to the witness. It is obvious that risks of suggestion attend either form of confrontation and increase the dangers inhering in eyewitness identification. But as is the case with secret interrogations, there is serious difficulty in depicting what transpires at lineups and other forms of identification confrontations…. The defense can seldom reconstruct the manner and mode of lineup identification for judge or jury at trial… Improper influences may go undetected by a suspect, guilty or not, who experiences the emotional tension which we might expect in one being confronted with potential accusers. Even when he does observe abuse, if he has a criminal record he may be reluctant to take the stand and open up the admission of prior convictions. Moreover any protestations by the suspect of the fairness of the lineup made at trial are likely to be in vain; the jury's choice is between the accused's unsupported version and that of the police officers present. In short, the accused's inability effectively to reconstruct at trial any unfairness that occurred at the lineup may deprive him of his only opportunity meaningfully to attack the credibility of the witness' courtroom identification....

State reports, in the course of describing prior identifications admitted as evidence of guilt, reveal numerous instances of suggestive procedures, for example, that all in the lineup but the suspect were known to the identifying witness, that the other participants in a lineup were grossly dissimilar in appearance to the suspect, that only the suspect was required to wear distinctive clothing which the culprit allegedly wore, that the witness is told by the police that they have caught the culprit after which the defendant is brought before the witness alone or is viewed in jail, that the suspect is pointed out before or during a lineup, and that the participants in the lineup are asked to try on an article of clothing which fits only the suspect....

The trial which might determine the accused's fate may well not be that in the courtroom but that at the pretrial confrontation, with the State aligned against the accused, the witness the sole jury, and the accused unprotected against the overreaching, intentional or unintentional, and with little or no effective appeal from the judgment there rendered by the witness – "that's the man."

Since it appears that there is grave potential for prejudice, intentional or not, in the pretrial lineup, which may not be capable of reconstruction at trial, and since presence of counsel itself can often avert prejudice and assure a meaningful confrontation at trial, there can be little doubt that for Wade the postindictment lineup was a critical stage of the prosecution at which he was as much entitled to such aid (of counsel) as at the trial itself. Thus both Wade and his counsel should have been notified of the impending lineup, and counsel's presence should have been a requisite to conduct of the lineup, absent an intelligent waiver....

The judgment ... is vacated and the case is remanded ... to the District Court for further proceedings consistent with this opinion.

Wade applies the Sixth Amendment right to counsel to lineups, requiring law enforcement officers to invite the defendant's counsel to attend any lineup that involves the defendant. Soon after that case, however, the Supreme Court recognized an important limit on this protection. In *Kirby v. Illinois* (1972), the Court considered a police-generated show-up identification that occurred at a police station two days after an alleged robbery. The defendant in that case, Thomas Kirby, challenged the identification procedure on the ground that, "No lawyer was present in the room," and Kirby was never "advised of any right to the presence of counsel." The Supreme Court rejected this challenge on the ground that a formal prosecution of Kirby had not been initiated – "whether by way of formal charge, preliminary hearing, indictment, information, or arraignment" – at the time of the procedure. Since "a person's Sixth and Fourteenth Amendment right to counsel attaches only at or after the time that adversary judicial proceedings have been initiated against him," the right to have counsel present during an identification did not apply. See Chapter 8.

UNITED STATES v. ASH
413 U.S. 300 (1973)

Case Summary

In-person lineups require logistical effort on the part of police, particularly if, after *Wade*, they must include defense counsel. A simpler way for police to obtain a pretrial identification is through a photographic lineup. That's what occurred in *United States v. Ash*.

After a man "wearing a stocking mask" robbed a bank in Washington, D.C., police arrested Charles Ash for the crime. Ash was indicted and assigned counsel. "Shortly before the trial, an FBI agent and the prosecutor showed five color photographs" to the witnesses, without notice to Ash. "Three of the witnesses selected the picture of Charles Ash." After being convicted of the robbery, Ash appealed. He argued that the Sixth Amendment required the government to permit his counsel to attend the photographic identification procedures – a "critical stage" of the prosecution.

The Supreme Court, thus, had to resolve the following question: "whether the Sixth Amendment grants an accused the right to have counsel present whenever the Government conducts a post-indictment photographic display, containing a picture of the accused, for the purpose of allowing a witness to attempt an identification of the offender."

In reaching the conclusion that Ash's Sixth Amendment rights were not violated, the Court emphasized important differences between the scenario in *Wade* (a live lineup) and a photographic lineup that included a picture of the accused. One obvious difference is that the defendant (Ash) was not present at the photographic lineup, but the Court did not rest its opinion on that point.

Instead, the Court emphasized that the key distinction between a live lineup and a photographic one was the ability to reconstruct the procedure at a later trial. The Court pointed out that, in *Wade*, the government had argued "that if counsel was required at a lineup, the same forceful considerations would mandate counsel at other preparatory steps in the 'gathering of the prosecution's evidence,' such as … the taking of fingerprints or blood samples." The *Wade* Court, however, rejected that contention, recognizing "that there were times when the subsequent trial would cure a one-sided confrontation between prosecuting authorities and the uncounseled defendant." Thus, counsel need not be present at the taking of "fingerprints, hair, clothing, and other blood samples," because, as the *Wade* Court had explained:

> "Knowledge of the techniques of science and technology is sufficiently available, and the variables in techniques few enough, that the accused has the opportunity for a meaningful confrontation of the Government's case at trial through the ordinary processes of cross-examination of the Government's expert witnesses and the presentation of the evidence of his own experts."

Interpreting these comments from *Wade*, the majority in *Ash* explained: "If accurate reconstruction [at trial] is possible, the risks inherent in any confrontation still remain, but the opportunity to cure defects at trial causes the confrontation to cease to be 'critical.'"

The *Ash* Court concluded:

> "We are not persuaded that the risks inherent in the use of photographic displays are so pernicious that an extraordinary system of safeguards is required. We hold, then, that the Sixth Amendment does not grant the right to counsel at photographic displays conducted by the Government for the purpose of allowing a witness to attempt an identification of the offender."

B. DUE PROCESS

In addition to *Wade*'s application of the Sixth Amendment right to counsel to certain identification procedures, the Supreme Court gradually crafted due process restrictions on the admissibility of evidence generated through unnecessarily suggestive identification procedures. The next case provides a review of those additional protections and identifies an important limit on their scope.

PERRY v. NEW HAMPSHIRE
565 U.S. 228 (2012)

Justice GINSBURG delivered the opinion of the Court.

I
A

[Police responded to an early morning call that someone was breaking into cars in an apartment building parking lot. One of the responding officers, Nicole Clay, located Barion Perry "standing between two cars" "holding two car-stereo amplifiers in his hands." Parry told the officer he found the amplifiers on the ground. While one of the officers stood with Parry in the parking lot, another interviewed the witness to the break ins, Nubia Blandon. When the officer asked Blandon for a description of the person she saw, Blandon "pointed to her kitchen window and said the person she saw breaking into [a car] was standing in the parking lot, next to the police officer. Perry's arrest followed this identification."] About a month later, the police showed Blandon a photographic array that included a picture of Perry and asked her to point out the man who had broken into [the] car. Blandon was unable to identify Perry.

B

Perry was charged in New Hampshire state court with one count of theft by unauthorized taking and one count of criminal mischief. Before trial, he moved to suppress Blandon's identification on the ground that admitting it at trial would violate due process. Blandon witnessed what amounted to a one-person showup in the parking lot, Perry asserted, which all but guaranteed that she would identify him as the culprit.

The New Hampshire Superior Court denied the motion....

At the ensuing trial, Blandon and Clay testified to Blandon's out-of-court identification. The jury found Perry guilty of theft and not guilty of criminal mischief....

II

A

The Constitution, our decisions indicate, protects a defendant against a conviction based on evidence of questionable reliability, not by prohibiting introduction of the evidence, but by affording the defendant means to persuade the jury that the evidence should be discounted as unworthy of credit. Constitutional safeguards available to defendants to counter the State's evidence include the Sixth Amendment rights to counsel; compulsory process; and confrontation plus cross-examination of witnesses. Apart from these guarantees, we have recognized, state and federal statutes and rules ordinarily govern the admissibility of evidence, and juries are assigned the task of determining the reliability of the evidence presented at trial. Only when evidence "is so extremely unfair that its admission violates fundamental conceptions of justice," have we imposed a constraint tied to the Due Process Clause.

Contending that the Due Process Clause is implicated here, Perry relies on a series of decisions involving police-arranged identification procedures. In Stovall v. Denno (1967), first of those decisions, a witness identified the defendant as her assailant after police officers brought the defendant to the witness' hospital room. At the time the witness made the identification, the defendant—the only African-American in the room—was handcuffed and surrounded by police officers. Although the police-arranged showup was undeniably suggestive, the Court held that no due process violation occurred. Crucial to the Court's decision was the procedure's necessity: The witness was the only person who could identify or exonerate the defendant; the witness could not leave her hospital room; and it was uncertain whether she would live to identify the defendant in more neutral circumstances.

A year later, in Simmons v. United States (1968), the Court addressed a due process challenge to police use of a photographic array. When a witness identifies the defendant in a police-organized photo lineup, the Court ruled, the identification should be suppressed only where "the photographic identification procedure was so unnecessarily suggestive as to give rise to a very substantial likelihood of irreparable misidentification." Satisfied that the photo array used by Federal Bureau of Investigation agents in Simmons was both necessary and unlikely to have led to a mistaken identification, the Court rejected the defendant's due process challenge to admission of the identification. In contrast, the Court held in Foster v. California (1969) that due process required the exclusion of an eyewitness identification obtained through police-arranged procedures that "made it all but inevitable that the witness would identify the defendant."

Synthesizing previous decisions, we set forth in Neil v. Biggers (1972), and reiterated in Manson v. Brathwaite (1977), the approach appropriately used to determine whether the Due Process Clause requires suppression of an eyewitness identification tainted by police arrangement. The Court emphasized, first, that due process concerns arise only when law enforcement officers use an identification procedure that is both suggestive and unnecessary. Even when the police use such a procedure, the Court next said, suppression of the resulting identification is not the inevitable consequence.

A rule requiring automatic exclusion, the Court reasoned, would "go too far," for it would "keep evidence from the jury that is reliable and relevant," and "may result, on occasion, in the guilty going free."

Instead of mandating a per se exclusionary rule, the Court held that the Due Process Clause requires courts to assess, on a case-by-case basis, whether improper police conduct created a "substantial likelihood of misidentification." "Reliability of the eyewitness identification is the linchpin" of that evaluation, the Court stated in Brathwaite. Where the "indicators of a witness' ability to make an accurate identification" are "outweighed by the corrupting effect" of law enforcement suggestion, the identification should be suppressed. Otherwise, the evidence (if admissible in all other respects) should be submitted to the jury.

Applying this "totality of the circumstances" approach, the Court held in Biggers that law enforcement's use of an unnecessarily suggestive showup did not require suppression of the victim's identification of her assailant. Notwithstanding the improper procedure, the victim's identification was reliable: She saw her assailant for a considerable period of time under adequate light, provided police with a detailed description of her attacker long before the showup, and had "no doubt" that the defendant was the person she had seen. Similarly, the Court concluded in Brathwaite that police use of an unnecessarily suggestive photo array did not require exclusion of the resulting identification. The witness, an undercover police officer, viewed the defendant in good light for several minutes, provided a thorough description of the suspect, and was certain of his identification. Hence, the "indicators of the witness' ability to make an accurate identification were hardly outweighed by the corrupting effect of the challenged identification."

B

Perry concedes that, in contrast to every case in the Stovall line, law enforcement officials did not arrange the suggestive circumstances surrounding Blandon's identification. He contends, however, that it was mere happenstance that each of the Stovall cases involved improper police action. The rationale underlying our decisions, Perry asserts, supports a rule requiring trial judges to prescreen eyewitness evidence for reliability any time an identification is made under suggestive circumstances. We disagree.

Perry's argument depends, in large part, on the Court's statement in Brathwaite that "reliability is the linchpin in determining the admissibility of identification testimony." If reliability is the linchpin of admissibility under the Due Process Clause, Perry maintains, it should make no difference whether law enforcement was responsible for creating the suggestive circumstances that marred the identification.

Perry has removed our statement in Brathwaite from its mooring, and thereby attributes to the statement a meaning a fair reading of our opinion does not bear. As just explained, the Brathwaite Court's reference to reliability appears in a portion of the opinion concerning the appropriate remedy when the police use an unnecessarily suggestive identification procedure. The Court adopted a judicial screen for reliability as a course preferable to a per se rule requiring exclusion of identification evidence whenever law enforcement officers employ an improper procedure. The due process check for reliability, Brathwaite made plain, comes into play only after the defendant establishes improper police conduct. The very purpose of the check, the Court noted, was to avoid depriving the jury of identification evidence that is reliable, notwithstanding improper police conduct.

Perry's contention that improper police action was not essential to the reliability check Brathwaite required is echoed by the dissent. Both ignore a key premise of the Brathwaite decision: A primary aim of excluding identification evidence obtained under unnecessarily suggestive circumstances, the Court said, is to deter law enforcement use of improper lineups, showups, and photo arrays in the first place. Alerted to the prospect that identification evidence improperly obtained may be excluded, the Court reasoned, police officers will "guard against unnecessarily suggestive procedures." This deterrence rationale is inapposite in cases, like Perry's, in which the police engaged in no improper conduct....

Perry's argument, reiterated by the dissent, thus lacks support in the case law he cites. Moreover, his position would open the door to judicial preview, under the banner of due process, of most, if not all, eyewitness identifications. External suggestion is hardly the only factor that casts doubt on the trustworthiness of an eyewitness' testimony. As one of Perry's amici points out, many other factors bear on "the likelihood of misidentification" —for example, the passage of time between exposure to and identification of the defendant, whether the witness was under stress when he first encountered the suspect, how much time the witness had to observe the suspect, how far the witness was from the suspect, whether the suspect carried a weapon, and the race of the suspect and the witness. There is no reason why an identification made by an eyewitness with poor vision, for example, or one who harbors a grudge against the defendant, should be regarded as inherently more reliable, less of a "threat to the fairness of trial," than the identification Blandon made in this case. To embrace Perry's view would thus entail a vast enlargement of the reach of due process as a constraint on the admission of evidence.

Perry maintains that the Court can limit the due process check he proposes to identifications made under "suggestive circumstances." Even if we could rationally distinguish suggestiveness from other factors bearing on the reliability of eyewitness evidence, Perry's limitation would still involve trial courts, routinely, in preliminary examinations. Most eyewitness identifications involve some element of suggestion. Indeed, all in-court identifications do. Out-of-court identifications volunteered by witnesses are also likely to involve suggestive circumstances. For example, suppose a witness identifies the defendant to police officers after seeing a photograph of the defendant in the press captioned "theft suspect," or hearing a radio report implicating the defendant in the crime. Or suppose the witness knew that the defendant ran with the wrong crowd and saw him on the day and in the vicinity of the crime. Any of these circumstances might have "suggested" to the witness that the defendant was the person the witness observed committing the crime.

C

In urging a broadly applicable due process check on eyewitness identifications, Perry maintains that eyewitness identifications are a uniquely unreliable form of evidence. We do not doubt either the importance or the fallibility of eyewitness identifications. Indeed, in recognizing that defendants have a constitutional right to counsel at postindictment police lineups, we observed that "the annals of criminal law are rife with instances of mistaken identification."

We have concluded in other contexts, however, that the potential unreliability of a type of evidence does not alone render its introduction at the defendant's trial fundamentally unfair. See, e.g., Kansas v. Ventris (2009) (declining to "craft a broad exclusionary rule for uncorroborated statements obtained from jailhouse snitches," even though "rewarded informant testimony" may be inherently untrustworthy); Dowling v. United States (1990) (rejecting argument that the introduction of evidence concerning acquitted conduct is fundamentally unfair because such evidence is "inherently unreliable"). We reach a similar conclusion here: The fallibility of eyewitness evidence does not, without the taint of improper state conduct, warrant a due process rule requiring a trial court to screen such evidence for reliability before allowing the jury to assess its creditworthiness.

Our unwillingness to enlarge the domain of due process as Perry and the dissent urge rests, in large part, on our recognition that the jury, not the judge, traditionally determines the reliability of evidence. We also take account of other safeguards built into our adversary system that caution juries against placing undue weight on eyewitness testimony of questionable reliability. These protections include the defendant's Sixth Amendment right to confront the eyewitness. Another is the defendant's right to the effective assistance of an attorney, who can expose the flaws in the eyewitness' testimony during cross-examination and focus the jury's attention on the fallibility of such testimony during opening and closing arguments. Eyewitness-specific jury instructions, which many federal and state courts have adopted, likewise warn the jury to take care in appraising identification evidence. See, e.g., United States v. Telfaire (C.A.D.C. 1972) (per curiam) (D.C. Circuit Model Jury Instructions) ("If the identification by the witness may have been influenced by the circumstances under which the defendant was presented to him for identification, you should scrutinize the identification with great care.") The constitutional requirement that the government prove the defendant's guilt beyond a reasonable doubt also impedes convictions based on dubious identification evidence.

State and federal rules of evidence, moreover, permit trial judges to exclude relevant evidence if its probative value is substantially outweighed by its prejudicial impact or potential for misleading the jury. In appropriate cases, some States also permit defendants to present expert testimony on the hazards of eyewitness identification evidence....

Given the safeguards generally applicable in criminal trials, protections availed of by the defense in Perry's case, we hold that the introduction of Blandon's eyewitness testimony, without a preliminary judicial assessment of its reliability, did not render Perry's trial fundamentally unfair.

.... Finding no convincing reason to alter our precedent, we hold that the Due Process Clause does not require a preliminary judicial inquiry into the reliability of an eyewitness identification when the identification was not procured under unnecessarily suggestive circumstances arranged by law enforcement....

One protection against unreliable identification evidence referenced by the Supreme Court in *Perry v. New Hampshire* is an "eyewitness-specific jury instruction." The Court specifically cites the instruction from the *Telfaire* case:

UNITED STATES v. TELFAIRE
469 F.2d 552 (D.C. Cir. 1972)

APPENDIX: MODEL SPECIAL INSTRUCTIONS ON IDENTIFICATION

"One of the most important issues in this case is the identification of the defendant as the perpetrator of the crime. The Government has the burden of proving identity, beyond a reasonable doubt. It is not essential that the witness himself be free from doubt as to the correctness of his statement. However, you, the jury, must be satisfied beyond a reasonable doubt of the accuracy of the identification of the defendant before you may convict him. If you are not convinced beyond a reasonable doubt that the defendant was the person who committed the crime, you must find the defendant not guilty.

Identification testimony is an expression of belief or impression by the witness. Its value depends on the opportunity the witness had to observe the offender at the time of the offense and to make a reliable identification later.

In appraising the identification testimony of a witness, you should consider the following:

(1) Are you convinced that the witness had the capacity and an adequate opportunity to observe the offender?

Whether the witness had an adequate opportunity to observe the offender at the time of the offense will be affected by such matters as how long or short a time was available, how far or close the witness was, how good were lighting conditions, whether the witness had had occasion to see or know the person in the past.

(2) Are you satisfied that the identification made by the witness subsequent to the offense was the product of his own recollection? You may take into account both the strength of the identification, and the circumstances under which the identification was made.

If the identification by the witness may have been influenced by the circumstances under which the defendant was presented to him for identification, you should scrutinize the identification with great care....

(4) Finally, you must consider the credibility of each identification witness in the same way as any other witness, consider whether he is truthful, and consider whether he had the capacity and opportunity to make a reliable observation on the matter covered in his testimony.

I again emphasize that the burden of proof on the prosecutor extends to every element of the crime charged, and this specifically includes the burden of proving beyond a reasonable doubt the identity of the defendant as the perpetrator of the crime with which he stands charged. If after examining the testimony, you have a reasonable doubt as to the accuracy of the identification, you must find the defendant not guilty."

Studies of persons convicted but later cleared by DNA evidence point to erroneous identification testimony as a primary culprit, occurring in about 70% of those cases.

ACKNOWLEDGEMENTS

Writing a casebook is a daunting task. We have lots of people to thank. Most importantly, thanks to all our wonderful Criminal Procedure students (#TeamCrimPro) whose interest in the topic, patience, and perceptive questions and comments make us better teachers every semester. Special thanks to the students who enthusiastically embraced the first edition of this book as part of a multi-year process of generating this more polished and comprehensive edition. Finally, thanks to the judges, researchers, and practitioners whose work we draw on and especially those who offered feedback on specific sections of the casebook, including Kami Chavis, Lisa Griffin, Carissa Hessick, Brooks Holland, Jennifer Laurin, Paul Marcus, and Chris Slobogin. All errors remain ours (primarily Bellin's).

We plan to periodically update the book with new editions. Please send suggestions or corrections to jbellin@wm.edu

Made in the USA
Las Vegas, NV
03 December 2024

13268544R00332